FUNDAMENTALS OF PHARMACOLOGY
Volume – I

Dr. K.G. BOTHARA
M.Pharm., Ph.D.
Principal, Sinhgad Institute of Pharmacy,
Narhe, Pune - 411041

Dr. K.K. BOTHARA
M.B.B.S.

FUNDAMENTALS OF PHARMACOLOGY (VOL-I)　　　　ISBN: 978-81-923503-0-1
First Edition : JULY 2012
© : Dr. K.G. Bothara

The text of this publication, or any part thereof, should not be reproduced or transmitted in any form or stored in any computer storage system or device for distribution including photocopy, recording, taping or information retrieval system or reproduced on any disc, tape, perforated media or other information storage device etc., without the written permission of Author with whom the rights are reserved. Breach of this condition is liable for legal action.

Every effort has been made to avoid errors or omissions in this publication. In spite of this, errors may have crept in. Any mistake, error or discrepancy so noted and shall be brought to our notice shall be taken care of in the next edition. It is notified that neither the publisher nor the author or seller shall be responsible for any damage or loss of action to any one, of any kind, in any manner, therefrom.

Published By :　　　　　　　　　　　　　　　　　　　　　　　　　　**Printed By :**
NIRALI PRAKASHAN　　　　　　　　　　　　　　　　　　**Repro Knowledgecast Limited**
Abhyudaya Pragati, 1312, Shivaji Nagar,　　　　　　　　　　　　　　　　　　　　　**Thane**
Off J.M. Road, PUNE – 411005
Tel - (020) 25512336/37/39, Fax - (020) 25511379
Email : niralipune@pragationline.com

DISTRIBUTION CENTRES

PUNE
Nirali Prakashan
119, Budhwar Peth, Jogeshwari Mandir Lane
Pune 411002, Maharashtra
Tel : (020) 2445 2044, 66022708
Fax : (020) 2445 1538
Email : bookorder@pragationline.com

MUMBAI
Nirali Prakashan
385, S.V.P. Road, Rasdhara Co-op. Hsg. Society Ltd.,
Girgaum, Mumbai 400004, Maharashtra
Tel : (022) 2385 6339 / 2386 9976,
Fax : (022) 2386 9976
Email : niralimumbai@pragationline.com

DISTRIBUTION BRANCHES

NAGPUR
Pratibha Book Distributors
Above Maratha Mandir, Shop No. 3, First Floor,
Rani Jhanshi Square, Sitabuldi, Nagpur 440012,
Maharashtra, Tel : (0712) 254 7129

BENGALURU
Pragati Book House
House No. 1,Sanjeevappa Lane, Avenue Road Cross,
Opp. Rice Church, Bengaluru – 560002.
Tel : (080) 64513344, 64513355,
Mob : 9880582331, 9845021552
Email:bharatsavla@yahoo.com

JALGAON
Nirali Prakashan
34, V. V. Golani Market, Navi Peth, Jalgaon 425001,
Maharashtra, Tel : (0257) 222 0395
Mob : 94234 91860

KOLHAPUR
Nirali Prakashan
New Mahadvar Road,
Kedar Plaza, 1st Floor Opp. IDBI Bank
Kolhapur 416 012, Maharashtra. Mob : 9855046155

CHENNAI
Pragati Books
9/1, Montieth Road, Behind Taas Mahal, Egmore,
Chennai 600008 Tamil Nadu, Tel : (044) 6518 3535,
Mob : 94440 01782 / 98450 21552 / 98805 82331
Email : bharatsavla@yahoo.com

RETAIL OUTLETS
PUNE

Pragati Book Centre
157, Budhwar Peth, Opp. Ratan Talkies,
Pune 411002, Maharashtra
Tel : (020) 2445 8887 / 6602 2707, Fax : (020) 2445 8887

Pragati Book Centre
676/B, Budhwar Peth, Opp. Jogeshwari Mandir,
Pune 411002, Maharashtra
Tel : (020) 6601 7784 / 6602 0855
Email : pbcpune@pragationline.com

Pragati Book Centre
Amber Chamber, 28/A, Budhwar Peth,
Appa Balwant Chowk, Pune : 411002, Maharashtra,
Tel : (020) 20240335 / 66281669
Email : pbcpune@pragationline.com

Pragati Book Centre
917/22, Sai Complex, F.C. Road, Opp. Hotel Roopali,
Shivajinagar, Pune 411004, Maharashtra
Tel : (020) 2566 3372 / 6602 2728

PBC Book Sellers & Stationers
152, Budhwar Peth, Pune 411002, Maharashtra
Tel : (020) 2445 2254 / 6609 2463

MUMBAI
Pragati Book Corner
Indira Niwas, 111 - A, Bhavani Shankar Road, Dadar (W), Mumbai 400028, Maharashtra
Tel : (022) 2422 3526 / 6662 5254
Email : pbcmumbai@pragationline.com

PREFACE

Paul Ehrlich's concept that protozoal diseases could be cured by the administration of synthetic chemicals which selectively react with the target tissue of the protozoa rather than that of the host and Domagk's later expansion of this view to the treatment of bacterial diseases with the introduction of prontosil were the prominent landmarks in the birth of modern chemotherapy. The accuracy and the depth of clinical applications of these chemotherapeutic agents were further sharpened due to new inventions in the molecular biology which are increasingly involved to explain the mechanisms of action of many new chemotherapeutic agents. These broad area of pharmacology presented together with necessary data on the chemistry, absorption, excretion, tolerance and toxicity of the drugs are expected to provide a proper understanding of both, the value and limitations of the drug therapy.

In the last two decades, pharmacology attained a status of a basic medical science due to tremendous achievements in both, basic pharmacology and its clinical applications. Many of the changes in pharmacology are reflected in the new foundations and techniques which can be exploited in the synthesis of drugs as well as in their application to the clinical problems. We have incorporated this latest information available without growing appreciably in size. This is reflected particularly in the chapters on the treatment on cancer, organ transplantation and cardiovascular diseases.

Much progress has been achieved in cardiovascular therapy over the past 20 years. Extensive research, in which the academic community and the pharmaceutical industry co-operated with and stimulated each other, has resulted in the development of new drugs affecting cardio-vascular system. These phases of evolution can be witnessed in the chapters on the treatment of cardio-vascular diseases.

Many new drugs have been added to the list through many advances, especially on chemical front. Unfortunately the clinical complications and limitations of each such invented drug, often make the choice of the drug difficult, if the basic principles of pharmacology are not clear. Hence separate chapters (i.e., protein-binding; immuno-modulators) have been added in certain fields to better understand newer concepts or to correlate the relevant data.

The authors are greatly indebted to their colleagues for their generous help and criticism. We wish to place on record our sincere thanks to the publisher, Mr. D.K. Furia for his kind co-operation.

Suggestions from all corners of the profession are welcome. Authors are responsible for any deficiencies or errors that have remained and would be grateful if readers would call them to our attention.

AUTHORS

CONTENTS

SECTION - I : GENERAL PRINCIPLES

1. Introduction   1.1 – 1.10
- 1.1 Introduction   1.1
- 1.2 Definitions   1.3
- 1.3 Aspects of Pharmacology   1.4
- 1.4 Routes of Administration   1.6

2. Pharmacokinetic Aspects of Drug Action   2.1 – 2.12
- 2.1 Introduction   2.1
- 2.2 Structure of a Biological Membrane   2.1
- 2.3 Processes in Drug Absorption   2.3
- 2.4 Distribution of Drugs   2.8
- 2.5 Storage Depots   2.11
- 2.6 Excretion of Drugs   2.11

3. Pharmacodynamic Aspects of Drug Action   3.1 – 3.16
- 3.1 Introduction   3.1
- 3.2 Physico-Chemical Parameters and Drug Action   3.1
- 3.3 Physiological Factors   3.12
- 3.4 Formulation Factors   3.15

4. Drug Metabolism   4.1 – 4.22
- 4.1 Introduction   4.1
- 4.2 Metabolic Biotransformation of Drugs : (Phase I Reactions)   4.4
- 4.3 Conjugation Reactions (Phase II Reactions)   4.10
- 4.4 Factors Influencing Metabolic Pathways of Drug   4.20
- 4.5 Inducers of Drug Metabolism   4.20
- 4.6 Inhibitors of Drug Metabolism   4.20
- 4.7 Pharmacodynamic Factors   4.22

5. Protein Binding   5.1 – 5.10
- 5.1 Introduction   5.1
- 5.2 Body Proteins   5.2
- 5.3 Forces Involved in Drug-Protein Interaction   5.2
- 5.4 Factors Affecting Drug-Protein Binding   5.3

	5.5	Mathematical Derivations Related to Drug-Protein Complex	5.4
	5.6	Methods Employed to Detect the Drug-Protein Interaction	5.5
	5.7	Pharmacological Significance of Drug-Protein Interaction	5.5
	5.8	Effect of Displacement of Bound Drug	5.8
	5.9	Drug Persistence	5.9
	5.10	Drug Allergy	5.9
	5.11	Substances that Apparently do not Interact with Plasma-Proteins	5.10
6.	**Receptors**		**6.1 – 6.18**
	6.1	Introduction	6.1
	6.2	Classification	6.3
	6.3	Types of Receptor	6.4
	6.4	Receptor Site Theories	6.8
	6.5	Forces Involved in Drug-Receptor Interactions	6.9
	6.6	Spare Receptors	6.10
	6.7	Silent Receptors	6.11
	6.8	Factors Affecting the Drug-Receptor Interactions	6.11
	6.9	Non-Receptor Mediated Actions of the Drugs	6.13
	6.10	Drug Antagonism	6.14
	6.11	Other Receptor-Linked Pharmacological Events	6.17
7.	**Drug Dependence**		**7.1 – 7.12**
	7.1	Introduction	7.1
	7.2	Terminology	7.3
	7.3	Mechanisms Involved in Tolerance Development	7.4
	7.4	Mechanisms Involved in Evoking Withdrawal Syndrome	7.4
	7.5	Classification	7.5
8.	**Screening and Testing of Drugs**		**8.1 – 8.6**
	8.1	Introduction	8.1
	8.2	Types of Screening Methods	8.2
	8.3	Screening Methods for Detection of Some Activities	8.3
9.	**Drugs and Immunity**		**9.1 – 9.12**
	9.1	Introduction	9.1
	9.2	Complement	9.3
	9.3	Immune Mechanisms	9.3
	9.4	Factors Affecting Immunity	9.4

9.5	Fate of Immunoglobulins	9.5
9.6	Hypersensitivity Reactions	9.5
9.7	Drugs Used in Immunization	9.11

10. Principles of Toxicology   10.1 – 10.8

10.1	Introduction	10.1
10.2	Manifestations of Toxicity	10.1
10.3	Animal Toxicity Testing	10.3
10.4	Treatment of Poisoning	10.5
10.5	Heavy Metal Poisoning	10.6

11. Drug-Interactions   11.1 – 11.8

11.1	Introduction	11.1
11.2	Mechanisms of Drug Interaction	11.2

SECTION - II : DRUGS ACTING ON AUTONOMIC NERVOUS SYSTEM

12. Neurohumoral Transmission   12.1 – 12.14

12.1	Introduction	12.1
12.2	Nervous System	12.2
12.3	Neuro-Chemical Transmitters	12.3
12.4	Autonomic Nervous System	12.3
12.5	Divisions of Autonomic Nervous System	12.4
12.6	Acetylcholine and Epinephrine as Neuro-Transmitters	12.11
12.7	Neuro-Transmitters Present in Central Nervous System	12.13

13. Cholinergic Agonists   13.1 – 13.10

13.1	Introduction	13.1
13.2	Pharmacology of Acetylcholine	13.1
13.3	Cyclic Analogues of Acetylcholine	13.4
13.4	Cholinergic Receptors	13.5
13.5	Metabolism of Acetylcholine	13.7
13.6	Cholinomimetics or Cholinergic Agonists	13.7

14. Anti-Cholinesterases   14.1 – 14.14

14.1	Introduction	14.1
14.2	Cholinesterase Inhibitors	14.2
14.3	Structural Features of Cholinesterase Enzyme	14.2

14.4	Classification of Anticholinesterases	14.3
14.5	Absorption and Metabolism	14.10
14.6	Therapeutic Uses	14.11
14.7	Cholinesterase Reactivators	14.13
14.8	Limitations of Oximes	14.14

15. Anti-Muscarinic Agents — 15.1 – 15.10

15.1	Introduction	15.1
15.2	Natural Alkaloids	15.1
15.3	Mechanism of Action	15.2
15.4	Absorption, Distribution and Excretion	15.3
15.5	Adverse Reactions	15.3
15.6	Chemistry	15.4
15.7	Pharmacology of Antimuscarinic Drugs	15.5
15.8	Semisynthetic and Synthetic Analogues of Atropine	15.8
15.9	Therapeutic Uses of Antimuscarinic Agents	15.9

16. Neuromuscular Blockers — 16.1 – 16.14

16.1	Introduction	16.1
16.2	Neuromuscular Transmission	16.1
16.3	Nicotinic Cholinergic Receptors	16.2
16.4	Classification	16.3
16.5	Structure-Activity Relationship	16.11
16.6	Absorption, Distribution and Excretion	16.11
16.7	Therapeutic Uses	16.11
16.8	Toxic Effects	16.11
16.9	Competitive Versus Depolarising Agents	16.12
16.10	Centrally Acting Muscle Relaxant	16.12
16.11	Therapeutic Uses	16.14

17. Drugs Affecting Ganglionic Transmission — 17.1 – 17.8

17.1	Introduction	17.1
17.2	Ganglionic Transmission	17.1
17.3	Ganglionic Stimulants	17.4
17.4	Nicotine	17.5
17.5	Ganglionic Blockers	17.6
17.6	Absorption, Fate and Excretion	17.7
17.7	Side Effects	17.8
17.8	Therapeutic Uses	17.8
17.9	Limitations	17.8

18. Sympathomimetic Drugs   18.1 – 18.28
    18.1 Introduction   18.1
    18.2 Biosynthesis of Neurotransmitter   18.3
    18.3 Synaptic Interactions   18.3
    18.4 Pharmacological Actions of Catecholamines   18.5
    18.5 Metabolism   18.5
    18.6 Adrenoceptors   18.7
    18.7 Classification   18.9
    18.8 Structure-Activity Relationship   18.11
    18.9 Mechanism of Action   18.12
    18.10 Direct-Acting Adrenergic Agonists   18.12
    18.11 Absorption, Fate and Excretion   18.16
    18.12 Side-Effects   18.16
    18.13 Selective α–Receptor Stimulants   18.17
    18.14 Selective β_1-Adrenergic Stimulants   18.17
    18.15 Selective β_2–Adrenergic Stimulants   18.18
    18.16 Indirect Acting Adrenergic Agonists   18.19
    18.17 Mixed-Action Adrenergic Agonists   18.23
    18.18 Therapeutic Uses of Sympathomimic Amines   18.23
    18.19 Adrenergic Receptor Structure   18.25
    18.20 Second Messengers   18.25

19. Adrenoceptor Blocking Agents   19.1 – 19.20
    19.1 Introduction   19.1
    19.2 Drugs Affecting Biosynthesis of Norepinephrine   19.2
    19.3 Drugs that Prevent Storage of Catecholamines   19.3
    19.4 Drugs that Prevent the Release of Catecholamines   19.4
    19.5 Drugs that Block the Interaction of Norepinephrine with the Receptor Sites or Adrenergic Antagonists   19.6
    19.6 α-Adrenoceptor Blocking Agents   19.7
    19.7 Therapeutic Uses of α-Receptor Blocking Agents   19.13
    19.8 β–Adrenoceptor Blocking Agent   19.14

SECTION - III : DRUGS ACTING ON CENTRAL NERVOUS SYSTEM

20. Neuropharmacology   20.1 – 20.10
    20.1 Introduction   20.1
    20.2 Cellular Biology of Brain   20.1
    20.3 Brain Compartments   20.3

20.4	Central Neurotransmitters	20.5
20.5	Blood-Brain-Barrier	20.7

21. General Anaesthetic Agents — 21.1 – 21.10

21.1	Introduction	21.1
21.2	Stages of Anaesthesia	21.2
21.3	Preanaesthetic Medications	21.3
21.4	Mechanisms of Action	21.4
21.5	Classification of General Anaesthetic Agents	21.5
21.6	Volatile General Anaesthetic Agents	21.5
21.7	Intravenous (Basal) Anaesthetics	21.8
21.8	Narcoanalysis	21.8
21.9	Dissociative Anesthesia	21.10
21.10	Premedications	21.10

22. Local Anaesthetic Agents — 22.1 – 22.10

22.1	Introduction	22.1
22.2	Mechanism of Action	22.1
22.3	Structural Features of a Local Anaesthetic Agent	22.4
22.4	Pharmacology	22.5
22.5	Metabolism	22.5
22.6	Adverse Reactions	22.6
22.7	Sites of Action of Local Anaesthetics	22.6
22.8	Classification of Local Anaesthetic Agents	22.8
22.9	Individual Local Anaesthetic Agents	22.8

23. Sedative – Hypnotic Agents — 23.1 – 23.14

23.1	Introduction	23.1
23.2	Classification	23.2
23.3	Barbiturates	23.2
23.4	Benzodiazepines	23.6
23.5	Acyclic Hypnotics Containing Nitrogen	23.11
23.6	Cyclic Hypnotics Containing Nitrogen	23.12
23.7	Alcohols and Aldehydes	23.13
23.8	Acetylene Derivatives	23.14
23.9	Miscellaneous Agents	23.14

24. Epilepsy and Its Treatment   24.1 – 24.12

24.1	Introduction	24.1
24.2	Types of Epilepsies	24.2
24.3	Mechanisms of Epileptogenesis	24.5
24.4	Mechanism of Action of Anticonvulsant Drugs	24.5
24.5	Classification of Anti-Convulsant Drugs	24.6
24.6	Anticonvulsant Barbiturates	24.7
24.7	Hydantoins	24.8
24.8	Oxazolidinediones	24.9
24.9	Succinimides	24.10
24.10	Acetylureas	24.10
24.11	Benzodiazepines	24.11
24.12	Sodium Valproate (Valproic Acid)	24.11
24.13	Iminostilbenes	24.12
24.14	Carbonic Anhydrase Inhibitors	24.12
24.15	Miscellaneous Agents	24.12

25. Aliphatic Alcohols   25.1 – 25.4

25.1	Introduction	25.1
25.2	Absorption, Fate and Excretion	25.1
25.3	Mechanism of Action	25.2
25.4	Pharmacology	25.2
25.5	Adverse Reactions	25.3
25.6	Treatment of Alcoholism	25.3
25.7	Methanol (Methyl Alcohol)	25.4

26. Anxiolytic Agents   26.1 – 26.6

26.1	Introduction	26.1
26.2	Treatment of Anxiety	26.1
26.3	Barbiturates	26.2
26.4	Propanediols	26.2
26.5	Diphenylmethane Derivatives	26.3
26.6	Antidepressant Agents	26.3
26.7	Adrenergic β-Receptor Blocking Agents	26.3
26.8	Benzodiazepines	26.3
26.9	Miscellaneous Agents	26.6

27.	**Central Nervous System Stimulants**		27.1 – 27.12
	27.1	Introduction	27.1
	27.2	Therapeutic Applications of CNS Stimulants	27.1
	27.3	Limitations of CNS Stimulants	27.1
	27.4	Classification	27.2
	27.5	Analeptics	27.2
	27.6	Methylxanthines	27.3
	27.7	Central Stimulant Sympathomimetics	27.5
	27.8	Miscellaneous Agents	27.7
	27.9	Hallucinogens or Psychodelics or Psychotomimetics	27.8
28.	**Psycotropic Drugs**		28.1 – 28.22
	28.1	Introduction	28.1
	28.2	Classification	28.3
	28.3	Antipsychotic Agents (Major Tranquillizers or Neuroleptics)	28.3
	28.4	Mechanism of Action of Neuroleptic Agents	28.4
	28.5	Phenothiazines	28.6
	28.6	Rauwolfia Alkaloids	28.9
	28.7	Butyrophenones	28.11
	28.8	Miscellaneous Agents	28.11
	28.9	Antimanic Agents	28.12
	28.10	Antidepressants	28.13
	28.11	Tricyclic Antidepressants	28.15
	28.12	Monoamine Oxidase Inhibitors	28.19
	28.13	Miscellaneous Agents Having Considerable Mao-Inhibiting Activity	28.22
	28.14	Therapeutic Usefulness of MAO-Inhibitors	28.22
29.	**Drug Therapy in Parkinsonism**		29.1 – 29.6
	29.1	Introduction	29.1
	29.2	Levodopa	29.3
	29.3	Inhibitors of Aromatic L-Amino Acid Decarboxylase	29.4
	29.4	Dopamine Agonists	29.4
	29.5	Amantadine Hydrochloride	29.6
	29.6	Anticholinergic Agents	29.6
	29.7	Propranolol	29.6
30.	**Opioid Analgesics and Antagonists**		30.1 – 30.16
	30.1	Introduction	30.1
	30.2	Narcotic or Opioid Analgesic Agents	30.2
	30.3	Morphine-Like Opioid Agonists	30.3

30.4	Therapeutic Uses of Opioid Agonists	30.9
30.5	Mechanism of Action of Opioid Agonists	30.10
30.6	Opioid Receptor	30.12
30.7	Partial Opioid Agonists	30.13
30.8	Opioid Antagonists	30.15
30.9	Therapeutic Uses of Opioid Antagonist	30.15
30.10	Antitussive Agents	30.16

SECTION - IV : DRUG TREATMENT OF RHUMATIC DISEASES

31. Drugs For Rheumatic Diseases — 31.1 – 31.14

31.1	Introduction	31.1
31.2	Classification	31.5
31.3	Salicylic Acid Derivatives	31.5
31.4	Para-Amino Phenol Derivatives	31.8
31.5	Pyrazolon Derivatives	31.9
31.6	Indole Acetic Acid Derivatives	31.10
31.7	Propionic Acid and Phenylacetic Acid Derivatives	31.11
31.8	Fenamates	31.12
31.9	Miscellaneous Agents	31.12
31.10	Treatment of Gout	31.13

SECTION - V : AUTACOIDS

32. Prostaglandins — 32.1 – 32.10

32.1	Introduction	32.1
32.2	Nomenclature of Prostaglandins	32.2
32.3	Biosynthesis of Prostaglandins	32.3
32.4	Catabolism	32.6
32.5	Pharmacology	32.7
32.6	Mechanism of Action	32.9
32.7	Therapeutic Uses of Prostaglandins	32.10

33. Polypeptides of Pharmacological Importance — 33.1 – 33.8

33.1	Introduction	33.1
33.2	Angiotensins	33.1
33.3	Pharmacology	33.3
33.4	Mechanism of Action	33.4
33.5	Angiotensin Antagonists	33.4

33.6	Plasmakinins	33.6
33.7	Neuropeptides	33.7
33.8	Other Polypeptides	33.8

34. Cyclic Nucleotides — 34.1 – 34.4

34.1	Introduction	34.1
34.2	Cyclic-AMP	34.1
34.3	Biosynthesis, Release and Metabolism	34.1
34.4	Cyclic-GMP	34.3
34.5	Purinoceptors	34.4

35. Serotonin and Its Antagonists — 35.1 – 35.6

35.1	Introduction	35.1
35.2	Biosynthesis, Metabolism and Elimination	35.1
35.3	Pharmacology	35.3
35.4	Serotonin Receptors	35.4
35.5	Melatonin (N-Acetyl-5-Methoxy Tryptamine)	35.5
35.6	Serotonin Antagonists	35.5

36. Histamine and Its Antagonists — 36.1 – 36.16

36.1	Introduction	36.1
36.2	Biosynthesis, Storage and Catabolism	36.2
36.3	Histamine Release	36.3
36.4	Histamine Liberation	36.4
36.5	Histamine Receptors	36.4
36.6	Physiological Actions of Histamine	36.6
36.7	Histamine Antagonists	36.9
36.8	H_1-Receptor Blocking Agents	36.10
36.9	Cromolyn Sodium	36.13
36.10	H_2-Receptor Blocking Agents	36.14
36.11	Absorption, Fate and Excretion	36.16
36.12	Therapeutic Uses	36.16
36.13	Inhibitors of H^+- K^+-ATpase Pump	36.16

*	**Sample Questions**	S.1 – S.3
*	**Index**	I.1 – I.14

SECTION - I : GENERAL PRINCIPLES

INTRODUCTION

1.1 INTRODUCTION

In ancient time, a number of effective and useful naturally occurring substances were discovered for protection against the evils of disease and suffering. According to Sir John Gaddum (1900 - 1965), when man first used a plant extract to guard himself against the symptoms of the disease, Pharmacology was thus born. The term, pharmacology (the Greek pharmakon = a drug or medicine; logus = science or treatise), but, could not be documented in the medical literature until Samuel Dale, in 1693, first introduced this term.

At a very early stage in the history of pharmacology, therapeutics was mainly coiled around the concept of magic. It was Hippocrates (460 - 370 B.C.) who first realized disease as an abnormal reaction of the body rather than a punishment from God. The ancient communities from China, India, Egypt and Greece had maintained the records of drugs which were locally used at that time (4000 B.C.) The latter period saw the gradual use of more complex formulation. In Rome, at that time (A.D. 131 - 201), Galen who was a Greek pharmacist-physician first introduced the concept of polypharmacy. There was a general tendency to prescribe the mixtures containing many drugs though they were not, in fact, needed. Patients had to suffer more from the side effects of the drugs. Paracelsus (1493 - 1541) was the first to openly criticize the Galenic system of polypharmacy. He mainly stressed and adviced others to use a single component mixtures wherever possible. During the same period, in 1497, the first official pharmacopoeia was published at Florence. During the sixteenth century, there was an intelectual awareness and curiosity almost about in every field of knowledge.

During 17th and 18th century, alongwith chemistry, equally of course, many of the most important advances in the knowledge of the physiology of circulation, central nervous system, hormones and enzymes in the body boosted up the growth of pharmacological thought in the profession.

The isolation, purification and indentification of the active substances, cataloguing of their properties and the synthesis of both existing and new molecules were the foundation upon which the basic pharmacology was built up.

In 1806, Serturner (1783 - 1841) reported the isolation of morphine from the opium poppy. It was then followed by isolation of a series of active principles like, emetine by Pelletier, quinine by Carentou, strychnine by Magendie and in 1856, cocaine by Wohler. For the studies on drugs, the crude methods were replaced by scientific and rational methods, due to the efforts of Francois Magendie (1813 - 1878), who came to be known as "Father of experimental medicine". The first laboratory to be devoted exclusively to a study of Pharmacology came out in 1849. It was set up by Rudolf Buchheim in Estonia.

During the last decade of nineteenth century, people in U.S.A. started realising the importance of pharmacology. 'American society for pharmacology and experimental therapeutics' was founded in 1908 by Dr. Abel. During this period, Sir Henry Dale (1875 -1968) and Paul Ehrlich (1854 - 1915) were credited for their valuable discoveries and contribution to the pharmacology. Sir Dale's work was in connection with histamine, the ergot alkaloids and functioning of CNS. While Ehrlich was considered as "Father of Chemotherapy". The modern era of chemotherapy began after 1935, with the introduction of sulphonamides and antibiotics. Prior to this, during the period 1919 to 1935, many organic compounds of low therapeutic index were present in the market. The importance of pharmacology as an independent science was acknowledged in Britain when the 'British Pharmacological Society' was formed in 1931.

After World War II, the rate of introduction of new drugs was phenomenal. This was the most fruitful time for pharmacology to get miraculous agents in different categories like, analgesics, barbiturates, local anesthetic, antibiotics, sulphonamides etc. Due to this extraordinary growth in the number of medicinal agents (about 200 new drug products per year) and inadequate testing procedures prevailing at that time, history witnessed many disasters due to the use of dangerous formulations; the thalidomide tragedy is an example. The magnitude and consequences of many commonly encountered adverse drug reactions could not be justified due to the incomplete and unrepresentative data.

In 20th century, an emphasis has been given to design such experiments to focus closely on mechanisms of action of drugs. Toxic effects of drugs are frequently a function of the dose-response relationship. The importance of quantification of drug action (QSAR) has also been realised. In the last fifty years, there has been an excellent growth in medical knowledge. Today we live in an era of a *"drug explosion"*. According to the report of the Task Force on Prescription drugs, 1969, around 70 new drug products are introduced per year due to adaption of a rational approach. With the advanced knowledge of the basic pharmacology and biochemistry, it is now possible to design new drugs which can control and cure disease. Unfortunately, the choice of the best drug in any particular situation is often difficult due to large number of drugs available and their adverse reactions. Hence whenever we use drug, we engage in an experiment with a desire to achieve maximum effectiveness and safety.

Besides this, manifestations of that disease on the behavioural and psychological components of an individual can not be neglected. The utilisation and correct interpretation of various clinical tests and laboratory data is a must qualification in the present life. In order to develop novel potent and less toxic medicinal agents, the knowledge of other allied fields of pharmacology (i.e. pharmacogenetics, biochemical pharmacology, molecular pharmacology and medicinal chemistry) is desired.

1.2 DEFINITIONS

With the recent advances in pharmacology, many terms have been documented in the literature and are commonly used to explain or interprete the mechanism of action of the drug. It would not be unjustifiable if we start with the definitions of such terms, to make easy further discussion.

(a) Drug :

The term 'drug' is derived from the French, "drogue" which means a dry herb. It may be any substance either of natural or synthetic origin, employed for the diagnosis, prevention or treatment of a disease. Certain drugs may also be used for the maintenance of normal healthy condition of the body. Drug does not impart a new function to the body cells but just alters the rates of on-going biochemical reactions to alleviate the symptoms of disease.

(b) Pharmacology :

This term involves :

(i) Screening of biological activity on an isolated organ or intact animal,

(ii) Study of nature and systematization of such responses.

(iii) Alongwith mechanism of action.

In the above definition, biological activity may be of beneficial or harmful nature. The beneficial effects may further be confirmed on animal (pre-clinical) and human (clinical) studies. The harmful effects may be examined by acute and chronic toxicity studies.

(c) Pharmacokinetics :

The term implies the relation of pharmacological response to the various factors affecting absorption, distribution, metabolism and excretion of the drug.

(d) Pharmacodynamics :

The term describes the dose-response relationship of drug alongwith its interaction with the receptor sites.

(e) Pharmacotherapeutics :

It is an application of the knowledge of pharmacodynamics to the treatment of disease.

(f) Chemotherapy :

It describes the specific drug treatment of various infections in human caused by microorganisms.

(g) Therapeutic Index :

It describes on the quantitative terms, the relationship between the dose of a drug required to produce undesired (LD_{50} = median lethal dose) and desired (ED_{50} = median effective dose) effects.

$$\text{Therapeutic index} = \frac{LD_{50}}{ED_{50}}$$

It is also termed as margin of safety or selectivity. The selectivity of action may be manifested at different levels of biological system. The greater the degree of selectivity, the more valuable will be the drug.

(h)

Biological responses obtained when two or more drugs of the same pharmacological class are given, may be categorized as

(i) Additive responses : An additive effect is said to occur when the combined effect of two drugs equals to the sum of effects of each agent if given alone, and

(ii) Synergistic response : This term is used when the combined effect of two drugs is greater than the sum of effects of each agent when given alone.

(i) Antagonism :

It is the interference in the biological response of one agent by another.

(j) Allergy :

The exaggeration of unusual biological response affecting organs other than the target tissue which occurs only in a small percentage of individuals is termed as allergy.

(k) Idiosyncrasy :

It is an abnormal reactivity or response to a drug due to some genetic disorder in the patient.

(l) Hypersensitivity :

If the person correlates well with the dose of a drug which is unexpectedly less than the prescribed, the person is said to be hypersensitive to that drug.

(m) Hyporeactivity :

If a drug produces its usual pharmacological response only at unusually large dose, the person is said to be hyporeactive to that drug.

(n) Tolerance :

If the hyporeactivity or decreased sensitivity to the drug is due to the repeated or chronic administration of the drug, the patient is supposed to develop tolerance against the drug.

(o) Immunity :

When a reduced sensitivity or resistance to the drug action arises due to the body's natural defence mechanisms (e.g. antibody formation), it is termed as development of immunity.

(p) Mutagenesis :

If any heritable change occurs in genetic material of a person, of whatever origin, it is known as mutagenesis.

1.3 ASPECTS OF PHARMACOLOGY

The ultimate biological response of a drug is influenced by many factors. The prominent amongst them, are

(1) Pharmacokinetic factors,

(2) Pharmacodynamic factors,

(3) Factors governing hypersensitivity and tolerance, and

(4) Pathological and genetic factors.

The drug therapy may be intended for either a complete cure of the disease or as a prophylactic measures (prophylaxis means 'favouring protection').

(a) Drug Receptor Interactions :

The pharmacological response of a drug is obtained when the drug reacts or interacts with the complementary chemical groupings of a biologically important integral part of the organism, known as *receptor*. The selectivity of action of a particular drug can be explained through the drug receptor interactions. Many receptor species for different categories of drugs have been identified and characterised. These include, muscarinic and nicotinic cholinergic receptors, opioid receptors, benzodiazepine receptors, adrenergic receptors etc.

The cells of the body are bathed in fluids having different ions and proteins held at remarkably constant concentrations. The drug receptor interaction conveys the complex language of extracellular stimuli to the cells into a simpler language of ionic, electrical and chemical signals. The receptor structure is quite stable and the potency or selectivity of action could be altered by making slight modifications in the structure of the drug.

Following types of receptor systems have been identified –

(1) Membrane bound receptor system : e.g., *cholinergic receptors, benzodiazepine receptors, digitalis receptors etc.*

(2) Receptors acting through second messenger : Example includes that of adrenergic receptors.

(3) Intra-cellular receptors : Examples include, steroid receptors and Ca^{++} receptor protein which is known as *calmodulin*.

(b) Drug Receptor Binding :

Once the drug reaches in viscinity to receptor sites, it must form bonds with the receptor before it can initiate a response. Drug receptor interactions involve one or more of the following types of bonding.

(1) Hydrogen bonding
(2) Ionic bonding
(3) Vander Waals forces
(4) Hydrophobic binding forces and
(5) Covalent bonding.

(c) Acceptors and Binding Sites :

Receptors are not necessarily uniformly distributed throughout the tissues. Similarly the same receptor may react with the drugs of other categories if used in higher dosages. Hence, untoward effects are likely to appear.

The term acceptor denotes such sites of drug loss where the drug binds but not leads to a biological response. In some texts, acceptors are also described as silent receptor. For example, only a small fraction (0.001 - 0.01 %) of the d-tubocurarine administered, is responsible for its selective biological action by its interaction with receptors limited to the end plate region of the motor nerves and voluntary muscles.

(d) Accessibility :

Biological barriers govern the pharmacokinetic aspects of drug action. These barriers include plasma membrane, lysosomal and mito-chondrial membranes, placental membrane, blood brain barrier etc. Lipid solubility, molecular shape and size, stability and ionization constant of the drug are some of the factors which affect the accessibility of the drug to the receptor sites and thus helps to obtain selective action.

(e) Potency :

In a series of compounds, if one drug is more effective than another at the same or lower dose, it is said to be more potent than the another agent. The difference in the potencies of two drugs of the same pharmacological class may be due to the differences in the affinities, intrinsic activities, pharmacokinetic and pharmacodynamic aspects or binding abilities of the drugs to the plasma proteins.

Selectivity of action and toxicological profiles of the drug are also given weightage while assigning therapeutic value to the more potent drugs. Obviously a drug of low potency but high selectivity will be always preferred.

(f) Drug Antagonism :

The activity of an agonist drug may be specifically blocked by other agents. Such agents are known as *antagonists* to the drug. Antagonist can bind with the receptor surface (i.e., it possesses affinity for the receptor) but cannot evoke pharmacological response (i.e., lacks intrinsic activity). Thus in a liberal sense, they may be considered as very weak agonists. Examples include that of atropine which is a selective muscarinic cholinergic blocker while d-tubocurarine antagonises only the nicotinic actions of acetylcholine. In most of the cases, particulary in competative antagonism, the antagonist shares in common, most of the structural features of the agonist.

(g) Structure Activity Relationship Studies :

To exhibit the same pharmacological response, drugs must possess some structural features or physicochemical properties in common alongwith the same special arrangement of such groups. SAR studies, thus, not only help to recognise such common structural features but also give an idea about probable structure of the receptor. After getting the in-sight of drug-receptor interactions, the knowledge of SAR studies can be utilised in designing more potent, more selective, yet less toxic drugs.

(h) Dose-response Relationship Studies:

When a new drug shows some promising activity during screening, it becomes necessary to find out its therapeutic usefulness. An approximation about its ED_{50} value (i.e. effective dose$_{50}$) can be made by studying the relationship between drug dose and its effect on simple, isolated preparations of tissues in vitro. A typical S shaped curve is obtained when response is plotted against log dose value.

1.4 ROUTES OF ADMINISTRATION

The biological response of a drug is a function of its concentration at the sites of action. To sustain the action for a desired period of time, the dosage form should be designed in such a manner to maintain sufficient concentration of the drug in the bio-phase. To achieve this goal, the rate and extent of drug absorption from the dosage form (bioavailability) and the rate of its clearance from the receptor sites (elimination) should be properly balanced. This is more applicable to the drugs having a low therapeutic index where fluctuations in the plasma drug concentration may lead either to therapeutic failure or drug toxicity.

Many factors influence the rate and extent of drug absorption from formulation. Prominent amongst them, include :

(a) surface area for absorption
(b) drug's physical and chemical properties.
(c) its desired site of action.
(d) blood flow to the site of absorption.
(e) pH at the absorpting sites.
(f) the drug volume and dosage interval.
(g) the general state of the patient.
(h) formulation factors alongwith the number and order of adding excipients.
(i) route choosen for administration of drug.

If the large surface area is available, the drug rapidly reaches into the bio-phase. Hence, at the areas like, skin, intestinal mucosa or pulmonary alveolar epithelium, the drugs are very rapidly absorbed.

The following table illustrates various routes of administration of drug. They can be employed depending upon the need and convenience of the patient.

Table 1.1 : Routes of administration

Route	Site of administration
1. Oral (Enteral route)	Buccal, sublingual gastro intestinal tract, rectal
2. Inhalation	Nose, lung
3. Topical	Skin, conjunctivae, otic canal, vagina
4. Parenteral	Intradermal Subcutaneous Intramuscular Intravenous Intra arterial Intralymphatic Intrathecal Intraperitoneal Intraventricular
5. Miscellaneous	Subdural Hypospray Iontophoresis

(a) Oral Route :

It is the most favoured route of administration holding number of advantages in its account. From the patient's point of view, it is a cheap and convenient dosage form. From the clinical point of view, absorption of drug by this route is rapid due to thin and extremely large surface area of the epithelium of intestine. The commonly used oral dosage forms include, solutions, suspensions, tablets, capsules or coated tablets. The drug absorption is rapid in solutions while it is slow if the drug is administered in the form of coated tablet. Liquid dosage forms are designed for the convenience of the children and other patients who due to their health problems or unwillingness cannot ingest solid dosage forms. The pH at the sites of absorption also plays an important role in drug absorption. Most of the drugs are either weak acids or weak bases. Since drug is absorbed mainly in it's unionized form in GIT, acidic drugs are rapidly absorbed in stomach while basic drugs are rapidly absorbed in small intestine.

Disadvantages of Oral Route :

(i) Fluctuations or irregularities in the bioavailability of the drug are likely to be encountered due to the presence of dietary material in the GIT.

(ii) The drug from GIT is absorbed in the blood which carries the drug first to the liver. Since the liver is a major site of drug metabolism, a substantial amount of drug absorbed, may be metabolised or stored in the liver leading to loss of drug during the first pass through liver. Hence oral route is not advisable in the emergency conditions where quick action is desired. For example, propranolol, a β-blocker or organic nitriles undergo appreciable losses during their first pass through liver.

(iii) Oral route is not preferable for drug which undergo structural changes or degradation due to the varying degree of acidity and alkalinity of the digestive juices or due to the action of intestinal digestive enzymes. Certain drugs, upon oral administration may irritate the gastric mucosa. If needed, these drugs can be administered orally in the form of enteric coated tablets so as to release the drug specifically at the site of absorption.

(b) Sublingual Administration :

This dosage form is designed specifically to avoid the substantial loss of the drug due to destruction in gastrointestinal fluid or due to presystemic metabolism. The tablet is generally small, flat and oval in shape and can be placed under the tongue to release the drug. The drug absorption takes place through venous drainage to the superior vena cava without first pass through the liver.

Since the drug is not lost in the hepatic metabolism, this dosage form is effective in lower dose and rapid absorption of drug entitles this route, to be used in emergencies. Sublingual tablets of many drug have been formulated. Examples include, progesterone, nitroglycerin, isoprenaline etc.

(c) Rectal Administration :

This route of administration is generally employed to treat local conditions as hemorrhoids or to achieve systemic absorption through the rectal mucous membrane for nauseating drugs. The drug can be administered in the form of suppositories, soft-gelatin capsules or enemas. This route can also be used in unconscious patients where oral administration of drug is not possible. Generally to achieve same pharmacological action, rectal dose should be doubled than the oral dose for most of the drugs, because about 50% of the rectal dose, after absorption, will pass through liver before entering into circulation.

(i) Suppositories : Variety of bases ranging from cocoa butter to polyethylene glycol derivatives are employed to prepare suppositories. The absorption pattern is often irregular and incomplete. Some drugs if given in the form of suppositories, may even cause irritation of the rectal mucosa.

Examples of drugs administered by suppositories include, theophylline to treat the nocturnal spasm of asthma; ergotamine to treat migraine when vomiting is present and benzocaine to treat haemorrhoids.

(ii) Enema : This is dosage form where drug is presented in the form of solution or suspension in water or some other vehicle. The anaesthetic bromethol can be given by this route.

(d) Inhalation :

This route of administration, is intended for the substances in gaseous form or designed in spray or aerosol forms. Due to the large surface area and extensive blood flow, rapid drug absorption occurs through the pulmonary epithelium and mucous membrane of the respiratory tract (i.e. trachea, bronchi, bronchioles etc.)

The anaesthetics gases like ether, nitrous oxide are administered by inhalation. Similarly certain drugs like decongestants, bronchodilators etc. can also be given by this route to achieve local effects. Drugs having their sites of action in CNS (e.g. nicotine) can also be administered by inhalation using smoke as a vehicle.

Insufflation is seldom used as a method of drug administration where absorption occures through the nasal mucous membrane.

(e) Topical Administration :

Topical application may be applied to the skin to treat the local dermatological disorders. Due to the thick layer of stratum corneum, the drug applied rarely gains an access to the systemic circulation. Topical application of drugs is possible to the mucous membranes of conjunctiva, nasopharynx, oropharynx, colon, urethra, urinary bladder or vagina. For topical application, the drug may be presented in various formulations, including ointments, pastes, creams, liniments and lotions. Absorption occurs through the sebaceous glands. This slow and erratic pattern of absorption can be enhanced by suspending the drug in an oily vehicle and rubbing it into the skin (i.e. inunction). If the skin is cut or damaged, the drug gets absorbed sufficient to produce systemic effects and would likely to be toxic.

A sustained and controlled release of drug into the systemic circulation is possible when the 'drug-patch' that releases drug from a reservior is applied behind the ear where body temperature and blood flow enhance the release and absorption of the drug. Scopalamine and nitroglycerine patches are available. The compact, dense horny layer like, stratum corneum may also act as a drug-reservoir, particularly for highly lipophilic drugs. Percutaneous absorption of drug is considerable, if the drug is applied to the areas of the skin where stratum corneum layer is very thin.

Certain drugs which are poorly absorbed by topical application, can be forced to get absorbed into the skin by means of a direct electric current. This process is known as *iontophoresis* which is seldom used.

(f) Vaginal Administration :

This method is advisable for the compounds which can be absorbed through the vaginal mucous membrane and can be safely used to treat local vaginal infections. The drug can be administered in the form of a pessary or a tablet.

(g) Parenteral Administration :

In emergencies or in cases where drug undergoes substantial metabolism in GIT or first-pass through liver, the drug can be given by a route which directly carries the drug into the body fluids. Drugs administered parenterally (par-beyond; enteral-intestinal), with an exception of intra-arterial route, possibly escape from the first pass in the liver. For all types of parenteral administration, sterile precautions are needed to be performed.

(i) Subcutaneous Administration : This route is restricted only for drugs that do not irritate the tissues. The drug is usually injected by inserting a hypodermal needle into the loose tissues located immediately below the dermis. The dose of drug needed, is approximately half to that of oral dose. The rate of release of the drug from intramuscular or subcutaneous sites can be slower down by using an oily vehicle (e.g. hormones) or by complexing it with other poorly soluble agents such as benzathene. Penicillin G can be complexed with benzathene to form a depot preparation (subcutaneous implant). The biological half-life of a drug can be prolonged by an inclusion of a small quantity of vasoconstrictor (e.g. epinephrine) to reduce blood supply at the site of administration.

Subcutaneous administration is usually employed for the drug whose presence at the sites of action is desired for prolonged period of time. Example includes that of insulin. A more rapid and extensive distribution in the case of subcutaneous administration of large volume of the drug solution can be achieved by addition of Hyaluronidase which acts as a spreading agent. A controlled and sustained release of the drug can be obtained by implanting a sterile compressed drug pellet into the subcutaneous tissues.

(ii) Intramuscular injection : The drug can be injected intramuscularly by inserting the needle through the layers of the skin deep into skeletal muscles usually into the deltoid muscle in the shoulder or the gluteus muscle in the buttocks. The release of drug occurs by simple diffusion from the drug depot to the plasma and process is concentration gradient dependent. This route is suitable for insoluble substances which can be administered in the form of suspension. The rate of release from suspension is generally slow, resulting into a prolonged duration of action. This route can also be employed for drug solutions which are tissue-irritant, if injected subcutaneously. Since the injection is made deep into the muscles, the injection may be painful.

(iii) Intravenous injection : This route carries the drug directly into the vein and then to the heart. From heart, it is then circulated to the tissues. Since the drug is instantly carried to its sites of action, the onset of drug action can be very rapid. Hence, intravenous administration generally should be made slowly and with constant monitoring of the responses of the patient.

The quickness with which drug reaches its sites of action, is advantageous in treating the emergency cases or in the induction of anaesthesia. This route is also useful in administration of the drugs which upon, subcutaneous administration leads to irritation of the tissues.

In intravenous administration, the drug may be directly injected into the vein over a short period of time (as a bolus) or over a period of hours (as an infusion) Infusion permits the intravenous administration of large volume of drug solution which has a narrow therapeutic range or has a short biological half-life value. Infusion is preferred in acute therapy where sustained and controlled plasma concentration of drug is necessary.

(iv) Intra-arterial injection : The drug is injected into the artery just near to the site of action. Precaution is to be taken to tie off the collateral arteries below the site of injection. This route is seldom used and is restricted for the diagnostic organ studies in human (arteriography). Recently this route has been tried for the administration of antineoplastic agents.

The most prominent advantage of arterial administration is injecting the drug quite close to the desired site of action. This may also lead to adverse effects if drug is injected in overdose.

(v) Intraperitoneal injection : The drug is injected into the peritoneum which provides very large surface area. First-pass hepatic losses are possible since the drug enters the circulation through the portal vein. It is seldom used route for drug administration.

(vi) Intrasternal injection : This route is employed only in the cases where intravenous injection is not possible due to unavailability of vein. A special type of sternal puncture needle is needed for this injection which is inserted into the marrow of the sternum. The drug injected by this route gives almost immediate response.

(vii) Intrathecal injection : To treat an acute CNS infection or to induce spinal anesthesia, the drug may be injected into the subarachnoid space (intrathecal) to get the effects on the spinal nerves and meninges. A high concentration of drug in the interspinous spaces of the spinal cord can be achieved by this route. For example, streptomycin can be injected intrathecally to treat tuberculous meningitis.

(viii) Intraventricular injection : Many drugs due to their poor lipophilicity, can not cross the blood brain barrier and hence can not reach to the CNS. Such drugs can be administered directly into the cerebrospinal fluid by intraventricular injection. The drug is injected into the cerebral ventricles which are filled by the cerebrospinal fluid. This route enjoys wide acceptance in the experimental neuropharmacology.

(ix) Hypospray : The technique involves painless administration of a fine stream of a drug solution of almost microscopic size through the dermis into the tissue. The process does not involve the use of a needle and the administration is done with the application of a high pressure. Thus it resembles, in its characteristics, with the subcutaneous injection.

PHARMACOKINETIC ASPECTS OF DRUG ACTION

2.1 INTRODUCTION

The potency of drug and its duration of action are influenced mainly by the pharmacodynamic and the pharmacokinetic aspects of the drug. To reach the site of action (i.e. receptor sites), the drug has to cross several body compartments. Biological membranes or cell-membranes serve to demorcate the boundaries of body's intercompartmental system. Obviously then, these cell membranes play an important role in evaluation of clinical merits and demerits of a drug by influencing its absorption, distribution, metabolism and excretion pattern. Hence, it becomes necessary to learn about the physicochemical properties of cell membrane. Beside this, the drug molecules due to the differences in their size, shape, solubility, degree of ionisation and partition coefficient may differ quantitatively in their biological response.

Biological membranes vary from single layer of cells (as in intestinal epithelium) to several layers of cells (as in skin). Let us gather some basic information about the structure and functions of biological membrane to understand better, the pharmacokinetic aspects of drug action.

2.2 STRUCTURE OF A BIOLOGICAL MEMBRANE

The living cells are capsulated and permeated by biological membranes or cell membranes. It is composed of protein-lipid continuous structure intermittently interrupted with water filled pores. Its thickness ranges from 60 A° to 100 A°. It contains specific molecular gates and pumps that enable it to function as a highly selective permeable barrier across which, there is a ceaseless movement of nutrients, metabolites and regulatory substances.

Singer and Nicolson have proposed a fluid mosaic model of a cell-membrane. According to them, the membrane consists of a double layer of protein and lipid. The lipid bilayer is bound on both sides by proteins, focusing ionic and polar group on both, inner and outer sides.

The intrinsic and extrinsic surface of membrane have a fairly rigid and restricted molecular motion. While lipoidal core is quite fluid, with a high degree of molecular motion of loosely oriented hydrophobic chains. This is probably due to the membrane proteins which are free to diffuse laterally in the lipid core. The volume ratio of lipid to

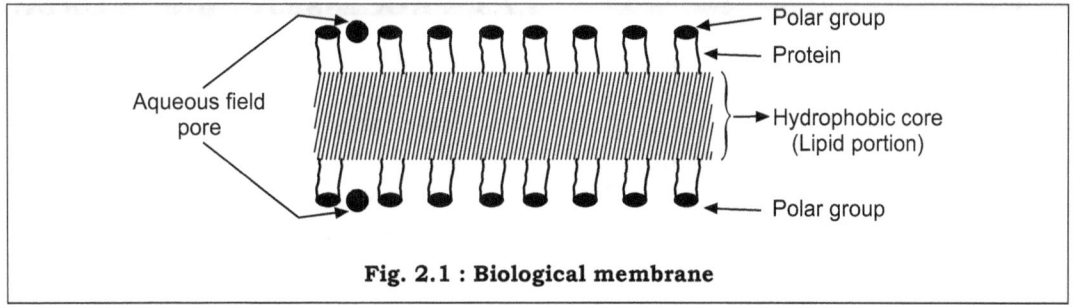

Fig. 2.1 : Biological membrane

proteins in membrane vary from 1:4 to 4:1. Both these constituents of membrane are held together by many noncovalent interactions. If the drug is lipophilic, its transport across the membrane is governed by lipoidal core whereas very small ionic or polar drugs get clearance through the pumps or gates in protein layer. The protein layer also serves the function of energy transducers, receptors and enzymes. With the help of these receptors, the cell membrane controls the biological communication where it can receive external stimuli and reciprocate them by generating signals. The biochemical functions and bioelectric properties of the cell membrane thus influence the means of communication and mechanisms of drug transport to the cell interior. These transport processes have many important roles to play. They include,

(a) to regulate cell environment and to maintain it favourable for vital cell interaction,

(b) to extract and store fuels and building blocks for maintainance and pipe out toxic metabolites,

(c) to generate, propogate and terminate ionic fluxes that are essential for excitability of nerves and muscles.

By interrupting or interferring in one or more above mentioned roles, many drugs exihibit their therapeutic or toxic effects. These transport processes thus permit, promote and direct the entry of molecules and ions across the membrane. The drug molecule may enter the cell through one of the following ways,

(i) Lipid soluble molecules of any size can easily cross the barrier. Lipid solubility and ease of penetration run parallel with each other upto certain limit. If lipophilicity is increased further, the drug absorption is retarded due to retention of drug molecules in the lipoid core. In most of the cases, it also leads to an increase in toxicity.

(ii) Very small water molecules and ions (e.g. K^+, Cl^-), enter into the cell through the aqueous gates present in the protein layers.

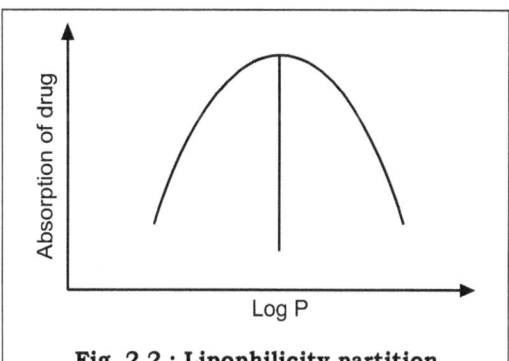

Fig. 2.2 : Lipophilicity partition coefficient

(iii) Water soluble molecules and ions of big size can not diffuse the cells readily. They are transported using specialized transport mechanisms. Their transport is facilitated by the formation of a loose complex with a carrier of protein nature. Such complex can then, easily diffuse across the membrane through lipoidal core to release the free drug. Such transport aided by carrier proteins bears resemblance with enzyme substrate interactions in several ways. For example,

(a) The transport is steriospecific : Such transport mechanisms are very selective and identify the required substrate easily.

(b) It is saturable : Since the number of such carrier proteins is limited, beyond a particular limit the rate of absorption can not be increased by increasing the concentration of drug.

(c) If drug having some structural similarity are given, both drugs will compete for the same binding sites on the carrier protein. This will lead to a sort of competitive inhibition of transport of one drug by another.

(d) Depending upon the utilization of energy or the change in free energy of the transported species, these transport processes are categorized either as passive or active.

The passive transport does not utilize energy whereas the active transport utilises energy and the change in free energy of the transported species is positive. Both these mechanisms may operate simultaneously.

(e) The bioelectrical properties (e.g., electrical potential across the membrane) may influence the transport of charged species.

2.3 PROCESSES IN DRUG ABSORPTION

The main processes by which a drug molecule crosses the natural barriers are –

(a) Simple diffusion

(b) Diffusion of ions across the membrane.

(c) Facilitated diffusion

(d) Active transport

(e) Pore transport

(f) Filtration

(g) Phagocytosis and pinocytosis.

(a) Simple diffusion : The drugs that are absorbed from gastro-intestinal tract cross the intestinal endothelium by simple diffusion. This process can be defined as, it is the flow of drug across a cell-membrane from a solution of higher concentration (C_A) to the solution of lower concentration (C_B) without energy utilization. The important features of simple diffusion are –

(i) It depends and proceeds along a concentration gradient.

(ii) It does not involve energy expenditure.

(iii) Partition coefficient plays a governing role in the transport of lipophilic drugs by this process.

(iv) The transport of ionic or polar drugs by this process is influenced by the difference in pH on both the sides of the membrane.

(v) The process terminates as soon as the concentration of free drug is same on the both sides of the membrane (i.e. at equillibrium).

Simple diffusion can be expressed mathematically using Fick's law, which is as follows :

$$\frac{dm}{dt} = -DA\frac{dc}{dx} \quad ...(2.1)$$

where,

$\frac{dm}{dt}$ = rate of drug diffusion, (T)

A = Surface area of the absorbing membrane

dc = Difference in solute concentration on both sides of the membrane.

dx = membrane thickness

(i.e. $\frac{dc}{dx}$ = concentration gradient)

D = Proportionality constant.

Here D is distribution coefficient. It includes all other factors that may affect drug absorption, e.g. physical properties of drug, nature and condition of the absorbing membrane. Movement of GIT membrane facilitates the contact of drug molecules with the absorbing surface. This leads to an increased absorption of drug. Food in the stomach interferes in the drug absorption, hence drugs that inhibit gastric emptying (e.g. atropine, amphetamine, morphine etc.) may decrease the rate of absorption.

If we replace $\frac{D}{dx}$ by another term, P (i.e. diffusion constant), equation (2.1) can be rewritten as,

$$T = -PA.dc \quad ...(2.2)$$

Fick in 1885, derived this equation and now it is known as Fick's law of diffusion. The minus sign indicates the passage of a drug from the area of higher concentration to the area of lower concentration. The continuous removal of the drug molecules from the serosal side of the intestinal wall by blood circulation tends to keep the concentration on the other side always negligible. This serves as an additional driving force for the transport of drug molecules.

The rate of diffusion of a drug is a function of an area of absorbing surface. It is much greater in the small intestine due to its folding and refolding into valves of Kerckring and villi. It thus provides an absorbing area of some 4500 m^2.

The pH difference across the cell membrane and the dissociation constant (pKa or pKb) of drug also govern the rate of drug absorption. Since most of the drugs are either weak acids or weak bases, their acidity value (ratio of ionised and unionised forms) is dependent upon pH and pKa. Hence, the dissociation constant plays a vital role in determining the ability of drug to cross cell-membranes. e.g. barbiturates.

(b) Diffustion of ions across the membrane : Sometimes, a potential difference develops which leads to polarisation of biological membrane. One side of the membrane becomes positively charged and other side gets associated with negative charges. When a positively charged ion (i.e. cation) comes in contact with the positively charged face of the membrane, it will be kicked away from the membrane. Similarly anions will be driven away by negatively charged face of the membrane in the opposite direction. This process works on the forces of repulsion and naturally does depend upon the electrochemical concentration gradient i.e. on bioelectrical properties of the membrane generated due to polarisation of the membrane.

(c) Facilitated diffusion : As the name indicates, it is an accelerated movement or diffusion of molecules that can not be justified by their lipophilicity or molecular size. This diffusion proceeds generally along the concentration gradients. Such diffusion is termed as downhill diffusion (i.e. from higher concentration to lower concentration). Downhill diffusion requires no net expenditure of energy. A series of acceptor-donar macromolecules carry out this diffusion. But sometimes, facilitated diffusion also trains away molecules against concentration gradient. This is known as uphill diffusion where energy is expended. Uphill diffusion is also termed as Active transport.

The accelerated diffusion of drug molecules is brought out by carrier macromolecules which oscillate back and forth across the cell-membrane. The loose complex is formed between carrier and drug molecule. Arriving at another side, loose complex dissociates to relieve the molecule and carrier returns back to lift again a new passenger. The process to certain degree, exhibits substrate specificity. Facilitated diffusion can be well illustrated with the example of transport antibiotics like, Valinomycin or Gramicidin A. The eight carbonyl oxygens of the four valine residues in Valinomycin skeleton, face inward, forming a cage within which, potassium ions can easily be held by co-ordinate bonds. Thus, potassium ions can get entry through the hydrophobic interior of the membrane and enjoy 'sound-sleep' within a mosaic of hydrophobic side chain of the antibiotic. Gramicidin A acts as transport antibiotic by forming channels that transverse the membrane.

Limitations of this process include :

(a) its saturable nature due to limited number of carrier macromolecules and

(b) competitive inhibition of transport of one drug by the presence of another drug bearing similar structural features.

(d) Active transport : Some substances diffuse across the biological membrane at much more faster rate that can not be accounted on the basis of their lipid solubility or molecule size. This transport which proceeds against the concentration gradient and utilizes a series of specilized carrier moieties is termed as Active transport of drug.

This carrier aided transport system is characterized by

(i) Utilization of energy supplied by metabolic activity of membrane,

(ii) Proceeds against the concentration gradient.

(iii) Absorption rate is independant of concentration.

The mechanisms that bring these and similar movements are often termed as pumps, e.g. Ca^{++} ATPase pump, Na^+-K^+-ATPase pump etc. Under the conditions of unavailability of energy, the material thus transported, drifts back again until equilibrium on both sides of the barrier reaches.

Active transport is identical in most of the aspects with facilitated transport. The only difference exists between facilitated transport and active transport is, former does not utilize energy (i.e. proceeds along concentration gradient) i.e., down bill diffusion. Whereas the latter process proceeds against the concentration gradient i.e. uphill diffusion and needs energy consumption. In the case of ionic molecules, transport may occur against an electrochemical potential gradient. The exact mechanism of active-transport is still not clear but it would appear that, on the mucosal surface side of GIT, carrier proteins forms a loose complex with the drug molecule. This complex trains away

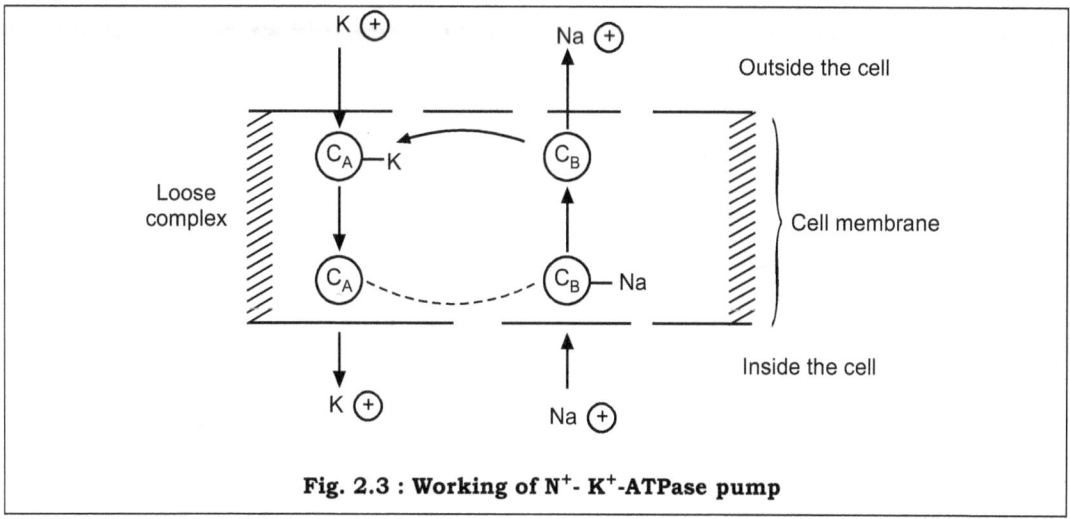

Fig. 2.3 : Working of N^+-K^+-ATPase pump

the drug molecule to the serosal side where the complex dissociates to relieve its passenger. The carrier may then return back to the mucosal surface empty handed or may pick up another molecule during its journey back to mucosal side. Before picking up another molecule, it is involved in an energy consuming chemical reaction that converts the carrier protein (C_A) into a new form (C_B). The new form C_B, releases that molecule to mucosal side and undergoes a spontaneous change to its original form, C_A.

Limitations of Active Transport :

(a) Active transport is site specific as well as a substrate specific process. It means that special carrier channels are appointed to carry particular type of chemical structures. Similarly these substrates are usually absorbed from their corresponding specific sites located in a limited segment of the small intestine. For example, ileum is a site of diffusion for bile acids.

(b) Since carrier channels with a specific carrier molecules are allotted to transport drugs from particular chemical structural class, the carrier system becomes saturated,

(i) If the drug is present at higher concentration or /and

(ii) If another substrate of close structural similarity is simultaneously administered.

(c) Substrates that interfere with cell-metabolism or in energy generation, may cause non-competitive inhibition of active transport system.

Active transport plays an important role in renal tubule reabsorption, secretion of H^+ into the stomach, accumulation of iodide ions in the thyroid gland, absorption of glucose, amino acids, some vitamins and metabolites in intestine, absorption processes across placenta and blood brain barrier.

The active transport of glucose across biological membrane is aided by sodium ions. The glucose molecule and sodium ion both, bind to a specific carrier protein. This complex when enters the cell, the sodium ion is then effluxed out through the operation of Na^+-K^+- ATPase pump. Such aided type of transport mechanism is termed as co-transport.

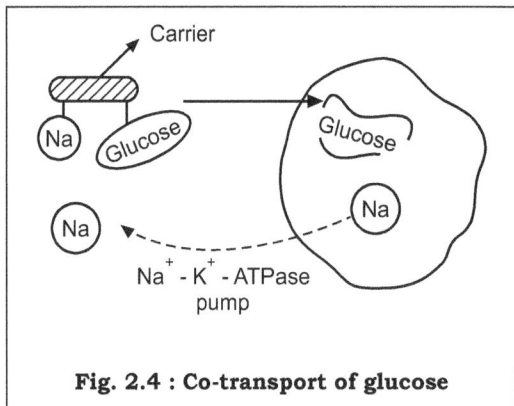

Fig. 2.4 : Co-transport of glucose

Na^+-K^+- ATPase pump is widely distributed in the cell membranes and especially present in high number in different secretory cells alongwith excitable tissue such as nerve and muscle cell. It is mainly concerned with the transport of amino acid and glucose, nerve excitability and maintainance of cell-volume. The enzyme, Na^+-K^+-ATPase was discovered in 1957 by Jens Skou in the cell-membrane. It hydrolyses ATP molecule to release energy necessary for functioning of this pump. The enzyme and the pump, both are tightly bound with the plasma membrane. The hydrolysis of ATP molecule needs the presence of Na^+, K^+ and Mg^{++} ions.

The phosphorylation reaction is catalysed by Na^+ and Mg^{++} ions whereas the dephosphorylation needs the presence of K^+ ions.

The Na^+-K^+-ATPase enzyme is the pharmacological receptor for digitalis. Digitalis like drugs bind to the external surface of the enzyme. Cardiac glycosides induce conformational changes and inhibit dephosphorylation reaction of the Na^+ - K^+ - ATPase enzyme.

(e) Pore transport : The aqueous filled pores or channels are present across the cell-membrane. The diffusion of small sized polar molecules is mainly governed by these channels. The diameter of these pores was estimated to be near about 4°A which serves as a major limitation to the transport process. It is an example of passive diffusion where the rate of transport depends upon the concentration of drug and does not utilize energy. Various electrolytes, urea, low molecular weight sugars etc. are transported by this mechanism.

(f) Filtration : The natural membrane consists of numerous pores of different sizes embedded in it, which generally control the diffusion of small sized molecules of water-soluble or lipid-insoluble substances. If a mechanical pressure (hydrostatic pressure) is imposed on the biological membrane, the drug molecules will ooze out to the other side. Such transport mechanism is termed as filtration . It means,

Filtration = Simple diffusion + Hydrostatic pressure

The hydrostatic force arises due to the pressure of a drug solution (solvent drug) at one side of the membrane which imposes its pressure at the site of absorption. These pores may have electrical charges that may influence the diffusion of charged bodies, like cations or anions.

In summary, there are then, three possible routes through which a polar substance can be passively transported across a membrane. These are —

(i) Diffusion down a concentration gradient (polar transport)

(ii) Diffusion down a gradient of electric potential (ion transport)

(iii) Filtration

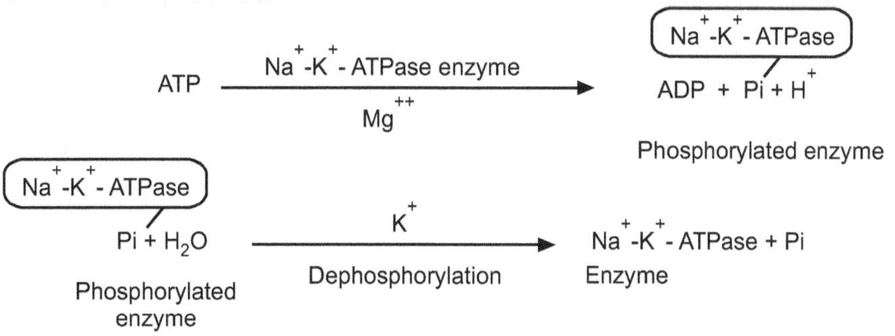

$$ATP \xrightarrow[Mg^{++}]{Na^+-K^+-ATPase\ enzyme} \boxed{Na^+-K^+-ATPase} + ADP + Pi + H^+$$

Phosphorylated enzyme

$$\boxed{Na^+-K^+-ATPase} + Pi + H_2O \xrightarrow{K^+} Na^+-K^+-ATPase + Pi$$

Phosphorylated enzyme   Dephosphorylation   Enzyme

Fig. 2.5

(g) Phagocytosis and Pinocytosis : Droplets of extracellular fluid alongwith solute molecules are carried into the cell through the formation of vacuoles.

Phagocytosis is described as cell eating process whereas pinocytosis is referred as cell drinking process. Both these processes are the examples of engulfing of extracellular fluid and substances dissolved in it. Phagocytosis can carry relatively macromolecules (such as proteins) into the cell, whereas pinocytosis has limitation for carrying large molecules.

Principle behind these processes has been exploited to develop new drug delivery system. Recently techniques have been developed to envelope drug molecules by 'liposomes' which can be engulfed by the cells through pinocytosis.

2.4 DISTRIBUTION OF DRUGS

If a drug is administered into the body, blood circulation serves as a transport system for it, to reach at its site of action. The drug diffuses to different compartments of the body. Water constitutes an important part of these body compartments. On an average water makes up about 70% of the adult body mass. Out of about 50 litres of water present in the body, about 25 litres of water is present in the intracellular fluid while remaining 25 litres is a part of extracellular fluid.

In adult male and female, the figures describing various aqueous compartments differ slightly. Once a drug is administered into the body, it diffuses into various body compartments. The concentration of a free drug present in the plasma water is always in equillibrium to the drug concentration present in the tissues. Hence calculation of drug concenration in the plasma water gives us an idea about the effective drug concentration. The latter is approximately estimated by calculating 'Apparent volume

Table 2.1

Body Compartment	Amount of Water Present in Litre
1. Intracellular fluid	25.0
2. Extracellular fluid	
(a) Blood plasma	05.0
(b) Fluid Interstitial	15.0
(c) Inaccessible water present in bone tissue	05.0
	50.0 litre

of distribution' (Vd) of a drug. It is defined as 'the fluid volume in which a drug seems to be dissolved'.

A known amount of drug is administered intravascularly. Sufficient time (e.g., 1 hour) is allowed to pass, for proper drug distribution and equilibration to occur. Then a sample of blood is analysed to determine the drug concentration in the plasma water.

Apparent volume of distribution of a drug (Vd)

$$= \frac{\text{Total amount of drug administered (mg) intravascularly}}{\text{Drug present in plasma water (mg/L)}}$$

This calculation assumes that the drug is not inactivated or degraded during metabolism or is not lost through protein binding or excretion.

The Vd calculation gives an idea about distribution pattern of a drug. For example, a drug having Vd of approximately 12 L is well distributed throughout the extracellular fluid. Such drug is unable to penetrate the cell due to low concentration of a drug per unit volume of extracellular fluid. With some restriction, one can say that, greater the Vd value, greater is the diffusibility of the drug e.g., highly lipophilic drugs like, thiopental, cyclopropane. Considerable fraction of such drugs is stored in fat depots. Similarly, drugs with Vd value of 3L are distributed only in the limited areas of the body, like, vascular compartments.

Thiocyanate, radioactive iodide, sucrose, insulin and radioactive bromide salts are routinely used in Vd calculations to estimate the extracellular fluid volume.

Factors Affecting Apparent Volume of Distribution:

Following are the factors that influence the distribution of a drug in the body.

(i) capacity of drug to get bind with plasma proteins.
(ii) the partition coefficient of a drug.
(iii) pKa or pKb values of a drug.
(iv) rate of blood flow to particular tissue.
(v) tissue's perfusion rate
(vi) the extent of capillary permeability at particular tissue.
(vii) the extent of drug loss in metabolism and excretion.

Table 2.2

Drugs	Vd value (litres)	Compartments in which drug is distributed
1. Heparin, furosemide, clofibrate	5	Vascular system
2. Tolbutamide, ampicillin, aspirin, gentamycin	10-20	Plasma water and interstitial fluid
3. Methyldopa, prednisolone, nitroglycerin	21-45	Throught extracellular fluid
4. Propranolol, nortriptylene, imipramine	> 70	Binding or sequestration of the drug

Similarly the ratio of extracellular fluid volume to tissue water differs from tissue to tissue. This may also affect Vd calculation of the drug. The vital organs like, liver, kidney and brain are enjoying a rich blood supply. This will lead to a more rapid distribution of drug from the plasma into the interstitial fluid of these organs.

Limitations in the Interpretation of Vd Values :

(a) In calculation of Vd value, it is supposed that very little or no drug is deactivated during metabolism or is lost through tissue binding or excretion. This ideal behaviour is not observed by drugs so that no real distribution pattern of drug can be guessed by using Vd value.

(b) Most of the drugs get bound with plasma proteins or tissue components in a form of reversible complex. This leads to a reduction in the free drug concentration present in the plasma-water. If a substantial fraction of the drug is bound to plasma protein, the reversible nature of this binding may lead to fluctuations in concentration of drug in various body compartments. It generates errors in the calculation of Vd values.

(c) Lipophilic drugs (e.g. thiopental, cyclopropane), have an affinity for the fatty tissues of the body. They may get extensively stored in the fat depots due to their high partition coefficient. As a result, their Vd values are very much greater than the entire fluid volume of the body.

The major fraction of the dose administrered, is shared by the prominent organs like heart, kidney, liver and brain. This occurs during the first or initial phase of distribution. In a complex biological system like that of human body, the extent of drug absorption is determined by

(a) The physico-chemical properties of the drug.

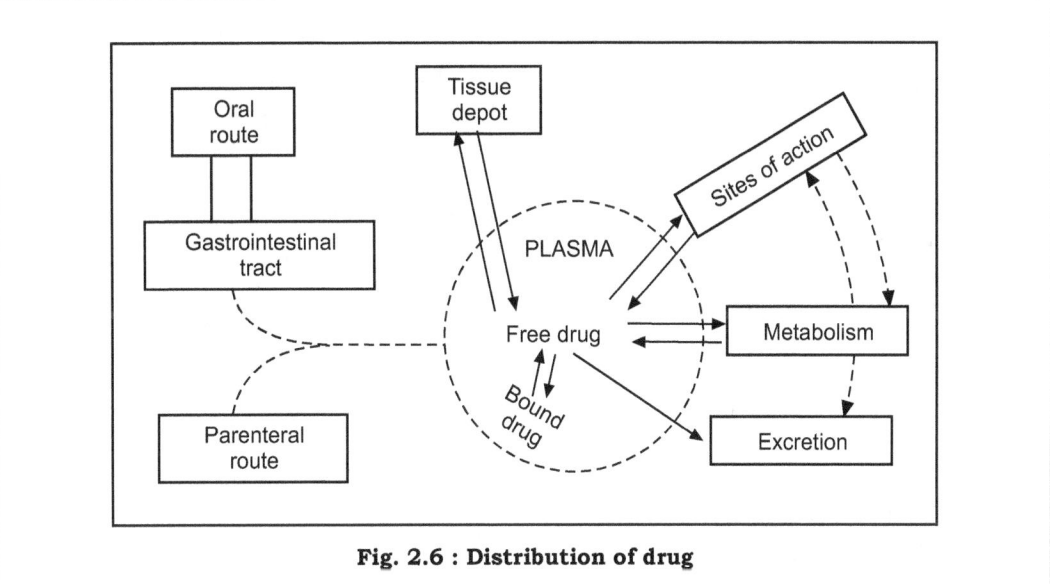

Fig. 2.6 : Distribution of drug

(b) Factors related with physiology of the patient. Once the drug reaches to its site of action, the other probable routes which lead to inactivation of drug can he categorised as under :

(i) A considerable amount of drug may be retained by reversible storage depots.

(ii) The drug may undergo certain metabolic alteration by biological enzyme system that may result into more or less active form.

(iii) Before a drug gets a chance to act on its site of action, it may be excreted unchanged or in the form of its metabolite.

2.5 STORAGE DEPOTS

Plasma proteins, certain tissues, neutral fat, bone and transcellular fluids (gastrointestinal tract, bronchi, gland and kidney) are found to act as drug reservoirs or storage sites for the drug.

The drug stored in these depots is in equilibrium with that in plasma and is released as the plasma concentration falls below its therapeutic concentration. Thus, plasma concentration of the drug is maintained, which sustains and prolongs the duration of action of the drug.

(i) Plasma proteins : Approximately 6.5% of blood constitutes protein fraction, of which about 50% is albumin. Most of the drugs bind to plasma proteins in the albumin fraction; binding to other plasma proteins, generally occur to a much less extent. Albumin has a net negative charge but can interact with anions as well. The binding generally involves ion-ion interactions that is further strengthened by the presence of secondary bindings like hydrogen bonding, Vander Waal's forces, etc. The protein binding is found to be a reversible process.

Protein binding reduces diffusion of the drug to the sites of action, metabolism and excretion. The size of drug-protein complex is larger and hence can not pass through glomerular filtration which prolongs its duration of action. Protein binding also delays the metabolism of the drug.

(ii) Tissue reservoirs : Since fat constituents around 10% (starvation) to 50% of the total body weight, it serves as a main storage site for drugs having a high partition coefficient (lipophilicity). e.g. barbiturate, adrenergic blockers, neuromuscular blocking agent (Hexafluoronium) etc.

(iii) Bone : Heavy metals (like lead or radium), divalent metal ions, chelating agents and antibiotics (tetracycline group) are the examples of the compounds which are retained by bones.

2.6 EXCRETION OF DRUGS

The termination of drug effect is caused by biotransformation (i.e., alteration in the structure of a drug due to the metabolic enzymes or due to other biochemical processes) and excretion.

Many weak acids or basic drugs do not present in their ionized form. Similarly many drugs are highly lipophilic in nature. These features assure slow elimination of such drugs. Metabolism usually tends to produce such drug metabolites which are more polar and hence can be excreted readily from the body.

For the most part, kidneys serve as a major site of elimination of drugs and their metabolites from the body. One or more of the transport systems - filtration, diffusion, secretion or active transport may be employed for excretion. Other sites like, milk, saliva, sweat, tears, bile, intestine, lungs and skin also participate. The various volatile anaesthetics, alcohol, paraaldehyde and other clinically used gaseous inhalants are excreted by lungs. Skin excretes the metalloids like, Arsenic and Lead in minute quantities. Occurrence of skin rashes may be due to the deposition of Arsenic in the hair follicles. If lactating mothers are placed under the treatment of drugs like, morphine, sulphonamides or certain antibiotics, these drugs may be excreted out in the milk. Heavy metals and purgatives like cascara sagarda and senna are reported to be excreted from intestine, alongwith the faeces. Whereas certain drugs like, Erythromycin and Novobiocin are excreted in the bile juices.

Little quantity of drug is excreted by the organs other than kidneys. Hence their contribution in the elimination process is not considerable.

PHARMACODYNAMIC ASPECTS OF DRUG ACTION

3.1 INTRODUCTION

The process by which a drug is released in the body from its dosage form is known as 'absorption'. Since the duration and the intensity of drug action is a function of rate at which the drug is absorbed, an understanding of the factors which influence the rate of absorption of drug is necessary.

Factors affecting accessibility of drug to the active sites :

(i) Concentration of the drug administered.
(ii) Physical state of the drug.
(iii) Particle size.
(iv) Route of administration.
(v) Drug solubility.
(vi) Physico-chemical parameters of drug.
(vii) Area of absorbing surface.
(viii) Factors related with physiology of the patient.
(ix) Factors related with dosage form.

3.2 PHYSICO-CHEMICAL PARAMETERS AND DRUG ACTION

Physico-chemical parameters of the drug play an important role in governing the rate of absorption. These parameters include; Lipid solubility, dissociation constant, pH-partition theory, dissolution rate, Donnan membrane equilibrium principle, salt form, effective surface areas, crystal form, complexation, viscosity, surface active agents and drug stability in gastrointestinal tract. These parameters explain effects of bioactive compounds. The effect of modifications in the molecular structure of a drug can be interpreted in terms of its physico-chemical parameters involved. These parameters are closely related to the interaction of the drug with its environment.

According to E.J. Ariens, the physico-chemical parameters of a drug can be divided into three main categories.

(a) Parameters which are an expression of the hydrophobic aggregation forces in operation at site of action:

These includes partition coefficient, surface activity, Rf value and the partial vapour pressure of a drug solution. The hydrophobic forces represented by these parameters give relatively large contribution to binding energy. By variation in the size of the groups, one can gradually change the partition coefficient of drug in body compartments.

(b) Parameters that are an expression of the charge distribution in the molecule and thus of the electrostatic (ionic) forces in operation at the site of action :

These parameters include, redox potential, the base or acid dissociation constants, the electronic polarization, dipole movements, an inductive field effect and the resonance effect (especially in conjugated systems), the capacity of chelate formation and H-bond formation and finally the characteristics in IR and NMR spectra. Electrostatic forces represented by these parameters give a relatively low contribution to binding energy. They contribute more to the selectivity in the drug-receptor interactions and are essentially involved in substrate activation in enzymes and conformational orientation necessary for the induction of a stimulus in the macromolecular receptor skeleton.

(c) Parameters that are an expression of 'Spacial arrangement' of the molecule :

These parameters represent spacial arrangement of various groups in the drug molecule and play a role in the possible steric hindrance at the intramolecular level. The location, size, volume and charge of particular groups are described by these parameters. They are also termed as steric parameters.

The intensity of the pharmacological response elicited by many drugs is probably directly related to the concentration, or activity of a drug in the immediate vicinity of the receptor site in the body. Since it is not possible to measure this concentration directly, the study of physico-chemical parameters presents a picture of indirect measurements of the concentration of a drug at receptor site. It follows, therefore that drug molecules exert their effects by influencing receptor sites in the living systems through their physico-chemical parameters.

$$\text{Biological response of drugs} = f(\text{physicochemical parameters of drug})$$

$$= f(\text{hydrophobic forces} + \text{eleotronic forces} + \text{steric forces})$$

... (3.1)

(I) Parameters which are an Expression of the Hydrophobic Aggregation Forces :

(i) Lipophilicity : The relationship of lipophilicity with narcotic activity dates back to almost a century. Using a series of simple neutral organic compounds, Meyer and Overton, postulated the parallelism between, the values of partition coefficients and narcotic potencies of these agents.

The partition coefficient value (π) expresses the relative free energy change occurring when a drug molecule moves from one phase to another. It means, a positive value of π suggests that the drug favours organic (lipoidal) layer while a negative value implies that it prefers an aqueous phase. An excellent correlation between partition coefficients determined in CCl_4 / 0.1 N HCl solvent system and gastric absorption rate for different barbiturates was established.

The partition coefficient determined in the solvent system having pH nearly in the range of pH at the site of absorption gives a better understanding of drug absorption. Hence partition coefficient serves as a good physicochemical guide to estimate % absorption of the drug.

Increase in lipophilicity of a drug, beyond its optimum (i.e. log P_o), leads to its deposition into the first lipoidal biomembrane or macromolecule with which, it comes in contact. A sort of parabolic relationship (Fig. 2.2) exists between biological activity and partition coefficient values of drugs whose biological activity is dependent mainly upon lipophilicity (e.g. CNS depressants). This implies that drugs having log P, far fluctuating from optimum log P value, in either direction, would not be effective CNS depressants, other forces being equal. Similarly the ionization of drug to a certain extent does not affect the narcotic activity if it is compensated with enough lipophilicity. Table 3.2 encloses a survey of different categories of drugs (with special attention to CNS acting drugs) and the relationship of their activity with the log P_o value of respective class.

Table 3.1

	Barbiturate	Partition coefficient	% absorption
1.	Barbital	0.7	12
2.	Phenobarbital	4.9	17
3.	Butethal	11.7	24
4.	Cyclobarbitone	13.9	24
5.	Pentobarbital	28.0	30
6.	Secobarbital	50.7	40

Table 3.2

	Class	Log P_o	Comment
1.	Volatile anaesthetics	2.35	At pH = 7.4
2.	Hypnotics - Barbiturates - Carbamates - Alcohols	Near 2.00	At pH = 7.4
3.	Nitrous oxide	0.43	At pH = 7.4
4.	Ether	0.89	At pH = 7.4
5.	Antipsychotic agent	2.40 ± 0.8	At pH = 7.4
6.	Tricyclic antidepressants	2.15 ± 0.7	At pH = 7.4
7.	Hallucinogens - LSD analogs - Phenylamines - Amphetamines	3.14	At pH = 6
8.	Steroids - Testosterone - Progesterone - Deoxycorticosterone	 3.29 3.87 3.08	Should possess CNS depressant activity

From the above table, it can be concluded that the log values in the range of 1.5 to 3.0, serve as a passport for the easy entry into the brain, where these drugs may produce sedative effects.

This statement serves as an important clue in designing the drugs where CNS depression is an undesirable effect. e.g. antihistamines. New drugs can be developed utilizing the lipophilicity, as minimum as possible and thus avoiding the log P values in the range of 1.5 - 3.00.

Lipophilicity governs the CNS penetration of a drug. Certain drugs disturb the brain function and may exhibit lethal effects. Toxicity of such agents was found to mainly governed by their lipophilic character. In summary, log P is a parameter of major importance in drug development.

Log P Calculations :

(a) can supply guidelines in the development of novel bioactive agents and

(b) become useful in toxicological estimations.

(ii) Partial vapour pressure of a drug solution : This parameter is of importance in describing the activity of structurally nonspecific drugs. These drugs do not need receptors for their activity and hence they enjoy a wide structural variations. Their SAR can not be framed out so their biological effects are defined in terms of the physical properties of drugs involved. Volatile anesthetics constitute an example from this category. Cyclopropane, diethyl ether, chloroform and nitrous oxide, though having different structures, all are good general anesthetics.

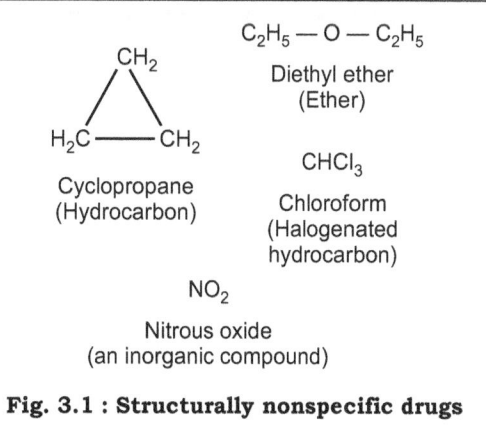

Fig. 3.1 : Structurally nonspecific drugs

The structurally nonspecific drugs do not act on specific receptors. Instead, they penetrate and accumulate into the cell membranes. They interfere, by chemical or physical means, with enzyme systems, may change the permeability of the membrane (Opening or closing the channels or pores) to ions and may modify carrier transport systems, or other fundamental cellular processes.

Ferguson suggested in 1939 that the potency of structurally nonspecific drugs was governed by their thermodynamic activity. This quantity is a measure of the proportion of the molecules which are free to react with enzyme systems, nerve membranes and other biologically important sites. The molecules which are not free to act in this way, are reacting with one another, with the molecules of the solvent or with the molecules of other solutes. It follows, therefore, that the thermodynamic activity of a drug in solution is not determined entirely by its total concentration. In the case of volatile anesthetics administered with air or oxygen, the thermodynamic activity is proportional to the relative saturation of a drug (a).

The relative saturation of drug is defined as P_t/P_o for volatile drugs and gases.

Relative saturation (a) = P_t/P_o ...(3.2)

Where,

P_t = Partial pressure of a drug in solution or in the gaseous mixture and

P_o = Vapour pressure of the pure drug at the same temperature.

For non-volatile drugs of limited solubility, the relative saturation (a), is given by

Relative saturation (a) = S_t/S_o, ...(3.3)

S_t = Molar concentration required to produce the biological effect and

S_o = Molar solubility of the drug.

Ferguson's theory predicts that the anaesthetic agents will show the same degree of biological activity if their concentrations are adjusted so that their thermodynamic activities are equal (or relative saturation values (a) are equal). This theory is equally applicable to substances other than anesthetics and it was originally applied to insecticides and antibacterial substances. Following tables illustrates the application of Ferguson's principle. i.e. Compounds with different structural features exhibit the same biological activity to the same extent, if their relative saturation values are in the same range.

Table 3.3 : Relative saturation values of some anesthetics

Compound	Partial pressure (At anesthetic concentration) (P_t)	Vapour Pressure (P_o)	Relative Saturation (P_t/P_o)
Nitrous oxide	760	59,300	0.01
Ethylene	610	49,500	0.01
Acetylene	495	5,17,000	0.01
Ethyl chloride	38	1,780	0.02

Table 3.4 : Bactericidal concentrations of miscellaneous organic compounds toward Salmonella typhosa

Compound	Bactericidal concentration (S_t)	Solubility (S_o)	Relative saturation (S_t/S_o)
Thymol	0.0022	0.0057	0.38
Aniline	0.17	0.40	0.44
Propanaldehyde	1.08	2.88	0.37
Methyl ethyl ketone	1.25	3.13	0.40
Cyclohexanol	0.18	0.38	0.47

(II) Parameters that are an Expression of the Charge Distribution in the Molecule :

(i) Ionization : Most of the drugs are either weak acids or weak bases. The rate of absorption of a drug which is capable of existing both, in ionized and unionized form, is dependent upon the concentration of its unionized form rather than on its concentration.

The unionized form is a function of both, dissociation constant (pKa or negative logarithm of acidic dissociation constant) and the pH of the environment at the site of action. The relationship is represented by Henderson-Hasselbach equation.

For acidic drugs

$$pKa - pH = \log(C_u/C_i) \quad ...(3.4)$$

For basic drugs

$$pKa - pH = \log(C_i/C_u) \quad ...(3.5)$$

Where, C_i and C_u are the concentration of the ionized and unionized drug fractions, respectively. Following tables illustrate an effect of pH on the intestinal absorption of weak acids and weak bases in rat.

Table 3.5

Drug	pKa	% absorption
Acidic drugs :		
o-nitrobenzoic acid	2.2	00
Salicylic acid	3.0	59
5-nitrosalicylic acid	2.3	6.0
Barbital	7.8	28
Basic drugs:		
Ephedrine	9.7	4.0
m-nitroanilline	2.5	76
Tolazolin	10.3	7.0

Table 3.6 : pKa values of some drugs

Acidic drugs	pKa scale	Basic drugs
Sulphonic acids	1	Antipyrin
Benzyl penicillin	3	
Aspirin	3	
Benzoic acid	4	
Phenyl butazone	4	
	5	Amidopyrin
Sulphadiazine	7	Reserpine
Barbital	8	Morphine
Sulphapyridine	8	Quinine
Diphenhydantoin	9	Procaine

Table 3.7

Drugs	pKa	% absorption pH 1	% absorption pH 8
1. Phenolsuphothalin	< 2.0	00	00
2. Salicylic acid	3.0	61	31
3. Thiopental	7.6	46	--
4. Secobarbital	7.8	30	--
5. Caeffine	0.8	24	--
6. Antipyrine	1.4	14	--
7. Aniline	4.6	06	56
8. Dextromorphan	9.2	00	16
9. Quinine	8.4	00	18

It can be seen that a solution of weak acid, aspirin (pKa = 3.5) in the stomach (pH = 1.0) will be more than 99% unionized and since unionized form is lipid soluble, it will get more easily absorbed in the stomach. Quinine, a weak base (pKa = 8.5) in solution in stomach (pH = 1.0) would have only one out of 10,000,000 molecules in unionized state, hence would be most unabsorbable in stomach. Similar type of comparison has been tabulated in the table 3.7. The table illustrates the percentage absorption of various acidic and basic drugs at regions having pH 1 and pH 8.

From the above table, it is clear that the % absorption is high in cases where pKa value of a drug and pH value at the site of absorption favour the predominance of unionized form of the drug. Inspite of the fact that certain drugs exist in unionized state, they are poorly absorbed due to their low lipid solubility. The distribution or partition coefficient of drug in unionized state between fat-like solvents (such as chloroform) and water or an aqueous buffer mixture, nearly at the pH of the site of absorption gives an idea about the lipophilicity of the drug. The co-ordinated effect of pKa and lipid solubility of a drug on its absorption led to the development of erythromycin propionate. The pKa value to erythromycin is 8.6 while that of ester is 6.9. Since the partition coefficient of ester form is about 180 times larger than of erythromycin, the ester yields 2-4 times higher blood level than does erythromycin. These observations are in accordance to Handerson-Hasselbach equation.

For rapid intestinal absorption of a weakly acidic drug, a minimum pKa value in the range of 3 is sufficient. Weak basic drugs, for rapid intestinal absorption, on the other hand, would need pKa value approximately of 8. Assuming a mean bulk pH of 6.5 for intestinal environment, minimum ratio of unionized to ionized fractions of total drug concentration, required for rapid absorption, would be

1: 3000 for weak acidic drugs.

1: 30 for weak basic drugs.

This difference in the ratio of unionised to ionised fractions indicates that the intestinal barrier is more permeable to the ionized form of weak acids than to the ionized form of weak bases. This observation is contradictory to the concept of a passive lipoidal sieve model of a barrier. To avoid this confusion, it was assumed that, a zone with an effective or virtual pH of 5.3 may be located at the surface of intestinal mucosa that governs the degree of ionization of a drug. In the light of this assumption now the ratio of unionized to ionized drug molecules would be 1: 3000 for both acidic and basic drugs.

(ii) Complexation : Complexation offers a protection against increased solubility and degradation or metabolism to drug. When the drug is administered into the body, a fraction of it, forms a complex with a suitable agent. Generally such reactions are of reversible nature. The magnitude of dissociation constant controls the equilibrium between complex drug and free drug. Such complexes may also arise unintentionally as a result of drug interaction with an excipient or with endogenous substances. Complexes can not cross the natural membrane barriers hence render the drug biologically ineffective. Thus, extent of complex formation for a drug affects the bioavailability of the drug. The rate of absorption is therefore, totally dependent upon the concentration of free drug molecule, i.e. the diffusible drug.

Due to the reversibility of complexation, there always exists an equilibrium between the free drug and the drug complex. Such equilibrium is represented below :

$$\text{Drug + Complexing agent} \rightleftharpoons \text{Drug complex} \quad \ldots (3.6)$$

Complexation reduces the rate of absorption of the drug but does not affect the total availability of it, because the absorption of the free drug molecules shifts the equilibrium to the left causing the free drug molecule to be released from the drug complex.

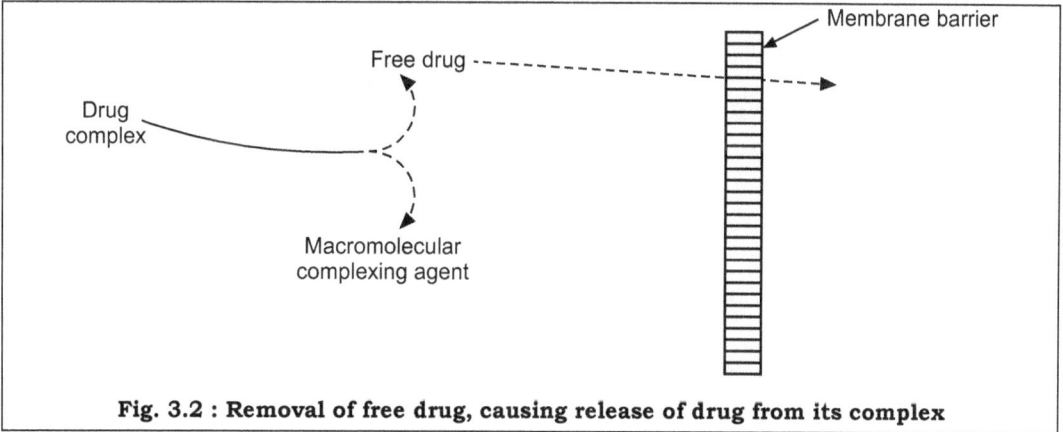

Fig. 3.2 : **Removal of free drug, causing release of drug from its complex**

Examples of Drug-macromolecule complex formation :

(a) Phenobarbital forms a nonabsorbable complex with polyethylene glycol - 4000. The dissosiation rate of phenobarbital tablets containing PEG - 4000, is only one-third to that of control tablets.

(b) Amphetamine carboxymethyl-cellulose is yet another example of nonabsorbable complex.

(c) Tetracycline family is known for its complex forming ability with divalent and trivalent cations, like Ca^{++} ions. It leads to retention of a fraction of a drug into ineffective form.

(d) Calcium is an important constituent of the mucous membrane of GIT. The complexation of this calcium with agents like, EDTA, increases the permeability of the membrane, probably due to widening of space between closely placed epithelial cells by removal of intermittently placed Ca^{++} ions. Therefore, the presence of EDTA, increases the absorption of mannitol, quaternary ammonium compounds of sulfanilic acids and heparin, which are very poorly absorbed in ordinary conditions.

(iii) Hydrogen bonding : Electronegative atoms when present in the structure of a drug, have a tendency to form either intramolecular or intermolecular hydrogen bonds with the nearby hydrogen atoms. Such electronegative atoms include, F, Cl, Br, I, N, O and S.

Though H-bonds are relatively weak bonds their presence may have profound effects on the biological activity of a drug e.g.

(a) 1-Phenyl -3-methyl -5-pyrazolone shows no analgesic properties while 1 phenyl -2,3-dimethyl-5-pyrazolone (Antipyrine) is a well known analgesic agent. This effect appears to be best explained by the fact that the first compound through intermolecular H-bonding forms a linear polymer.

The resulting large attractive force between the molecules lowers the solubility, especially in the nonpolar solvents which are not capable of breaking the H-bonds.

On the other hand, antipyrine can not form H-bonds and has only comparatively weak attractive forces between its molecules and hence it is freely soluble in nonpolar solvents. Thus, antipyrine is adequately soluble in both polar and nonpolar solvents and has the proper partition characteristics to penetrate the CNS.

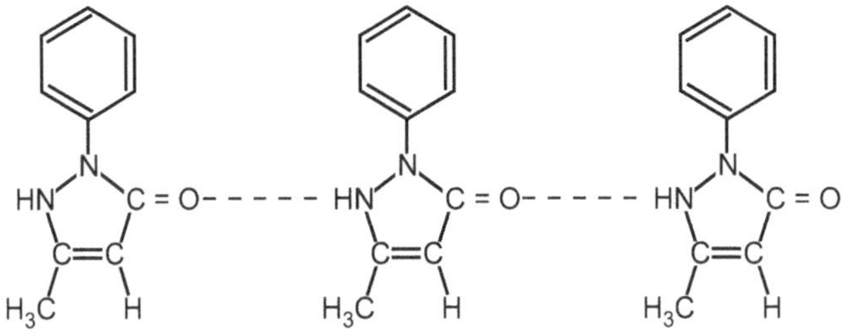

Intermolecular hydrogen bonding
1-Phenyl-3-methyl-5-pyrazolone

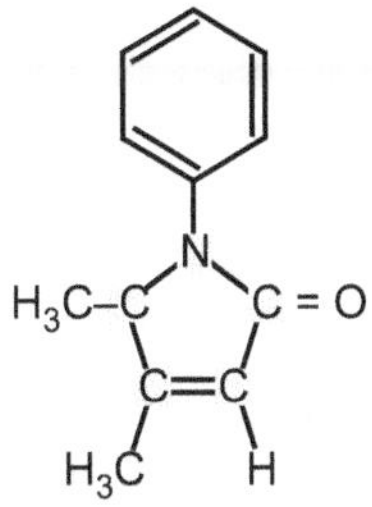

1-Phenyl-2,3-dimethyl-5 pyrazolone (Antipyrine)

(b) Salicylic acid (O-hydroxy benzoic acid) has quite an appreciable antibacterial activity, but the para isomer (P-hydroxybenzoic acid) is inactive. The reason may be the ability of salicylic acid to form intramolecular H-bonds.

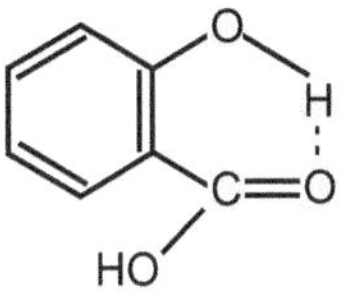

Salicylic acid

The m and p isomer can form only intermoleculear H-bonds.

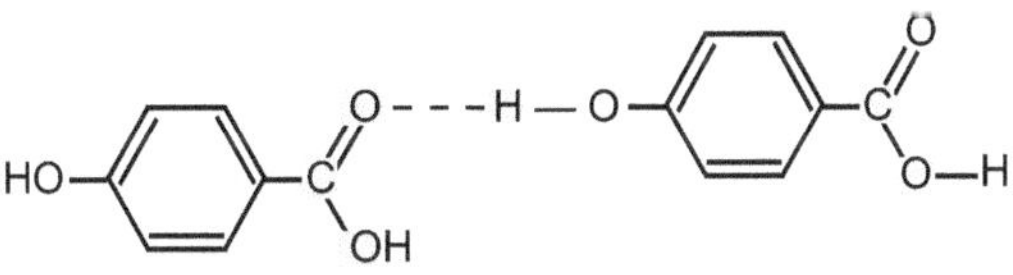

p-Hydroxybenzoic acid (dimer)

Salicylic acid is less soluble in water than the p-isomer and its partition coefficient (benzene / water) is approximately 300 times greater, while p-hydroxy benzoic acid has low partition coefficient and hence low antibacterial activity. In salicylic acid, intramolecular H-bond has the phenolic hydroxyl group masked but the carboxylic acid group is free and can function as an antibacterial agent similar to benzoic acid.

(c) The nucleic acids, fundamental reproductive units of cells, provide an important example of molecules held together by specific hydrogen bonds. The genetic code of the cell, which constitutes the instruction for the synthesis of the cell's proteins, is contained in the cell nucleus, in the form of DNA. The code consists of sequences of four purine and pyrimidine bases, like adenine-thymine; guanine-cytosine. These purine pyrimidine pairs are held together by specific hydrogen bonds.

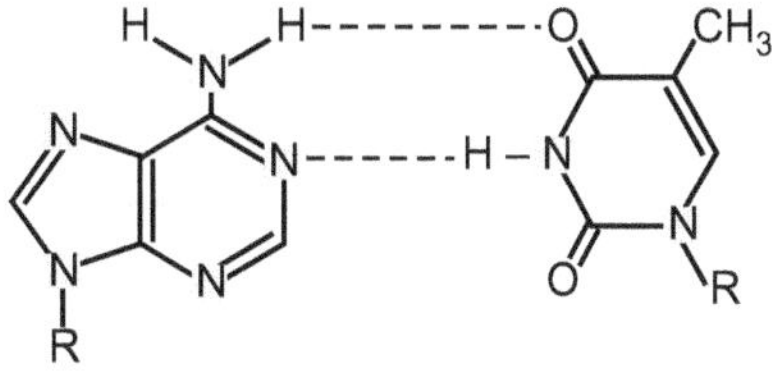

Adenine **Thymine**

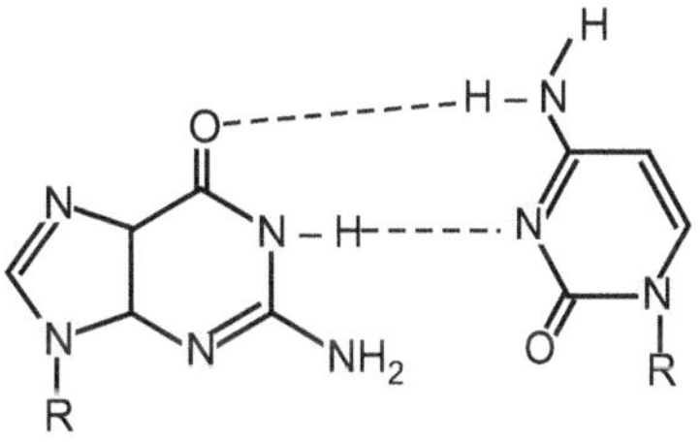

Guanine **Cytosine**

Thus, H-bonds play a key role in maintaining the structural integrity of the base pairs of DNA.

(iv) Oxidation-Reduction potentials : The tendency of a compound to give or to receive electrons, is measured quantitatively by its oxidation-reduction potential or redox potential.

Since the oxidation-reduction potential applies to a single reversible ionic equilibrium which does not exist in a living organisms, the correlation between redox potential and biological activity can only be drawn for the compounds of very similar structure and physical properties. Following are the examples :

(a) The optimum bacteriostatic activity in quinones is associated with the redox potential at + 0.03 volt, when tested against Staph aureus.

(b) The biological activity of riboflavin is due to its ability to accept electrons and is reduced to the dihydro form. This reaction has a potential of $E_o = -0.185$ volt. By retaining most of the structural features and altering its redox potential, one may develop compounds antagonistic to riboflavin. Kuhn prepared the analogue, in which the two methyl groups of riboflavin were replaced by chlorines and having a potential of $E_o = -0.095$ volt. Its antagonistic properties are due to the dichloro-dihydro form, being a weaker reducing agent than the dihydro form of riboflavin. It may be absorbed at specific receptor sites but not have a negative enough potential to carry out the biological reductions of riboflavin.

Riboflavin, $E_o = -0.185$ V

Riboflavin analogue, $E_o = -0.095$ V

(c) The optimum anthelmintic activity in a series of substituted phenothiazines is associated with E_m potential of 0.583 V (acetic acid-water) which could lead to maximum formation of semiquinone ion (a radical ion) at physiological pH. The semiquinone facilitates an essential biological electron transfer reaction, producing a toxic or paralyzing effect.

The necessity of a free 3rd or 7th position in the phenothiazine nucleus for significant anthelmintic activity and the inactivity of phenothiazine tranquilizing drugs (2-substituted-10-dimethyl amino-propyl phenothiazines) is only due to the difficulty of correlating redox potential and activity.

(III) Parameters that are an Expression of Spacial Arrangement of the Molecule :

The location, size and volume of the different groups present on the molecular skeleton are collectively described by their steric parameters. Since the interaction of a drug with its site of action involves the mutual approach of two molecules, steric factors have some role to play in any attempt to produce a comprehensive correlation of drug structure and activity.

Steric interactions are not easily translated and they need not to be always clear and hence are difficult to quantify.

In order to evoke the pharmacological action, a drug must approach the receptor and fit closely to its surface, hence a drug must possess a high degree of structural specificity or sterioselectivity to initiate a response at a particular receptor. e.g. in diethylstilbestrol, only trans-diethyl stilbestrol is estrogenic drug while the cis-isomer is virtually inactive.

In open chain compounds, all possible conformations are not equally manifested by the drug due to the steric complications at all times. Hence by virtue of the ability of such compound to interact in a different and unique conformation with different biological receptors, may result into multiple biological effects. e.g. acetylcholine may react in its extended conformational form with the muscarinic receptor and quasi-ring form, may react with nicotinic receptor.

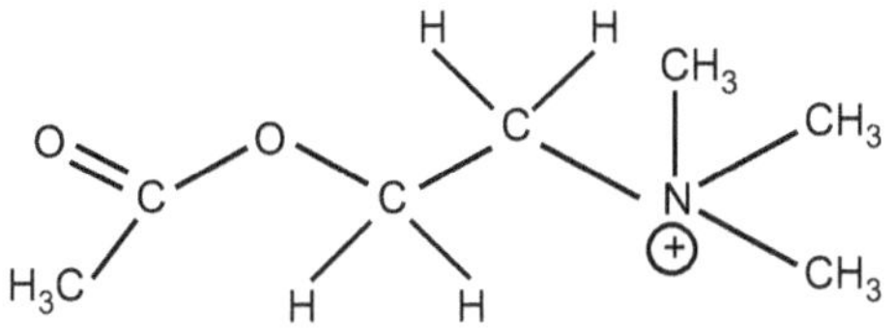

Acetyl choline in extended conformation

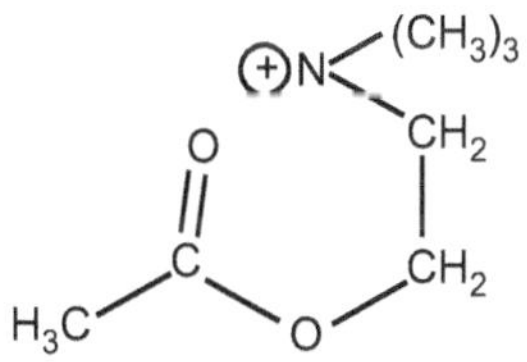

Acetyl choline in quasi-ring conformation

3.3 PHYSIOLOGICAL FACTORS

Bioavailability assessment now, stands as a professional responsibility for pharmacists and pharmaceutical manufacturers since, though highly effective, a new drug product may face clinical failure due to bioavailability variations caused by number of factors. Some of these factors affecting bioavailability are tabulated in the next table.

Table 3.8

Factor	Variable
I. Physiological :	Age, sex, physical state of patient, time of administration, gastric emptying, intestinal transit rate, pathophysiological state of GIT, food-drug and drug-drug interactions etc.
II. Dosage form :	Particle size, polymorphic form, solvent, hydrate, salts, esters, complex solubility characteristics, manufacturing methods etc.

In comparison to an extensive work devoted to the effects of dosage form related factors on the bioavailability of large number of drugs, a meagre attention has been paid towards physiological factors.

The presence of various physiologic material in GIT facilitates the digestion and absorption of nutrients as well as drugs. The anatomical arrangement and mechanical force provided by GIT structure further promote the absorption. Hence variations in the basic parameters that govern the GIT function, may influence the absorption of drugs in a positive or a negative way.

(a) Area of absorption : Various segments of the GIT differ as to the total epithelial surface area available for absorption. Stomach, small intestine and large intestine are the three major segments of GIT. The small intestine has the maximum available surface area. The presence of villi in the region of small intestine, increases manyfold, the area for absorption. Some drugs possess low solubility pattern or are released slowly if given through enteric coated or sustain-release dosage form. Drugs that escape from the stomach or small intestine may get absorbed in the large intestine.

(b) Effect of pH on absorption of drug : With slight variations, the pH of GIT fluids in the various segments are : In stomach; pH ranges from 1 to 3, in small intestine; pH ranges from 5 to 8, and in large intestine region; pH remains to be near 8. Thus, there are significant differences in the pH values of the fluids, in which the absorption sites for different drugs exist. These differences in pH at various sites naturally then influence the site and rate of passive absorption of drugs.

The pH of the gastric fluids are subject to a great deal of variation. The physiological factors predispose a large intrasubject variation depending upon the state of a person. e.g. Gastro-intestinal functions including the gastric secretions are very much different in the fasting and nonfasting conditions. In pathological conditions like, duodenal or gastric ulcers, the pH appears to decrease. Since many drugs are either weakly acidic or basic compounds, their absorption in GIT is governed, more or less, quantitatively by pH partition theory. The absorption of weakly basic drugs, such as, antihistamines and antidepressants is favoured in the small intestine where they exist mainly in a non-ionised form whereas the acidic gastric fluids tend to promote the absorption of weakly acidic drugs such as sulphonamides and non-steroidal anti-inflammatory agents. Besides this, many drugs may increase the gastric secretions or may neutralize the gastric secretion, thus affecting the pH range of a particular segment of GIT.

(c) Effect of gastric emptying : The small intestine region offers very suitable environment for absorption of many drugs because –

(i) it has a maximum available surface area necessary for absorption.

(ii) the physicochemical properties of a drug matches closely with the pH environment of this region.

(iii) it provides the facilitated absorption due to the presence of active carrier mechanisms.

Since most of the drugs are optimally absorbed from the small intestine, any factor that delays stomach emptying has the potential of delaying the absorption of an orally administered drug. Similarly prolonged residence of the drug in the stomach may have varying effects on stability of drugs (that are prone to chemical degradation in the stomach) and the lipophilic character of the dissolved molecules.

The effect of presence of food on drug bioavailability need not to be over emphasized. The volume of the meal, its composition and viscosity, the acidity of the duodenal contents etc., have their influence over the rate of drug absorption. The effect of food on drug absorption may involve the water and lipid solubility of the drug, the nature and temperature of the food, formation of drug food precipitate, saturation of the active carrier system, as well as the effect of food on gastrointestinal pH, motility and blood flow. The decreased blood flow may, in turn, diminish the concentration gradient across the intestinal mucosa, which is required for optimal absorption of drugs transported into the blood by a passive diffusion process.

Table 3.9 : Drugs affecting the rate of gastric emptying or intestinal motility

1. Antacids
2. Anticholinesterases
3. Atropine and anticholinergic agents
4. Antiparkinsonian agents
5. Antihypertensives
6. Antihistaminics
7. Narcotic analgesics
8. Nonnarcotic analgesics
9. Laxatives
10. Sympathomimetic amines
11. Tricyclic antidepressants
12. Prostaglandins
13. Nitrites
14. Phenothiazines
15. Caffeine
16. Iproniazid
17. Metoclopramide

(d) Effect of drugs : The presence of many drugs may affect the rate of absorption of other drugs either :

(i) by affecting the rate of gastric emptying via local or central mechanisms or

(ii) by affecting intestinal motility. Such drugs are enlisted into the following table.

(e) Effect of intestinal motility : The mechanical function served by the peristaltic movements of GIT promotes drug absorption by

(i) increasing the contact points between the drug solution and the epithelial surface area.

(ii) and helping in the rapid dissolution of drugs from their solid dosage forms.

Some drugs may affect the intestinal motility. For example antispasmodic agents (e.g. papaverine and its synthetic analogues) decrease the motility and may cause decreased or delayed absorption of other drugs. Cholinergic drugs, on the other hand, may increase the motility and enhance the absorption of other drugs.

(f) Drug-food interactions : The presence of food may have varying effects on the absorption of drug. For example, the absorption of drug on to the food components, chelation of drug by polyvalent metal ions such as calcium and magnesium and complexation with food may result into :

(i) Reduced drug absorption

(ii) Delayed drug absorption

(iii) Absorption unaffected, and

(iv) Increases drug absorption

(i) Reduced drug absorption : Some of the drugs whose absorption is reported to be reduced due to dietary conditions of the patient are listed below :

Penicillins, Levodopa, Tetracyclines, Rifampicin.

(ii) Delayed drug absorption : e.g. Furosemide, Barbiturates, Sulphonamides, Acetaminophen, Digoxin, Cephalosporines etc.

(iii) Drugs whose absorption may be unaffected by food : e.g. Theophylline, Prednisone, Diazepam etc.

(iv) Increased drug absorption : e.g. Propranolol, Metaprolol, Nitrofurantoin, Riboflavin, Propoxyphene, Griseofulvin, Hydralazine etc.

(v) The rate of absorption of some drugs like, salicylic acid, barbital, haloperidol and chlorpromazine, were not affected by fasting until after approximately 20 hours.

(vi) Effect of food on drug distribution : Plasma proteins act as carriers for drug movement through the circulation. A number of nutritional metabolites derived from food are found to affect plasma protein binding of the drugs like free fatty acids, nonpolar amino acids (e.g., tryptophan) and lysolecithin. The nutrient molecules may influence drug plasma protein binding, resulting into a lack of available protein binding sites to transfer the drug through the plasma.

(vii) Effect of food on drug metabolism : In fact, very less attention has been paid to this aspect. According to some reports available, the phenacetin and antipyrine metabolism in GIT and/or during its first pass through the liver, is increased by sprouts and cabbage. It thus results into the decreased bioavailability of these drugs. The half life of theophylline increases due to high carbohydrate contents of the diet and decreases due to high protein rich diet.

(viii) Effect of normal gastrointestinal components : Bile salts, mucin, hydronium ion and enzymes are the normal constituents of GIT. These agents may cause some physicochemical changes in the drug molecule prior to its absorption. These changes like, complexation or structural modification, may influence the rate of absorption and thus affect the activity of the drug.

3.4 FORMULATION FACTORS

The drug is administered into the body through various dosage forms. Some are given orally, some are to be applied externally while others are to be injected into the various body layers. Each such dosage form has its own sets of advantages and disadvantages. Hence, the formulation factors markedly influence the rate and extent of absorption of drugs. These factors mainly include, particle size, manufacturing methods employed, route of administration, time of administration etc.

Route of administration mainly governs the rate and extent of absorption, distribution, metabolism and elimination of the drug. The activity and toxicity spectra and the dose amount of drug also differ due to the route of administration. This is particularly true with potent drugs like morphine and digoxin.

Gastric emptying has its own impact on drug absorption. Hence whether the drug is administered before the meal or after the meal governs the onset of action of drug. Some drugs may cause irritation of GIT. Such drugs have to be administered after meal. Most of the drugs are rapidly absorbed when given under fasting condition. This describes how the time of administration influences the rate of absorption of drug.

Although many routes exist for the administration of the drug, the most popular route is the oral route. With respect to the rate of drug absorption, the various dosage forms for oral administration can be ranked as follows :

Increases the rate of absorption of drug
- Aqueous solutions
- Emulsions
- Soft gelatin capsules
- Suspension
- Powder
- Granules
- Hard gelatin capsule
- Tablet
- Coated tablet

❖ ❖ ❖

DRUG METABOLISM

4.1 INTRODUCTION

Whenever a drug is administered into a body, it undergoes structural changes resulting into an increase in the polarity and water solubility of the drug. These molecular modifications carried out by a battery of enzyme systems present in the body, are grouped under the term, biotransformation or metabolism. The earlier concept of detoxification is now replaced by metabolism. Metabolism increases hydrophilic character (i.e., water solubility) of the drug and thus facilitates its elimination from the body. Hence, in addition to excretion and tissue redistribution, metabolism plays an important role in governing the intensity and duration of effect of drugs. This biochemical modification of the drug-structure by the host enzyme systems serves as a major mechanism by which the drug action is terminated. This termination is achieved due to :

(i) Production of either less active or inactive metabolites or/and

(ii) More rapid rate of drug clearance from the body due to its increased polarity.

Brodie and co-workers were first to recognize the affinity of microsomal enzymes to attack on lipophilic drugs. Their excretion from the body is accelerated by their modification to more hydrophilic variations. The microsomal enzymes serve the function of metabolic tools and exert a well defined influence on the distribution and elimination pattern of the drug. Thus, the drug-enzyme interactions are the part of the way by which foreign substances are handled by the living system.

The drug metabolism usually ends into the formation of metabolites with

(i) reduced pharmacological activity e.g., Aspirin, pentobarbital.

(ii) equipotent pharmacological activity e.g., Amphetamine is a metabolite of methamphetamine or morphine is a metabolite of codeine.

(iii) increased pharmacological activity. This happens in case of pro-drugs e.g., the antineoplastic agent, cyclophospbamide.

(iv) Sometimes metabolites may be quite toxic. In such cases, the organism provides the means to increase their hydrophilicity further so that the stay of such toxic metabolite in the body can be cut short.

Considering the drug elimination as a first order reaction, one can easily quantify the rate of drug disapperance from the body, in terms of its biological half-life ($t\frac{1}{2}$). It can be defined as 'the time required to reduce the amount of drug administered to its one half'. With the knowledge of $t\frac{1}{2}$ value, one can compare the elimination rates of drugs from same pharmacological series and can determine the dosage schedule of drugs.

The metabolism of any drug is generally characterized by two phases of reaction, namely metabolic transformation (biotransformation) and conjugation.

Metabolic bio-transformations or bio-transformations are enzyme induced reactions where drug may undergo a wide variety of oxidation, reduction and hydrolysis reactions, resulting into an introduction or unmasking of functional groups. This leads to the formation of more polar and water soluble metabolites. Sometimes metabolites accumulating in plasma may influence the rate of biotransformation of the unchanged drug.

If the biotransformation or phase I reactions fail to increase the polarity of the molecule to the desired extent, the drug molecule serves as the centre for the second phase of metabolism, i.e. conjugation. Conjugation reactions are a sort of biosynthesis by which the drug or its metabolites are combined with endogenous molecules or groups, such as glucuronic acid, sulphate, amino acids, acetyl group or methyl group. This turns the molecule, more polar, less lipid soluble and therefore it is readily excreted out.

Most drugs metabolise at least to some extent, by both phases of metabolism. e.g., aspirin undergoes hydrolysis (metabolic biotransformation) to give salicylic acid which is then conjugated with glycine to form salicyluric acid (conjugate), that is readily excreted out.

Some drugs are considered bio-chemically inert as they have been excreted unchanged. They do not utilize the metabolic machinery of the body. For example, barbitone, diethyl ether are excreted unchanged by active transport mechanisms of kidney.

The principal aim in studying the drug metabolism is to identify the pathways by which drugs are transformed in the body and to ascertain the importance of each pathway and the intermediate.

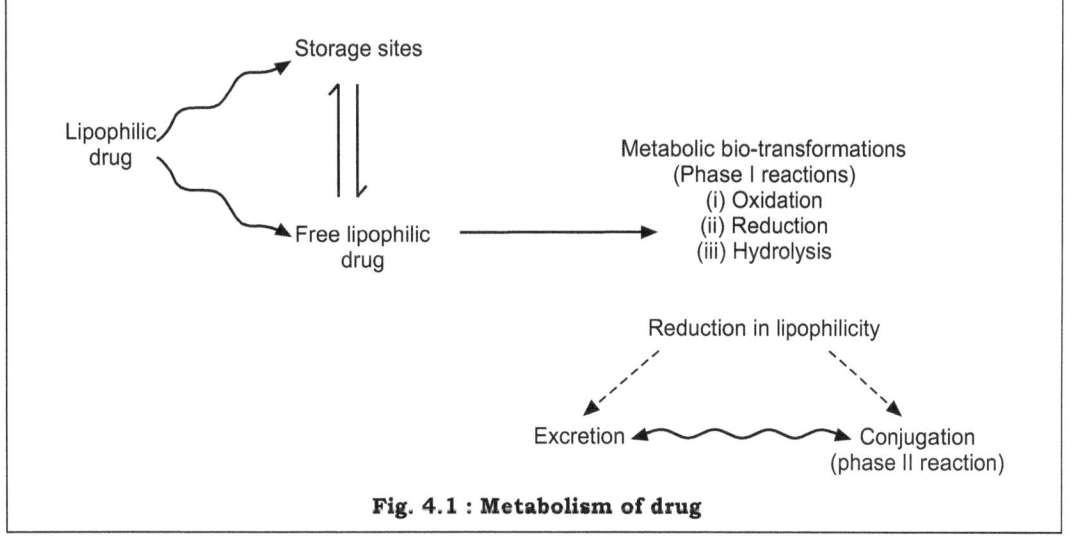

Fig. 4.1 : **Metabolism of drug**

The endoplasmic reticulum of mammalian cells plays an important role in drug metabolism. A variety of enzymes that carries out a large number of vital cellular functions and detoxification are located in the endoplasmic reticulum. This intracellular membrane is richly endowed with the monooxygenase system which catalyses various oxidation reduction reactions involved in drug metabolism. Monooxygenase reactions take place on or near the outer surface of the membrane. Cytochrome P-450 is deeply exbedded in the membrane but a small portion is open to the surface. The exposed region contains the catalytic and substrate binding sites. The endoplasmic reticulum is equipped with a set of oxidation/reduction enzymes (microsomal enzymes) and conjugation enzymes, whereas the hydrolytic enzymes are mainly present in the plasma.

Cytochrome P-450, molecular oxygen, a reducing agent (NADPH) and Mg^{++} ions are the basic requirements for monooxygenase enzyme system. The system consists of an undetermined number of species of cytochrome P-450 linked with NADPH cytochrome P-450 reductases. Cytochrome P-450 can be defined as 'any hemoprotein that has an ability to show a peak absorbance at 450 nm', when it is reduced and reacts with carbon monoxide to form a complex. The term includes either a single molecular species or a group of cytochromes. At least 15 different cytochromes of P-450 type have been identified. They differ in substrate selectivity, molecular weight, catalytic ability, immunological reactivities, electrophoretic mobility or response to enzyme inducers.

The enzyme inducers that cause an increase in the activity of microsomal enzymes include, phenobarbital, steroidal hormones and 3,4-benzpyrene.

A conclusive evidence about the presence of cytochrome P-450 and its role in drug metabolism was documented in 1962 due to the efforts of G.R. Williams of Johnson Foundation for Medical Physic, University of Pennsylvania. Sato and Omura provisionally named the carbon-monoxide binding pigment as cytochrome P-450.

Cytochrome P-450 hemoproteins are present in relatively higher concentration in liver and adrenals. In adrenal cortex, hemoprotein functions in mitochondria to hydroxylate steroids. The location of cytochrome P-450 is not restricted to microsomes of liver but they have been reported to be present in microsomes of the kidney, intestinal mucosa, lung, brain, skin, testis, and placenta. Spleen, gonads, eye and leukocytes also exhibit less significant cytochrome P-450 activity. Some higher plants alongwith yeasts, molds and bacteria also have cytochrome P-450 activity.

Table 4.1 : Cytochrome P-450 activity in various organs

Organ	Relative activity (%)
Liver	100
Lung	20-30
Kidney	09
Intestine	07
Placenta	05
Adrenal gland	02
Skin	01

The electron transfer chain present in monooxygenase system is dependant upon :

(a) NADPH (reduced nicotinamide adenine dinucleotide phosphate) is a source of electrons.

(b) cytochrome P-450 is a hemoprotein.

(c) NADPH-cytochrome P-450 reductase enzyme catalyses the oxidation of NADPH to release protons. The reductase enzyme is a FAD and FMN containing flavoprotein. The flavoprotein transfers an electron to cytochrome C or other electron acceptor (e.g., menadione, methylene blue) if they are present at the site. Another electron is consumed for the conversion of $2H^+$ to $2H$.

(d) Phosphatidylcholine is necessary for electron transport from NADPH to cytochrome P-450. The monooxygenase system is thus a multicomponent, membrane bound enzyme. Cytochrome b_5 is yet another microsomal hemoprotein which sometimes participates in metabolism of drugs.

4.2 METABOLIC BIOTRANSFORMATION OF DRUGS : (Phase I reactions)

If we consider the animal body as a complex reaction vessel, the drug molecule undergoes various oxidation, reduction and hydrolysis types of reactions.

Depending upon the nature and localization of the enzymes which catalyse these reactions, metabolic biotransformations are further classified as :

(a) Biotransformations that are catalysed by the enzymes of endoplasmic reticulum of the liver and other tissues or the microsomal drug metabolising enzymes,

(b) Biotransformations catalysed by nonmicrosomal mammalian enzymes i.e., enzymes present in the mitochondria, lysosomes or cytoplasm of the tissues or in the blood plasma, and

(c) Biotransformations catalysed by intestinal microflora.

Very often a drug is subjected to several competing pathways simultaneously and the extent of formation of the various metabolites depends on the relative rates of these interactions.

Among the many enzymes associated with the endoplasmic reticulum, is a group of enzymes known as drug metabolising enzymes. These include,

(i) Mixed function oxidases

(ii) Reductases and

(iii) Esterases

The simple metabolic biotransformations carried out by above enzymes, are followed by conjugation, e.g. an alkyl side chain of a drug may be oxidised to an alcohol which then forms a conjugate with glucuronic acid or an ester may be hydrolised to its acid form which then, is coupled with glycine.

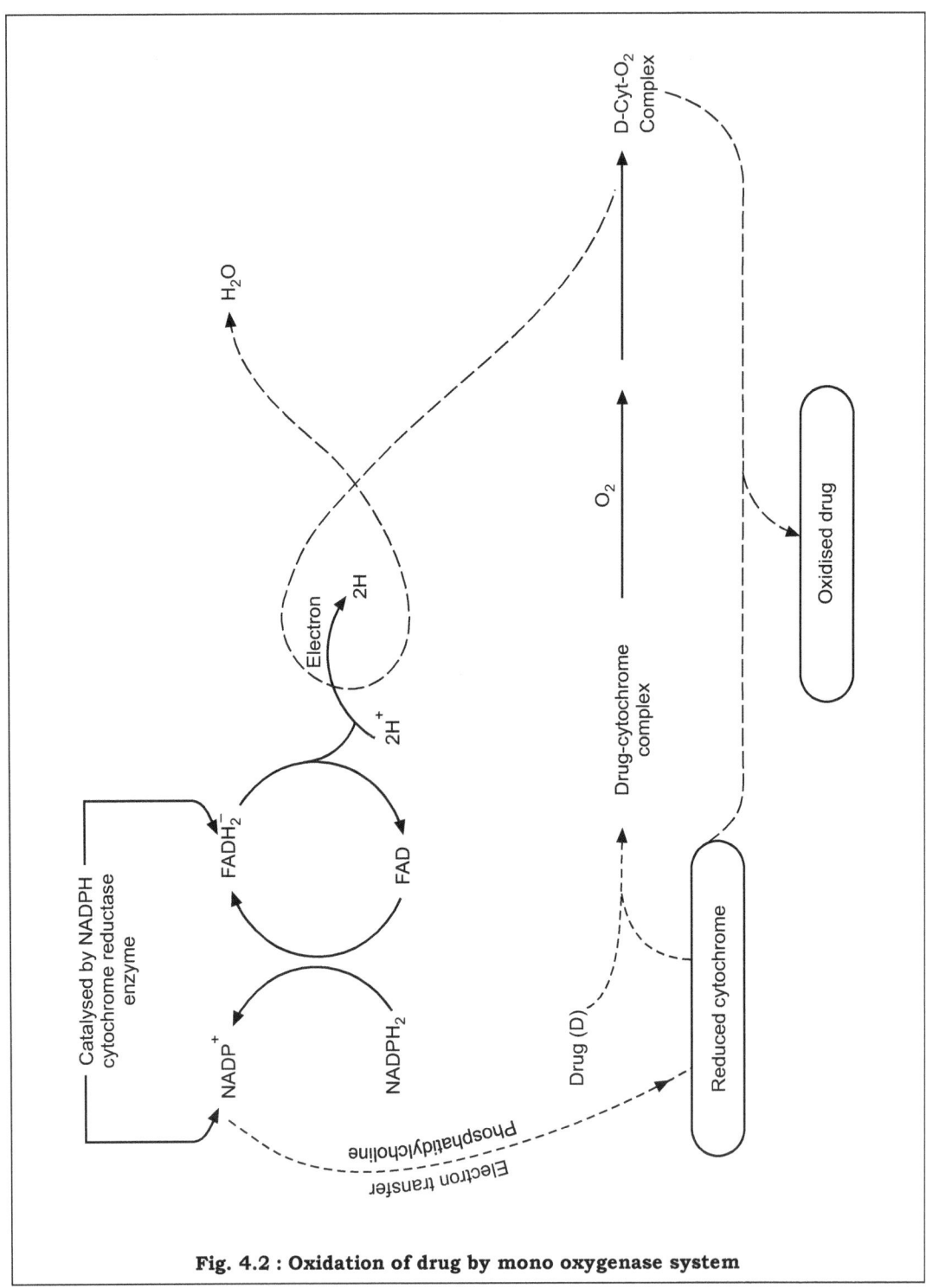

Fig. 4.2 : Oxidation of drug by mono oxygenase system

[A] OXIDATION

Examples :

(i) Ethanol : Ethanol, in mammals, is rapidly oxidised by liver alcohol dehydrogenases to a toxic intermediate, acetaldehyde. This is a reversible reaction. The latter is rapidly oxidised to acetic acid by acetaldehyde oxidase and other enzymes. This reaction is irreversible and proceeds faster than the former. Acetic acid, then may enter the tricarboxylic acid cycle and reaches to final stage of oxidation to CO_2.

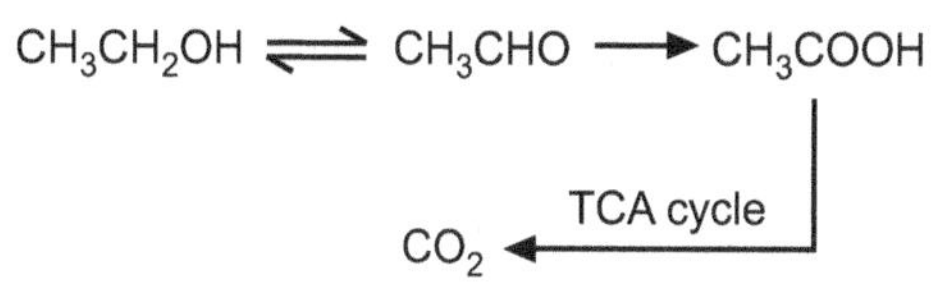

$$CH_3CH_2OH \rightleftharpoons CH_3CHO \longrightarrow CH_3COOH$$

$$CO_2 \xleftarrow{\text{TCA cycle}}$$

(ii) Chloral hydrate : Chloral hydrate is biotransformed to trichloroacetic acid by an aldehyde dehydrogenase enzyme.

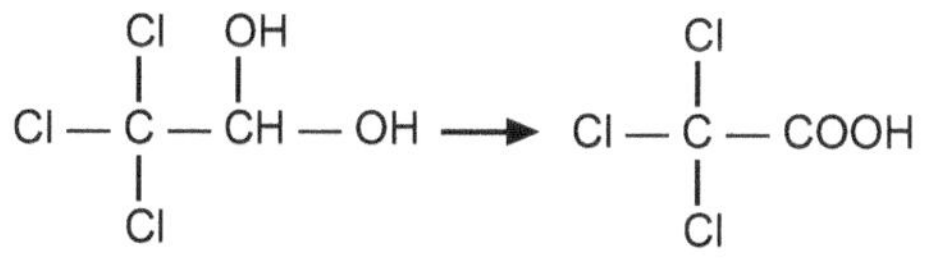

Chloral hydrate $\longrightarrow$ **Trichloroacetic acid**

(iii) Methadone :

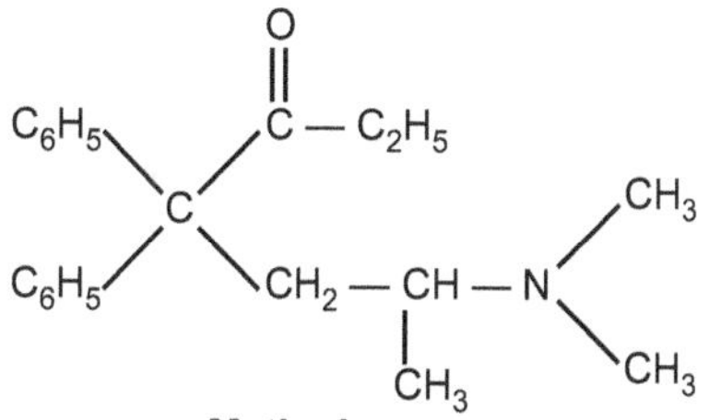

Methadone

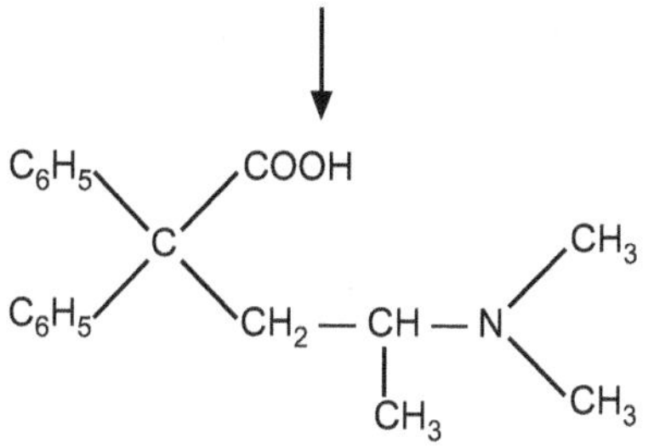

↓

Methadone metabolite

(iv) Steroidal drugs :

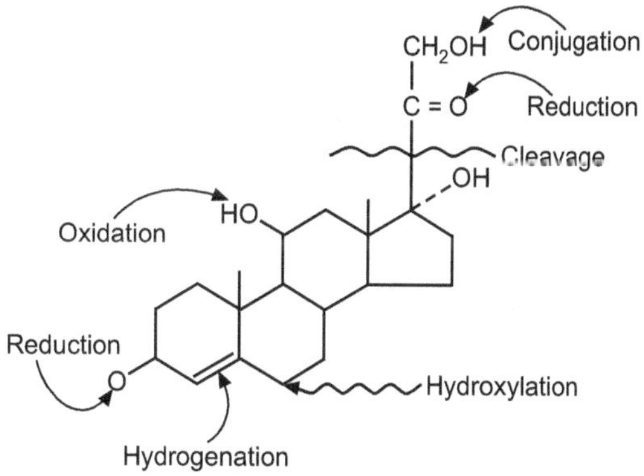

(structure showing Oxidation, Reduction, Hydrogenation, Hydroxylation, Cleavage, Reduction, Conjugation)

(v) Sulfoxidation :

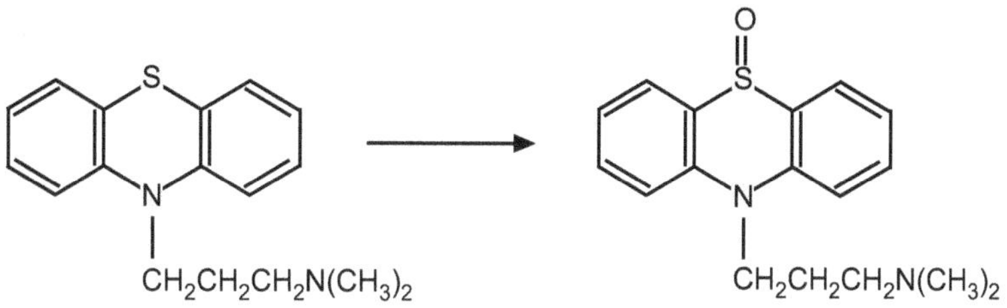

Chlorpromazine $\longrightarrow$ **Chlorpromazine sulfoxide**

(vi) Side chain oxidation :

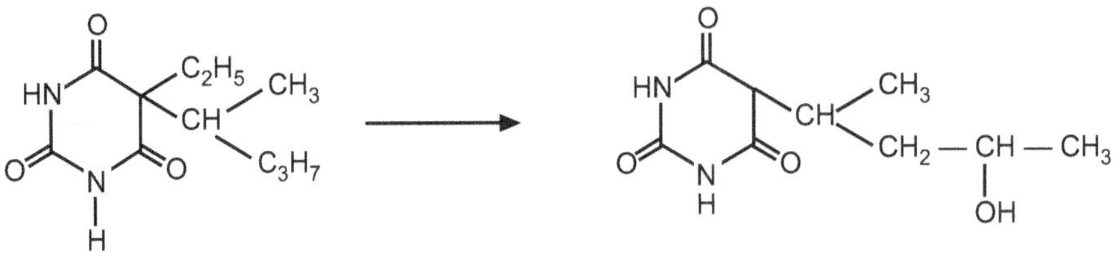

Pentobarbital → **Pentobarbital alcohol**

(vii) Other oxidative reactions : These include sulphur atom replacement reaction and ring foramtion. Former is an important and significant metabolic reaction for thiobarbiturates and for phosphorothionate insecticides.

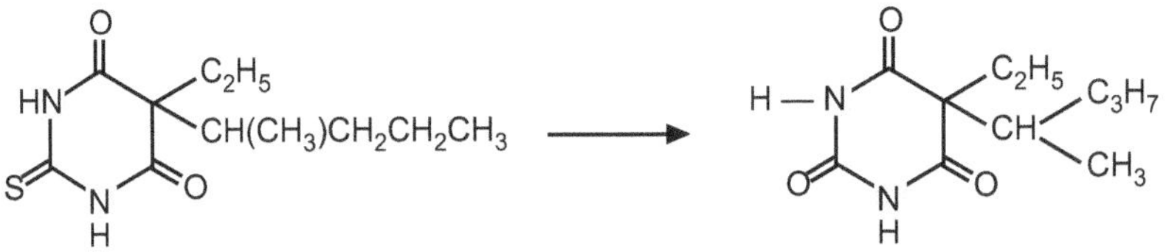

Thiopental → **Pentobarbital**

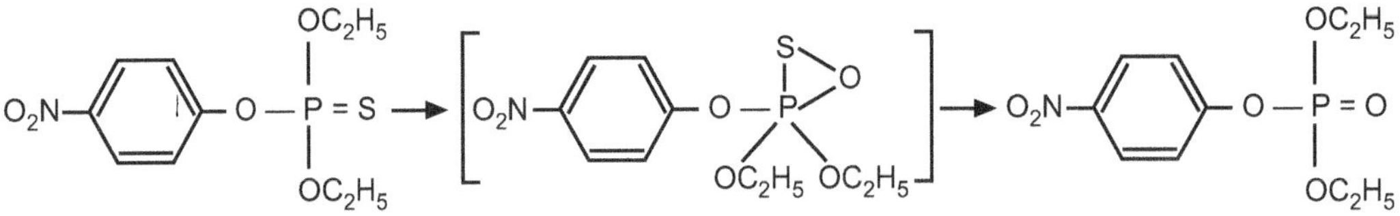

Parathion
Low anticholinesterase activity

Paraxon
High anticholinesterase activity

Parathion through a ring formation reaction, is transformed to a very toxic compound, paraxon, (an active cholinesterase inhibitor in mammals) by the liver microsomes.

(B) REDUCTION

This process plays an important role in the metabolism of many drugs containing carbonyl, nitro and azo moieties. Bioreduction of carbonyl compounds generate alcohol derivatives while nitro and azo reduction leads to amino derivatives.

Since the hydroxyl and amino groups are much more susceptible to conjugation than the functional groups of the parent compounds, reductive processes facilitate the drug elimination.

Examples :

(i) Chloramphenicol

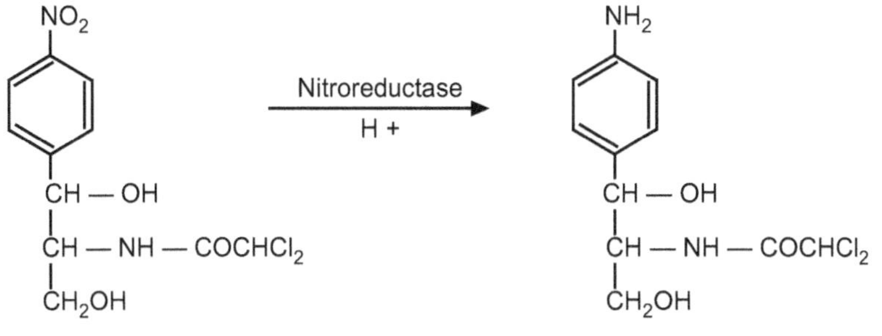

Chloramphenicol →(Nitroreductase, H+) Metabolite

Chloramphenicol: NO_2-C$_6$H$_4$-CH(OH)-CH(NH-COCHCl$_2$)-CH$_2$OH

Metabolite: NH_2-C$_6$H$_4$-CH(OH)-CH(NH-COCHCl$_2$)-CH$_2$OH

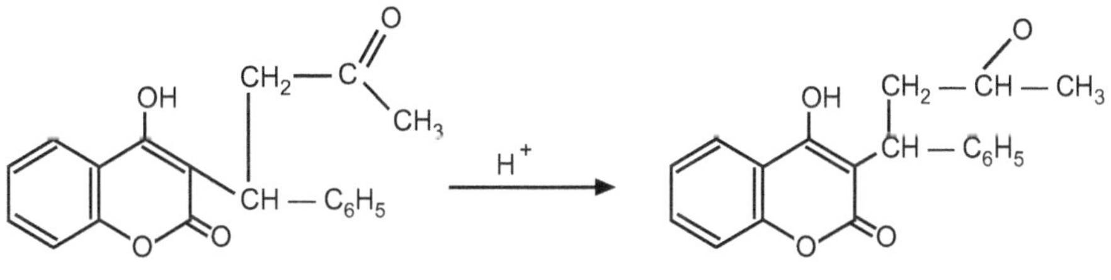

(ii)

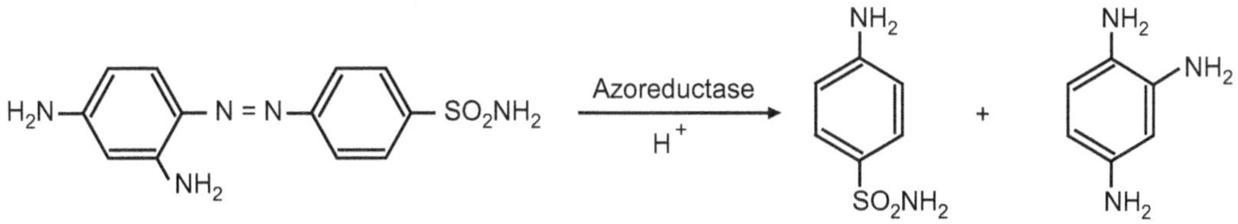

Prontosil →(Azoreductase, H+) Sulphanilamide + triaminobenzene

Prontosil: H_2N-C$_6$H$_3$(NH$_2$)-N=N-C$_6$H$_4$-SO$_2$NH$_2$

Sulphanilamide: NH_2-C$_6$H$_4$-SO$_2$NH$_2$

(iii)

Warfarin →(H+) Metabolite

(iv)

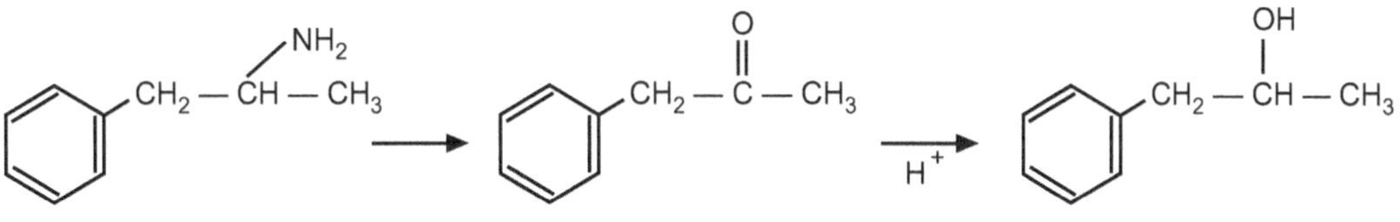

Amphetamine: C$_6$H$_5$-CH$_2$-CH(NH$_2$)-CH$_3$ → Phenylacetone: C$_6$H$_5$-CH$_2$-CO-CH$_3$ →(H+) 1-Phenyl-2 propanol: C$_6$H$_5$-CH$_2$-CH(OH)-CH$_3$

[C] HYDROLYTIC REACTIONS

The metabolism of ester and amide linkages in many drugs is catalysed by hydrolytic enzymes present in liver, kidney, intestine, blood and other tissues. The metabolic products formed, namely carboxylic acids, alcohols, phenols and amines, generally are polar and functionally more susceptible to conjugation and excretion than the parent ester and amide drugs. Amide hydrolysis appears to be mediated by liver, microsomal amidases, esterases and deacylases.

Examples :

(i) Aspirin → Salicylic acid + Acetic acid

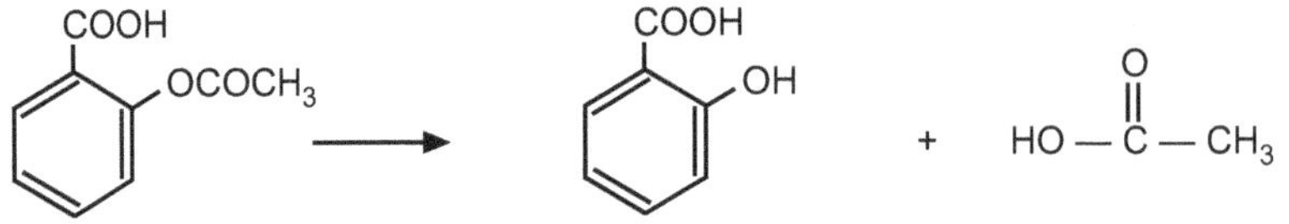

(ii) Carbamazepine → Metabolite

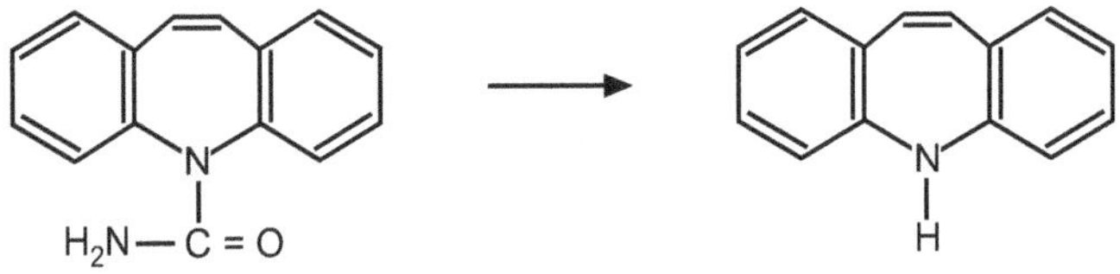

(iii) Lidocaine → (dealkylated metabolite)

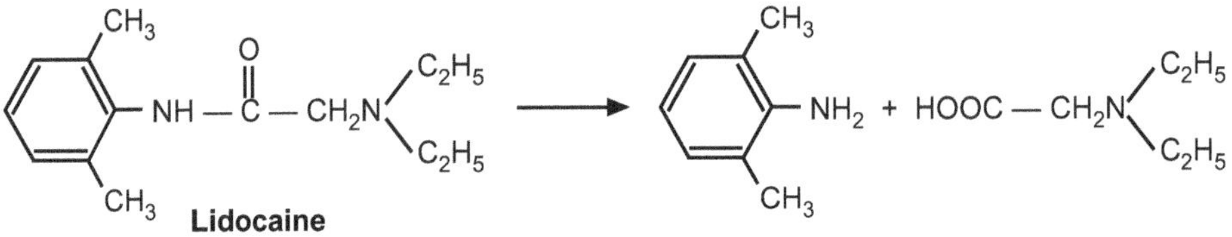

(iv) Clofibrate → P-chlorophenoxyisobutyric acid

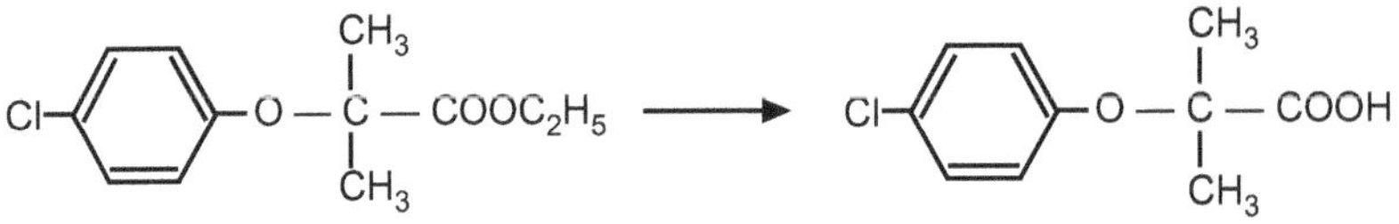

(D) OTHER IMPORTANT REACTIONS

(i) N-dealkylation :

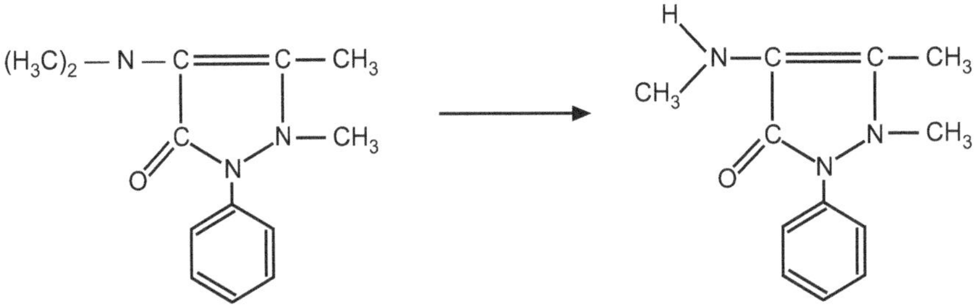

Aminopyrine → Metabolite

(ii) O-dealkylation :

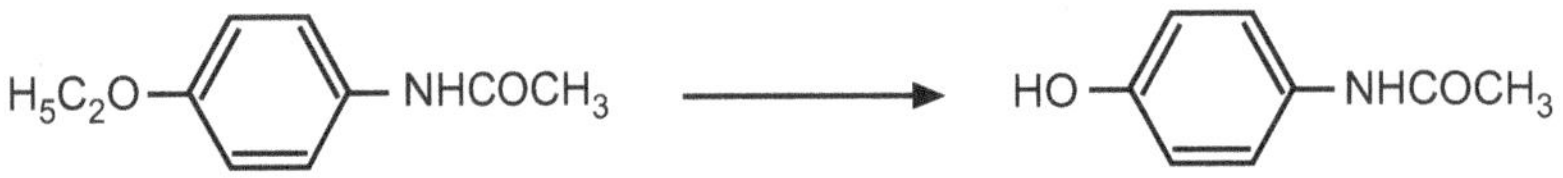

Acetophenetidin → Metabolite

(iii)

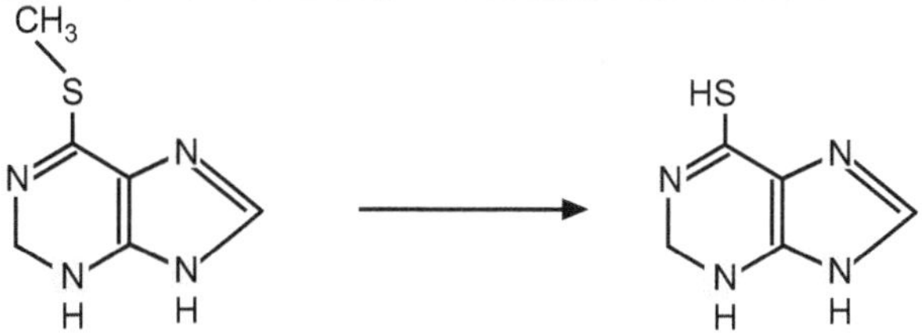

6-methyl thiopurine → 6-mercaptopurine

(iv) **Aromatization :**

Cyclohexene carboxylic acid → Benzoic acid

4.3 CONJUGATION REACTIONS (Phase II Reactions)

Metabolic transformations or phase I reactions do not always produce hydrophilic (more polar and hence water soluble) or/and pharmacologically inactive metabolites. Such metabolites undergo further metabolic process known as conjugation or phase II reactions, resulting into deactivation and excretion of the inactive conjugates.

Phase II reactions are classified mainly into :

(a) Attachment of small, polar and ionizable endogenous molecules like, glucuronic acid, sulphate, glycine or glutamine to the phase I metabolite.

(b) Methylation and acetylation which do not generally increase water solubility but serve mainly to terminate the pharmacological activity.

(c) Conjugation with phosphate, glycosides or other amino acid is the pathway of minor importance.

Thus, phase II reactions include –

(I) Glucuronic acid conjugation

(II) Sulfate conjugation

(III) Glutathione or mercapturic acid conjugation.

(IV) Conjugation with glycine, glutamine and other amino acids.

(V) Methylation

(VI) Acetylation

(VII) Nucleoside and nucleotide formation.

(I) Conjugation with Glucuronic Acid :

The reaction involves the condensation of the drug or its metabolite with the activated form of a readily available glucuronic acid, Uridine diphosphate glucuronic acid (UDPGA). The soluble fraction of liver contains enzymes that catalyse the synthesis of UDPGA from glucose - 1- phosphate.

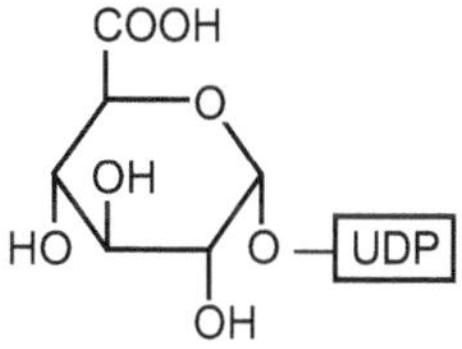

UDP-α-D Glucuronic acid (UDPGA)

Glucuronic acid conjugation proceeds into two steps :

(1) Formation of UDPGA

(2) Subsequent transfer of the glucuronic acid from UDPGA to various acceptors e.g.,

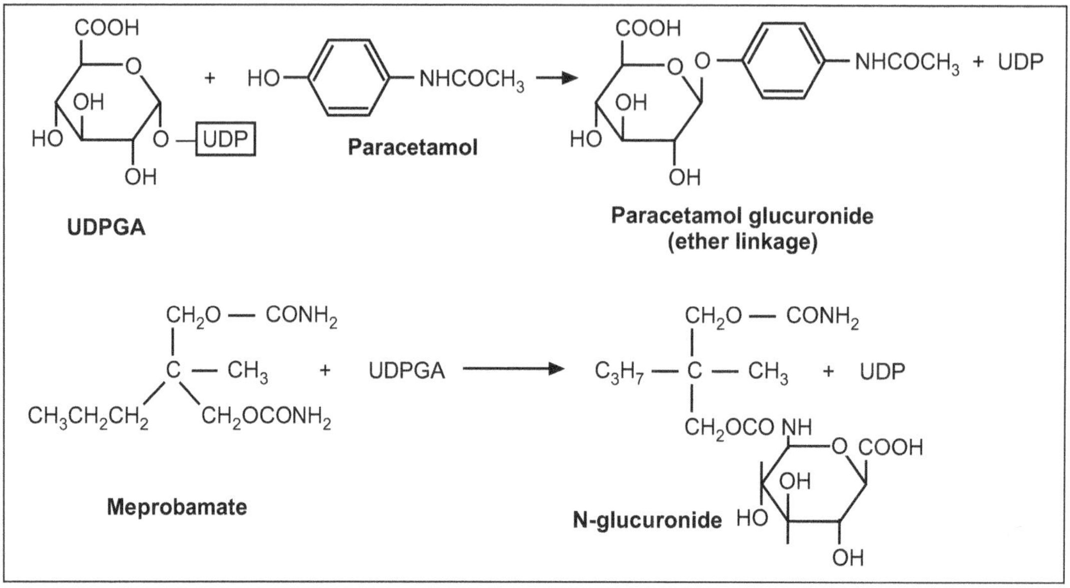

[Reaction schemes shown: UDPGA + Paracetamol → Paracetamol glucuronide (ether linkage) + UDP; Meprobamate + UDPGA → N-glucuronide + UDP]

Aromatic amines and sometimes sulfhydryl group can also be conjugated. Sulfhydryl compounds form S-glucuronides. They are acid labile.

The transfer of the glucuronic acid from UDPGA to an appropriate substrate is catalysed by microsomal enzymes called as UDP-glucuronyltransferases, present mostly in the liver but may also occur in other tissues like kidney, Intestine, skin, lung and brain. The metabolites are excreted in the bile and subsequently into the small intestine, from which, they may be reabsorbed.

Glucuronide conjugation results in increased water solubility, ionizability and deactivation of the substrate activity. Thus, all the objectives desired for drug disposal are achieved in one step.

Types of Compounds Forming:

(a) Alcohols and phenols :

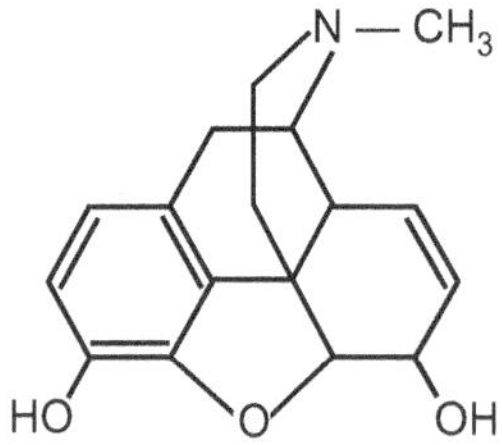

[Structures: Morphine, Paracetamol, Chloramphenicol]

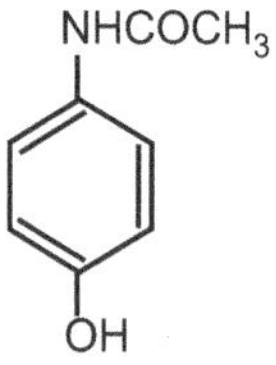

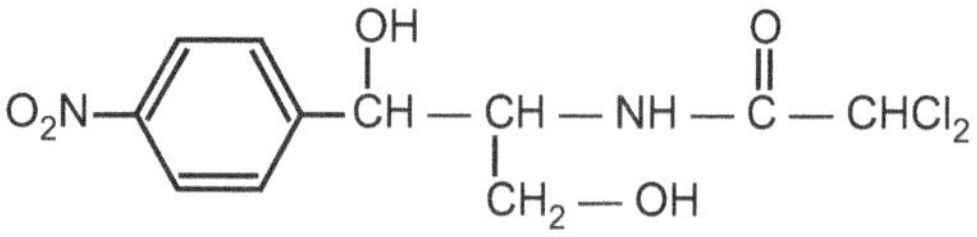

These drugs form ether type glucuronides.

(b) Compounds containing carboxylic group :

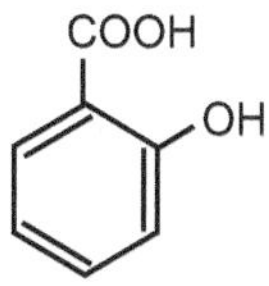

Salicylic acid 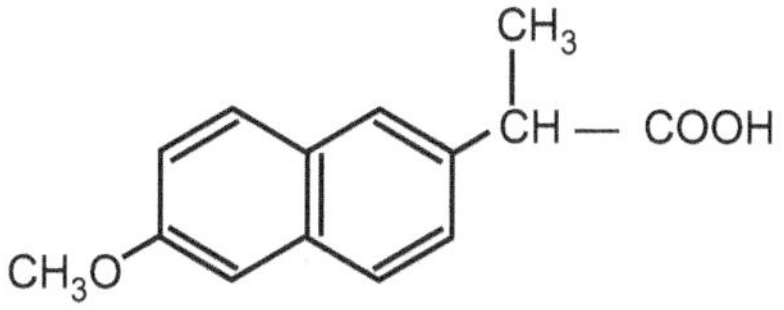   **Naproxen** 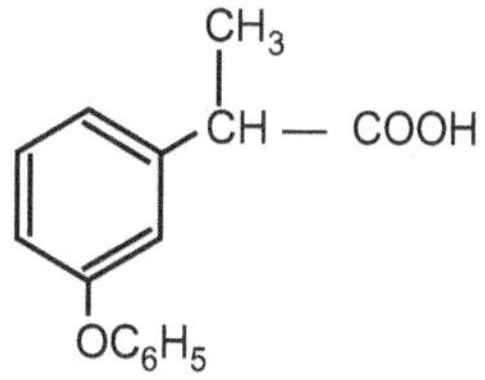   **Fenoprofen**

These drugs form ester type glucuronides.

(c) Aromatic amines :

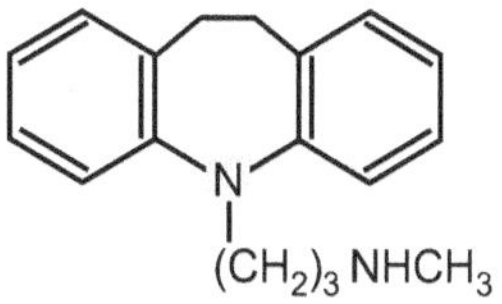

Desipramine 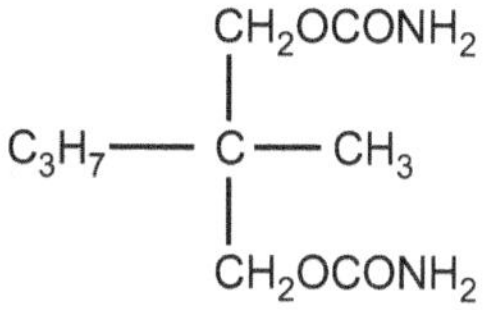   **Meprobamate** 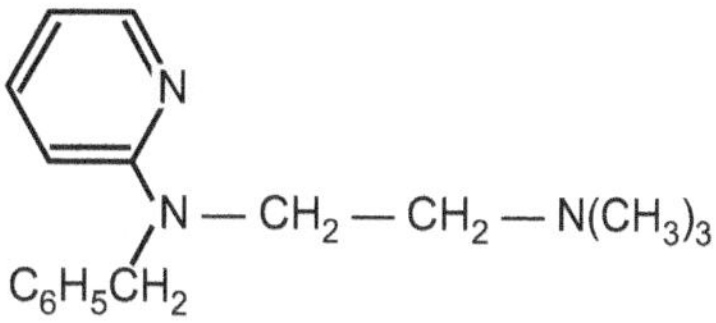   **Tripelennamine**

These drugs form N-glucuronide.

(d) Compounds containing sulfhydryl group :

Methimazole   **Propylthiouracil**   **Diethylthiocarbamic acid**

These drugs form S-glucuronides.

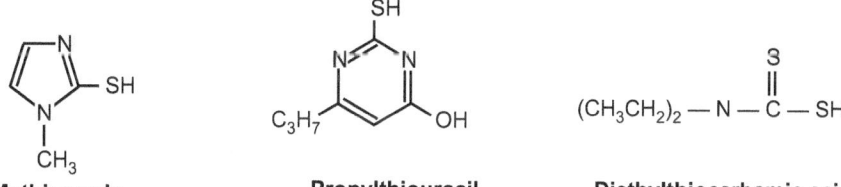

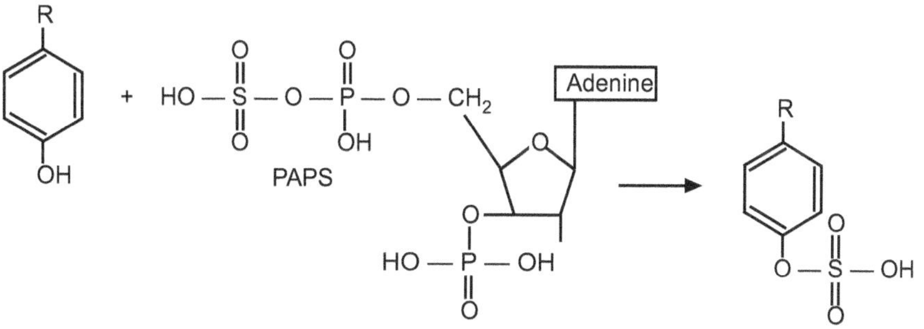

PAPS

Sulfate conjugate
+ 3'-phosphoadenosine-5'-phosphate

Glucuronidation of one functional group is usually sufficient to effect excretion, diglucuronide conjugates usually do not occur. An enzyme, β-glucuronidase can easily hydrolyse the drug-glucuronide conjugate.

$$\text{Drug-glucuronide} \xrightarrow{\beta\text{-glucuronidase}} \text{Free drug + Glucuronic acid}$$

This enzyme is present virtually in all tissues but mucosa of jejunum possesses a quite significant amount. The free drug liberated from the conjugate is reabsorbed from GIT. This reabsorption prolongs the life of the drug in the body.

[II] Sulphate Conjugation :

Sulphate conjugates are formed by the reactions of phenolic and aliphatic hydroxyl group and of certain amino groups with an activated form of sulfate through an ether linkage. Hence they are also termed as "etheral sulfates". Sulphate conjugation generally results into highly polar compounds that are readily excreted in the urine. The soluble fraction of liver contains the enzymes that catalyse the sulfur activation and transfer of sulfate to the substrate.

The sulfate moiety is present in activated state in 3'- phosphoadenosine - 5'-phosphosulfate (PAPS). The sulfotransferase enzyme then catalyses the transfer of sulfate group to the phenolic acceptor.

The sulfotransferase enzymes are structure specific. Hence, for different substrates, specific sulfotransferase enzymes catalyse the reactions.

[III] Glutathione or Mercapturic Acid Conjugation :

The metabolically generated reactive eletrophilic species manifest their toxicity (e.g. tissue necrosis, carcinogenicity, mutagenicity, teratogenicity etc.) by combining covalently with nucleophillic groups present in vital cellular proteins and nucleic acids. For example, epoxide formation may occur in the metabolic process of compounds with an aromatic ring. The epoxide then either can be converted enzymatically to a diol or can react with glutathione.

Mixed function oxidase

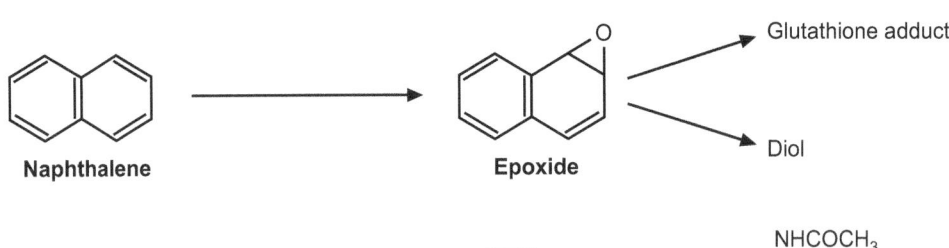

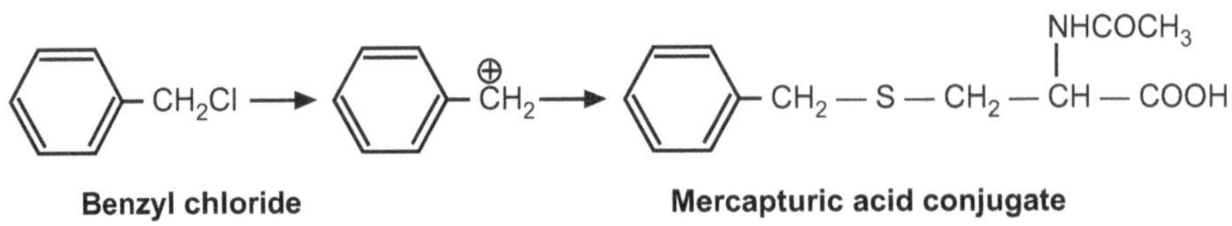

(2) **Naphthalene** → **Epoxide** → **1-Napthyl mercapturic acid** (S—CH₂—CH(NHCOCH₃)—COOH)

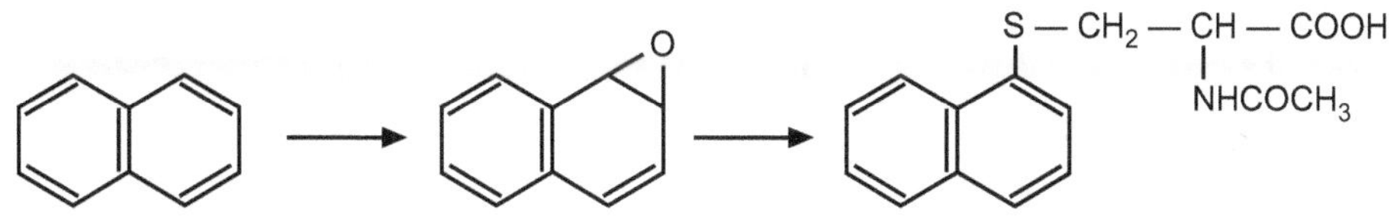

(3) **Paracetamol** (NHCOCH₃, OH) → (N=COCH₃, =O quinone imine) → **Mercapturic acid derivative** (NHCOCH₃, OH, S—CH₂—CH(NHCOCH₃)—COOH)

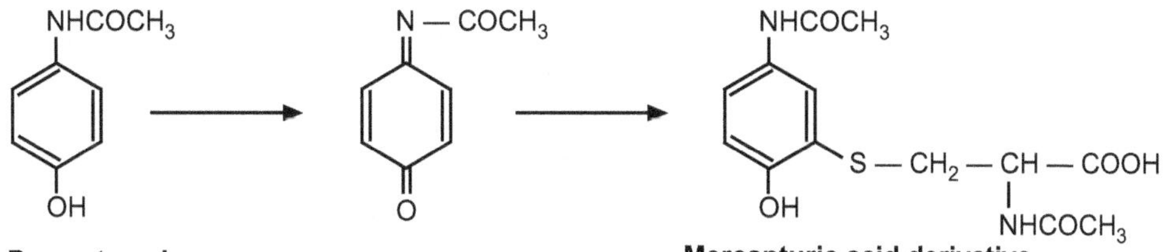

Thus, aromatic hydrocarbons, halogenated or nitrated aromatic hydrocarbons are eventually excreted in urine as conjugates with an acetylated cysteine residue (i.e. as mercapturic acid derivative). Thus, glutathione conjugation is an extremely important pathway which protects vital cellular constituents from a large variety of toxic epoxide intermediates.

The enzymes, glutathione - s - transferases, catalyse the formation of mercapturic acid derivatives. These enzymes can be isolated from the supernatant fractions of rat liver homogenate. Glutathione first reacts with an activated substrate to form Glutathione adduct.

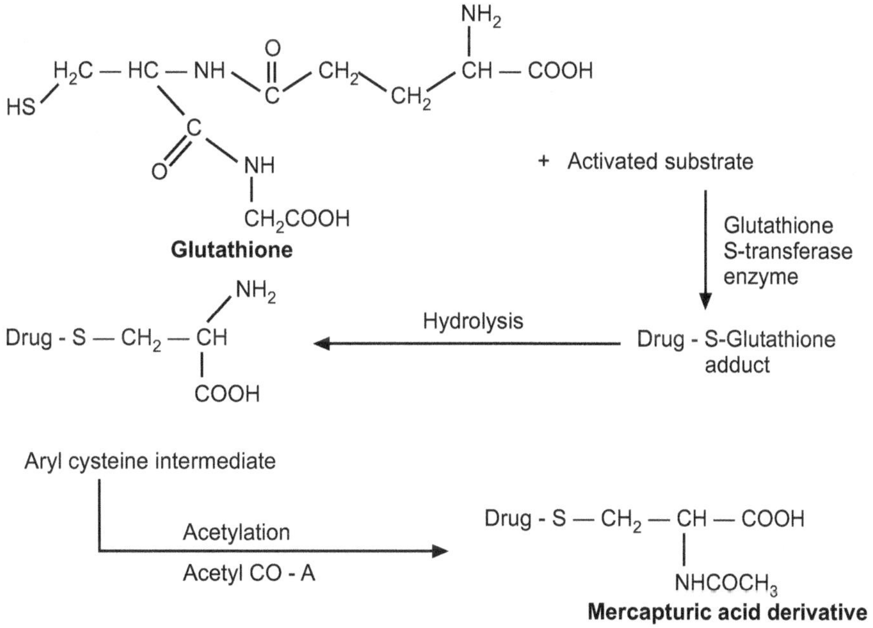

Glutathione (HS—CH₂—CH(NH—CO—...)—CO—NH—CH₂COOH structure with glutamate portion CH₂—CH₂—CH(NH₂)—COOH)

+ Activated substrate

↓ Glutathione S-transferase enzyme

Drug - S-Glutathione adduct

← Hydrolysis

Drug - S — CH₂ — CH(NH₂) — COOH
Aryl cysteine intermediate

→ Acetylation / Acetyl CO-A

Drug - S — CH₂ — CH(NHCOCH₃) — COOH
Mercapturic acid derivative

(a)

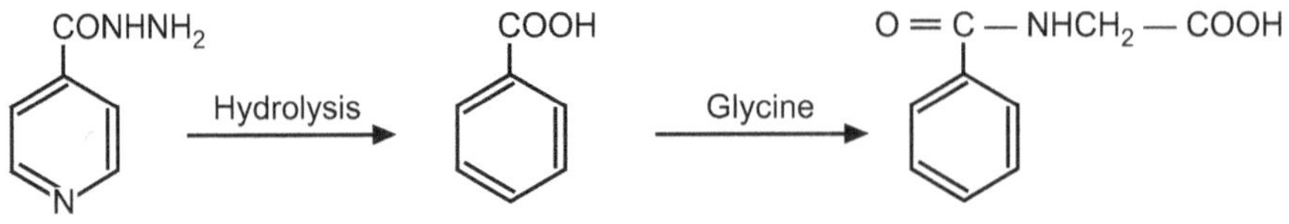

Isoniazid (CONHNH₂ on pyridine) —Hydrolysis→ Isonicotinic acid (COOH on pyridine) —Glycine→ Glycine conjugate (O=C—NHCH₂—COOH on pyridine)

(b)

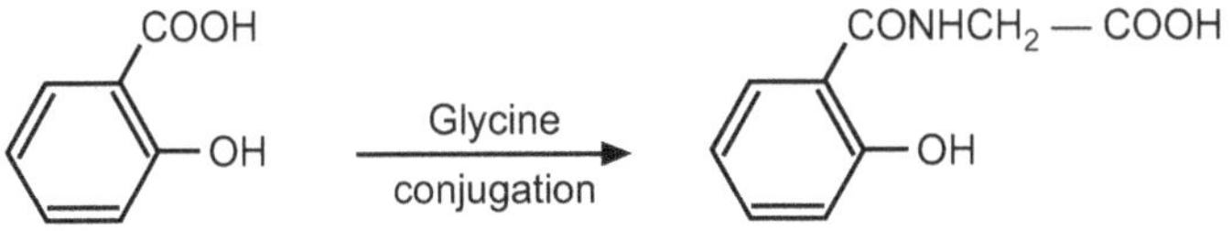

Salicylic acid (COOH, OH on benzene) —Glycine conjugation→ Glycine conjugate (CONHCH₂—COOH, OH on benzene)

(c)

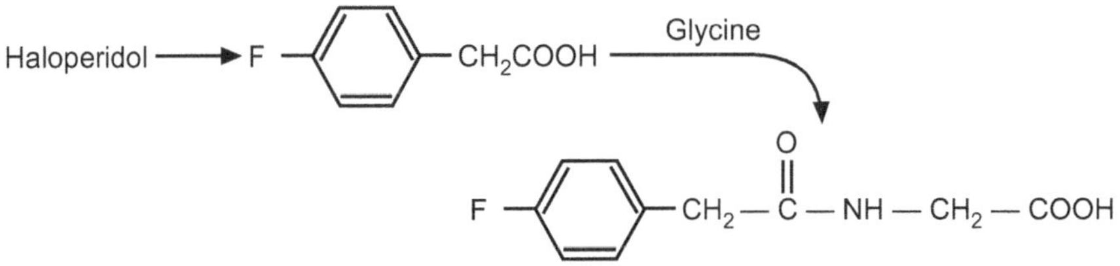

Haloperidol → F—C₆H₄—CH₂COOH —Glycine→ F—C₆H₄—CH₂—C(=O)—NH—CH₂—COOH (Glycine conjugate)

The glutathione adduct undergoes hydrolysis to form aryl cysteine derivative. The final, mercapturic acid derivative is obtained through the acetylation of cysteine amino group.

[IV] Conjugation with Glycine, Glutamine and Other Amino Acids:

The amino acids, glycine, taurine and glutamine are utilized by mammalian system to conjugate drugs containing carboxyl group. Conjugation with ornithine is also reported but appears to be restricted to birds.

In contrast to glucuronic acid, glycine and glutamine are not converted to activated form. Instead the carboxylic acid substrate is activated with ATP to form Acyl CoA complex. This complex then reacts with glycine and glutamine to form conjugate and free acyl CoA.

[V] Methylation:

Methylation involves s-adenosyl-methionine that serves as a methyl donar. There are number of methyl transferase enzymes present in the body.

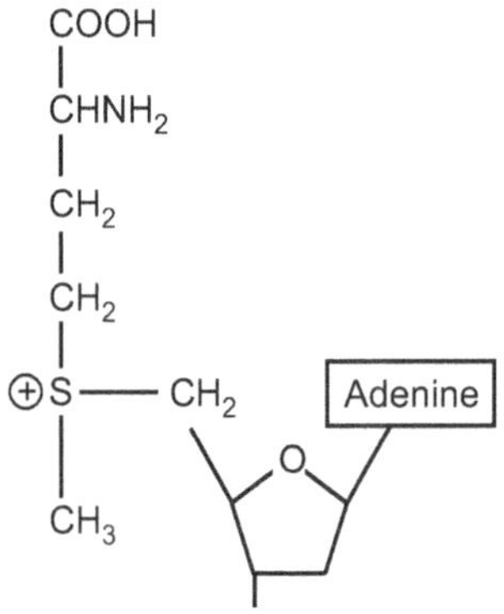

```
   COOH
    |
   CHNH₂
    |
   CH₂
    |
   CH₂
    |
  ⊕S——CH₂——[Adenine]
    |        \_O_/
   CH₃
```

**S-adenosylmethionine
(a methyl group donar)**

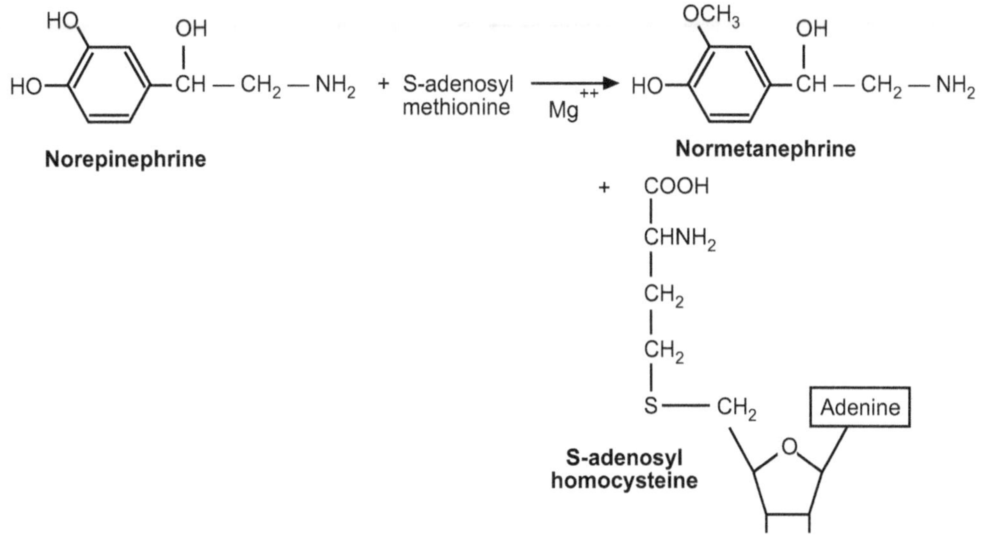

Norepinephrine + S-adenosyl methionine →(Mg²⁺) Normetanephrine + S-adenosyl homocysteine

Methylation differs from other conjugation pathways in that,

(i) it is of greater significance in the metabolism of endogenous compounds. e.g., catechol-O-methyl transferease enzyme catalyses the transfer of a methyl group to a phenolic hydroxyl function of catecholamines.

The reaction requires Mg^{++} ions and catechol nucleus is methylated at meta position.

(ii) it, in some cases, may result in the products having greater pharmacological activity than the parent molecule.

In all these methylation reactions, methionine transfers its methyl group via an activated intermediate, S-adenosyl-methionine, to the substrate, under the influence of methyl transferase enzymes.

These enzymes include,

(i) Catechol-O-Methyl transferase : It catalyses O-methylation of catechol-amines.

(ii) Hydroxyindole-O-Methyl transferase : It catalyses O-methylation of substrates other than catecholamines.

It is found only in pineal gland. S-adenosylmethionine serves as a methyl group donar. But Mg^{++} ions are not required. Amongst the endogenous substances, serotonin undergoes metabolism by this pathway.

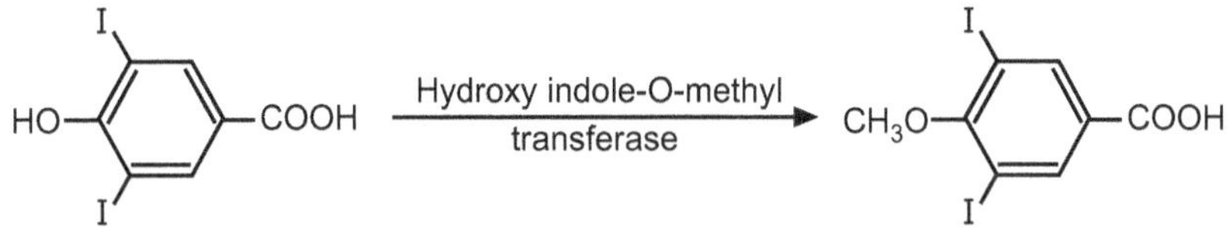

4-hydroxy-3,5-diiodo benzoic acid →(Hydroxy indole-O-methyl transferase) (methylated product)

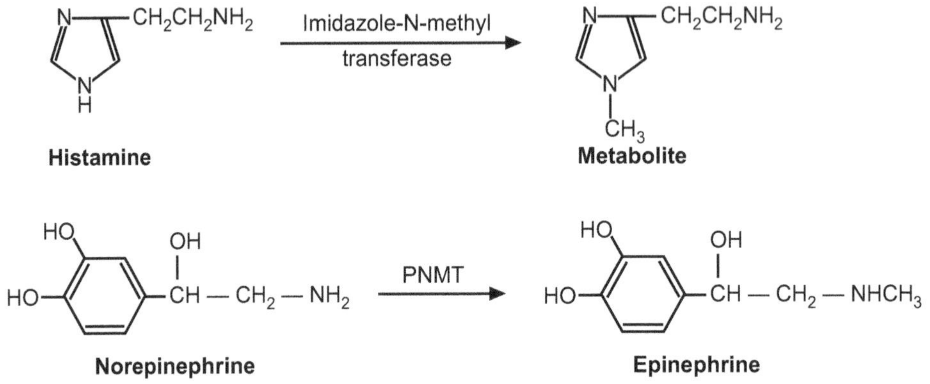

Histamine —[Imidazole-N-methyl transferase]→ Metabolite

Norepinephrine —[PNMT]→ Epinephrine

(iii) N-methylation of numerous amines has been known. It is catalysed by substrate-specific enzymes e.g., histamine is methylated by Imidazole-N-methyl transferase or norepinephrine is converted to epinephrine by the enzyme, phenylethanolamine N-methyl transferase (PNMT).

PNMT is abundant in the soluble fraction of adrenal medulla and is also present in heart and brain.

(iv) S-methyl tranferase : It catalyses S-methylation reactions e.g.

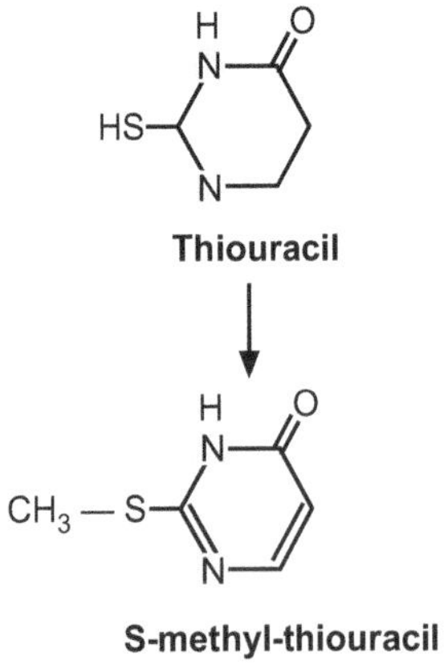

Thiouracil ↓ S-methyl-thiouracil

[VI] Acetylation :

Acylation reactions serve as an important metabolic route for drugs containing 1° amino groups, sulphonamides, hydrazines and hydrazides, which upon acylation, get converted to their corresponding amide derivatives. The acylated conjugates are generally nontoxic and inactive. Not all acetylated metabolites are more water soluble than the parent compound. For example, risk of kidney damage is always associated in the prolonged treatment with sulphonamides due to the relative insolubility of their acetylated conjugates.

Coenzyme A reacts with a carboxylic acid to form acyl-CoA derivative. The transfer of acyl group from acyl CoA, to a suitable acceptor is catalysed by N-acetyltransferase enzymes present mainly in hepatic reticuloendothelial cells. These enzymes display broad substrate specificity.

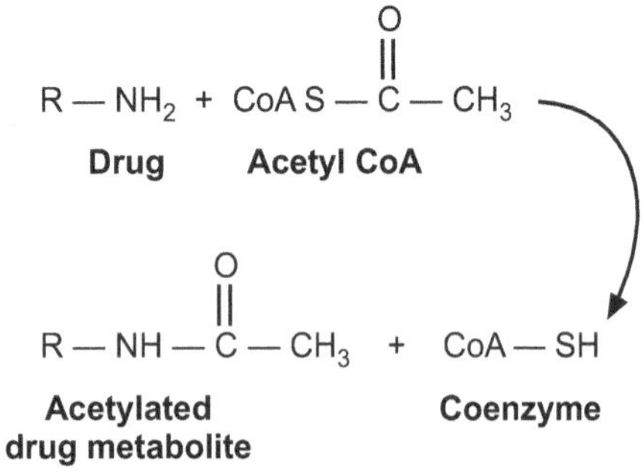

$$R-NH_2 + CoAS-\overset{O}{\underset{\parallel}{C}}-CH_3$$
Drug   Acetyl CoA

$$R-NH-\overset{O}{\underset{\parallel}{C}}-CH_3 + CoA-SH$$
Acetylated drug metabolite   Coenzyme

(1) Aliphatic 1° amines :

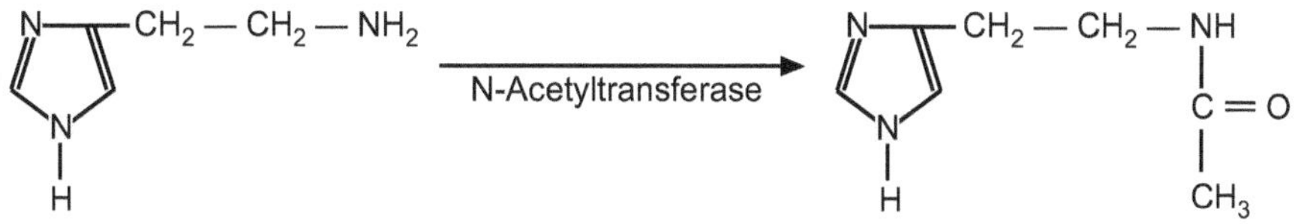

Histamine →(N-Acetyltransferase)→ N-acetyl histamine

(2) Aromatic amines :

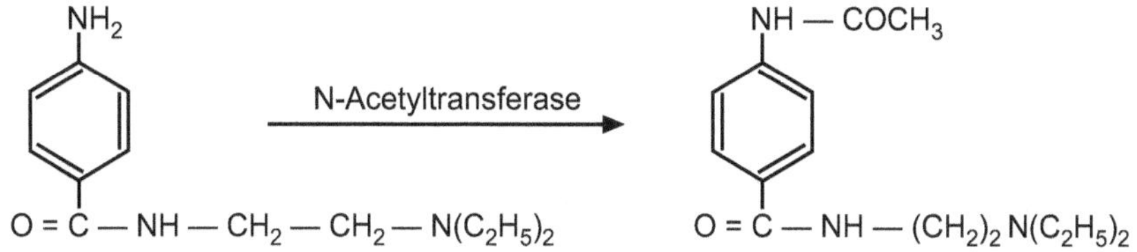

Procainamide →(N-Acetyltransferase)→ N-acetyl procainamide

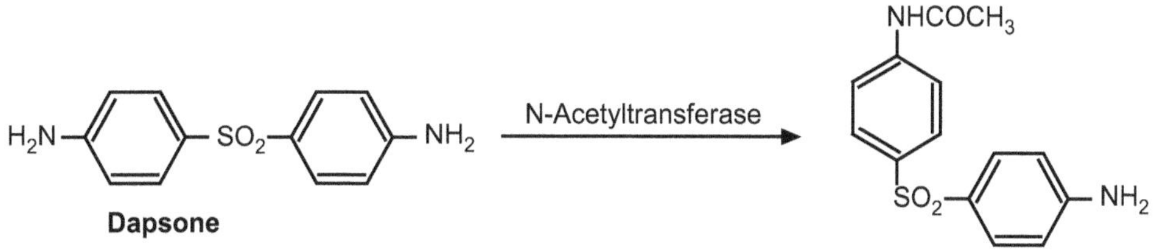

Dapsone →(N-Acetyltransferase)→ N-acetyl dapsone

(3) Sulphonamides :

Sulphapyridine →(N-Acetyltransferase)→ N-acetyl sulphapyridine

(4) Hydrazines and Hydrazides :

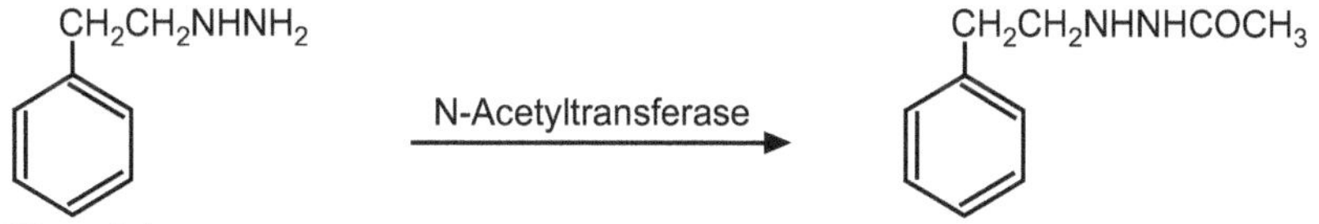

Phenelzine →(N-Acetyltransferase)→ N-acetyl phenelzine

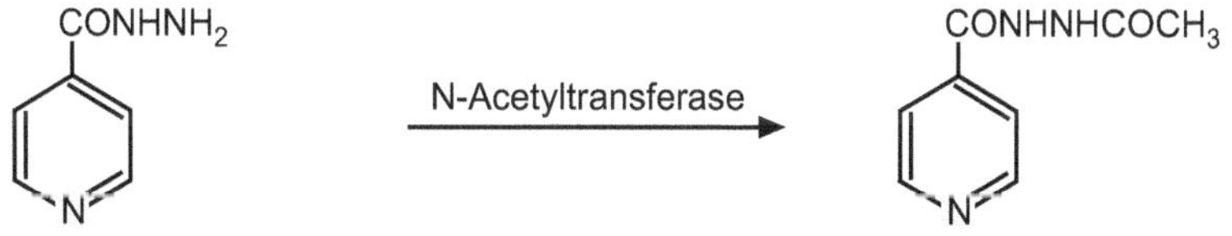

Isoniazid →(N-Acetyltransferase)→ N-acetyl isoniazid

In all these cases, the endogenous carboxylic acid (i.e. acetic acid) is used to conjugate exogenous substance (i.e. drug). Similarly an exogenous carboxylic acid is also able to form complex with co-enzyme A and the complex then, can form conjugates of endogenous amines (e.g. glutamine, glycine etc).

(i)

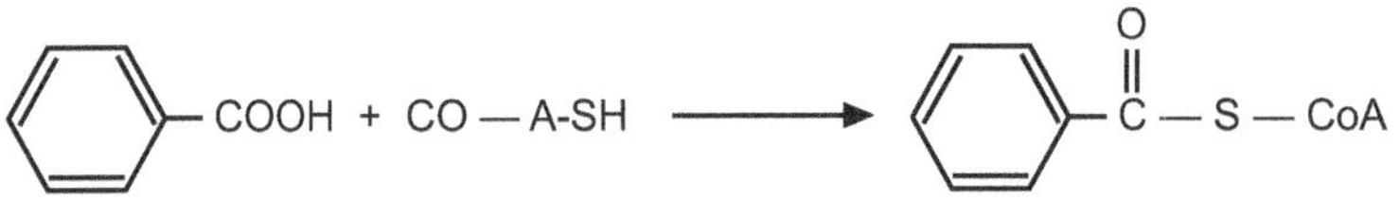

Ph—COOH + CO—A-SH ⟶ Ph—C(=O)—S—CoA

Benzoic acid

(ii)

Ph—C(=O)—S—CoA + H_2N—CH_2—COOH ⟶ Ph—C(=O)—$NHCH_2COOH$ + CoA-SH

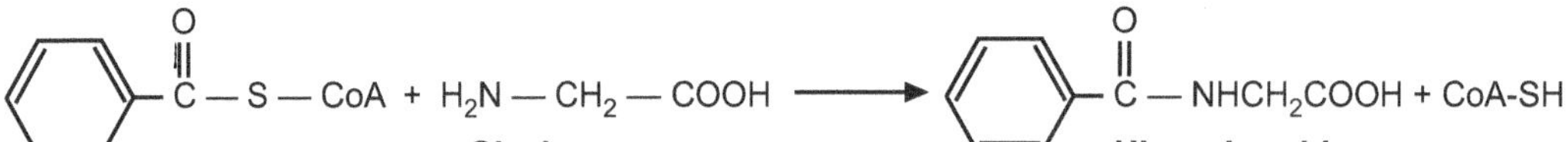

Glycine   **Hippuric acid**

Similar to acetylation, formylation reactions are also reported.

(VII) Nucleoside and Nucleotide Formation :

Addition of ribose and phosphate to the drug or its metabolite containing purine or pyrimidine nucleus, results in the formation of nucleoside or nucleotide.

Certain sugars like ribose, through an activited form, reacts with drugs to form ribonucleosides, ribonucleotides. The drugs that undergo this metabolic pathway should have either purine or pyrimidine nucleus.

6-mercaptopurine   +   **5-phosphoribosyl-1-pyrophosphate (PRPP)**

It is an activated form of ribose

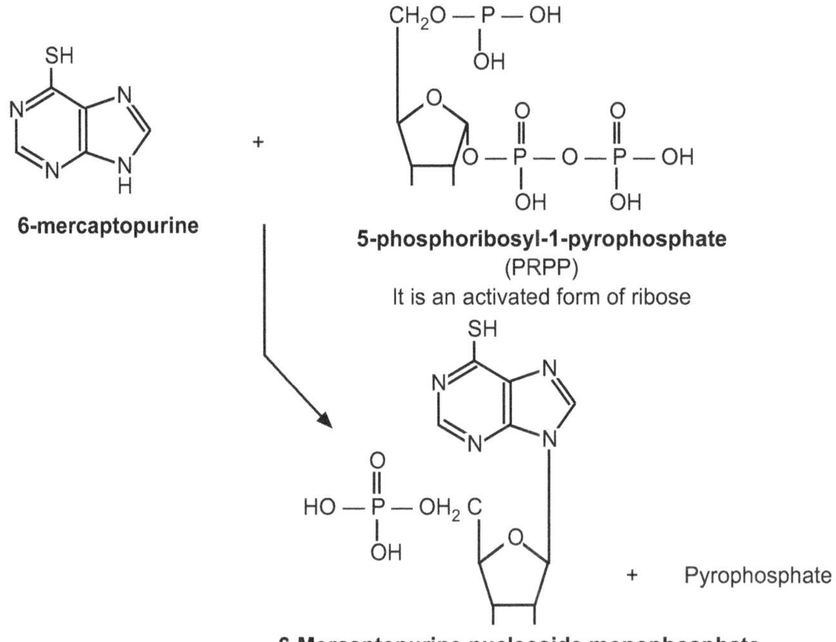

⟶ **6-Mercaptopurine nucleoside monophosphate** + Pyrophosphate

[Iproniazid, Phenelzine, Isocarboxazide structures]

Beside starvation and parenchymal liver damage, some drugs on chronic long term use, may depress the microsomal drug-metabolizing system. Such drugs include, oxyphenbutazone, nortriptyline, methylphenindate and allopurinol.

4.7 PHARMACODYNAMIC FACTORS

These factors include :

(i) Effect of protein-binding on drug metabolism,

(ii) Effect of urinary pH on drug metabolism, and

(iii) Effect of drug synergism.

(i) Effect of protein binding : The protein-bound fraction of the drug in the plasma is not available for drug-receptor interaction. It neither can show any biological response, nor it undergoes metabolism. The plasma protein-drug complex acts as a storage depot from which drug is slowly released into a free form. This free form can easily diffuse into the tissue to show the activity and then undergoes metabolism. Hence higher the affinity of drug towards the plasma-proteins, lower will be the rate and extent of drug metabolism. e.g. the oxidation of phenylbutazone and acetylation of sulphonamides were found to be reduced due to their protein binding affinity.

(ii) Effect of urinary pH : During urinary excretion, the chances of tubular reabsortion of drug are more if favourable pH condition is not present. For example, basic drugs (or metabolites) can easily be excreted through urine, if the urinary pH is in the acidic range. Similarly acidic drugs (or metabolites) can easily be excreted through urine, if the urine pH is in basic range.

(iii) Drug synergism : An increase in activity (or toxicity) of one drug by administration of another drug is known as drug synergism. This may be due to a competitive inhibition of metabolism of one drug by another. A knowledge of such synergism is necessary specially when the multi-drug prescription is dispensed.

Examples of drug synergism are scattered throughout the literature. e.g. desmethylimipramine inhibits the metabolism of amphetamine and thus potentiates and prolongs its activity.

Some drugs may compete with each other for the binding sites on the plasma protein. While doing so, they may displace other drugs from plasma protein. This results into an unexpected rise in the plasma concentration of the displaced drug. Naturally, the pharmacological activity and metabolism of such displaced drug is also amplified.

PROTEIN BINDING

5.1 INTRODUCTION

The reversible binding of drug with non-specific and non-functional sites on the body proteins without showing any biological effect is called as *Protein Binding.*

A drug molecule, to less or more extent, has a capacity to enter into specific combination with plasma-proteins. These molecular interactions play an important role in deciding the intimate nature of drug action. For example, using paramecia as test organism, Busck, in 1906, observed the inhibitory effects of serum on the photodynamic and other toxic properties of certain dyes. This inhibition was attributed to the formation of dye-albumin complexes. Moore and Roaf reported that protein binding of volatile anaesthetics, ether and chloroform make them more soluble in plasma than in saline. Rabbit serum has excellent binding properties towards various drugs.

Drug molecules in blood are present in two forms :

(a) Free form : This form is pharmacologically active. It is diffusible and available for both, metabolism and excretion.

(b) Bound form : It is non-diffusible (being complexed with plasma-proteins) and hence inactive. It acts as reservoir of drug.

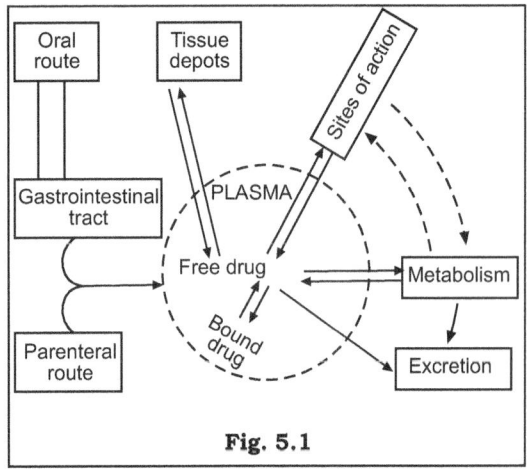

Fig. 5.1

The free drug diffuses into various body compartments through biological membranes and barriers. It is consumed at sites of action for physiological effects, for metabolism and excretion.

Numerous alliances of drug molecule with different body proteins are possible. The one which is responsible for pharmacological response, is known as *'Primary interaction'* whereas all other interactions fall under the term, *'Secondary interactions'*. These secondary alliances are responsible for side-effects and storage of drug. It means the key fits many locks but there is only one door.

The body proteins which take part in binding are mainly available in blood and to small extent in tissues. They function as a specially designed transport system for the regulated distribution of drugs throughout the body.

5.2 BODY PROTEINS

Human plasma is a circulating fluid tissue. The protein portion occupies about 7% (or 200 gm) of total volume (3000 ml) of plasma. Albumin is the most important protein fraction which constitutes about 59% of total body proteins. On the basis of differences in size, shape, composition, physical and chemical properties, over 25 distinct proteins are categorised into different groups or fractions.

Table 5.1

Fraction	Major components
I	Fibrinogen
II	γ-globulins
III-0	$β_1$ – lipoprotein
III-1, 2, 3	Isoagglutinins, plasmin, thrombin
IV-1, IV-4	Various α- and β-globulins and several enzymes
IV-7	Metal combining $β_1$-globulin
V-1	Bilirubin-containing $α_1$ –globulin
V	Albumin

(a) Fibrinogen : It is not generally involved in binding with drugs except certain substituted naphthoquinones. It forms loose complexes and requires drug at comparatively higher concentration.

(b) γ-globulins : No specific reactivity of γ-globulins in drug binding has been witnessed. They are more involved in highly specific protein-protein interactions e.g., immune responses.

(c) α- and β-globulins : These include enzymes like choline esterase, peptidase, lipase and amylase. Due to their lipoidal nature, they can easily form conjugates with steroids, phospholipids and other non-polar molecules.

(d) Albumin : It is the most important protein fraction involved in binding of drugs and scatters greatest diversity in drug-protein interactions. Albumin has a molecular weight of 69,000. At blood pH 7.4, it has a net negative charge. It has about 109 cationic and 120 anionic residues. Hence, it can interact with both, anion as well as cation. It is a macromolecule, composed of many hundreds of amino acids. It is the side-chain of composite amino acid structure that possesses the functional groups necessary for attracting and binding of the drug molecules. For example, epsilon amino groups of lysine residues and phenolic groups of tyrosine residues actively participate in binding of drug by albumin. Beside this, many and varied sites, capable of binding, exist in albumin.

Large molecule size (either due to inclusion of aromatic rings or due to increase in chain-length) contributes to increase an affinity of albumin towards drug molecule. This has been observed with penicillins, sulphonamides and barbiturates.

5.3 FORCES INVOLVED IN DRUG-PROTEIN INTERACTION

Drug binds with plasma-proteins which hinder their access to the sites of drug action, metabolism and excretion. It remains stored in an inactive form. Thus, drug molecules not only form alliances with the receptors responsible for their pharmacological action but also interact with several other secondary receptors in the body tissues. In the plasma, plasma-proteins play the role of secondary receptors.

Drug molecule binds with proteins through two different modes.

(a) Primary Binding :

A firm binding results through primary binding. This is an ionic interaction in which an ionised form of the drug molecule interacts with the charged molecule of the plasma-protein.

(b) Secondary Binding :

The primary binding alone, is not sufficient for plasma-protein to hold the drug molecule. It is to be supplemented with other secondary binding forces. These forces mainly operate between the non-ionic part of drug and non-polar portion of protein molecule.

The forces involved in secondary binding are :

(1) Hydrogen bonding

(2) Hydrophobic bonding

(3) Van der Waals forces.

(1) Hydrogen bonding : A sort of electrostatic union always exists between a hydrogen atom and an electronegative atom. This bonding can be illustrated as :

$$A - F \ldots\ldots\ldots H - B$$
$$A - O \ldots\ldots\ldots H - B$$

The hydrogen atom may be a part of drug molecule or the plasma-protein. This is an example of *intermolecular hydrogen bonding*.

(2) Hydrophobic bonding : According to the principle of 'like dissolves like', the hydrophobic portion of drug molecule always has a tendency to avoid an aqueous phase. Hydrophobic bonding results through this tendency. Actually bond formation does not take place but association of two hydrophobic portions occur to form micelle like structures in order to avoid water.

Thus, an attraction of non-polar portion of drug molecule towards non-polar portion of another molecule results through their unwelcome reception to water, is known as *hydrophobic bonding*.

(3) Vander Waals forces : This force operates mainly between dipole and induced dipole portions of the molecules. This is categorised as a weak binding force. All the above mentioned secondary binding forces help a non-ionised drug molecule to bind with plasma-protein e.g. steroidal drugs, like hydrocortisone.

There are usually one or two primary binding sites available per protein molecule with several possible secondary sites. The characteristics of each such site depend not only upon the properties of its ionic residues but are also influenced by the properties of neighbouring non-ionic groups, and upon surface configuration and steric hindrances offered to approaching molecules.

5.4 FACTORS AFFECTING DRUG-PROTEIN BINDING

These factors are categorised as :

(a) Physical factors,

(b) Chemical factors, and

(c) Physiological factors.

(a) Physical factors : The pH of blood, ionic strength and temperature are top amongst the list of physical factors. They affect the degree of drug binding in plasma by affecting the number of binding sites available per protein molecule.

(b) Chemical factors : Polarity of drug molecule increases its affinity for protein. For example, salicylic acid binds more strongly with protein than benzoic acid due to increase in number of sites for primary binding.

Similarly, an increase in non-polar portion of drug molecule through addition of non-polar substituent or by lengthening the side-chain results into more firm binding due to increase in number of sites for secondary binding.

Table 5.2

Drug	No. of binding sites per protein molecule (η)	Association constant $K \times 10^4$
Phenol	Negligible	Negligible
Benzoate	0.3	1.5
Salicylate	0.4	3.0

Table 5.3

Compound	η	$K \times 10^4$
Octanol	4.5	3.0
Octyl sulphate	4.5	60.0
Dodecanol	4.5	15.0
Dodecyl sulphate	8.5	120.0

Such enhancement is due to an interaction between the lipophilic portions of drug and protein. Plasma proteins, while interacting with small molecules, exhibit a high degree of structural specificity. The specific structural features of thyroxine analogues necessary for binding with thyroxine binding albumin fraction have been well characterised.

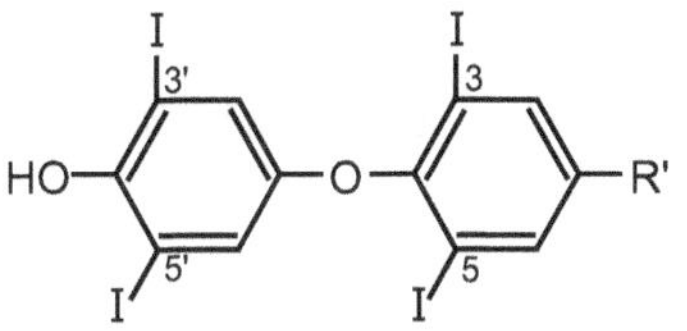

Thyroxine; $R' = -CH_2 - \underset{\underset{NH_2}{|}}{CH} - COOH$

The following structural features favour more efficient binding with plasma-proteins.

(1) A diphenyl ether nucleus.
(2) A free phenolic hydroxyl function.
(3) An ionised moiety separated by about three carbon atoms away from aromatic ring.

In general, the extent of binding of any substance to plasma-proteins is greatly influenced by its partition coefficient value. Other factors which determine the extent of protein binding include decrease in albumin concentration, dose of drug given, route of administration, pathological conditions and genetic factors. These factors affect the number and type of protein binding sites. For example, the protein binding of phenytoin found to increase two times in a healthy person than that in nephrotic or uremic patient.

5.5 MATHEMATICAL DERIVATIONS RELATED TO DRUG-PROTEIN COMPLEX

In most of the cases, the drug-protein complex formation is a reversible reaction, and hence is governed by the law

Protein + Unbound drug $\underset{k_2}{\overset{k_1}{\rightleftharpoons}}$ Protein : Drug

1   1   1 : 1

...(5.1)

If P_u = Unbound plasma-protein concentration

D_u = Unbound or free drug concentration, and

PD = Protein-drug complex concentration.

Then, the equilibrium constant k, can be calculated by :

$$k = \frac{k_1}{k_2} = \frac{(PD)}{(P_u)(D_u)} \quad ...(5.2)$$

Using experimental models, the concentration of bound and free drug can also be determined or may be known.

The average number of drug molecules bound per protein molecule (r) can then be calculated by :

$$r = \frac{\text{Moles of drug bound}}{\text{Total moles of plasma-protein}}$$

$$r = \frac{(PD)}{(PD) + P_u}$$

$$= \frac{k(P_u)(D_u)}{k(P_u)(D_u) + (P_u)} \quad ...(5.3)$$

$$r = \frac{k(D_u)}{k(D_u) + 1} \quad ...(5.4)$$

If 'η' equals to total number of binding sites on each protein molecule then equation (5.4) can be rewritten as :

$$r = \frac{\eta k(D_u)}{1 + k(D_u)} \quad ...(5.5)$$

This is the expression that is identical with the Langmuir isotherm.

Similarly, the fraction of the total bound drug in plasma (β) can also be calculated by

$$\beta = \frac{[DP]}{[D]}$$

$$= \frac{1}{1 + \frac{1}{\eta k(P_T)} + \frac{[D_u]}{\eta [P_T]}} \quad ...(5.6)$$

where,

[DP] = Concentration of bound drug in plasma,

[D] = Total drug concentration,

P_T = Total protein concentration.

5.6 METHODS EMPLOYED TO DETECT THE DRUG-PROTEIN INTERACTION

Sometimes, the activity of a drug may change suddenly in its magnitude. This may be due to either :

(a) Fluctuation in the concentration of free drug due to its binding to, or release from plasma-proteins, or

(b) Change in the thermodynamic activity of drug.

Different methods have been documented in literature to demonstrate the presence of an interaction between drug and plasma-protein. All are coiled around three basic principles :

(i) Methods based upon reduction in free drug concentration :

(a) Dialysis,

(b) Ultra-filtration,

(c) Differential adsorption,

(d) Osmotic pressure, surface tension, vapour pressure and freezing point,

(e) Biological activity.

(ii) Methods based upon alteration of drug properties :

(a) Solubility,

(b) Diffusion,

(c) Stabilization,

(d) Electrophoresis,

(e) Spectrophotometry.

(iii) Methods based upon alteration of protein properties or behaviour :

(a) Precipitation,

(b) Stabilization of protein,

(c) Viscosity, electrophoretic mobility, sedimentation rate and other related properties.

The chemical reactivity of many plasma-proteins differ and is dependent largely upon their amino acid compositions and physical characteristics.

5.7 PHARMACOLOGICAL SIGNIFICANCE OF DRUG-PROTEIN INTERACTION

Depending upon their structural features, most drugs interact at their therapeutic concentration with one or more of the plasma-proteins. This may give rise to different possibilities like :

(1) Drug bound to plasma-protein is pharmacologically active and can penetrate the sites of drug action.

(2) When only unbound or free drug is active, then protein binding may :
  (a) act as a reservoir of drug and prolong the duration of action,
  (b) facilitate the distribution of drug throughout the body,
  (c) retard the excretion of drug,
  (d) lower the therapeutic concentration of the drug by not allowing a sufficient concentration of free drug to develop at the receptor site,
  (e) unbound drug is freely diffusible and the drug-protein complex is generally confined to the circulating plasma.

"Proteins Investigated" : S, serum (or whole plasma); F, plasma fractions; A, albumin fraction (impure); A*, crystalline albumin; (b), bovine; (c), cat; (ch), chicken; (d), dog; (f), frog; (g), goose; (ho), horse; (h), human; (p) pig; (r) rabbit; (s) sheep.

"Methods" : B, biological action; C, conductivity; D, dialysis; DA, differential adsorption; Di, diffusion; E, electrophoresis; EA, enzyme activity; EM, electrophoretic mobility; FP, freezing point; OP, osmotic pressure; P, precipitation; Sb, stabilization (of drug); So, solubility; SP, stabilization (of protein); SR, sedimentation rate; ST, surface tension; Sy, spectrophotometry; U, ultrafiltration; V, viscosity; VP, vapour pressure.

(bac.) bacteria; (c.g.) cat gut; (cl) clotting time; (f.h.) frog heart; (hem.) hemolysis; (m.a.) mouse assay; (r.h.) rabbit heart.

O, none; S, interaction, in an experiment with serum, where the specific protein interacting was not further identified; A, A*, interaction wich albumin (impure) or crystalline albumin; G, interaction, with globulin fraction.

"Ease of Reversibility" : +, definitely reversible by simple means, e.g. dilution; (+), probably reversible by simple means, not proved definitely; —, apparently not reversible by simple means.

"Complex dissociated by" : Lists of special reagents which seem to dissociate the complex without denaturation of the protein.

Table 5.4

	Substance	Protein investigated	Method	Primary interaction with	Ease of reversibility	Complex dissociated by
1.	Iron	F (h), S (h)	B, (bac)	G (β_1-pseduo) in IV—7	(—)	pH < 5
2.	Glucose	S (b), S (h)	U, E	S, O		
3.	Cholesterol	S (h)	E	G		

contd...

4.	Estrogens	S (b, r, h)	P, D	S	(+)	Vigorous acid hydrolysis
5.	Ascorbic acids	S (h)	E	A	(+)	
6.	Vit. K	S (h)	E	A		
7.	Nicotinamide	S (h)	E	G		
8.	Riboflavin	S (h)	E	G (eu-)		
9.	Thiamine	S (h)	E	O		
10.	Barbiturates	S (h)	E	A	(+)	
11.	Heparin	F (h, ho)	E, B (cl.)	A	(+)	
12.	PAS	S (h), A(b)	U	A	(+)	
13.	Salicylate	S (h, b)	D	S	(+)	
14.	Atropine	S (b, r)	D, B (c.g.)	S	(+)	Citrate, peptone
15.	Caffeine	S (ho)	D	S	(+)	
16.	Cocaine	S (b, ho, r)	D	S	(+)	High pH with ether
17.	Epinephrine	S (h)	SB	S		
18.	Morphine	S (h)	D	S	(+)	Citrate, peptone

[A] Effect of Protein Binding on Drug Distribution :

(i) Protein bound drug is unable to penetrate membranes and is confined to the circulating plasma. It cannot diffuse to the site of action or metabolise in other compartments.

Only free drug can cross biological membranes. This transfer is mainly influenced by partition coefficient and concentration gradient of the free drug. Protein binding, therefore, by acting as reservoir of drug, can decrease the rate of drug disappearance from general circulation. When required it dissociates to release free drug and maintains a steady state concentration level of free drug. It thus compensates the loss of free drug by excretion or metabolism e.g., the affinity and extent of binding of different sulfonamides enable these drugs to be classified into long and short acting categories. Sulfamethoxydiazine strongly binds with plasma-proteins. Hence, it is a long acting drug, whereas sulfathiazole weakly binds to proteins resulting into its short duration of action.

(ii) Protein binding of drug slows the rate of distribution of drug into peripheral compartments.

(iii) Placenta is a demarcation line between the maternal and the foetal circulation. Hormones such as thyroxine, is not required in foetus before the appearance of foetal endocrine glands. Since the placenta is not permeable to the proteins, protein binding of thyroxine limits its access to the foetal circulation.

(iv) Ferrous ions are transported to the bone marrow with transferin, a β-globulin. They are utilised in the formation of haemoglobin but are toxic when they are not bound in the plasma.

(v) Protein binding of a drug may project misleading conclusions, if two drugs of the same pharmacological category, are compared on the basis of concentration of drug in the plasma.

[B] Effect of Protein Binding on Drug Metabolism :

In general, the drug present in the unbound form is available for metabolic processes. Hence, the rate of metabolism is inversely proportional to the extent of protein binding of a drug.

[C] Effect of Protein Binding on Drug Elimination :

Even though renal blood supply consists of both, bound and free drug, only the free drug is filterable through the glomerular filter. The concentration of free drug in the glomerular filtrate equals to the concentration of free drug in the plasma. Hence, the drug elimination via the kidneys is influenced by the extent of plasma-protein binding of a drug.

Glomerular filtration rate of a drug

$$\propto \frac{1}{\text{Extent of protein binding}}$$

It means that increased protein binding decreases the rate of elimination of a drug, resulting into prolonged biological half-life. But it does not hold true, if the rate of dissociation of drug-protein complex is high. For example, the rate of dissociation of penicillin-protein complex is considerably high. Hence, penicillin can be completely removed from the blood during single passage through the kidneys.

5.8 EFFECT OF DISPLACEMENT OF BOUND DRUG

There are obvious occasions where drugs bounded with plasma-proteins can be partially or completely liberated by another drug. This leads to increase in pharmacological response of the displaced drug due to an increase in the concentration of free drug in plasma and biophase. In such cases, the dissociation constant and the apparent volume of distribution determine the rate of excretion of the displaced drug.

The effect of displacement could be sudden if the binding exceeds 90-95%. For example, in the case of a drug which is 98% bound, a displacement of 2% drug will lead to a substantial 100% increase in the unbound drug concentration in plasma. In such cases, if the volume of distribution (V_D) is large the effects may be minimal. Serious toxic effects may appear if V_D is small. This is due to a significant rise of drug concentration in plasma and biophase.

Some drugs may exert an indirect biological effect by displacing other drugs from plasma-proteins. This can reasonably be attributed to competition between the drugs that are known to act on same physiological receptors or that share some common structural features.

Examples include :

(1) Sulphonyl urea anti-diabetic agents displace insulin from its complex with protein.
(2) Atropine displaces pilocarpine.
(3) Salicylates and sulphonamides displace bilirubin.
(4) Acetylcholine displaces carbonic ester inhibitors from their complex with the plasma cholinesterases.
(5) Similarly, benzoates and salicylates displace thyroid hormone.

The impairment of the binding capacity of plasma-proteins (e.g. hypoalbuminemia) may be a significant factor in justifying an unusual sensitivity or resistance to drugs. Moderate hypo-albuminemia may be caused by a number of diseases and conditions such as cancer, myocardial infarction, pregnancy, prolonged immobilisation, G.I.T. disorders etc. Severe hypoalbuminemia is observed in severe burns, liver and renal impairments. In renal impairment, decreased binding of acidic and neutral (but not basic drugs) drugs to plasma-protein is found.

5.9 DRUG PERSISTENCE

Beside plasma-proteins, tissue proteins also exhibit an affinity for certain drugs. They thus provide drug depots outside the plasma. This process obviously is reversible. The effective intracellular protein concentration is considerably higher for certain body organs, e.g. liver, lung, spleen, muscles etc. They have much higher affinity for certain drugs which include emetine, suramin, quinacrine and organic arsenicals and antimonials. For example, quinacrine, an antimalarial drug, after 4 hours of administration, shows a 2000 fold concentration in liver than in plasma. After 14 days of daily administration, the concentration of drug in liver touches to 20,000 times to that in plasma. It is not entirely clear whether albumin or a globulin is primarily involved in it.

5.10 DRUG ALLERGY

An allergy arises due to antigen-antibody interaction, which itself can be interpreted in terms of protein-protein interaction. Landsteiner has developed a method of producing an artificial drug antigen (by coupling particular drug to protein through diazolinkage) which can be utilised to get specific antibody responses in experimental animals. Strychnine, epinephrine, aspirin, sulphonamides are among the drugs which have been tried. In many cases, only albumins qualify themselves to act as antigens but purified globulins could not give expected results.

5.11 SUBSTANCES THAT APPARENTLY DO NOT INTERACT WITH PLASMA-PROTEINS

Though most of the drugs bind with plasma-proteins, there still remain a short list of substances which are least interested in forming association with plasma-proteins.

This list includes :

(a) Sodium and potassium ions,

(b) Nitrous oxide,

(c) Thiamine,

(d) Histamine and choline,

(e) Streptomycin.

These agents interact with plasma-protein weakly if at all.

RECEPTORS

6.1 INTRODUCTION

To exhibit the same pharmacological action, the two drugs must share certain structural features in common alongwith the same spatial arrangement of such groups. Such requirement cannot logically be explained unless it is assumed that for a drug, in order to produce its pharmacological action, it must react or interact with the complementary chemical groupings of a biologically important integral part of the organism known as *receptor*.

Paul Ehrlich (1842-1912), the father of chemotherapy and J.N. Langley (1852 – 1926) a physiologist, were among the first to express the concept about the existence of receptive substances or more simply, receptors in the body organs. This concept was elaborated further by A. J. Clark in 1937. He considered the receptors as the dominant loci of drug action, which are not fixed. Receptors are devices at which drugs interact to initiate a series of complex events that is latter amplified to give biological response. In most of the cases, the drug-receptor interaction is a unimolecular reversible process which is brought to the end by drug metabolism and its elimination from the body.

Biological activity of a drug is the result of its interaction with receptor(s). The **biological response** may consist of both, the **therapeutic effect** and **adverse**

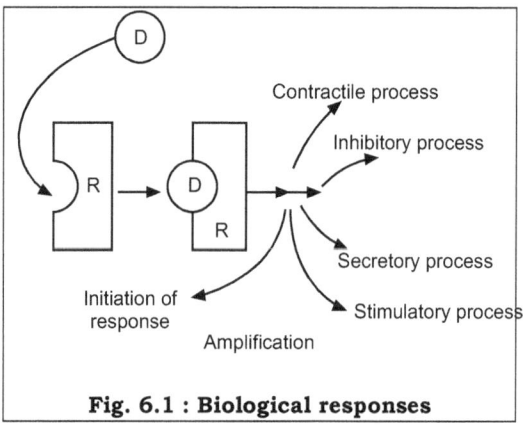

Fig. 6.1 : Biological responses

effects. Thus, initiation (acceleration) or inhibition (diminish) of the bio-chemical or ionic processes is associated with the drug-receptor interaction. Single drug may generate multiple responses or distinct drugs may share same family of receptors to initiate or inhibit a common response.

The term receptor denotes a relatively small region of a macro-molecule which may be –

(a) **An enzyme :** For example, digitalis utilizes Na^+ - K^+ - ATPase enzyme as its receptor.

(b) **A structural component of a cell membrane :** CNS depressants in general, get deposited in the cell membrane to exhibit their activity, e.g. general anesthetics, sedative – hypnotic agents etc.

(c) **Carrier proteins :** Steroidal and thyroidal drugs bind with intracellular receptor moieties, which then carry the drug into the cell nucleus to cause changes in the expression of genetic machinery.

(d) Genetic material : Many anti-cancer drugs act at the level of DNA or RNA.

Thus to initiate the biological response, the drug should possess structural features that are necessary to fire the receptor. By virtue of such interactions with receptors, drugs do not create new effects but merely modulate the rates of ongoing bio-chemical reaction. A classic example involves opiate receptors. In 1975, the endogenous peptides (e.g., endorphins), that interact with opiate receptors, were identified. Morphine and other narcotic analgetic agents merely mimick endorphins by combining with opiate receptors. Thus, in simple pharmacological words, a drug cannot impart a new function to a cell but is potentially capable of altering the rate at which any bodily function proceeds.

Receptor serves as a device through which an immensely complex language of extra-cellular stimuli is translated to the cell and is reciprocated in terms of ionic, electrical and chemical signals. In terms of Newton's third law, if one considered the signals of extra-cellular environment as 'action', then the receptors serve as a media through which 'reaction' is propagated. The mechanism of drug action and development of resistance, tolerance and super-sensitivity can best be explained with the help of the receptor concept. By knowing the chemical features of a series of compounds eliciting same pharmacological response, the shape, size and charge distribution of the active sites present on the receptor surface can easily be imagined. For example, the endplate region of a skeletal muscle fiber contains large number of receptors with a high affinity for the neurotransmittor, acetylcholine. They are known as nicotinic cholinergic receptors. A nicotinic receptor has a molecular weight of 250,000. It is found to be an oligomer, composed of 5 sub-units $\alpha_2 \beta \gamma \delta$ each a glycoprotein), embedded in the lipid bilayer of the cell-membrane. Three sub-units are fused to form an ion channel. The cholinergic drugs may bind with the 4th subunit to open or to close this ion channel, thus influencing the transmembrane ion flux and membrane potential.

Recently, radio-actively labelled compounds of high selectivity were developed to search and to measure the drug binding sites on receptor surface and to determine localization, population and purification of receptor per cell.

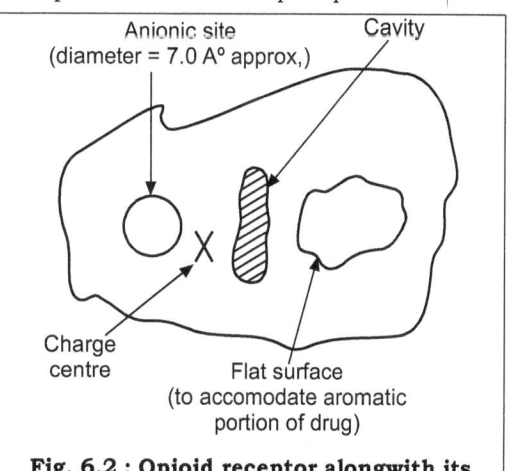

Fig. 6.2 : Opioid receptor alongwith its active drug-binding sites

The ability of a drug to bind to the receptor is termed as 'affinity of the drug for the receptor'. While the drug ability to elicit its pharmacological response is termed as its 'intrinsic activity or efficacy'.

Intrinsic activity defines the drug whether it is an agonist, an antagonist or a partial agonist. For example, when a drug molecule possesses a high affinity as well as high intrinsic activity, it is known as 'agonist'. Those having a high affinity but poor intrinsic activity, are known as 'antagonists' and drug having an affinity equal or less than that of the agonist but with less intrinsic activity is termed as *partial agonist*'.

If efficacy (intrinisic activity) for a full agnosist is considered equal to one (1), that of antagonist, it will be nearly equal to zero (0). Partial agonists also change receptor conformation but not to the extent necessary to result in full efficacy. Hence, the intrinisic activity of partial agonist ranges between zero to one. In fact, many weak partial agonists were used as competitive antagonists.

6.2 CLASSIFICATION

The existence of receptors for a wide variety of pharmacological categories of drugs, has been confirmed. The cholinergic agents act though cholinergic receptors that are further sub-divided on the basis of effects and selective antagonists. For example, some of the actions of cholinergic agents are mimicked by muscarine, an alkaloid whereas the remaining actions are mimicked by another alkaloid nicotine. Hence, the receptors through which former actions are propagated and which are blocked by atropine, are known as 'muscarinic receptors' while the receptors blocked by curare, are termed as 'nicotinic receptors'.

Similarly in 1948, Ahlquist observed that the tissues he examined, carried two kinds of adrenergic responses. He sub-divided the adrenergic receptors into α-receptors and β-receptors. α-receptors are mainly associated with excitatory processes and β-receptors are mainly associated with inhibitory processes, except their action on heart. Lands etal proposed further sub-division of the β-receptors into $β_1$ and $β_2$ receptors. $β_1$ receptors are involved in certain intestinal smooth muscle responses and stimulate cardiac muscle and lipolysis. $β_2$ receptors are predominantly located in bronchi, uterus and blood vessels.

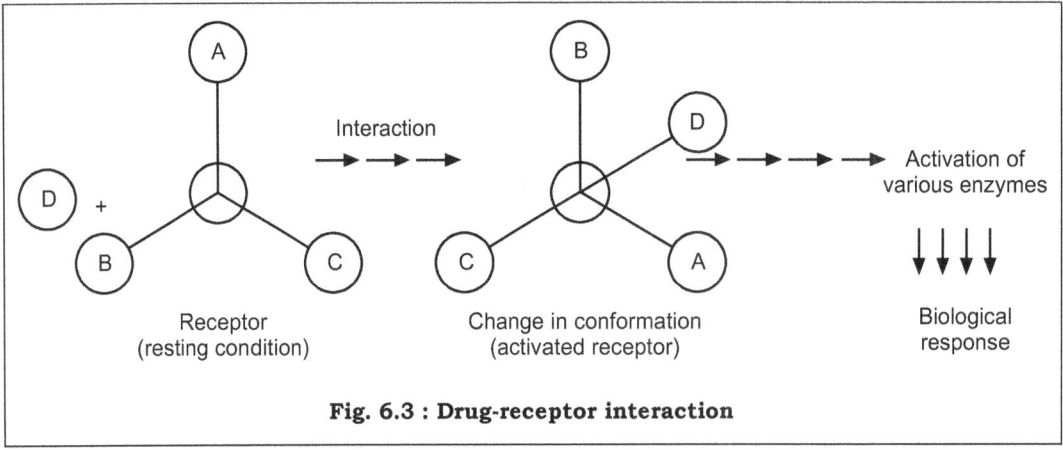

Fig. 6.3 : Drug-receptor interaction

Similarly, α-receptors are categoriezed as either α_1 or α_2 receptors. α_1-receptors are present on post-synaptic receptor sites of smooth muscle and gland cells while α_2-receptors are present on nerve terminal and also on post-synaptic cells in several tissues. On the similar lines, histaminic receptors are sub-divided into H_1 and H_2 receptors and benzodiazepine receptors into BZ_1 and BZ_2 receptors.

6.3 TYPES OF RECEPTOR

(a) Membrane Bound Receptor Systems:

The cells of the body are bathed in fluids whose major constituents are held at remarkably constant concentrations over a long period. The signals from the extra-cellular environment are translated to the cell in terms of fluctuation in ionic, electrical or chemical properties of the cell-membrane. Certain hormonal and neurotransmitter receptors are associated with structural and functional elements of the cell by relatively weak covalent bonds and may be solubilized and isolated by treatment with non-ionic detergents, without the loss of their binding properties. Receptors for several neuro-transmitters (e.g., acetylcholine, γ-amino butyric acid, glycine etc.) are themselves associated with ion channels or ionophores, in the cell membranes.

Cholinergic receptors, for example, are an integral part of the post-synaptic membrane of the cholinergic nerve. Stimulation of the nerve results in the release of acetylcholine from the presynaptic nerve endings. The interaction of released acetylcholine with receptors results in the opening of Na-ion channels and Na^+ flows inwards. The influx of sodium ions, coupled with other ionic processes, leads to change in trans-membrane electrical potential, as a result of change in the state of specific ionophore or ion conductance modulator.

The ionophore is a protein that is distinct from the receptor, perhaps of the molecular weight 43,000. The receptor and ionophore are strongly associated in the native membrane.

Besides acetylcholine, insulin, ACTH, glucagon and epinephrine, all appear to bind with their plasma-membrane bound receptor sites.

(b) Receptors Acting Through Second Messenger System :

Receptors for a number of hormones and neurotransmitters function by regulation of the concentration of the intracellular second messenger, cyclic adenosine 3', 5' monophosphate (cyclic AMP) through the activation of intracellular adenylate cyclase. The role of cyclic AMP in the propogation of intracellular signals was proposed by late

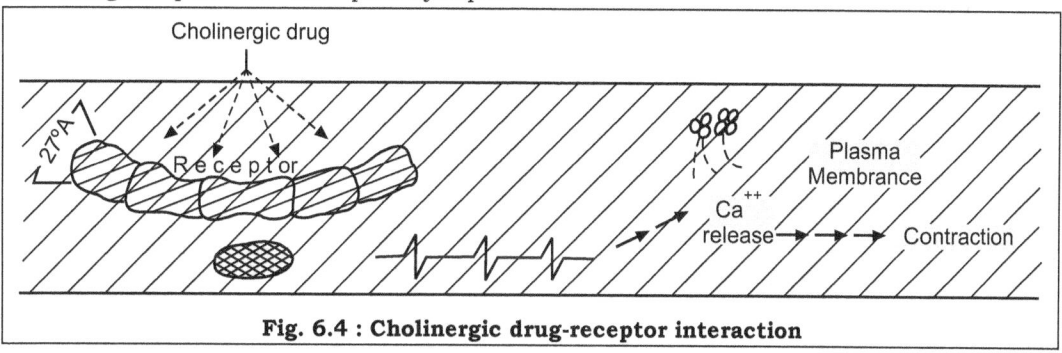

Fig. 6.4 : Cholinergic drug-receptor interaction

Earl Sutherland and his colleagues. He postulated that cyclic-AMP plays the role of second messenger in the activation of β-adrenergic, glucagon and various other hormone system. c-AMP illucits a variety of effects, both at the cytoplasmic and nuclear level.

Yet another second messenger is cytoplasmic calcium ions. They regulate some functions directly and regulate others only when they are bound to the intracellular Ca^{++} dependent regulatory protein, calmodulin.

Generally each mole of calmodulin forms a complex with four moles of Ca^{++} ions. Many drugs can also bind with calmodulin and may interfere in the activation of several enzyme systems regulated by calmodulin. These drugs have the structural features as shown below.

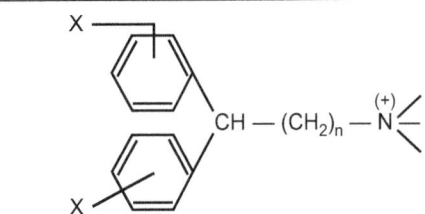

Fig. 6.5 : Structural features necessary to interact with calmodulin

Many drugs lead to the activation of adenylate cyclase. They include, $β_1$, $β_2$-adrenergic drugs, H_2-histaminic agents, adrenocorticotropic hormone, glucagon (probably G_2-receptors), and prostacycline. Similarly, receptors that inhibit adenylate cyclase, include, $α_2$-adrenergic, muscarinic and opioid receptors.

The stimulatory or inhibitory receptors (acting through second messenger) are embedded in the plasma-membrane. They face the exterior side of the membrane.

The enzyme catalytic site (adenylate cyclase) is on separate protein, which faces the interior of the cell. If the adenylate cyclase is activated, it catalyses the conversion of ATP and Mg^{++} ions into cyclic AMP. Ns GTP causes activation of adenylate cyclase and Ni GTP causes its inhibition. c-AMP is the active factor that stimulates or activates various c-AMP dependent protein kinases. c-AMP action is terminated by the phosphodiesterase enzymes which destroy c-AMP.

The action of a wide variety of hormones and drugs is operated through the Ca^{++} signals, generated by cytosolic Ca^{++} ion concentration. The signal generation leads to the rapid breakdown of membrane inositol phospholipids into inositol triphosphates and diacylglycerol. Inositol triphosphate mobilizes Ca^{++} ions from bound Ca^{++} intra-cellular stores. Thus, it acts as a messenger for the intracellular mobilization of Ca^{++}. Besides this, Ca^{++} influx is also stimulated to increase cytosolic Ca^{++} ion concentration. The binding of cytosolic Ca^{++} with intracellullar Ca^{++} dependent regulatory protein, calmodulin causes initiation of phosphorylation of target proteins. Another breakdown product, diacylglycerol causes activation of protein kinase C. The latter, independently, initiates phosphorylation of different chains of target proteins. Thus, the drug-receptor interaction may lead to an increase or decrease in the intra-cellular concentration of either c-AMP or calcium ions, resulting into an activation or termination of dependent bio-chemical reaction. The biological response thus obtained, is said to be propagated through second messenger system.

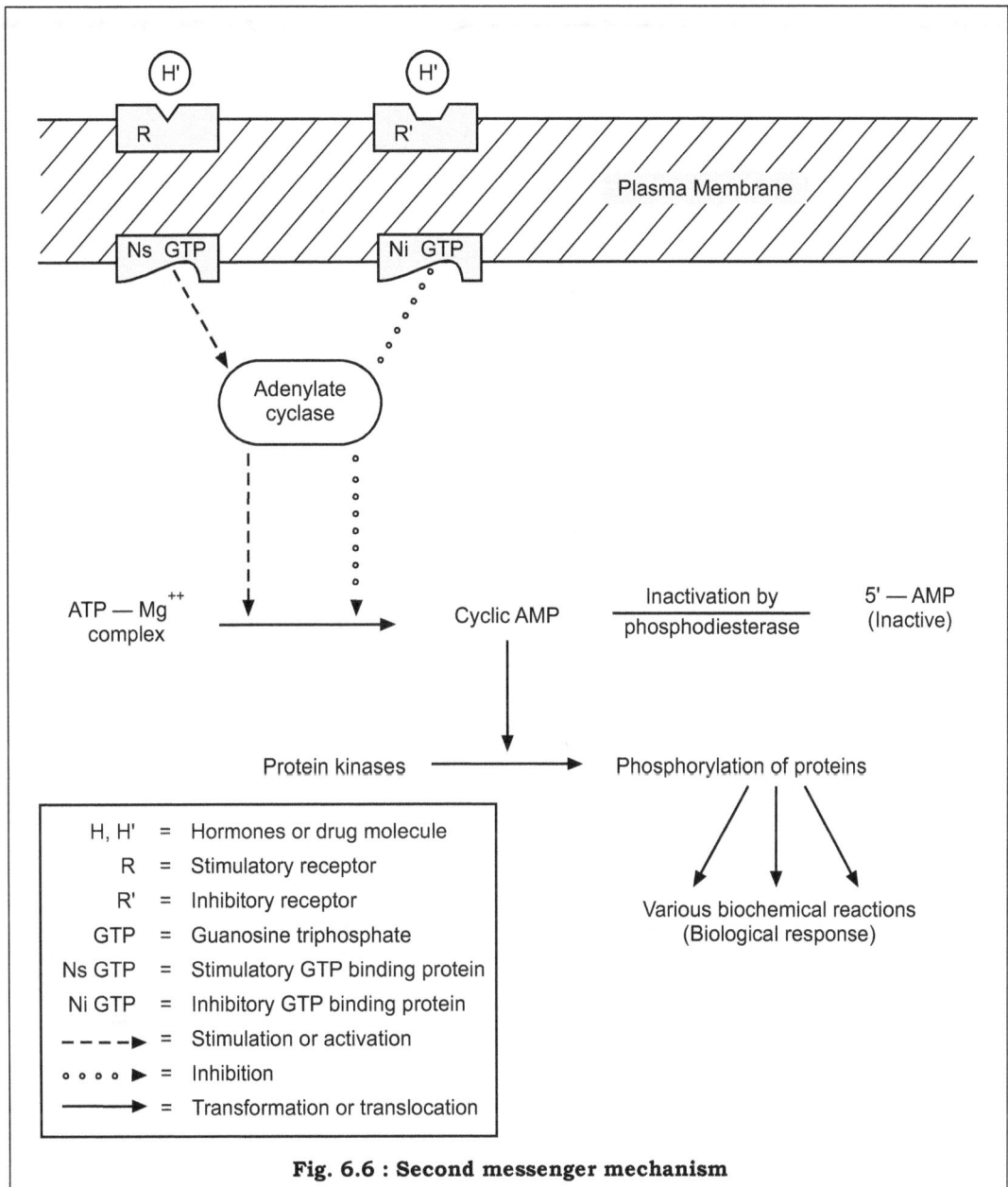

Fig. 6.6 : Second messenger mechanism

(c) Intracellular Receptors :

Intracellular receptors play a dominant role in the mechanism of actions of the steroid and thyroid hormones, vitamin A and vitamin D. After entering the drug into the cell, it forms complex with specific cytoplasmic binding proteins (receptors). The drug-receptor complex undergoes a conformational change and is thereby activated.

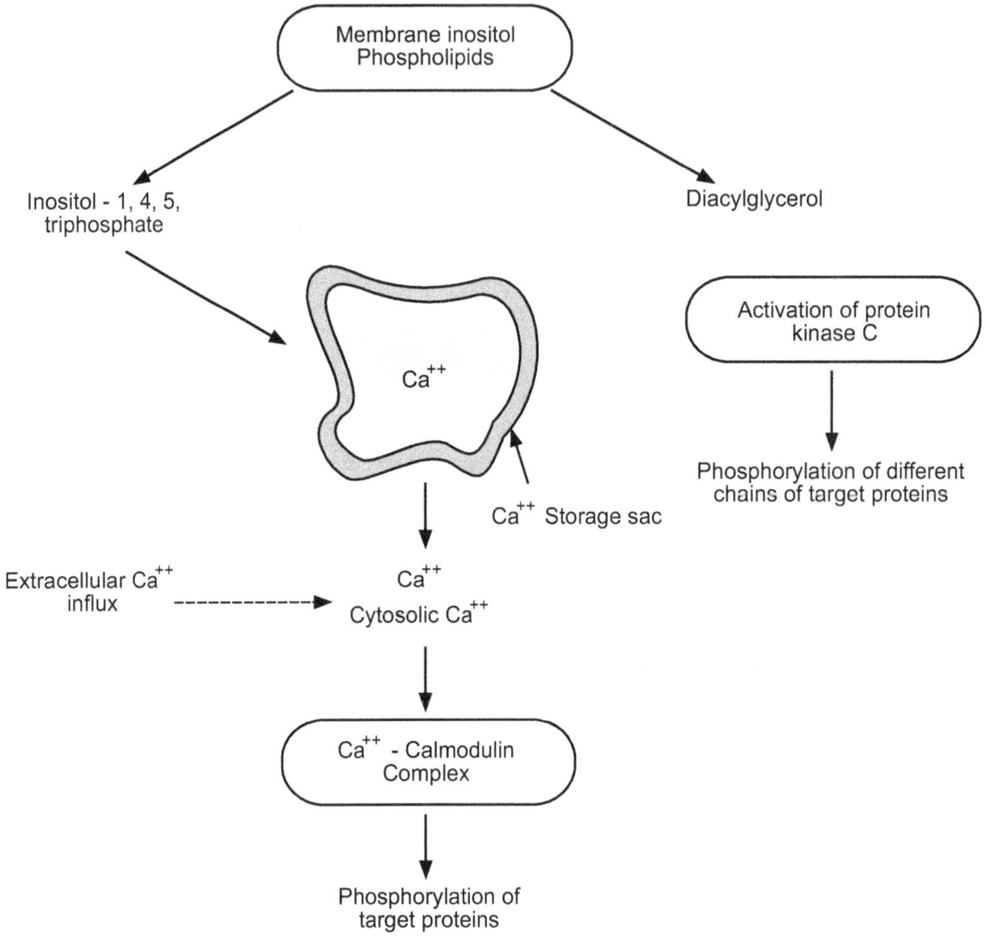

Membrane inositol Phospholipids
Inositol - 1, 4, 5, triphosphate
Diacylglycerol
Ca^{++}
Activation of protein kinase C
Phosphorylation of different chains of target proteins
Ca^{++} Storage sac
Extracellular Ca^{++} influx
Ca^{++}
Cytosolic Ca^{++}
Ca^{++} - Calmodulin Complex
Phosphorylation of target proteins

Fig. 6.7 : Mechanism of Ca^{++} - dependent hormone action

Drug receptor complex
Nucleus
Chromatin
D
R
D
R
Nucleus
D
R
Carrier receptor
Drug chromatin binding

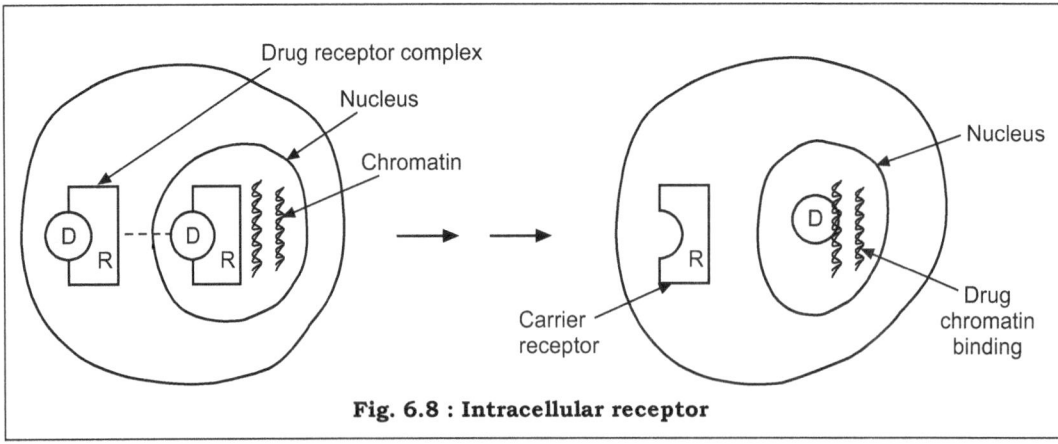

Fig. 6.8 : Intracellular receptor

This activated complex then enters into the nucleus and releases the free drug. The drug molecule then binds to the acceptor sites on nuclear chromatin. Here the receptor behaves as if it is a carrier protein, hence some workers consider chromatin as an actual or true receptor. The drug binding to the chromatin results in an increase or decrease in the production of certain RNA's and m-RNA's along with the corresponding enzymes and other proteins which cause the biological response.

Receptors that act by different primary mechanism can be co-ordinated at other levels.

6.4 RECEPTOR SITE THEORIES

(a) Occupation Theory :

The pharmacological response of a drug molecule is a function of dose, number of receptors available and its intrinsic activity. The rate of combination of drug and receptor can therefore be expressed as under -

Rate of combination of drug with receptor
$$= K_1 [R] \times [A]$$

where,

K_1 = Association constant

R = Concentration of the receptors not occupied by drug molecules and

A = Concentration of drug molecules or dose.

Similarly, the rate of dissociation of the drug-receptor complex is given by the following expression

Rate of dissociation of drug-receptor complex = $K_2 [RA]$

where,

K_2 = dissociation constant.

[RA] = concentration of receptors occupied by the drug.

At equilibrium,
$$K_1 [R] \times [A] = K_2 [RA]$$

This relationship can be more conveniently expressed by taking account of the fact that [R] + [RA] is the equal to [r] = total concentration of receptors. Thus,

$$K_1 [A] [r] - [RA] = K_2 [RA] \quad \ldots (6.1)$$

Or
$$\frac{[RA]}{[r]} = \frac{K_1 [A]}{K_1 [A] + K_2}$$

$$= \frac{1}{1 + K_2/K_1 [A]} \quad \ldots (6.2)$$

Here, $\frac{K_2}{K_1}$ can be replaced by,

KA = equilibrium constant. It is reciprocal of the drug's affinity for the receptors. The term $\frac{[RA]}{[\gamma]}$ represents the fraction of the total number of receptors occupied by the drug. When [RA] = [γ], i.e. all the receptors are occupied and the response is thus proportional to its intrinsic activity, α.

Thus, relative response will be equal to -

$$\frac{[RA]}{[\gamma]} = \frac{\alpha}{1 + KA/[A]} \quad \ldots (6.3)$$

(b) Rate Theory :

Paton and Rang in 1965 proposed that the most important factor determining drug action is the rate at which drug-receptor combination takes place.

At equilibrium, the rates of combination and dissociation of drug-receptor reactions are same and equation (6.1) can be re-written as :

$$\frac{K_1 [A] ([r] - [RA])}{[\gamma]} = \frac{K_2 [RA]}{[\gamma]} \quad \ldots (6.4)$$

By simple mathematical manipulation from equation (6.3), it can be shown that

Rate of receptor occupation
$$= \frac{K_2}{1 + \frac{KA}{[A]}} \quad \ldots (6.5)$$

When the response is proportional to the number of receptors occupied, the equation (6.3) of occupation theory is important and when the response is proportional to the rate of receptor occupation rather than to the proportion of receptors occupied, equation (6.5) of rate theory is important.

(c) The Induced-fit Theory of Enzyme-Substrate Interaction :

This theory states that after combination, the substrate induces a change in conformation of the enzyme, leading to an enzymatically active orientation of groups. e.g., acetylcholine may interact with the regulating protein and alter the normal forces which stabilize the structure of the protein, thereby producing a transient rearrangement in the membrane structure and a consequent change in its ion regulating property.

(d) Macromolecular Enzyme Perturbation Theory :

According to this theory, Belleau proposed that interaction of small molecules of drug or a substrate with a macromolecule (such as the protein or a drug receptor) may lead either to specific conformational perturbations (SCP) or to non-specific conformational perturbation (NSCP).

A SCP (specific conformation) possesses intrinsic activity and would result into biological response.

If a NSCP occurs, no stimulant response would be obtained and an antagonistic or blocking action may be produced. If a drug possesses features which contribute to formation of both, a SCP and a NSCP, an equilibrium mixture of the two complexes may result, which would account for a partial stimulant action e.g. alkyl trimethyl ammonium ions.

$$[CH_3 - (CH_2)_n - N^+(CH_3)_3]$$

Lower alkyl trimethyl ammonium ions, (n = upto 4) alter the receptor structure in a specific perturbation, thus stimulate the muscarinic receptor. With 'n' in between 8 to 12, an antagonistic action is observed due to non-specific conformational perturbation while intermediate, (n = 5 to 8) derivatives act as partial agonists.

6.5 FORCES INVOLVED IN DRUG-RECEPTOR INTERACTIONS

To initiate a biological response, the drug must form bonds with the receptor surface. When the drug is administered into the body, it passes into the biophase, (i.e., an area in viscinity to receptor surface). When it attains a critical concentration level in biophase, it starts forming bonds with the receptor surface. The different types of binding forces that may exist in drug-receptor interactions are as follows :

(a) Covalent Bonding :

Covalent bond is a strong and stable bond. The stability of this type of bond hardly permits the formation of an easily reversible drug-receptor complex at body temperature. Only when the receptor is inactivated by an irreversible antagonist, there is the formation of covalent bond e.g. the enzymes acetylcholinesterases are irreversibly inactivated by a number of phosphate esters. Similarly antineoplastic or antibiotic drugs act mainly through the formation of covalent bonds resulting into long-lasting inhibition of cell replication.

(b) Hydrogen Bonding :

An important type of bonding between drugs and receptors is a weak and easily broken hydrogen bond. Since many drugs contain hydroxyl, amino, carboxyl and carbonyl groups, they can form hydrogen bonds with the complementary groups present on the receptor surface. H-bonding aids in creating a reasonably stable drug-receptor complex. The reduced potency of many sulphur analogues of oxygen-containing drugs has been attributed to the reduced ability of sulphur to form H-bond.

(c) Electrostatic Bonding :

The receptor surface has a number of ionizable groups at physiological pH. These ionized groups (e.g. carboxyl, hydroxyl, phosphoryl, amino etc.) easily interact with the ionized groups of the drug molecule. The charged ions produced by the drug molecules may be attracted to the charged groups within the receptor site. For example, in acetylcholine molecule, the positively charged quaternary nitrogen may be attracted to the negative charged ionized carboxyl group present in the receptor site.

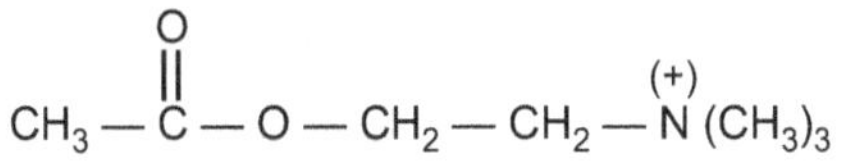

$$CH_3 - \overset{\overset{O}{\|}}{C} - O - CH_2 - CH_2 - \overset{(+)}{N}(CH_3)_3$$

Acetyl choline

The strength of ionic bond diminishes in proportion to the square of the distance between the ionic species.

(d) Dipole-dipole and Ion-dipole Interactions :

These forces are generally associated alongwith electrostatic bondings.

$$\overset{(+)}{R_4N} \text{-----------------} NR_3$$

Ion-dipole interaction

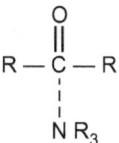

Dipole-dipole interaction

(e) Hydrophobic Forces :

Most of the drug molecules have non-polar portion (alkyl or aryl groups) which may combine with non-polar section of the receptor site through hydrophobic forces. It is a reversible type of bonding that liberates energy.

(f) Vander Waals Forces :

It occurs less frequently than hydrophobic forces. It can occur only when the receptor and a portion of the drug form a perfect fit, which bring the atoms in close proximity. e.g., in acetyl-choline-cholinesterase interaction, methyl groups of drug moledule, are atttached to enzyme surface through Vander Waals forces.

Table 6.1

	Bond type	Strength Kcal/mol
1.	Covalent	40 - 140
2.	Ionic	5 - 10
3.	Hydrogen	1 - 7
4.	Dipole - dipole	1 - 7
5.	Hydrophobic	1

6.6 SPARE RECEPTORS

In most of the cases, the biological response is a function of total number of receptors that are occupied or activated by drug molecules. But in certain cases, it has been observed that a relatively small fraction of the available receptors, if occupied, may result into the maximal biological response of which, the tissue is capable. Furchgott (1954) showed that only 1% of the total receptors have to be occupied in order to get the maximum response. Here the remaining 99% receptors, even if occupied or unoccupied, do not make any difference. Such receptors are known as spare *receptors or reserved receptors*. These receptors are not qualitatively different from non-spare receptors. Myocardium is said to contain a large number of spare receptors. They are not inactive receptors. An agonist can easily turn on the spare receptor to get a response but the maximum effect is attained as soon as the desired number of receptors have been activated.

6.7 SILENT RECEPTORS

The binding sites of any origin, that can retain the drug molecules, without initiating the biological response, are known as *silent receptors* e.g. the adsorption sites on plasma-proteins can be categorised as silent receptors. The binding of drug on plasma-protein does not evoke the response. It delays the release of free drug into the plasma, hence the drug-effect and drug-metabolism. Thus, silent receptor prolongs duration of action of drug. Some drugs may displace another drug from the silent receptors resulting into an unexpected rise in the plasma concentration of that drug. Thus, promotion and potentiation of drug effect occurs due to competitive affinity of two drugs for the same silent receptors. By a proper controlled change of chemical environment, one can activate the silent receptors to get the biological response.

6.8 FACTORS AFFECTING THE DRUG-RECEPTOR INTERACTIONS

The basis of attempts to design compounds of similar biological activity not only involves the presence of common functional groups in compounds but also such groups should be in same specific spatial relationship to each other. This consideration has led to the study of following important factors which affect the drug-receptor interactions.

(1) Isosterism :

Groups of atoms which impart similar physical or chemical properties to a molecule due to similarities in size, electronegativity or stereochemistry are referred under the general term of isostere. For example, the molecules N_2 and CO, both possess total 14 electrons and show similar physical properties. Examples of isosteric pairs which possess similar steric and electronic configurations are : sulphonamide ($SO_2 NR^-$) and the carboxylate (COO^-) ions, ketone (C=O) and sulphone (SO_2) groups; Divalent ether (–O–), sulphide (–S–), amine (–NH–) and methylene ($–CH_2–$) groups. Although dissimilar, electronically they are sufficiently alike in their steric nature to be frequently interchangeable in drugs.

Applications in design of drugs :

(i)

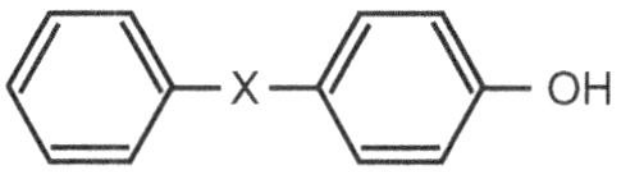

⌬—X—⌬— OH

Antibacterial activity

X=S, Se, O, NH or CH_2

(ii)

$$R - X - CH_2 - CH_2 - N \begin{matrix} R' \\ R' \end{matrix}$$

Cholinergic blocking agents

X = — COO, — CONH or — COS

(a) Compounds may be altered by isosteric replacement of atoms or groups in order to develop analogues or to act as antagonists to normal metabolites.

(b) When a group is present in a part of a molecule where it may be involved in an essential interaction or may influence the reactions of neighbouring groups, isosteric replacement sometimes produces analogues which act as antagonists. In the field of antineoplastic agents. e.g.,

$$\underset{R}{\underset{\substack{1 \\ N}}{\overset{\substack{3 \\ N}}{\bigvee}}}\underset{5}{\overset{\substack{4 \\ 6}}{\bigvee}}\underset{7}{\overset{\substack{H \\ N 9}}{\bigvee}}8$$

Adenine; R = –NH$_2$ } Metabolites
Hypoxanthine; R = –OH

6-Mercaptopurine; R = –SH–

Antimetabolite

On the similar lines, the hydroxyl group of folic acid, if replaced by the amino group leads to aminopterin, an antagonist useful in the treatment of certain types of cancer.

(2) Steric Features of Drugs :

In order to evoke the pharmacological action, a drug must approach the receptor and fit closely to its surface. Hence a drug must possess a high degree of structural specificity or stereoselectivity to initiate a response at a particular receptor. e.g. in diethylstilbestrol, only trans-diethylstilbestrol is estrogenic in action while cis-isomer is almost inactive. The role of geometrical isomers in drug activity is illustrated in the Fig. 6.9.

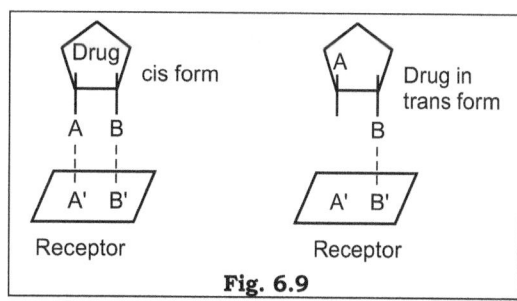

Fig. 6.9

To activate the receptor, if functional groups, A and B of the drug molecule have to interact with the complementary groups A' and B' of the receptor, then only cis-isomer will have the biological activity. For example, in the series of antihistamines, represented by the following formula (e.g., triprolidine), only cis-isomers are effective.

$$\begin{matrix} Ar' \\ Ar \end{matrix} C = CH - CH_2 - N \bigcirc$$

Antihistaminics

Just like geometric isomers, in certain rigid systems, (where rotation around the bonds is difficult), conformational isomers also show significant differences in biological activity due to differences in affinity as well as intrinsic activity towards the receptor. The conformation of a drug plays an important role in the two point or three point attachement of drug to the receptor surface. A change in the conformation leads to change in interatomic distances between bioactive groups of the drug resulting into diminished biological response. For example, in the following figure A and B represent the bioactive moieties.

In open chain compounds, all possible conformations are not equally manifested by the compounds (due to steric complications) at all times. Hence, by virtue of the ability of such compounds to interact in a different and unique conformation with different biological receptors, may result in multiple biological effects e.g. Acetylcholine may react in its extended conformational form with the muscarinic receptor and in quasi-ring form, may react with nicotinic receptor.

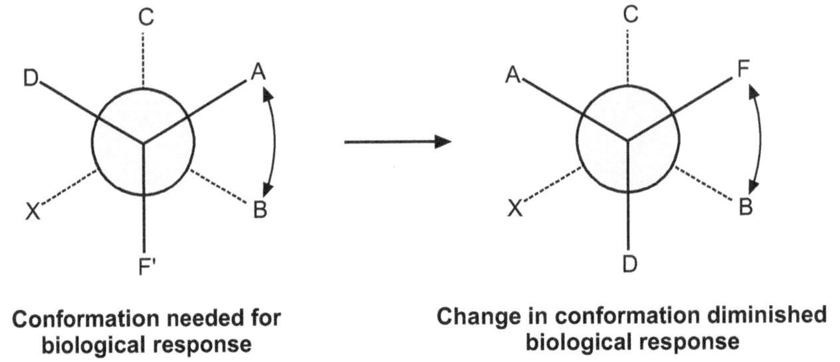

[Fig. 6.10 — Conformation needed for biological response → Change in conformation diminished biological response]

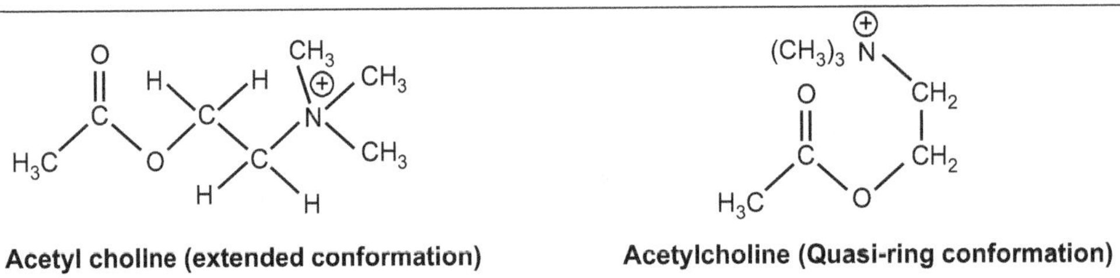

[Fig. 6.11 — Acetyl choline (extended conformation); Acetylcholine (Quasi-ring conformation)]

Similarly, histamine acts at H_1 and H_2 receptors with different conformational forms. The drug molecule always tries to exist in the conformational form which is most stable. The interaction of histamine with H_1 – receptor or H_2 – receptor is governed by different conformational forms.

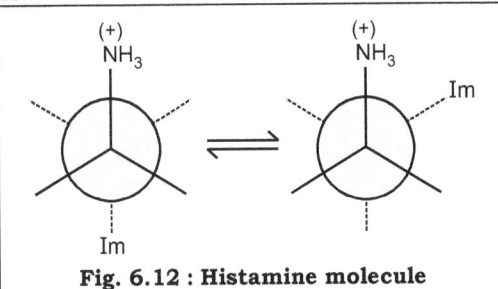

Fig. 6.12 : Histamine molecule
(Im = Imidazole ring)

(3) Optical Isomers and Biological Activity :

Optical isomers, particularly diastereo isomers (i.e. compounds with two or more asymmetric centers), exhibit similar chemical reactions but different physical properties. Since the physical properties are important in drug distribution, metabolism and interaction with the receptor, the biological properties of such isomers may also be different.

We may expect from the definition of optical isomers i.e. enantiomers (that compounds having identical physical and chemical properties except for their ability to rotate the plane of polarised light) that they may have the same biological activity. However, this is not the case with many of the enantiomers, e.g., the laevo form of morphinan possesses an analgetic activity while the dextro from (dextro methorphan) is having cough depressant activity.

6.9 NON-RECEPTOR MEDIATED ACTIONS OF THE DRUGS

Several drugs do not act by virtue of combination with receptors. They may interact specifically with small molecules or ions that are normally or abnormally present in the body. This can be explained with the following examples.

(a) The chelators or chelating agents form strong bonds with specific metallic cations and form chelate. The therapeutic neutralisation of gastric acid by an antacid (base) is a good example.

(b) In 'counterfeit incorporation mechanism' techniques, certain drugs which are structural analogoues of normal biological constituents may get incorporated into cellular components and bio-chemical chain reactions of the organisms and thereby alter their function. The clinical utility of this technique has already been tried in cancer chemotherapy.

(c) The biological activity of drugs acting on the central nervous system (e.g. general anaesthetic agents) could not be correlated well, with their structures. It suggests a relatively non-specific bio-chemical mechanism of action, since their individual potencies correlate well with their oil : water partition coefficients. Lipophilicity, the relationship of which, with narcotic activity dates back to almost a century, thus enjoys the importance over the concept of drug-receptor interaction.

A series of opioid compounds ($\log P_o = 1.32 \pm 0.80$) and a natural product, Nicotine ($\log P = 0.45$) are expected to possess low narcotic potency, on account of their low log P values. On the contrary, these agents are known to cross blood-brain-barrier and enter the CNS very rapidly to exert their effects. This observation may be explained by saying that –

(i) Even though they reach in low amounts in CNS due to their low log P value, these agents are so potent (i.e. high intrinsic activity) that optimum lipophilicity requirement is not a barrier to their action.

(ii) Or there must be some sort of facilitated transport mechanism which is structure specific. Only selected agents enjoy this amenity and Nicotine fulfils the structural requirement to get transported to CNS via facilitated mechanisms.

For categories listed in table 6.2, it can be said in general that, the lop P values in the range of 1.5 to 2.5, serve as a passport for the easy entry into brain where these drugs may produce sedative effects. This serves as an important clue in designing the drugs where CNS depression is either a desirable or undesirable effect.

6.10 DRUG ANTAGONISM

In terms of intrinsic activity, antagonists can be defined as 'those having high affinity towards the receptor but have poor or zero intrinsic activity'. The relative concentrations and affinities of agonist and antagonist result into competitive antagonism of drug action. Antagonists only occupy the receptor sites due to their high affinity value but they cannot activate the receptor due to their poor intrinsic value. In most of the cases, attachment of bulky group (R), at the bio-active part of agonist structure results into an antagonistic effect.

Table 6.2

S.N.	Category	Log* P_o	Comment
1.	Volatile anesthetics	2.35	
2.	Hypnotics : - Barbiturates - Carbamates - Alcohols	Near 2.00	
3.	Antipsychotic agents	2.40 ± 0.87	
4.	Tricyclic antidepressants	2.15 ± 0.65	
5.	Steroids : - Testosterone - Progesterone - Deoxycorticosterone	 3.29 3.87 3.08	Should possess CNS depressant activity
6.	Hallucinogens	3.14	at pH 6

Log* P_o = log of partition coefficient value, calcauated at pH 7.4.

Example :

(i) 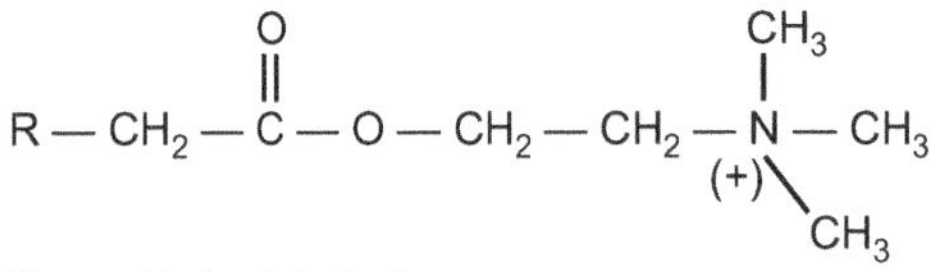 $R-CH_2-\overset{O}{\underset{\|}{C}}-O-CH_2-CH_2-\underset{(+)}{N}(CH_3)_3$

R = H; Acetyl choline

R = Bulky group; cholinergic antagonist

(ii)

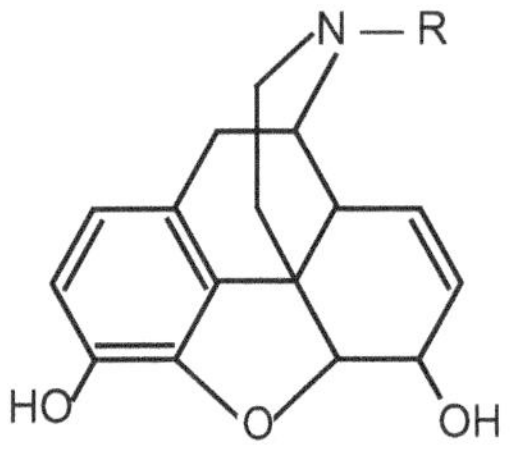

R = CH_3; Morphine

R = $-CH_2-\triangleleft$; Narcotic antagonist

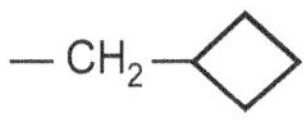

A knowledge of drug antagonism is necessary in the design of drug combination preparations. The mechanism of action of many drugs can be easily explained on the basis of antagonism of the endogenous agonists. For example,

(a) Anticancer drugs — Some drugs from this category act as anti-metabolites.

(b) Antihistaminic agents — These agents act by either preventing the release or blocking the receptor sites of endogenous histamine.

(c) Analgesic agents, Hypnotics and Diuretics — Their effectiveness is mainly due to their ability to antagonise the activity of endogenous stimulants

(d) Vitamines and the corresponding anti-vitamins.

Types of Antagonism :

The following figure presents a scheme of classification of various types of antagonisms exhibited by different drugs.

(a) Competitive antagonism : A competitive antagonist shifts the dose-response curve to the right and does not have intrinsic activity. Since it is a competitive antagonism, by increasing the concentration of agonist, one can easily reverse the antagonism. The converse is also true.

Schild (1947) devised an index of activity (pAx), on the basis of which, the potency of a competitive antagonist can be evaluated. The pAx value can be defined as 'the negative logarithm of the molar concentration of the antagonist required to reduce the effect of a multiple dose (x) of the agonist to that of a single dose'. In case of a potent antagonistic agent, the dose required to cause antagonism will be small. Hence, its pAx value will be large.

(b) Non-competitive antagonism : A non-competitive antagonist acts on different channels of receptors than that of agonist. Through exertion of opposite actions, antagonist depresses the response to the agonist. This permits the usual lack of specificity with respect to the agonist. The antagonist needs not to be a structural relative of the agonist. Example is that of papaverine (a spasmolytic) which antagonises the spasmogenic activity of different types of spasmogens as histamine, acetylcholine, norepinephrine, serotonin etc.

Since the agonist and antagonist do not act on the same receptor systems, the inhibitory action of the antagonist cannot be overcomed by increasing the concentration of agonist. Hence, it is said that they act in an irreversible fashion. Example is phenoxybenzamine, an α-adrenergic blocker. It is used to treat hypertension caused by catecholamine release. The following pairs illustrate other examples of non-competitive antagonism.

1. Nicotine and atropine
2. Strychnine and curare
3. PABA and aminopterine

The evaluation of potencies of non-competitive antagonists is done on the pD'x scale. The pD'x value can be defined as 'the negative logarithm of molar concentration of the antagonist which is required to reduce the maximum effect of the agonist to $\frac{1}{x}$ of that which it exerts in the absence of the antagonist'. Some non-competitive antagonists act as sensitizers rather than inhibitors by increasing the response of a tissue to the agonist.

Types of Antagonism

- Antagonism between drugs in the pharmacodynamic phase (i.e. at drug-receptor interaction level)
  1. Competitive anatagonism
  2. Non-competitive antagonism
  3. Functional and physiological antagonism
- Antagonism between drugs in the pharmacokinetic phase
  - Chemical anatagonism

Fig. 6.13 : Classification scheme for Antagonisms

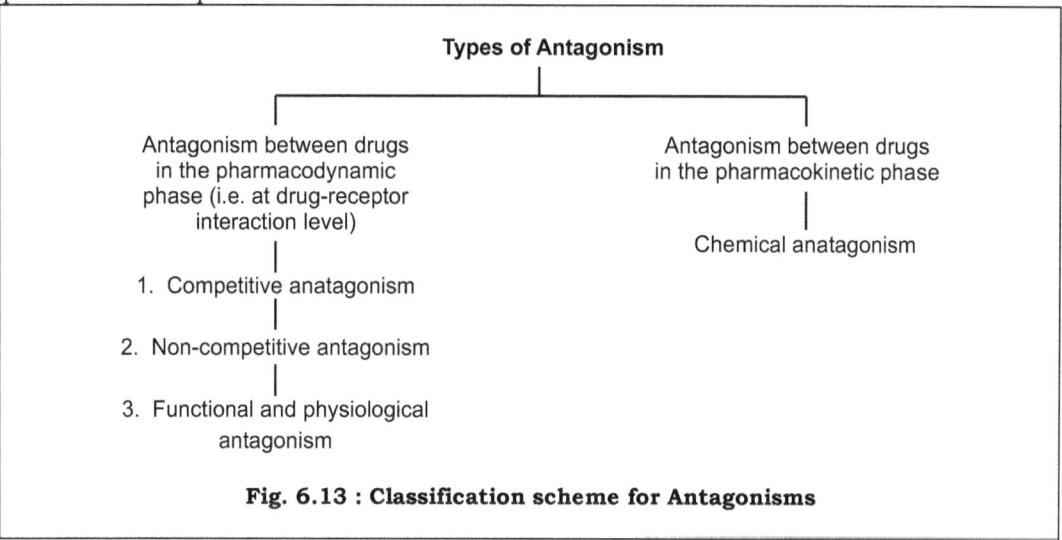

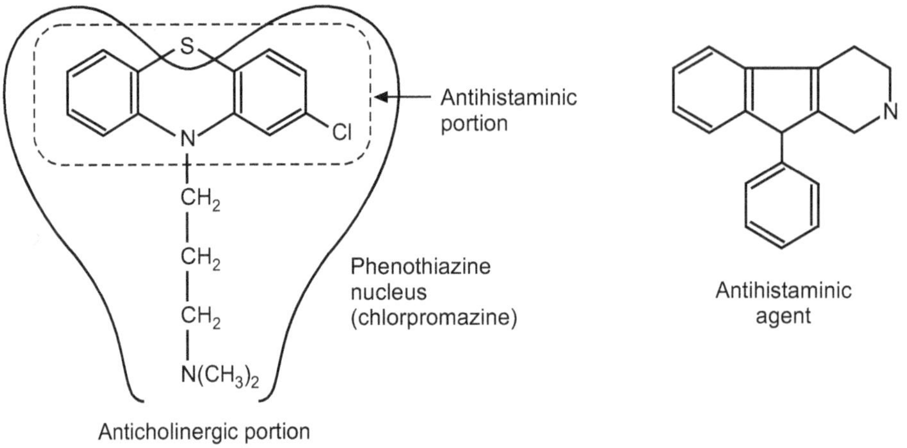

Fig. 6.14 : Structural resemblance between neurotransmitters and their antagonist

(c) Chemical antagonism : These are neutralisation reactions. Here the effect of agonist is terminated by a chemical inactivation of agonist by antagonist. Examples include :

1. A basic protein, protamine is used to inactivate an acidic anticoagulant, heparin.
2. In heavy metal poisoning, chelating agents are used as effective antidotes. They chemically interact with toxic metals to form non-toxic complexes.
3. The mechanism of action of various antacids is based upon chemical antagonism.

(d) Functional and physiological antagonism : In the body, various functions of different organs are governed by hemostatic mechanisms. Opposing regulatory pathways control many physiological functions. When two agonists acting on a same tissue organ; change a particular biological function in opposite directions, it is called as functional antagonism. For example, agonist agents like, cholinergic (spasmogen) and β-adrenergic (spasmolytics) agents exert opposite activities on bronchial smooth muscles. When both opposing agonists give rise to their actions by acting on different tissues, it is known as physiological antagonism. For example, an increase in blood sugar concentration resulting due to catabolic activities of glucocorticoids is physiologically inhibited by insulin.

6.11 OTHER RECEPTOR-LINKED PHARMACOLOGICAL EVENTS

(a) **Tachyphylaxis**, tolerance, refractoriness or desensitization, all these terms can be explained as a diminished response of the receptor for the same dose of a drug. If the drug treatment is continued for a prolonged period of time, a time comes where the dose of the drug has to be increased to achieve the same intensity of pharmacological response.

One can say that the patient has developed tolerance to the drug. The term tolerance can be defined as 'decreased sensitivity of the patient to the drug due to its prior exposure'. This state of desensitization is usually referred to as refractoriness.

At the non-receptor level, tolerance develops due to the over activation of drug-metabolising enzymes resulting into an increase in drug metabolism. At receptor level, various mechanisms operate independently to develop the tolerance. These include -

1. Changes in the properties of drug binding sites of receptor.
2. Changes in the number and structure of receptors.
3. Due to prolonged exposure to the drug, receptor may get damaged and get converted into an inactive state.
4. Receptor may be delinked from its amplification unit.
5. Under certain disease conditions, degradation of receptor structure is reported. For example, in myasthenia gravis, autoantibodies cause destruction of nicotinic cholinergic receptors, leading to impaired neurotransmission in skeletal muscles. Similarly in asthma, or allergic rhinitis, circulating antibodies degrade the β_2-adrenergic receptors in several patients.
6. Sometimes genetically-linked receptor deficiencies may occur.
7. In some cases, drug-metabolites may inhibit the functioning of one or the other receptor components.

At certain occasions, receptors develop the capacity of auto-regulation in which chronic increase or decrease in agonist concentration reflects in decrease (i.e. down regulation) or increase (i.e. up regulation), respectively in the receptor concentration. It is particularly true for hormones like, insulin, catecholamines, angiotensin etc. These hormones can also regulate the functioning of other receptors. For example, steroid hormones can regulate uterine catecholaminergic receptors whereas β-receptors in heart can be governed by thyroid hormones.

(b) **Hyperreactivity** or supersensitivity is just a reversed condition to that of tolerance or desensitization. Supersensitivity means an increased biological response when same dose of the drug is administered. This is particularly true where antagonists are recommended for long-term treatment. The increase in the biological response is due to synthesis of additional receptors or activation of additional drug-binding sites on the receptors. The synthesis of additional receptors is only possible during development and ageing process. Hence under chronic antagonist treatment, generally very young and ageing persons share better chance to develop hyperreactivity to the drug.

(c) **Withdrawal symptoms:** Most of the drugs acting on CNS show adverse effects if they are discontinued during the therapy. Generally these drugs should be discontinued gradually. Instead of stopping the dose instantly, the dose should be reduced gradually. The adverse effects emerging due to immediate withdrawal of the drug are known as *withdrawal symptoms*. The drugs acting on CNS may exhibit their pharmacological actions by affecting biosynthesis, storage, release or metabolism of the neurotransmitters. Receptor has a flexible nature. If the drug is continued for a long-term, receptor gradually changes its structure and adjusts itself to coop up with the presence of the drug. The drug now becomes an essential part of the receptor-environment. The presence of the drug is now needed for the proper functioning of receptor. In such a set-up, if the administration of the drug is stopped immediately, the receptor environment gets disturbed. The receptor could not function properly. The consequences of this, results in adverse reactions. These reactions are known as *withdrawal symptoms*. They continue to occur till the receptor manages to adjust itself to this newly changed atmosphere (i.e. drug-free atmosphere).

DRUG DEPENDENCE

7.1 INTRODUCTION

Drug addiction is a problem of severe concern. Many attempts involving social awareness programmes could not achieve the expected decrease in the addiction cases. Millions of people habitually ingest both, the active ingredients and their numerous synthetic preparations for their CNS effects. Such drugs which are regularly used for non-medial purposes, are known as 'drugs of abuse'. These drugs produce their effects mainly on mood, thought and feeling, and are thought to give pleasure or relief from anxiety, tension or pain.

Despite adverse social and medical consequences, drug addicts consume these drugs for non-therapeutic purposes. If it is continued for a considerable long-period, the person becomes dependent on the drug. The normal functioning of the person needs the presence of that particular drug. This situation is termed as drug dependence or compulsive drug use. If the person is deprived of the drug-dose, a feeling of abnormality arises due to drug hunger. General symptoms include, restlessness, tremor, apprehension and a general sense of unease. The drug addict in such a situation will try to get the drug at any cost, legally or illegally and poses social problems. In 1957, WHO defines the term, Drug addiction as "It is a state of periodic or chronic intoxication produced by the repeated consumption of the drug".

As per the directions issued by WHO (1964), a more general term, drug dependence is used to cover the conditions previously described as habituation and addiction.

The list of drugs which are commonly abused, include opioids, alcohol, barbiturates, local anesthetics, anesthetic gases, caffeine, nicotine, phencyclidine, CNS stimulants and volatile solvents.

In the above list, almost every drug has some actions on central nervous system. Hence, it can be said that most of the drugs of abuse are from the category of "CNS—acting drugs". Repeated administration of these drugs cause a change in neuronal environment and results into adaptive change in the CNS. The nervous system of the person becomes so much dependent on the drug that normal functioning can only continue in the presence of the drug. The person is said to be physically dependent on the drug.

An abrupt withdrawal of the drug in such a situation, leads to the occurrence of withdrawal symptoms or abstinence syndrome. Generally withdrawal of all CNS-depressant drugs affect the CNS in the opposite sense, and cause hyperexcitatory reactions. The withdrawal symptoms of any drug are always unpleasant and troublesome to the health of the patient.

The principles underlying the treatment remains same for most of the types of withdrawal symptoms. These include :

(a) Substitution of another long-acting pharmacologically equivalent drug for the original drug of abuse. The daily dose of the substituent drug can be estimated from the response of the substituent needed to suppress the withdrawal syndrome.

(b) The dose thus decided for the initial period of withdrawal becomes the stabilization level dose. Once stabilization level is established, a gradual tapering of that dosage over a period of days or weeks is continued.

(c) The gradual withdrawal of the substituted drug is followed by supportive treatment. The rehabilitation employed usually involve hospitalization and psychotherapy. Other measures include gastric suction, acidification of urine to facilitate the excretion of the drug (e.g. phencyclidine) and artificial ventilation to overcome respiratory depression. Anxiety and seizures constitute as a withdrawal symptom, for most of the CNS depressant drugs. Diazepam is most commonly employed to treat both these symptoms.

The chronic administration of CNS-acting drugs, if discontinued, may result into withdrawal symptoms. One drug that sometimes induces physical dependence but which is not from the category of 'CNS-acting' drugs, is furosemide. The physical dependence is as severe as it is in any opiate or alcohol addict. The withdrawal of furosemide results in idopathic oedema in the women patient.

Furosemide

On the gross-level, the withdrawal symptoms may be clearly divided into :

(a) In case of morphine and related analgesics, the withdrawal symptoms are due to generalized hyperexcitability of the somatic and autonomic nervous systems, and

(b) While a number of sedative-hypnotic drugs alongwith some tranquilizers, after abrupt withdrawal, leads to the psychotic behaviour and tremors.

Drugs act by altering the rates of ongoing biochemical reactions. In the chronic administration of the drug, the cell-environment becomes familiar with the drug. Due to adaptive nature of the body, the enzyme tends to reset back the drug-induced change in the rate of biochemical reactions. As a result, there is a decline in the drug-action. The drug is likely to become progressively less effective. In order to achieve the original intensity of action, the dose of the drug has to be increased. This is the phenomenon of tolerance. There is an appreciable degree of similarity between the tolerance and bacterial resistance to antibiotics. The development of highly resistant strains of bacteria is due to their long-term exposure to a specific antibiotic. Hence, some people consider the tolerance as a form of drug-resistance.

The tolerance may be either dispositional or cellular type. Former results due to either decreased absorption or increased metabolism and excretion of the drug. Thus, interference in the pharmacokinetic properties of the drug after its chronic administration may result into dispositional tolerance. For example, the rate of metabolic hydroxylation of meprobamate is doubted only after one week of use. Similarly the increased metabolism of opioids after chronic administration may lead to shorter duration and decreased intensity of drug-actions. While cellular tolerance occurs due to changes in the receptor number present on cell, for that drug. Thus, pharmacodynamic interference at cellular level is responsible for the development of cellular tolerance. Both these types of tolerance develops ultimately due to the presence of reduced concentrations of the drug at the sites of drug-action.

For the drugs having multi-dimensional activities, tolerance need not be exhibited equally against all the actions of the drug. For example, in case of pethidine which has analgesic and atropine like activities, tolerance develops only against analgesic effect while atropine like activity remains unaffected.

Other categories of drugs like anti-cholinergics, imipramine, chlorpromazine etc. also leads to physical dependence and development of tolerance, if administered chronically.

Physical dependence may be categorised of either physical or psychological (habituation) origin. In physical dependence, the normal functioning of certain vital processes in the body becomes dependent either on the drug or its metabolites. For example, if the use is discontinued, barbiturates develop fits and chronic alcoholics suffer from psychosis known as 'delirium tremens'. Whereas, the best known examples of psychological dependence include, caffeine and tobacco. Physical dependence for a particular drug cannot occur without tolerance but a development of tolerance cannot be always interlinked with physical dependence.

7.2 TERMINOLOGY

(a) Cross-tolerance : When a person develops a tolerance against a particular drug, he also exercises tolerance against other drug belonging to the same pharmacological class of the previous agent. For example, if a tolerance to barbiturate is developed, the person develops tolerance against most of the general CNS depressants including that of alcohol and volatile anesthetics. This is known as a 'phenomenon of cross-resistance'. The drugs among which cross-tolerance develops, need not be structurally related with each other. Specific cross-tolerance exists in the members of the same pharmacological class while in non-specific cross tolerance, the chronic use of first drug leads only to partial tolerance to other drugs.

(b) Tachyphylaxis : In simple terms, tachyphylaxis implies a case of rapidly developed tolerance. During chronic exposure to certain agents, the cell-environment tends to adopt the drug, comparatively more rapidly. Such rapid adaptation may be seen in both, an isolated organ preparation and less frequently in the whole animal. Tachyphylaxis is also reported to occur in cases where the drug dissociates very slowly from the binding sites on its receptors.

(c) Sensitization : The term describes a situation just opposite to that of tolerance. Here a chronic administration of the drug causes a gradual increase in the intensity of drug-action until a maximum response is attained. The nature of the response does not change in sensitization.

Sensitization differs from anaphylactic shock. The mechanisms involved in sensitization operate just in the opposite directions to that in tolerance development. Sensitization for a particular drug results due to progressively increased concentration of a drug at the sites of drug-action. This is achieved by either pharmacokinetic changes (an increased absorption and distribution or decreased metabolism and/or elimination of the drug) or pharmacodynamic alterations (increase in receptor population). Sensitization is also reported to occur due to drug-interactions, where one drug may act as a sensitizing agent for other by increasing its affinity as well as intrinsic activity for the receptors.

Sensitization can be easily seen in the functioning of denervated structures, when they are exposed to the action of exogenous neurotransmitters. For example, denervated striated muscles respond in an exaggerated fashion to cholinergic analogues.

7.3 MECHANISMS INVOLVED IN TOLERANCE DEVELOPMENT

Tolerance, in simple words, means resistance to the drug action. In chronic administration, the drug effects decline, if the same dose is continued. This is examplified with the use of drugs affecting autonomic nervous system. These drugs exhaust the stores of neurotransmitters necessary for the drug-effects. Repeated doses of drug exhaust the stores of neurotransmitter at a much faster rate than the rate of re-filling of the storage granules (i.e., the rate of metabolism of neurotransmitter becomes more than the rate of biosynthesis of neurotransmitter). As a result, there is a fall in the neurotransmitter level needed to propogate the drug-effects. It results into a decline in the intensity of drug activity.

According to Collier (1966), there exists silent receptors alongwith pharmacologically active receptors. Silent receptors cannot evoke any pharmacological response. Repeated administration of the drug causes inactivation of pharmacologically active receptors resulting into an increase in the number of silent receptors and decrease in the number of pharmacologically active receptors. (The situation is just reverse in sensitization phenomenon). The overall effect is a progressive increase in the effective dose of the drug. This condition is termed as *tolerance*.

7.4 MECHANISMS INVOLVED IN EVOKING WITHDRAWAL SYNDROME

Many theories have been postulated to explain the genesis of withdrawal symptoms. The most promising ones include -

(a) Goldstein and Goldstein in 1968 proposed an enzyme induction theory. According to this theory, the drug decreases the rate of biosynthesis of neurotransmitter directly or indirectly by inhibiting an enzymse which catalyses that biosynthesis. Due to the adaptive nature of the body, feedback mechanisms are put into action. The enzyme, inhibited by the drug, undergoes conformational changes and then catalyses the reaction at such a rate to overcome drug-induced decrease in the level of neurotransmitter. (i.e. now the rate of biosynthesis is increased than the normal rate to counter balance the drug-induced decrease). Conformational changes may involve an increase in the number of enzymes. If the drug is abruptly withdrawn, the feedback mechanisms take their own time to re-adjust the rate of biosynthesis of neurotransmitter. Meantime, the excess synthesis of neurotransmitter leads to the occurrence of withdrawal of symptoms which continue until the enzyme activity falls to a new steady state.

(b) In the same year, 1968, Martin proposed a homeostatic and redundancy model. According to Martin, whenever vital cellular pathways or processes are blocked or inhibited by the drug, alternative secondary pathways or processes emerge to serve the need of the body function. This is well in correlation with the adaptive nature of the body. In case of chronic administration of the drug if primary pathways are blocked, body has to sought out alternative pathways. It is quite logical. If the drug is discontinued, the primary pathways regain their original capacity. Withdrawal syndrome may result due to functioning of both, alternative pathway and restored primary pathway. The syndrome continues until the functioning of alternative pathway ceases or blocking of primary pathway by reusing the same drug.

Since the drugs of abuse produce the effects that are pleasurable, novel or tension relieving, these drugs are liberally used in depressive and anxiety disorders. Many individuals who wish to build up antisocial personality, usually are the victims of drugs of abuse. If the person becomes physically dependent on these drugs, he has to undergo substitution drug-therapy to discontinue the habit. The drugs of substitution should have a long duration of action. Such a list of drugs include, methadone, phenobarbital, chlordiazepoxide, etc. Such drugs do have their own withdrawal symptoms, but these symptoms are generally less severe, although are more protracted or prolonged due to longer half-lives of the drugs. This principle serves as a basis for the selection of a drug for the substitution treatment of physical dependence for both, opioids and CNS depressants. In case of patients taking large doses of longer acting benzodiazepines, the treatment does not involve substitution therapy.

Once a tolerance is developed to the euphorigenic effects of the drug, the addict seems to be dysphoric and depressed till the dose is not increased. Each such successive increase in the dose of drug is associated with a substantial increase in the toxicities. It interferes in the normal functioning of the organs and if present in sufficient concentration, the drug may cause a direct organ damage.

7.5 CLASSIFICATION

The various drugs which after chronic administration, produce a state of physical dependence, can be classified into eight classes.

These include :
(a) Opioids
(b) General CNS depressants
(c) Amphetamines and other sympathomimetic agents
(d) Nicotine
(e) Caffeine
(f) Hallucinogens
(g) Arylcyclohexylamines (phencyclidine)
(h) Inhalants (nitrous oxide, ethyl ether and volatile solvents)

The withdrawal symptoms associated with many of these classes are rebound hyperexcitability.

(a) Opioids :

The term 'opioids' refers to all natural as well as synthetic narcotic analgesics having morphine-like activity. The most abused drugs from this category include morphine, heroine and pethidine.

Opioids reduce pain, aggression and sexual drives and regular use is associated with a complaint of constipation. To escape the legal definitions, many drugs having slight structural variations from the existing narcotics have been synthesized. Atleast six of such derivatives of feritanyl nucleus have been identified from the market.

An abrupt discontinuation of the use of opioids may lead to occurrence of irritability, nausea, vomiting, intestinal spasm, diarrhoea, insomnia, anorexia, an increase in heart rate and blood pressure. In certain cases, chilliness accompanied by severe sweating is also reported. Pain in the bones and muscles of the back are also characteristics. An administration of opioid immediately suppresses these withdrawal symptoms. Some of the opiate withdrawal symptoms correlate well with the signs of increased cholinergic activity. Similarly hyperactivity in the locus ceruleus or increased noradrenergic turnover is responsible for other symptoms. In extreme cases death of the addict occurs due to active respiratory depression alongwith pulmonary oedema.

Generally long-acting opioids may be used to suppress the withdrawal symptoms. Methadone, in that sense, is a 'drug of choice'. Due to special cross-tolerance, it can easily block the euphoric effects of the street heroin. Methadone itself leads to physical dependence. The withdrawal symptoms are less intense but more protracted. The complete withdrawal of the methadone takes about 2 3 weeks. The withdrawal symptoms can be suppressed by using chlordiazepoxide, a long-acting antianxiety agent.

Cyclazocine, yet another long-acting opioid can be used in similar fashion to methadone. Other longer-acting opioid under trials is methadyl acetate or 1-α-acetyl methadol (LAAM). Once given, it can suppress the withdrawal symptoms for about 72 hours. As with methadone, it is quite effective orally.

Clonidine exerts antihypertensive action by acting primarily on presynaptic α_2-adrenergic receptors. Some of the autonomic withdrawal symptoms of opioids can be suppressed by Clonidine.

Unlike methadone, it has no narcotic action and is not addiction producing drug. Other α_2-adrenergic agonists (e.g., guanabenz) have also been tried and found useful in some of the opioid withdrawal symptoms.

The use of opioid antagonist during the phase of opiate dependence immediately leads to the occurrence of withdrawal symptoms. The opioid antagonist, such as naloxone, if given, it blocks the opioid receptor and inhibits the access of the opioid to the receptor sites. Thus, a phase of endogenous discontinuation of drug exists which leads to withdrawal symptoms. Until the antagonist is eliminated, the syndrome cannot be suppressed even using larger doses of opioid. On the contrary, the opioid in larger doses may lead to other complications.

(b) General CNS Depressants :

The term general CNS depressant (for further discussion in this chapter) includes, barbiturates, benzodiazepines, alcohol, meprobamate, glutethimide, methaqualone and related drugs.

(i) Barbiturates : Over a century, barbiturates are in the clinical field and in varying doses, possess many activities like, sedative, hypnotic, muscle relaxant, anticonvulsant and anesthetic, in different forms. The first experimental evidence about the physical dependence to barbiturates dates back in the early 1950s. This led to the replacement of barbiturates by newer drugs which include glutethimide, methaqualone, meprobamate and chlordiazepoxide. There are marked similarities between the withdrawal symptoms seen with barbiturates and those seen with other general CNS depressants. These include, anxiety, insomnia, and rebound increase in rapid eye-movement (REM) sleep pattern. In severe cases, delirium may be associated with tonic-clonic seizures. But abrupt withdrawal of general CNS depressants that have been used in higher doses over prolonged period is not advisable. It may sometimes be life-threatening, if not properly controlled.

Since they act on the ascending reticular formation of the brain stem, psychic dependence alongwith physical type, is likely to occur. Due to easier availability and low price, secobarbital sodium is the most commonly used drug of abuse. Methaqualone and diazepam are also used frequently.

The doses of shorter-acting barbiturates are to be repeated more frequently due to their short-duration of action. Hence, physical dependence more rapidly develops with shorter-acting barbiturates than with long acting barbiturates. The withdrawal symptoms include, nausea, vomiting, anxiety, anorexia, insomnia, muscle twitching, delirium, fits and possibly status epilepticus Barbiturate addicts and alcoholics share some of the symptoms in common which include slurring of the speech, sluggishness of thought and muscular inco-ordination. Hence, barbiturate addicts easily develop cross-tolerance to alcohol. In the patients, addicted with sedative-hypnotic drugs, tolerance develops mainly due to a rapid-enzymatic degradation of drug.

As usual long acting drug should be used to suppress the abstinence syndrome. Pentobarbitone, in a dose level of 200-400 mg every six hourly, is a suitable drug of substitution. Besides barbiturate withdrawal syndrome, pentobarbital orally, can be successfully used to suppress the withdrawal symptoms of glutethimide, paraldehyde, chloral hydrate, meprobamate and alcohol. The dose of the substitute drug is then gradually tappered down. At the end of the second week, it can be completely withdrawn.

(ii) Alcohol : The word, *'alcohol'* has its origin from the Arabic word, al-koh'1.

The alcohol content of naturally fermented wines varies from 8 -12%. The small intestine is the main site of alcohol absorption, though a part may be absorbed from the stomach. Presence of food generally delays its absorption. Similarly, absorption is also delayed if the alcohol is either in dilute solution or concentrated form. In the concentrated form, the delayed absorption is due to inhibition of gastric peristalsis.

The chronic administration of alcohol leads to harmful effects on the liver. Health problems arise due to acute hepatitis, chronic hepatitis, portal cirrhosis of the liver, alongwith pancreatits, gastritis and thiamine depletion. The chronic ingestion of alcohol causes an increase in the hepatic microsomal enzyme activity. Most of the ingested alcohol is metabolized in the liver to acetaldehyde and then to acetate. The latter is finally converted to carbon-dioxide and water.

Withdrawal symptoms of alcohol involve anxiety, coarse tremors, weakness, abdominal cramps. In some cases, patient may develop severe tremors and in rare cases fits also.

The most commonly used drug in the treatment of chronic alcoholism is disulfiram. It is to be taken orally in doses of about 500 mg daily. After taking disulfiram, the patient becomes intolerant to alcohol. Unpleasant symptoms develop which include, nausea, sweating, flushing, violent headache, palpitation, hypotension and respiratory embarrassment. Depot preparation of disulphiram are also now available.

Disulfiram causes an accumulation of acetaldehyde by inhibiting aldehyde dehydrogenase enzyme in the liver. The enzyme is responsible for further metabolism of acetaldehyde to the acetate form. The accumulation of acetaldehyde above certain limits, leads to toxic symptoms. Disulfiram also inhibits a whole range of other enzymes.

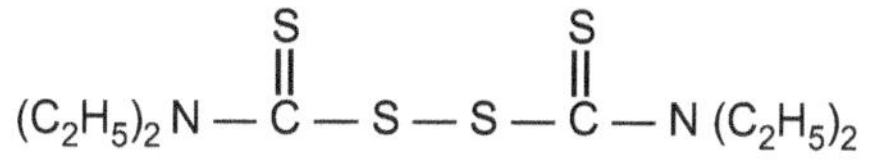

$$(C_2H_5)_2 N - \overset{\overset{S}{\|}}{C} - S - S - \overset{\overset{S}{\|}}{C} - N (C_2H_5)_2$$

Disulfiram

Certain drugs like, citrated calcium carbimide (Ca = N — C ≡ N), sodium valproate and clomethiazole are also effective and considerably reduce the intensity of the abstinence syndrome. Citrated calcium carbimide has the same mode of action as disulfiram. It is usually used in a dose of 50 mg once or twice a day. In some cases, it is reported to cause hypothyroidism. In addition to psychotherapy, tranquillizer like chlordiazepoxide, diazepam or flurazepam may also be used.

The nutritional deficiencies and any dehydration resulting due to alcoholic diuresis should be treated with the injection of β-complex or thiamine alone and by giving attention to the fluid balance. The chances of developing pneumonitis may be nullified by the administration of antibiotics.

(iii) Benzodiazepines : The programme for synthesis and screening of thousands of benzodiazepine derivatives has been launched after the introduction of chlordiazepoxide, the first benzodiazepine into the market. They have been adviced in the treatment of psychoses and share other activities also, like anxiolytic, anticonvulsant, muscle relaxant etc. They enjoy additional advantages of low acute toxicity and freedom from peripheral side-effects. But in the recent years their therapeutic value in the long-term treatment has been questioned due to their potential to produce tolerance and physical dependence.

The benzodiazepines, unlike other antiepileptic drugs, are effective against all types of seizures. Clonazepam and diazepam are the benzodiazepines, commonly employed in the treatment of epilepsy.

They could not become the drugs of choice in the long-term antiepileptic treatment only because of their ability to develop tolerance. Tolerance may be developed either due to pharmacokinetic or pharmacodynamic factors. It has been shown that the plasma-levels of a number of benzodiazepines does not alter during the development of anticonvulsant tolerance. Hence, pharmacodynamic mechanisms of tolerance production may dominate in case of benzodiazepines.

An abrupt withdrawal of benzodiazepine after a long-term treatment may lead to the occurrence of withdrawal symptoms. These symptoms include, confusions, psychotic reactions and epileptic fits. Hence, it is advised to use benzodiazepines only for a short-term treatment, i.e., generally less than 3-4 weeks. The intensity of withdrawal symptoms depends upon the dose and duration of benzodiazepine used. Generally short-acting drugs (e.g. lorazepam, alprazolam, triazolam) lead to more intense withdrawal symptoms than medium acting (temazepam) and long-acting (chlordiazepoxide, nitrazepam, flurazepam) benzodiazepines. Other withdrawal symptoms which generally occur, include rebound anxiety, tension and insomnia.

(c) Amphetamines and Other Sympathomimetic Agents :

Originally amphetamine was introduced as antidepressant agent. Later it finds its use in the treatment of obesity and narcolepsy. Other amphetamine-type drugs include, methamphetamine, phenmetrazine, methylphenindate, dexamphetamine, diethylpropion, glutethimide and methylprylon.

Table 7.1 Neuropharmacological Screening

Albino rat → Sex : Male and Female; Weight : 100 - 120g. Route : Intraperitoneal; pH; 6.8 to 7.0

Category	Parameter	Normal Score	5-CPPTH 100	5-CPPTH 200	N3₁ 100	N3₁ 200	NB₅ 100	NB₅ 200
Awareness	Alertness	4	4	3	3	2	2	1
	Visual Placing	4	4	4	4	3	3	2
	Passivity	0	3	3	3	2	3	2
	Stereotypy	0	0	0	0	1	0	1
	Grooming	4	3	3	3	2	3	3
Mood	Vocalization	0	0	0	0	0	0	0
	Restlessness	0	0	0	0	1	1	2
	Irritability	0	0	0	0	0	0	0
	Fearfullness	0	0	1	1	1	1	1
Motor Activity	Reactivity	4	3	3	4	3	3	2
	Spontaneous act	4	3	3	3	3	2	2
	Touch Response	4	4	4	4	3	4	3
	Pain Response	4	4	4	4	4	4	4
CNS excitation	Straub Response	0	0	0	0	0	0	0
	Startle Response	0	0	0	0	0	0	0
	Tremour	0	0	0	0	0	0	0
	Twitching	0	0	0	0	0	0	0
	Convulsion	0	0	0	0	0	0	0
Posture	Body Posture	4	4	4	4	4	4	3
	Limb Posture	4	4	4	4	4	4	4
Motor incor\ⁿ.	Staggering gait	0	0	0	0	1	1	2
	Abnormal gait	0	0	0	0	0	0	1
	Righting reflex	0	0	0	0	1	1	2
Muscle tone	Limb tone	4	4	4	4	4	4	4
	Grip strength	4	4	4	4	4	4	4
	Body sag	0	0	0	0	0	0	1
	Body tone	4	3	3	3	3	3	3
	Abnormal tone	4	3	3	3	3	3	2
Reflexes	Pinna	4	4	4	4	4	4	4
	Ipsilateral	4	4	4	4	4	4	4
	Corneal	4	4	4	4	4	4	4
Autonomic Profile	Pupil size	4	4	4	4	4	4	4
	Palpebral opening	4	4	4	4	4	4	3
	Exophthalamus	0	0	0	0	0	0	0
	Urination	0	0	0	0	0	0	0
	Salivation	0	0	0	0	0	0	0
	Hypothermia	0	0	0	0	0	0	0
	Piloerection	0	0	0	0	0	0	0
	Writhing	0	0	0	0	0	0	0
	Skin colour	4	4	4	4	4	4	4
	Heart rate	4	4	4	4	3	3	2
	Respiratory rate	4	4	4	4	4	4	4
	No. of animals used		2	2	2	2	2	2
	Dose mg/kg		100	200	100	200	100	200

Dose form : Water suspension with the help of Tween 80.
Control group was given 0.9 % saline intraperitonelly (1 ml/100 g)

The score card showing the results obtained in the neuropharmacological screening procedure of Irwin, for some new hydantoin derivatives

The combination of amphetamine and barbiturates produces more elevation of mood than either drug alone. Many marketed preparations contain barbiturates, aspirin, or phenacetin alongwith amphetamine. While hallucinations have been reported to occur when amphetamine is used in combination with cannabis.

Yet another interesting drug having similar pharmacological background with amphetamine is cocaine. Cocaine, a local anesthetic agent, discovered in 1860, produces the effects more quickly and more intensively. (-) Cathinone which is an active ingredient in freshly gathered leaves of the Khat shrub, also belongs to 'amphetamine type' class. Among the amphetamines, methamphetamine is the most widely abused agent. All these amphetamine type drugs act as indirect central and peripheral sympathomimetics.

These agents produce marked euphoria, a sense of enhanced physical and mental strength and insomnia. They act as dopaminergic agonist and block the re-uptake processes for neurotransmitter in adrenergic nervous system. The withdrawal symptoms usually consist of depression, hyperphagia and tiredness.

(d) Nicotine :

Nicotine and caffeine in small doses produce mainly a psychological dependence. Posselt and Reiman, in 1828, reported the isolation of nicotine in a pure form, from the leaves. Now, it is available in a number of different forms like tobacco smoking, intranasal and buccal forms. On an average, nicotine content in a cigarette varies from 0.05 to 2.0 mg. In the non-addicts, about 60 mg acute doses of nicotine may lead to life-threatening effects. The physiological effects of nicotine appear to propagate mainly through nicotinic receptors and dopaminergic pathways. These involve nausea, vomiting and an increase in the plasma concentration of several hormones and neuro-transmitters. These effects can be blocked by mecamylamine. However, muscarinic or adrenergic blockers fail to do so.

In body, nicotine is metabolised to a inactive metabolite, continine.

In the chronic cigarette smokers, the enzyme activity in the intestinal mucosa and the liver is stimulated by the components of tobacco smoke. Similarly the chances to develop coronary artery disease and lung cancer are multiplied due to regular use of tobacco.

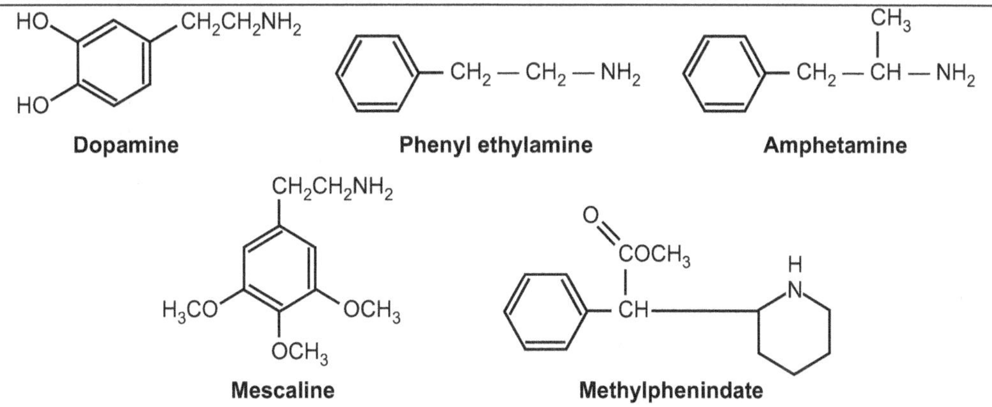

Fig. 7.1 : Some Amphetamine-like drugs

Abrupt withdrawal of nicotine use may result into drowsiness, restlessness, anxiety, irritability, insomnia, difficulty in concentrating and GIT complaints.

(e) Caffeine :

The beverages like tea, coffee and cocoa owe their stimulant effects due to the active ingredient, caffeine.

The stimulant effects of caffeine and theophylline are mainly due to an increase in c-AMP in central nervous system. An increase in coronary blood flow and myocardial activity is also reported which may sometimes result into palpitations and ectopic beats. These agents also lead to diuresis due to decreased tubular reabsorption.

(f) Hallucinogens (Psychotomimetics, Psychedelics or Psychotogens) :

On the chemical basis, hallucinogens can be divided into two classes :

(i) The indole alkylamine class : This class has its structural resemblance with 5-hydroxytryptamine. Examples include, lysergic acid diethylamide and its analogues, psilocin and psilocybin etc.

(ii) β-phenylethylamine class : This class is structurally related with mescaline, an alkaloid which is obtained from the Mexican cactus, Lophophora williamsii. It is abused to cause hallucinations. Examples of this class include, mescaline, 3, 4-methylenedioxy amphetamine (MDA), 5-methoxy-3, 4-methylenedioxy amphetamine (MMDA) etc.

Hallucinogens of Class I, are of very low acute toxicity and very rarely in overdoses, project life-threatening effects. Their sites of actions scatter from the cortex to the spinal cord. LSD is not a therapeutic agent. It constitutes an important part of all ergot alkaloids. It is odourless, tasteless and colourless substance which is equally effective by both, orally as well as parenterally (I.V.).

Though tolerance develops rapidly, the drug can be abruptly withdrawn without any withdrawal syndrome. Thereafter the patient should be treated with antianxiety agents in a supportive and familiar environment.

LSD exerts its central effects by acting on presynaptic serotonergic receptors resulting into decrease in the release of serotonin. It's actions are partly due to antagonism to serotonin, while on some receptor sites, it mimics the actions of serotonin. It can also interact with both, tryptaminergic and adrenergic receptors within CNS. As a result, overall effects produced by LSD cannot be related with each other in a co-ordinated fashion (i.e. hallucination). During LSD episode, the firing rate of serotonergic neurons which comprise the dorsal raphe nuclei of brain stem is sharply reduced. A large dose of phenothiazine is preferable to control the psychotic episodes produced by LSD.

Other dangerous hallucinogens from LSD class are diethyltryptamine (DET), dimethyltryptamine (DMT) and dipropyl-tryptamine.

The other agents, psilocin and psilocybin are also potent hallucinogens which are active alkaloids isolated from the Mexican "magic mushrooms".

(g) Arylcyclohexylamines :

Phencyclidine constitutes as a unique hallucinogen from the series of phenylcyclohexylamines. It was introduced into the market in 1957 as an anesthetic agent. But soon, its hallucinogenic effects were observed. In 1965, the drug was banned for human use but was continued to be used as veterinary anesthetic. Presently no one uses if for veterinary purpose also. At present its structural relative, ketamine is used as an anesthetic in man.

At the cellular level, it increases the synaptic concentrations of dopamine, serotonin and norepinephrine by inhibiting their re-uptake processes. This results into psychotic behaviour, convulsion and in severe cases, coma.

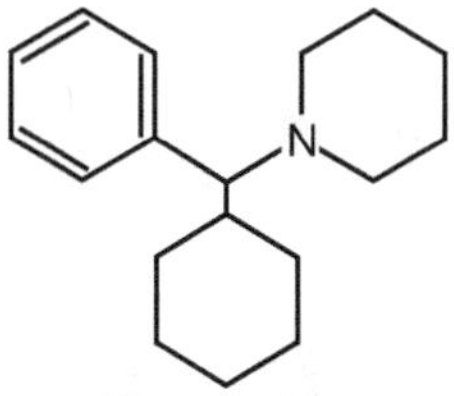

Phencyclidine

In the acute toxicity due to phencyclidine, the unabsorbed drug from the stomach can be removed by a continual nasogastric suction. The treatment with antipsychotic agents is supplemented with the use of diazepam to control the occurrence of seizures.

(h) Miscellaneous Agents :

Drug dependence is reported to occur with the repeated inhalation of some anesthetic gases (like nitrous oxide and diethyl ether) and some organic solvents like chloroform and toluene. Other agents which constitutes household spice, nutmeg, caffeine and aspirin-phenacetin-caffeine tablets also develop dependence.

Table 7.2

Sr. No.	Drug of abuse	Withdrawal symptoms	Substituent drug
1.	Opioids	Nausea, vomiting, irritability insomnia, diarrhoea, intestinal spasm and an increase in heart rate and blood-pressure.	Methadone, clonidine
2.	Barbiturates	Rebound increase in REM sleep, insomnia, anxiety, delirium, tonic-clonic seizures.	Phenobarbital.
3.	Alcohol	Same as barbiturates.	Long acting benzodia-zepines, sodium valproate, clomethiazole, multi-vitamin injections, and antibiotics.
4.	Amphetamines	Depression, hyperphagia and tiredness.	Chlorpromazine diazepam.
5.	Nicotine	Irritability, anxiety, restlessness, insomnia, headache, drowsiness, GIT complaints and difficulty in concentrating.	Buffered nicotine chewing gum.
6.	Hallucinogens	No serious withdrawal symptom.	Anti-anxiety agents, barbiturates and phenothiazines.
7.	Phencyclidine	Fearfulness, tremors, facial twitches and hypertension.	Diazepam, Hydralazine.
8.	Benzodiazepines	Anxiety, tremulousness or severe insomnia.	Longer-acting benzodiazepines.

SCREENING AND TESTING OF DRUGS

8.1 INTRODUCTION

A new drug can be obtained from either natural or synthetic source. A synthetic drug may be achieved either by :

(i) A simple molecular modification of the structure of pre-existing, clinically evaluated drug; or

(ii) Route of synthesis designed on the knowledge of receptor structure (i.e. rational approach), or

(iii) Random approach with no particular therapeutic aim in mind.

The medicinal chemists play a key role in pharmaceutical research. Their ultimate goal is to synthesize such novel biological compounds which will be more potent and least toxic than their clinically available relatives. Once, such new drugs arrive in the pure form, the next logical thought off-course, is to carry out pharmacological studies to detect the therapeutic activity.

A firm conclusion cannot be drawn, if such studies lack systematic background. These studies generally involve a battery of tests for rapid detection of activity. These tests provide a direct, both, qualitative and quantitative relationship to the desired therapeutic activity. An ideal objective of all such studies, is to find the remedy on the human diseases. These studies are generally carried out :

(a) to find out effective therapy to cure a diseased condition, and

(b) to search out other possible areas of clinical applications for the new drug.

For such studies, a thorough knowledge of diseases, pathophysiology and pharmacology is of vital importance. Such studies which are adopted to detect the effects of a drug (may be of natural or synthetic origin), on intact animal or isolated organs, are grouped under the term, *Screening*. Screening is a large scale experimental data-bank which involves parameters that are related with functioning of almost every important organ system. The interpretation of the data obtained, guides the investigator in deciding the direction of further studies. It permits a rapid recognition of active compounds from the series and inert or toxic compounds can be readily rejected. Thus, screening is such a facility by which compounds can be evaluated for many activities at once.

8.2 TYPES OF SCREENING METHODS

Screening involves, both, scanning and evaluation. There are three kinds of screening programs for pharmaceuticals, depending upon the experimental requirements for different types of drugs.

A. Simple Screening :

It does not involve interconnected multiple test procedures. It just employs a single test or perhaps two similar tests to evaluate the activity of the test compounds. For example, determination of sugar concentration in the blood or urine samples of the treated persons would be a sufficient criteria to evaluate the hypoglycemic activity of a drug under testing.

B. Blind Screening :

It is generally employed to evaluate the fields of activity (in qualitative as well as in quantitative terms) for the series of compounds, having no previous pharmacological background. It involves a battery of tests, in order to screen out the pharmacologically active fraction of a series. It also helps to differentiate the main activity from other subsidiary activities, associated with the test drug. The tests are also of multiple purposes rather than for single purpose.

The screening procedure proposed by Irwin, is an excellent method, to obtain clues of activity on CNS and any other field of activity of a test compound. Before undertaking a detailed pharmacological testing, it becomes imperative to understand whether the test compound should be studied further or should be rejected. If it is worthy for further attention, which pharmacological properties are associated with it.

The general observation for blind screening includes the recording of :

(i) the species, the sex, the weight and the age of the animal used, and

(ii) the name of the test substance, solvent, dose, route and time of administration should also be noted down.

The profile is broadly categorized into three sections -

(a) Behavioural profile

(b) Neurological profile

(c) Autonomic profile

Each section is further sub-divided into 3 or 4 parameters :

The effects of the test compounds on the animals are ranked on a scale having the markings of nine degrees. i.e. from 0 to 8. The base score for normal signs or effects is 4, while score below 4 is considered as subnormal response (decrease in the intensity or negative side) and those above 4, is considered as supernormal response (increase in the intensity or positive side). Similarly, the base score for abnormal sign is 0 and maximum score is 8.

Generally, the time interval chosen between two successive observations related to each parameter, may be one of the following :

(a) 5 or 10 or 15 or 30 minutes.

OR

(b) 1 or 2 or 4 or 8 or 24 hours.

It depends upon the potency and type of activity associated with the drug. Usually the test compound is administered by minimum two different routes.

Irwin's method, not only helps to detect psychotropic or neuro-muscular activity but can also be useful to search CNS side-effects or toxicities associated with the test compound.

C. Programmed Screening :

It is the next stage of blind screening. As soon as active compound/s is/are found in the blind screening programme, or when the activity of definite type is anticipated for a series of compounds, a well defined and direction oriented test program for that particular activity is sketched out. It is known as *programmed screening*. The aim of such screening is to confirm quantitatively the presence of activity alongwith potential side-effects, if any. Therefore, tests and methods that are modifiable into quantitiable procedures have to be adopted. Thus, programmed screening serves as a preface to the detailed pharmacological studies of the most promising compounds.

8.3 SCREENING METHODS FOR DETECTION OF SOME ACTIVITIES

Using Irwin's method, one can easily detect the presence of neuropharmacological activities, like central stimulation, central depression, motor inco-ordination, irritability, myorelation, analgesia, anesthesia or convulsion. A brief review of the methods generally employed to detect the presence of activities other than described above, is given in the points ahead.

(a) Test on the Guinea Pig Isolated Ileum :

Since the guinea pig ileum consists of quite a good number of muscarinic cholinergic receptors, various activities like, cholinergic, anticholinergic, ganglion-stimulant, ganglion-blocking, histaminic, antihistaminic, serotonin-like, antiserotonin can be easily tested on it. Acetylcholine will cause contraction of ileum muscles whereas anticholinergic agents will antagonise this action.

The test compound is added alone to the tissue bath and is also added in the presence of acetylcholine (or for that matter, histamine, serotonin or nicotine). If it has agonist action, it will potentiate the effect of neurohormone. Whereas if it antagonises the effect of neurohormone, it will have lytic action for that particular hormone. The parasympatholytic activity may also be evidenced by mydriasis and by inhibition of the secretions of the alimentary tract (e.g., saliva, gastric juice etc.). The ganglion-blocking activity is guessed by the dilation of the pupil in mammals. Hexamethonium dibromide is generally used as a drug for comparison.

Table 8.1

Behavioural profile	Neurological profile	Autonomic profile
(i) Awareness	(i) CNS excitation	(i) Optical signs
(ii) Mood	(ii) Posture	(ii) Secretary signs. e.g. salivation, urination.
(iii) Motor activity	(iii) Motor inco-ordination (iv) Muscle tone (v) Reflexes	(iii) General signs. e.g. skin colour, heart rate, respiratory rate.

Similarly sympatholytic activity may be recognised, usually by the effect of the test compound on the blood pressure of the cat.

(b) Antihistaminic Activity :

For in vitro testing, the antihistaminic activity of the test compound is evaluated on:

(i) isolated guinea pig ileum;

(ii) isolated guinea pig lung;

(iii) isolated guinea pig tracheal chain.

For invivo testing, the drug is injected to the unanesthetized guinea pig through the jugular vein (Preziosi, 1958). With a time gap of 5 minutes, a series of histamine (0.5 mg) injections by the same route is given. It continued with a gap of 5 minutes per action until the death of the animal. The activity of drug against following properties of histamine can be evaluated.

(i) Protection against intravenous or aerosolised histamine-induced lethal effects.

(ii) Antagonism of vasodepressor response to histamine in anesthetized dog, and

(iii) Protection against capillary permeability, cutaneous reactions and edema caused by histamine.

(c) Analgesic Activity :

The present tests for analgesia generally depend upon a delayed response to a noxious stimulus after the administration of the test compound. The test compound can be given either subcutaneously or intravenously. The noxious stimulus may be of mechanical or thermal or electrical origin.

Table 8.2

	Stimulus	Procedure
(a)	Mechanical	An artery clip in thin rubber is applied to the tail-end for about 30 secs.
(b)	Thermal	The mouse is placed for 15 secs on a hot-plate, maintained at 55°C.
(c)	Electrical	A shock of 15 volts is applied to the tail three times for 100 msec.

(d) Cardiovascular Activity :

The cardiovascular tests are usually performed on cats. Similarly, the aorta of the rabbit is very sensitive for the evaluation of some drugs for their properties to affect the heart and vascular system.

(i) Cardiotonic activity : The inotropic action can be assessed on the thin papillary muscle removed from right ventricle of the cat heart (Bennett etal, 1958). Drugs can be screened for cardiotonic properties by the administration to the bath and recording the amplitude and frequency of contractions.

The time for attainment of the maximum effect is also recorded.

(ii) Antihypertensive activity : The renal hypertension is produced by the constriction of both renal arteries in a dog. The antihypertensive effect of the drug is evaluated by using mean arterial blood pressure as a parameter. Similarly, the determination of systolic and diastolic blood pressure and heart rate may also be useful to evaluate the activity.

(iii) Antifibrillatory activity : Fibrillation may be produced by acetyl choline, aconitine, epinephrine, veratridine, or electrically. The induction or abolition of an arrhythmia by subsequent administration of the drug, is the basis of all the testing methods. The antifibrillatory activity is compared with the activity of classic antifibrillatory agent, quinidine. Quinidine increases both, the refractory period of cardiac muscle and the threshold of response to electrical stimulus.

An index of antifibrillatory activity

$$= \frac{\text{Activity of test drug} \times LD_{50}}{\text{Activity of quinidine} \times LD_{50} \text{ of quinidine}}$$

(e) Hypoglycemic Activity :

For the testing purposes, white rats, dogs and rhesus monkey are the animals of choice. Hypoglycemic activity is usually expressed as the blood-sugar lowering effect of the compound. Hence, before any test, food should be withdrawn 18 hours before to ensure stable blood-sugar regulation. Generally, the test compound is administered either by gastric intubation or by intravenous route. The latter involves either a single dose injection given within a few minutes or a slow infusion. The activity of the drug can be evaluated by comparing with a standard oral hypoglycemic compound or with insulin or with a placebo.

Frawley and Shelley suggested the use of both, normal and diabetic subjects for short term evaluation of new drugs. For this, after the administration of drug, the blood samples are periodically withdrawn at the times, 1 hour, 2 hours, 3 hours, 5 hours, and 7 hours (duration of the experiment is of seven hours). The blood samples are usually taken by puncture of the tail veins. To prevent the glycolysis, the blood sample is immediately mixed with fluoride or oxalate and is sent to the laboratory for blood sugar determination. A graph is then plotted using time of sampling, expressed in hours against the lowering in level of blood sugar (ordinate), expressed as mg/100 ml.

(f) Antimicrobial Activity :

The invitro and invivo screening methods for antimicrobial activity should be designed in such a way to get an adequate information about the stability, the nature of activity (whether it is bacteriostatic or bacteriocidal) and its antimicrobial spectrum. The most commonly used techniques for the evaluation of antimicrobial activity are –

(i) *Agar diffusion*

(ii) *Turbidimetric methods :*

    (a) Serial dilution technique;

    (b) Photometric technique.

(iii) *Respirometric method :* This is comparatively a new technique. A dose dependent property of most of the antimicrobial agents to inhibit the respiration of the microbial cells, is the basis of this technique.

For the determination of the antimicrobial spectrum, either an agar diffusion or a serial dilution technique is generally employed to know the minimum inhibitory concentration (MIC). The former method, though more economical in terms of time, personnel and material required, is much less precise than the latter.

The synergistic antimicrobial action can be evaluated by the serial dilution method in fluid media where one agent is present in a constant concentration and the other is serially diluted.

Finally before clinical trials, the drug is given to the experimentally infected animals. For such protection tests in laboratory animals, mice are the most economical animals.

(g) Antiviral Activity :

The various screening methods for antiviral activity involve cell culture procedures, embryonated egg tests, titration techniques, actual animal infections and assays based on inhibition of viral specific enzymes. Unfortunately, there is an apparent lack of predictability in the most commonly utilised antiviral screening methods. Hence, careful selection of the proper screening methods plays an important role in the evaluation of the activity.

Many viruses form plaques in the favourable cell system. In such cases, the inhibition of plaque formation is an effective means of detecting antiviral activity. But some viruses where plaques or cytopathic effects are not readily seen, antiviral activity can be evaluated in the light of following properties :

   (i) The agglutination of red cells by influenza virus : This property is used to evaluate the antiviral activity of some benzimidazole derivatives.

   (ii) In one of the qualitative method, the extent of multiplication of a virus in a culture can, in most cases readily be demonstrated by immunofluorescence.

The potency of the antiviral agent can be guessed by its minimum inhibitory concentration (MIC) value which is the least amount of test compound that will still retain the activity. An individual cell destruction (cytopathogenic effect) and the toxicity of the compound for the host cell are also studied.

(h) Sex Steroids :

Bioassay methods play an important role for the evaluation of gonadal hormones. The most widely used bioassay methods for oestrogenic substances are based on vaginal cornification (Allen and Doisy) and uterine weight changes (Rubin et al). While for progestins, the evaluation is based upon the proliferation of rabbit endometrium (Allen and Corner). This test is performed on immature female rabbits and grading is done from 0 to +4. The carbonic anhydrase determination in endometrial cells (Pincus etal) also gives good dose-response curve.

For evaluation of androgenic activity, the screening methods based upon the response of the chick or capon comb and the weight increase of the accessory sex organs of the castrated male rat enjoyed wide acceptance.

Antifertility activity : In male, the antifertility agents may cause sterility by inducing oligospermia or formation of nonfunctional spermatozoa. In female, inhibition of ovulation or fertilization, interference with the transport or implantation of the fertilized ovum and the destruction of the early implanted embryo are the stages where antifertility action is exerted.

Ovulation, transportation, fertilization and implantation of the fertilized ovum need co-ordinated events. These events depend upon a very fine balance between the gonadal hormones. The antifertility agents act by disturbing and disorganising the gonadal hormones-dependent system.

DRUGS AND IMMUNITY

9.1 INTRODUCTION

The human body is composed of many important systems viz. respiratory system, vascular system, urinogenital system, central nervous system etc. All these systems are distinct and apparently compact entities which operate in a very systematized and composite manner. Any disturbance in the functioning of these vital systems due to disease or infection, may put life of the person in trouble. Hence, there exists a natural defence mechanism in each individual to protect itself from external pathogens as well as internal offenders. This mechanism is operated through the immune system. Unlike other systems in the body, immune system is non-compact and diffusely spreads throughout the body. It acts at both, cellular and humoral levels.

The attacking injurious stimulus may be :

- **(a) physical** : heat, cold, humidity, radiation etc., or
- **(b) chemical** : acids, alkali, poisons etc., or
- **(c) biological** : parasites, pathogenic micro-organisms.

Body first tries to prevent the entry of external offenders by executing certain non-immunogenic, non-specific mechanisms. These mechanisms include, barriers of physical nature, body secretions, (e.g. lysozymes, interferon, lactoferrin etc.) storage in the lymph nodes, coughing and excretion. Secretions like puspiration, sebum, ear wax etc. contain unsaturated fatty acids which are bacteriocidal and protective in nature. If these mechanisms fail to defend the body from the infecting organism then the second line of defence defends the host. This constitutes the immune system. It imparts a resistance or tolerance against the internal or external offenders.

The developed resistance or immunity operates in two different ways.

(a) Cellular immunity : If the immunity is brought about by the production of specially modified cells, (T-cells), then it is called as *cellular immunity*. T-cells may be of different types, e.g. memory cells, helper cells, effector cells, suppressor cells or killer cells.

(b) Humoral immunity : It operates through the synthesis of soluble plasma proteins (immunoglobins). If the developed resistance is due to production of circulating antibodies, the immunity is known as *humoral immunity*. It is operated through immunoglobins of different types e.g., IgG, IgM, IgA, IgD, IgE, which have their subclasses also.

The concept of immunization basically involves an interaction between an offender (antigen) and an ingredient of the body's defence system (antibodies) which is capable of specifically reacting with it. The infecting organism acts as an antigen, which after being introduced into the body, induces the production of a specific antagonist. In most of the cases, the antagonist is an antibody that remains in the blood even after complete neutralization of antigenic action. In future, whenever it comes across that antigen, it immediately recognizes the antigen and tries again to expel or destroy it. The antigen-antibody complex neutralizes antigen toxins and various damaging factors. The termination of antigenic action results through various mechanisms like, agglutination, precipitation, flocculation or lysis of the antigen. The antigens which stimulate the production of antibodies, are also known as immunogens. Similarly, the antigens which lead to hypersensitivity reactions (or allergy) through antigen-antibody interactions, are called as allergens.

The antibodies are produced in response to the presence of antigen in the body (exception is isoantibodies which are naturally occurring antibodies in the human circulation). For one molecule of immunogen or antigen, millions of specific antibodies are formed and released into the body fluids. They are found in the serum, lymph and other body fluids. The blood plasma or serum retains higher amounts of antibodies. They are also known as immunoglobulins because they are associated with the gammaglobulin fraction of the plasma (all immunoglobulins present in the circulation or other body fluids are not necessarily be of antibody nature). The immunoglobulins (Ig) have been categorized into five types, namely IgG, IgM, IgA, IgD and IgE. The presence of yet another type, IgT is a subject of current studies. Hypersensitivity of allergic reactions results due to the interaction of antigen with IgE antibodies. Hence, IgE antibodies are also, called as 'reaginic antibodies or reagins'.

About 80% of serum antibodies are present in the form of IgG. The antibodies of IgG types also predominate at rest of sites in the body.

Various approaches have been made to classify the antibodies. Accordingly they can be classified atleast in three different ways :

1. On the basis of their source : auto-antibodies, heteroantibodies etc.

2. On the basis of immunological reactions: Antibodies may be categorised as precipitins, lysins, agglutinins, flocculins, opsonins, neutralizing etc.

3. On the basis of their biological properties : Cytotropic antibodies, Homocytotropic antibodies, Heterocytotropic antibodies etc.

In most of the cases, antigens are of protenious nature. Polypeptides including glyco- and mucoproteins may act as antigen. Similarly lipopolysaccharides and complex carbohydrates may also lead the production of antibodies. Beside this even bacteria, virus, erythrocytes and other cells possess antigenic properties. Generally, low molecular weight proteins do not act as antigens. They can induce allergic reactions only after lodging with a carrier protein. The complex of such silent or incomplete antigen with a carrier protein results into an active antigen. The incomplete antigen was termed as hapten by Landsteiner, signifying an attachment. The carrier protein may be serum albumin, polypeptides or even an amino acid residue. Examples of hapten include penicillin, sulphonamides, some steroids etc.

In certain cases, entry of antigen does not induce the production of corresponding antibodies. Instead the immunological memory of that antigen is retained through the agency of thymus dependent lymphocytes or T-cells. These cells are scattered throughout the body. These cells have surface receptors that allow them to recognize the specific antigen. On re-exposure to the same antigen, T-cells immediately recognise it and terminates its antigenic properties. As this reaction takes comparatively a longer time to manifest, it is called as delayed or tuberculin type of reaction.

Artificial immunization may also be achieved. This can be done either by administration of small amounts of antigen (active immunization) or of the corresponding antibodies (passive immunization) to the patient.

Higher levels of antibodies at the time of exposure to antigen, can be achieved in active immunization. Hence it is not needed to be repeated again. These are the advantages of active immunization over the passive immunization. On the other side, passive immunization is quite safe and does not involve the complications of developing allergy or other non-specific toxic reactions. Passive immunization generally involves transfer of only immunoglobulins. The passive immunization can also be achieved by the administration of immune effector cells but the process is technically a bit difficult.

The antigens or more specifically agglutinogens present on the cell membranes of erythrocytes belong to either Antigen A or Antigen B. In 1900, Karl Landsteiner (hapten fame) utilized this difference as a basis for the classification of human blood into four major groups, O, A, B and AB.

Many of the signs of immune reaction show similarity with inflammatory symptoms. If antibody fails to differentiate its antigen from the body's own cells and products, it may result into autoimmune diseases. Autoimmunity plays an important role, at least to some extent in Addison's disease, myasthenia gravis, rheumatic fever and in some skin diseases.

9.2 COMPLEMENT

The complement is not an antibody. It normally occurs in the plasma serum of all animals. It is necessary for the immunolysis of erythrocytes and gram-negative bacteria. In some cases, the antigen-antibody complex cannot get activated unless it combines with complement. The complement fixation leads to the activation of antibody. Such antibodies that need complement fixation in order to evoke immune response, are known as complement fixing antibodies. The immune response may be evoked through phagocytosis, cytolysis, chemotaxis etc.

Complement, a naturally occurring substance in the plasma serum, is thought to be composed of atleast 11 components. These components are designated by letters C1 to C9. All these are either α or β globulins with the possible exceptions of C1q and C8 which are γ globulins.

9.3 IMMUNE MECHANISMS

Immunization is induced to get protection against many infectious agents and may utilise either inactivated (killed) cells or live material.

Immune mechanisms operate through the antibodies that circulate in the blood and lymph. Specific immunity develops due to existence of different types of lymphoid cells which are derived from the thymus and bone marrow. Two different types of lymphoid cells exist in both, the blood as well as in peripheral lymphoid tissues. These are:

(a) T-cells : These cells induce cellular immunity.

(b) B-cells : These cells mediate serological immunity.

Cellular immunity due to T-cells arise due to their direct cytotoxic interactions and the release of various effector substances or lymphokinines. While serological immunity is caused by the presence of monoclonal immunoglobulins on the surface of B-cells.

Besides this, blood itself contains a natural, high molecular weight protein, propeidin which is an effective killer of a number of gram-positive and gram-negative bacteria. This bacteriocidal action needs the presence of magnesium ions. Propeidin is considered as distinct from normal antibodies.

Various proteolytic enzymes that can be isolable from the tissue extracts exhibit immunological action.

For example, lysozymes can lead to bacteriocidal action due to their attack on bacterial cell-wall. The cell-wall ruptures resulting into the release of the contents of the cell machinery.

Lysozomes are released from the polymorphs and pulmonary macrophages in response to the injury. They also occur in the conjunctival secretions, nasal and intestinal mucus as well as in the saliva.

Interferon is a protein which can be produced by many types of cells under the stimulus by various kinds of inactivated viruses. The release of interferon imparts a resistance to the person against the attack of viral infection. Generally, a person once infected with one virus, develops a resistance against other viral infections. This phenomenon is known as *viral interference.*

When cells are exposed to antigen the very first time, cells take their own time to produce the corresponding antibodies to inactivate that antigen. The latent period for production of antibodies may consume about 3-4 days or more. Hence, the primary response of the host against the antigen usually remains less exaggerated. After this latent period, antibody titre in the body increases potentially. Hence, at this point, if the patient is re-exposed to same antigen, the secondary response results. This response is of vigorous nature and can be termed as booster response.

9.4 FACTORS AFFECTING IMMUNITY

Various factors have been found to affect the functioning of normal immune mechanisms in the body. These factors are listed below :

(a) Genetic factors : For certain diseases, the body need not develop resistance. The immunity is already in existence since from birth and is gained through the hereditary characteristics. This natural immunity or innate immunity could be gene linked. For example, guinea pigs are susceptible to, diphtheria but rats are resistant to the disease probably by a genetic mechanism. This resistance can possibly be linked with an increased number of lysozomes present in the cytoplasm of macrophages.

(b) Racial differences : The susceptibility to various diseases in persons varies according to racial differences. But the diagnosis of influence of racial factors is difficult due to the interference of environmental factors. Examples include that of Nigroes who are resistant to yellow fever for which white men are susceptible.

(c) Age differences : Immune mechanisms operate with maximum efficacy during adolescence. They are weak at the two extremes of the life i.e., foetal life and in old aged people. Naturally the effects of infectious agents in these classes are more severe. Several infections result in severe damage if occurred in the infancy because immune mechanisms are in developing stage. For example, severe damages including, deafness, heart lesions, cataract may occur in the foetus if it is attacked by German measle virus. This is mainly due to less weakly developed interferon defence mechanism. However increase in the age, does not mean an increased resistance against the disease.

(d) Hormonal factors : Homeostatic mechanisms exist in the body to co-ordinate balancing between various body fluids and secretions. Hormones are known to control these homeostatic mechanisms. Hence, hormonal disturbances either in up or down directions, lead to the changes in the susceptibility towards various diseases. Examples include :

1. Insulin deficiency leads to an increased susceptibility to streptococci infections, tuberculosis and urinary tract infection.

2. Addison's disease and Cushing's syndrome are found to occur more readily in patients suffering from hypothyroidism.

3. Patients under a long-term cortisone therapy are more prone to certain diseases including rheumatic artihritis, Hodking's disease etc.

9.5 FATE OF IMMUNOGLOBULINS

Initially immunoglobulins are derived from B-lymphocytes and plasma cells in very low amounts. The presence of antigen may lead to an acceleration in the rate of synthesis. Usually only one class of immunoglobulins is initially synthesized by a given immunocyte and a clone of immunocytes synthesizes a specific type of immunoglobulins.

Details are not available about the catabolism of immunoglobulins. In most of the cases, they are likely to be destroyed and eliminated by GIT route. Liver serves a major site where this degradation occurs. Rarely immunoglobulins undergo fragmentation and eliminated through urine.

9.6 HYPERSENSITIVITY REACTIONS

The antibodies produced by the host defence mechanism, protect the host against the action of antigen by neutralizing the antigen-toxins. However, exceptionally, with response to specific agents or under certain conditions, the antigen-antibody interaction may provoke an unusual and exaggerated reaction, damaging the host body tissues. This altered response of the host tissues is known as *hypersensitivity or allergy.* The antigen involved in this process is known as *allergen or sensitizer.*

The various types of hypersensitivity reactions are classified as :

Type I (anaphylactic) reactions.

Type II (cytotoxic) reactions.

Type III (toxic complex) reactions, and

Type IV (delayed hypersensitivity) reactions.

Type I Reactions :

Type I hypersensitivity reactions include anaphylactic shock and atopic diseases. They are mediated by humoral antibodies and depend primarily on the interaction of antigen with IgE antibodies (reagin antibodies).

(a) Anaphylaxis or Anaphylactic Response :

The term, anaphylaxis (which means removal of protection) was first coined by Richet and Portier in 1902 to describe a hypersensitivity reaction which was in exaggerated form. It results due to parenteral administration of fluids containing sensitizing antigens or haptens. It leads to an intense systemic and general reactivity resulting into sneezing, dyspnea, cyanosis, convulsions and sometimes in death.

During the sensitization induced by an allergen, a specialized class of humoral antibodies are formed. These antibodies belong to IgE type and also are called as reagin antibodies. They have a high affinity for mast cells and basophil granulocytes. Beside their presence in the circulation (i.e. basophils), mast cells are fixed in connective tissue and IgE antibodies which attach to them are often described as homocytotropic antibodies. They get retained on the mast cells or basophil receptors through the binding of reversible nature.

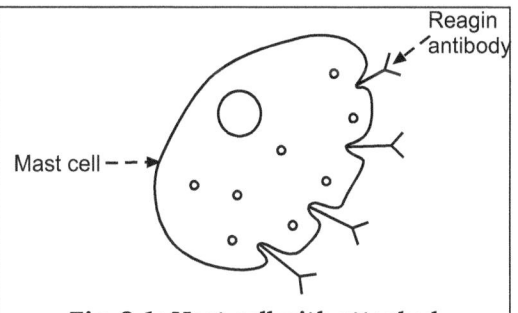

Fig. 9.1: Mast cell with attached reagin molecules

The binding of IgE antibodies occurs through their Fc constituents with the receptors. Then the antigen molecule binds with the reagin molecules attached on the mast cells, in such a way to cross-link the adjacent reagin molecules. Here the initial step of anaphylaxis is completed. Thereafter, whenever the host is re-exposed to the same antigen, exaggerated reaction occurs due to degranulation (rupturing of storage granules) of the mast cells. The activated membrane enzymes cause an increased influx of calcium ions and a fall in the concentration of c-AMP or rise in c-GMP. These changes bring out degranulation of the mast cells and are necessary to release chemical mediators responsible for anaphylaxis. These mediators include histamine, serotonin, slow releasing substance of anaphylaxis (SRS-A), bradykinins, prostaglandins, platelet activating factor, eosinophil chemotactic factor of anaphylaxis (ECF-A) and heparin.

Chemical mediators in anaphylaxis :

1. Histamine plays the most prominent role in anaphylaxis. It is present in the mast cells in the form of its precursor, histidine. Histidine is stored in the bound form with a heparin protein complex.

2. Slow releasing substance of anaphylaxis (SRS-A) has a molecular weight of about 500 daltons. It has bronchoconstrictory activity in man which makes it to play an important role in asthamatic condition. Chemically its properties are similar to that of an unsaturated acid.

3. Plasmakinins (e.g., bradykinin) have histamin-like activities and lead to bronchoconstriction and increased capillary permeability.

4. Prostaglandins as we know, play an important role in inflammatory conditions. They are released in response to tissue damage either due to injury or anaphylaxis. In some way, they are connected with humoral regulation of bronchial tone. In anaphylaxis, they are released reciprocally with SRS-A.

5. Platelet activating factor contributes indirectly by inducing the release of autacoids like, histamine and serotonin from the platelets.

6. Eosinophil chemotactic factor of anaphylaxis (ECF-A) is a normal constituent of mast cell. It is a tetrapeptide in nature. It encourages the migration of polymorphs and eosinophils to the site of reaction.

7. Heparin : Heparin does not play any role in anaphylatic shock. It is a normal constituent of the mast cell, which helps in the storage of histidine. It is released into the anaphylaxis due to degranulation of mast cells.

Treatment of anaphylaxis :

Chemical mediators of anaphylaxis are released due to degranulation of mast cells which occurs as a result of either a fall in the concentrations of c-AMP or a rise in c-GMP. An increase in the c-AMP level stabilizes store granules of mast cells. Hence any attempt, (or drug therapy) to increase the c-AMP level or to decrease c-GMP level, will result into the prevention of the occurrence of anaphylactic shock.

Generally, β-adrenergic receptor agonists (e.g. adrenaline, isoproterenol, salbutamol etc.) administration lead to an increase in the concentration of c-AMP. Since α-adrenergic receptor simulation leads to a decrease in c-AMP level, α-adrenergic blockers (e.g. thymoxamine) also increase the c-AMP levels. Certain drugs maintain the c-AMP level by blocking phosphodiesterase enzymes which metabolise c-AMP. These drugs include aminophylline and disodium-cromoglycate (Intal). Besides this, antihistamines and steroidal therapy is aimed to reduce the severity of attack. In all the therapies, oxygen inhalation leads to better improvement of the patient's health.

(i) Adrenergic drugs : β_1-Adrenergic agonists activate the enzyme, adenylate cyclase. The activation of this enzyme enhances the production of c-AMP. Some adrenomimetic drugs more specifically, β_2-adrenergic agonists (e.g. terbutaline, salbutamol) have bronchodilatory activity. This effect is useful in the relief of asthmatic condition .

(ii) Antihistaminics : Since histamine plays a prominent role in allergic manifestations, antihistaminic therapy always creates beneficial effects. For this purpose, more specifically, H_1-receptor blockers are used.

Besides H_1-blockers, some drugs like, ketotifen and cromolyn sodium also find use in the treatment of allergic reactions. Ketotifen, a potent antianaphylactic agent acts primarily by inhibition of chemical mediators. Chemically, it is a benzocycloheptathiophene derivative and acts as an antagonist of histamine.

Cromolyn sodium (sodium cromoglycate) is one of the commonly used drug in the therapy of anaphylaxis. It was first synthesized in 1968 and chemically it is related to a naturally occurring compound known as Khellin. It has a pharmacological profile similar to ketotifen. It appears to inhibit antigen-linked release of histamine and leukotrienes from the mast cells.

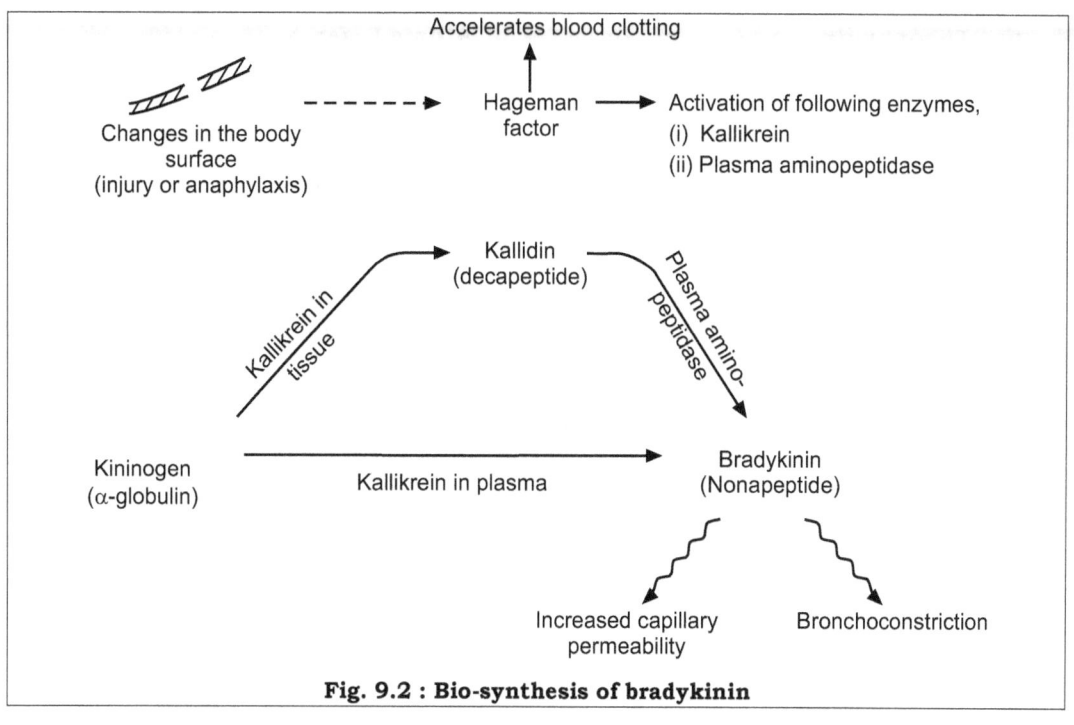

Fig. 9.2 : Bio-synthesis of bradykinin

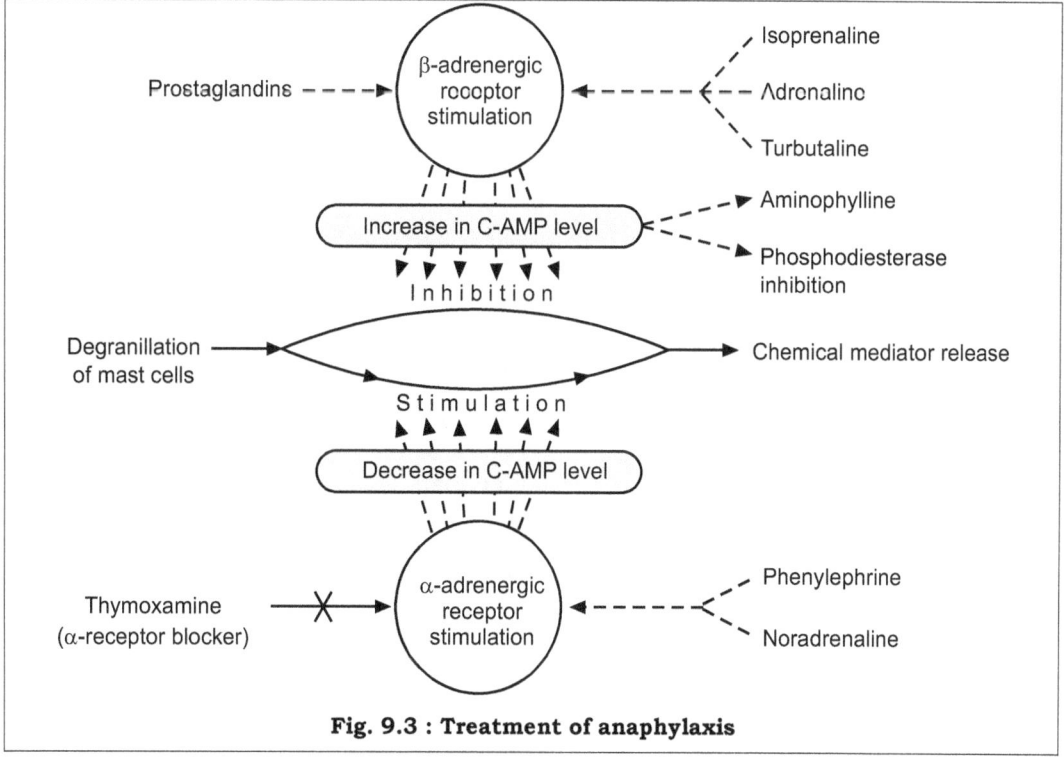

Fig. 9.3 : Treatment of anaphylaxis

(iii) Theophylline : Certain drugs stabilize mast cells by maintaining a steady-state level of c-AMP. They inhibit phosphodiesterase enzymes which are responsible for the metabolism of c-AMP. Thus, these drugs exhibit indirectly, an adrenomimetic action and inhibit degranulation of the mast cells. Examples include, aminophylline and cromolyn sodium (Intal).

(iv) Diethylcarbamazine : It is basically an antihelmintic drug. Its spectrum of activities showed that it also inhibits the antigen-induced release of SRS-A from the mast cells. Hence, it can be used to get partial relief in asthmatic conditons.

(v) Cholinergic blockers : Bronchoconstriction is one of the major symptom in anaphylactic shock and asthama which is caused by histamine released during these reactions. The lung and peripheral airways are innervated by cholinergic nervous systems. Hence, cholinergic agents may influence the regulation of diameter of these airways. Cholinergic blockers lead to bronchodilation. This property entitles cholinergic blockers to reserve a seat in the treatment of Type-I hypersensitivity reaction. One of such agents, administered by inhalation is Ipratropium bromide. It is a quaternary isopropyl derivative of atropine.

(vi) Steroidal therapy : In severe conditions when other drugs do not give satisfactory results, cortico-steroidal therapy is undertaken. These drugs recover very quickly the weakened pulmonary function and reduce to the appreciable level, the severity of recurrent attacks.

(b) Atopic Diseases :

Atopy is a spontaneous form of immediate hypersensitivity which does not result into harmful effects into normal (non-atopic) individuals. Anaphylactic shock attacks almost all vital organs of the body and can be considered as a state of systemic anaphylaxis whereas in atopic diseases, the functioning of only restricted areas of the body are affected. Hence atopic diseases, in simple words, can be considered as a state of local anaphylaxis.

A strong hereditary predisposition, eosinophilia and a natural tendency to disappear with age are some of the characteristics of atopic diseases. In some cases, eosinophilia (an increase in blood eosinophil count) serves as a basis of diagnostic test for these diseases. The examples of atopic diseases include asthma, hay fever and urticarial dermatitis.

(i) Asthma : It is characterised by paroxysmal attacks of difficult respiration. The symptoms include constriction of the bronchial muscles, oedema of the bronchial mucosa and cynosis.

(ii) Hay fever : It is a type of hypersensitivity that occurs in persons sensitive to a variety of pollens. Symptoms of the disease include, sneezing, running nose, itching and irritation of the nose and eyes, profuse lachrymation and photophobia.

(iii) Urticaria (urticaria = nettle) : The disease is characterised by a widespread eruption of firm, pink or white wheals, accompanied by intense itching. The disease appears for a short duration and disappears within few hours.

Type II Reactions :

This type of hypersensitivity reaction results when antigen utilizes a host cell as a platform for its stay. Hence, antigen antibody interaction not only results into the destruction of antigen but also that of host cell. Therefore type II reactions are known as cytotoxic reactions. Examples include the case of Apronal, a hypnotic drug. If administered, it gets accommodated by platelets and acts there as an antigen. Naturally this leads to destruction of platelets and results into thrombocytopenic purpura. Hypersensitive reactions if occurred during blood transfusions can also be categorised under type-II reaction.

Type III Reactions :

Depending upon the quantity of antigen or antibody involved, these reactions are classified into -

(a) reactions in which antigen is in excess. Example is serum sickness and

(b) reactions in which antibodies are in excess. These reactions are examplified by Arthus reaction.

(a) Serum sickness : This reaction is associated with an antigen in excess and leads to the production of soluble type of immune (i.e. antigen-antibody) complexes. These complexes fix on complement and get deposited during their circulation in the blood vessels. This results into acute inflammatory and tissue damaging type of responses. Symptoms vary according to the severity. These include fever, urticaria, rashes, painful and swallon joints, lymphadenopathy, and glomerullonephritis with albuminuria. The myocardium is also vulnerable to attack of inflammatory origin. The immunoglobulines IgM, IgG1 and IgG2 have ability to produce serum sickness, in the descending order.

Type IV Reactions (Cell-mediated Immune Reactions) :

Type-I, Type-II, and Type-III reactions occur immediately after the introduction of an antigen. All these reactions are mediated by humoral antibodies. On the contrary, type IV reaction is delayed for about 12 - 24 hours after the antigen has been introduced. Type-IV reaction is mediated by sensitized lymphoidal cells (specific T-lymphocytes). As this reaction is provoked after a longer time lag, it is also called as delayed type of hypersensitivity response (DHR) or tuberculin type hypersensitivity.

In delayed hypersensitivity, the antigen reacts with a specific T-lymphocyte instead of with humoral antibody. The complex undergoes a multiple division to give rise to several lymphoblasts. The immunity develops due to these cells and lymphokines.

When lymphocytes and macrophages (macrophages are fixed, mononuclear phagocytic cells having protective action against invading micro-organisms) from blood circulation of a guinea pig, already sensitized to Mycobacterium tuberculosis are transferred to the guinea pig, previously unexposed to Mycobacterium tuberculosis, the latter develops a hypersensitivity reaction, if tuberculin or purified protein derivative of tubercle bacilli (antigen) is injected to them. Hence, Type-IV reaction is also known as tuberculin type hypersensitivity.

Other examples of Type-IV reactions include, contact dermatitis, transplant rejection etc.

9.7 DRUGS USED IN IMMUNIZATION

(a) Immuno stimulating Agents :

Under normal circumstances or in diseased conditions, if the body's natural defence system fails to fight against the offender, certain drugs can be used to increase body's resistance against it. These agents are categorised as :

(i) Agents commonly used for active immunization : These include DTP, tetanus toxoid and various vaccines (e.g., BCG vaccine, typhoid vaccine, cholera vaccine, yellow fever vaccine etc.)

(ii) Agents available for passive immunization : The list includes Gas gangrene, antitoxin, diphtheria antitoxin, tetanus immunoglobulin etc.

(b) Immuno-modulating Agents :

These agents can be used to increase the immunity of patients who have either selective or generalized immunodeficiency. These agents are indicated in the treatment of :

  (i)   Immunodeficiency disorders,

  (ii) Chronic infectious diseases, and

  (iii) Neoplastic diseases.

Examples of this category include, interferon, levamisol, BCG vaccines, thymosine and transfer factor. Thymosine is a protein obtained from epitheloid component of the thymus gland while transfer factor is a small RNA molecule or peptide (having molecular weight of about 5000), derived from normal human lymphoid cells.

(c) Immunosuppressive Agents :

If a transplantation of a tissue is carried out, the recipient's body does not readily accept it. The recipient treats the graft as an invading pathogen. Immune reactions commence and result into rejection of the transplanted tissue. In such cases, suppression of the immune system of the recipient is needed to save his life. The drugs for this purpose are known as *immunosuppressants*. Many drugs may shoulder this property as one of their side-effects.

The immunosuppression may or may not be reversible. Other factors like physical, physiological, psychological, nutritional or environmental conditions also govern the situation.

The immunosuppression leads to an increased susceptibility to bacterial, fungal and viral infections. This is due to the absence of specific T-cells which are an important component of the immune system.

Sometimes the patient suffers from a very weak functioning of immune system. This is known as immunedeficiency. Immunosuppression has to be artificially brought about by using the drugs whereas immunedeficiency exists naturally. When it is genetically transmitted, it is called as *primary immunedeficiency,* while if it arises due to other factors (e.g. malnutrition, malignancy, irradiation, or metabolic diseases), it is known as *secondary immunedeficiency.*

Table 9.1 : Immunosuppressive agents

	Category	Examples
1.	Corticosteroids	Dexamethasone, beclomethasone.
2.	Alkylating agents	Cyclophosphamide, nitrogen mustard, chlorambucil, mechlorethamine.
3.	Folic acid analogues	Aminopterin, amethopterin.
4.	Purine analogues	Azathiopurine, 6-mercaptopurine.
5.	Antibiotics	Chloramphenicol, streptomycin, mitomycin C, actinomycin.
6.	Miscellaneous	Aspirin, promethazine, thalidomide, Cyclosporin A.

❖ ❖ ❖

PRINCIPLES OF TOXICOLOGY

10.1 INTRODUCTION

The human body is a complex living system. Naturally, any drug that has been given for a specific purpose does not exert selectively that action alone. To less or more extent the desired action is always associated with undesired effects or side-effects. Since these effects are not necessary for that therapeutic indication, their occurrence may place limitations on the use of the drug. The study of such undesired effects which occur with the therapeutic dose (and not with overdose) of the drug comes under 'toxicology'. The term, toxicology is derived from :

toxikon means poison and
logos means account

Of course, no drug is free from the adverse effects. The right dose differentiates a poison and a remedy. Hence, if the beneficial effects dominate the side-effects, then that drug is of medicinal value. Toxicological studies give us an idea about the ratio of risks to benefits. The toxicological studies assess the therapeutic value of newly discovered drug. If the drug does not fit into the standards, the search for safer drug is continued. Sometimes, the adverse effects of a drug may be wrongly interpreted as symptoms of disease. Treatment of poisoning due to overdoses of chemicals may sometimes pose problems. The study of toxicology offers answers to these and similar problems.

The toxic effects produced by a drug may be categorised as :

(a) Pharmacological effect : Barbiturates may cause excessive depression of CNS.

(b) Biochemical effects : Penicillins in sensitive patients cause allergic manifestations.

(c) Pathological effects : Many drugs exhibit hepatotoxicity and or nephrotoxicity e.g. acetaminophen and

(d) Genotoxic effects : These effects involve alteration of genetic material. These effects are more likely to be associated with neoplastic agents.

If these effects are severe, the patient may die within a short time. Sometimes, the administered drug may not be toxic but during its metabolism, it may be biotransformed in the toxic, mutagenic or carcinogenic metabolites. The changes produced by these metabolites can be complex and damaging not only to one organ or tissue, but may be to different cells.

10.2 MANIFESTATIONS OF TOXICITY

(a) Phototoxicity :

Some drugs when externally applied to skin, may get converted into potent allergens due to exposure to the ultraviolet and/or visible radiation. Chlorpromazine, nalidixic acid, sulfonamides and tetracyclines are some examples of such phototoxic drugs.

(b) Systemic Toxicity :

Many drugs have CNS side-effects as the prominent feature of their systemic toxicity. The intensity of these effects governed mainly by the lipophilicity of the drug. Systemic toxicity also affects other organs like, liver, kidney, lung, circulatory system etc.

(c) Organ Failure :

In severe cases, a drug may cause degeneration or death of the cells. If this degeneration is within a limit, organ or tissue has regeneration capacity to recover this damage. But if cell-death occurs to more extent, it can lead to necrosis and organ failure. It is irreversible damage and can not be recovered by body's own compensatory mechanisms.

(d) Immunotoxicity :

The interaction of a drug with the immune system can give rise to two types of toxicities :

(1) During the interaction, the drug may damage immune system functionally. The immunodeficiency thus develops. The body's natural resistance to infection is decreased and the person can easily affected by infections. This is called as an increased susceptibility of a patient to infection.

(2) The immune system is activated due to the presence of drug (allergen). The allergen is responsible for the antigen-antibody interactions that provoke the typical manifestations of allergy. The drug or its metabolite, combines with an endogenous protein to form antigen. After a latent period (atleast 1 - 2 weeks), a competent antibody is formed to interact with the antigen. The antigen-antibody complex (or immune complex), then adhere to tissue sites and induces local damage by macrophages and neutrophils.

Many drugs can induce allergic reactions in sensitive patients. These include, insulin, sulphonamides, penicillins, cephalosporins, quinidine etc.

Based on the mechanism of immunological involvement, the allergic responses have been divided into four types.

(e) Idiosyncracy :

It is a hypersensitivity to the particular drug which occurs only in small percentage of the individuals. The unusual effects of the drug arise in the patient due to certain genetic defects. For example many black males, when treated with primaquine, suffer from hemolytic anemia.

The idiosyncratic toxicities can be studied under following heads :

- **(i) Dose - dependent reactions :** e.g. Aspirin, penicillins etc.
- **(ii)** Dose-independent reactions.
- **(iii) Toxicogenetic reactions :** Due to inheritance or mutagenic effects, such toxicity arises.
- **(iv) Immuno toxicity :** These include, an anaphylactic shock, bronchial asthma, urticaria and various skin reactions.

Table 10.1

Type	Antibody involved	Target tissues	Symptoms
Type - I (Anaphylactic reactions)	IgE	Respiratory tract (asthma) Vasculature (anaphylactic shock) Skin (urticaria)	Edema Vasodilation Inflammation
Type - II (Cytolytic reactions)	IgG and IgM	Circulatory system	Hemolytic anemia Granulocytopenia
Type - III	IgG	Vascular endothelium resulting into serum sickness	Urticaria arthritis lymphadenopathy fever.
Type - IV (Delayed hyper sensitivity)	These reactions are mediated by sensitized T - lymphocytes and macrophages.		

(f) Teratogenicity :

Adverse drug effects are more evident in the fetus and neonate. Hence the drugs that have capacity to cross the placental barrier eventually pose a potential threat to the developing fetus. Thalidomide-tragedy is the famous case. Thalidomide is a sedative which induces sleep without residual hangover. Many pregnant women under the thalidomide treatment, gave birth to grossly deformed infants. Since from them, teratogenicity testings (teras, a Greek work meaning monster) were strictly adopted for every drug. For such testing, rabbit is the animal of choice.

The drugs that can cross the placenta (and may endanger the fetus, if taken during pregnancy), include, androgens, antithyroid drugs, estrogens, aminopterin, methotrexate, barbiturates, phenytoin, chloroquin, chloropromazine, isoniazid, methadone, nitrofurantoin, phenylbutazone, salicylates etc. Barbiturates can induce hemorrhagic disease in the new-born.

Some drugs may act as reproductive toxins for males. For example, a long-term anticancer treatment with alkylating agents exposes the patient to the risk for sterility. Similarly, parasympatholytic agents, upon chronic administration, may lead to impotency.

(g) Carcinogenicity :

Carcinogenicity is the capacity of drug to induce cancer in the subjects under treatment. This property is more linked with the repeated (i.e. chronic) administration. Hence, two years toxicity program is generally prescribed for the testing of carcinogenicity of a drug. Though rat and mouse are preferred for this test, dog is a really suitable species for more prolonged testings.

One can not launch clinical trials for a new drug, until the reports for all above tests in animals as well as on healthy volunteers appear to be negative.

10.3 ANIMAL TOXICITY TESTING

The toxicological tests for a new drug, that are to be performed on animals, are sketched out in the following figure :

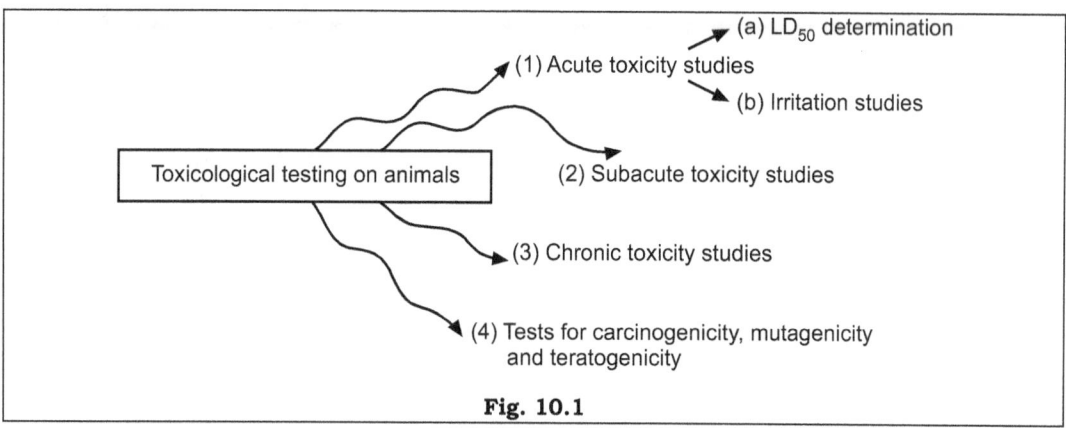

Fig. 10.1

(1) Acute Toxicity Studies :

Acute toxicity can be studied by delivering a single dose (or an overdose) for short period through either oral or intravenous route. Acute toxicity testing is generally done by the determination of median lethal dose (LD_{50}) of the drug. It is defined as the dose expected to cause a 50% response in a population, tested for the lethal response. A quantal dose-response relationship curve is used to find out LD_{50} value of a drug.

Determination of LD_{50} demands the use of relatively large number of animals. Generally rat and mice are the animals of choice but rabbit or guinea pig may also be used. To the animal choosen, the drug is administered orally or intraperitoneally at several doses in the lethal range. The resultant mortalities are observed for a set time period, usually 1 - 2 weeks. A dose-response curve is constructed by plotting logarithm of dose (on x-axis) versus the % of the population killed by the drug in probit units. A probit of 5 corresponds to a 50% response.

LD_{50} value of a drug helps us to fix up the upper limit for the daily dose to be given to the patient. As far as toxicological studies are concerned, it conveys less information than does the ratio of lethal to effective dose ($LD_{50} : ED_{50}$). This ratio is also known as therapeutic index. Similarly LD_1 and LD_{99} can easily be calculated from the equations worked out to determine LD_{50} value. LD_1 value gives an idea about the maximal nonlethal dose in animal studies.

(2) Subacute Toxicity Studies :

These studies are usually carried out on two species, namely rat and dog. The duration of studying the drug effects is extended to about three months in which the toxicity is studied at three different dose levels. The administration of sublethal dose search out side-effects like vomiting, tremors, catatonia or changes in autonomic function.

(3) Chronic Toxicity Studies :

The treatment of certain diseases necessitate a prolonged administration of drugs. Chronic toxicity studies expose out the toxicities, if any associated with such treatment. These studies are carried out by administering relatively small quantities of drug over a long period of time. Thus, chronic effects may arise from the slow accumulation of the toxic substance or its metabolities in the body or summation of acute effects. Each dose of drug produces slowly a reversible or irreversible type of tissue damage. Hence, it is the injury which accumulates rather than the toxic substance.

The procedure involves the administration of the drug to the animals for atleast twice as long as human patients will need it. In most cases, duration of treatment is fixed to two years. The dose administered, is higher than the pharmacologically desired dose. The drug is given preferably two species, one of which should be non-rodent.

Chronic toxicity studies are used to evaluate the potential of a new drug for it's teratogenic, mutagenic and carcinogenic properties. These studies are also accompanied with regular haematological examination, biochemical tests for liver and kidney function and for state of electrolyte balance.

(4) Special Tests :

Though chronic toxicity tests expose out the possibility for a drug to cause neurotoxicity, teratogenicity, carcinogenicity or mutagenicity, special tests for these toxic syndroms are needed to be carried out.

10.4 TREATMENT OF POISONING

The treatment of toxic symptoms arising due to the overdose of any drug, primarily involves maintenance of respiration and cardiovascular function. Measures should also be taken to treat imbalances in fluid and electrolyte levels.

Antidote therapy plays an important roie in the management of poisoning. Unfortunately it does not give positive results in the treatment of all poisoning cases. Hence, beside antidote treatment, supportive therapy is also utilised in the treatment of poisoning cases. It includes,

(a) Vomiting :

If the poisoning occurs due to orally ingested substance, a logical approach is to clear off that substance from the stomach. Vomiting is generally induced by either taking syrup of ipecac or by injecting apomorphine, 0.066 mg/kg subcutaneously. In absence of emetics, vomiting can be induced mechanically by stroking the posterior pharynx. For prompt emesis, it is better to take 1-2 glasses of water before hand.

Emesis is contraindicated if corrosives, strychnine, petroleum distillates are ingested and during coma.

(b) Gastric Lavage:

It is used in the cases where emesis does not work. It involves the insertion of a tube into the stomach of the patient and washing the stomach in order to remove the unabsorbed poison. Oral passage is easier but in adults, nasal route may also be utilised. The fluid generally used for lavage may be water, normal saline or one-half saline solution. The process is effective as long as six hours after the ingestion of a poison and should be repeated until the washing comes free from poison.

(c) Chemical Adsorption:

Once the poison has been removed maximally from the stomach by emesis, the traces of poison left in stomach can be removed by using activated charcoal. It easily adsorbs drug to the surface through irreversible fashion, thereby preventing its further absorption and poisoning.

It is administered usually as a slurry, suspended in water. It may either be given orally or by lavage. The amount of activated charcoal to be used, is determined in such a way to achieve a charcoal : drug ratio of 10:1.

(d) Purgation :

An aim of every therapy used in the treatment of poisoning is to neutralize or reduce the manifestations arising due to such poisoning. Purgatives are also employed in order to reduce absorption of the poison by hastening its passage through GIT. Saline cathartics are usually preferred due to their prompt action and less side-effects.

(e) Forced Diuresis :

To treat barbiturate and other intoxications, other options are also open. These include forced osmotic diuresis and alkalinization of the urine.

(f) Antagonism :

The drugs having the capacity to block the action of the poison, can be utilized. Such drugs are known as antidotes. They are broadly divided into categories on the basis of their mechanism of action.

(i) Some antidotes have opposite physical, chemical or pharmacological property to nullify the effect of the poison. In such cases, problem arises if the duration of action of poison and antidote, does not match each other. If duration of action of antidote is more, it may lead to poisoning with the antidote.

(ii) Some antidotes fix-up the poison molecules by forming a complex with it. They are also known as chelating agents. Chelating agents possess a high degree of selective affinity for certain metallic ions.

Heavy metals can not be metabolized in the body. During their stay, they combine with vital functional groups, necessary for normal physiological functions. The toxicity arising due to this ligand formation, may be dealt with chelating agents. Chelating agents can prevent or reverse toxic effects by forming soluble chelates (complexes) with the heavy metals. Thus, they enhance the excretion of the metals.

(g) Dialysis :

Peritoneal dialysis and hemodialysis are usually employed techniques in the life-threatening intoxication, in the blood, the poison may bind to several cells and plasma-protein. The rate of elimination of such poison, therefore, is governed by the rate of dissociation of the poison from its binding sites.

(i) Hemodialysis (Artificial kidney) : It is much more effective dialysing technique than peritoneal dialysis. It can be used to treat intoxication due to barbiturates, glutethimide, methanol, salicylates etc. Generally nephrotxic agents can not be dialysed.

(ii) Peritoneal dialysis : Though it is less effective than the hemodialysis, it is generally used to enhance the rate of elimination of the toxic elements from the body. The poisoning resulting due to overdoses of many exogenous poisons may be treated using this technique.

(h) Blood Transfusion :

When all the approaches to remove poison from the blood fails then blood transfusion remains the only solution. Similarly if hemoglobin is converted to methemoglobine due to the toxic action of drug present, the life of the patient comes in danger. In such cases of methemoglobinemia, the circulating blood has to be replaced. Blood transfusion is an effective therapy to supply normal hemoglobin that can train oxygen to the tissues at required level.

10.5 HEAVY METAL POISONING

To function various physiological activities smoothly and in co-ordinated fashion, a number of metals are essential. Depending upon their need, some are required in appreciable quantity whereas some metals are needed in trace amounts. Due to some reasons, if the concentration of metals in the biophase exceeds than that is required, toxic effects start appearing. These toxic effects can be accounted on the basis of interaction of the metal with specific functional groups (ligands) on the macromolecules (i.e. enzymes or receptors) in the cells. Due to this interaction, macromolecule can not catalyse the functions, vital to the existence of the cell. Metal generally interacts with functional groups like, amino, carboxyl, phenolic, phosphoric and sulfhydryl moieties. The interaction with such vital functional groups (ligands) leads to disruption of energy production and ion regulation. Adverse reactions of metals are also reported. For example, the heavy metals like, cadmium, lead, mercury, arsenic, tin and cobalt can lead to immunosuppressive effects. Similarly arsenic, chromium and nickel may cause cancer in humans.

In the treatment of intoxication due to heavy metals, chelating agents play a dominating role. All such compounds that can form complexes (chelates) with the heavy metals and have a common property to prevent or reverse the binding of metallic cations to body ligands, are collectively referred under the term, chelating agents. Chelating agents generally consist of N, O or S as ligand atoms. The ligand atoms entrap the metal ion and form a complex with it by co-ordinate bonds. The bond is often indicated by an arrow. The head of an arrow is directed away from the atom (ligand) which donates the electron pair needed for formation of the bond. The stability of chelate (complex) formed varies with the metal and ligand atoms. A large number of drugs can form metal chelates. Chelate formation may be a part of their mechanism of action against the diseases for which they are intended.

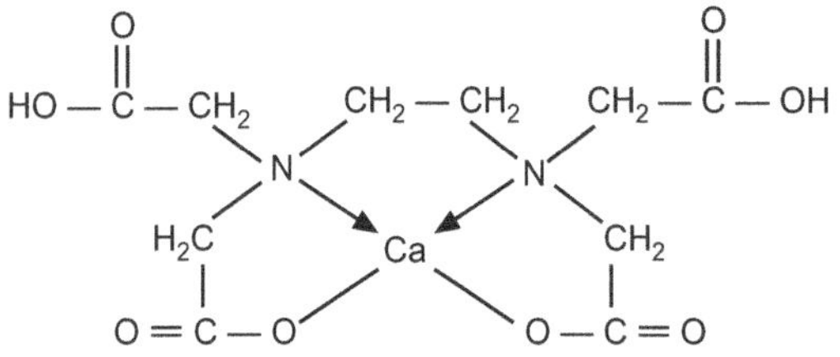

Calcium is complexed with EDTA

(a) Arsenic Poisoning :

Arsenic as such is not needed for the body. It does not catalyse any biological function. It is the trioxide form, in which arsenic is usually present. The most severe form of arsenic toxicity involves erythrocyte hemolysis. Similarly kidney and liver damage may occur. Dimercaprol, a chelating agent, may be used in the treatment of arsenic poisoning.

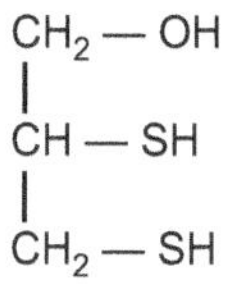

2, 3-dimercaptopropanol (BAL) or dimercaprol

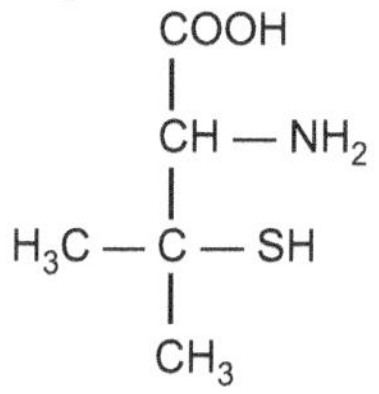

Penicillamine

In toxic symptoms, arsenic can cause uncoupling of mitochondrial oxidative phosphorylation. This uncoupling is known as arsenolysis, Since it inhibits the functioning of many vital enzymes, almost every important organ is affected by arsenic poisoning. Besides dimercaprol, oral penicillamine may also be given to treat the poisoning. But to treat severe arsenic induced nephropathy, renal dialysis is the only solution.

(b) Mercury Poisoning :

Mercury constitutes as an important part of the chemical structure of many diuretics, antiseptics, antibacterials and laxatives. It has a high affinity for sulphur. Hence mercury readily forms covalent bonds with sulfhydryl groups and inactivates the enzymes containing sulfhydryl group. Thus, presence of mercury can easily retard the normal cell metabolism.

Dimercaprol and penicillamine which contain a sulfhydryl group can be routinely used to treat intoxication due to either inorganic or elemental mercury. N-acetyl-D, L-penicillamine appears to be more potent and safer than the former agents. In severe case, hemodialysis may also be employed.

(c) Lead :

Human exposure to lead is primarily from food, environmental and industrial sources. It is mainly absorbed into the circulation from GIT and respiratory system. In body lead is mainly deposited in liver, kidney and bones. The chronic exposure to lead results into gastrointestinal, neuromuscular, CNS, hematological and renal toxicities.

Lead as such is not essential for life. The intoxication of lead can be treated by using one of the three chelating agents : Edetate calcium disodium ($CaNa_2$ EDTA), dimercaprol and D-penicillamine. The lead-EDTA complex is non-toxic, water soluble and hence is rapidly excreted. Usually at the start, the combination of edetate calcium disodium and dimercaprol is used. This is followed by oral penicillamine, continued for a long term.

(d) Cadmium :

It occurs in nature in association with zinc and lead. After absorption, kidney retains higher concentration of cadmium than do any other tissue. This accumulation leads to renal tubular damage. Liver also shoulders considerable deposition of cadmium.

Intoxication leads to nausea, dizziness, diarrhoea, chest pain and irritation of the upper respirator tract. Treatment commences with respiratory support and steroidal therapy. Chelating agent like, edetate calcium disodium can be used whereas, dimercaprol should not be used, due to its nephrotoxicity. Vitamin D is recommended for the treatment of associated orthopedic problems.

(e) Iron :

Body has a considerable amount of iron, circulating in the plasma. The plasma circulating iron can not exhibit toxic reactions because the presence of natural chelating, agent, transferrin in the blood. It protects the body from the toxic actions of the circulating iron. Iron, if absorbed into circulation in excess amounts, may lead to toxic manifestations. These include, irritation of GIT, pneumonitis, convulsions and coma. Hepatic damage is also reported to occur.

Deferoxamine is an effective chelating agent in treating the systemic iron toxicity.

(f) Cyanide Poisoning :

Even though cyanide does not come under the term "heavy metals", the treatment of cyanide poisoning deserves a special attention. Cyanogenic compounds if ingested orally, may release hydrogen cyanide due to their hydrolysis in GIT. The cyanide ion impairs several vital cellular functions. For example, there occurs impairment of tissue oxygen utilization due to inhibition of cytochrome oxidaze enzyme. The blood runs deficient of oxygen. The patient suffers from hypoxia followed by ataxia, coma and death.

There is a need of two-fold therapy in the treatment of cyanide poisoning. i.e., (1) the cyanide ions present in the circulation should immediately be converted into a nontoxic form and (2) attempts should be made to reverse the condition of hypoxia i.e. placing the patient in the oxygen-riched atmosphere and a quick conversion of methemoglobin to hemoglobin should be effected. The treatment involves the use of amyl nitrite by inhalation or sodium nitrite by injection. These agents serve the second purpose. The subsequent intravenous adminstration of sodium thiosulfate facilitates the conversion of free cyanide ions to nontoxic thiocyanate form. Thiocyanate can readily by excreted in the urine.

DRUG-INTERACTIONS

11.1 INTRODUCTION

On theoretical grounds, every drug strictly follows its own pharmacological pattern. Differences in the response to the drug if occur, may be due to the interference of the individual's personal characteristic features. The problem becomes more severe, when the person is subjected to multi-drugs therapy. For example, a hospitalized patient may be exposed to on an average, six to eight drugs. In fact many illnesses and deaths have been reported to occur due to vigorous in vivo interactions between the drugs administered. This is mainly due to the alteration in the pharmacological effects of drugs which are expected to occur on the basis of the effects seen when these drugs are used alone.

The effect of one drug may be altered by another concurrently administered substance which may be another drug, an excipient, food, environmental or chemical contaminant. This alteration in the pharmacological effect of the drug occurs due to the interference of another substance at pharmacokinetic (absorption, distribution, metabolism and elimination), pharmacodynamic (drug receptor interactions) and pharmaceutical patterns of the drug. The overall result is the change in either the prophylactic,, therapeutic or diagnostic action of the drug. In addition, pharmacologically induced changes in a patient may render him sensitive or resistant to the effects of another drug. In some cases, more than one mechanism are involved in the development of drug-interactions e.g. antacids.

Drug-interactions may lead to an increase or decrease in the action of either or both interactants. Sometimes interaction does not cause any change or a totally new effects may be seen. Thus, the patient may be exposed to an adverse drug reaction, a potentiated therapeutic effect or a therapeutic failure.

The drug interactions may or may not be dangerous. The drug interactions can be employed, in a beneficial way, in the treatment of hypertension, i.e., one agent causes a decrease in the cardiac output while other lowers the peripheral vascular resistance. Whereas dangerous effects are expected when the drug interactions occur in the following categories.

    anticoagulants
    monoamino oxidase inhibitors
    oral hypoglycemic agents
    cytotoxic drug treatment,
    digitalis-like drug
    antiepileptic agents.

These drug-interactions include in hemorrhage, hypoglycemic coma, seizures or a hypertensive state.

Though drug interactions are classified on the basis of the severity of the toxic effects, many factors influence this severity. These factors include, a state of the disease, dose, route and duration of drug administration, renal and hepatic clearance etc. Depending upon these features, a minor interaction in some patients, may become of major importance while a major interaction will end with no toxic effects.

Thus, in the light of knowledge of drug interactions, a physician can easily recognize the margin of safety of the drug. He can take steps to prevent the expected drug interaction by either adjusting the dose or schedule of drug administration or by using another suitable drug.

11.2 MECHANISMS OF DRUG INTERACTION

As we know, the drug-interactions usually result due to the interference of another substance in the pharmacokinetic, pharmacodynamic or pharmaceutical properties of the drug. The net result of these interferences is either increased or decreased free drug (or active drug metabolite) concentration at the receptor site. Various mechanisms have been proposed to explain the commonly occurring drug interactions. In some cases, more than one mechanism operate or overlapping of many mechanisms can also be seen.

(a) Interference During Absorption Process :

Certain drugs (e.g., procainamide) exhibit short biological half-life due to high first-pass metabolism in the liver. If their absorption is retarded due to the influence of another drug, their therapeutic plasma level could not be achieved. Several cases of physical as well as chemical incompatibilities have been recognised. For example, phenothiazines, amphotericin B, sodium nitropruside etc. are reported to be light-sensitive.

Direct chemical interactions are possible particularly when the concentrations of both the interactants are high. Thus, carbenicillin and gentamicin interact each other. Similarly antihistaminics, protamine and phenothiazines due to their basic nature may counteract heparin's effects. Protamine, a protein may be used to neutralize excessive effects of heparin. Due to the chelating property of tetracyclines, their absorption is retarded when antacid or iron is present. The ionic nature of the aminoglycosidic antibiotics may hinder the absorption of many drugs. Similarly the adsorptive ability of the resins, such as, cholestyramine limits the absorption of thyroxine and corticosteriods. Kaolin, having same capacity, adsorbs drugs like lincomycin. Bentonite, yet another adsorbent prevents the absorption of rifampin by same mechanism.

The activity of many catecholamines decreases due to their oxidation in intravenous solutions. Antacids alter the pH at the sites of absorption in GIT and hence the absorption of several drugs by affecting their ionization.

The microbial flora of gastrointestinal tract is disturbed due to the antibiotic administration resulting into inhibition of vitamin k synthesis by intestinal microflora. The effectiveness of an oral anticoagulant (i.e. vitamin k antagonists) will definitely be increased if an antibiotic is concomitantly administered. Antibiotic administration also leads to an increase in absorption of the drugs which are partly metabolised by intestinal microorganisms. Barbiturates reduce the gastrointestinal absorption of bishydroxy coumarin and griseofulvin by increasing their GIT metabolism.

Table 11.1 : Chemical or physical incompatibility

Drug	Incompatible with
(1) Penicillin G	ascorbic acid, dexamethasone, amphotericin B, lincomycin.
(2) Chloramphenicol	erythromycin, tetracyclines, vancomycin, barbiturates.
(3) Amphotericin B	tetracyclines, penicillin G, diphenhydramine.
(4) Lincomycin	penicillin G, phenytoin.
(5) Erythromycin	tetracyclines, barbiturates, phenytoin, vitamin B-complex.
(6) Kanamycin	sulfisoxazole, barbiturates, heparin, methicillin.

(b) Alterations in Gastric Emptying Time :

(1) Some drugs may alter the rate at which other drugs are transported across the mucosal membrane by either altering gastrointestinal motility or gastric emptying time. Spasminogens, like, cholinergic drugs will lower down the absorption of digoxin whereas antispasmodic agents (atropine-like drugs) will increase its absorption.

(2) Imipramine impairs the absorption of levodopa by delaying gastric emptying time which results in increased metabolism of levodopa. Phenytoin and other anticonvulsants also interfere in the absorption of folic acid.

(3) Laxatives increase the intestinal motility; thus they affect the rate of tablet disintegration, dissolution of tablet constituents and the contact time with the absorptive surface.

(4) The degree of absorption of iron and penicillins varies with the degree of gastric acidity. For example, iron is best absorbed in highly acidic conditions. Hence, presence of food makes the differences in the absorption process.

(5) Naturally occuring purines and pyrimidines present in the food may hinder the absorption of purine and pyrimidine antimetabolites by competing for same transport mechanism. Similarly many fat soluble drugs (vitamins A, D, E and K) may be retained in the fatty portion of the meal or concurrently administered fatty compounds like castor oil or mineral oil. In these cases, surface-active agents may promote absorption.

(6) By interfering transport across membranes, the action of antihypertensive agents may be minimised or reversed by tricyclic antidepressants and some antihistaminic agents.

Table 11.2 : Drugs altering intestinal motility

Antacids	Laxatives
Phenothiazines	Narcotic analgesics
Antihypertensives	Caffeine
Histamine blockers	Iproniazid
Cholinergic drugs	Piperazine derivatives

(7) Many drugs impair the absorption of other drugs by exerting structural changes in the intestinal mucosa. Villus atrophy is reported to be caused by phenoformin, neomycin, mefenamic acid and α-methyl dopa, leading to the malabsorption of certain drugs. The absorption of propranolol, trimethoprim and others has been promoted in the state of malabsorption.

(8) Neomycin minimises absorption of vitamin A by disruption of the lipid micelles.

(9) By changing the pH at the absorption sites in GIT, the absorption of many drugs can be altered. This results due to the change in their partition co-efficient due to change in the physiological pH. For example, the absorption of weakly acidic drugs (e.g., salicylates, nitrofurantion, phenylbutazone and nalidixic acid) can be retarded with the elevation of pH and that of weakly basic drugs (e.g., ephedrine, amphetamines, quinine) is lowered down with lowering the pH.

(c) Plasma-Protein Binding :

Plasma proteins and other components of blood including cellular elements offer the sites for drug binding. Most of the drugs are reversibly bound to these plasma or tissue proteins. The plasma protein bound fraction of the drug remains unavailable to evoke-pharmacological response. Only the free or unbound drug can leave the vascular compartment and initiates the pharmocological activity. The extent of protein binding is governed by the number of such binding sites available, affinity of drug for these binding sites and the plasma concentration of drug.

In many cases, displacement of bound fraction of one drug by another is reported. Such displacement results into an increase in the concentration of unbound fraction of the former drug causing potentiation of its pharmacological activity. Naturally the rate of metabolism and excretion of displaced drug also enhances. Generally acidic drug having a long biological half-life and a small volume of distribution promptly displace other drugs from plasma-proteins.

(1) Many non-steroidal antiinflammatory agents (e.g. phenylbutazone) promptly displace warfarin and tolbutamide.

(2) The activity of sulfonylurea oral hypoglycemic agents (e.g. tolbutamide) is potentiated due to their displacement from plasma proteins by sulfaphenazole.

(3) The displacement of methotrexate by many acidic drugs (salicylates) leads to unexpected rise in its toxic effects causing pancytopenia. Similarly the gastrointestinal and hematologic toxicities of pamaquine dramatically increases if it is given simultaneously or shortly after quinacrine.

(4) Drugs having high affinity constants for protein binding may displace endogenous substances. Bilirubin is displaced by this mechanism.

Table 11.3 : Acidic drugs acting as potential displacer

Sulfonamides	Nonsteroidal anti-inflammatory agents
Penicillins	Clofibrate
Furosemide	Nalidixic acid
Barbiturates	Tranquillizers
Phenytoin	Warfarin

Since in most cases major fraction of the drug (95 - 98%) remains protein bound, the pharmacological response is mainly due to the very minor fraction of the drug, present in the free form. Hence, a minor percentage change in the extent of protein binding (2 - 5%) results in doubling or trebling of the concentration of free drug. This invites chances of drug toxicities to occur.

(d) Induction of Drug-metabolic Enzymes :

In the case of drugs having high "first-pass" value (e.g. oxyphenbutazone, lidocaine), drugs which influence hepatic blood flow or liver disease such as propranolol, (which decreases liver blood flow) may play an important role. Similarly drugs that increase hepatic blood flow, such as glucagon, phenobarbital may lead to enhanced clearance of oxyphenbutazone or lidocaine.

Many drugs induce or inhibit the activity of microsomal enzyme. These enzymes metabolise drugs by various mechanisms, including dealkylation, deamination, sulphoxidation, aromatic hydroxylation, side-chain oxidation, azo link reduction and conjugation reactions. Generally an induction of enzyme activity occurs due to an increase in the rate of synthesis of drug metabolising enzymes.

About 200 drugs are known that induce the metabolism of other drugs alongwith their own. Their enzyme-inducing capacity is governed by their potency and dose. Phenobarbital tops in the list since it induces the metabolism of more than 60 different drugs including itself. When such induction is not desired, it can be replaced by other agents like diazepam and chlordiazepoxide which do not cause enzyme induction in humans.

(1) Rifampin increases the metabolism of aminosalicylic acid, isoniazid, estrogens, methadone, hexobarbital and tolbutamide.

(2) Barbiturates (e.g. phenobarbital) can induce the metabolism of several drugs such as, quinidine, warfarin, bishydroxycoumarin etc.

In the case of most oral hypoglycemic agents, lidocaine, phenoxy benzamine, propranolol and cyclophosphamide, the metabolites still retain the pharmacological activity. In such cases enhancement of the rate of metabolism may sometimes result into potentiation of the activity.

Besides this, species differences and genetic factors may play an important role in determining an individual response to such enzyme inducers.

Table 11.4 : Some drug-metabolising enzyme inducers

Spiranolactone	Meprobamate
Barbiturates	Phenylbutazone
Antihistamines	Alcohol
Rifampicin	Imipramine
Griseofulvin	Chlorpromazine
Tolbutamide	Nikethamide

(e) Inhibition of Drug-metabolism :

A number of drug interactions are reported to occur due to the inhibition of an enzyme which catalyses metabolism of first-drug or by competing the first drug for the same drug metabolizing enzyme. Inhibition of drug metabolism results into potentiation of biological effects and toxicities except in cases where the activity is due to active drug metabolite. Hence the consequences of inhibition of metabolism are almost opposite to those seen with enzyme induction.

(1) Allopurinol, a xanthine oxidase inhibitor, inhibits the metabolism of antipyrine, 6-mercaptopurine and azathioprine. Profound bone-marrow toxicity occurs with the intensification of the effects of the latter drugs. But the metabolism of phenylbutazone or warfarin is not affected which are also oxidised by hepatic microsomal enzymes.

(2) The metabolism of tolbutamide is inhibited by many drugs, including phenyl butazone, salicylates, bishydroxycoumarin and some sulphonamides. Hence in the diabetic persons, a safe anticoagulant like, phenindione should be used which does not affect drug metabolism.

(3) Disulfiram, phenylbutazone, bishydroxycoumarin and antituberculosis drugs potentiate the effects of phenytoin to the toxic level by inhibiting its metabolism.

(4) The metabolism of many drugs like tolbutamide, bishydroxy coumarin, chloropropamide and diphenylhydantoin may be inhibited by chloramphenicol.

(5) Glutethimide inhibits the biosynthesis of cortisol by inhibiting the enzyme involved in 2 α-hydroxylation of cholestetol.

Table 11.5 : Some inhibitors of drug-metabolism

Chloramphenicol	Nialamide
Pargyline	Androgens
Quinacrine	Chlorpropamide
MAO inhibitors	Sulfonyl areas
Allopurinol	Oral contraceptives

(6) Mono-amino oxidase inhibitors (MAO inhibitors), nonspecifically inhibit other enzyme systems and may potentiate the effects of CNS depressants, phenothiazines, tricyclic antidepressants, antihypertensive agents and hypoglycemic agents.

(7) Dextroamphetamine inhibits the metabolism of hexobarbital.

(f) Interferences During Renal Excretion:

Body employees various mechanisms for the elimination of the drug and its metabolites. The excretion through urine and bile are of major clinical importance. Mainly ionized or polar drugs are excreted in the bile either intact or after conjugation. Glucuronization constitutes a major pathway in the conjugation process.

Drug interactions are reported to occur due to significant alterations in the urinary excretion pattern of drugs by other substances. Here the interacting drug may act by causing increase or decrease in the rate of glomerular filteration, tubular reabsorption, change in the pH conditions within the tubules or it may compete with other drugs for the tubular transport systems. Many acidic drugs for example, compete for the same transport system in the proximal tubules and reduce excretion of each other. Probenecid competes with indomethacin, penicillin and para amino salicylic acid. Similarly through a competitive process, phenyl butazone reduces the excretion of acetohexamide and chlorpropamide resulting into an intense hypoglycaemia.

The changes in urinary pH also alter the excretion of many drugs. These changes occur as a consequence of the disease condition or due to therapy with ammonium chloride, sodium bicarbonate or thiazides. For example, thiazide diuretics may cause systemic alkalosis with or without paradoxical aciduria resulting into quick renal clearance of basic drugs like, amphetamine, phentermine, mephentermine etc. Conversely carbonic anhydrase inhibitors may cause systemic acidosis with an alkaline urine resulting into rapid renal clearance of acidic drugs like phenobarbital or salicylic acid. Thus, a change in urine pH brings about major alteration in the rate of renal clearance of the drug thereby increasing or decreasimng the concentration of free drug of its receptor sites.

Diuretics more specifically, influence the concentration of various electrolytes and pH of body fluids. This ultimately results in the alterations in the absorption, distribution and renal clearance of different drugs resulting sometimes into fatal interaction. For example, the activity of cardiac glycosides is potentiated in the state of hypokalemia produced by some of the diuretic agents, laxatives, carbenoxolone sodium or carbenicillin. Similarly hyperkalemia if produced, may potentiate the conditions of skeletal muscle disorder and myocardial toxicity.

Table 11.6 : Enhancement of excretion of some drugs

In acidic urine	In alkaline urine
Amphetamine	Phenobarbital
Phentermine	Salicylic acid derivatives
Pethidine	Streptomycin
Quinidine	(all acidic drugs)
Procainamide	
(all basic drugs)	

(g) Drug Synergism :

Some drug-interactions occur due to synergistic effect between the drugs concurrently administered. The synergistic effect is said to occur when the combined effects of two drugs is greater than the sum of the effect of each drug given alone. The drugs usually belong to different chemical categories and are given to initiate same pharmacological response. Examples of synergistic drug effect include,

(1) Salicylates, propranolol and mono amino oxidase inhibitors potentiate the hypoglycemic action of oral hypoglycaemic agents.

(2) Barbiturates, narcotic analgesics and antihistaminic agents synergise the CNS depressant action of alchool.

(3) Propranolol and guanethidine lead to bradycardia when they are simultaneously administered with digitalis.

(h) Pharmacodynamic Interactions :

The pharmacological response of a drug or of its active metabolite is a function of the free drug concentration of the active form at its receptor sites. The non-specific drugs may act on the different pharmacological receptors. The unwanted effects arised due to their lack of specificity may potentiate or antagonise the effects of other drugs. Examples include,

(1) Phenothiazines are effective α-adrenergic antagonists.

(2) The activity of antihypertensive agents is potentiated with the concurrent use of either MAO inhibitors, CNS depressants, or diuretics.

Table 11.7 : Agonist - Antagonist interactions

Agonist	Antagonist(s)
Acetyl choline	Atropine, curare.
Narcotic analgesics	Naloxone.
Histamine	H_1-receptor and H_2-receptor blockers.
Vitamin K	Coumarin anticoagulant derivatives.
α - adrenergic drugs	Phenothiazines, imipramine.
Curare	Kanamycin, neomycin, streptomycin and gentamicin.
Muscarnic cholinergic agents	Antihistaminics, tricyclic antidepressants, phenothiazines.

(3) The anticholinestrases (e.g. neostigmine, physostigmine) potentiate the effects mediated through cholinergic nervous system.

(4) In the patients undergoing insulin therapy, propronolol (β-blocker) administration may lead to hypoglycemic reactions by blocking β-receptor mediated metabolic effects of epinephrine.

(5) Many general anesthetics sensitize the myocardium to the arrhythmogenic action of catecholamines.

(i) Antibiotic Interactions:

Drug interactions have been documented due to non-rational combination of different antibiotics. One should not present a combination of a bacteriostatic drug with a bacteriocidal agent. Besides this, a combination of gentamicin and carbenicillin is not advised due to their ability to chemically inactive each other. Whereas miconazole and amphotercin B are antagonist of each other.

(j) Miscellaneous Reactions:

(1) On parenteral administration, (epinephrine interferes in and reduces the absorption of local anesthetics).

(2) While determining the response of a patient to antigens by intradermal skin-tests, systemic, glucocorticoids and antiallergy drugs may interfere in the results.

(3) Reserpine and guanethidine deplete myocardial stores of norepinephrine and make such patients supersensitive to the effects of infused norepinephrine.

SECTION - II : DRUGS ACTING ON AUTONOMIC NERVOUS SYSTEM

NEUROHUMORAL TRANSMISSION

12.1 INTRODUCTION

According to the theory of neurohumoral transmission, specific chemical agents are responsible for transmission of nerve impulse across most synapses and neuroeffector junctions. These agents are known as neurohumoral transmitters. The concept of 'chemical neuro-transmission' was first proposed by Dale and co-workers, instead of 'electrical transmission hypothesis'. The release of transmitter substances occur when the nerve impulse elicits the responses at smooth, cardiac and skeletal muscles, exocrine glands and postsynaptic neurons. These neurotransmitters cross the synapse or the neuro-effector junction to initiate activity in another neurone or in a muscle or a gland cell by interacting with the post-synaptic receptors. A clear understanding of the impulse transmission therefore, is essential to study the pharmacology of the drugs acting on autonomic nervous system.

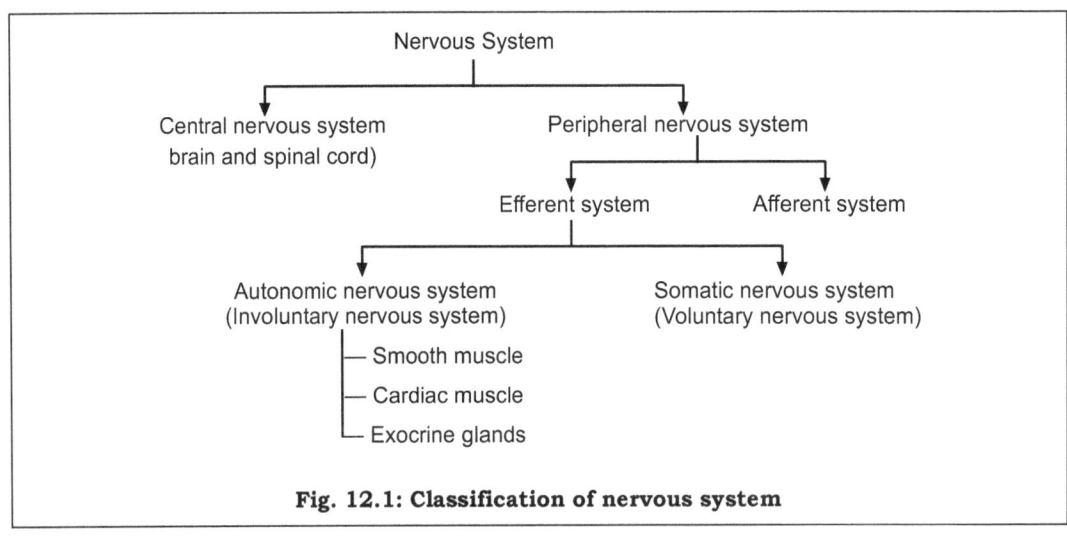

Fig. 12.1: Classification of nervous system

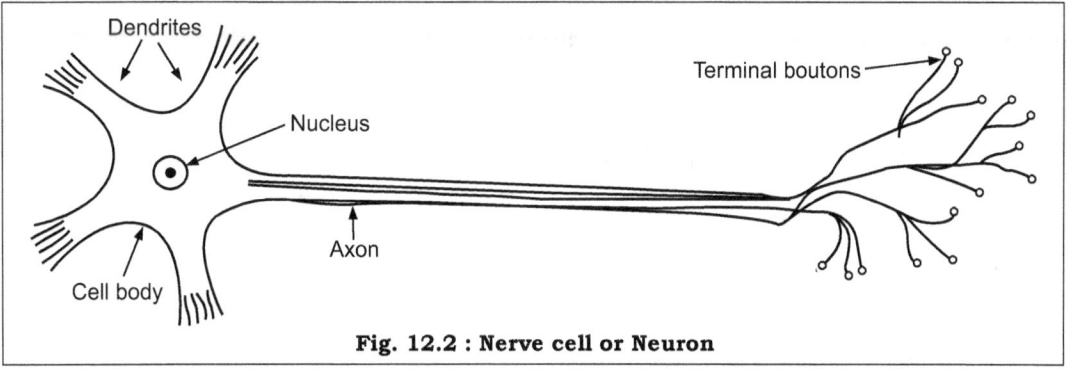

Fig. 12.2 : Nerve cell or Neuron

12.2 NERVOUS SYSTEM

Principally, the nervous system may be described as a device of,
(1) Receiving information (i.e., sensory input),
(2) Processing information (i.e. integration), and
(3) Transmitting information (i.e., motor output).

The sensory nerve fibres carry the information from organs to CNS and also termed as afferent nerves. Similarly the motor nerve fibres convey the message from CNS to the organ and also are known as efferent nerves.

The fundamental unit of a nervous system is the neuron or a nerve cell. Each neuron consists of a nucleus and a cell body from which, stems an extensive network of branches, the axon - (long process) and the dendrite - (short process).

The surface membrane of a neuron consists of a semipermeable layer of lipoproteins. The composition of salt solution inside the membrane is usually different from that on the outside. This is due to differences in the permeability of the membrane to the various ions like Na^+, K^+, Ca^{++}, Cl^-, HCO_3 etc.

In the resting state, the inside of neuronal membrane is more negative than the outside. This normal situation is known as resting state or polarised state. When any exogenous stimulus is applied; a change in the electrical activity occurs within the neuron. At the point, where an exogenous stimulus attacks, the inside of neuronal membrane becomes positive than the outside. As a result, local action currents are set up, which have the effect of transferring the area of reversed polarization to an adjoining region of the nerve while normal resting conditions are re-established in the previous stimulated area.

In this way, the patch of reversed polarization is transmitted alongwith the nerve. The process is continued until the whole length of the nerve has been visited by the impulse. The nerve impulse, in other words jumps from one patch to other patch. As soon as this impulse reaches the terminal boutons, it activates the influx of extracellular Ca^{++} ions. These ions, upon their entry in the cytoplasm lead to the release of intracellular Ca^{++} ions from the sacs present on sarcoplasmic reticulum. When the cytoplasmic concentration of Ca^{++} ions reach a threshold value, the storage granules for neuro-transmitter get ruptured and a discrete amount of neuro-transmitter is discharged from the presynaptic nerve endings into the synaptic cleft. The synaptic cleft or junctional cleft is generally about 200 – 400 A° wide but in some blood vessels, it may be as wide as 10,000 A°.

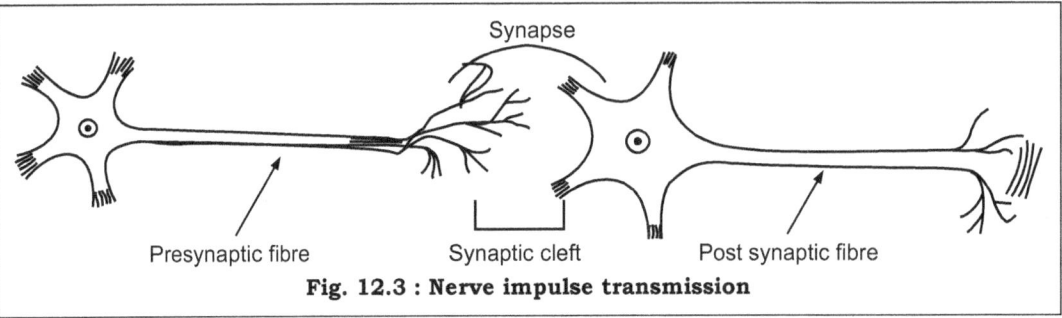

Fig. 12.3 : **Nerve impulse transmission**

The transmitter, then diffuses across the synaptic space and binds to the receptor sites present on the cell body of post-synaptic neuron. This binding causes conformational changes in these receptors, which in turn, produce a change in ion-permeability of the axon-membrane of post-synaptic neuron. As a result, local action currents are set up into the post-synaptic neuron. The post-synaptic axon branches many times upon entering the effector tissue forming a plexus among the innervated cells. The release of neuro-transmitter from post-synaptic nerve terminals into the neuro-effector space then leads to the biological response in a muscle or a gland cell. This synapse between a motor neutron and effector cell is also termed as a neuro-effector junction.

Once the neuro-transmitter has interacted with the receptors, it is either removed by active uptake processes back to the terminal boutons of pre-synaptic or post-synaptic neuron or by surrounding glial cells where it is destroyed by metabolic deactivation.

12.3 NEURO-CHEMICAL TRANSMITTERS

Following are the examples of chemical agents that act as neuro-chemical transmitters in nervous system.

(a) Aspartic acid, taurine, glycine, gama amino butyric-acid (GABA), and glutamic acid. These can be grouped as amino acids.

(b) Acetylcholine, dopamine, tyramine, norepinephrine, epinephrine, histamine, serotonin (5 HT). These can be grouped as amines.

(c) **Miscellaneous** : Peptide substance P, ATP, c-AMP, c-GMP, prostaglandin E, enkephalins, neurotensin cholecystokinin etc.

Neuro-transmitters have an ability to initiate the impulse propagation. Certain substances do not initiate the process of impulse transmission but can modify it. Such substances are termed as modulators of transmission. For example, most of the autonomic drugs act either by mimicking or modifying the actions of the neurotransmitter released by autonomic fibers at either synaptic cleft or effector cells. Besides this, the nerve cell is provided with a number of feed-back control systems which regulate the biosynthesis, release and metabolism of the neurotransmitter and thus exercise a control over the biological response.

12.4 AUTONOMIC NERVOUS SYSTEM

The autonomic nervous system controls all involuntary actions aimed to maintain the constancy of the internal environment. It provides a homeostasis required for the regulation of all metabolic changes which are essential for life. The ANS is termed as the visceral, vegetative or involuntary nervous system. In the periphery, it functions through nerves, ganglia and plexuses and regulates autonomic functions which are not under the conscious control. These include, breathing, regulation of the cardiovascular system, glandular secretions, digestion, body temperature and metabolism. Except skeletal muscles, all innervated organs of the body are supplied with efferent nerves of ANS, while skeletal muscles are provided with somatic nerves. Thus, ANS is essentially a motor system. The sensory fibers are numerous than autonomic motor nerves and they pass into the cerebrospinal axis via either somatic nerves or various ramifications of ANS without synaptic interruption.

Hypothalamus is a principal control center for organization and co-ordination of the autonomic nervous system. The cells of the adrenal medulla constitute an integral part of the ANS, which upon activation, release epinephrine and norepinephrine into the circulation.

12.5 DIVISIONS OF AUTONOMIC NERVOUS SYSTEM

The autonomic nervous system controls tissues, e.g. glands, smooth muscles and cardiac muscles that are not under voluntary control. It consists of two main divisions :

(a) Sympathetic nervous system and

(b) Parasympathetic nervous system.

Both these divisions have essentially opposite actions. The sympathetic nervous system is associated with catabolic effects whereas parasymapathetic nervous system is characterized by its anabolic effects.

The principal neuro-transmitter present in parasympathetic nervous system is acetyl choline.

(i) The preganglionic and post-ganglionic fibers of the parasympathetic nerves liberate acetyl choline.

(ii) The preganglionic fibers and some postganglionic fibers (e.g. salivary glands) of sympathetic nerves liberate acetyl choline.

(iii) All autonomic ganglia and skeletal muscle end plate region need acetyl choline as a neuro-transmitter to evoke biological response. The end plate is a specialized region of the muscle with which the terminal ramifications of the motor nerve fibers are associated. The ganglionic transmission is a highly complex process and several secondary transmitters or modulators either enhance or diminish the sensitivity of the postganglionic cell to acetylcholine.

Stimulation of parasympathetic nervous system induces the constriction of the pupils and bronchi, decrease in heart activity and an increase in the activity of the digestive system - salivation and GIT secretions are promoted, the motility of the intestine is increased.

Similarly the principal neurotransmitters present in the sympathetic nervous system include epinephrine (adrenaline), norepinephrine (noradrenaline) and dopamine. The postganglionic fibers of the sympathetic nerves with few exceptions, bring about their effects by the liberation of norepinephrine.

Stimulation of the sympathetic nervous system causes dilation of the pupils, acceleration of rate of (positive chronotropic) and the force of (positive inotropic) heart contraction, peripheral vasaconstriction, glycogenolysis, inhibition of intestinal motility and of gastroinestinal secretory activity (except salivary gland).

When the transmitter substance reacts with the post-synaptic receptors, it may produce either excitation or inhibition. The action of the transmitter results in selective increase or decrease in ionic permeability of membrane for ions. In inhibition, there is a negligible change in the ion potential and the fiber remains at near to the resting potential, thereby preventing the fibre to get in an excited position.

The transmitters in the neurons are in a state of flux, being continuously biosynthesized, released and metabolized, thus producing profound changes in the activity of the nerves. The nerves in the peripheral nervous system are classified on the basis of their function into,

(1) Sensory (afferent) neuron,
(2) Motor (efferent) neuron and
(3) Internuncial neuron.

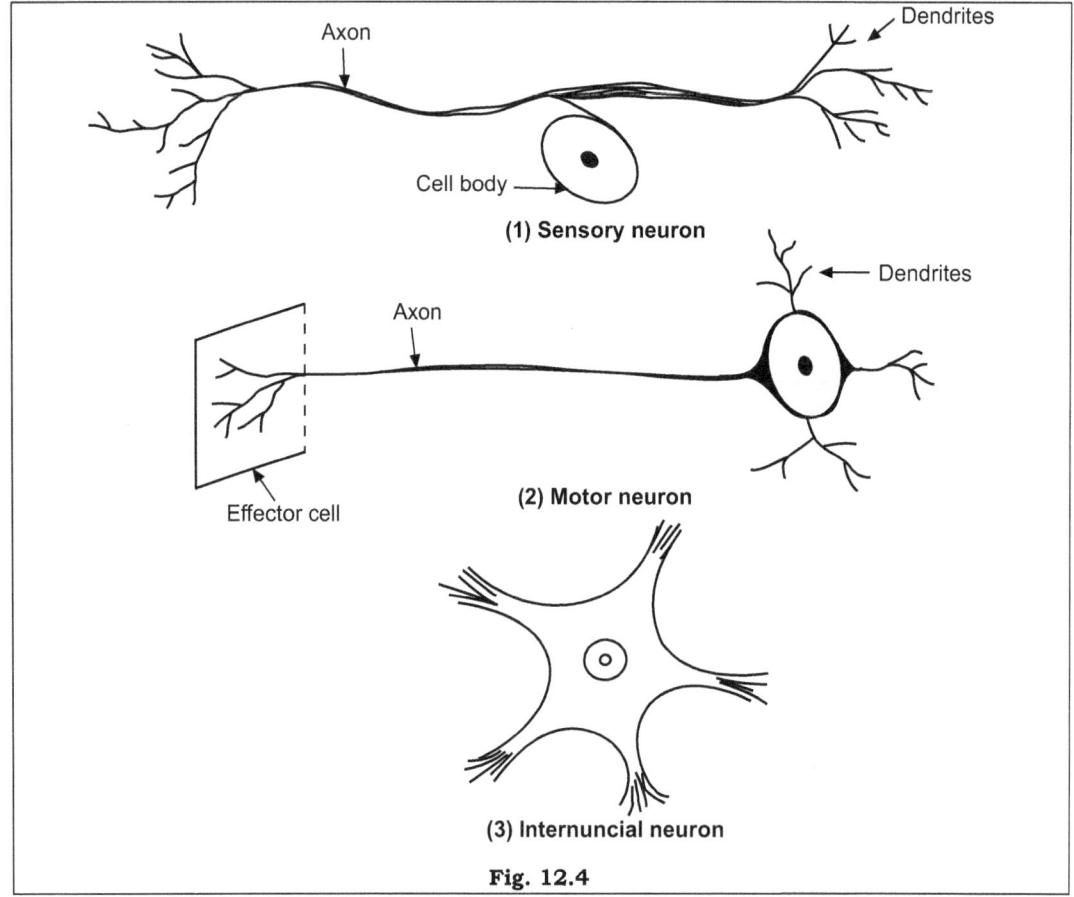

Fig. 12.4

Many neuro-transmitters play an important role in the propogation of the nerve impulse in the sensory neurons. These include substance P, somatostatin, vasoactive intestinal polypeptides and cholecystokinin.

H — Arg — Pro — Lys — Pro — Gln — Gln — Phe — Phe — Gly — Leu — Met — NH$_2$

Substance P

Sensory neurons transmit impulses from CNS to or towards the muscle or tissues.

Internuncial neurons are located in CNS and they transmit impulses from sensory to the motor neurons.

The efferent (motor) nervous division of ANS can be broadly categorised into,

(a) Parasympathetic (or craniosacral) division and,

(b) Sympathetic (or thoracolumbar) division.

This classification is mainly based upon type of neuro-transmitter that predominates in each division.

(a) Parasympathetic Nervous System :

Acetyl choline is the neuro-transmitter which propagates impulse transmission in the parasympathetic division. Besides this, acetylcholine also functions as a neurotransmitter in,

(i) Motor nerves to skeletal muscles and

(ii) Certain neurons within CNS.

Reid Hunt and Taveau (1906) were first to report the properties of acetylcholine. In 1921, Otto Loewi, a German pharmacologist identified the nervous stimulation of the heart as a chemically mediated event. Loewi then, alongwith Navratil demonstrated in 1926 that acetylcholine functions as a neuro-transmitter in cholinergic nerves. This was later confirmed by Dale and Feldberg in 1934 on stimulation of vagal fibers to the stomach.

The three important responses mediated by acetylcholine in man or laboratory animals include :

(1) Contraction of smooth muscles.

(2) Cardiac inhibition and

(3) Peripheral vasodilation.

Since upon stimulation, parasympathetic nerve fiber liberates acetylcholine, the parasympathetic division is also termed as cholinergic nervous system. The terms cholinergic and adrenergic were first presented by Dale to denote neurons that release acetylcholine and norepinephrine respectively.

Acetylcholine is biosynthesized by the acetylation of choline molecule. Choline itself has a weak parasympathomimetic activity and upon injection, causes a fall in blood pressure. Acetylcholine is about 10,000 times more active than choline molecule.

Acetylcholine is biosynthesized in the nerve terminals as shown in Fig. 12.5.

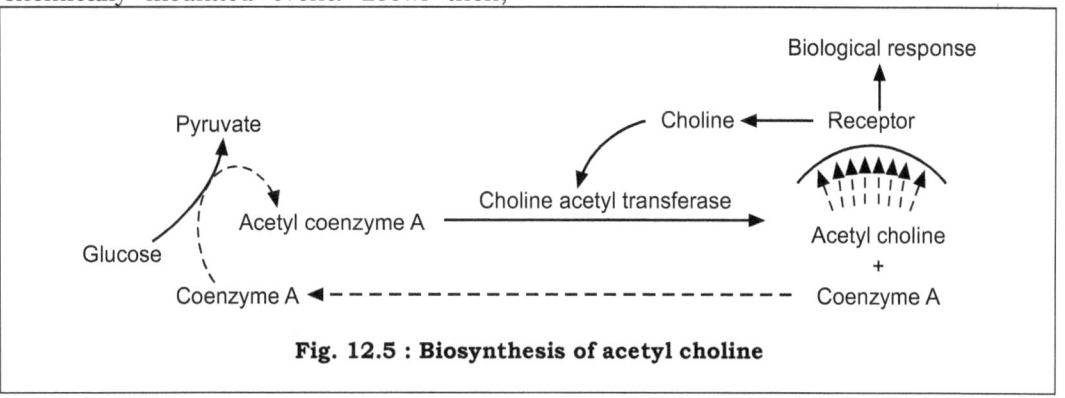

Fig. 12.5 : Biosynthesis of acetyl choline

Active transport mechanisms are involved in picking up choline molecules from the extrasynaptic fluid into the axoplasm. This transport is dependent upon the intracellular concentration of Na^+ and K^+ ions. The choline molecule is acetylated in the cytoplasm by acetyl coenzyme A which is biosynthesized in the mitochondria present in the nerve terminal. The acetylation of choline is catalyzed by choline acetyl transferase enzyme. The enzyme is synthesized within the perikaryon and has a molecular weight of about 68,000. In peripheral cholinergic nerves, it is usually present in higher concentrations. As soon as acetylcholine is synthesized, it is sequestered within the synaptic vesicles.

The cholinergic nervous system consists of preganglionic and postganglionic fibers. The proganglionic fibers have their origin in midbrain, medulla oblongata and the sacral part of the spinal cord. Thus, the principal site of control and co-ordination of both sympathetic and parasympathetic nervous system is hypothalamus. The hypothalamus alongwith cerebral cortex serves as a locus of integration of the entire autonomic nervous system. Hypothalamus also plays an important role in the regulation of gastrointestinal, cardiovascular, sexual, emotional and the functioning of limbic system.

The biosynthesized acetylcholine is stored within the synaptic vesicles immediately inside the membrane of the nerve terminal. Each vesicle is expected to contain about 5,000 – 10,000 molecules of acetylcholine. The number of such vesicles present in the nerve terminal varies in different organs. For example, a motor nerve terminal may contain 3,00,000 or more synaptic vesicles.

When an impulse reaches to nerve terminal, depolarization causes an activation of calcium ionophose which allows an influx of extracellular calcium ions within the cytoplasm. The entry of extracellular calcium ions is an essential step for the rupturing of storage vesicles of almost all neuro-transmitters. The extracellular calcium then leads to the release of acetyl choline from the vesicles. Four calcium ions are taken up for each molecule of acetylcholine released. The ruptured synaptic vesicles are again re-shaped to store fresh neuro-transmitter.

The vesicular release of acetylcholine is reported to be inhibited by excess of magnesium ions. The released acetylcholine alongwith extracellular calcium ions then mobilize intracellular calcium ions from the sacs present on sarcoplasmic reticulum. The increase in the concentration of free intracellular calcium ions then activates calmodulin dependent myosin light chain kinase and phosphorylation of myosin, in turn, creates the conditions that initiate muscle contraction. In general, minimum concentration of calcium ions needed to evoke muscle contraction is estimated to be 10^{-6} mol/l.

In contrast to other cholinergically innervated organs, the cardiac impulse conduction system (i.e., S-A node, atrium, A-V node and the His-perkinje system) has its own activity where the conduction of impulse can be influenced but not initiated by autonomic nervous system. In cardiac cell, cholinergic influence results into inhibitory response due to hyperpolarization. The hyperpolarization results due to the increased permeability of the axon membrane to potassium ions.

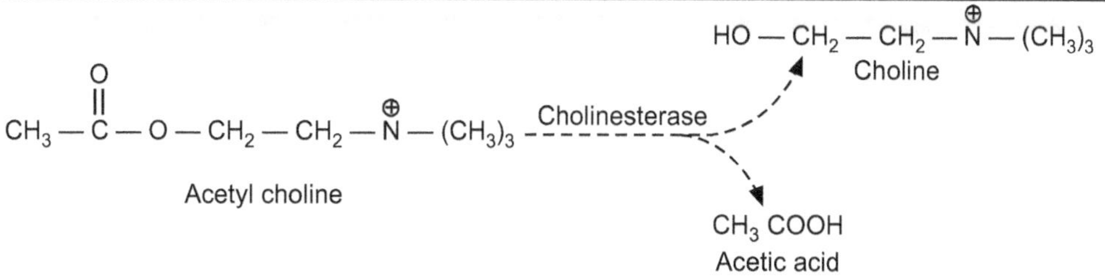

$$CH_3-\overset{O}{\underset{\|}{C}}-O-CH_2-CH_2-\overset{\oplus}{N}-(CH_3)_3 \xrightarrow{\text{Cholinesterase}} \begin{array}{l} HO-CH_2-CH_2-\overset{\oplus}{N}-(CH_3)_3 \\ \text{Choline} \\ \\ CH_3COOH \\ \text{Acetic acid} \end{array}$$

Acetyl choline

Fig. 12.6 : Hydrolysis of acetylcholine

In parasympathetic division, a preganglionic fiber synapses with one or at the most two postganglionic neurons. The synapses are located very close to or within the organ innervated. Due to the limited distribution, parasympathetic preganglionic neurons can affect only specific organ and do not influence a wide region of the body. In contrast to this, sympathetic synapses are located in the vertebral and prevertebral ganglia. Hence, a single sympathetic preganglionic fiber may synapse with 60 to 189 postganglionic neurons provided to a widely separated regions of the body. Naturally upon activation, sympathetic nervous system can evoke and influence the biological activities of the whole body. The area of functioning of parasympathetic division is thus limited and involves accumulation and preservation of body resources. While sympathetic division regulates body compartments of vital importance and prepares the person in the conditions of stress and emergencies. Its stimulation results in a generalized somatic or mass relax action. The free acetylcholine present in blood and other tissues, gets quickly hydrolyzed by either e-cholinesterase (present in erythrocytes) or s-cholinesterase (present in serum). Upon hydrolysis, acetylcholine is converted into acetic acid and choline molecule.

The cholinesterase enzyme is present in high concentration in the synapses of both, cholinergic and somatic nerves and striated muscle. Hydrolysis occurs in the immediate vicinity of the nerve ending. At the neuromuscular junction, hydrolysis occurs at the end plate region after acetylcholine has initiated the muscle twitch. In the autonomic ganglia, cholinesterase is usually present in the preganglionic fiber. While serum esterase is present in glial cells, plasma, liver and at other sites.

Cholinesterase enzyme presents in two different forms.

(i) Simple oligomers of a 70,000 dalton catalytic subunit, and

(ii) Elongated forms of, complex structure.

The cholinesterases are not very selective enzymes. Both these types hydrolyse a large number of esters, both of, choline and other carboxylic acids. Cholinesterase is one of the most efficient enzyme present in the body. It can hydrolyse about 3×10^5 acetylcholine molecules per mole per minute.

During hydrolysis, acetylcholine binds with the enzyme surface through tetrahydral orientation. The tetrahydral intermediate then gets converted first to choline and then to acetic acid.

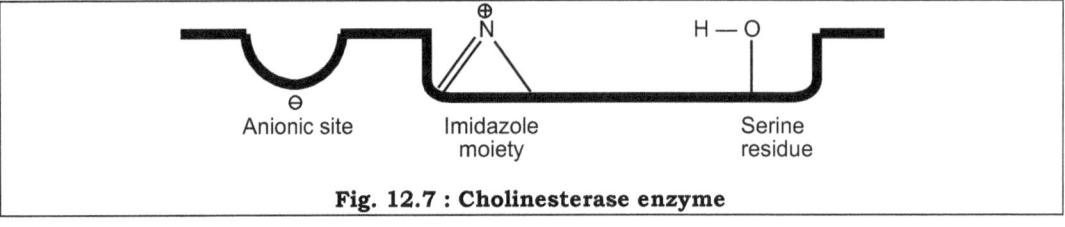

Fig. 12.7 : Cholinesterase enzyme

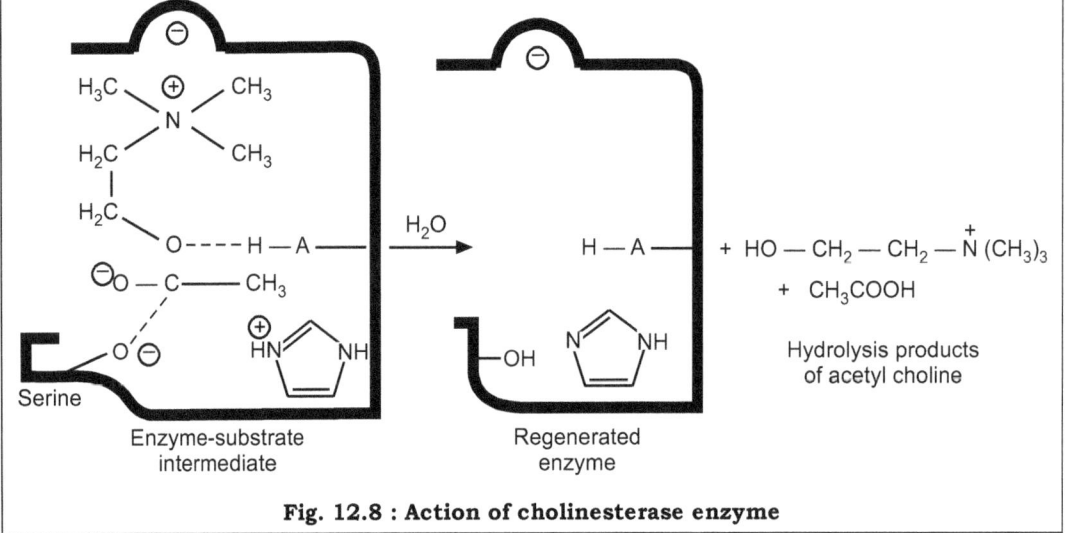

Fig. 12.8 : Action of cholinesterase enzyme

If the enzymatic hydrolysis of acetylcholine is inhibited, it will lead to prolongation and protentiation of neurotransmitter action. This can be done by the inhibition of cholinesterase enzyme.

Muscarine is a naturally occurring plant alkaloid, obtained from the poisonous mushroom, Amanita muscaria. Its actions on the smooth muscle, cardiac muscles, exocrine glands and its vascular effects are very much alike to that exhibited by acetyl choline. Similarly nicotine, yet another alkaloid, mimics the actions of acetylcholine on autonomic ganglia and the adrenal glands. Hence, it was proposed that acetylcholine exhibits some of its action via muscarinic receptors while remaining actions are propagated through the nicotinic receptors.

Cis-L-(+) muscarine

Nicotine

Muscarinic receptors are further subdivided into M_1 and M_2 depending upon the selectivity of certain agonists and antagonists. The nicotinic cholinergic receptor is a protein of five sub-units (i.e. $\alpha_2\ \beta\ \gamma\ \delta$) having a molecular weight of about 280,000 and is embedded into the cell surface membrane.

The actions of acetylcholine thus, are classified into :

(I) Muscarinic Actions :

These include,

(1) Cardiac inhibition

(2) Peripheral vasodilation

(3) Contraction of the eye pupils

(4) Increased salivation and increased flow of most secretory glands and

(5) Contractions and peristaltic action of the GIT and urinary tract.

All muscarinic actions are antagonised by atropine.

(II) Nicotinic Actions :

Nicotinic receptors occur at striated muscle and at autonomic ganglia. Nicotine first stimulates and then paralyses all autonomic ganglia. The nicotinic actions are thereby involved in the stimulation and maintenance of tone of the skeletal muscle. These actions are not antagonised by atropine.

(b) Sympathetic Division :

Epinephrine, norepinephrine and dopamine are the principal neurotransmitters present in the sympathetic nervous system. In many cases, synaptic transmission may be mediated by the release of more than one neurotransmitter.

Dopamine is a predominant transmitter in the human extrapyramidal system, mesocortical and mesolimbic neuronal pathways. The first evidence for nor-epinephrine as a principal neurotransmitter in ANS was given by Euler in 1946. The sympathetic system is distributed to effector cells throughout the body. It is also called as thoracolumbar division because the preganglionic neurons of sympathetic nervous system have their cell bodies in the thoracic and lumbar regions of the spinal cord. The synaptic ganglia are categorised into,

(a) Paravertebral.

(b) Prevertebral and

(c) Terminal.

This classification is based upon their sites of location. The terminal ganglia are few in number and consist especially of those connected with the urinary bladder and rectum.

In most instances, the sympathetic and parasympathetic divisions act as physiological antagonists. Exception is male sexual organ where both divisions act to promote sexual function. The sympathetic system is normally active at all times and by stimulating mental alertness, respiration, energy, production and heart activity, it prepares the person for 'fight or flight' situation. Receptors for a number of hormones including norepinephrine and autocoids, function by regulation of the concentration of the intracellular second messenger, cyclic adenosine -3', 5'- monophosphate (cyclic AMP) through the activation of intracellular adenylate cyclase. Cyclic AMP was discovered by Suderland and coworkers in 1956.

Epinephrine and norepinephrine catalyse many of the responses of the autonomic nervous system. The biosynthesis of epinephrine occurs in the nerve terminals using tyrosine as a starting material. This scheme of biosynthesis was first proposed by Blaschko in 1939. Phenylalanine is converted to dopamine in cytoplasm via two intermediates. The hydroxylation of tyrosine to dopa is generally regarded as the rate-limiting step in the biosynthesis of catecholamines. To meet increased demands for norepinephrine, acute regulatory mechanisms are available at nerve terminals to activate tyrosine hydroxylase enzyme.

The biosynthesized norepinephrine is stored in the synaptic vesicles or chromaffin granules which are about 0.05 to 0.2 μm in diameter. In these vesicles, catecholamine is present alongwith ATP in the molecular ratio of 4:1. The vesicles may contain other substances like ascorbic acid, enzymes, chromogranin proteins and endogenous peptides. The release of stored norepinephrine requires ATP and magnesium ions and is blocked by reserpine like drugs. The release is effected by the process of exocytosis which is influenced by a number of cytoplasmic proteins. These proteins include, calmodulin, tubulin, neurin (actine-like), and stenin (myosin-like). *l*-norepinephrine is released almost exclusively at the postganglionic sympathetic nerve endings. While adrenal medulla releases a mixture of both, i.e., *l*-norepinephrine and *l*-epinephrine.

After the exocytosis, the neuro-transmitter is released into the synaptic cleft. It crosses the synaptic cleft and releases at the adrenergic receptors present at post synaptic neuron. The action of epinephrine at the myoneural junction is blocked by ergotamine. The transmitter action is terminated by a number of processes. These include,

(a) Re-uptake mechanisms carry the neuro-transmitter into the nerve terminals or glial cells.

(b) Part of the neuro-transmitter diffuses out into the surrounding tissue fluid and blood circulation where it is metabolized by catechol-O-methyl transferase (COMT) enzymes.

(c) And part of the neuro-transmitter is attacked by mono amino oxidase (MAO) enzymes present in the mitochondria of the nerve terminal and it results into the metabolic deactivation of neuro-transmitter.

MAO and COMT enzymes are present in almost every vital organ of the body. The highest concentration of these enzymes is reported in brain, liver and kidney.

12.6 ACETYLCHOLINE AND EPINEPHRINE AS NEURO-TRANSMITTERS

Acetylcholine and epinephrine are the neuro-transmitters of major importance which lead the list of parasympathetic and sympathetic neuro-transmitters respectively. An element of structural similarity is shared between these neuro-transmitters.

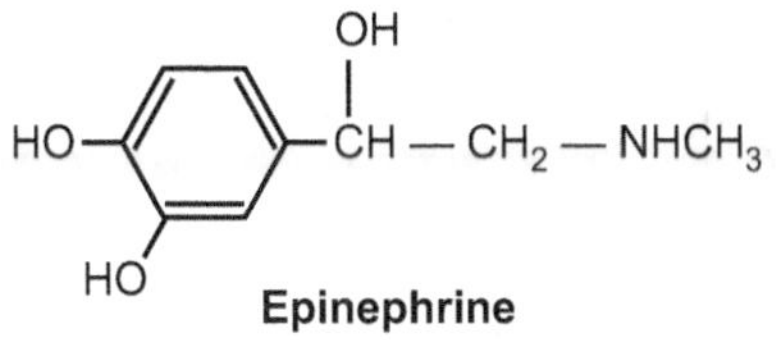

Epinephrine

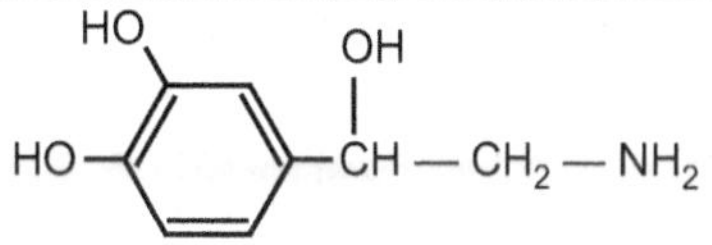

HO-C₆H₃(OH)-CH(OH)—CH₂—NHCH₃

Norepinephrine

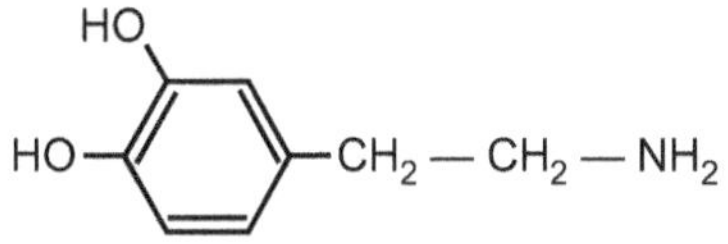

HO-C₆H₃(OH)-CH(OH)—CH₂—NH₂

Dopamine

HO-C₆H₃(OH)-CH₂—CH₂—NH₂

The replacement of H-atom present on β-carbon of choline molecule by a catechol nucleus results into formation of a dimethyl derivative of epinephrine. Thus, by an introduction of catechol nucleus in a choline molecules, the parasympathetic activity is shifted into acetylcholine sympathomimetic activity. The following table illustrates the points of differences between the sympathetic and parasympathetic divisions of ANS.

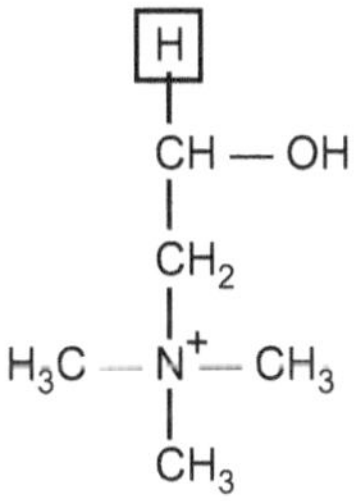

The sympathetic fibers to sweat glands and to certain blood vessels provided to skeletal muscles, release acetylcholine and hence the effect of stimulation of both the divisions at these target sites is similar. For example, in salivary glands, both divisions upon activation leads to an increase in saliva production.

Some organs are innervated only by sympathetic nervous system. These include, most blood vessels, spleen, sweat glands etc.

Choline

H—CH—OH—CH₂—N⁺(CH₃)₃

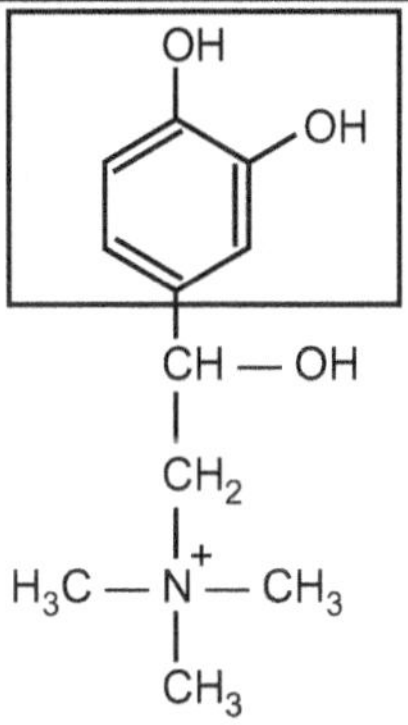

N, N-dimethyl epinephrine

Fig. 12.9 : Structural similarity between epinephrine and choline part of

Table 12.1 : Difference between parasympathetic division and sympathetic division

S.N.	Parasympathetic division	Sympathetic division
1.	Craniosacral division.	Thoracolumbar division.
2.	Acetylcholine is a principal neuro-transmitter.	Epinephrine and norepinephrine are principal neuro-transmitters.
3.	Emerges at segmental level S_2 to S_4 of spinal cord.	Emerges at segmental level of T_1 to L_2 or L_3 of spinal cord.
4.	Ganglia are small and suited very close to the structures innervated.	Ganglion contains neurons that are distributed to a number of organs.

5.	Effects are localized and limited and affects only a small region of the body.	Influences a wide region of the body.
6.	It is involved mainly in storage and preservation of body resources.	Prepares the person to face emergency cases.
7.	In rare cases, c-GMP is used as second messenger.	Operates through c-AMP which acts as second messenger.
8.	In the organs, innervated by both these divisions, effects upon stimulation of parasympathetic system are exactly opposite to that obtained after the stimulation of sympathetic system.	

12.7 NEURO-TRANSMITTERS PRESENT IN CENTRAL NERVOUS SYSTEM

Alongwith acetylcholine and norepinephrine, other neuro-transmitters which function in the CNS include, dopamine, epinephrine, serotonin, glycine, gamma amino butyric acid, glutamic acid, aspartic acid, taurine, histamine, substance P, enkephalins and ATP.

It is usually difficult to establish an identity of any other substance as a candidate to function as neurotransmitter in CNS. Many drugs affect CNS functioning by influencing the release, action or metabolism of the neuro-transmitters. In such cases, it can not be judged easily whether the altered CNS pattern is due to involvement of new neuro-transmitter or due to modulating effect of drug given. It can be decided by developing such specific agents that will block the specific form of the nervous activity in CNS which was supposed to be operated by the drug which was claimed to be a new neuro-transmitter.

Acetylcholine has been searched out in the brain cortex, limbic system, extrapyramidal nuclei and reticular formation. It regulates the sensory functions, short term memory, the classical phase of sleep and elimination of hormones, especially vasopressin.

Norepinephrine acts as a neurotransmitter in limbic system, reticular formation, locus coeruleus, hypothalamus and medulla oblongata. It is involved in thermoregulation, memory, motor activity and vegetative functions.

Dopamine is present at higher concentration in the extrapyramidal nuclei and limbic structures. It regulates motor activity, emotional tone, memory and release of hormones.

Serotonin is a mediator which influences thermoregulation, learning, classical phase of sleep, analgesia and sensory functions. It is present in limbic system, hypothalamus, spinal cord and Raphe nuclei. Lysergic acid diethylamide (LSD) interferes in and reduces serotonin turnover in the brain. This explains the basis of hallucinogenic action of LSD. The depression of serotonin activity results in the inhibition of visual and other sensory inputs.

CNS Depression :

CNS excitation occurs as a result of the release of excitatory neuro-transmitters like acetylcholine, catecholamines, dopamine, glutamic acid etc. Similarly CNS depression arises either due to,

(a) Inhibition of the release of CNS excitatory neuro-transmitter.

OR

(b) Release of inhibitory neurotransmitter which then stimulates inhibitory responses. The inhibitory neurotransmitters include, serotonin, glycine, taurine and gamma-amino butyric acid (GABA).

Glycine :

It acts as a inhibitory neutransmitter predominantly in the reticular formation. Strychnine appears to antagonise selectively the glycine responses but fails to antagonise the effects mediated by GABA.

Taurine :

It uniformly depresses the functioning of CNS except the cortex where it has very weak depresant action.

GABA :

Though it has a widespread depressory action on the various regions of CNS, its main sites of action involve local inter-neurons in the brain and presynaptic sites within the spinal cord. Its presence in brain was first reported in 1950.

Many drugs lead to excessive CNS stimulation (convulsant action) mainly due to the blockadge of inhibitory nerve-channels mediated by GABA. For example, the action of benzodiazepines is linked with the potentiation of the functions of receptor-chloride ionophore systems that are regulated by GABA. The activation of chloride ionophore causes influx of chloride ions which carry impulses through the channels that are regulated by GABA.

Table 12.2 : Some of the neuro transmitters present in CNS

Acetylcholine: $CH_3-C(=O)-O-CH_2-CH_2-\overset{\oplus}{N}-(CH_3)_3$	Norepinephrine: (3,4-dihydroxyphenyl)–CH(OH)–CH$_2$–NH$_2$
Epinephrine: (3,4-dihydroxyphenyl)–CH(OH)–CH$_2$–NHCH$_3$	Dopamine: (3,4-dihydroxyphenyl)–CH$_2$–CH$_2$–NH$_2$
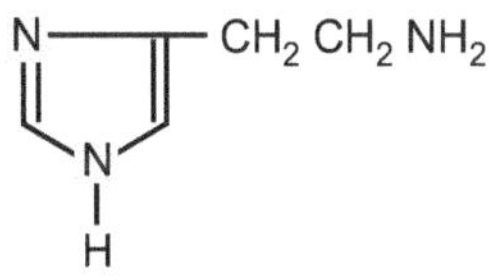 Histamine: imidazole–CH$_2$CH$_2$NH$_2$	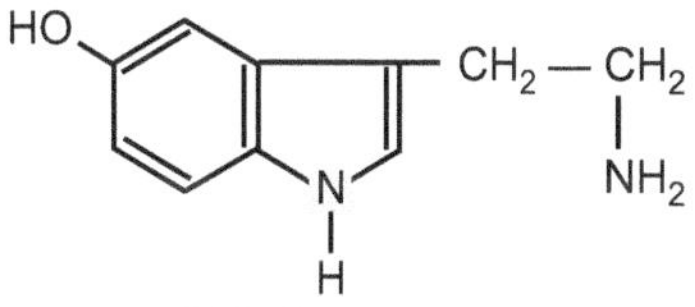 5-Hydroxytryptamine (Serotonin): 5-hydroxyindole–CH$_2$–CH$_2$–NH$_2$
Glycine: NH$_2$–CH$_2$–COOH	Aspartic acid: H$_2$N–CH(COOH)–CH$_2$–COOH

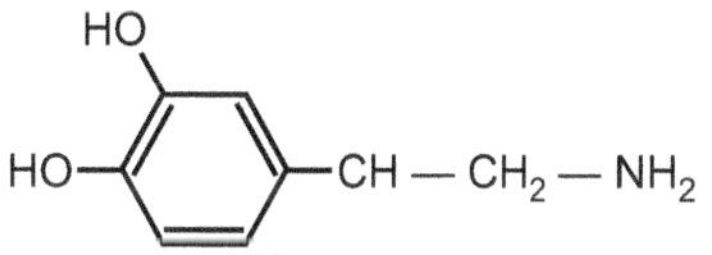

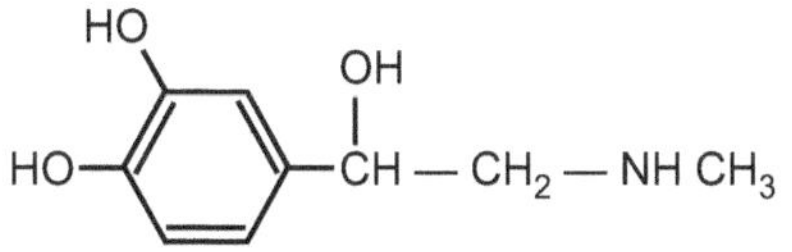

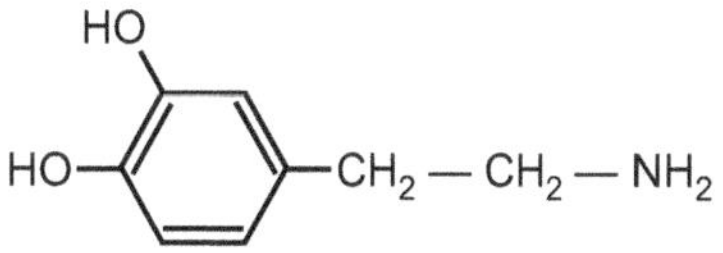

$H_2N - CH - CH_2 - CH_2 - COOH$
         |
       $COOH$
Glutamic acid
	$H_2N - CH_2 - CH_2 - CH_2 - COOH$
	γ-aminobutyric acid

H – Tyr – Gly – Gly – Phe – Met – OH **Methionine enkephalin**	H – Tyr – Gly – Gly – Phe – Leu – OH **Leucine enkephaline**
H – Arg – Lys – Pro – Pro – Gln – Gln – Phe – Phe – Gly – Leu – Met – NH_2 **Substance P**	

CHOLINERGIC AGONISTS

13.1 INTRODUCTION

The nervous system which regulates many of the body's vital functions is divided into two branches, the somatic system, which controls the activity of skeletal (voluntary) muscles, and the autonomic system which is concerned with the involuntary activities. It is subdivided into sympathetic and parasympathetic divisions. The parasympathetic division of the autonomic nervous system employs acetylcholine (ACh) as a neurotransmitter to propagate its nerve impulse. Acetylcholine is one of the most important and most widely distributed neurotransmitter present in the human body. Hence, the parasympathetic division is also called as cholinergic nervous system. The drugs which exhibit similar pharmacological actions on tissues to that of ACh, are termed therefore, as parasympathomimetic or cholinergic agonists whereas the drugs which antagonise the ACh activity (by interfering in its biosynthesis, release metabolism or with its interaction with receptors) are termed as parasympatholytic or cholinergic blocking agents or anticholinergic agents. Acetylcholine occurs in animals, both vertebrate and invertebrate, and in plants.

13.2 PHARMACOLOGY OF ACETYLCHOLINE

Acetylcholine was first synthesized by Baeyer in 1867. In general, stimulation of parasympathetic nervous system induces constriction of pupil and bronchi, decrease in heart activity and an increase in the activity of digestive system i.e. salivation and other GIT secretions are promoted. Motility of the intestine is also increased.

$$H_3C-\overset{O}{\underset{\|}{C}}-O\mid CH_2-CH_2\mid \overset{\oplus}{N}\begin{cases}CH_3\\CH_3\\CH_3\end{cases}$$

Acetyl group | Ethylene bridge | Quaternary ammonium cation (onium group)

Fig. 13.1 : Acetylcholine

Following are some of the important chemical features of acetylcholine molecule :

(i) Chemically it is an ester of acetic acid and choline, an amino alcohol.

(ii) On the structural basis, it offers three sites for molecular modifications :

(a) acetyl group,

(b) ethylene bridge and

(c) quaternary ammonium group.

(iii) The quaternary ammonium group (i.e. onium group) is linked by an ethylene bridge to an ester group.

(iv) Acetylcholine is stable in acidic solutions but it is very unstable in alkaline media.

(v) Free acetylcholine present in the tissue fluids and circulation, is rapidly hydrolysed to acetic acid and choline by cholinesterase enzyme.

Muscarine is a naturally occurring plant alkaloid, obtained from a poisonous mushroom, *Amanita muscaria*. Its actions on the smooth muscles, cardiac muscles, exocrine glands and its effects on vasculature are similar to that produced by ACh. Similarly nicotine, yet another alkaloid present in tobacco, mimicks the actions of ACh on autonomic ganglia and the adrenal glands. Hence it was proposed that ACh exhibits some of its actions via muscarinic receptors while remaining actions are propagated through nicotinic receptors.

Muscarinic receptors are also reported to be present at cortical and subcortical sites within the CNS and in autonomic ganglia. At these receptor sites, the effects of ACh are dose dependent and are blocked by atropine. Hence, atropine is regarded as a blocker of muscarinic actions of acetylcholine. Muscarinic receptors are further subdivided into M_1 and M_2 depending upon the selectivity of certain cholinergic agonists and antagonists. These receptors are present at both, presynaptic and post-synaptic sites. The presynaptic muscarinic receptors, when stimualted, may inhibit the release of neurotransmitter from the nerve terminals into the synaptic cleft. They do not differ in chemical specificity from the post synaptic muscarinic receptors. M_1 receptors are found in ganglia and CNS, whereas M_2 sites are present on the post-synaptic effector organs. The nicotinic receptors are present at striated muscle and at autonomic ganglia. They are also present in CNS alongwith some muscarinic receptors. The nicotinic actions involve, stimulation and maintenance of tone of the skeletal muscle. These actions are not antagonised by atropine. Nicotinic actions at autonomic ganglia are antagonised by hexamethonium and related drugs whereas at neuromuscular junction of skeletal muscle, they are antagonised by tubocurarine. At nicotinic receptor sites, acetylcholine produces stimulant effects in small doses whereas large doses of acetylcholine lead to receptor inhibition.

(a) Cardiovascular System :

If acetylcholine is injected intravenously, the muscarinic effects of acetylcholine are predominantly seen on cardiovascular system. These effects include :

(i) Vasodilation.

(ii) Decrease in the heart rate (negative chronotropic effect) and decrease in the force of heart contraction (negative inotropic effect).

(iii) Decrease in the force of heart contraction (negative inotropic effect).

Low doses acetylcholine are sufficient to produce vasodilation including the pulmonary and coronary vasculature. This is brought about mainly by the stimulation of muscarinic receptors present in the endothelial cells of vasculature. The vasodilatory effect of acetylcholine on peripheral vasculature is very marked but is quickly terminated. The latter two effects of acetylcholine can be observed only in higher doses. In heart, cholinergic innervation is provided mainly to the sinoarterial node, atrioventricular node and the atrial muscles. The activation of this innervation leads to an increase in the permeability of cardiac fibres to potassium resulting into a decrease in the activity of S-A node.

The effects of acetylcholine on cardio-vascular system just described, sometimes may be reversed by the release of catecholamines from the adrenal medulla and from sympathetic ganglia. This release may be due to the stimulation of nicotinic cholinergic receptor sites present in these organs.

(b) Smooth Muscle :

At moderate doses, acetylcholine stimulates the muscarinic receptors present on the smooth muscles of GIT, urinogenital and respiratory tract, and eye resulting into contraction of these muscles. The increased muscle tone of GIT may lead to nausea and vomiting. The lacrimal, salivary, gastric, pancreatic, and sweat glands are also stimulated. The motility of gall bladder and bile duct is also increased.

The stimulatory effects of acetylcholine can be explained on the basis of an increase in the permeability of the muscle cell to Na^+ and Ca^{++} ions which results into a depolarization of the cell membrane. When acetylcholine reacts with the post-synaptic receptors, it may produce either excitation or inhibition.

The action of the transmitter results in selective increase or decrease of ionic permeability of membrane for ions. The ratio of permeability for K^+ to that of Na^+, if increased may lead to hyperpolarization (as in cardiac cells) and if decreases, may cause depolarization (as in smooth muscle cells). For example, high concentration of acetylcholine may lead to the complete heart block due to hyperpolarization.

Thus, enhanced permeability to monovalent cations, an increase in the concentration of intracellular calcium ions, an increase in the concentration of guanosine - 3', 5'-monophosphate (cyclic GMP) or the inhibition of adenylate cyclase enzyme are some of the mechanisms associated with muscarinic receptor stimulation. Investigations in the role of c-GMP started from 1960. It is widely distributed in the tissues. It is present at higher concentration in cerebellum and particularly in retina.

Due to the quaternary cationic nature, acetylcholine, at low doses, can not readily reach the skeletal muscles embedded by the fatty layers. Hence at low doses, the nicotinic actions of acetylcholine are not prominant. At large doses, acetylcholine can stimulate nicotinic receptors present in both, sympathetic and parasympathetic ganglia.

Acetylcholine is poor therapeutic agent since it gets easily hydrolysed by cholinesterase enzyme. Clinically, its use as acetylcholine chloride, is restricted in ophthalmic surgery to obtain rapid and complete miosis during cataract removal. For this purpose, 0.5 to 2.0 ml of 10 mg/ml solution of acetylcholine chloride can be applied locally.

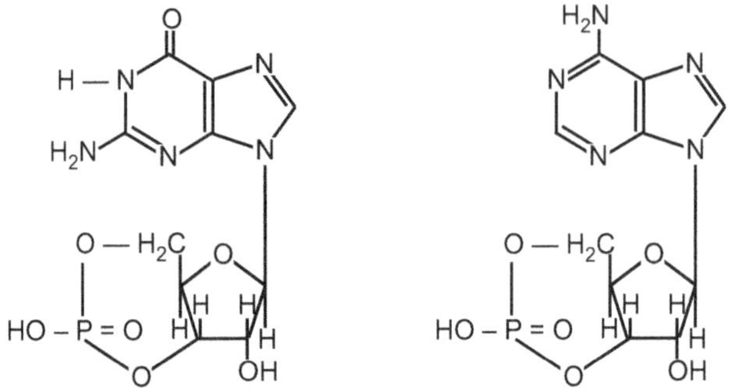

Fig. 13.2 : Important cyclic nucleotides

Structure-Activity Relationship :

(i) Any change in the ethylene bridge may affect the chemical stability of acetylcholine molecule.

(ii) A cationic ammonium group is essential for the manifestation of both muscarinic and nicotinic receptor activities. If one or more of the methyl groups on nitrogen atom are replaced by hydrogen or ethyl group, both activities are reduced.

(iii) The quaternary nitrogen atom itself may be replaced by arsenic, antimony, phosphorus or sulphur atom without the loss of all acetylcholine-like activities.

(iv) Ing in 1949 proposed that for maximal muscarinic activity, there should not be more than four atoms between the nitrogen and terminal C-atom.

(v) If bulky substituents are placed on the terminal C-atom of acetyl group, through a firm binding and 'Umbrella effect', these substituents block the access of acetylcholine to the receptor. This results in the antimuscarinic activity. Examples include, benzilylcholine, tropylcholine etc.

(vi) Carbachol and acetyl-β-methylcholine are the cholinergic agonists acting chiefly at muscarinic receptors while propionylcholine and acetyl α-methylcholine act chiefly at nicotinic cholinergic receptors.

13.3 CYCLIC ANALOGUES OF ACETYLCHOLINE

Muscarine is a cyclic analogue of acetylcholine, devoid of nicotinic receptor activity. It has a quaternary ammonium group but does not possess an ester function. Hence, it is not enzymatically metabolized by cholinesterase enzyme. This explains its long duration of action. If administered in sufficient concentration, it reaches the CNS by crossing blood-brain-barrier and evokes cortical arousal.

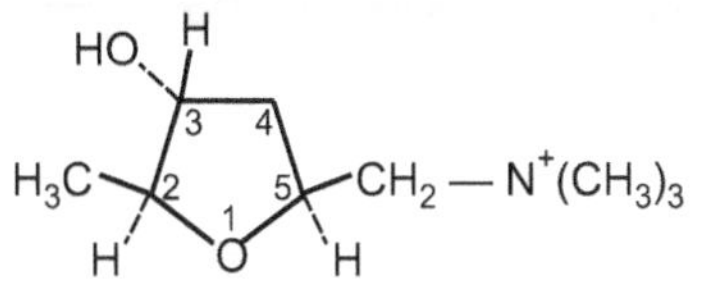

Cis-L-(+) muscarine

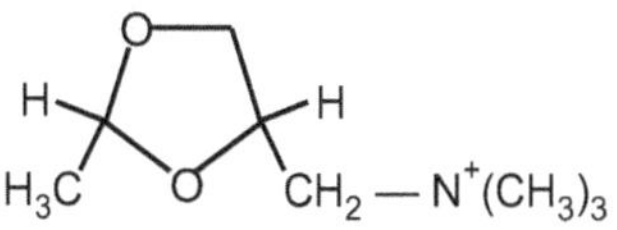

2-methyl-4-trimethyl ammonium - methyl-1,3-dioxolone

Fig. 13.3 : Cyclic analogues of acetylcholine

The above structures, alongwith the rigid size requirements for the esters of choline, also indicate steric and conformational requirement for optimal fit on the muscarinic receptors. For example, Acetyl-β-methyl choline adopts following conformation.

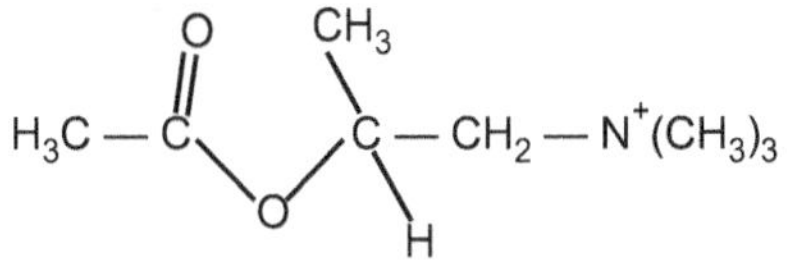

Acetyl-β-methylcholine

13.4 CHOLINERGIC RECEPTORS

From the SAR studies, the structure of a cholinergic receptor is predicted as shown in the Fig. 13.4.

The negative charge at the anionic site of the receptor may result from the ionization of a dicarboxylic amino group (i.e., aspartic or glutamic acid) present in the receptor. The quaternary ammonium group forms an electrostatic bond with this anionic site. The ester or other group capable of forming H-bond interacts at the esteratic site through H-bonding.

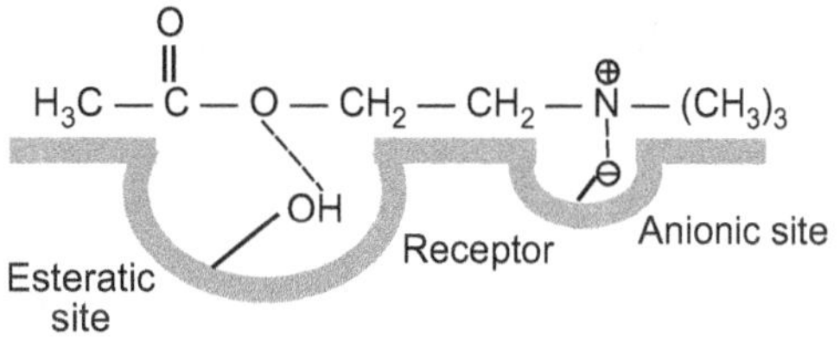

Fig. 13.4 : Cholinergic receptor

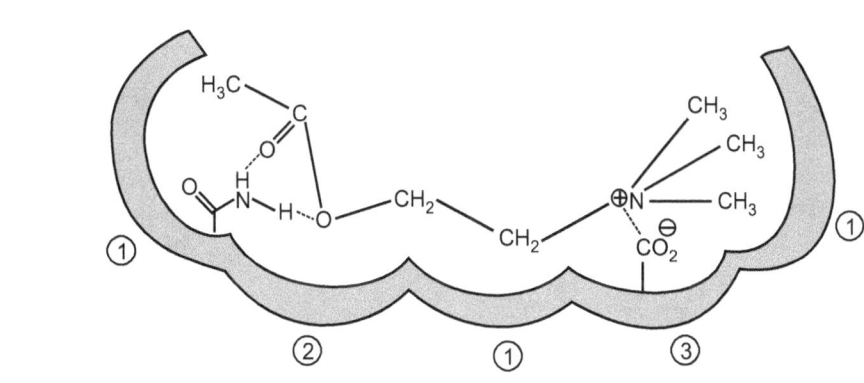

(1) : Region of hydrophobic binding (van der Waal's forces)
(2) : Region of H - bonding
(3) : Region of ionic bonding

Fig. 13.5 : Acetyl choline - receptor interactions

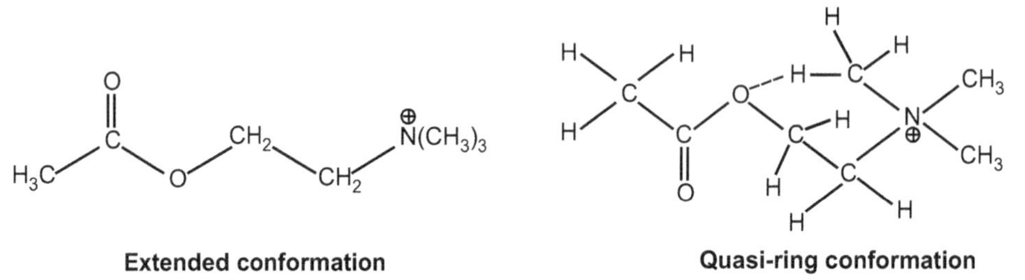

![Fig. 13.6 : Conformations of acetylcholine](extended and quasi-ring conformations)

Fig. 13.6 : Conformations of acetylcholine

Since the tissues containing muscarinic receptors are extremely complex, binding studies between acetylcholine analogues and cholinesterases were made. They indicate that the methyl groups present on N-atom alongwith the acetyl methyl group are bound to the receptor by both hydrophobic and vander Waal's forces. This binding assures a close fit of the molecule to the receptor as shown in Fig. 13.5.

But due to the free rotation around most of its covalent bonds, acetylcholine can exist in a large number of conformations. The following two structures represent extremes in all such possible conformations (Fig. 13.6).

The structure of any drug can be categorized into an essential part (necessary for better intrinsic activity) and a supporting part (necessary for better affinity and pharmacokinetic properties). The supporting structure also helps to bring the essential structure in the correct three-dimensional arrangement with respect to the receptor surface.

The essential as well as supporting structures, both differ in their conformations with regard to the action of acetylcholine on muscarinic and nicotinic receptors. For example, acetylcholine is present in an extended conformational form when it fits on muscarinic receptor while it adopts quasi ring conformation when it acts on nicotinic cholinergic receptors.

While in another hypothesis, Beckett proposed that, the muscarinic receptors contain one anionic and two cationic sites as shown in Fig. 13.7.

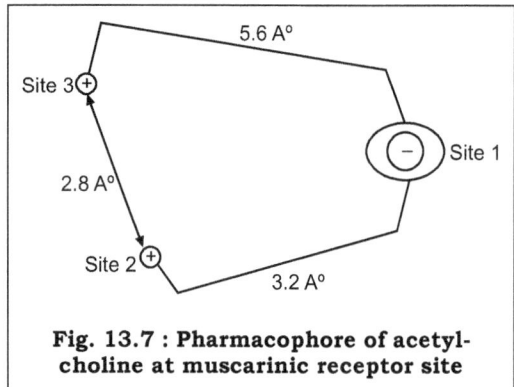

Fig. 13.7 : Pharmacophore of acetylcholine at muscarinic receptor site

The anionic binding site (site 1) accommodates the quaternary nitrogen of muscarine. The site 2 or a H-bonding site is for ether oxygen of muscarine or acetylcholine while the site 3 can interact with the carbonyl group of acetylcholine or the ether oxygen of dioxolone or with the alcohol group of muscarine as shown in Fig. 13.8. Although acetylcholine has three reactive sites, only two sites are necessary for the various actions of the compound.

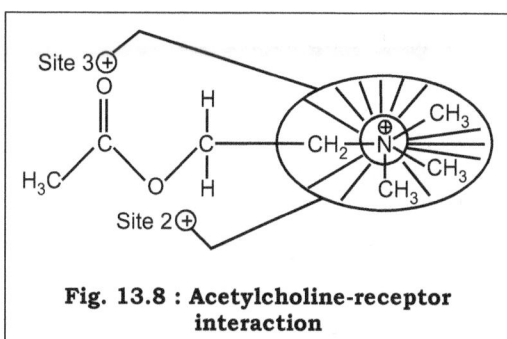

Fig. 13.8 : Acetylcholine-receptor interaction

13.5 METABOLISM OF ACETYLCHOLINE

The free acetylcholine present in the blood and other tissues, gets quickly hydrolyzed by either e-cholinesterase (present in erythrocytes) and s-cholinesterase (present in the serum). Dale (1914) first proposed the concept of enzymatic destruction of acetylcholine in the blood and other tissues. Serum cholinesterase is also known as butyrocholinesterase while e-cholinesterase is also termed as acetylcholinesterase. The cholinesterases are not very selective enzymes. A number of other s-cholinesterases share some of the properties of e-cholinesterases. Both these types hydrolyse a large number of esters, both, of choline and of other carboxylic acids.

13.6 CHOLINOMIMETICS OR CHOLINERGIC AGONISTS

The cholinomimetics have as their primary action the excitation or inhibition of autonomic effector cells that are innervated by post-ganglionic parasympathetic nerves. They differ from acetylcholine in,

(1) their selectivity on muscarinic and nicotinic receptors.

(2) their chemical stability.

(3) their resistance to hydrolysis by cholinesterases and

(4) their duration of action.

On the structural basis, the cholinomimetic agents can be divided into,

(a) Acetylcholine and several synthetic choline esters.

(b) Naturally occurring and synthetic alkaloids.

(c) Cholinesterase inhibitors or anticholinesterases and

(d) Ganglionic stimulants.

The last two categories do not act at post-ganglionic cholinergic effector sites and produce their effects by acting in an indirect way. Hence in this chapter, only the first two categories will be discussed.

(a) Acetylcholine and Synthetic Choline Esters :

Acetylcholine is a poor therapeutic agent since it gets easily hydrolized. This disadvantage necessitated the synthesis of more analogues with a prolonged duration of action. Efforts were made to obtain acetylcholine analogues with a thought that if a structure contains an enzymatically nonhydrolysable group, it will evoke a more prolonged action. The pharmacological spectrum of activity of all choline esters is essentially identical with acetylcholine.

(i) Methacholine : This compound was first synthesized in 1929 by Hunt and his associates by incorporating a methyl group β to the quaternary nitrogen atom in acetylcholine molecule.

$$H_3C-\overset{O}{\overset{\|}{C}}-O-\overset{CH_3}{\overset{|}{CH}}-CH_2-\overset{\oplus}{N}(CH_3)_3\ X^-$$

Acetyl-β-methylcholine (Methacholine)

It has a prominant muscarinic activity and is almost devoid of nicotinic activity. Its absorption from GIT is quite poor and irregular. It is usually hydrolysed by acetylcholinesterase but not by butyrocholinesterase. During absorption, it is also partly destroyed by gastric secretions.

Though methacholine chloride is now rarely used clinically, it can be used

1. in the treatment of glaucoma to supplement the effect of other anticholinesterase and

2. for the diagnosis of atropine poisoning. For this, the drug is given subcutaneously in the dose of 10-30 mg. If the drug fails to stimulate muscarinic receptors, it confirms the poisoning by atropine.

The adverse effects are usually due to the stimulation of muscarinic receptors and include, nausea, urination, defecation, marked bronchoconstriction etc.

(ii) Carbachol : It was first synthesized by Kreitmar in 1932. In carbachol, the acetyl methyl group of acetylcholine is replaced by $-NH_2$ group. Thus, it contains carbamic ester linkage than the acetic acid ester linkage and hence it is more resistant to hydrolysis by cholinesterases. Its muscarinic effects are prominantly seen on GIT, urinary bladder and iris. Carbachol retains considerable nicotinic activity particularly on autonomic ganglia, adrenal medulla and skeletal muscle.

$$H_2N-\overset{\overset{O}{\|}}{C}-O-CH_2-CH_2\overset{\oplus}{N}(CH_3)_3$$

Carbachol

Clinically carbachol is used to

(i) relieve urinary retention.

(ii) ocular disorders to lower intraocular pressure in the treatment of glaucoma as 1-1.5% solution.

(iii) Bethanechol (Urecholine) : It is a commonly used muscarinic agent in urology. Chemically, it is carbamic acid ester of β–methylcholine and possesses structural features common to both, methacholine and carbachol. It was first synthesized in 1932. Structurally, it is the urethane of methacholine.

$$H_2N-\overset{\overset{O}{\|}}{C}-O-\overset{\overset{CH_3}{|}}{CH}-CH_2-\overset{\oplus}{N}(CH_3)_3$$

Bethanechol

It is a stable ester which is not succeptible to hydrolysis by cholinesterases. It has chiefly muscarinic activity and acts selectively on GIT and urinary bladder. Upon oral administration, it is readily absorbed.

Clinically it is used in the treatment of urinary retention, orally (30 mg) or subcutaneously (5 mg). Quinidine and procainamide may antagonise the effects of Bethanechol, if administered together. Various adverse reactions include, sweating, flushing, salivation, epigastric diastress and abdominal cramps.

All above synthetic choline esters find their applications in,

(a) Gastrointestinal and urological disorders,

(b) Opthalmologic disorders and

(c) Glaucoma.

Adverse Reactions :

All synthetic choline esters should never be administered by intravenous route. They are usually administered preferably by oral or by subcutaneous route. The usual side-effects include, salivation, diarrhoea, profuse sweating, headache, bladder pain, vomitting and severe gastro intestinal cramps.

Contraindications :

These synthetic derivatives of acetylcholine are contraindicated in patients suffering from peptic ulcer, bronchial asthma, hypotention, presence of organic urinary tract or gastrointestinal obstruction.

(b) Naturally Occurring and Synthetic Alkaloids :

Muscarine is a prototype of naturally occurring alkaloids having cholinergic activity at muscarinic receptors while nicotine is a prototype having similar activity to that of cholinergic nicotinic receptor stimulation. All these alkaloids are structurally more complex than choline esters. But the distance between the bioactive positions in alkaloids is kept similar to that in acetylcholine. It thus allows a firm attachment of the alkaloidal structure on the cholinergic receptor.

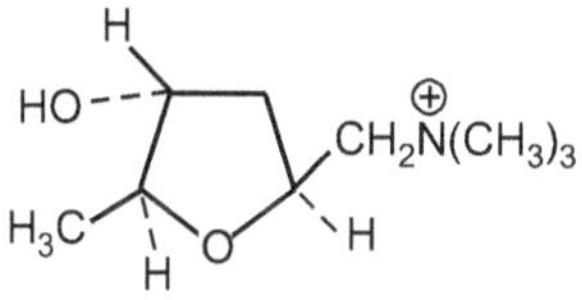

Cis-L-(+) muscarine

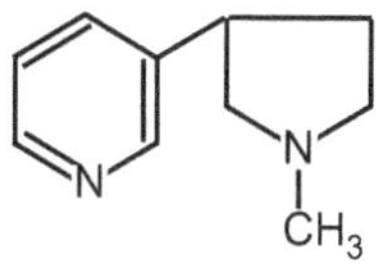

Nicotine

Nicotine mainly acts on the cholinergic receptors present in ganglia, striated muscles and CNS. Nicotine first stimulates and then depresses the receptors. At high dose, it is a powerful convulsant drug, stimulating the vomiting centre, the respiratory centre and several hypothalamic centres as well.

Various alkaloids from both, natural and synthetic origin, having cholinomimetic effects include, Muscarine, nicotine, pilocarpine, oxotremorine, arecholine, deanol, furrethonium etc.

(i) Pilocarpine : It is a liquid alkaloid, isolated in 1875 from the leaves of species of Pilocarpus. Various species of Pilocarpus are found in South and Central America and West Indies. Since its nitrate salt is not hygroscopic, clinically it is used in the form of its nitrate salt. It prominantly acts on the muscarinic sites and does not possess nicotinic cholinergic activity. In higher concentration however, it leads to hypertension and tachycardia mainly due to its nicotinic actions on sympathetic ganglia and adrenal medulla, releasing norepinephrine and epinephrine into circulation. Clinically it is used to induce miosis and to lower down intraocular pressure in the treatment of glaucoma (a condition arised due to increased intraocular pressure resulting by impaired drainage or excessive secretion of aqueous humour).

It induces miosis within 15-20 minutes after topical administration. Opthalmic solutions of both pilocarpine hydrochloride and pilocarpine nitrate are available. The nitrate is employed as a 0.25 – 2.0% solution. It can cross the blood-brain-barrier and evokes cortical activation response. The drug can be delivered in the form of sustained release formulations. For example, soft contact lens reservoirs, polymer emulsions etc.

(ii) Oxotremorine : It is a synthetic alkaloid and acts as potent muscarinic cholinergic agonist in the periphery and CNS. In CNS, its actions lead to cortical arousal response. Since most of its effects resemble closely with the symptoms of parkinsonism, it is used as an investigative tool in the drug design of effective antiparkinsonian agents.

(iii) Arecholine : It is a natural alkaloid obtained from the betel nut, the seed of Areca catechu. It has prominant, muscarinic actions but its nicotinic actions are considerably weak.

(iv) Deanol : Clinically deanol is used to increase the rate of biosynthesis of acetylcholine in brain. Hence, its use in the treatment of mild mental depressive state and of schizophrenia is beneficial.

Furtrethonium is yet another synthetic choline ester. A non-alkaloidal indirect acting cholinomimetic drug is metoclopramide. It has two fold actions :

(1) In CNS, it antagonises the effects of dopamine.

(2) At periphery it acts as cholinomimetic agent by increasing the concentration of acetylcholine at muscarinic synapses.

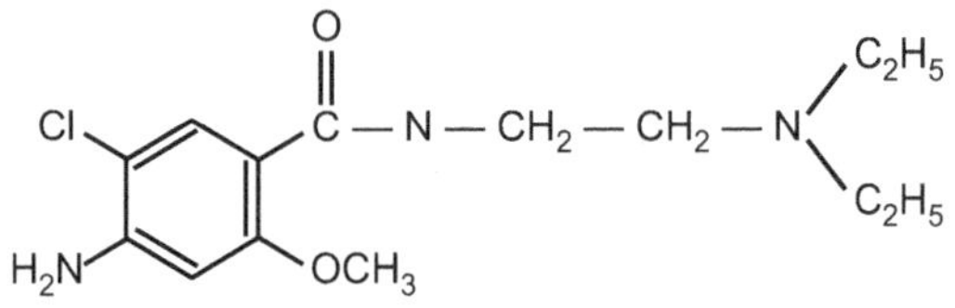

Metoclopramide

❖ ❖ ❖

ANTI-CHOLINESTERASES

14.1 INTRODUCTION

The cholinesterase enzyme terminates the biological activity of acetylcholine by hydrolyzing acetylcholine into acetic acid and a choline molecule, thus limiting the turnover time of acetylcholine to 150 microseconds. The hydrolysis of acetylcholine occurs through deacetylation reaction which is catalysed by cholinesterase enzyme.

The cholinesterases present in the human body can be broadly categorised into,

(a) Acetylcholinesterase or e-cholinesterase or true cholinesterase or specific cholinesterase and

(b) Butyrocholinesterase or s-cholinesterase or pseudocholinesterase or non-specific cholinesterase.

The specific acetylcholinesterase is found in R.B.C., in the brain and other nerve tissues. It is present in high concentration on presynaptic sites, post-synaptic membrane sites and at motor nerve end plate regions of cholinergic nervous system. At presynaptic sites, its role is to regulate the acetylcholine levels in cholinergic nerve terminals. It is also located in autonomic ganglia and certain cholinergic synapses in the CNS. The non-specific or butyrocholinesterase is present in plasma, glial cells, intestine and other organs. The cholinesterases present in different species or organs sometimes bear basic differences and need not be identical.

These enzymes are mainly located in the outer basement membrane of the synapses and in the neuro-muscular junctional cleft. They are also reported to be present in the cisternae of the endoplasmic reticulum.

Sometimes cholinesterase enzymes have been located in such regions where they can not claim the role of 'acetylcholine-killer' (Ach-killer). In such cases, they are supposed to be tied up with some independent activities like,

(a) to control the membrane permeability and

(b) to control the blood level of fatty substances.

$$CH_3-\overset{O}{\underset{\|}{C}}-O-CH_2-CH_2-\overset{\oplus}{N}(CH_3)_3 \xrightarrow{\text{Cholinesterase}} CH_3COOH + HO-CH_2-CH_2-\overset{\oplus}{N}(CH_3)_3$$

Acetylcholine   Acetic acid   Choline

Fig. 14.1 : Hydrolysis of acetylcholine

14.2 CHOLINESTERASE INHIBITORS

Cholinesterase inhibitors, as the name indicates, increase the concentration of the acetylcholine at the receptor sites by inhibiting its metabolism by cholinesterases, resulting into prolongation and potentiation of acetylcholine activity at both, muscarinic and nicotinic receptors. They do so mainly through competitive antagonism and hence often resemble with acetylcholine in structure.

The unhydrolysed acetylcholine accumulates and exerts its actions. Hence, cholinesterase inhibitors are also termed as indirectly acting cholinomimetic agents.

The activation of muscarinic receptors results into various muscarinic effects which include miosis, contractions of smooth muscles, diarrhoea, vasodilation, bradycardia, nausea, vomiting, salivation, perspiration, lacrimation etc. All these effects can be blocked by administration of muscarine blocker like, atropine.

The activation of nicotinic receptors by high levels of accumulated acetylcholine results into generalised muscle twitching followed by the muscle weakness and ganglionic stimulation. The activation of nicotinic receptors present in the autonomic ganglia and adrenal medulla leads to the release of catecholamines which may further alter the cardiovascular function.

Some anticholinesterases have an independent direct cholinomimetic action of their own while some may cause neuromuscular blockade. The toxic effects of some drugs may be due to their in-vivo metabolism to toxic metabolites.

14.3 STRUCTURAL FEATURES OF CHOLINESTERASE ENZYME

Cholinesterase constitutes an example of one of the most effective enzyme systems present in the body. It is a tetramer having a molecular weight of about 80,000. The cholinesterase molecule consists of three important sites namely, anionic, cationic and esteratic site.

The anionic site is formed by an ionized gamma-carboxylate group of a glutamic acid residue and is stereospecific. The cationic site possesses hydroxyl group probably that of tyrosine residue. While the esteratic site consists of two imidazole groups (Im_1 and Im_2) from histidine moieties and a serine residue.

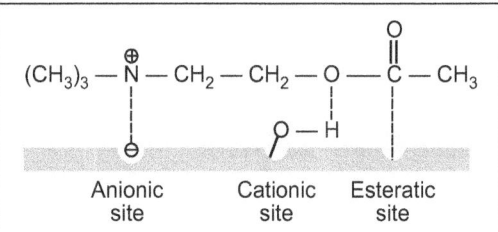

Fig. 14.2 : Possible interactions between acetylcholine and cholinesterase enzyme

The process of hydrolysis of acetylcholine, thus occurs in the following steps :

I. The imidazole group Im_2 of histidine, accepts a proton from a serine hydroxyl group at the esteratic site, creating a strong nucleophile while OH - from tyrosine just serves as binding site to ether oxygen of the acetoxy group of acetylcholine.

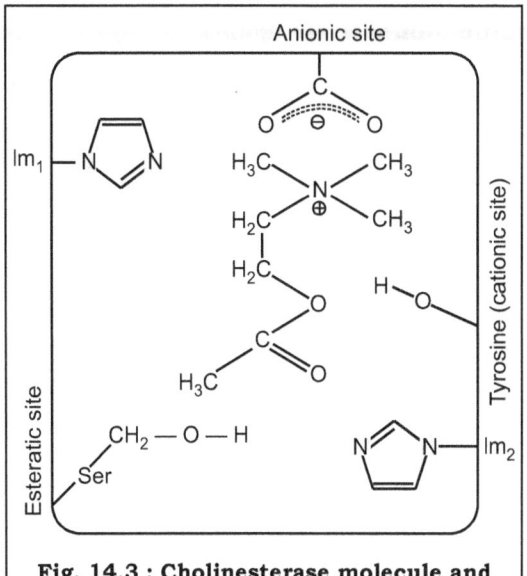

Fig. 14.3 : Cholinesterase molecule and acetylcholine

II. The anionic site of the enzyme binds with the quaternary nitrogen of the acetylcholine through both ionic and hydrophobic forces. The latter binding force is provided by the presence of three methyl groups which are present on the nitrogen. The activated serine, being a strong nucleophile, then attacks on the C-atom of carbonyl group of acetylcholine resulting into a tetrahedral intermediate. This intermediate is very short-lived and its collapse results into the release of choline molecule, leaving the acetylated serine residue on the enzyme.

III. The choline molecule can readily dissociate from the anionic site, since it is bound only by Vander Waals forces and hydrophobic forces. The acetyl group however, forms a covalent bond with the nucleophilic group (activated serine residue) of the enzyme. The acetylated enzyme then undergoes a conformational change which brings the acetylated serine in close proximity to the second imidazole (Im_2) residue. In presence of a water molecule, the second imidazole residue catalyzes hydrolysis of acetylated serine to give acetic acid and serine residue. This step is rate limiting step which occurs at a very rapid rate and the enzyme is thereby efficiently regenerated back.

The cholinesterase enzyme from a purified sample of OX red blood cell is found to hydrolyse 3×10^5 molecules of acetylcholine per minute.

14.4 CLASSIFICATION OF ANTICHOLINESTERASES

The anticholinesterases are classified into :

    I. Reversible anticholinesterases

   II. Irreversible anticholinesterases.

(I) Reversible Anticholinesterases :

They bear a structural resemblances to acetylcholine. Hence, they are capable of interacting with the anionic and esteratic sites of cholinesterase enzymes and receptors as well. They have a great affinity for the active sites but no intrinsic activity. This produces the temporary inhibition of the enzyme. Hence, they are termed as reversible anticholinesterases. In contrast to other reversible cholinesterases, edrophonium forms a reversible complex only with the anionic site and hence has a shorter duration of action.

The reversible anticholinesterases can be further sub-divided into

(a) Naturally occurring : E.g. physostigmine.

(b) Synthetic analogues : E.g. Neostigmine, pyridostigmine, ambenonium, miotine, demecarium, edrophonium and benzpyrinium.

Reversible cholinesterase inhibitors may delay the hydrolysis of acetylcholine from 1-8 hours.

Table 14.1: Some reversible anticholinesterase agents

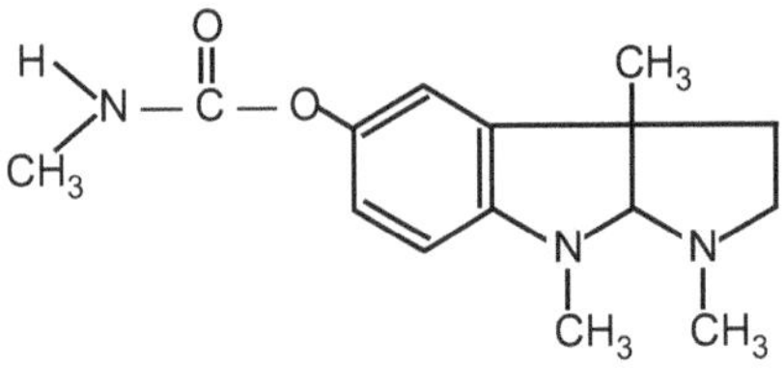 Physostigmine	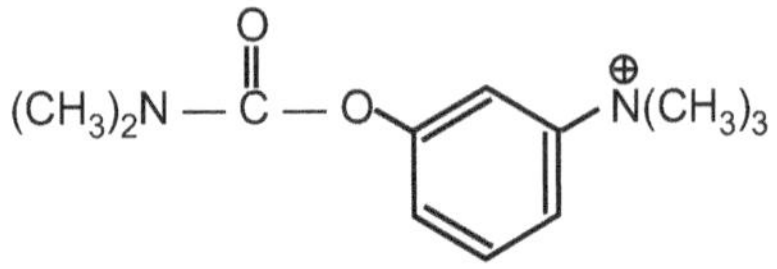 Neostigmine
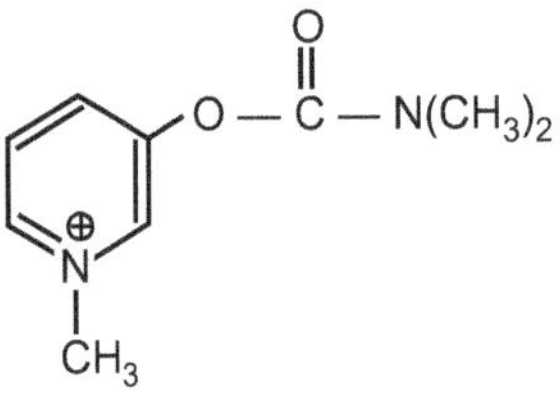 Pyridostigmine	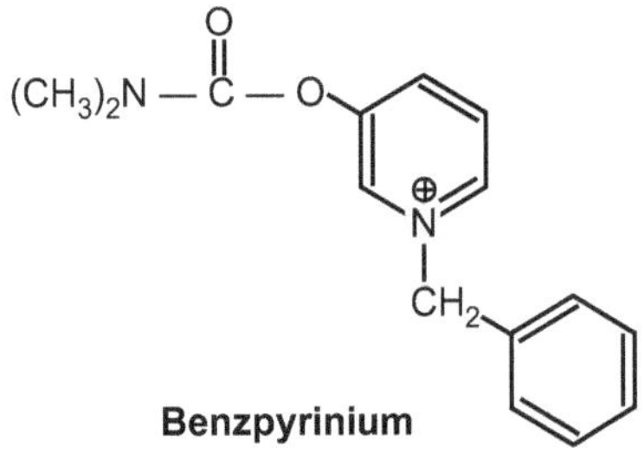 Benzpyrinium
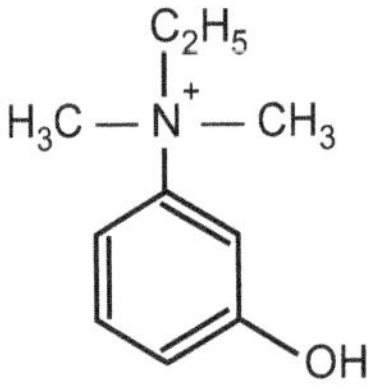 Edrophonium	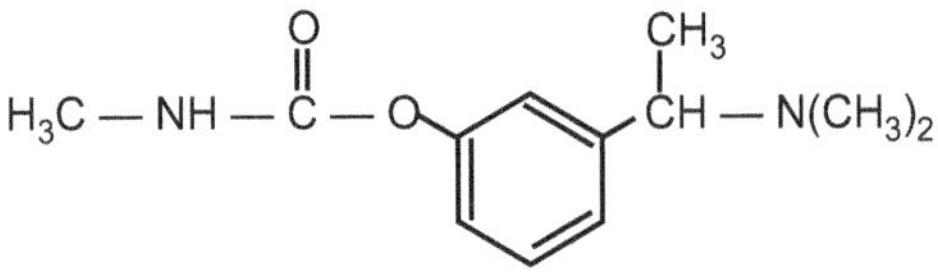 Miotine
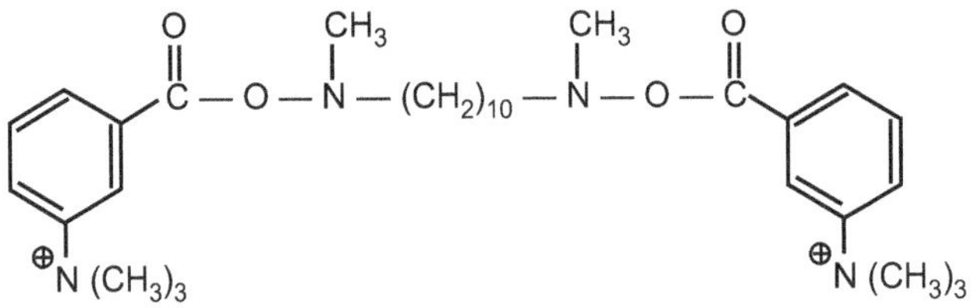 Demecarium (bisneostigmine)	

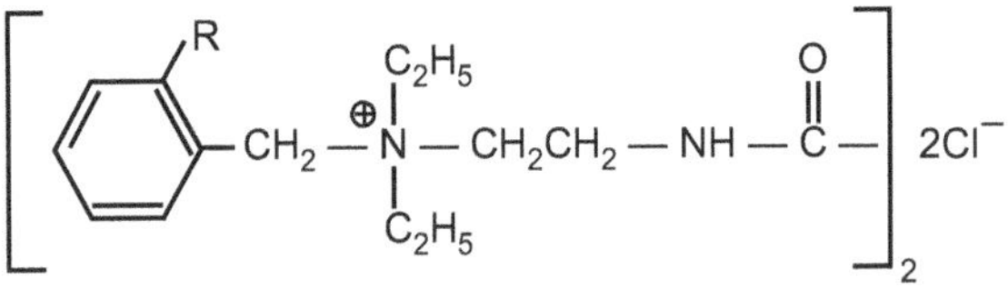

Ambenonium chloride; R = – Cl
Methoxyambenonium chloride; R = – OCH$_3$

(a) Physostigmine (Eserine) :

It is a naturally occuring alkaloid, isolated from the Calabar bean, the dried ripe seeds of Physostigma venenosum. The alkaloid content of these seeds is estimated to be 0.15%. It was named as physostigmine by Jobst and Hesse when they isolated it in a pure form in 1864. Its structure was elucidated in 1925 by Stedman and Barger. Chemically, it is a methylaminocarbamic acid ester of oxyphenyl attached to two heterocyclic rings. The first clinical use of physostigmine was made by Laqueur in 1877 to treat glaucoma.

It reversibly antagonises the activity of cholinesterase enzyme. It also competitively antagonises the action of curare on skeletal muscle by increasing the concentration of acetylcholine. If administered in large doses, it can cross blood-brain-barrier and reaches the CNS where it first stimulates and then depresses the CNS. It is for this reason, it was replaced in the treatment of myasthenia gravis by other cholinesterase inhibitors having quaternary amino function which do not significantly reach the CNS.

In general, physostigmine is a powerful stimulant to the organs innervated by cholinergic nerves. It can inhibit the cholinesterase enzymes when present in the concentrations as low as 10^{-6} moles.

(b) Synthetic Analogues :

The anticholinesterase activity associated with physostigmine, a naturally occurring alkaloid, serves as a stimulus to carry out a systematic investigation of a series of substituted phenyl esters of alkyl carbamic acids. Aeschlimann and Reinert developed a series of carbamic acid esters devoid of the heterocyclic rings and screened out neostigmine, a most promising member of the series which was introduced into clinical practice in 1931. Upto 1950, many series of heterocyclic, aromatic and naphthyl carbamates were synthesized and evaluated for anticholinesterase activity.

These synthetic reversible anticholinesterases fall into two chemical groups, namely,

(i) Carbamates and

(ii) Monoquaternary and bis-quaternary amines.

(i) Carbamates : Neostigmine, pyridostigmine, benzpyrinium, miotine, constitute examples of this category. Carbamates are water soluble and can be represented by following general formula,

$$R_2 - \underset{\underset{R_1}{|}}{N} - \underset{\underset{}{\overset{\overset{O}{\|}}{}}}{C} - O - R_3$$

Carbamates

where,

R_2 and R_3 = H atom or organic radicals

R_3 = aromatic amine or ring containing quaternary nitrogen

Generally the ester linkage

$$-N - \overset{\overset{O}{\|}}{C} - O -$$

(R_1 R_2 — N — C — O is attached meta to nitrogen atom present in the aromatic ring (R_3). Moving the position of the carbamic ester to ortho or para position however does not increase the potency of the compound.

(ii) Neostigmine : It is the first synthetic carbamate ester which is employed clinically. The drug does not cross easily Blood-Brain- Barrier and exerts its anticholinesterase activity mainly at peripheral sites. The presence of quaternary N-atom qualifies the drug to activate both, muscarinic and nicotinic receptor sites due to which it is preferred for its effects at the neuromuscular junctions.

Neostigmine has some direct acetylcholinomimetic activity. It can cause direct stimulation of nicotinic receptors on skeletal muscles. This property explains its anticurare activity. The dose required to remove a curare block is some what higher than that needed to increase the amplitude and duration of end-plate potenials. The anticurare activity of neostigmine can be attributed to both the quaternary nitrogen and to the carbamate ester group. Neostigmine does not evoke direct action on the autonomic effector organs. For oral administration, the drug is presented in the form of neostigmine bromide.

(ii) Edrophonium:

Like neostigmine, edrophonium also possesses a direct stimulant action on the skeletal neuro-muscular junction. It has a very powerful anticurare action. It acts competitively and displaces curare from the receptor sites present on the motor end-plate. It is the most widely employed agent to reverse curare induced paralysis of skeletal muscles. In contrast to other reversible anticholinesterases, it interacts only at anionic site of the enzyme and hence possesses much shorter onset and duration of action than neostigmine.

(iii) Pyridostigmine : Pyridostigmine and benzpyrinium, both are yet other examples of carbamate esters. They have slightly longer duration of action and exhibit good oral absorption pattern. They are quite safe and possess less side-effects after oral absorption.

(iv) Ambenonium and demecarium : These are the examples of bis-quaternary compounds. They have greater duration of action and have about 6 – 7 times more potent anticholinesterase activity than neostigmine.

Structure-Activity Relationship of Reverisble Anticholinesterases :

(i) The distance across the ether oxygen and nitrogen atom is approximately same as that between the ether oxygen and nitrogen atom in acetylcholine.

(ii) The size and nature of the substituents on the tertiary or quaternary nitrogen atom play an important role in determining the potency of the molecule.

(iii) In-vivo, the carbamate esters can inhibit the enzyme for about 3 - 4 hours. The absence of carbamyl group results into less potency and shorter duration of action, e.g. edrophonium.

(iv) The phenyl carbamate moiety may not be needed for anticholinesterase activity. Demecarium serves as an exception.

(v) The presence of bisquaternary moiety results in an increase in the anticholinesterase potency and duration of activity. e.g., demecarium, ambenonium etc.

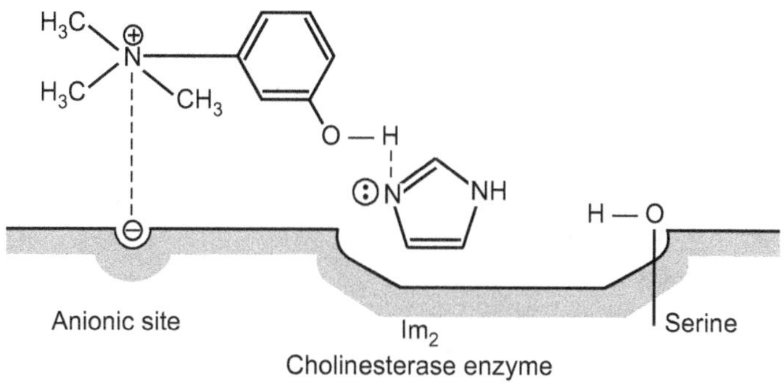

Fig. 14.4 : Edrophonium – enzyme interaction

(vi) The two heterocyclic rings of physostigmine are not essential for anticholinesterase activity. During hydrolysis, the phenolic fragment of this drug is eliminated, leaving the carbamoyl group attached to the enzyme. The rate of hydrolysis of carbamoyl group is about 60 times less than the rate of hydrolysis of acyl group of acetylcholine.

II. Irreversible Anticholinesterases:

The organic esters of phosphoric acids had been used as insecticide from many years. Clermont, in 1854, first reported the synthetic accounts of a highly potent agent from the organophosphate series. It was named as TEPP (i.e., tetraethyl pyrophosphate). The interest in its anticholinesterase activity was arosed mainly due to the work of Schrader on organophosphate series and recommended their use as chemical warfare agents during World War II due to their potent cholinesterase inhibiting activity.

The organophosphates are not specific in their action. Along with cholinestrases, other carboxylic esterases are also inhibited like, the lipases, trypsin enzymes. Most of these compounds are equally effective against both the types of cholinesterases.

Organophosphorus compounds combine only with esteratic site of cholinesterases and the esteratic site is phosphorylated. The hydrolysis of this phosphorylated site, however, is extremely slow which produces a long term inhibition of cholinesterases. In contrast to other organophosphorus compounds, echothiophate possesses a quaternary nitrogen. It differs from rest of the organophosphrous agents in following points.

(a) Echothiophate does not cross readily blood-brain-barriers and does not cause central effects, and

(b) It forms complex with both anionic and esteratic sites and hence is much more potent.

$$(CH_3)_3 - \overset{\oplus}{N} - CH_2 - CH_2 - S - \overset{\overset{O}{\uparrow}}{P} - (OC_2H_5)_2$$

Echothiophate

A number of phosphate, pyrophosphate and phosphonate esters apparently react irreversibly with cholinesterase by forming phosphate ester with the esteratic site. Because the rate of hydrolysis of the phosphorylated enzyme is measured in hours, these compounds are therefore termed as 'irreversible anticholinesterases'. The hydrolysis rate of the phosphorylated serine is extremely slow and hydrolysis to the free enzyme and phosphoric acid derivative is so limited that the inhibition is considered irreversible.

The process of cholinesterase inhibition by organophosphorous compounds is two step reaction. The compound forms a reversible complex with the enzyme in the first step, which can readily dissociate back into active enzyme and the compound.

The reversible complex then immediately is converted into an irreversible complex. The esteratic site of the enzyme gets firmly phosphorylated. The stability of this phosphorylated enzyme causes hydrolysis to proceed very slowly. Various other enzymes present in the liver, kidney and other tissues can also be nonspecifically blocked by organophosphate compounds.

Organophosphorus compounds are very lipid-soluble which enable them to reach the CNS and exert central effects, except echothiophate which possesses, ionic nature due to the presence of quaternary amino group.

Parathion was synthesized by Schrader in 1944. Both, parathion and melathion are thionophosphates and are virtually inactive when tested for cholinesterase inhibiting activity in-vitro. When administered, they are converted in-vivo to the active metabolites in which the sulfur atom is replaced by oxygen.

Due to their high lipophilicity, these compounds can easily penetrate into the CNS and give rise to pronounced central effects. The sulfur containing organophosphates undergo metabolic changes yielding sulphones and sulphoxides. These metabolites are inactive and possess high toxicity.

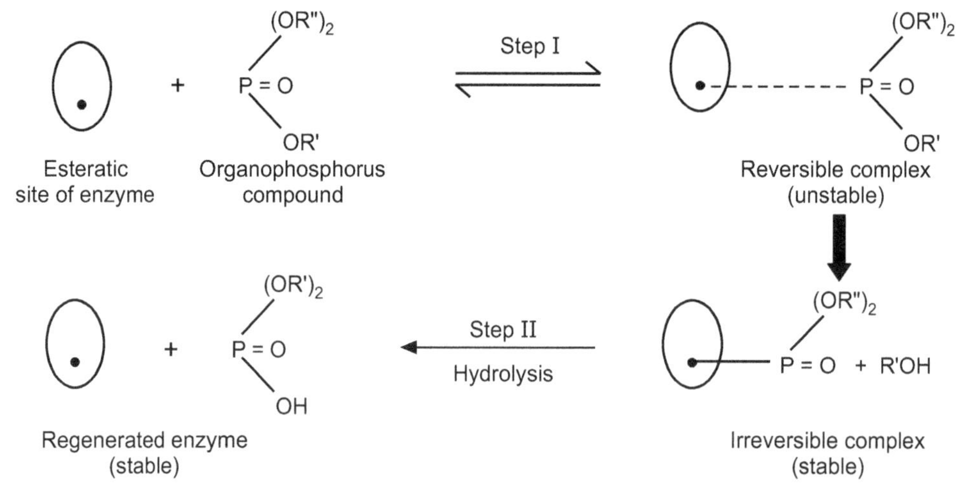

Fig. 14.5 : Action of irreversible anticholinesterase

Table 14.2 : Some irreversible anticholinesterase agents

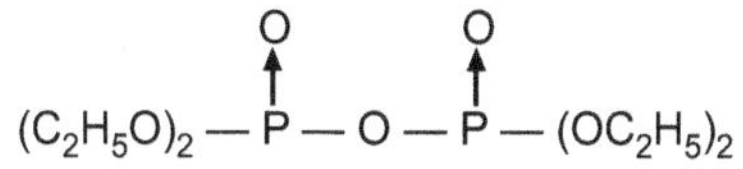

Tetraethyl pyrophosphate

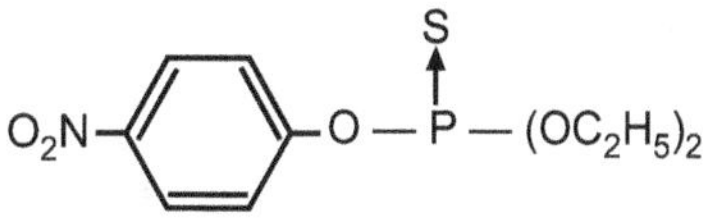

$(C_2H_5O)_2-\overset{\overset{O}{\uparrow}}{P}-O-\overset{\overset{O}{\uparrow}}{P}-(OC_2H_5)_2$

Parathion

$O_2N-\underset{}{\bigcirc}-O-\overset{\overset{S}{\uparrow}}{P}-(OC_2H_5)_2$

Melathion

$(CH_3O)_2-\overset{\overset{S}{\|}}{P}-S-\underset{\underset{\underset{O}{\|}}{CH_2-C-OC_2H_5}}{CH}-\overset{\overset{O}{\|}}{C}-OC_2H_5$

Paraoxon

$O_2N-\underset{}{\bigcirc}-O-\overset{\overset{O}{\uparrow}}{P}-(OC_2H_5)_2$

Dipterex

$(CH_3O)_2-\overset{\overset{O}{\uparrow}}{P}-\underset{OH}{CH}-\underset{Cl}{\overset{Cl}{C}}-Cl$

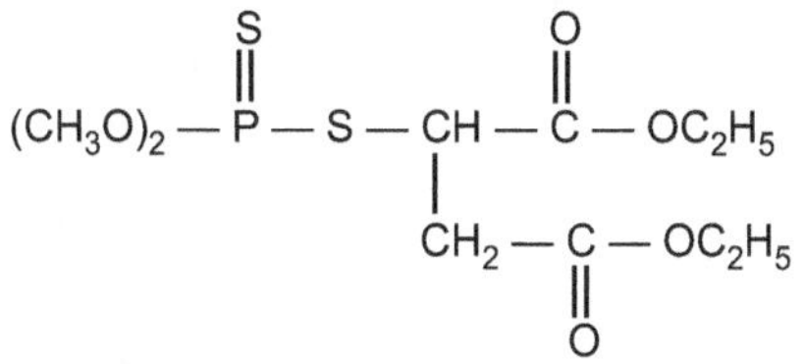

Schradran

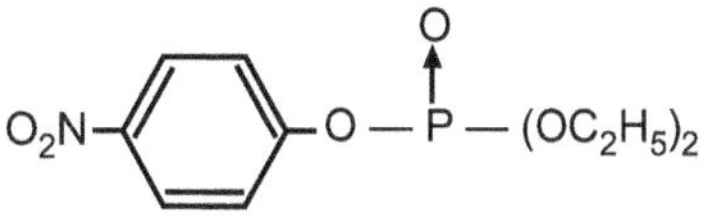

$[(CH_3)_2N]_2-\overset{\overset{O}{\uparrow}}{P}-O-\overset{\overset{O}{\uparrow}}{P}-[N(CH_3)_2]_2$

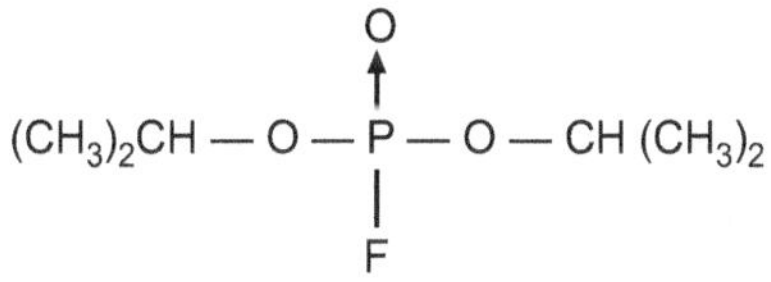

Di-isopropylfluorophosphate

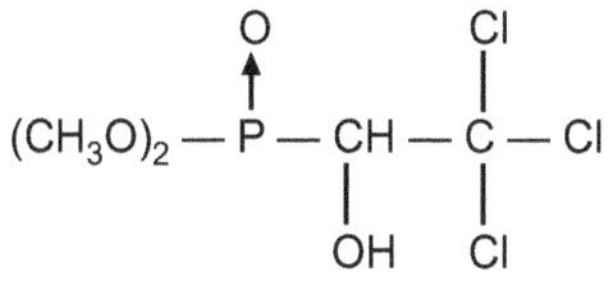

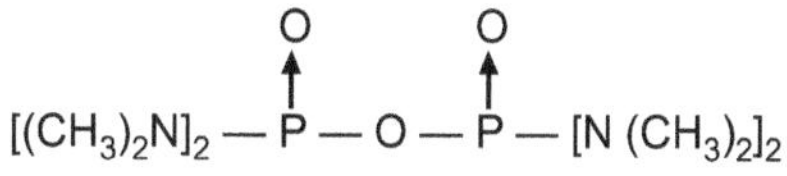

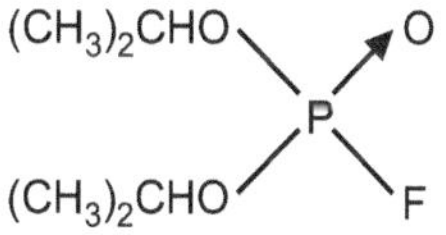

$(CH_3)_2CH-O-\underset{F}{\overset{\overset{O}{\uparrow}}{P}}-O-CH(CH_3)_2$

Isoflurophate

$(CH_3)_2CHO\diagdown \overset{\nearrow O}{\underset{\diagdown F}{P}}$
$(CH_3)_2CHO\diagup$

Mipafox

$(CH_3)_2CHNH\diagdown \overset{\nearrow O}{\underset{\diagdown F}{P}}$
$(CH_3)_2CHNH\diagup$

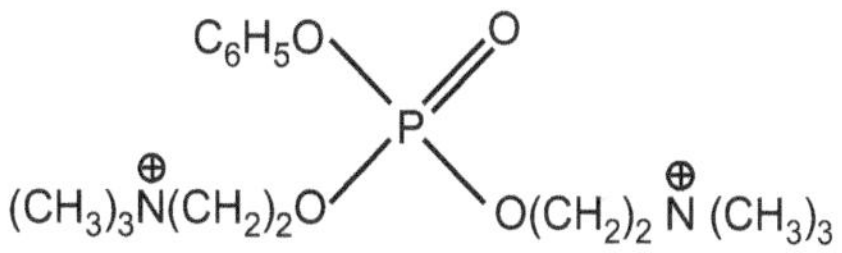

Phenoxyphosphoryl dicholine

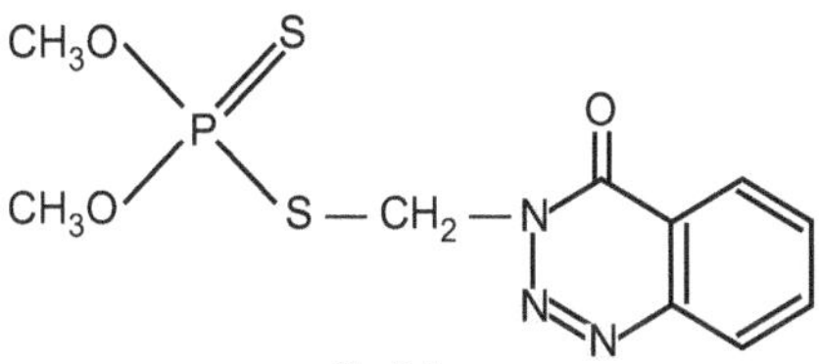

$C_6H_5O\diagdown \overset{\nearrow O}{\underset{\diagdown O(CH_2)_2\overset{\oplus}{N}(CH_3)_3}{P}}$
$(CH_3)_3\overset{\oplus}{N}(CH_2)_2O\diagup$

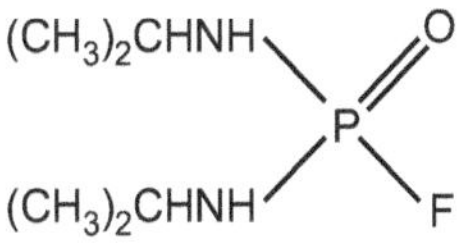

Guthion

$CH_3O\diagdown \overset{\nearrow S}{\underset{\diagdown S-CH_2-N}{P}}$
$CH_3O\diagup$
(attached to benzotriazinone ring)

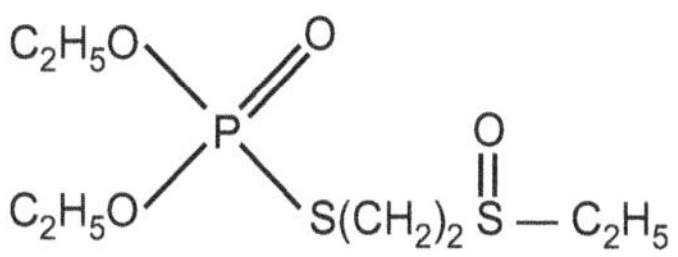

Isosystox

$C_2H_5O\diagdown \overset{\nearrow O}{\underset{\diagdown S(CH_2)_2\overset{\overset{O}{\|}}{S}-C_2H_5}{P}}$
$C_2H_5O\diagup$

Structure-Activity Relationship of Irreversible Anticholinesterases :

A general formula for these compounds is as follows :

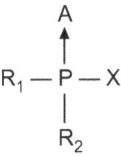

where R_1 = alkoxyl

R_2 = alkoxyl, alkyl or tertiary amine,

X = A good leaving group,

e.g. F, CN, p-nitrophenoxy.

(i) A is usually oxygen or sulphur, but may also be selenium. When A is other than oxygen, biological activation is required before compound becomes effective.

(ii) X is good leaving group when the molecule reacts with the enzyme.

(iii) The quaternary organophosphorous compounds are the most potent members of this category.

(iv) The R moiety imparts lipophilicity to the molecule and contributes its absorption through the skin. If it is methyl or ethyl, it inhibits the enzyme for several hours. If R is secondary or tertiary alkyl group, the inhibition of the enzyme is so strong that, body has to synthesize new enzymes to restore the cholinesterase activity.

(v) In alkoxy series, compounds containing fluorine atom are the most potent agents. In general, monalkoxy substituted compounds are more effective anticholinesterases than the symmetrical dialkoxy compound.

These compounds are very toxic to humans and must be handled with extreme caution. Toxic symptoms include nausea, vomiting, excessive sweating, salivation, miosis, bradycardia, low blood pressure and respiratory difficulty which is usually the cause of death. The respiratory failure is mainly due to,

(a) excessive salivary and branchial secretions.

(b) bronchoconstriction.

(c) neuromuscular blockade of the respiratory muscles and

(d) respiratory failure due to the central effects.

Alongwith the depression of the respiratory centres, central effects include disturbances of sleep, tremor, ataxia, hallucination, coma, convulsions and death. Due to the widespread distribution of cholinergic neurons throughout the CNS and periphery regions, if used in high doses, they prove to be fatal. Hence, they are also known as nerve poisons or nerve gases. Even though they do not exist in gaseous state, they can be distributed in the aerosol form for better absorption.

14.5 ABSORPTION AND METABOLISM

The carbamate anticholinesterases having a tertiary amine, are readily absorbed after oral administration and due to their nonionic nature, get well distributed in the body fluids. While carbamates with a quaternary amine, due to their ionic nature, are poorly absorbed from GIT. Some drugs like, neostigmine or pyridostigmine are effectively absorbed if their oral dose is increased significantly.

Due to the high lipophilicity, irreversible anticholinesterases can be readily absorbed from GIT, subcutaneous tissues and mucous membrane and distributed in the body compartments. The naturally occurring alkaloid, physostigmine and most organophosphorous compounds readily enter the CNS.

The various metabolizing enzymes present in the plasma, kidney, liver and lungs detoxify the carbamates and the organophosphorous compounds into inactive products. Metabolites of neostigmine, pyridostigmine and edrophonium alongwith a significant amount of parent compounds are eliminated through the urine while organophosphorous compounds are metabolized by specific enzymes known as paroxonase.

14.6 THERAPEUTIC USES

The cholinesterase inhibitors find their clinical uses mainly due to their following basic properties :

(1) They activate muscarinic receptors by accumulating acetylcholine at the receptor sites.

(2) Activation of nicotinic receptor sites leads to stimulation, followed by depression or paralysis of skeletal muscles.

(3) Activation of muscarinic receptors in the CNS leads to stimulation followed by depression of the centrally governed cholinergic effects.

The cholinesterase inhibitors are recommended under following condition,

(a) glaucoma.
(b) myasthenia gravis.
(c) curare induced neuromuscular blockade.

(a) Glaucoma :

It arises due to the increased intraocular pressure of aqueous humor due to either increased secretion of humor or drainage block. If remains untreated, the increased intraocular pressure may damage the optic disc at the juncture of the optic nerve and retina and may lead to permanent blindness. The primary glaucoma is categorized into,

angle closure glaucoma
and open angle glaucoma.

Short acting agents such as physostigmine or neostigmine is applied locally as 0.25 –1.0% solution to the eye in the treatment of primary angle-closure glaucoma. Sometimes these agents are used in combination with pilocarpine. Recently the use of non-selective β-adrenergic blocker like timolol, is also tried successfully in the treatment of open-angle glaucoma. If either short-acting cholinesterase inhibitor or timolol fails to cure glaucoma, then other long-acting anticholinesterases (e.g., demecarium, paraoxon or echothiophate) or certain carbonic anhydrase inhibitor may be effective.

The primary ocular effects of these agents are mainly due to the accumulation of acetylcholine at muscarinic receptor sites and include, miosis, fall in intraocular pressure, dimness of vision, eyelid twitch and cataract.

(b) Myasthenia Gravis :

These agents can be used for both, diagnosis and treatment of myasthenia gravis, a skeletal muscle disorder. It is a chronic disease arising due to failure of acetylcholine to attain effective concentration at end-plate region of the skeletal muscle. This results into a weak muscle tone and easy muscle fatiqueness. If remains untreated, in severe conditions, it may result into a permanent muscular paralysis.

The muscles of head and neck are first affected followed by dysphagia and dysarthria. The etiology of the disease include morphological, electrophysiological or bio-chemical abnormalities in the end-plate region due to genetic alteration in the thymic cell function. An autoimmune reaction is generated which leads to the cholinergic receptors degradation with subsequent decrease in the receptor population at the end-plate region.

Use of anticholinesterases lead to an accumulation of acetylcholine at the end-plate region resulting into increased contact time of ACh in the synapses. Though it is so, the administration of choline or acetylcholine as such, does not help to recover the condition. Both, edrophonium and neostigmine can be used for the diagnostic purpose and to differentiate myasthenic crisis (condition due to inadequate therapy) from cholinergic crisis (condition due to overdose of cholinesterase inhibitor). Neostigmine does not enter the CNS and it has its own direct cholinomimetic action. These advantages lift neostigmine as a drug of choice in myasthenia gravis. It mainly acts by,

(i) Direct cholinomimetic action on skeletal muscles.

(ii) Inhibiting cholinesterases and increasing residence time for acetylcholine and

(iii) Increasing blood potassium level by shifting potassium from the muscles.

Orally it may be used in the dose range of 10 - 350 mg depending upon the severity of the condition. It may also be given intravenously or intramuscularly to potentiate the effects or in cases where oral administration is not possible. In larger doses, effects are so potentiated that depression or neuromuscular blockade is reported to occur due to persistent depolarization of the cell-membrane. The side-effects are mainly due to activation of muscarinic receptors which can be minimised by the use of atropine.

At neuromuscular junction, sympothomimetic amines potentiate the action of acetylcholine, resulting into a decurarizing action against fatigue. Hence, ephedrine sometimes, may be orally administered with a dose of 25 - 30 mg thrice a day. In long-term treatment, to reduce frequency of doses, usually long-acting agent like pyridostigmine is preferred over neostigmine.

The curare-induced neuromuscular blockade and myasthenia gravis share some features in common. Hence, the drugs having decurarizing activity will be equally effective in the treatment of myasthenia gravis. This concept was confirmed by Mary Walker, who successfully employed physostigmine in the treatment of the disease. Similarly other anticholinesterases act as decurazing drugs and by increasing the concentration of acetylcholine, break the neuromuscular blockade through competitive antagonism.

In severe condition, alongwith the drug treatment, other measures such as thymectomy and corticoidal therapy, if employed, may improve the situation. On the other hand, quinine if given, antagonises the cholinomimetic effects at skeletal muscle and is contraindicated in myasthenia gravis.

(c) GIT and Urologic Disorders :

Neostigmine enhances the muscle tone and peristalsis. Hence, it is used to treat the postoperative abdominal distention or urinary retention.

(d) In anesthesiology, anticholinesterases find their application to reverse the neuromuscular blockade, caused by non-depolarizing curare-like agents. In such cases, neostigmine, pyridostigmine and edrophonium are generally used.

The acute toxicity due to anticholinesterases mainly include the signs of muscarinic stimulation and can be treated well by atropine or scopolamine. Atropine in sufficient dosage, effectively antagonizes the actions at muscarinic receptor sites. While larger doses are needed for atropine to get entry in the CNS.

14.7 CHOLINESTERASE REACTIVATORS

When an irreversible anticholinesterase is used, it combines with cholinesterase and the hydroxyl (OH) group of the serine moiety gets phosphorylated. It was usually considered that water in body fluids attacks the phosphorylated serine residue and causes its hydrolysis. But the rate of hydrolysis is very slow and that a more effective dephosphorylating agent was required for rapid hydrolysis i.e. it involves the administration of a better nucleophile than water to attack the phosphorus atom and thereby eliminate or liberate the enzyme back to its original form, as shown in Fig. 14.6.

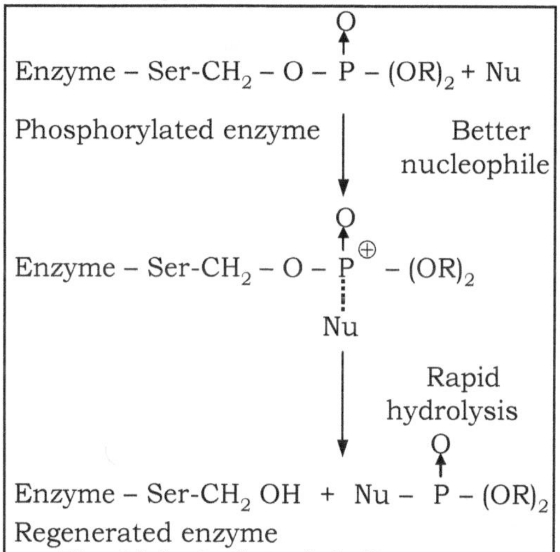

```
Enzyme – Ser-CH₂ – O – P(=O) – (OR)₂ + Nu
Phosphorylated enzyme          | Better nucleophile
                               ↓
Enzyme – Ser-CH₂ – O – P⁺(=O) – (OR)₂
                        ⋮
                        Nu
                               | Rapid hydrolysis
                               ↓
Enzyme – Ser-CH₂ OH  +  Nu – P(=O) – (OR)₂
Regenerated enzyme
```

Fig. 14.6 : Action of cholinesterase reactivator

The effective cholinesterase reactivator or antidotes for irreversible anticholinesterases developed are as follows :

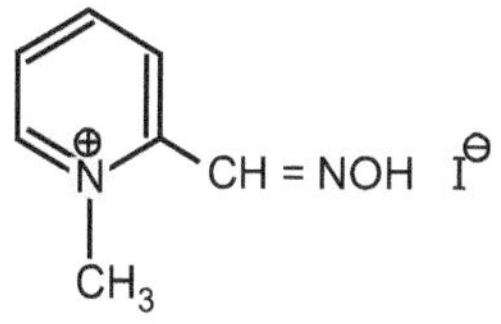

[Structure: N-methylpyridinium-2-CH=NOH I⁻]

2-pyridine aldoxime methiodide
(2-PAM or pralidoxime)

For a good reactivating property, the compound should have a strong nucleophilic nature. Wilson (1951) developed various hydroxylamine (H_2N-OH), hydroxamic acids (RCONHOH) and oximes (RCH = HOH) and evaluated their reactivating capacity. He found that these compounds promote the reactivation of the phosphorylated enzyme much more rapidly than does the in vivo natural hydrolysis. Pralidoxime, a most commonly used rectivator, is synthesized in 1955 by Wilson and Ginsburg. It is a quaternary amine and hence can not reach CNS. It can not reactivate centrally located cholinesterases. But, it has a good reactivating potency at neuromuscular junction and peripherally located muscarinic sites. It is available as a powder with a sterile water diluent and is usually administered by i.v. infusion. Other examples include,

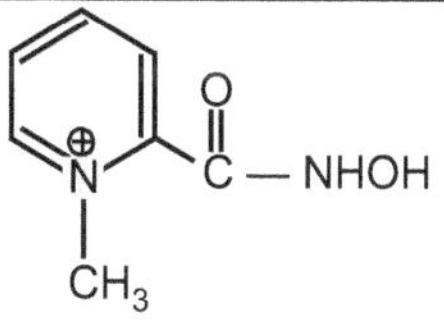

[Structure: N-methylpyridinium-2-C(=O)-NHOH]

2-Pyridine hydroxamic acid methiodide

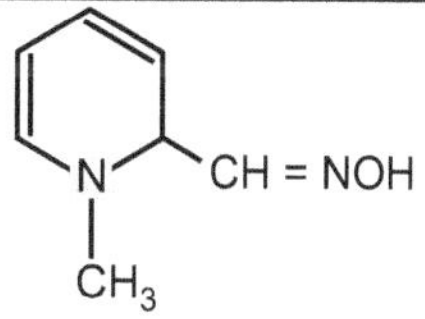

$$H_3C - \overset{O}{\underset{\|}{C}} - \overset{R}{\underset{|}{C}} = NOH$$

[Structure: Dihydropyridine-N-methyl-2-CH=NOH]

Dihydro 2-Pyridine aldoxime methiodide

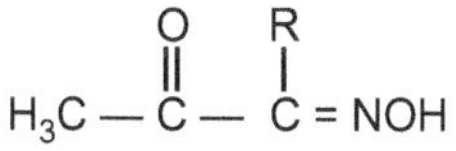

R = CH₃ ; Diacetylmonoxime
R = H ; Pyruvaldoxime

A number of bis–quaternary oximes were developed which were found to possess a good reactivating potency.

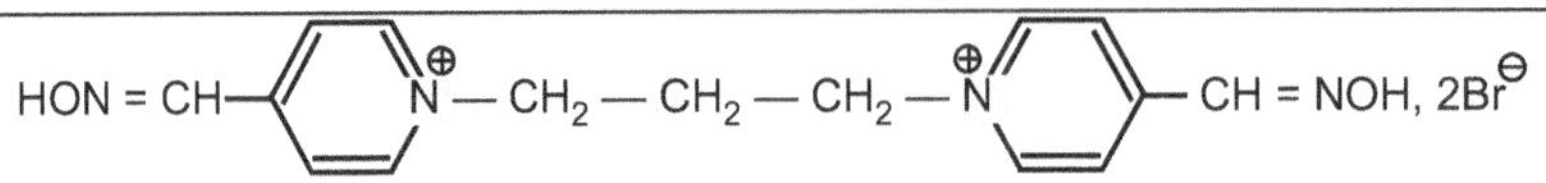

$$HON=CH-\text{[pyridinium]}-N^{\oplus}-CH_2-CH_2-CH_2-N^{\oplus}-\text{[pyridinium]}-CH=NOH, 2Br^{\ominus}$$

1, 3 bis (pyridinium - 4 - aldoxime) propane dibromide

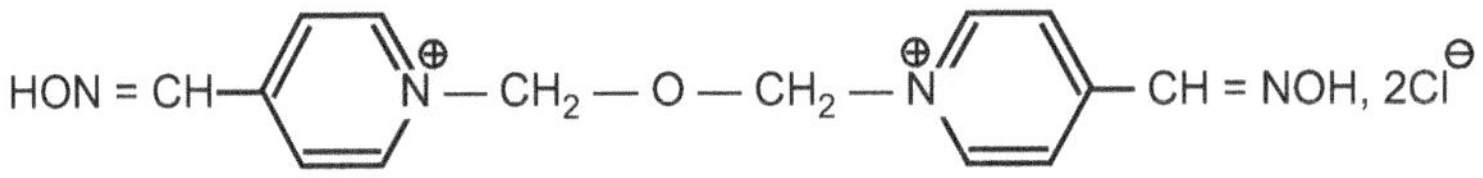

$$HON=CH-\text{[pyridinium]}-N^{\oplus}-CH_2-O-CH_2-N^{\oplus}-\text{[pyridinium]}-CH=NOH, 2Cl^{\ominus}$$

Obidoxime chloride (Toxogenin)

The reactivating property of oximes and hydroxamic acids invivo is well marked at the neuromuscular junction and autonomic effector sites. For example, the peripheral neuromuscular blockade can be reversed by pralidoxime. Due to the presence of a quaternary nitrogen in the structure, they can not reach the CNS and hence CNS effects of the drugs are insignificant.

To potentiate the action of oximes, atropine is also used alongwith. Atropine acts as a competitive antagonist for the accumulated acetylcholine at muscarinic sites.

14.8 LIMITATIONS OF OXIMES

(i) These are not effective if they are given immediately before or soon after the exposure to the inhibitor. The phosphorylated enzyme undergoes a fairly rapid process, called as 'ageing' (which probably involves the loss of an alkyl part of alkoxy group) as a result of which it becomes resistant to the action of the antidote.

The rate of ageing is governed by both, the nature of the enzyme and the anticholinesterase employed. Generally the organophosphonates containing tertiary alkoxy group are more suceptible to 'ageing' than are the primary or secondary congeners.

(ii) The reactivators are not very successful in restoring cholinesterase activity in CNS.

(iii) The oximes are not effective reactivators for the cholinesterase activity in CNS.

(iv) They are not effective against all organophosphonates the toxicity of few of which is actually increased by the oximes.

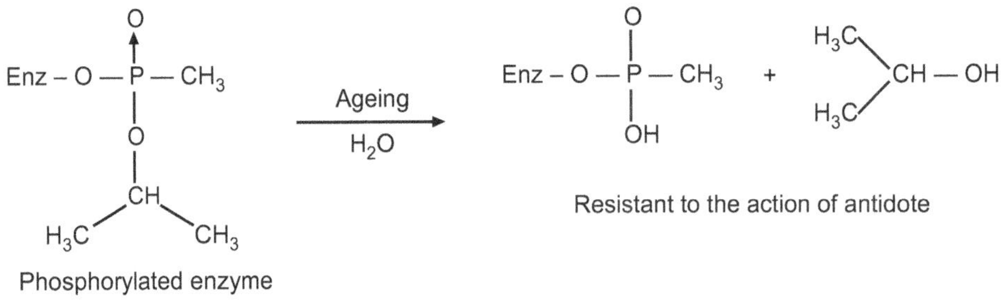

$$\text{Enz}-O-\underset{\underset{\underset{H_3C}{\overset{|}{CH}}}{\overset{|}{O}}}{\overset{\overset{O}{\uparrow}}{P}}-CH_3 \xrightarrow[H_2O]{\text{Ageing}} \text{Enz}-O-\underset{\overset{|}{OH}}{\overset{\overset{O}{\uparrow}}{P}}-CH_3 + \underset{H_3C}{\overset{H_3C}{>}}CH-OH$$

Phosphorylated enzyme Resistant to the action of antidote

Fig. 14.7 : Ageing process

❖❖❖

ANTI-MUSCARINIC AGENTS

15.1 INTRODUCTION

Two obvious approaches are there, to treat the conditions characterised by overstimulation of cholinergic nerves.

I. Use of agents that inhibit the synthesis or release of acetylcholine.

II. Use of agents that block the acetylcholine from reacting with the receptors.

Compounds that inhibit acetylcholine synthesis have been discovered but have not proved to be clinically useful. Hemicholinium is such a drug that interferes with acetylcholine biosynthesis. While drugs that block the interaction of acetylcholine with the receptor, however, are widely employed in medicine. These drugs are of three types.

(a) Those who block the transmission at parasympathetic post-synaptic nerve terminals e.g., Atropine

(b) Those who block the transmission of sympathetic and parasympathetic ganglia. e.g., Hexamethonium

(c) Those who block neuromuscular junctional receptors in skeletal muscles. e.g., d-tubocurarine.

Such compounds have the opposite effects to that of cholinergic agonists and their administration should be characterised by decreased secretion of saliva and gastric juices, decreased motility of GIT and urinary tract and dilation of pupil. Because of their ability to relax smooth muscle, they are sometimes referred to as antispasmodic agents. Such compounds should have an affinity for cholinergic receptor but should lack intrinsic activity.

In this chapter, we shall focus our attnention mainly on the drugs that inhibit acetylcholine from reacting with muscarinic receptors i.e., atropine and its analogues.

15.2 NATURAL ALKALOIDS

A number of plants belonging to the potato family, the order Solanacea contains alkaloids which dilate the pupil. These alkaloids hence, were also referred to as the mydriatic alkaloids. They are present prominantly in the leaves of

Atropa belladonna (contain about 0.3% alkaloids)

Hyoscyamus niger (0.04% alkaloid) and Datura stramonium.

These alkaloids include atropine, scopolamine (hyoscine) and other alkaloids of minor importance.

Atropine and Scopolamine : The prototype of parasympathelytic series is atropine. It is the main alkaloid present in the leaves of Atropa belladonna. Due to its poisonous nature, Linneaus called it Atropa, after Atropos, the oldest of the Fates, who cuts the thread of life while the term Bella Donna (means a beautiful woman) was employed due to its local action in the eye causing pupil dilation (mydriasis). The mydriatic action was accidently discovered in 1776 by Daries.

Atropine, in a pure form, was first isolated in 1831 by Mein. Chemically it is an ester of tropic acid with tropanol. Now-a-days it is prepared synthetically. It is mainly used as a racemic mixture of (+) and (−) hyoscyamine.

Atropine (Tropanyl tropate)

Scopolamine and hyoscyamine are the main alkaloids present in the leaves of Hyoscyamus niger and Scopolia carmiolica. Scopolamine is also an ester of tropic acid with scopine. Scopine differs from tropine in having an additional oxygen bridge between C_7 and C_6 atoms. In both atropine and scopolamine, the pharmacologically active isomer is levorotatory.

Scopolamine (Scopinyl tropate)

In atropine, the *l*-isomer is more potent both, peripherally and centrally. However, the racemic mixture is preferred due to its chemical stability. While in scopolamine, only *l*-isomer is pharmacologically active and it is in this form, the drug is given. The inactive d-isomer is known as atroscine which has much weaker pharmacological activity. Both, atropine and scopolamine are the oldest known muscarinic blocking agents. In addition, scopolamine possesses a cerebral depressant activity in all therapeutic doses.

In CNS, muscarinic receptors are present mainly in striatum, hippocampus and cerebral cortex. Beside blocking muscarine receptors present at various sites, if administered in larger doses and with intra-arterial administration these drugs can antagonize ganglionic and neuromuscular transmission.

Many semisynthetic and synthetic congeners of the belladonna alkaloids have been synthesized in a hope to obtain parasympatholytic agents with greater selectivity, different duration of action and less side-effects. They have their pharmacological profiles, resembling very closely to that of atropine with only quantitative differences. Hence, atropine is considered as a prototype of all such compounds and will be discussed in detail.

15.3 MECHANISM OF ACTION

The antimuscarinic agents or atropine-like drugs antagonise the actions of acetylcholine at muscarinic receptors through competative antagonism. In therapeutic doses, they have little effect at nicotinic cholinergic receptors. However the synthetic antimuscarinic drugs, especially quaternary ammonium compounds interfere partly with ganglionic or neuromuscular transmission by inhibiting nicotinic receptors.

In CNS, these drugs block the muscarinic receptors present mainly in subcortical and cortical regions. Hence, the available acetylcholine naturally has to react with the nicotinic receptors present in subcortical, cortical and spinal cord region, accounting for the central effects of this class of drugs. For example, the sub-type, M_1-receptors are predominantly present in corpus striatum, cerebral cortex, hippocampus and at autonomic ganglia. Their activation results in generation of Ca^{++} fluxes and some phosphorylated derivatives of inositol. While the sub-type, M_2-receptors regulate the actions of acetylcholine in heart, cerebellum, ileum and at cholinergic and some adrenergic nerve terminals.

The main difference in cholinergic and anticholinergic agents appears to be the size of the acyl group.

$$R-\overset{\overset{O}{\|}}{C}-O-CH_2-CH_2-N(R')_2$$

In cholinergic compounds, R = small group.

In anticholinergic compounds, R = large group.

The large alkyl or aryl group (R), may not only increases the affinity of the blocking agent to the receptor but through an 'Umbrella effect' may also block the approach of acetylcholine to the receptor sites. The presence of free hydroxyl group in the acyl portion of the molecule further strengthens the binding of drug with the receptor. The administered antimuscarinic drug (with some losses due to diffusion at receptor sites) block the receptor sites through competitive antagonism, hence by increasing the concentration of acetylcholine at receptor sites may terminate the blocking action of these drugs.

In addition to acetylcholine, antimuscarinic drugs also are reported to decrease the responses of other neurotransmitters like, histamine, serotonin and norepinephrine, if given in large doses.

Beckett proposed that, the muscarinic receptors contain three bioactive positions comprising of one anionic and two cationic sites which are separated by optimal distances as shown in the following figure.

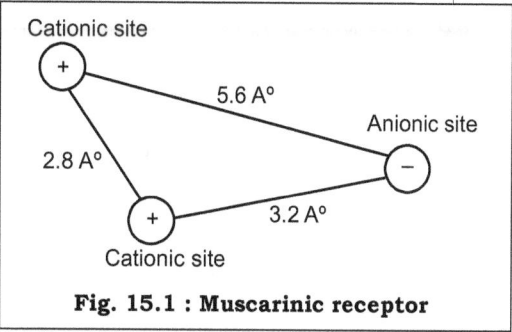

Fig. 15.1 : Muscarinic receptor

The antimuscarinic drugs also contain three bioactive groups which fit the receptor by interacting the corresponding sites present on the receptor surface. This drug receptor complex is comparatively stable and gets slowly degraded.

15.4 ABSORPTION, DISTRIBUTION AND EXCRETION

Belladonna alkaloids are rapidly absorbed from GIT and from all other sites except from the eye or intact skin. The synthetic quaternary ammonium derivatives, due to their ionic nature, are poorly absorbed (10 - 25%) after oral administration.

Once absorbed into circulation, these drugs get well distributed through all body compartments including placenta. Enzymatic hydrolysis followed by conjugation take place in liver. Atropine has a half-life of about 2.5 hours. About half the drug administered, appears unchanged in the urine while rest is hydrolysed to tropine which appears in its glucuronide form. Traces of atropine may be excreted through various secretions including milk.

15.5 ADVERSE REACTIONS

Atropine is usually administered in the form of atropine sulfate which can be taken orally (0.25 - 1.0 mg) or by subcutaneous injection.

The side effects are mainly due to its unselectivity for site of action and include nausea, vomiting, dry mouth, mydriasis, blurred vision, increase in the body temperature, tachycardia, constipation, urinary retention, delirium and convulsions. These side-effects are also shared by antihistaminics, antipsychotic drugs, tricyclic antidepressants, MAO inhibitors, Lithium and antiparkinson agents due to their same atropine - like behaviour.

15.6 CHEMISTRY

Anticholinergic compounds possess some structural similarity to acetylcholine but contain additional substituents that enhance their binding to the cholinergic receptors.

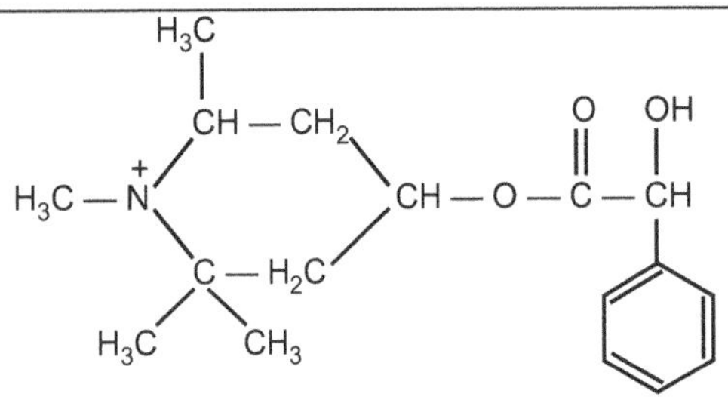

Eucatropine hydrochloride

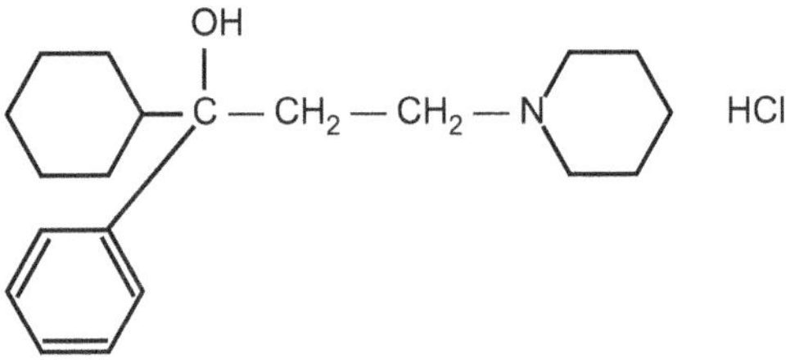

Trihexyphenidyl hydrochloride

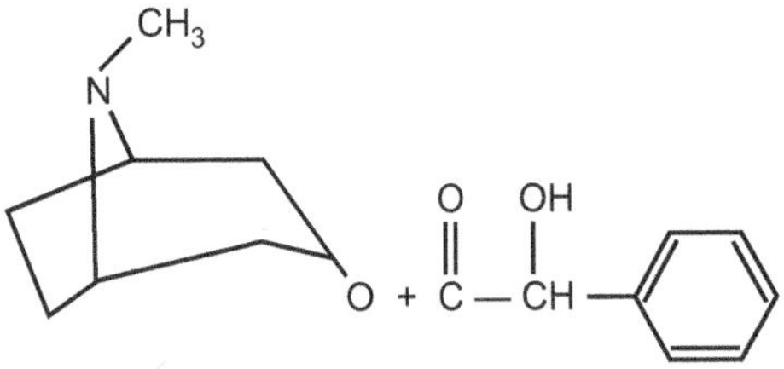

Homatropine

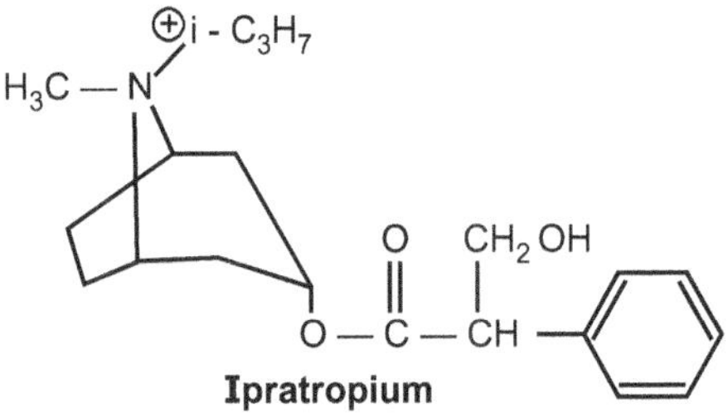

Ipratropium

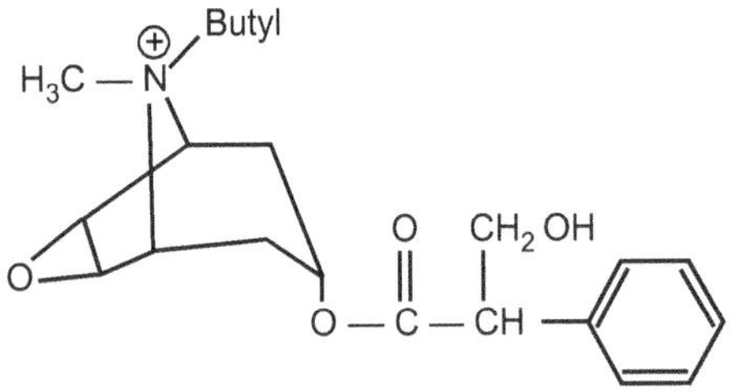

Buscopan bromide

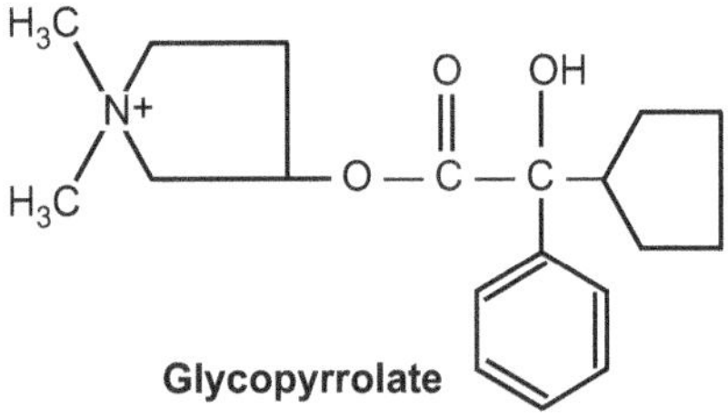

Glycopyrrolate

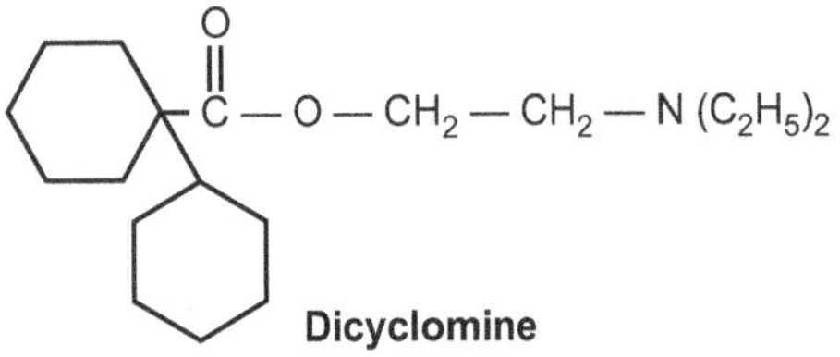

Dicyclomine

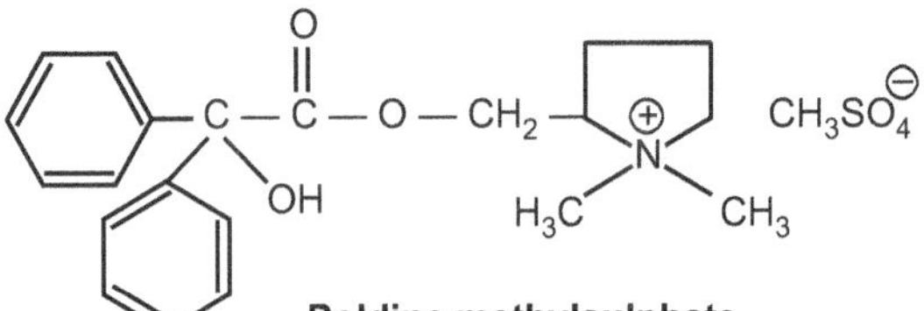

Poldine methylsulphate

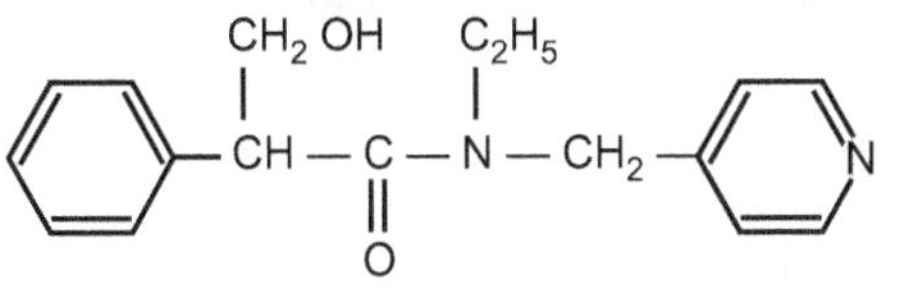

Structures

Tropicamide:

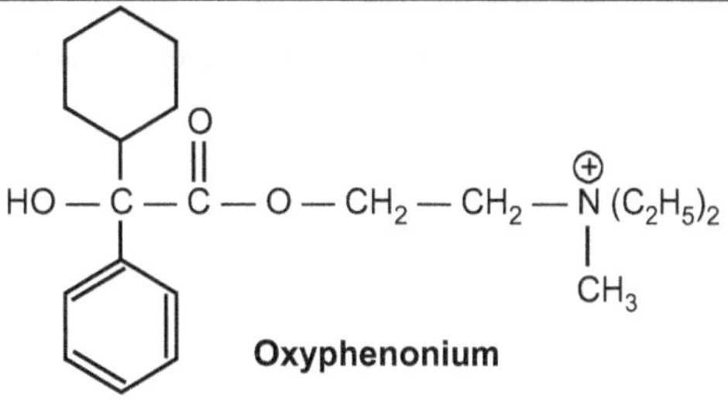

Ph–CH(CH₂OH)–C(=O)–N(C₂H₅)–CH₂–(pyridin-4-yl)

Oxyphenonium:

Cyclohexyl–C(OH)(Ph)–C(=O)–O–CH₂–CH₂–N⁺(C₂H₅)₂(CH₃)

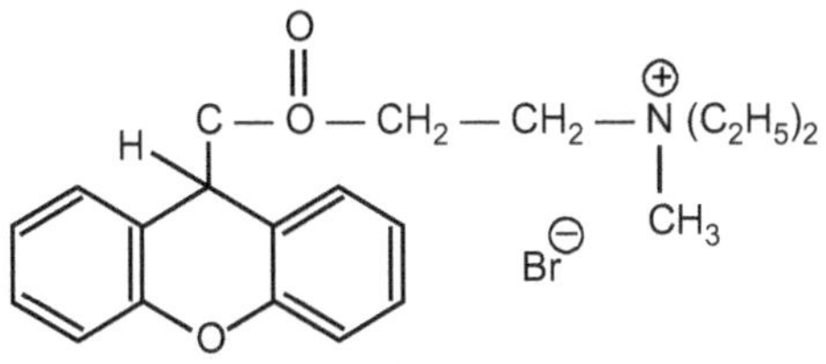

Methantheline bromide: (xanthene-9-yl)–C(=O)–O–CH₂–CH₂–N⁺(C₂H₅)₂(CH₃) Br⁻

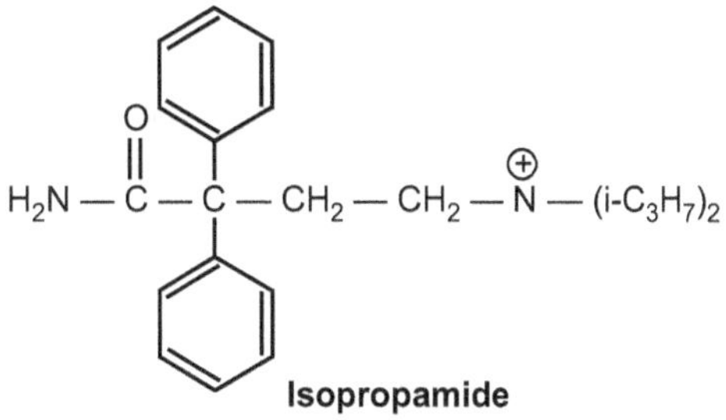

Isopropamide: H₂N–C(=O)–C(Ph)₂–CH₂–CH₂–N⁺(i-C₃H₇)₂

Structure-activity Relationship :

(i) The natural alkaloids, atropine and scopolamine are both tertiary amines and are esters of tropic acid. The high potency of these esters result from their ability to form H-bonding with a suitable group on the receptor, surrounded by the hydrophobic area.

(ii) An aromatic ring, an asymmetric carbon atom and an alcoholic hydroxylic group are essential features for anticholinergic agents. Neither tropine nor tropic acid is essentially required for the activity. Acetic acid, mandelic acid or benzilic acid can be used instead of tropic acid to produce simpler structures.

(iii) Minimum structure necessary for pure antagonistic activity is –

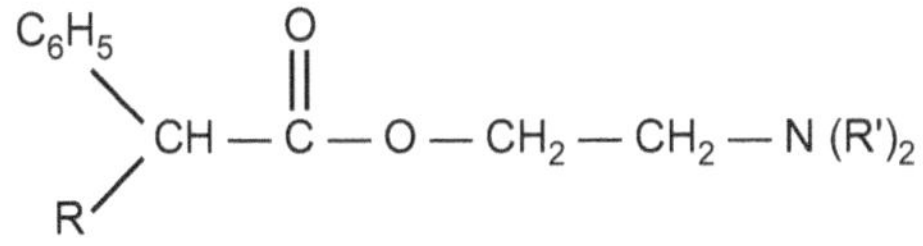

C_6H_5 \
     CH—C(=O)—O—CH₂—CH₂—N(R')₂ \
R /

Where, R = hydroxyalkyl, cycloalkyl or heterocyclic

R'= alkyl group

The larger acyl group ensures pure antagonistic activity.

(iv) The nitrogen atom in an antagonist need not be always quaternised. Since the pH at the receptor sites is acidic, this amino group gets protonated and carries a positive charge.

15.7 PHARMACOLOGY OF ANTIMUSCARINIC DRUGS

Natural Alkaloids : These alkaloids prevent the access of acetylcholine and other choline esters to muscarinic receptors sites. The pharmacology of atropine and atropine-like drugs can be studied under following heads.

(i) blockage at parasympathetic nerve terminals.

(ii) peripheral anti-muscarinic actions

(iii) anti-muscarinic effects in CNS, and

(iv) peripheral actions not due to antimuscarinic property.

(i) Blockage at Parasympathetic Nerve Terminals :

Ocular effects : The ocular effects can be observed after either local or systemic administration of the alkaloids. The muscles which cause constriction of the pupil (i.e. the circular smooth muscles of the iris and ciliary muscles) are connected to parasympathetic neurons in the third cranial oculomotor nerve. While the radial muscles of the iris are supplied by sympathetic nerves from superior cervical ganglion. Both the divisions are responsible for tonic activity of the muscles. By blocking the action of acetylcholine at sphincter, atropine causes dilation of pupil (mydriasis) due to unopposed action of norepinephrine at dilator pupillae. The wide pupillary dilation thus may result into photophobia. Due to narrowing of the irido-corneal angle in mydriasis, the drainage of the aqueous humour is hindered resulting into a rise in intraocular pressure. The paralysis of accomodation (cycloplegia) is also observed due to the inhibition of contraction of ciliary muscle by atropine. In cycloplegia the person looses near vision while the distant remains unaffected.

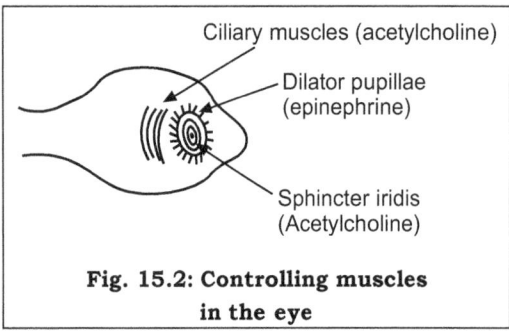

Fig. 15.2: Controlling muscles in the eye

Smooth muscles of GIT :

The gastrointestinal smooth muscles are under prominant parasympathetic control. Atropine leads to a decrease in the tone, amplitude and frequency of peristaltic contraction. Atropine-like drugs are used to tranquilize the gastrointestinal irritability, pylorospasm, gastric hyper motility and hyper irritable states of urinary bladder. Urinary retention occurs due to the inhibitory action on the destrusor muscle of the bladder. Though atropine and scopolamine have negligible effects on human uterus, they can relieve dysmenorrhea due to hypertonic uterus.

Glandular secretion:

The secretion of tears, sweat, saliva and digestive juices is decreased or abolished by the use of alkaloids. They also decrease volume and acidity of gastric juices. The inhibition of food-induced secretion of gastric juices by atropine was reported first by Sanozki in 1893. It causes a reduction in the vagal stimuli for acid and pepsin secretion. They have little effect on secretions by the pancreas, intestine or liver. Due to the suppression of the activity of salivary glands, these alkaloids lead to a state of dry mouth (xerostomia) and difficulty in swallowing.

Respiratory system:

The parasympathetic nerves to the bronchi are both motor and secretory in nature. Atropine inhibits the secretions of the nose, mouth, pharynx and bronchi and thus decreases the frequency of cough and laryngospasm. This activity alongwith the sedative property of scopolamine, promoted the use of alkaloids as pre-anesthetic agents. They also lead to relaxation of smooth muscles of bronchi and bronchioles resulting into bronchodilation. This helps to increase the volume of residual air in lungs. But they are less effective than epinephrine as far as bronchodilatory action is concerned.

Cardiovascular system:

Like on respiration, the effect of alkaloids on the circulation is dose-dependant. These alkaloids lead to either increase or decrease in heart rate which is dose-dependent. At low doses, atropine decreases the heart rate due to central vagal stimulus. At higher concentration, atropine removes the vagal control and thus potentiates the effects of sympathetic nerve stimulation in the myocardium, resulting into cardiac arrhythmia. In toxic doses, it abolishes the cardio-inhibitory reflexes and lead to A-V block due to overstimulation. In therapeutic doses however, atropine does not influence blood vessels and blood-pressure.

(ii) Other Peripheral Anti-muscarinic Actions :

The vascular bed in the body is prominantly under the influence of sympathetic nervous system. Hence these alkaloids do not influence blood vessels. But they antagonize the vasodilation caused by the administration of acetylcholine and its agonists. Their administration is usually accompanied by the rise of 1-2° F in body temperature. This is probably due to decrease in the sweat secretion and hence in the peripheral heat loss.

(iii) Anti-muscarinic Effects in CNS :

Acetylcholine operates both, excitatory and inhibitory mechanisms by interacting with muscarinic and nicotinic receptors distributed throughout the CNS. Hence atropine may cause both inhibitory and excitatory types of responses when reached into the CNS. This property entitles the alkaloid to be used in the treatment of motion sickness and parkinsonism. Scopolamine is about 8-9 times more active than atropine in this regard. The inhibitory responses of these alkaloids are due to their stabilizing efficacy on the neuronal membrane, resulting into a decrease in the response of excitatory neurotransmitters. They reduce the effect of cholinergic synaptic transmission and thus correct the symptoms of motion sickness and parkinsonism. The site of action is probably either on the cortex or on the vestibular apparatus.

Table 15.1: Pharmacology of antimuscarinic drugs

System	Pharmacological actions
1. Skin	Cutaneous blood vessel dilation (flushing) and rise in body temperature (pyrexia) due to inhibition of sweat gland functioning.
2. Ocular	Dilation of pupil (mydriasis); rise in intraocular pressure; paralysis of accomodation (cycloplegia).
3. GIT	Decrease in the tone and motility of muscles; decrease in glandular secretion.
4. Urinary bladder	Relaxation of ureter resulting into urine retention.
5. Respiration	Decrease in bronchial secretion; bronchodilation; increase in the volume of residual air.
6. Cardiovascular	Decrease in the heart rate at low doses and increase in the heart rate at higher doses.
7. CNS	Inhibitory responses at low concentration while when present in higher concentration leads excitation followed by depression.

The excitatory effects of alkaloids include stimulation of the medulla and higher cerebral centers resulting into increased respiration, restlessness, delirium and convulsions. In toxic doses, excitation is followed by depression, resulting into coma and medullary paralysis. Reversible anticholinesterases like physostigmine is useful in reversing these central effects.

(iv) Peripheral Actions not Due to Anti-muscarinic Property :

Following are some of the actions of these alkaloids which are exhibited without affecting peripheral muscarinic receptor sites.

Skin : Atropine, in larger doses, exerted vasodilation of cutaneous blood vessels due to either acting directly on the smooth muscles of blood vessels or causing local histamine release.

Heart : Atropine prolongs the refractory period by exerting quinidine like activity on cardiac cells.

Local anesthetic activity :

Due to its stabilizing property on the nerve membrane, atropine retains a considerable local anesthetic activity, comparable to that of procaine.

Beside these actions, atropine possesses antihistaminic activity.

15.8 SEMISYNTHETIC AND SYNTHETIC ANALOGUES OF ATROPINE

Atropine efficiently blocks all muscarinic responses mediated by acetylcholine. It is a potent muscarinic blocking agents and serves as a prototype of this class. However, if employed for chronic administration, its lack of selectivity may pose problems. Atropine administration is usually characterised by dryness of mouth, cycloplegia, photophobia and urine retention. Though these are not life threatening effects but are sufficient to disturb the patient, if chronic administration is desired. To overcome these problems, drugs having a good degree of specificity and selectivity are sought. A number of semisynthetic and synthetic simpler derivatives of atropine have been synthesized and evaluated for their antimuscarinic activity. Except oxyphencyclimine, a tertiary amine, all synthetic clinically employed antimuscarinic agents are substituted quaternary ammonium compounds. These quaternary amines are poorly absorbed after oral administration and are devoid of central effects. They enjoy comparatively longer duration of action and have greater potency at nicotinic receptors. Their ratio of ganglionic blocking to antimuscarinic activity is more than that of natural alkaloids.

Semisynthetic Compounds :

(a) Homatropine : It is a mandelic acid ester of tropine and is less active (about 1/10th to that of atropine), less toxic and has shorter duration of action. Due to its rapid onset of action, it is used in the form of its hydrobromide salt (2-5 %) solution for ophthalmological examination. Due to its antispasmodic action, it can be used as a supporting drug in the treatment of peptic ulcer.

(b) Homatropine methyl bromide : It is a quaternary ammonium compound having a strong ganglionic blocking activity.

(c) Atropine methonitrate : It is a quaternary ammonium derivative of atropine. It is used as 1% solution for ophthalmic examination.

(d) Methscopolamine bromide : It is a quaternary ammonium compound used chiefly in gastrointestinal disorders orally in the dose range of 2.5 - 3.0 mg.

(e) Hyoscine butyl bromide (Buscopan) : It is a quaternary ammonium derivative of hyoscine, possessing a good antispasmodic activity. Its use is indicated in dysmenorrhea, peptic ulcer and all gastrointestinal diseases characterised by increased muscle-spasm in the dose level of 20 mg four times a day.

Synthetic Compounds :

(a) Methantheline bromide : It has a more potent and prolonged action on GIT. It is usually administered in the dose range of 50-100 mg. In toxic dose, it may paralyze respiration by neuromuscular block.

(b) Oxyphenonium bromide : Chemically it is diethyl (2-hydroxy ethyl) methyl ammonium bromide-2-phenylcyclohexane glycolate. Methantheline and oxyphenonium are the drugs having highest ratio of ganglionic blocking to antimuscarinic activity. Its use is advised in the treatment of peptic ulcer. Side effects are few in therapeutic dose and include constipation, blurring of vision etc.

(c) Propantheline bromide : This quaternary ammonium compound is obtained by replacing the ethyl substituents on the N-atom in methantheline structure by isopropyl groups. It is more potent than methantheline and is one of the most widely used antimuscarinic agents. If administered in the dose of 15 mg, it remains active for about 6 hours.

(d) Synthetic tertiary amines :

(i) Cyclopentolate and tropicamide are the examples of synthetic tertiary amines used in ophthalmology.

(ii) Trasentin, dicyclomine, oxyphencyclimine and thiphenamil are some of the examples of synthetic tertiary amines used as antispasmodic agents. Trasentin, in addition, also possesses a mild local anesthetic action.

(iii) Trihexyphenidyl, a synthetic tertiary amine, however, is useful in the treatment of parkinsonism.

15.9 THERAPEUTIC USES OF ANTIMUSCARINIC AGENTS

(1) Ophthalmology : The local application of antimuscarinic drug to the eye is advocated for

(a) relieving pain in iris.

(b) breaking the adhesions between the iris and cornea after certain surgical procedures.

(c) ophthalmoscopic examination and

(d) the treatment of inflammatory states like, acute iritis and keratitis (i.e., inflammation of cornea). For these purposes, a 1% solution of atropine sulphate is usually used. Beside this, homatropine, eucatropine, scopolamine, cyclopentolate and tropicamide are commonly used drugs in ophthalmology. The short-acting drugs like cyclopentolate and tropicamide, are usually favoured when mydriasis alone, is required.

In some persons, atropine causes conjunctivitis due to local irritation to eyes. It can be corrected by using antihistaminic agents.

(2) Since these drugs decrease salivary and bronchial secretions (and few of them have sedative activity e.g., scopolamine), they are used as preanesthetic medication.

(3) They can be used as antispasmodic agents to relieve pain associated with biliary, intestinal and renal colic.

(4) They reduce gastric motility and acid secretion and due to their

antispasmodic action, prolongs the residential time of antacid tablets. Thus they provide favourable condition for healing in the patients suffering from peptic ulcer. The selective M_1-receptor blocker, pirenzepine, would be effective in peptic ulcer.

(5) These drugs induce bronchodilation and increase the volume of residual air. They decrease bronchial secretion and hence, are useful in the treatment of obstructive pulmonary diseases. In addition, atropine also prevents excessive sweating (hyperhydrosis), usually seen in pulmonary tuberculosis. Due to some systemic side-effects of atropine, it is now replaced by locally effective antimuscarinic agent, ipratropium bromide. Its use is indicated in chronic bronchitis.

(6) Cardiovascular system demands the use of atropine in the treatment of vagus induced acute myocardial infarction or nodal bradycardia. For this, atropine sulphate is given intravenously in a dose of 0.3-2.0 mg. It is also of value in treating the heart block due to cardiac glycoside poisoning.

(7) Atropine administration leads to a considerable increase in the capacity of urinary bladder.

(8) Atropine may also be used with partial success in the treatment of dysmenorrhea due to uterine hypertonicity.

(9) Its ability to block the action of acetylcholine in the CNS, suggests the use of atropine in the treatment of schizophrenia.

(10) Due to the central effects, atropine-like drugs are used to relieve some of the symptoms of vertigo, motion sickness and parkinsonism. In motion sickness and parkinsonism, there is an increase in the activity of acetylcholine or histamine or a decreased turnover of norepinephrine in the brain. Hence, the inhibitory action of these drugs on central synapses, serves the basis for the treatment of these disorders. Moreover, these drugs are also used to control the extapyramidal effects arising due to use of antipsychotic drugs.

The use of atropine-like drugs in the treatment of motion sickness and parkinsonism, now-a-days is less favoured due to the occurrence of other central side-effects. They have been replaced from the therapy mainly by *l*-dopa which control the disorders by compensating the level of dopamine in the striatum of the patient.

(11) These drugs may be used to reverse the effects of poisoning either from species of mushroom (in which muscarine and alkaloid is present in higher concentration) or by an overdose of anti cholinesterases.

They are also advocated in the cholinergic crisis, which occurs in myasthenia gravis due to inadequate treatment.

NEUROMUSCULAR BLOCKERS

16.1 INTRODUCTION

Acetylcholine produces its spectrum of biological activities by acting either on muscarinic cholinergic receptors or nicotinic cholinergic receptors. The actions of ACh on autonomic ganglia and skeletal muscles are thus due to activation of nicotinic receptors. These structures are stimulated by small doses of ACh and get depressed if ACh is administered in larger doses. Since nicotine also evokes same response on these systems, this action is referred to as the ganglionic or nicotinic action of acetylcholine.

The main source of nicotine is the plant, Nicotiana tabacum from potato family. The alkaloid is present in varying quantities (1-8%) in the dried tobacco leaves, in combination with malic and citric acids.

Pharmacology of Nicotine :

(a) In GIT, the alkaloid stimulates musculature and the activity of secretory glands.

(b) It depresses cardiac activity. Small doses of alkaloid cause an increase in blood pressure while in larger doses, it causes decrease in blood pressure.

(c) Both, autonomic ganglia and skeletal muscles are stimulated by small doses and paralysed due to larger doses of nicotine. Nicotine leads to repetitive excitation (fasciculation) followed by block of transmission in the neuromuscular junction. This results in neuromuscular paralysis.

16.2 NEUROMUSCULAR TRANSMISSION

The skeletal muscles are supplied with somatic efferent nerves. Depending upon the skill and delicateness of function assigned to skeletal muscle, the main nerve is linked with other nerves. For example, the nerve controlling the functioning of larger muscles of limb is interconnected with less number of other nerves while the nerve controlling a delicate function needs interconnections with several nerves to exercise fine control.

The axon loses its myelin sheath when the nerve comes in close contact with the muscle fiber and gets bifercated into several fine branches which penetrate the muscle cell membrane. The region of contact of the terminals of these branches with the muscle membrane is known as 'neuromuscular junction'.

The surface of muscle fiber that is near to the nerve terminals and is encircling the nerve terminal is known as 'end-plate' region which carries the sites for nicotinic receptors and cholinesterase enzyme. The gap between the nerve terminal and end-plate region is about 50 mm wide and may be termed as synaptic cleft.

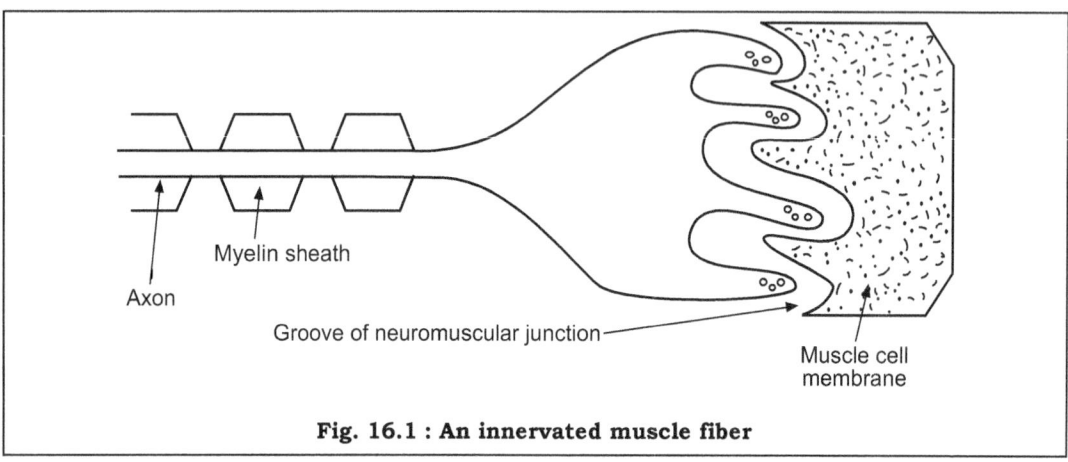

Fig. 16.1 : An innervated muscle fiber

The process is just similar to neurotransmission in other synapses. When the motor nerve is stimulated, an action potential is generated by the exchange of potassium and sodium ions. It travels along the length of the axon and reaches to nerve terminals. The activation of Ca^{++}-ionophore leads to influx of extracellular calcium into the nerve terminal. In response to Ca^{++}- influx, many storage vesicles get ruptured and release ACh into the synaptic cleft. The ruptured vesicles immediately reform and store the newly biosynthesized acetylcoline.

The released ACh then reacts with nicotinic receptor sites present on the junctional folds of end-plate region and causes opening of ion-channels resulting into development of local, graded currents in the membrane of muscle-fiber. These are termed as end-plate currents. They are generated due to increased inward Na^+ and outward K^+ conductances. When their summation attains adequate intensity, it can lead to excitation of the muscle which is followed by contraction of the skeletal muscle. The bound ACh is then hydrolysed by cholinesterase enzymes present in junctional folds to choline and acetate. This entire process of muscle contraction is completed within 2-3 m sec. and maintains its uniformity if repeated many times per second.

16.3 NICOTINIC CHOLINERGIC RECEPTORS

In vertebrate skeletal muscle, the end-plate region comprises of about 0.1 % of the total cell-surface. The end-plate region bears the sites for nicotinic cholinergic receptors. Recent studies revealed the structure of a nicotinic receptor. It consists of five subunits in the ratio of $\alpha_2 \beta \gamma \delta$. Only α-subunits are found to possess binding sites for ACh. These α-subunits have molecular weight of 40,000 daltons each, while β, γ and δ subunits are 50,000; 60,000 and 65,000 daltons peptides respectively. Thus, the receptor as a whole appears to be of about 2,50,000 daltons. These subunits are arranged in the cylindrical fashion (with a diameter of about 8 nm) leaving some space within them, to form an open channel like interior. The nicotinic receptors usually occur in pairs linked by a disulfide bridge between the delta sub-units.

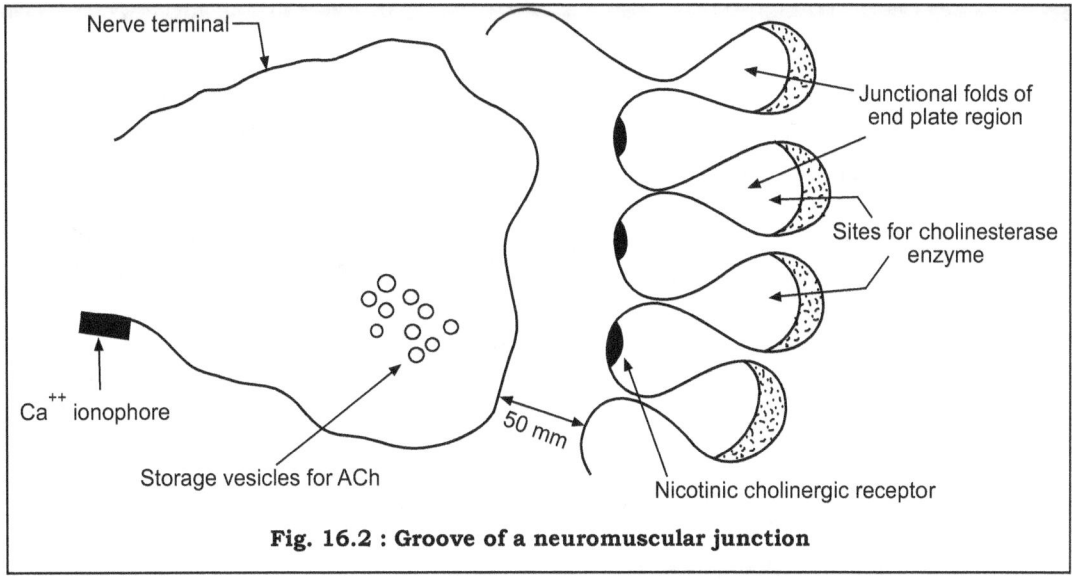

Fig. 16.2 : Groove of a neuromuscular junction

The receptor concentration in the end-plate region appears to be 8 - 10 thousand/μm^2. The binding of ACh to the receptor surface results into the opening of the ion-channel. The channel life-time depends mainly on the intrinsic properties of the drug used. For example, ACh-induced receptor activation leads to opening of ion-channel for about 1m sec. Anticholinesterase drugs prevent the degradation of ACh and extends its biological life. This results into increase in survival period of ACh. In such case, ACh will repetitively bind with the receptor and will cause repetitive ion-channel opening. Tetraethylammonium and 4-aminopyridine are the examples of drugs which increase the neuronal ACh release by prolonging duration of action potential at nerve terminal. Due to this, the number of vesicles which undergo rupture, increases resulting into more ACh release into neuromuscular junction. The bursts of miniature end-plate currents cause repetitive contractions of the skeletal muscle.

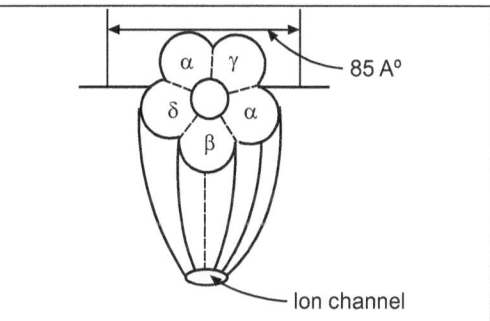

Fig. 16.3 : Arrangement of subunits in nicotinic receptors

16.4 CLASSIFICATION

Various neuromuscular blocking agents act by interferring with

(a) synthesis or release of ACh

OR

(b) ACh-receptor interaction.

Hence, they can be classified accordingly into :

I. Drugs that depress ACh junctional concentration.

(a) by inhibition of its synthesis or

(b) by inhibition of release.

Triethylcholine

$(C_2H_5)_3 - \overset{\oplus}{N} - CH_2CH_2OH$

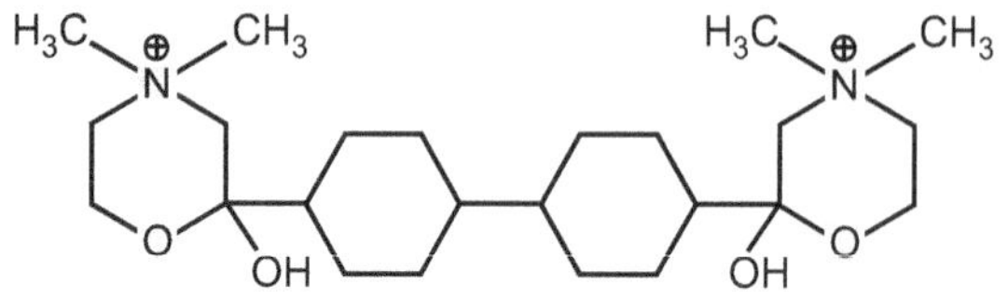

Hemicholinium, HC-3

II. Drugs that prevent the action of released ACh on receptors.
(a) by depolarizing the muscle end-plate region or
(b) by inhibiting depolarizing action of ACh.

III. Centrally acting muscle-relaxants.

I. (a) Drugs which Inhibit the Biosynthesis of ACh :

Choline, an aminoalcohol is needed for ACh biosynthesis. It is transported to the site of synthesis by intracellular transport mechanisms. Triethylcholine and hemicholiniums, due to their structural resemblance with choline, compete with the transport mechanisms and thus decrease the rate of synthesis of ACh.

Hemicholinium, a series of compounds synthesized by Schueler in 1955 compete with choline. Their inhibitory action is reversed by increasing the concentration of choline. The most extensively studied member of this series is HC-3. Both, triethylcholine and HC-3 could not be employed clinically due to their lack of selectivity. They impair the production of ACh in other cholinergic nerves and in brain tissues as well.

(b) Drugs which Inhibit the Release of ACh :

(i) The influx of extracellular Ca^{++} ions in nerve terminal leads to rupture of synaptic vesicles which release ACh. Hence, there exists a quantitative relationship between the concentration of Ca^{++} ions and amount of ACh released. Naturally, neuromuscular block can easily be obtained if Ach enough to generate post-junctional end-plate potential, is not released due to reduction in the amount of Ca^{++} ions. Potassium ions facilitate transmission by enhancing ACh release while magnesium ions have exactly opposite effects.

(ii) Ion-channel blockers : Many categories of drugs including, atropine, amino-glycoside antibiotics, local anaesthetics, barbiturates and some psychotropic drugs interfere with ACh-induced opening of an ion-channel. They bind to these receptor sites and cause narrowing of ion-channel passage which results into reduction in the muscle tone. They do not interfere in the release of ACh from prejunctional sites. The anaesthetic agents specifically stabilize the post junctional membrane with weak to moderate potencies and reduce the intensity of current flow. This activity of anaesthetic agents is synergistic with the action of competitive (non-depolarizing) neuromuscular blocking agents.

(iii) Botulinum toxin : Clostridium botulinum, an anaerobic organism releases toxins which are categorised into eight antigenically distinct types. Of these, the type A has been identified as the neurotoxic component of botulinum toxin. It has a molecular weight of about 900,000 daltons, of which the two polypeptide chains of about 150,000 daltons have been characterized. It is a potent inhibitor of the ACh release from the nerve terminals. This inhibitory action is effected by locking of the molecular gates through which ACh molecules are released from the nerve terminal into the synaptic cleft. The depression of the release of ACh from the motor nerve terminal results into neuromuscular paralysis. The botulinum toxin can cross blood-brain barrier and exerts its effects on CNS. However, it lacks the ability to cross placental barrier. In the persons affected by botulinum toxin, treatment with anticholine-sterases may improve and restore the strength and functioning of the muscles.

II. Drugs that Prevent the Action of Released ACh on the Receptor Sites :

(a) Depolarizing the Muscle End-plate Region : Both depolarizing blocking agents and competitive (non-depolarizing) blocking agents cause neuromuscular blockade by acting on the nicotinic receptor sites present in post-junctional membrane. The depolarizing agents are weak agonists of ACh having greater affinity and weaker intrinsic activity at the receptor sites. They bind to nicotinic receptor and depolarize the post-junctional membrane by opening the ion-channel. Due to their greater affinity, they may cause prolonged depolarization by repeated opening of ion-channels and make further depolarization by endogenous ACh impossible. This repeated excitation leads to muscular fasciculation and the loss of significant quantities of K^+ ions from the muscle cell. The continuous triggering of muscle excitation then causes a block of transmission followed by neuromuscular paralysis. These events can also be seen with very high doses of acetylcholine. Due to prolonged and repeated end-plate depolarization, a time comes when the depolarized area can not generate muscle action potential sufficient to cause muscle contraction.

The action of depolarizing muscle is manifested at an early stage by transient muscular fasciculation. This is followed by the paralysis of muscles of fingers and eyes. The larger muscles of limb and trunk are affected. Ultimately respiration ceases due to paralysis of diaphragm. During recovery the muscle regain their strength and function in the reverse order to that of paralysis.

Succinylcholine is the only agent from this category which is used clinically. It has more side-effects than competitive neuromuscular blockers.

(i) Succinylcholine : It was synthesized by Bovet et al in 1949 in order to create synthetic alternatives or substitutes for d-tubocurarine, a natural competitive neuromuscular blocker. As shown in the structure, succinylcholine is a twin structure comprising of two ACh molecules. It has a rapid onset and a short duration of action. It acts on the nicotinic receptors and initiates repeated depolarization of the end-plate region resulting into a brief period of muscle fasciculations. This is phase I which is followed by phase II, inducing neuromuscular blockade if the drug is administered repeatedly.

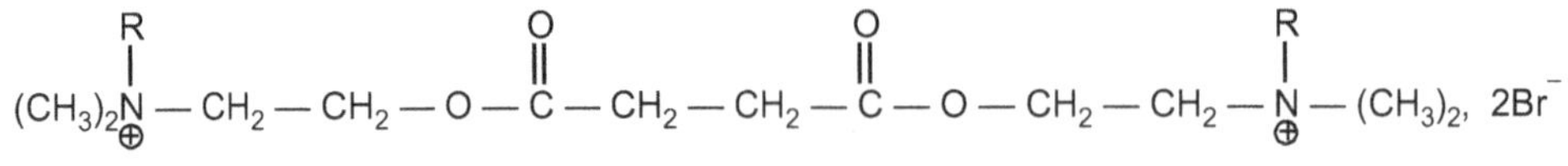

$$\underset{\underset{\oplus}{(CH_3)_2\overset{R}{\underset{|}{N}}}}{}-CH_2-CH_2-O-\overset{O}{\underset{||}{C}}-CH_2-CH_2-\overset{O}{\underset{||}{C}}-O-CH_2-CH_2-\underset{\oplus}{\overset{R}{\underset{|}{N}}}-(CH_3)_2, 2Br^-$$

Succinylcholine bromide ; R = – CH$_3$

Suxethonium bromide ; R = – C$_2$H$_5$

Succinylcholine has a very short duration of action (5 - 10 minutes). Its action is terminated due to its rapid hydrolysis by butyrocholinesterases present in plasma and liver. The main metabolite, succinylmonocholine still retains a weak competitive neuromuscular blocking activity. The drug undergoes a two step metabolism as shown in the Fig. 16.4.

The action of succinylcholine can be prolonged by administration of local anaesthetics which block butyrocholinesterase enzymes. The drug does not reach the CNS. Its prolonged administration may lead to an increase in intraoccular pressure due to its contractile action on extraoccular muscles.

Adverse effects include muscle fasciculation, muscle ache and pain, hyperkalemia, increase in intraoccular pressure and rise in blood pressure. The latter effect is due to stimulation of autonomic ganglia and not due to histamine liberation. Diazepam may be used to reduce muscle pain and spasm associated with the use of succinylcholine.

Succinylcholine is mainly used to prevent tetanic muscle contraction and for providing general muscle relaxation needed to carry out surgery. Its ethyl analogue, suxethonium bromide has similar properties as that of succinylcholine except that it gets hydrolyzed more rapidly than succinylcholine.

(ii) Decamethonium : It is an example of a series of compounds in which a polymethylene chain bridges two quaternary nitrogens. Such a series is known as methonium series and is represented as

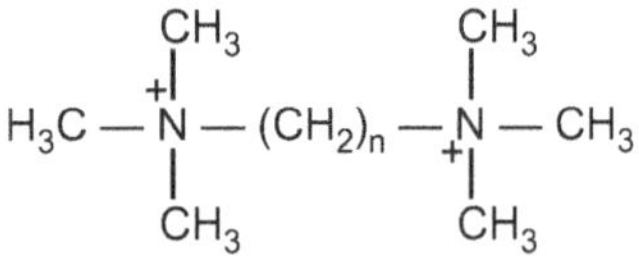

$$H_3C-\overset{CH_3}{\underset{\underset{CH_3}{|}}{\overset{+|}{N}}}-(CH_2)_n-\overset{CH_3}{\underset{\underset{CH_3}{+|}}{\underset{|}{N}}}-CH_3$$

Methonium series

Decamethonium is an effective neuromuscular blocking agent. In usual doses, it neither releases histamine nor it blocks autonomic ganglia. Its effectiveness as a depolarizing agent is due to the distance of separation between two quaternary nitrogens which is about 1.4 mm. This distance correlates closely with the distance covering two adjacent ACh receptors at the end-plate region.

$$(CH_3)_3 \overset{+}{N} - (CH_2)_{10} - \overset{+}{N} (CH_3)_3 ; 2Br^-$$

Decamethonium bromide

It is longer acting and more stable molecule than succinylcholine. It is not employed clinically.

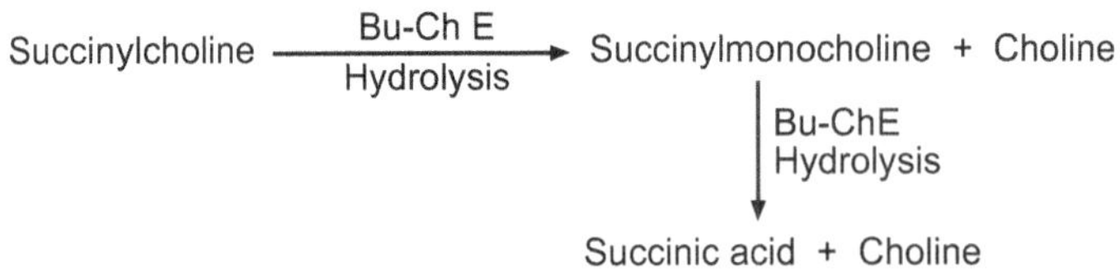

Succinylcholine $\xrightarrow[\text{Hydrolysis}]{\text{Bu-Ch E}}$ Succinylmonocholine + Choline
$\quad\quad\quad\quad\quad\quad\quad\quad\quad\quad\quad\quad\quad\quad\quad\downarrow$ Bu-ChE Hydrolysis
$\quad\quad\quad\quad\quad\quad\quad\quad\quad\quad\quad\quad$ Succinic acid + Choline

Fig. 16.4 : Metabolism of succinylcholine

(iii) Carbolonium bromide : It depolarizes the motor end-plate region mainly due to its anticholinesterase activity. Presently, it is not under clinical use.

(b) Drugs that Act by Inhibiting Depolarizing Action of Acetylcholine :

Acetylcholine released from the nerve terminal, binds to α-subunits of the nicotinic-cholinergic receptor and causes opening of an ion-channel. When the summation of end-plate currents attain adequate level (post-junctional end plate potential), it leads to the excitation of the muscle, followed by contraction.

If the end-plate receptor sites are already blocked by drugs having affinity but not intrinsic activity, endogenous ACh cannot bind to the receptor and hence can not depolarize the end-plate region. This will result into muscle relaxation due to neuromuscular block. Since these agents act competitively with endogenous ACh to occupy receptor sites, such drugs are known as competitive or non-depolarizing or anti-depolarizing or membrane stabilizing agents. Since they block competitively the transmitter's action on the receptor sites, the post-junctional membrane remains insensitive to the propagated nerve impulse and contraction does not occur. Examples of this category include, d-tubocurarine, Alcuronium, Pancuronium, Gallamine, Atracurium and β-erythroidine etc. Action of all these compounds can be reversed by increasing the concentration of ACh at receptor sites. This can be achieved by anticholinesterases.

(i) d-Tubocurarine : It is an example of various curare alkaloids which are found in plants of genera Menispermaceae and Strychnos. The term 'Curare' is used to describe various South American arrow poisons which possess neuromuscular blocking alkaloids. Currently d-tubocurarine is obtained mainly from the bark of Chondodendron tomentosum. Since at that time, the native were using bamboo tubes to store the crude preparation, the alkaloid was named as tubocurarine. The first clinical use of this crude alkaloid was done in 1932 by West to treat spastic disorders. The isolation, structural elucidation and determination of optical activity of the ingredient of the crude preparation was carried out in 1935 by King. Since 1942, its use for promoting muscle relaxation in general anaesthesia was continued on ever-increasing scale. Soon after, metocurine, a synthetic dimethyl analogue of tubocurarine was developed which was found to be three times more potent as muscle relaxant than d-tubocurarine.

d-Tubocurarine has a rapid onset of action, if given intravenously. It competitively binds to the end-plate region and reduces the frequency of channel-opening events resulting into flaccid paralysis. At therapeutic doses, it partially blocks the ganglionic transmission. Some of the side-effects of the drug can be explained by its capacity to liberate histamine from the mast cells. (These side-effects include bronchospasm, hypotension, excessive bronchial and salivary secretion etc.). In larger doses, d-tubocurarine blocks the transmission of both at autonomic ganglia and at adrenal medulla resulting into a fall in blood pressure and tachycardia. Histamine release is partly responsible for this hypotensive response. It also decreases the tone and motility of GIT and leads to an increase in intraoccular pressure.

Table 16.1 : Competitive neuromuscular blocking agents

(i)

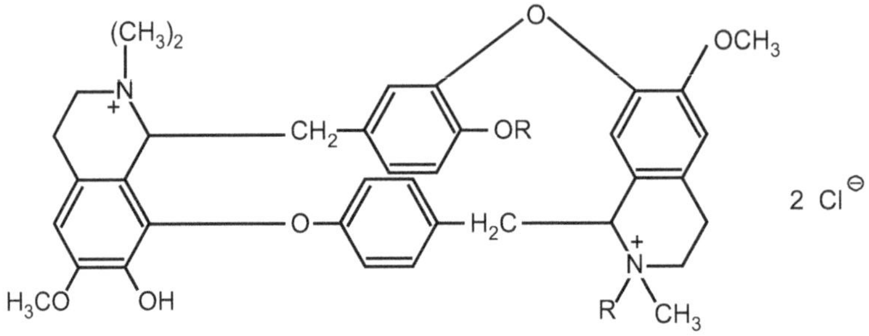

d-Tubocurarine chloride ; R = – H
Metocurine chloride ; R = – CH$_3$

(ii)

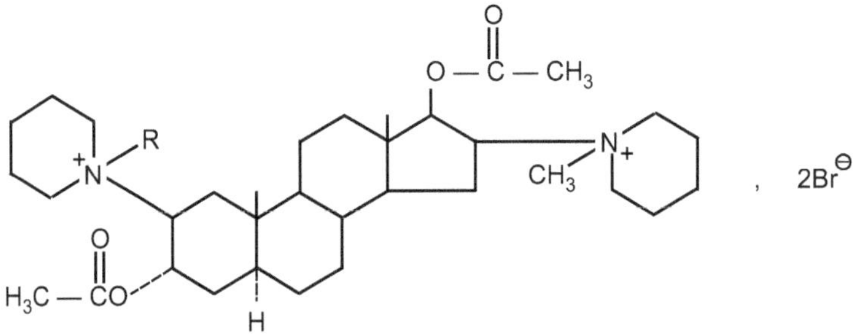

Pancuronium bromide ; R = – CH$_3$
Vecuronium bromide; R = – H

(iii)

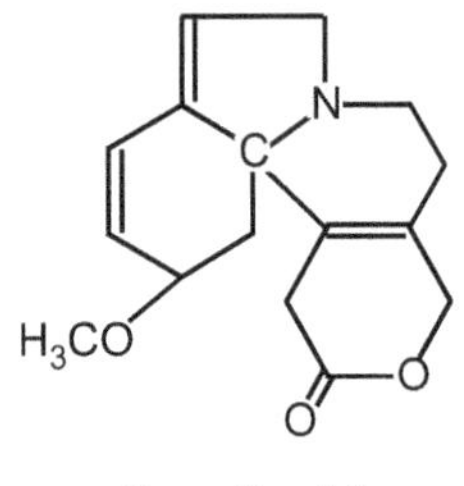

β-erythroidine

(iv)

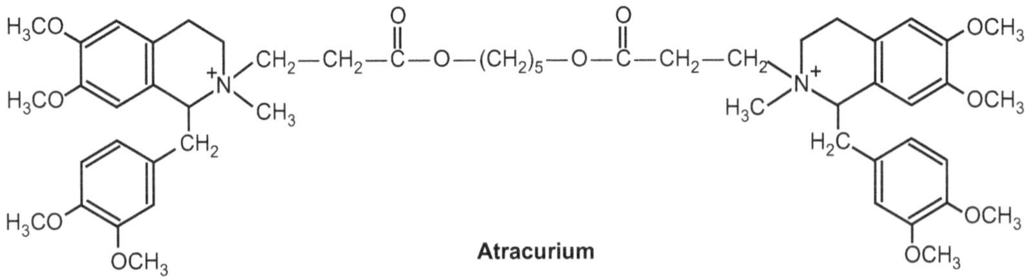

Atracurium

(v) Alcuronium chloride

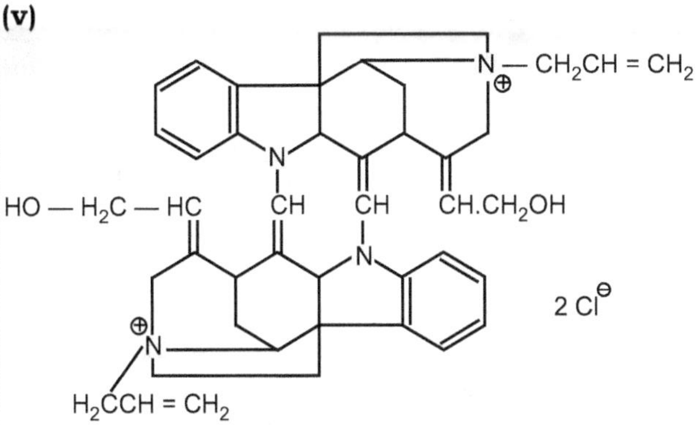

(vi) Gallamine triethiodide

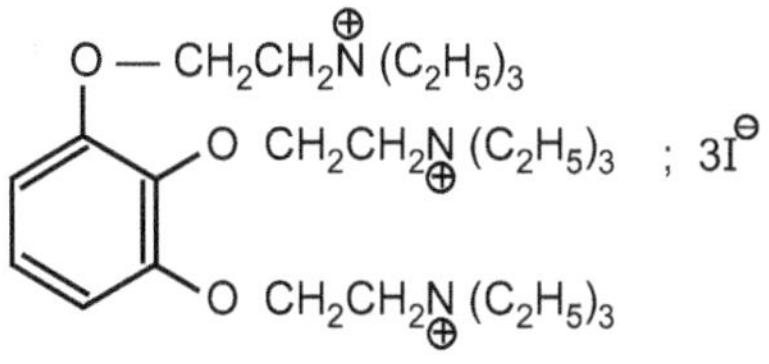

d-Tubocurarine and all other quaternary neuromuscular blockers lack an ability to enter the CNS. Hence, they do not exert central effects in man. They are used as muscle-relaxants in anesthesia mainly due to their peripheral effects at neuromuscular junction. For this purpose, d-tubocurarine chloride is administered 0.2 to 0.7 mg/kg of body weight for an adult either by i.v., or i.m. route. It is commonly used to relax muscles and thus to prevent dislocation and fracture associated with electroconvulsive therapy.

(ii) Gallamine : It is one of the member of a series, synthesized by Bovet and co-workers in 1946 in hope to avail synthetic substitutes for curare alkaloid. It is widely used as competitive neuromuscular blocking agent. It contains three quaternary nitrogens and block the muscarinic receptors of cardiac branches of vagus through atropine like action. This results into an increase in heart rate, blood pressure and develops occasional arrhythmias.

(iii) Pancuronium : This compound first synthesized in 1964 consists of a steroidal nucleus in which acetylcholine part is incorporated. It does not have steroidal activity. It is about five times more potent than d-tubocurarine as a blocker of neuromuscular junction. This activity is potentiated by ether. It has quite less ability to cause histamine liberation.

Vecuronium is a moderately short-acting and a bit potent analogue of pancuronium. The structure of vecuronium does lack the 2β methyl group present in pancuronium. It does not lead to release of histamine. It neither affects autonomic ganglia nor the vagal neuroeffector junctions.

(iv) Atracurium : It is another new synthetic derivative of curare and has intermediate duration of action. It is 3-4 times less potent than pancuronium and its neuromuscular blocking activity is potentiated by halothane. It is metabolized in plasma primarily by hydrolysis of the ester group or by disconnecting both quaternary nitrogens from each other. It possesses a half-life of about twenty minutes and has less ability to cause liberation of histamine.

(v) Dihydro-β-erythroidine : It is a semi-synthetic derivative of β–erythroidine, an alkaloid obtained from E. americana. From various semi-synthetic derivatives of β-erythroidine, the dihydro compound was found to be clinically useful muscle relaxant.

(vi) Baclofen : It is a newly introduced muscle relaxant used in the treatment of spasms associated with disorders that affect spinal cord.

$$H_2N - H_2C - \underset{C_6H_5}{CH} - CH_2\ COOH$$

Baclofen

Its structure is closely related to the structure of GABA, an inhibitory neurotransmitter present in CNS. After oral administration, the drug is rapidly absorbed and enters into the CNS where it may inhibit monosynaptic and polysynaptic spinal reflexes. About 35% of the administered drug appears unchanged in urine.

It can be used orally in a daily dose of 15 mg to treat spinal spasticity and spasticity associated with multiple sclerosis. If desired, the dose can be progressively increased upto 50 mg.

(vii) Dantrolene sodium : This agent is of special interest mainly due to its unique mechanism of action. It causes muscle relaxation by directly blocking the contractile mechanism of skeletal muscle fiber. It prevents both, the influx of extracellular calcium ions and the release of intracellular Ca^{++} ions from the sarcoplasmic reticulum. This results into blocking of excitation, contraction and coupling of skeletal muscles. It is not used as an adjuvant to anaesthesia due to its slow onset and longer duration of action. It has a half-life of 7-9 hours. Generally, the drug action is more pronounced on fast muscle fibers than slow muscle fibers. It is metabolised by liver microsomal enzymes and excreted mainly through urine and bile.

It is used orally in a dose of 12-25 mg, once a day, for the treatment of chronic spasticity due to spinal cord injury or multiple sclerosis. In the treatment of malignant hyperthermia, it is usually given intravenously.

Side-effects include drowsiness, diarrhoea, visual disturbances, hallucination and a dose-dependent muscle weakness. Hence it is contra-indicated in patients with liver disease or weakness of respiratory muscle.

(viii) Benzodiazepines : Beside having anxiolytic and anticonvulsant activities, some of the benzodiazepines possess muscle relaxant activity.

Diazepam, chlordiazepoxide and clonazepam are the most useful agents for the control of flexor and extensor spasms, spinal spasticity and multiple sclerosis. They are usually employed in the dose range of 15-60 mg.

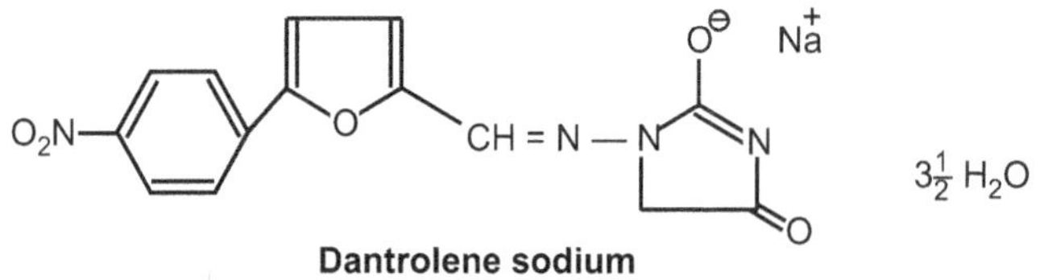

Dantrolene sodium

(ix) Some antipsychotic drugs like chlorpromazine and fonazine are also of value in the therapy of muscle relaxation. Fonazine, a phenothiazine derivative causes a non-specific arrest of histamine release.

16.5 STRUCTURE-ACTIVITY RELATIONSHIP

(i) The quaternary nitrogen moiety maintains cationic charge in minimally hydrated condition and confers good neuromuscular blocking activity.

(ii) The neuromuscular blockade can also be obtained with non-quaternerized compounds like nicotine.

(iii) Larger alkyl substituents at quaternary nitrogen hinder the attack of the drug molecule at receptor-sites.

(iv) Lipophilicity plays an important role in governing the access of molecule to the muscle membrane. More bulky and rigid molecules generally exhibit competitive type of activity while simple and flexible structure is found to be necessary for depolarizing type of muscle-relaxant activity.

(v) The distance between two quaternary nitrogens in the drug governs the activity. It should be near about 1.2 - 1.4 nm for optimal activity. Gallamine and β-erythroidine are exceptions to this rule. Quaternerization of nitrogen atom in β-erythoidine results in decline of activity.

(vi) The quaternary nitrogen atom can be substituted by arsenium, osmium, sulfonium, phosphonium and platinum with retention of muscle-relaxant activity.

16.6 ABSORPTION, DISTRIBUTION AND EXCRETION

In general, the quaternary ammonium compounds, due to their ionic nature are poorly absorbed after oral administration. From intramuscular sites, absorption is rapid and regular. Major amount of drug is eliminated through urine. Pattern of metabolism is not uniform in each type. Insignificant amount of the drug administered may be excreted through bile.

16.7 THERAPEUTIC USES

(i) Muscle-relaxants are employed as an adjuvant in surgical anaesthesia in order to carry out operations with ease. They are administered after the patient is anaesthesized.

(ii) They are used in the treatment of status epilepticus and to reduce painful muscle spasms of tetanus.

(iii) They can be used in various orthopedic operations.

(iv) Some of these agents are used in the treatment of spastic muscle disorders. These disorders involve an increased tone of muscle due to imbalance between the central and spinal control of muscle tone.

(v) d-Tubocurarine is particularly useful in the diagnosis of myasthenia gravis and conditions symbolized by immobility of joints.

16.8 TOXIC EFFECTS

Respiratory muscles, muscles of the eyes and digits may be attacked by these neuromuscular blockers. If these muscles get paralyzed, the patient may be exposed to fatal effects.

The ability of some competitive muscle relaxant to liberate histamine from the mast cells may lead to prolonged apnea, bronchoconstriction and cardiovascular side-effects of these drugs.

The acute toxicity by these drugs can be overcome by the administration of anticholinesterases, adrenaline, potassium chloride or antihistaminics. Artificial respiration proves to be beneficial in recovering the condition of the patient.

16.9 COMPETITIVE VERSUS DEPOLARISING AGENTS

The following table summarises some of the important points of differences between depolarizing and competitive types of neuromuscular blocking agents.

16.10 CENTRALLY ACTING MUSCLE RELAXANT

The muscle relaxants we studied just now, do so by acting peripherally at neuromuscular junctions. Yet another category of muscle relaxants exists which bring out their effects by their action on CNS. Muscle-relaxation is achieved by the suppression of some reflexes involving interneurons, mainly in the region of brain-stem, thalamus and basal ganglia. Hence, these agents are also termed as interneuronal blocking agents. The muscle-relaxation is effected without loss of consciousness. In therapeutic doses, these agents do not impair voluntary muscle activity.

Mephenesin, a phenoxypropanediol derivative, synthesized in 1946, serves as the prototype of this category of drugs. To minimize the side-effects of mephenesin, its derivatives have been prepared. But instead of muscle-relaxant nature, they proved to be good antipsychotic agents. Surprisingly diazepam an anxiolytic agent used in psychosis treatment, retains the muscle-relaxant activity. It appears therefore that since these drugs cause muscle-relaxation due to their central action, they also might have an action on emotional centres and hence can be useful agents in the treatment of psychotic disorders.

Table 16.2

Parameter	Depolarizing agents	Competitive agents
1. Neuromuscular block can be reversed by	Antidepolarizing agents but difficult to reverse	Anti-ChE, K^+-ions, adrenaline, depolarizing agent and ephedrine
2. Nature	Partial agonists	Competitive antagonists
3. Muscle twiches	Few muscle twiches followed by a flaccid paralysis	Flaccid paralysis not preceded by muscle twitches
4. Histamine	Do not liberate histamine	Liberate histamine

(1) Mephenesin : Berger and Bradley in 1946 prepared a series of glycerol ether derivatives, of which mephenesin is a centrally acting muscle-relaxant having highest activity. It depresses internuncial neurons in the CNS, which are involved in the control and maintenance of tone and movements of muscles. In therapeutic doses, it has membrane-stabilizing and analgesic activities. Muscle-relaxation is accompanied by depression of reflex activity and tremors.

It is administered orally (2-3 g) usually 3-4 times a day. It has a short duration of action. When given intravenously, mephenesin exposes the patient to risks of hypotension, haemolysis and haemoglobinuria. In comparison to mephenesin, its carbamate ester has a longer duration of action.

(2) Mephenesin derivatives : In order to increase the potency and minimize side-effects associated with mephenesin, series of compounds bearing structural resemblance with mephenesin have been prepared and were evaluated for their central muscle relaxant activity but vary in their capacity to produce sedation and analgesia, and their duration of action. These include methocarbamol, carisoprodol, phenyramidol, phenoglycodol, chlorzoxazone and chlormezanone. The latter two drugs can also be used as anxiolytics. Some of the above mentioned agents, due to their sedative property, (e.g., phenaglycodol) also find place in anticonvulsant therapy.

Table 16.3 : Some centrally acting muscle-relaxant

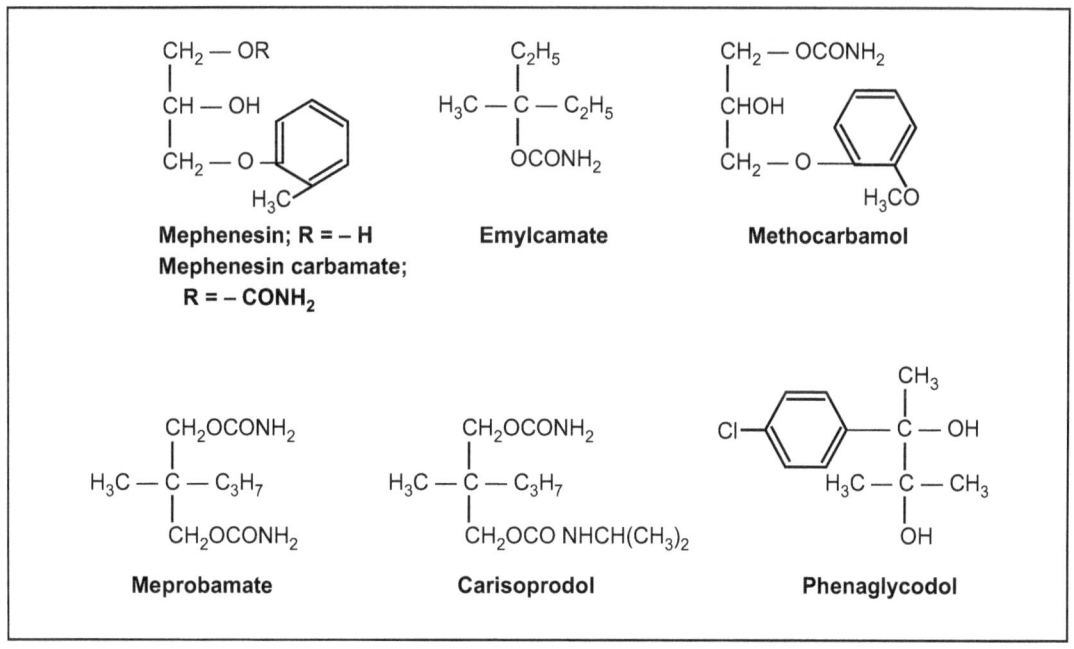

Structures

Styramate: C₆H₅–CH(OH)–CH₂–OCONH₂

Phenyramidol: C₆H₅–CH(OH)–CH₂–NH–(2-pyridyl)

Chlorzoxazone: 5-chloro-benzoxazol-2(3H)-one

Chlormezanone: 2-(4-chlorophenyl)-3-methyl-1,3-thiazinan-4-one 1,1-dioxide

Nefopam has a benzoxazocine structure and is developed as cyclized analogue of diphenhydramine. It lacks antihistaminic activity. Its muscle relaxant activity may be due to its interference with serotonergic transmission.

16.11 THERAPEUTIC USES

(i) Due to their centrally located site of action, these agents can be used to treat spasticity in spinal cord injury and multiple sclerosis.

(ii) As like peripheral neuromuscular blockers, these agents can be employed as an adjunct for induction of anaesthesia.

(iii) Muscle spasm induced due to inflammation, trauma and tetanus can be relieved by these agents.

(iv) Drugs having prominent anxiolytic action (e.g., diazepam and lorazepam) can be used to relieve muscle tension and pain in stress and anxiety.

The usual dose of centrally acting muscle relaxants varies according to the disorders and the agent choosen for its treatment. Generally for relaxing the muscles, the dose for following agents can be used.

Diazepam   – 10 mg i.v.

Chlordiazepoxide – 50 to 100 mg i.v./i.m.

Mephenesin   – 1.2 g per day orally

Meprobamate   – 1.2 g - 1.6 g per day orally

In these doses, these agents produce therapeutic effects which are associated with certain minor side-effects like, drowsiness, headache, blurred vision, general weakness and sedation.

DRUGS AFFECTING GANGLIONIC TRANSMISSION

17.1 INTRODUCTION

The balance, co-ordination and control of muscle movement and muscle tone is governed by the autonomic ganglia in the regions of mid-brain, cerebellum and spinal cord. Like in neuromuscular transmission, acetylcholine plays the role of main neurotransmitter also in autonomic ganglionic transmission. This is supported by the fact that d-tubocurarine, a neuromuscular blocking agent, can also cause the blockade of ganglionic transmission. In addition, there are several points of similarity between ganglionic and neuromuscular transmission. For example, the transmission in parasympathetic ganglia obeys the same presynaptic to postsynaptic cell relationship as that is seen in neuromuscular junctions. In most of the cases, however, transmission through autonomic ganglia is quite complex and may involve neurons interposed between the pre and post synaptic components. These neurons are therefore termed as interneurons.

In general, following categories of drugs can alter the transmission through the autonomic ganglia.

(a) drugs which inhibit either synthesis or storage of acetylcholine. Hemicholiniums is an example of this category.

(b) drugs which reduce or prevent the release of acetylcholine from preganglionic nerve fibers. Example is botulinus toxin.

(c) drugs which inhibit metabolism of acetylcholine by blocking cholinesterase enzymes. Example is physostigmine and

(d) drugs which potentiate or inhibit the interaction of acetylcholine with postganglionic receptor sites.

For better understanding of the action of various drugs which alter the transmission through the autonomic ganglia in either ways, a concise report about the events taking place during ganglionic transmission is presented below.

17.2 GANGLIONIC TRANSMISSION

The ganglionic synapse retains many of the characteristic features of neuromuscular synapses. However in sympathetic ganglia and some parasympathetic ganglia, a dopaminergic neuron is present in the region of synaptic cleft. The muscarinic receptors present on interneuron are activated by the acetylcholine released from preganglionic nerve ending. This, results into release of catecholamines (i.e., noradrenaline, adrenaline or dopamine) from the interneuron which then activate the postsynaptic α-adrenergic receptors. Thus, the dopaminergic interneuron if activated, results into characteristic catecholamine fluorescence spectrum and hence the interneuron may also be termed as a small intensity, fluorescent cell (SIF). At many places, its role is assigned to be of modulator of ganglionic transmission.

In neuromuscular junction, the end-plate region comprises only of nicotinic cholinergic receptors but in autonomic ganglia, both types i.e., muscarinic and nicotinic receptors are located on the postganglionic fiber. The post-ganglionic cell body also possesses receptor sites for autacoid (e.g., angiotensin, bradykinin, serotonin or histamine) which are brought near to the ganglionic membranes through circulation. Depending upon the type of autacoid reacting, these receptor sites may give rise to excitatory or inhibitory type of responses and modulate the ganglionic transmission.

The released acetylcholine thus reacts with muscarinic and nicotinic receptor sites present on the cell body, and with muscarinic receptor sites of SIF cell. The stimulation of nicotinic receptors leads to the generation of fast excitatory post-synaptic potential (fast EPSP).

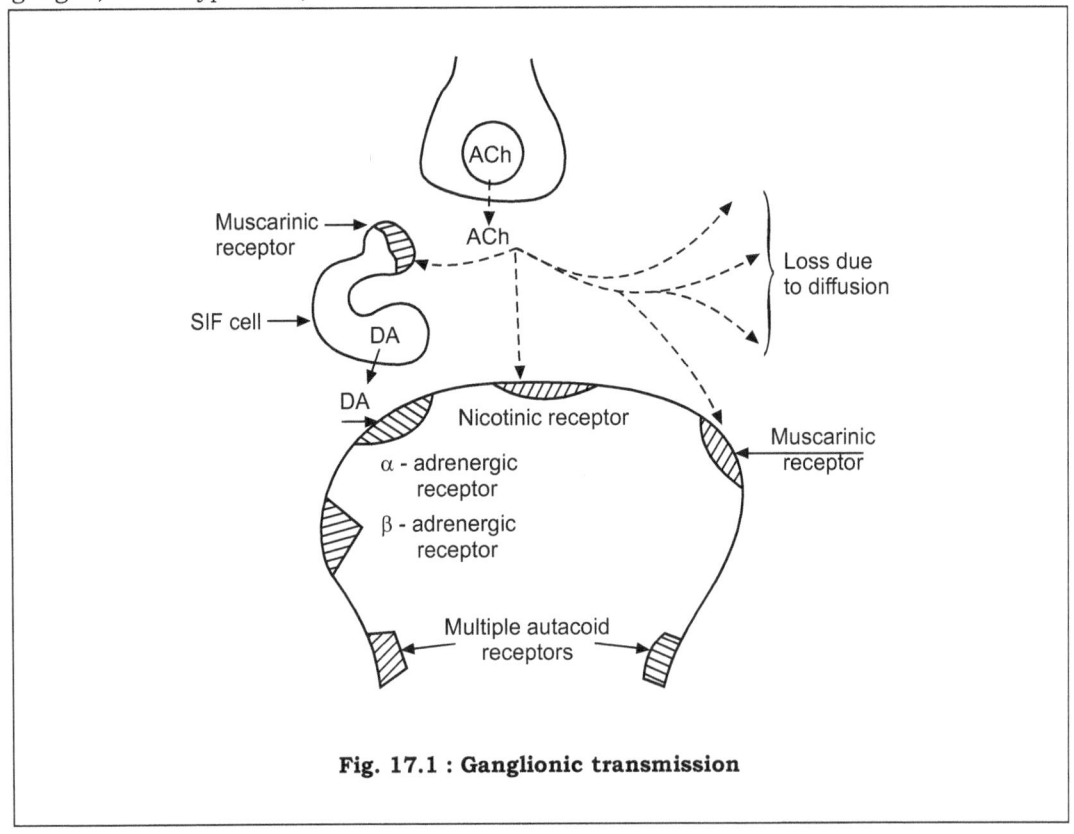

Fig. 17.1 : Ganglionic transmission

The events involved in fast EPSP are essentially similar to that which occur in neuromuscular junction. The release of catecholamine from SIF cell activates α–adrenergic receptor located on postganglionic cell body and leads to release of cyclic AMP. The accumulation of cyclic AMP in the ganglia causes a change in membrane permeability resulting into hyperpolarization of the cell. This hyperpolarization is responsible for the development of a slow inhibitory post synaptic potential (slow IPSP). A part of the acetylcholine released from the preganglionic nerve terminal, comes in contact with the muscarinic receptors present on the postganglionic cell-body, resulting into activation of these receptor sites. As a consequence, there is a release of cyclic GMP which is responsible for a slow excitatory post-synaptic potential.

Thus, the use of specific blockers of muscarinic and α-adrenergic receptors will alter secondary events like slow EPSP and slow IPSP but could not affect the fast EPSP.

The generation of fast EPSP is primary event and will only be influenced by drugs that block specifically nicotinic actions of acetylcholine.

Table 17.1: Ganglionic versus neuromuscular transmission

Ganglionic transmission	Neuromuscular transmission
1. Post ganglionic membrane possesses various types of (muscarinic, nicotinic, α- and β- adrenergic, etc.) receptors.	1. The end-plate region possesses only nicotinic receptors.
2. Ganglionic post-synaptic potential is more complex and consists of three phases : Fast EPSP, slow IPSP and slow EPSP.	2. End-plate potential is a simple partial depolarization. No such subsidiary mechanisms exist.
3. Cholinesterases (ChE) are present in preganglionic fibre and prevent further release of neurotransmitter.	3. Most ChE are concentrated at the end-plate region.
4. Diffusion and not the enzymatic hydrolysis is an important mechanism for terminating transmitter's action in ganglia.	4. Enzymatic hydrolysis is the most important mechanism for termination of ACh-action.
5. Hence anti-ChE agents are less effective at ganglionic synapses.	5. Anti-ChE agents are effective agents, employed to reverse the paralysis produced by anti-depolarizing substances.

Thus, ganglionic transmission consists of three sequentially followed mechanisms, as listed below :

(a) Fast excitatory post-synaptic potential (Fast EPSP) : This is the primary pathway which causes rapid depolarization of the postganglionic membrane due to the opening of ion-channel with an inward sodium ion current. The events and mechanism are essentially same as that in neuromuscular transmission. An action potential is generated when the initial EPSP attains a critical amplitude. The activation, in the similar fashion of multiple synapses, is required before transmission becomes effective.

In multiple synapses subsidary pathways are necessary to amplify or suppress the excitatory post-synaptic potential. They prove a device to limit the ganglionic stimulation. These include

(i) Slow inhibitory post-synaptic potential (slow IPSP) : This results due to hyperpolarization of post ganglionic sites by the activation of α-adrenergic receptor sites. The catecholamine released from SIF cell is mainly responsible for this.

(ii) Slow excitatory post-synaptic potential (slow EPSP) : This phase arises by accumulation of cyclic GMP due to the activation of post-ganglionic muscarinic sites. Cyclic GMP decreases K^+ conductance and causes slow EPSP.

17.3 GANGLIONIC STIMULANTS

Ganglionic stimulating agents can be categorised into :

(a) Drugs which stimulate ganglionic nicotinic receptors : These agents, including nicotine itself, do not have clinical applications. The stimulation of postganglionic nicotinic receptors lead to a rapid depolarization alongwith the generation of a fast excitatory post-synaptic potential. Their ganglionic stimulatory action is rapid in onset and can be blocked by competitive or non-depolarizing ganglionic blockers.

(b) Drugs which stimulate postganglionic muscarinic receptors : Muscarine, methacholine, McN-A-343 and reversible anticholinesterases are the examples of this category. They activate the postganglionic muscarinic receptor sites and give rise to slow EPSP. It takes a considerable period of time to attain critical amplitude which is necessary to evoke action potential. Hence, the excitatory effects of these drugs on ganglia are slow in onset and can be blocked by atropine-like drugs.

Ganglionic stimulation is mainly brought about by drugs which stimulate post-ganglionic nicotinic receptor sites. Beside this, they may stimulate the nicotinic receptors present on various other organs and produce a response of complex nature. For example, during their use

(i) Signs of adrenergic nervous system stimulation can be seen due to the release of adrenaline and noradrenaline from adrenal medulla and sympathetic nerve terminals.

(ii) Contraction of skeletal muscle may be observed due to their action on nicotinic receptors present at end-plate region of skeletal muscles.

(iii) Nausea and vomiting are the common side-effects observed due to the activation of nicotinic chemoreceptors in the aortic arch and carotid bodies and

(iv) Both excitatory and inhibitory types of responses arise due to activation of nicotinic receptors that are located in the CNS.

Nicotine, an alkaloid obtained from leaves of Nicotina tobacum, is a prototype of this series. The actions of other ganglionic stimulants are qualitatively similar to the actions of nicotine and bear only quantitative differences. Hence, a brief review of various actions of nicotine is presented below.

17.4 NICOTINE

It is one of the few natural liquid alkaloids. Its isolation from the natural source is first reported in 1828 by Posselt and Reiman. Demonstration of ganglion as it's site of action was given in 1889 by Langley and Dickinson. The biological effects produced by nicotine are generally of complex nature due to the simultaneous activation of nicotinic receptors located at different organs. Hence, the ultimate response at any one system represents the summation of both stimulant and depressant actions of nicotine.

Lobeline, a nicotine analogue was isolated from dried leaves of Lobelia inflata. Wieland in 1915, successfully isolated crystaline α-Lobeline which is the chief constituent of lobelia. Lobeline is less potent than nicotine in its pharmacological actions. Besides this, some synthetic compounds are also employed to cause ganglionic stimulation. These include tetramethyl ammonium (TMA) and 1,1-dimethyl-4-phenyl piperazinium (DMPP).

Pharmacology of nicotine : The alkaloid, at low doses, stimulates and at high doses depresses the functioning of many organs. This type of activity is known as biphasic action.

(a) Nicotine exerts a biphasic action at autonomic ganglia on adrenal medulla (i.e. discharge of catecholamines) and neuromuscular junction.

(b) Like acetylcholine, nicotine also stimulates a number of sensory receptors.

Table 17.2 : Ganglione stimulants

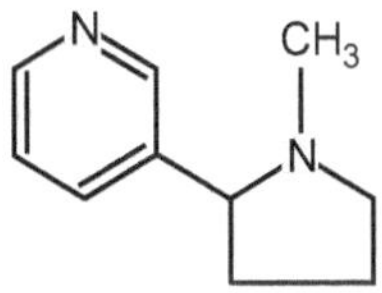

Nicotine

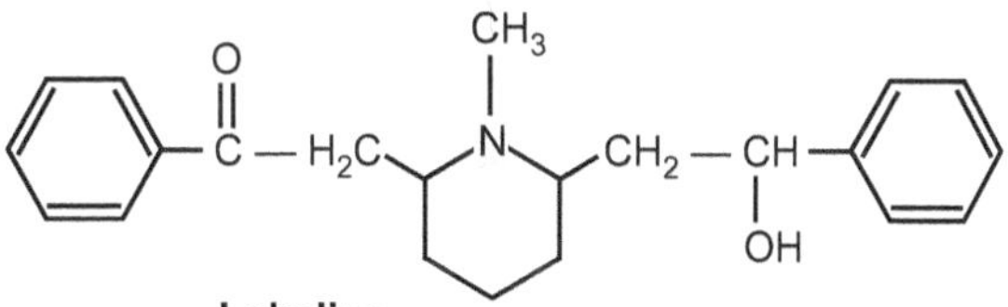

Lobeline

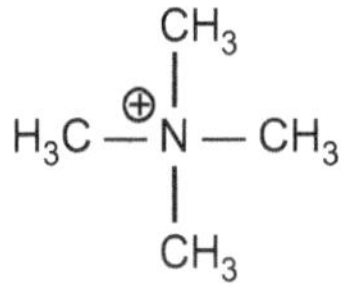

Tetramethyl ammonium (TMA)

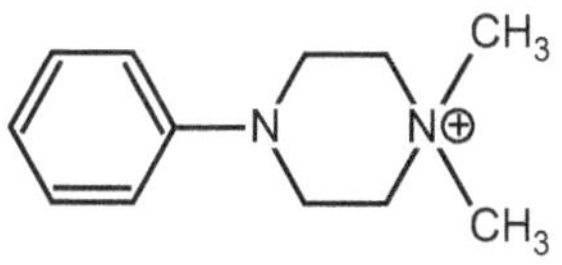

1,1 dimethyl- 4-phenyl piperazinium (DMPP)

(c) The effects on respiratory system are mainly central in origin. For example, in low doses, nicotine activates chemoreceptors located in aortic arch and respiratory centers. High doses of alkaloid cause direct stimulation of respiratory centers alongwith a generalized CNS stimulation. While in toxic doses, it causes CNS depression followed by death due to respiratory paralysis. The failure of respiration is due to the inhibition of respiratory centers in the brain stem as well as to a depolarizing blockade of neuromuscular junction of respiratory muscles.

(d) It causes the release of antidiuretic hormone from pituitary gland.

(e) Cardiovascular effects of nicotine are mainly due to the activation of
  (i) sympathetic ganglia,
  (ii) adrenal medulla
  (iii) sympathetic nerve endings and
  (iv) chemoreceptors of aortic and carotid bodies. The ultimate or overall effects of nicotine administration results in vasoconstriction, tachycardia and increase in blood pressure.

(f) GIT : The overall increase in the tone and muscle activity in GIT is mainly due to the combined activation of parasympathetic ganglia and cholinergic nerve endings.

(g) Exocrine glands : Nicotine first stimulates and then depresses the secretions of bronchial tract and salivary gland.

Nausea, vomiting and diarrhoea are seen as the side-effects after systemic absorption of nicotine and lobeline. They are caused due to central and peripheral actions of these alkaloids. They are readily absorbed from the mucous membranes of oral cavity, GIT and respiratory system. Liver serves as the main site of metabolism but the drug also undergoes metabolism in lung and kidney. Cotinine and nicotine-1'-N-oxide are the principal metabolites excreted through urine alongwith unchanged fraction of administered dose of nicotine. Half-life of nicotine, administered parenterally or by inhalation is estimated to be two hours, during which, it can readily cross blood-brain-barrier and placental barrier.

In 1913, Marshall, first reported the ganglionic biphasic action of tetraethyl ammonium (TEA). The synthetic analogue, DMPP is about 3-4 times more potent than nicotine. Both the synthetic analogues do not cause ganglionic blockade except when given in large intra-arterial doses.

17.5 GANGLIONIC BLOCKERS

Various drugs which exert blocking activity at autonomic ganglia can do so by
(i) acting presynaptically and affecting the neurotransmitter synthesis, release and re-uptake,
(ii) acting postjunctionally and
  (a) initially stimulating the ganglia by an ACh like action and then blocking the ganglia by a persistent depolarization. Blokade occur due to desensitization of cholinergic receptors sites. These agents are known as depolarizing ganglionic blockers.
  (b) blocking the ganglionic transmission either by inhibiting competitively the interaction between ACh and its receptor sites or closing the channel when it is open. These agents are known as competitive ganglion blocking agents.

(a) Depolarizing ganglionic blockers: Nicotine itself, is an example of this class. In small doses, nicotine stimulates all autonomic ganglia. But, if given in larger doses or during prolonged administration, nicotine causes an initial repetitive stimulation phase followed by blockade of ganglionic transmission due to persistant depolarization. The desensitization of the cholinergic receptor sites present on postganglionic cell-body is the main reason of ganglionic blockade. Beside nicotine, many drugs possess variable degrees of ganglionic blocking activity as a side-effect. The members of this class are not used clinically for this purpose.

(b) Competitive ganglionic blocking agents : It is a class of clinically employed ganglionic blockers. The fact that d-tubocurarine blocks the transmission of impulses in neuromuscular junction by competitively inhibiting the ACh-receptor interaction, stimulated the development of this series. The competitive ganglionic blocking action of hexamethonium, a prototype of this series was first reported by Paton and Zaimis in 1949. This is followed by development of other synthetic ganglion-blockers. The blocking action of hexamethonium is mainly due to its ability to occlude or to close the ion-channel which was opened due to ACh-receptor interaction. This leads into a reduction in the duration of current flow resulting into ganglionic blockade. While trimethaphan acts as competitive antagonist of ACh and blocks the receptor sites on post-ganglionic surface. Thus, the initial EPSP does not develop.

Hexamethonium, Azamethonium and pentolinium are the members of a series of bis-quaternary ammonium salts. Pentolinium has a longer duration of action than hexamethonium. The report about the effectivity of triethylsulfonium salts as ganglionic blockers, led to the development of trimethaphan. It has a very short duration of action; hence it is available only for parenteral administration (50 mg/ml). Trimethaphan, in high doses, can stimulate the release of histamine resulting into a direct vasodilation. Hence, it should be used with caution in patients with asthma or allergy. Another agent, mecamylamine was developed and studied in mid-1950s. Soon after, it was released into the market. It is as potent as hexamethonium but less potent than pentolinium, in its ganglionic blocking activity. Due to its nonquaternerized nature, it is well absorbed and distributed in various body compartments. It is able to penetrate the CNS and placental barriers. It is excreted unchanged by kidney. The main side-effects of mecamylamine include tremors, mental confusion, mania and depression, all of central origin. Pempidine is a newly introduced ganglionic blocker having simple structure. In larger doses, pempidine controls the release of acetylcholine from the preganglionic nerve terminals.

17.6 ABSORPTION, FATE AND EXCRETION

Most of the important agents of this category are quaternary or bis-quaternary ammonium salts. Hence, their absorption remains poor and unpredictable. Once absorbed, they are mostly retained in the extracellular space. They are not affected much by metabolizing enzymes and get excreted through urine in almost unchanged form.

17.7 SIDE EFFECTS

The side effects associated with their use are mainly due to their unselective blocking action and include, nausea, vomiting, dry mouth, anorexia, decrease tone and motility of GIT, xerostomia, anhydrosis, cycloplegia and postural hypotension. These side effects sufficiently disturb the patient and limit their chronic use.

17.8 THERAPEUTIC USES

(a) Because they reduce the level of sympathetic activity, they were once widely used in the treatment of hypertensive cardiovascular disease. Since the mechanism governing transmission in all autonomic ganglia remains same, their unselectivity of action leads to numerous side-effects. Hence they are now totally replaced by more selective and less toxic β_1-adrenergic blockers.

(b) They are used to produce controlled hypotension to minimize blood loss during plastic, neurological and opthalmic surgery or in operative procedures where extensive skin dissection is needed. Trimethaphan is a drug of choice due to its short duration of action. The hypotension can easily be reversed within few minutes of stopping the drug administration.

(c) Trimethaphan, pentolinium and mecamylamine can be used in the management of autonomic hyperreflexia or autonomic neurovegetative syndrome. This syndrome results due to excessive catecholamine discharge by the injuries of upper spinal cord. For the treatment α-adrenergic blockers can also be employed.

17.9 LIMITATIONS

(i) During prolonged administration, tolerance may develop and to achieve the same intensity of pharmacological response, one has to increase the dose of the drug.

Some patients, however, may show hypersensitive responses when exposed to the treatment of these drugs.

Table 17.3: Pharmacological actions of hexamethonium related drugs

System	Effects of ganglionic blockade
Salivary glands	decrease in the salivary secretion (xerostomia)
Sweat glands	decrease in perspiration (anhydrosis)
GIT	reduction in tone and motility
Urinary bladder	urine retention
Ciliary muscle	paralysis of accommodation (cycloplegia)
Iris	pupil dilation (mydriasis)
Arterioles	vasodilation, increase in peripheral blood flow, hypotension.
Veins	vasodilation, decreased venous return.
Heart	decreased cardiac output, tachycardia.

SYMPATHOMIMETIC DRUGS

18.1 INTRODUCTION

The sympathetic nervous system controls various important systems including cardiovascular, bronchial airway tone, muscular, metabolic etc. It prepares the organism against the conditions of stress, either physical or physiological origin. In addition to epinephrine, a large number of agents can mimic the responses obtained as a result of stimulation of adrenergic nerves. They bear structural resemblance with the neurotransmitter, epinephrine. Hence, they can be used to mimic or alter the functioning of sympathetic nervous system in several clinical disorders like hypertension, asthma, arrhythmia and various allergic conditions. Majority of these substances contain an intact or a partially substituted amino group and hence, also called as sympathomimetic amines.

These drugs, are divided into two broad categories according to their structures.

(a) Compounds with 3,4-dihydroxyphenyl nucleus or a catechol nucleus : They are termed as catecholamines.

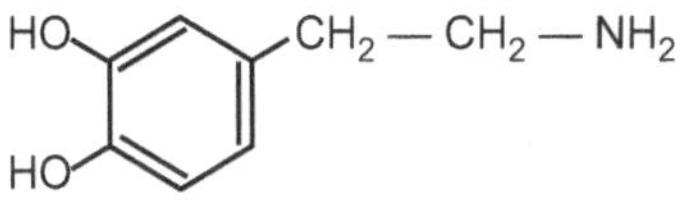

Dopamine

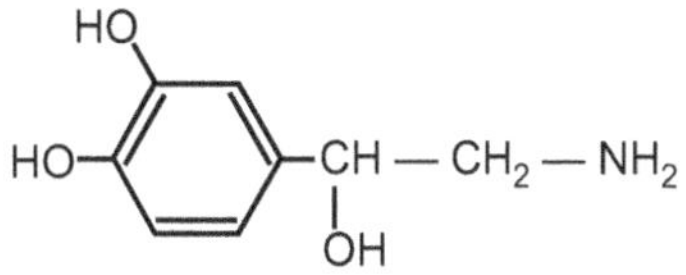

Norepinephrine (Noradrenaline)

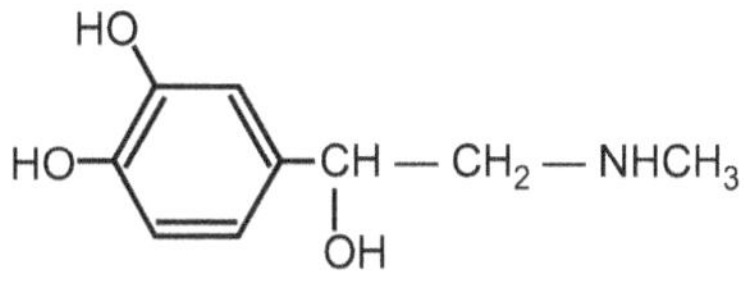

Epinephrine (Adrenaline)

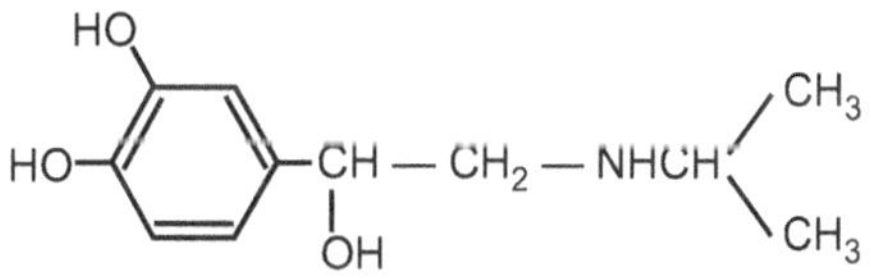

Isoprenaline (Isoproterenol)

(b) Compounds those lack hydroxy groups on phenyl ring : They are termed as noncatecholamines.

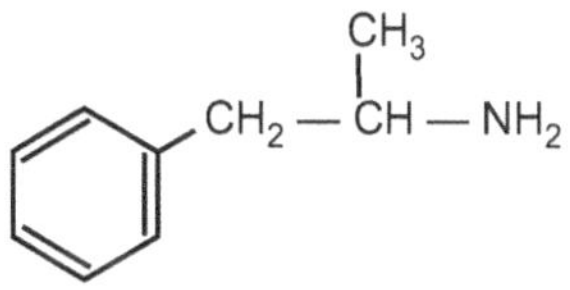

Amphetamine

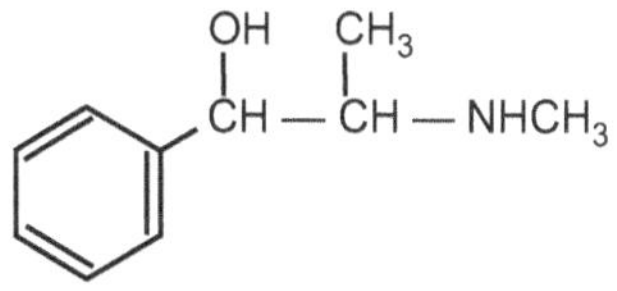

Ephedrine

With few exceptions, drugs which act on the adrenergic nervous system all possess some chemical elements of the endogenous agonist, epinephrine. Epinephrine, norepinephrine and dopamine are the naturally occurring catecholamines. They control most of the responses of this branch of the involuntary, autonomic nervous system. Many of the familiar responses of the "flight or fight" syndrome such as vasoconstriction or an increase in the heart rate, are due to stimulation of sympathetic nervous system.

Norepinephrine is the neurotransmitter present in the sympathetic nerves and in brain. It also serves as a precursor for the synthesis of adrenaline in the adrenal gland. Adrenaline is the hormone of adrenal medulla. It was first separated from the adrenal medulla by Abel and Crawform (1897) in the form of its polybenzoyl derivative. Japanese chemist, Takamine named it as adrenaline. It was first synthesized by Stoltz in 1904.

A large number of synthetic amines, structurally related to epinephrine were prepared and evaluated for the activity by Barger and Dale in 1910. They described the activity of these compounds as sympathomimetic. The racemic mixture thus formed, was resolved by Tullar in 1948. Upon resolution, dextro-epinephrine was found to be about one twelfth potent as levoepinephrine. Its role as a neurotransmitter in the sympathetic nervous system, was proposed by Elliott in 1904.

Dopamine, a third naturally occurring catecholamines, acts as a neurotransmitter in the basal ganglia of CNS. Dopamine-β-hydroxylase enzyme converts dopamine into norepinephrine. This enzyme is not present in the dopaminergic neuron. Hence, dopamine remains in its original form to carry out the function of neurotransmitter. For example, dopamine acts through dopaminergic neuronal mechanisms to dilate mesenteric and renal vascular beds.

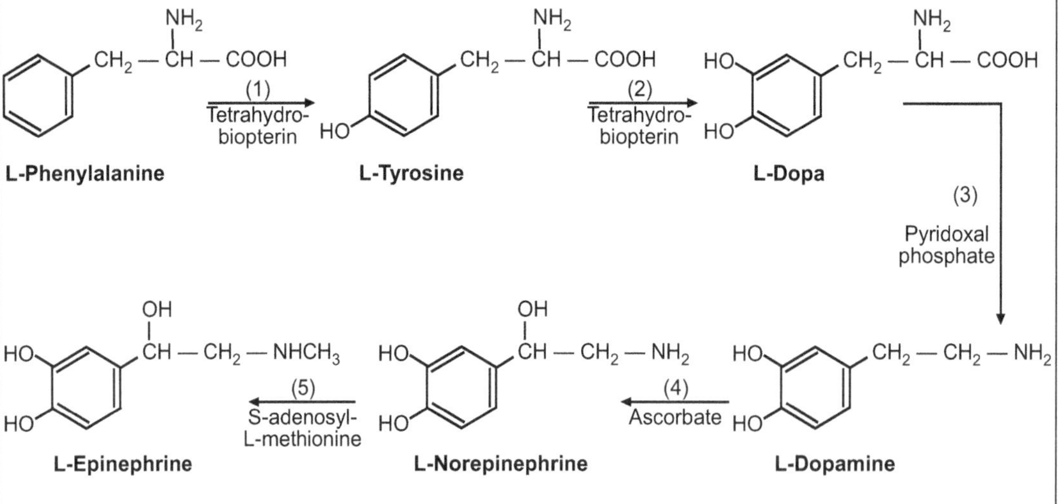

Fig. 18.1 : Biosynthesis of neurotransmitters

18.2 BIOSYNTHESIS OF NEUROTRANSMITTER

The Fig. 18.1 represents the biosynthetic pathway for norepinephrine and epinephrine in the nerve terminals.

The enzymes which catalyse the intermediate steps of biosynthesis of sympathetic neurotransmitter are denoted by the number present on the arrow. They are listed as below :

Enzymes participating :

1. Phenylalanine hydroxylase
2. Tyrosine hydroxylase
3. Dopa decarboxylase
4. Dopamine–β–oxidase
5. Phenylethanolamine–N–methyl-transferase.

These enzymes are synthesized within the cell bodies of the adrenergic neurons and are then transported along the axons to their nerve terminals. The activity of tyrosine hydroxylase is low and conversion of tyrosine to DOPA is a rate-limiting step in neuro-transmitter synthesis. The remaining enzymes are of generally low specificity. From step 1 to step 3, take place in cytoplasm. Dopamine, the end-product of step 3, then enters into the synaptic vesicles where it is converted into norepinephrine. Norepinephrine thus synthesized is then stored inside the nerve endings within the synaptic vesicles.

18.3 SYNAPTIC INTERACTIONS

1. When the impulse reaches to the nerve terminals, the membrane becomes more permeable for the influx of Ca^{++} ions. This causes the release of neurotransmitter from the synaptic vesicles through exocytosis. The transmitter migrates across the synapse and binds to its receptor sites upon the target organ.

2. After its interaction with the receptor, norepinephrine may be removed by the following routes :

(a) Norepinephrine is rapidly and efficiently 'reabsorbed' into the neuron i.e., nerve terminals and then into its storage sites. The greatest quantity of norepinephrine is removed in this way. This type of uptake (uptake-1) has strict ionic requirements, being completely dependent on the presence of Na^+ ions (and low concentration of K^+ ions) in the external surrounding medium. Similarly this uptake exhibits high steriochemical selectivity and operates against concentration gradient. Certain drugs like cocaine, imipramine selectively block this neuronal uptake and avail high concentration of norepinephrine in the synaptic cleft. **(see Fig. 18.2 on next page)**

(b) Extraneuronal uptake : In addition to neuronal uptake, there exists a second uptake process of norepinephrine from synaptic cleft to supporting tissues (glial cells). This process is not sterio-selective and is not inhibited by usual inhibitors of neuronal uptake. This extraneuronal uptake is reported to be inhibited by metanephrine and corticosteroids. The extra neuronal uptake can be regarded as transport and metabolism while neuronal uptake is transport and retention of neurotransmitter.

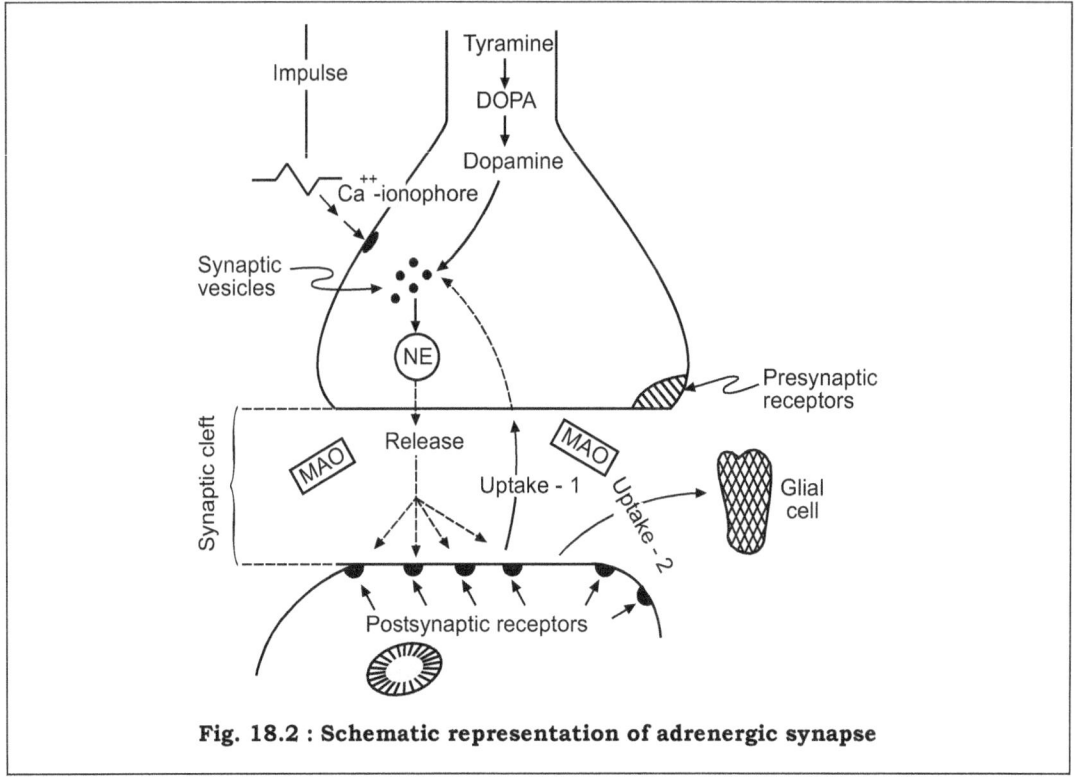

Fig. 18.2 : Schematic representation of adrenergic synapse

(c) Part of the neurotransmitter may also be lost due to its diffusion across the synaptic cleft : In the adrenergic synapses, diffusion mechanism is a route of minor importance in removing norepinephrine. The blood vessels, probably stand as an exception where the immediate disposition of released norepinephrine is accompanied largely by a combination of extra-neuronal uptake diffusion and enzymatic breakdown of neuro-transmitter.

The other routes of removing norepinephrine are metabolic in nature.

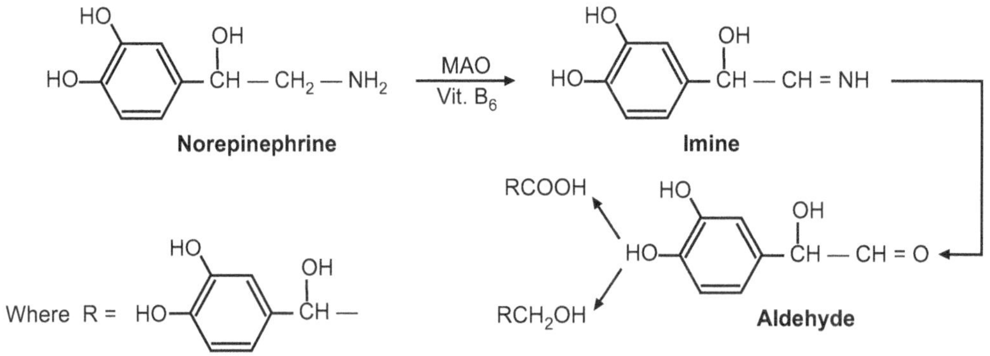

Fig. 18.3 : Metabolic inactivation of norepinephrine by monoamine oxidase enzyme

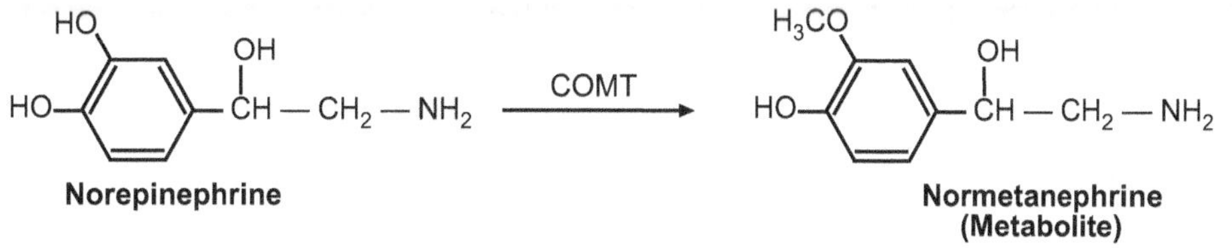

Norepinephrine —COMT→ **Normetanephrine (Metabolite)**

For example, norepinephrine through its interaction with cytoplasmic mono amino oxidase (MAO) enzymes is converted to the corresponding aldehyde which then non-enzymatically further oxidised.

Similarly, catechol-O-methyl transferase (COMT) enzyme methylates the m-hydroxy group of the phenyl ring of catecholamines, rendering them less active.

18.4 PHARMACOLOGICAL ACTIONS OF CATECHOLAMINES

1. They exert excitatory effects on smooth muscles present in blood vessels and on salivary as well as sweat glands.

2. They initiate inhibitory responses on smooth muscles of GIT, bronchial tract and blood vessels provided to skeletal muscles. Thus, the blood vessels get dilated to supply the skeletal muscles with more blood.

3. Depending upon the drug employed, the secretion of various endocrine glands either increases or decreases.

4. They exert excitatory effects on cardiac cells resulting into an increase in force of contraction (i.e., positive ionotropic effect) and an increase in the rate of contraction (i.e., positive chronotropic effect).

5. The increased level of catecholamines in the CNS leads to respiratory stimulation, alertness, an increase in psychomotor activity and a reduction in appetite.

6. Catecholamines promote glycogenolysis both in liver and skeletal muscles and cause an increase in the production of free fatty acids from adipose tissue.

Thus, catecholamines are responsible for the "flight or fight" syndrome and prepare the body to protect itself or to run away when threatened.

The adrenergic agonists all have pharmacological spectrum of activities similar to that of norepinephrine. Only quantitative differences are present.

18.5 METABOLISM

Monoamino oxidase (MAO) and catechol-O-methyl transferase are the main enzymes which metabolise the sympathomimetic drugs. About 6% of the administered dose of epinephrine or norepinephrine in man remains untouched by these main enzymes which then is excreted in its original form or in its conjugated form with sulfuric or glucuronic acid. Conjugation usually occurs at phenolic hydroxyl groups.

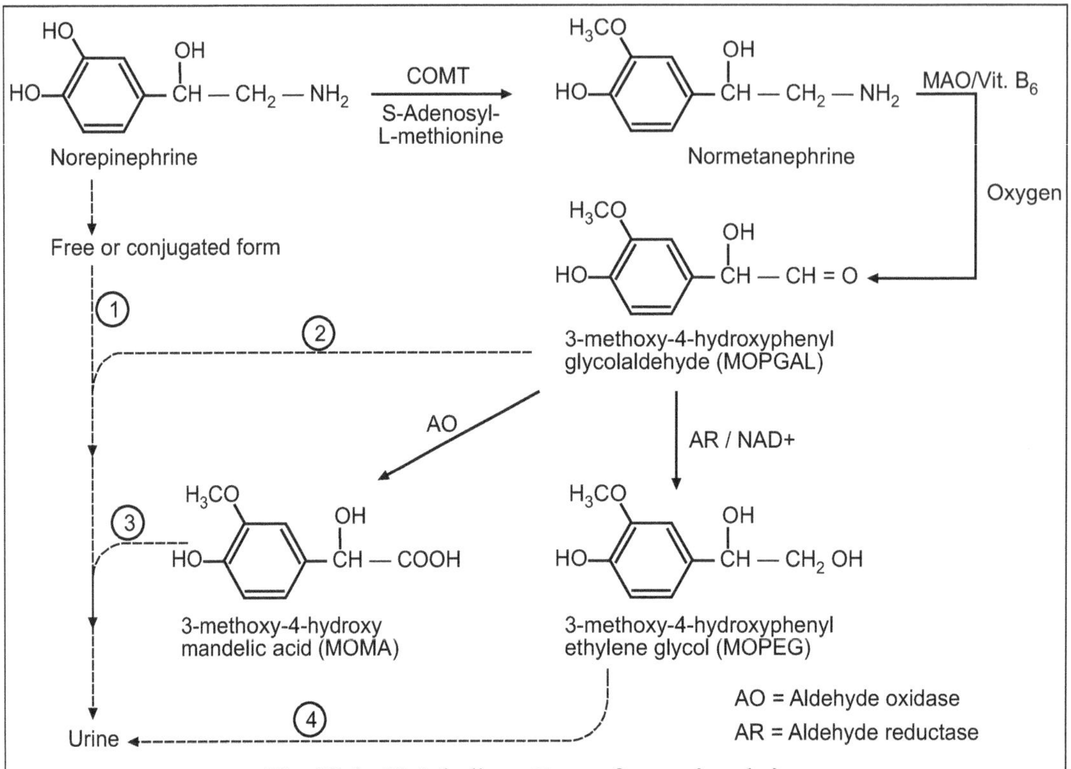

Fig. 18.4 : Metabolic pattern of norepinephrine

The major fraction of natural catecholamines is attacked by MAO and/or COMT. At periphery, they are preferentially oxidized to the acid and in the CNS, are reduced to glycol.

Thus, the principal metabolites of nor-epinephrine (MOPGAL, MOMA and MOPEG) are excreted through urine alongwith a free or conjugated form of unaltered norepinephrine. Of these, 3-methoxy-4-hydroxymandelic acid is the principal metabolite and the estimation of its content in urine can be taken as an index of catecholamine metabolism. On an average, about 70% of an administered dose of epinephrine or norepinephrine follow metabolism by COMT enzymes while only 20% favour the attack by MAO enzymes.

By using drugs which inhibit these metabolising enzymes, the duration and intensity of effects can be raised. For example, some agents can specifically block the MAO enzymes and are in clinical use under the name of MAO inhibitors. While only few agents can block the activity of COMT enzymes on circulating catecholamines but did not find clinical applicability. These include pyrogallol and tropolone derivatives.

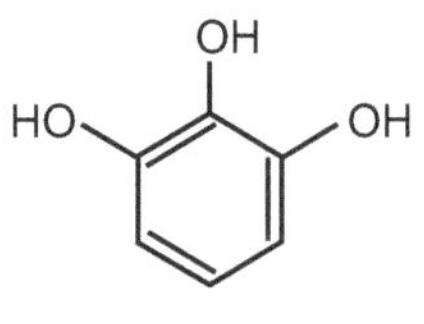

Pyrogallol

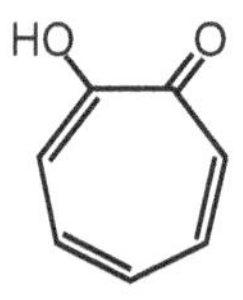

Tropolone

18.6 ADRENOCEPTORS

Upon discharge from nerve terminals, norepinephrine reacts with post-synaptic receptor sites to evoke its pharmacological response. In 1948, Ahlquist observed that, the tissues he examined, carried two kinds of adrenergic responses, i.e. alpha and beta responses, as shown in the following table.

Table 18.1 : Results of Ahlquist experiment

Group 1 responses (α-responses)	Group 2 responses (β-responses)
Vasoconstriction	Vasodilation
Contraction of Uterus	Relaxation of Uterus
Contraction of Ureters	Increased rate and force of heart beats
Contraction of Pupil	
Relaxation of Intestine	

From the table, it can be easily seen that (with the last response as an exception) α-responses are mainly excitatory in nature, while β-responses are inhibitory in nature. In general, inhibitory β-receptors can be activated at quite low concentration of catecholamines than that is needed to activate excitatory α-receptors.

Lands and co-workers in 1967, based on the differences in the cardiac and bronchial responses of the sympathomimetic agents, proposed a further sub-division of the β-receptors into :

(i) $β_1$-receptors, whose activation accounts for cardiac stimulation, lipolysis and intestinal relaxation effects of sympathomimetic drugs, and

(ii) $β_2$-receptors, whose activation accounts for relaxation in vascular bed, bronchial tree, uterus and ureter alongwith metabolic effects of sympathomimetic agents.

With an exception of $β_2$-receptors present in pancreas (which have excitatory response), the activation of most of the $β_2$-receptors is linked with the inhibitory responses. While the activation of $β_1$-receptors leads to the excitatory responses in general. The type of response is mainly governed by Ca^{++} ion fluxes at the nerve endings.

On the same line, α-receptors can be categorised into $α_1$- and $α_2$-receptors. $α_1$-receptors are present on postsynaptic receptor sites of smooth muscles of blood vessels and gland cells. While $α_2$-receptors are present on pre-and-post-synaptic sites on the nerve terminals and are also present in the CNS. The post-synaptic sites of $α_2$-receptor presence, include the tissues like brain, uterus, parotid gland and extra-synaptic region at some blood vessels.

The presynaptic $α_2$-receptors are present on the nerve terminal. Their activation leads to inhibition of neurotransmitter release (norepinephrine or acetylcholine) through negative feedback inhibitory mechanism. Their function is :

(i) to govern the release of neuro-transmitter, and

(ii) as per need, to alter the rate of synthesis of neurotransmitter.

Thus, the activation of $α_2$–receptors on the cholinergic nerve terminals within the intestinal wall leads to the inhibition of release of acetylcholine.

Table 18.2 : Distribution of receptor sub-types

β-receptor predominant	α-receptor predominance	α and β
Cardiac cells (β_1)	Blood vessels to	Coronary blood vessels
Metabolic effects	– skin	Skeletal muscle
– lipolysis (β_1)	– visceral region	Blood vessel
– glycogenolysis (β_2)	– brain region	Mucous membrane of alimentary tract
Bronchial muscles (β_2)		
Ciliary muscles (β_2)	– renal region	
Bladder muscles	Intestinal sphincter	
	Sweat gland	
	Bladder sphincter	
	Dilator pupillae	

Clonidine, yohimbin and α-methyl-norepinephrine are more effective on α_2-receptors than α_1-receptors. Phenylephrine, prazosin and methoxamine while act prominently on α_1–receptors.

Thus in tissues, the overall effect of the adrenergic nerve stimulation depends upon the population of α and β-receptors present in that organ.

For example, in cardiac cells, positive inotropic and positive chronotropic actions are due to the activation of β-receptors whereas α-receptors activation leads to ectopic excitation induced by sympathetic stimulation.

Tachyphylaxis or reduced response is a common problem encountered in the prolonged treatment of adrenergic drug. Upon continuous exposure, the receptors lose their efficiency resulting into decrease in the magnitude of biological response. This is known as desensitization, refractoriness, down regulation or tachyphylaxis. Various mechanisms are proposed to account for this event. Thus, tachyphylaxis may be due to :

(a) Feedback regulatory mechanisms governed by cyclic-AMP.
(b) Some receptors may undergo degeneration causing a decrease in total number of receptors.
(c) Receptors may be inactivated or blocked due to irreversible phosphorylation, or
(d) The correlation between the receptor and adenylate cyclase may get paralyzed.

Norepinephrine is the most active agent at α-receptor and the latter is least responsive to isoproterenol. The responses mediated through α-receptors are blocked by antagonists like phenoxybenzamine or phentolamine. The excitatory nature of α-receptors and inhibitory nature of β-receptors can easily be seen from the table 18.3.

Table 18.3 : Adrenergic responses

α–receptor mediated responses	β–receptor mediated responses
Vasoconstriction	Vasodilation
Mydriasis	Bronchial smooth muscle relaxation
Release of ACTH	
Uterine myometrial contraction	Uterine myometrial relaxation
Retractor penis contraction	Intestinal smooth muscle relaxation
Seminal vesicle contraction	Positive ionotropic effect on the heart
Pilomotor muscle contraction	
Orbital contraction	Positive chronotropic effect on the heart
Nictitating membrane contraction	
Intestinal smooth muscle relaxation	Hepatic glycogenolysis, Lipolysis

The β-receptor is most responsive to isoproterenol while the least responsive agent is norepinephrine. The β-receptor mediated responses remain unaffected by the usual α-adrenergic blockers and are blocked by agents like Nadolol or timolol.

18.7 CLASSIFICATION

Norepinephrine, epinephrine or isoproterenol-like drugs mimic the responses of adrenergic stimulation by acting directly on the receptor sites. While some agents when administered, do not act on the adrenergic receptors. They enter the adrenergic nerve terminals and cause stoichiometric displacement of norepinephrine from the synaptic vesicles. Their pharmacological responses are thus due to this displaced neurotransmitter. Thus, the adrenergic agonists can be conveniently divided into :

(a) Direct-acting Drugs :

These amines produce their pharmacological responses by their direct action on adrenoceptors. The actions produced are of rapid onset and short-lived. Most of the agents can influence both α- and β-receptors, thus ranging from pure α-agonist (phenylephrine) to pure β-agonist (isoproterenol). The intensity of their effects remains unaffected by the use of reserpine, cocaine or imipramine.

(b) Indirect-acting Drugs :

Tyramine does not act directly on the adrenoceptors. The fact that reserpine depletes tissues of norepinephrine (Bertler et al; 1956) indicated that tyramine acts by releasing endogenous norepinephrine.

Many sympathomimetic agents exert a large fraction of their effects by releasing (through displacement) norepinephrine from storage sites in the synaptic vesicles or from extra-vesicular binding sites. The responses of this released norepinephrine are prominently α-receptor mediated, slower in onset and generally longer lasting.

Examples of indirect acting drugs include tyramine, amphetamine etc. These drugs usually lack catechol nucleus. Indirect acting agents have little or no action in reserpinized animals. Cocaine or imipramine also lowers down the intensity of activity by inhibiting the drug-induced displacement and release of norepinephrine. Since these drugs lack the phenolic hydroxyl groups, the increased lipophilicity imparts pronounced central effects to these drugs. If given repeatedly, tachyphylaxis is likely to occur due to the depletion of norepinephrine stores.

(c) Mixed Action Drugs :

Many sympathomimetic drugs exert their actions partly by acting directly on the receptor sites and partly by their effect on the norepinephrine release. They are termed as mixed action drugs. Examples include –

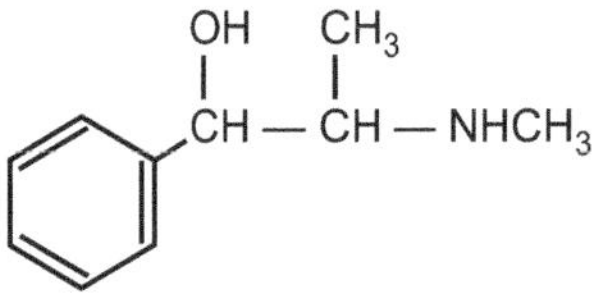

Ephedrine

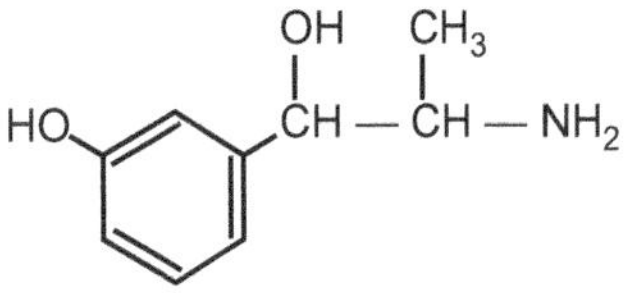

Metaraminol

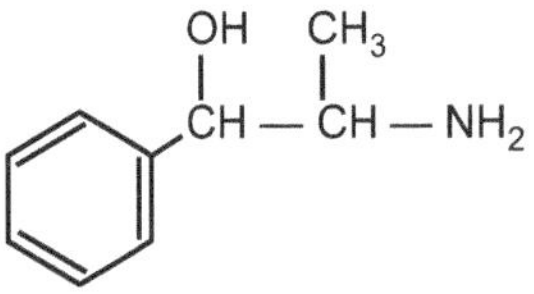

Phenylpropanolamine

They share structural features of both classes. The presence of cocaine, reserpine or imipramine only reduces (and not abolish) the intensity of their effects, where higher doses of these drugs will be needed to produce comparable effects.

Thus if we assume, the following skeleton essential for sympathomimetic activity.

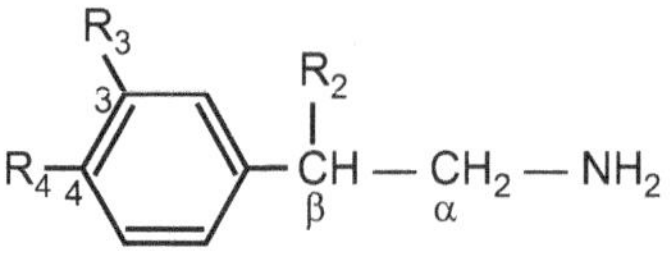

Then,

(i) Direct-acting drugs usually have $R_3 = R_4 = $ OH or OCH_3 and $R_2 = $ OH i.e.,

(ii) Indirect acting drugs will have only a hydroxyl group at β-carbon atom or no substitution at R_2, R_3 and R_4. They retain the phenylethylamine framework, and

(iii) Mixed action drugs share the structural features of both above classes.

Thus, Examples of direct-acting drugs include :
- norepinephrine
  (predominantly on α-receptor)
- epinephrine
  (on α, $β_1$, and $β_2$ receptors)
- isoprenaline
  (on $β_1$ and $β_2$ receptors)
- Tazolol
  (predominantly on $β_1$ receptor)
- Salbutamol
  (predominantly on $β_2$ receptor)
- Phenylephrine
  (predominantly on α-receptor)

Prototype of indirect-acting drugs is amphetamine.

Prototype of mixed action drugs is ephedrine.

The commonly used alpha blocking agent is dibozane or 1, 4 - (bis-1, 4-benzodioxan-2-yl-methyl) piperazine while the commonly used β-blocking agent is dichloroisoproterenol.

18.8 STRUCTURE-ACTIVITY RELATIONSHIP

[Structure: β-phenylethylamine skeleton with OH at position 3, numbered positions 1-6 on ring, R'' substituent, β-carbon with OH, α-carbon with R, attached to NHR']

[Structure: R—C$^\beta$(H)(R')—C$^\alpha$(CH$_3$)(R'')—NHR''']

Direct-acting Adrenergic Agonists :

β–phenylethylamine is the basic skeleton in these drugs.

(i) To act directly on the adrenoceptors, a compound must have –

  (a) Phenolic hydroxyl group at 3 and 4 positions,

  (b) a hydroxyl group at β-carbon, and

  (c) small substituents (H, CH$_3$, C$_2$H$_5$) may be placed on α-carbon atom.

(ii) The phenolic hydroxyl group can be successfully replaced by alkoxy (–OCH$_3$) or arylsulfonamide functions.

(iii) Direct acting agonist activity is enhanced by the presence of a hydroxyl group of the correct steriochemical configuration (i.e., leavorotatory) on the (β-carbon but is reduced by the presence of a methyl group on α-carbon. The presence of α-methyl group increases the duration of action by making the compound more resistant to metabolic deamination by MAO.

(iv) The presence of a hydroxyl group on β-carbon lowers the lipophilicity of the compound, thus decreasing the central effects associated with the drug.

Indirect-acting Adrenergic Agonists :

(i) Indirect-acting adrenergic agents do not contain the phenolic hydroxyl group (if R = phenyl), at 3,4-position. Hence, they are attacked upon by COMT enzymes. Lack of phenolic hydroxyl group increases lipophilicity. Thus, their oral effectiveness, duration of action and penetration into CNS is increased. In many such drugs, CNS effects are more prominent than their peripheral actions.

(ii) The absence of polar hydroxyl groups on phenyl ring results in a loss of direct peripheral sympathomimetic activity. These compounds therefore, have a higher ratio of central to peripheral stimulating properties.

(iii) An increased activity at α-receptor (vasoconstriction), is attributed to an absence of phenyl ring in the structure. Hence, such drugs are widely used as nasal decongestant.

(iv) β$_2$-receptor stimulation is prominant in drugs having large substitution at terminal nitrogen atom. These drugs are not deaminated by MAO enzymes. Other substituents like phenolic hydroxyl groups at 3 and 5 positions potentiate β$_2$-receptor stimulation.

18.9 MECHANISM OF ACTION

1. Direct-acting adrenergic agonists act directly on the adrenoceptors located in cellular plasma membranes. The responses mediated through β-receptor are mainly through cyclic-AMP. While α-receptor effects arise due to

(a) mobilization of Ca^{++} ions and/or the formation of inositol triphosphate resulting into activation of α_1-receptor, and

(b) inhibition of adenylate cyclase thus blocking the synthesis of cyclic-AMP is mainly due to the activation of α_2-receptor.

The overall effects of adrenergic stimulation arise as combination of responses mediated through the receptors and the effects of reflux homeostatic regulation of the organism.

2. Indirect-acting adrenergic agonists mimic the responses at the target organs by releasing the endogenous norepinephrine from its storage sites.

3. Some drugs do not have sympathomimetic actions of their own, but they can increase the concentration of neurotransmitter at the receptor sites present on the target organ. They do so by inhibiting either the attack of metabolizing enzymes (MAO inhibitors) on the neurotransmitter or re-uptake processes in the synapses.

18.10 DIRECT-ACTING ADRENERGIC AGONISTS

Norepinephrine, epinephrine and dopamine are the examples of naturally occurring direct-acting drugs while isoprenaline belongs to the synthetic series of compounds.

These compounds can influence both, α and β-receptors and vary in their affinities towards these receptors. Thus, norepinephrine is most active at α-receptors while isoprenaline is most active at β-receptors. This determines their pattern of pharmacological spectrum of activities. In these compounds, the presence of hydroxyl group on the β-carbon atom makes possible the existence of sterioisomers. In most instances, this hydroxyl group increases the affinity of the compounds for the receptor sites. The laevorotatory(–) isomers of both, norepinephrine and epinephrine are much more active than dextro-isomers. This is particularly true for β-adrenergic agonists than α-adrenergic agonists. In general, any substituent at α-carbon in the side-chain will inhibit metabolic deamination of the compound by MAO enzymes and will increase the duration of action. Compounds with dextro-rotatory substituent at α-carbon atom possesses more pronounced central effects than their laevo isomers. For example, d-amphetamine is more potent CNS stimulant than *l*-amphetamine.

Norepinephrine (Noradrenaline): HO-C6H3(OH)-CH(OH)-CH2-NH2 (with α and β carbons labeled)

Epinephrine (Adrenaline): HO-C6H3(OH)-CH(OH)-CH2-NHCH3 (with α and β carbons labeled)

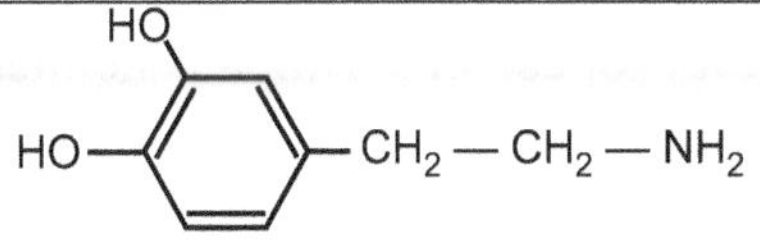

Dopamine: HO, HO-C₆H₃-CH₂-CH₂-NH₂ (3,4-dihydroxyphenyl)

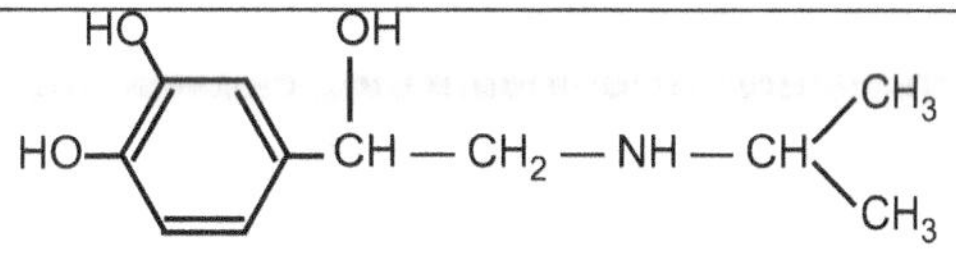

Isoprenaline: HO, HO-C₆H₃-CH(OH)-CH₂-NH-CH(CH₃)₂

All these agents have actions similar to epinephrine, the prototype of this series. Only quantitative differences exist among them. Hence, we shall study the pharmacological activities of epinephrine in detail. Whenever other compounds disobey the usual pharmacological pattern sketched out by epinephrine, mention will be made at that point.

(I) Epinephrine :

Epinephrine is a term official in USP while the same compound is known as adrenaline in British pharmacopoeia. It can activate and evoke the responses at both α-and β-adrenoceptors. Its prominent actions on the heart, vascular and other smooth muscles, are exploited for its clinical applications.

(a) Effects on Cardiovascular System :

Epinephrine has stimulatory effects on the heart. Acting through $β_1$ receptors present in cardiac cells, it leads to an increase in rate and force of heart contraction. As a result of these effects, oxygen consumption in the heart also increases. Vasoconstriction occurs in many vascular beds alongwith a marked constriction of the veins. As a result, the blood pressure rises rapidly where the rise in systolic pressure is more than the rise in diastolic pressure. This rise is immediately followed by a fall in blood pressure due to activation of $β_2$-receptors present in the vasculature. Unlike epinephrine, small doses of norepinephrine do not cause vasodilation or lower the blood pressure.

Table 18.4 : Direct-acting adrenergic agonists

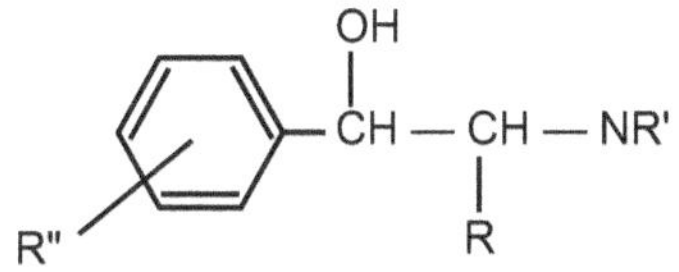

General structure: R''-C₆H₄-CH(OH)-CH(R)-NR'

Compound	R"	R	R'	Primary receptor site
Norepinephrine	3, 4-di OH	H	H	α
Epinephrine	3, 4-di OH	H	CH₃	α and β
Phenylephrine	3 – OH	H	CH₃	α
Isoproterenol	3, 4-di OH	H	– CH (CH₃)₂	β
Isoetharine	3, 4-di OH	– C₂H₅	– CH (CH₃)₂	β
Metaproterenol	3, 5-di OH	H	– CH (CH₃)₂	β
Metaraminol	3 – OH	CH₃	H	α

In general, epinephrine causes an increase in heart rate, stroke volume, cardiac output and venous return. These changes activate the parasympathetic (vagus) tone to the heart through caroticoaortic pressor receptive mechanism. The increased heart rate is lowered down due to the inhibitory action of vagus stimulation which causes reflex bradycardia. The ventricular muscles are least supplied with parasympathetic innervation. Hence, they remain unaffected by vagus stimulation. As a result, heart rate decreases while increase in stroke volume remains unaffected. The vagal interference in the cardiostimulant activity of epinephrine can be blocked by atropine. Epinephrine irritates myocardium and increased concentrations of the drug will elevate the possibility of cardiac arrhythmias.

(b) Smooth Muscles :

The pre-existing tone of the smooth muscle plays an important role in determining the action of epinephrine on smooth muscle. In general, it relaxes almost all varieties of smooth muscles, especially that of GIT and bronchial tract. The tone and frequency of muscle contraction is reduced. The sphincters (i.e. pyloric and ileocecal) get contracted. It inhibits the contraction of detrusor muscle of bladder resulting into urine retention. The relaxation of smooth muscles is affected by the following mechanisms.

(i) due to the activation of β_2 receptors on smooth muscle.

(ii) due to the activation of α_2-receptors which have inhibitory effects. These receptors are located at the presynaptic sites on terminal cholinergic (excitatory) neurons of Auerbach's plexus. The activation of α_2- receptors lead to inhibition of the release of acetylcholine.

(iii) due to the reduction in the cytoplasmic concentration of free calcium ions. The free Ca^{++} ions activates the calmodulin–dependent myosin light chain kinase and phosphorylation of myosin results into tension development.

Uterine smooth muscle contains both α- and β–receptors. Hence, response to epinephrine varies with dose and the stage of reproductive cycle. In non-pregnant women, epinephrine causes contraction of uterus (α-effect), but during last month of pregnancy, β_2-receptor mediated inhibition of tonic contractions of uterus predominates and epinephrine inhibits uterine tone and contraction. Hence, more selective β_2-receptor acting drugs can be used to minimize premature labour, e.g. turbutaline or ritodrine.

(c) Respiratory System :

Epinephrine is a potent respiratory stimulant alongwith its bronchodilating activity. These effects (particularly bronchodilation) are partly shared by selective β_2-receptor stimulants. Like isoprenaline, it also inhibits antigen-induced release of histamine. In large doses, pulmonary edema induced by direct acting drugs may become a cause of death of the patient.

(d) Central Effects :

The structures of direct-acting drugs consist of many polar groups. The low lipophilicity associated with these compounds accounts for their poor central effects. The exaggeration of their peripheral effects on the glycogenolysis, lipolysis and cardiorespiratory system leads to restlessness, headache and tremors in some patients receiving epinephrine.

(e) Metabolic Effects :

(i) Epinephrine increases oxygen utilization by 20 - 30% and promotes the breakdown of glycogen (glycogenolysis) to glucose-6–phosphate. Epinephrine is the most potent stimulator of hepatic glycogenolysis while isoproterenol is most potent stimulant of skeletal muscle glycogenolysis. Glycogenolysis is promoted by the activation of α_1, and β_1 receptors.

(ii) Epinephrine inhibits insulin secretion via activation of α–receptors and stimulates glycogen secretion via activation of β-receptors. Both these effects are carried out by epinephrine-induced accumulation of cyclic-AMP.

(iii) As a result of glycogenolysis, the blood sugar level may exceed the renal threshold (170 mg%) leading to a transient glycosuria.

(iv) Epinephrine through its action on receptors (α_1, β_1) in adipose tissues, activates triglyceride lipase which then cause the breakdown of triglycerides into free fatty acids and glycerol. Thus, lipolysis in adipose tissue is also mediated by cyclic-AMP.

(v) An increase in the basal metabolic rate alongwith its cardio-stimulant action, epinephrine causes a rise in body temperature.

(vii) Norepinephrine causes mild hyperglycemia and is usually effective only when large doses are administered.

(f) Miscellaneous Effects :

(i) Epinephrine causes dilation of pupil which is an expression of fear and allied emotional responses. It lowers the intraocular pressure.

(ii) It stimulates lacrimation and salivary glands.

(iii) By increasing the activity of factor V, epinephrine makes blood coagulation faster.

(iv) Epinephrine increases motor power of the muscle by promoting neuro-muscular transmission.

(v) It reduces the circulating plasma volume by directing the protein- free fluid to the extra-cellular space.

(II) Other Direct-acting Catecholamines:

Norepinephrine is the precursor amine of epinephrine. It acts as a transmitter in post-synaptic adrenergic nerves. Human adrenal medulla also releases minor portion of norepinephrine alongwith epinephrine.

Pharmacologically the laevo-norepinephrine isomer is important. It is a potent agonist at α–receptors and has little actions on β–receptors. In heart, norepinephrine acts on β_1–receptor and exerts cardio-stimulant action quite comparable to that produced by epinephrine. Other effects produced by epinephrine are weakly mimicked by norepinephrine.

Dopamine serves both the functions, i.e.

1. It is utilized as the precursor for the biosynthesis of norepinephrine and epinephrine. Hence, it retains the structural features necessary to activate adrenergic α and β receptors.

2. It acts as a neurotransmitter in some area of the CNS. Hence, some of the effects are recognized as 'due to dopamine only' type. For example, vasodilation in the renal, mesenteric, coronary and intra-cerebral vascular beds is thought to be linked with activation of specific dopamine receptors. Due to its low lipophilicity administered dopamine can not reach the CNS region to activate specific dopaminergic receptors located therein and thus lacks central effects.

The structure of dopamine exposes the drug to the attack of both, MAO and COMT enzymes. Hence, it is orally ineffective and possesses very short duration of action. In therapeutic dose, it has cardiostimulant activity similar to that of epinephrine. The systolic and pulse pressure increases whereas the peripheral resistance remains unchanged.

Isoproterenol is the most potent sympathomimetic amine that acts almost exclusively at β–receptors. It mimicks with more potency the β–receptor mediated responses of epinephrine and lacks α–receptor mediated responses. Its field of interest thus is restricted to the heart, metabolic effects, smooth muscles of bronchi, skeletal muscle, vasculature and alimentary tract. The drug is principally metabolized by COMT enzymes and sulphate conjugation. Since it is poorly metabolized by MAO enzymes, isoproterenol has duration of action longer than epinephrine. It is usually recommended for the relief in respiratory disorders and as a cardiac stimulant in heart block.

18.11 ABSORPTION, FATE AND EXCRETION

If administered orally, direct-acting sympathomimetic amines are rapidly conjugated and oxidised in the gastro-intestinal mucosa and liver which seriously limits their therapeutic use. Absorption occurs at a slow rate by inhalation and subcutaneous routes. Intra-muscular administration is visually effective.

The principal metabolizing enzymes are COMT and MAO which are aided by other enzymes present in liver, compounds with substituent at α–carbon are resistant to MAO attack while compounds missing phenolic hydroxyl group at 3-position escape from COMT influence. The metabolic pattern and principal metabolites which appear in urine are already dealt (Article 18.5).

18.12 SIDE-EFFECTS

The acute side-effects include nausea, vomiting, fear, anxiety, restlessness, headache, tachycardia, dizziness, weakness, anginal pain, hypertension, arrhythmia and respiratory difficulty. Palpitation is produced due to increased force of heart beats. Most of these effects can be linked with excessive sympathetic activity.

Serious toxicities like cerebral hemor-rahage or arrhythmia are reported to occur in patients already under the treatment of MAO inhibitors or tricyclic antidepressants. Doses in hypersensitive patients lead to severe hypertension.

18.13 SELECTIVE α-RECEPTOR STIMULANTS

Some adrenergic agents have a selective action on the α-adrenergic receptors with very weak activating action on the β-receptors. The clinical used agents from this class are phenylephrine and methoxamine.

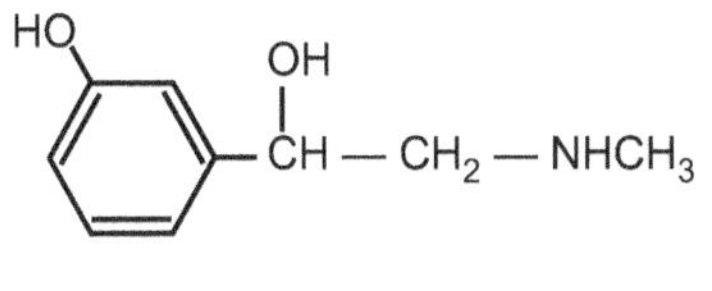

Phenylephrine

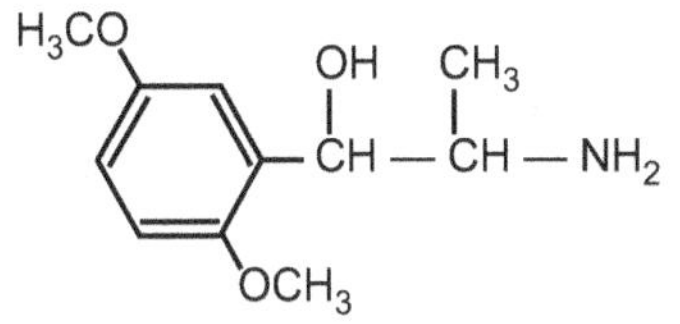

Methoxamine

Phenylephrine is a powerful $α_1$-receptor stimulant. An increase in blood pressure is mainly due to its vasoconstrictor action. Most vascular beds are constricted resulting into reduced blood flow except in coronary artery where blood flow increases. It lacks stimulant actions on heart and the CNS. It has a weak capacity to induce the release of norepinephrine from its storage sites. Methoxamine has similar properties to that of phenylephrine. They are mainly used as nasal decongestant, mydriatic or as a pressor agent in hypertensive states.

18.14 SELECTIVE $β_1$- ADRENERGIC STIMULANTS

With few exceptions, drugs that act on the β-receptors, all possess some chemical elements of similarity with the endogenous agonist, epinephrine. But this is not always true with α-adrenergic agonists or antagonists.

Tazolol has been claimed to be a selective $β_1$ agonist.

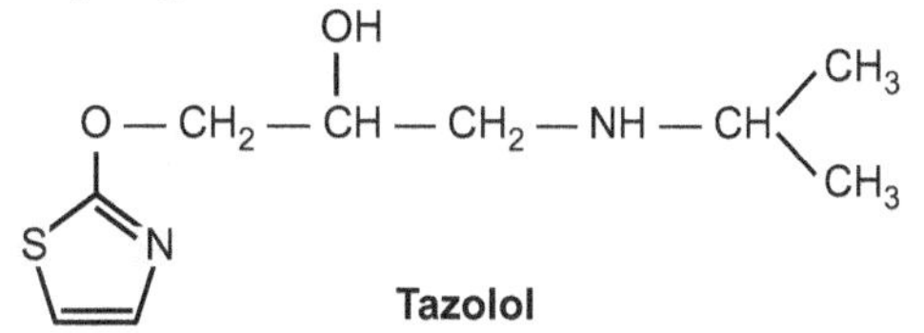

Tazolol

Mechanism of action of this compound is yet not clear and needs further studies. In general, if a phenylethylamine is supposed to be a prototype of direct acting drug, then it is the nature of nitrogen substituent that determines whether, it will act primarily at α- or β-receptor.

Dobutamine is yet another example of directly acting drug having selective affinity for $β_1$-adrenergic receptors. Chemical features include :

1. resemblance with dopamine, and
2. a bulky aromatic substituent on the nitrogen atom.

It has its major action on the heart ($β_1$ receptors). It causes a dose-dependent cardiostimulant action in patients with congestive cardiac failure. It does not activate dopaminergic receptors in renal vasculature.

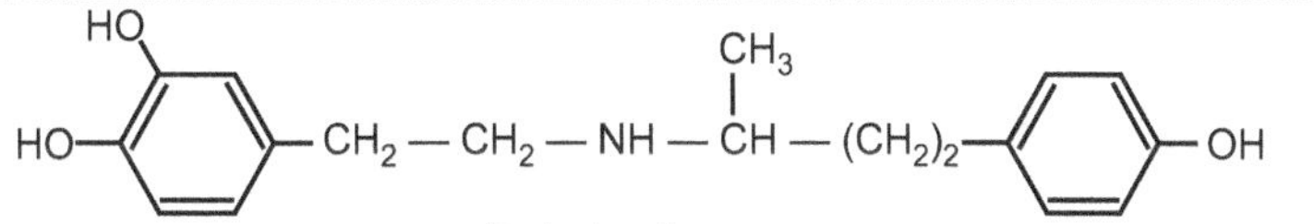

Dobutamine

18.15 SELECTIVE β₂-ADRENERGIC STIMULANTS

Isoproterenol is a prototype of drugs acting at both β_1 and β_2 receptors. Selective β_2-adrenergic agonists usually cause relaxation of

(i) bronchial smooth muscles
(ii) vasculature provided to skeletal muscles, and
(iii) uterine smooth muscle.

They are devoid of cardio-stimulant activity.

Based upon their pharmacological actions, selective β_2-agonists are used for :

(a) the symptomatic treatment of respiratory disorders due to the bronchospasm, and
(b) the inhibition of premature uterine contraction to delay the labour.

Table 18.5 : Selective β₂-Agonists

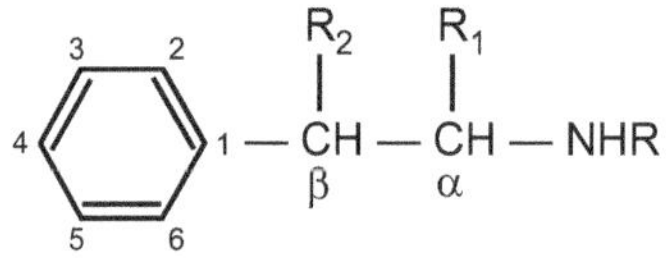

General formula for β₁-agonists

Compound	Phenyl ring	R₂	R₁	R
Metaprotorenol	3-OH, 5-OH	OH	H	— CH(CH₃)₂
Isoetharine	3-OH, 4-OH	OH	C₂H₅	— CH(CH₃)₂
Isoxsuprine	4-OH	OH	CH₃	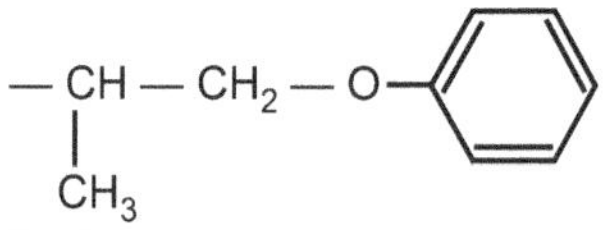 — CH(CH₃) — CH₂ — O — C₆H₅
Nylidrin	4-OH	OH	CH₃	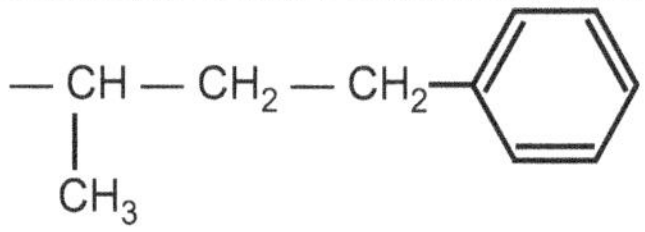 — CH(CH₃) — CH₂ — CH₂ — C₆H₅
Ritodrine	4-OH	OH	CH₃	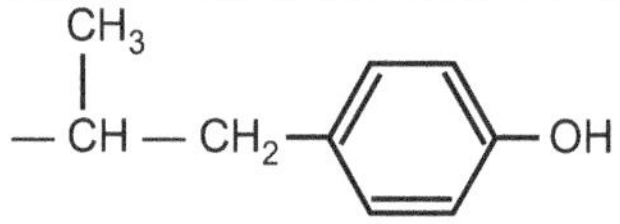 — CH(CH₃) — CH₂ — C₆H₄ — OH
Terbutaline	3-OH, 5-OH	OH	H	— C(CH₃)₃
Salbutamol	3-CH₂OH, 4-OH	OH	H	— C(CH₃)₃
Fenoterol	3-OH, 5-OH	OH	H	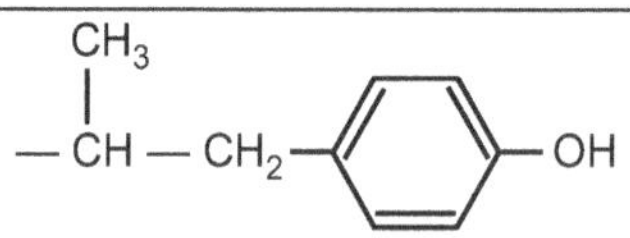 — CH(CH₃) — CH₂ — C₆H₄ — OH
Soterenol	3-NHSO₂CH₃, 4-OH	OH	H	— CH(CH₃)₂

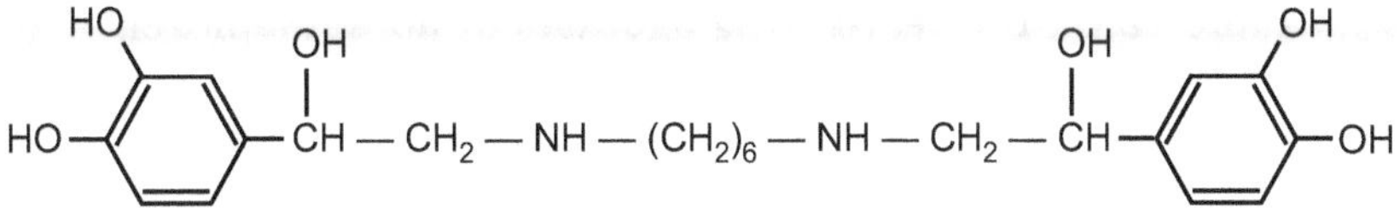

Hexoprenaline structure:

HO-, HO- (on benzene ring) — CH(OH) — CH₂ — NH — (CH₂)₆ — NH — CH₂ — CH(OH) — (benzene ring with OH, OH)

Hexoprenaline

Continuous exposure to β_2-agonists results in the reduced response (tachyphylaxis) in the bronchial muscles. This can be corrected by using glucocorticoids. Most of these drugs can be administered orally or by inhalation. They have longer duration of action than isoproterenol. After absorption they improve the respiratory function and cause bronchodilation which is beneficial in conditions like asthma and other bronchospastic diseases. To arrest premature labour, they can be given by intravenous route.

These drugs are excreted in urine usually as conjugates of glucuronic acid. Side-effects associated are not serious and include nausea, vomiting, nervousness, palpitation, tachycardia and hypertension.

After the introduction of salbutamol in 1968, many long acting selective β_2-agonists have been synthesized. Few of them which are employed clinically include carbuterol, quinterenol, rimiterol, salmefamol, tretoquinol and hexoprenaline.

Hexoprenaline (1970) has prolonged duration of action due to its slow rate of metabolism.

It is reported that metabolites of hexoprenaline still retain β_2-agonist property.

In general,

(i) An α–CH$_3$ group is necessary for preferred vascular effects.

(ii) If α-CH$_3$ group is dropped, more selectivity for bronchial β_2-receptors is obtained, and

(iii) A fairly large N-substitution is needed for both these effects.

18.16 INDIRECT ACTING ADRENERGIC AGONISTS

This class is comprised of non-catecholamines. Most of these drugs retain phenylethylamine skeleton. The following structure is representative of indirect-acting drugs.

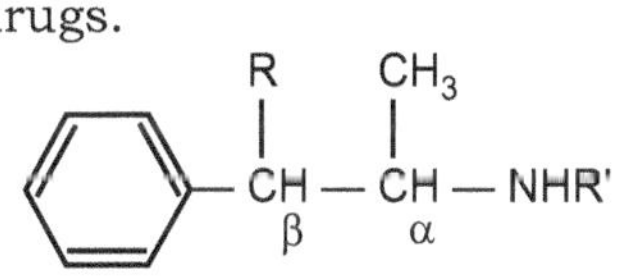

Phenyl — CH(R)(β) — CH(CH$_3$)(α) — NHR'

Where, R = H or OH

R' = H, CH$_3$, or heterocyclic ring.

The structural features of this category of compounds include :

(i) lack of phenolic hydroxyl group which makes these compounds resistant to the attack of COMT enzymes.

(ii) presence of α-methyl group which makes these compounds resistant to the attack of MAO enzymes, and

(iii) increased lipophilicity due to the absence of polar phenolic hydroxyl groups and due to the presence of α-methyl group. These compounds pass more readily through Blood-Brain-Barrier.

Table 18.6 : Indirect-acting agonists of norepinephiren

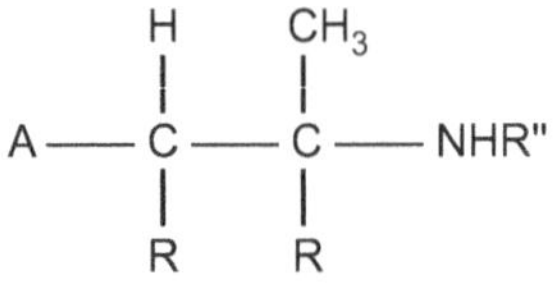

$$A-\underset{\underset{R}{|}}{\overset{\overset{H}{|}}{C}}-\underset{\underset{R'}{|}}{\overset{\overset{CH_3}{|}}{C}}-NHR''$$

Compound	A	R	R'	R''
1. Phenylpropanolamine	C_6H_5	OH	H	H
2. Amphetamine	C_6H_5	H	H	H
3. Methamphetamine	C_6H_5	H	H	CH_3
4. Phentermine	C_6H_5	H	CH_3	H
5. Chlorophentermine	p – Cl C_6H_4	H	CH_3	H
6. Methoxyphentermine	p – CH_3O C_6H_4	H	CH_3	H
7. Cyclopentamine	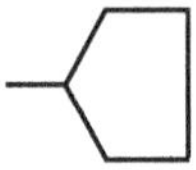 (cyclopentyl)	H	H	CH_3
8. Propylhexedrin	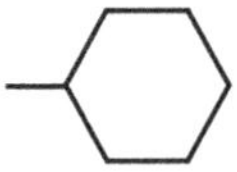 (cyclohexyl)	H	H	CH_3

The effects of above structural features of these compounds are reflected in :

(a) oral effectiveness and longer duration of action, and

(b) a higher ratio of central to peripheral actions.

In some compounds, the lipophilicity can be further increased by replacing the benzene ring by a 5 or 6-membered saturated ring by naphthalene or by an aliphatic chain.

As already mentioned, indirect-acting drugs do not interact (with some exceptions), with the receptor sites. Their pharmacological activity is mainly due to their ability to displace norepinephrine from its storage sites. Since norepinephrine has more prominant action on α–adrenergic receptors, indirect-acting drugs have their actions mainly centered on α–receptor stimulation. For example, bretylium and guanethidine are employed as antihypertensive agents.

They act by affecting the storage and release of norepinephrine.

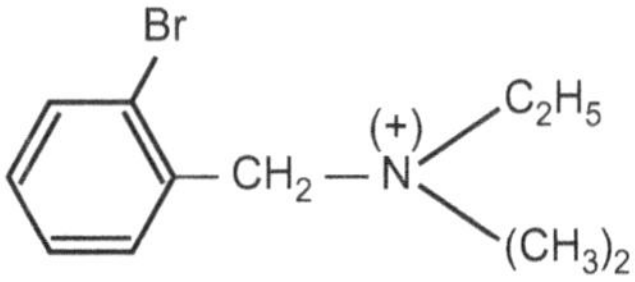

Bretylium

In addition to the actions that mimic adrenergic responses, a number of indirect-acting drugs have an anorexic or appetite supressing action. In attempts to modify the phenylethylamine structure to provide anorexic activity without pronounced CNS stimulation, compounds were prepared in which the amino nitrogen is a part of heterocyclic system. But these attempts failed to separate totally the two effects.

Amphetamine is a prototype of this class. It shares most of its pharmacological effects with other members except quantitative differences. Hence it will be dealt in detail in the following section.

Amphetamine :

Amphetamine, the term describes a racemic β–phenylisopropyl amine. Alongwith its peripheral adrenergic (α, and β–responses) actions, it is a powerful cerebrospinal stimulant. The dextroisomer dexamphetamine) is about twice as active as racemic amphetamine. Usually l-isomer is more active at peripheral sites while the CNS effects are mainly due to d-isomer. In addition to these effects, amphetamine also has an anorexic action and can be used in the treatment of obesity. In higher doses, it induces the release of dopamine from extra-pyramidal sites resulting into stereotypy (i.e., repetitive and purposeless movements). Parahydroxyamphetamine, one of its derivative, lacks CNS activity and possesses α–receptor stimulant activity. It is a powerful vasoconstrictor. It, alongwith its derivatives constitute a separate class, comprising the compounds useful as nasal decongestants.

Pharmacology:

1. Cardiovascular effects :

Amphetamine has moderate cardio-stimulant activity. When orally administered, it causes an increase in both systolic and diastolic blood pressures.

2. Smooth muscles :

In its actions on the smooth muscles, amphetamine follows the footprints of epinephrine. Variable effects are obtained on the smooth muscles of GIT and uterus. At latter, amphetamine usually has excitatory effect.

3. CNS:

More specifically, the CNS stimulant effects of amphetamine are due to its dextroisomer, which is about 3-4 times more active than l-isomer in this regard. Amphetamine is reported to be most potent sympathomimetic CNS stimulant drug. It mainly arouses reticular activating system, medullary and cortical region. As a result, there is a feeling of alertness, awakefulness, an increase in motor and speech activity and an increase in rate and depth of respiration. It also potentiates the analgetic action of opioids. Its anorexic activity is mainly due to its action on lateral hypothalamic feeding centre.

In higher doses, amphetamine induces the release of dopamine and 5-hydroxytryptamine in the brain which accounts for stereotypy and psychotic abnormalities in the patients. Since most of the actions of amphetamine are due to its ability to displace norepinephrine from its storage sites, over dosage, or prolonged administration will exhaust norepinephrine stores. This will lead to fatigue and mental depression. Tachyphylaxis is one of the problems associated with the continuous use of these drugs.

Methamphetamine has marked CNS stimulant properties with very few peripheral α– or β–receptor mediated actions.

4. Metabolic effects:

In therapeutic doses, amphetamine - like drugs do not affect the basal metabolic rate. In humans, a slight fluctuation on either side in the metabolic rate is reported.

Absorption, Fate and Excretion :

Most of the indirect-acting drugs are orally effective. Upon absorption they are uniformly distributed in tissues and can cross blood-brain-barrier to reach the CNS area in significant proportion. In liver, they are primarily metabolized by p-hydroxylation and N-demethylation. These metabolites appear in the urine in the form of their conjugates. Amphetamine when appears in the urine, the excretion pattern include : conjugate of hydroxylated metabolite (3%) + conjugate of deaminated derivative (25%) + unaltered drug (35%). Urinary pH, of course may influence the pattern of excretion.

Adverse Effects :

Acute toxicities associated with these drugs include :

(a) Peripheral effects :

Nausea, vomiting, dry mouth, diarrohea, headache, palpitation, anginal pain, hypertension, arrhythmia etc.

(b) Central effects :

Restlessness, tremors, insomnia, hyperactivity, euphoria, fever etc.

Tolerance and dependence are reported to develop with amphetamine.

Specific uses of these drugs include:

(a) In the treatment of narcolepsy (irresistable desire to sleep) and cataplexy (extreme muscular weakness). Both these conditions do not involve the loss of consciousness.

(b) Some of them are clinically used as anorexic agents in the treatment of obesity, and

(c) In the treatment of attention-deficient, hyperactive disorders in the children.

Some clinically used amphetamine - like **drugs in the treatment of obesity (anorexigenic agents) :**

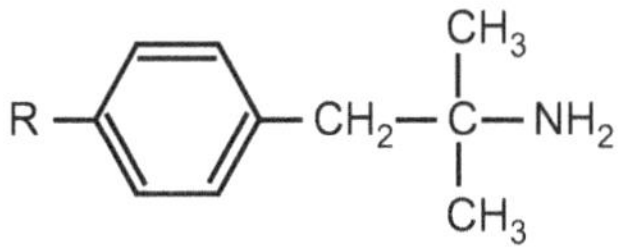

Phentermine; R = H

Chlorphentermine; R = Cl

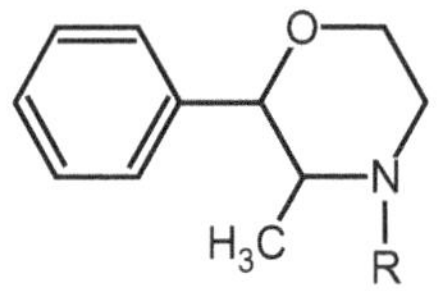

Phenmetrazine; R = H

Phendimetrazine; R = CH$_3$

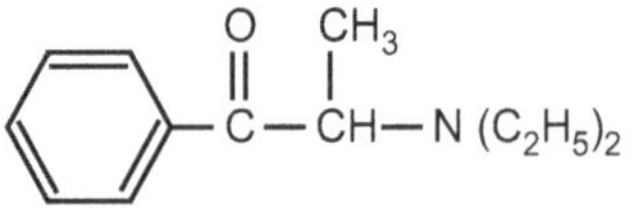

Diethylpropion

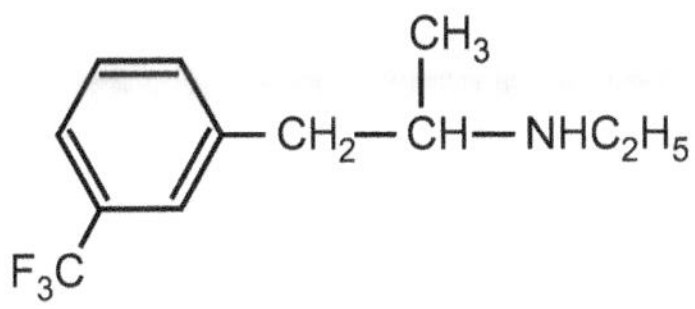

Fenfluramine

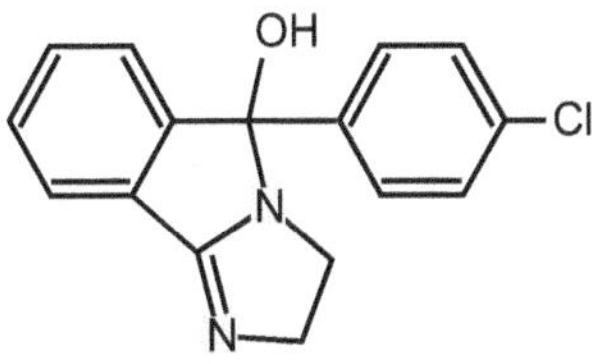

Mazindol

18.17 MIXED-ACTION ADRENERGIC AGONISTS

These compounds act both, directly with the receptor sites and partly by the release of endogenous norepinephrine. The characteristic features of these drugs include oral effectiveness, longer duration of action and more pronounced CNS effects. Some agents from this category, due to their vasoconstrictor action, are employed clinically as nasal decongestant. The prototype drug of this series is ephedrine. Other important examples include mephentermine, hydroxy-amphetamine and metaraminol.

Ephedrine occurs naturally in various plants of the genus Ephedra. Near 1925 it was introduced into modern medicine. Today it is mainly obtained through synthetic route. Out of four isomers, only *l*-ephedrine and racemic mixture are used clinically.

Peripherally it stimulates both α and β-adrenergic receptors. It has marked central action which is less pronounced than amphetamine. It also induces the release of endogenous norepinephrine.

Hence, like amphetamine, tachyphylaxis is also likely to occur in the continuous use of ephedrine. It is mainly used in the treatment of :

(i) nasal congestion of allergic origin, and,

(ii) patients suffering periodic attacks of complete heart block (Stokes-Adams Syndrome).

Due to the vasoconstrictive properties, following compounds are also used as nasal decongestant.

The adverse effects of mixed-action drugs are quite similar to but less intensive than those of amphetamine like drugs.

18.18 THERAPEUTIC USES OF SYMPATHOMIMIC AMINES

(I) Use of Vascular Effects :

1. The activation of α-receptors by sympathomimetic agents leads to vasoconstriction. Hence they are applied locally in surgical procedures.

(a) to control superficial hemorrhage by reducing capillary oozing, and

(b) for better visualization of the area to be operated.

The vasoconstrictive (α-response) action of these agents, qualifies them to be used as nasal decongestion when applied topically to nasal and pharyngeal mucosal surface.

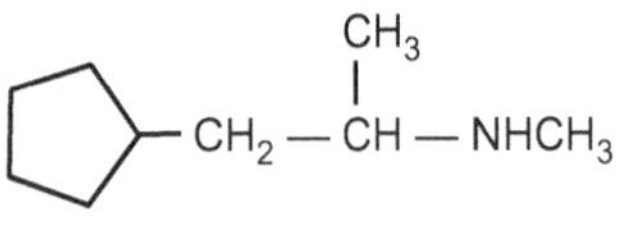

Cyclopentamine: cyclopentyl-CH$_2$-CH(CH$_3$)-NHCH$_3$

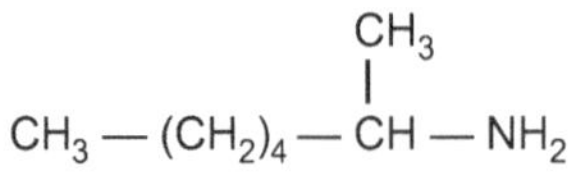

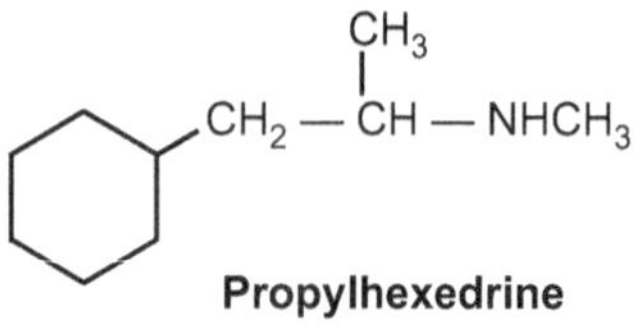

Tuaminoheptane: CH$_3$-(CH$_2$)$_4$-CH(CH$_3$)-NH$_2$

Propylhexedrine: cyclohexyl-CH$_2$-CH(CH$_3$)-NHCH$_3$

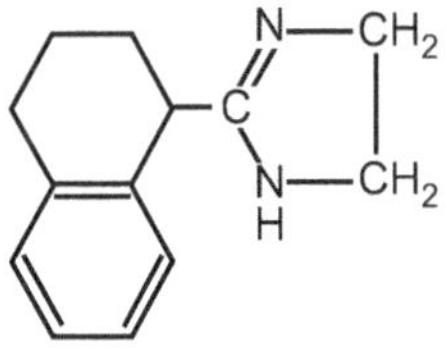

Tetrahydrozoline

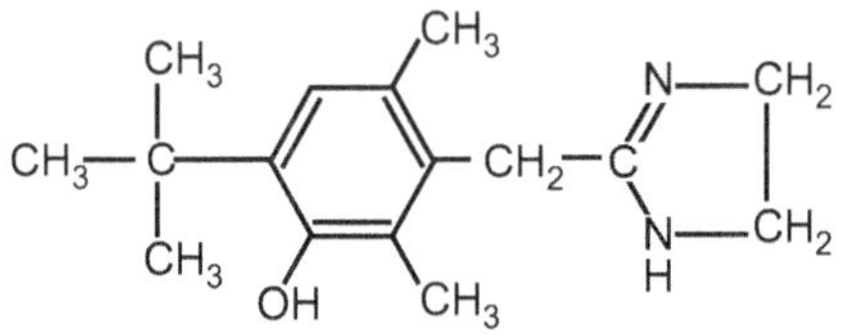

Oxymetazoline

In addition, they also relax the smooth muscles of bronchial tract (β$_2$-response) and relieve bronchospasm in respiratory disorders.

2. Their ability to antagonise the histamine-induced effects, increases their efficacy in the treatment of asthma. They can be employed also in the treatment of urticaria, serum sickness and other allergic conditions where histamine dominates the scene.

Shock is a condition which arises due to inadequate tissue perfusion. It is an outcome of acute peripheral vascular failure. They can be used to treat most forms of shocks, e.g., cardiogenic shock, anaphylactic shock etc. For example, dopamine is used in the treatment of cardiogenic shock.

3. They can be used alongwith local anesthetics for –

   (a) localization and prolongation of anesthetic activity, and
   (b) preventing fall in blood pressure, a possible danger associated with spinal anesthesia.

Their utility in anesthesia is mainly due to their α–mediated responses.

4. The sympathomimetic amines with prominent α–receptor activity can be used to correct the hypertensive crisis associated with certain drug-therapy. While the sympathomimetic amines with prominent β-receptor agonistic activity can be employed to prevent cardiac arrest in Stokes–Adams syndrome.

5. These drugs are used to dilate the pupil in ophthalmological examination. Like other mydriatics, their use is neither accompanied with an increase in intra-ocular pressure nor with cycloplegia.

6. Amphetamine-like drugs, due to their pronounced CNS effects can be used in the treatment of :

   (a) Narcolepsy,
   (b) Cataplexy,
   (c) Parkinsonism,
   (d) Obesity, and
   (e) Hyperkinetic syndrome.

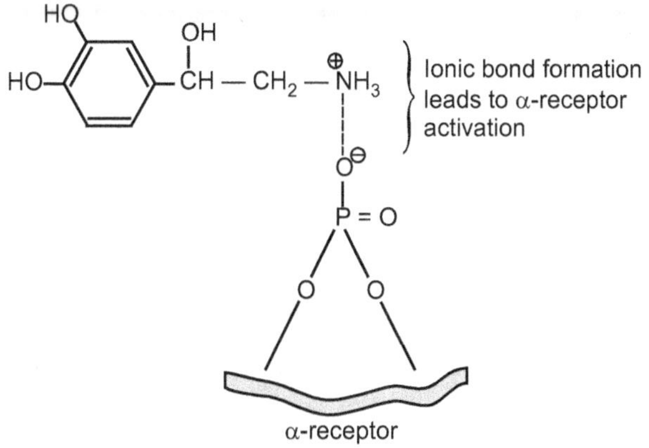

Fig. 18.5 : α-receptor activation

18.19 ADRENERGIC RECEPTOR STRUCTURE

One of the most effective compound acting chiefly at α–receptor is norepinephrine. The more bulky the substituent on nitrogen, α-receptor activity decreases and β–receptor activity increases, as it is revealed in isoproterenol.

The α–receptor carries a negatively charged group (probably a phosphate) which will then react with the positively charged ammonium nitrogen.

The prosthetic group of α–receptor resembles in structure with c-AMP molecule. Bulky substituents present on nitrogen would hinder the attack of positively charged nitrogen on phosphate anion. Hence, isoproterenol has less affinity for α–receptor.

The hydroxylated benzene ring is important for attachment to β–receptor. Belleau suggested that β–receptor bears a resemblance to the prosthetic group of COMT enzymes. The binding of β–agonists with the receptor involves the chelation process.

18.20 SECOND MESSENGERS

Receptors for a number of hormones and autocoids function by regulating the concentration of the intracellular second messengers. In most cases, adrenergic responses are mainly due to an increase or decrease in the concentration of second messenger, cyclic adenosine 3', 5'–monophosphate (cyclic AMP) through the activation or inhibition of the membrane-bound enzyme, adenylate cyclase.

Cyclic-AMP or cyclic-GMP (guanosine monophosphate) are the examples of cyclic nucleotides which act as second messenger. Chemically nucleotide is an ester of phosphoric acid with a pentose sugar already linked with a purine or pyrimidine base. For example, GMP nucleotide is formed due to esterification of phosphoric acid with guanosine.

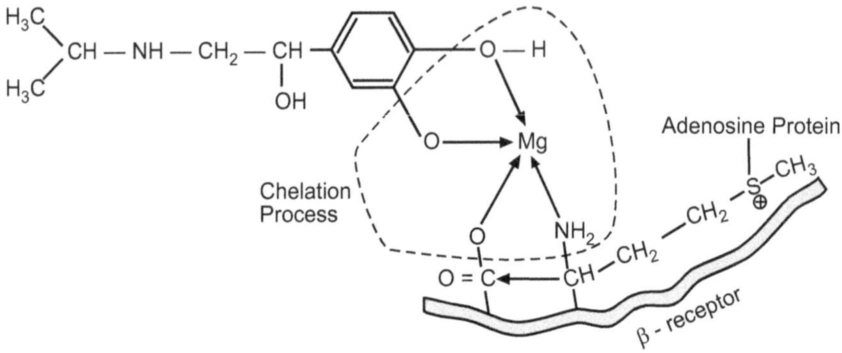

Fig. 18.6 : β-receptor activation

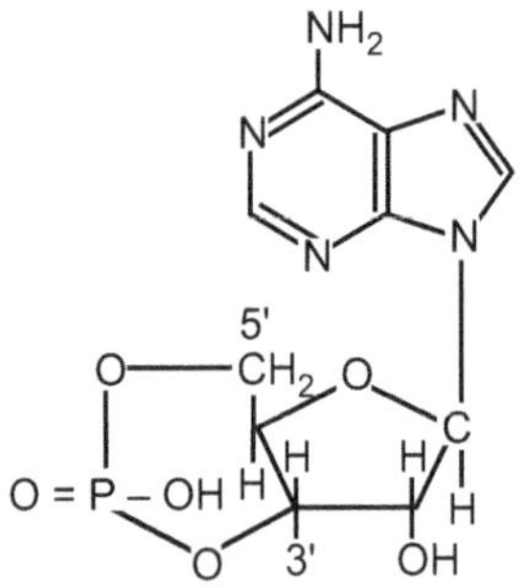

Fig. 18.7 : Cyclic adenosine 3'- 5'-monophosphate (c-AMP)

Cyclic AMP :

Its presence in the tissues was first recognized by Sutherland and his co-workers in 1956, while studying the metabolic effects of epinephrine. He proposed that, since epinephrine is unable to enter the cell, its intracellular effects are carried out by c-AMP.

Cyclic-AMP plays an important regulatory role in body to control the rates of a number of cellular processes. In hormone action, the biological effects are mediated with a high amplification inside the cell by c-AMP. Adenylate cyclase and hormone (e.g., epinephrine) receptors are considered to be proteins. They are embedded in lipid matrix of the cellular membrane in such a way that adenylate cyclase faces the intracellular fluid, whereas the receptor faces the extra-cellular fluid. The activation of adenylate cyclase enzyme leads to the formation of c-AMP from Mg^{++}–ATP complex. An additional protein appears to mediate this conversion is guanosine triphosphate (GTP). Similarly, phosphodiesterase enzyme metabolises c-AMP to inactive

5'-AMP. Thus, it limits the accumulation of cyclic AMP in the tissues.

The function of cyclic AMP is to regulate the activity of a class of enzyme, protein kinases, which activate a wide variety of reactions which are characteristic of the hormone involved.

For example, in case of epinephrine, responses observed, may include increased cardiac contractility, smooth muscle relaxation, glycogenolysis, inhibitory effect on the secretion of insulin etc.

Some hormones bring out their effects by increasing the c-AMP concentration in target cell. While some hormones bring about their effects by decreasing the c-AMP concentration in the target cell. Thus, hormones which increase the concentration of c-AMP include, epinephrine, prostaglandin E, glucagon, ACTH, LH, vasopressin, thyroid stimulating hormone etc.

While hormones which decrease the c-AMP concentration include, insulin, prostaglandin F_2 and melatonin.

In the expression of many hormonal effects, Ca^{++} ions play an important role in the activation of protein kinases by c-AMP. These protein kinases when activated, modulate the activities of different proteins in different organs by phosphorylating them and bringing about different physiological responses.

Cyclic AMP and c-GMP, both are the examples of cyclic nucleotides. Their role has been confirmed or suspected in diversified field ranging from hypertension to contraception.

Talbutamide, in some instances has been reported to antagonise the effects of c-AMP on protein kinases.

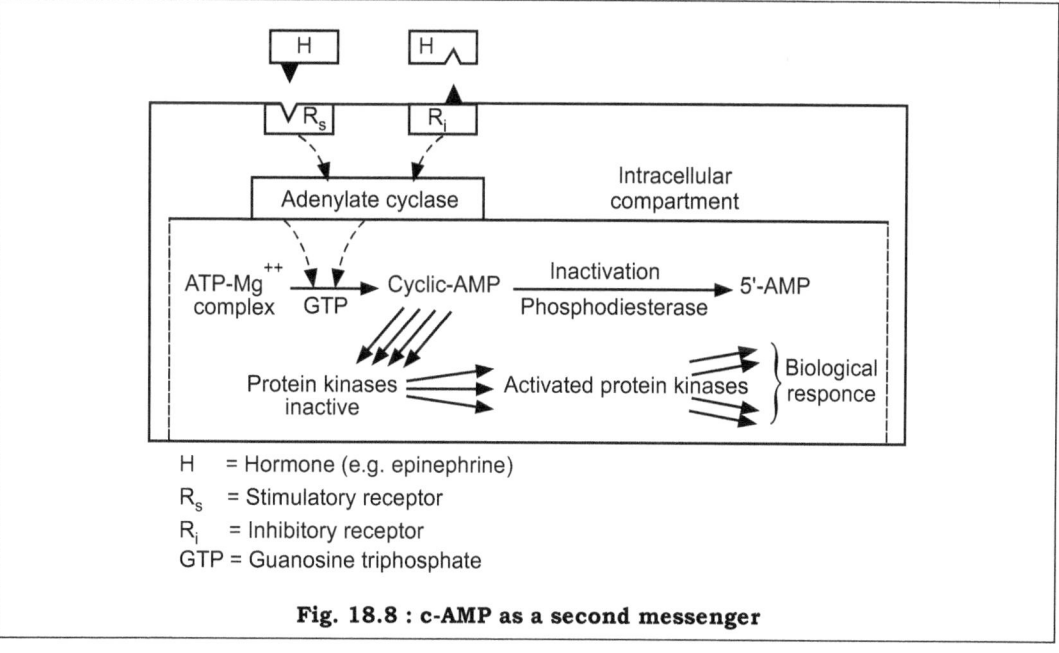

Fig. 18.8 : c-AMP as a second messenger

Cyclic GMP:

The discovery about the presence of c-AMP was followed immediately by investigation about the presence of another cyclic nucleotide, cyclic GMP (1960).

This nucleotide was found to be widely distributed in the tissues particularly, in retina and cerebellum. It is, in some cases, linked with the inhibitory responses of acetylcholine and its accumulation appears to be due to the activation of presynaptic receptors (e.g. α_2-adrenergic presynaptic receptors).

Table 18.7 : Drugs affecting c-AMP accumulation

Parameter	Accelerated	Inhibited
Synthesis	β–receptor agonist	Lithium
Metabolism	Insulin	Papaverine, theophylline

Pentobarbital induces a decrease in cerebellum level of c-GMP while d-amphetamine is reported to increase its concentration.

ADRENOCEPTOR BLOCKING AGENTS

19.1 INTRODUCTION

The sympathetic nervous system is intimately involved in the control of homeostatic mechanisms. It is activated mainly during the conditions of stress, exercise or in cardio-deficient mechanisms. Hence, drugs which interfere with the proper functioning of this system are virtually of therapeutic value in the treatment of hyperactivity of cardiovascular system, e.g. hypertension.

Such agents are conveniently divided into :

(a) Drugs that prevent the biosynthesis of catecholamines.
   e.g., α-methyl dopa.
(b) Drugs that prevent storage of catecholamines.
   e.g. reserpine.
(c) Drugs that prevent release of catecholamines.
   e.g. bretylium.
(d) Drugs that degenerate sympathetic nerve endings.
   e.g. 6-hydroxydopamine.
(e) Drugs that, block the interaction of norepinephrine with the receptor sites (antagonists).
   e.g. α-adrenoreceptor blockers.
      β-adrenoreceptor blockers.
(f) Drugs that block the sympathetic neurons.

Drugs that prevent the bio-synthesis, storage and release of norepinephrine cannot antagonise the activity of catecholamines which reach the circulation from exogenous source. They can reduce the impulse traffic in the peripheral sympathetic nerves non-specifically at both α and β-receptors. They are also able to inhibit the action of indirect-acting sympathomimetic drugs.

While the antagonists at receptor sites, exhibit selectivity in the blockade. For example,

α-receptor blockers will cause vaso-dilatation.

$β_1$-receptor blockers will cool down the heart functioning, and

$β_2$-receptor blockers concentrate their attention mainly to bring about broncho constriction.

Thus, α- and $β_1$-receptor blockers find their role in the therapy of hypertension. While $β_2$-blockers or non-selective β-antagonists, due to their bronchoconstrictory activity are disqualified for the use in the patients suffering from asthma or other allergic conditions.

All such adrenoceptor blocking agents to limited degrees, can also influence parasympathetic nervous system. This explains the origin of some side-effects like blurred vision, dry mouth etc. associated with their use.

The adrenoceptor blocking agents reduce the effects of sympathetic nerve stimulation by both, endogenous and exogenously administered adrenomimetics. Due to their structural similarity with the endogenous catecholamines, they block the receptor activation by competitive mechanism. They all possess, affinity for the adrenoceptors but have little or zero intrinsic activity necessary to activate these receptors.

19.2 DRUGS AFFECTING BIOSYNTHESIS OF NOREPINEPHRINE

These drugs act by inhibiting various enzymes which are involved in the biosynthesis of norepinephrine. Tyrosine and dopa are the principal intermediates in the biosynthesis of neurotransmitter. Drugs having structural resemblance with these intermediates will then, naturally compete with the enzymes which convert these intermediates into norepinephrine.

They get acted upon by enzymes instead of tyrosine and dopa resulting into false neurotransmitter instead of norepinephrine. These false neurotransmitters usually have less potency than norepinephrine which explains the reduced sympathetic tone.

Inhibitors of each enzyme have been studied but major effects are observed only with drugs that act on the hydroxylation of tyrosine (a rate-limiting step).

Examples of drugs from this class include,

(a) α-methyl-m-tyrosine :

It competes with tyrosine for tyrosine hydroxylase enzyme which catalyses the conversion of tyrosine to DOPA (a rate determining step). Due to structural similarity with tyrosine, it is consumed during the biosynthetic pathway of norepinephrine. The false neurotransmitter thus produced is metaraminol, some of which may then be hydroxylated to α-methyl norepinephrine.

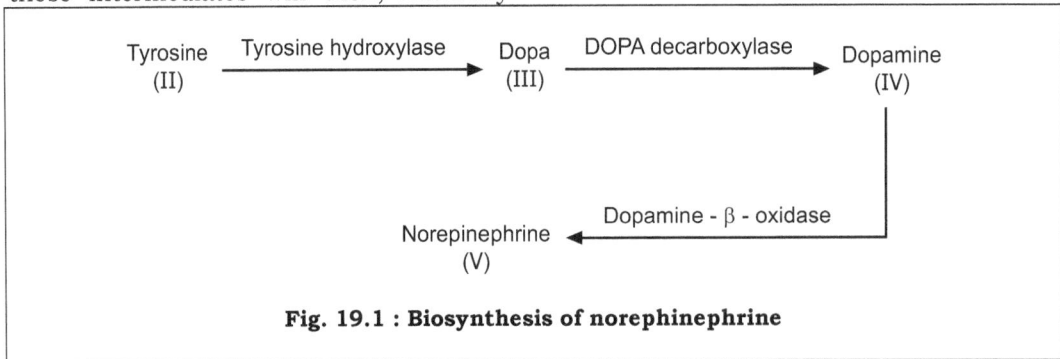

Fig. 19.1 : Biosynthesis of norephinephrine

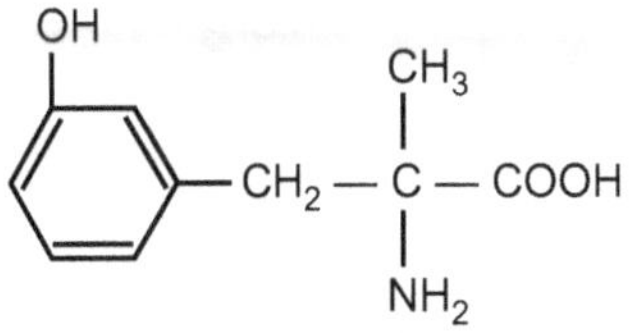

α-methyl-m-tyrosine

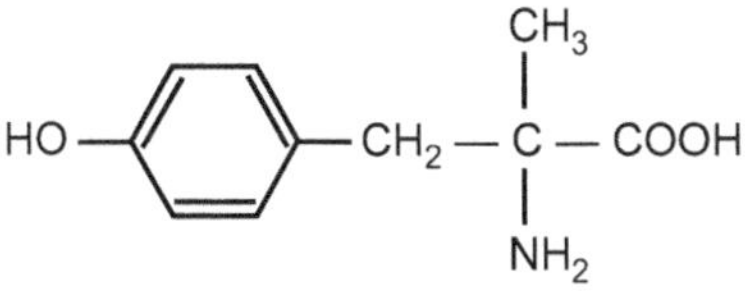

α-methyl-p-tyrosine

Both these agents cause major depletion of norepinephrine and dopamine in both CNS and periphery. They are of no value in the treatment of hypertension but may be used in the management of pheochromocytoma.

(b) α-methyl dopa :

It competes with dopa as a substrate for dopa decarboxylase, an enzyme which is involved in the biosynthesis of dopamine, norepinephrine and serotonin. Since the rate of decarboxylation of α-methyl dopa is considerably slower than that of dopa, it ties up the enzyme for a longer period of time and is effective inhibitor of the biosynthesis of norepinephrine. Instead of norepinephrine, α-methyl norepinephrine is formed which has weak central as well as peripheral action.

Since it is a potent agonist at α_2-receptors in the CNS, it causes an inhibition of central sympathetic outflow.

It depletes tissue stores of norepinephrine. Its antihypertensive effect results from a decrease in cardiac output and peripheral resistance. Its use is also suggested in the treatment of malignant carcinoid and phaeochromocytomas.

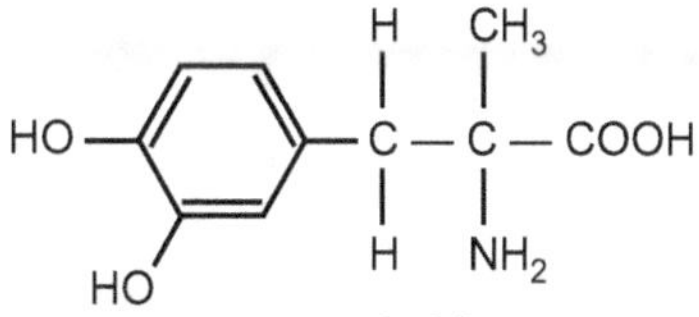

α-methyldopa

The side effects associated with its therapy include, nasal stuffiness, gastrointestinal upset, jaundice, agranulocytosis, edema, postural hypotension and reactions of allergic basis. It enters the CNS quite readily. The CNS effects include, sedation, vertigo, extra pyramidal signs and psychic depression.

(c) Dopamine hydroxylase may be inhibited by a variety of compounds including disulfiram.

$$(C_2H_5)_2-N-\overset{\overset{S}{\|}}{C}-S-S-\overset{\overset{S}{\|}}{C}-N(C_2H_5)_2$$

Disulfiram

19.3 DRUGS THAT PREVENT STORAGE OF CATECHOLAMINES

Cocaine interferes with norepinephrine uptake at the neuron and thus increases the concentration of norepinephrine at the receptor sites. Reserpine depletes the neuronal storage sites. Released norepinephrine is then metabolised by MAO enzymes.

Reserpine :

It is an example of rauwolfia alkaloids obtained from the roots of Rauwolfia serpentina from Apocynaceae family. It acts centrally to produce a tranquillizing action and peripherally to deplete stores of catecholamines and 5-hydroxy tryptamine. It paralyzes the functioning of storage visicles, which thereafter loose interest to store newly synthesized norepinephrine. This neuro-transmitter then escapes into cytoplasm where most of it, is deaminated by intraneuronal MAO enzymes. Probably by blocking the ATP-Mg^{++} dependent mechanism, it also lowers down the uptake of norepinephrine in isolated chromaffin granules. At all these sites of actions, reserpine exhibits cumulative effect upon repeated administration. Upon chronic administration, tissues become hypersensitive to catecholamines due to adaptive changes in the adrenoceptor. In some patients extra-pyramidal effects can also be seen.

Once, reserpine was one of the most favoured antihypertensive drug. It is also reported to cause arteriolar dilation. The mild sedative and tranquillizing effect of reserpine may contribute to its antihypertensive action.

Reserpine has prominent action on GIT. It increases motility and tone accompanied with abdominal cramps and diarrhoea. It promotes gastric acid secretion and the cases of ulceration and hemorrhage are reported due to chronic administration of the drug. It may induce sodium and water retention that can progress to frank congestive cardiac failure.

19.4 DRUGS THAT PREVENT THE RELEASE OF CATECHOLAMINES

A number of antihypertensive agents exert their activity by affecting the storage and release of norepinephrine. Examples include, bretylium, guanethidine and xylocholine.

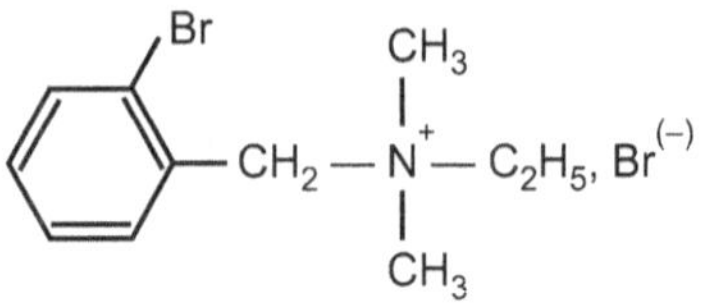

Bretylium bromide

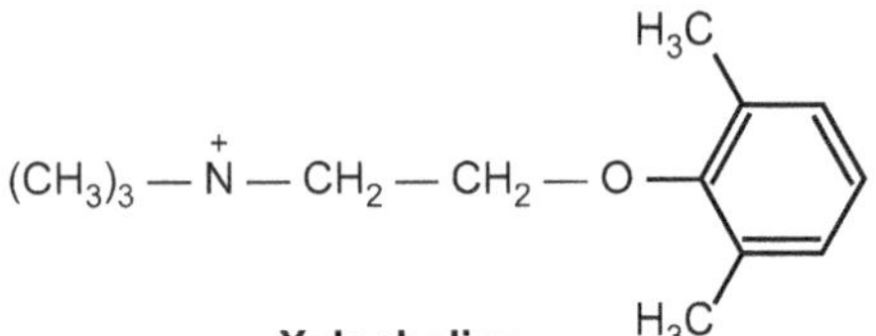

Xylocholine

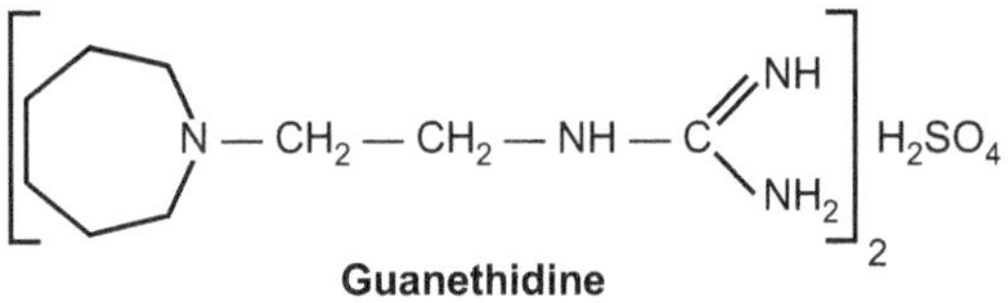

Guanethidine

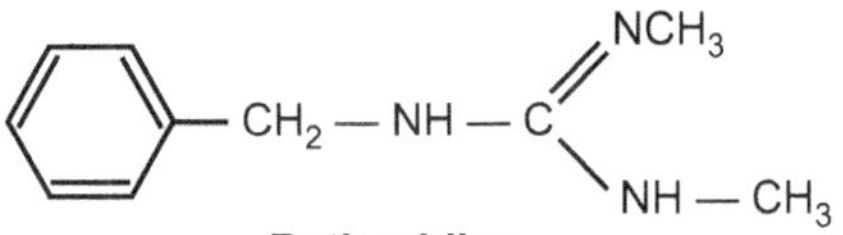

Bethanidine

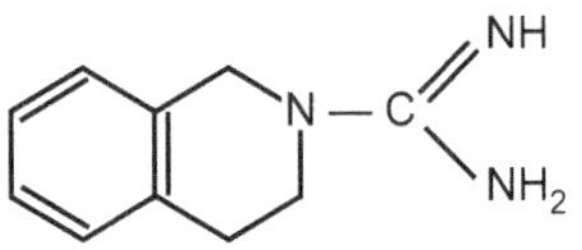

Debrisoquine

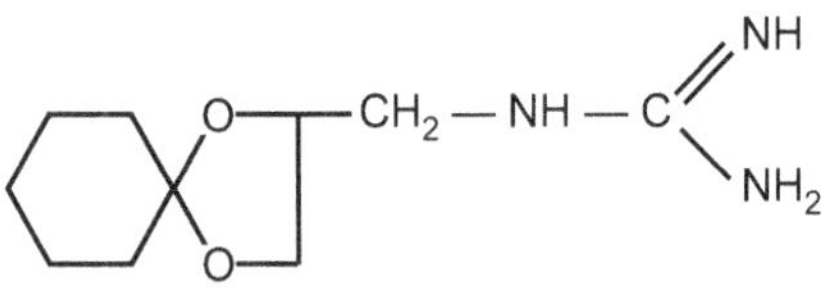

Guanadrel

(a) Bretylium :

The drug was discovered in 1960. Its absorption from GIT is poor and unpredictable. Bretylium utilizes the same transport system which is involved in re-uptake of norepinephrine into the nerve terminals and reaches in the nerves. Its accumulation in adrenergic nerve fibres causes, local anesthetic effect at that site resulting into prevention of release of norepinephrine in response to nerve impulse. Bretylium induced blockage of uptake of catecholamines into nerve terminals, potentiates the actions of circulating catecholamines. The transport system utilized by bretylium and guanethidine to reach in the nerve terminals is blocked by drugs like amphetamine or imipramine resulting into reverse or inhibition of the activity of bretylium or gaunethidine.

Side effects include nasal stuffiness, breathlessness, diarrhoea, postural hypotension, muscular weakness and mental changes. In many patients, tolerance is also reported to occur.

Clinically bretylium is known for its antihypertensive and antiarrhythmic properties.

(b) Guanethidine :

In most of the properties, it resembles with the bretylium except the fact that it, itself acts as a false transmitter and released by nerve stimulation, resulting into a decrease response. It prevents both the storage (reserpine-like) and release (bretylium-like) of the endogenous amines causing depression of the functioning of post-ganglionic adrenergic nerves. The actions of both, direct and indirect acting sympathomimetic amines are reduced at α- and β-adrenoceptors. It has a local anesthetic effect at the nerve terminal sites.

Guanethidine does extensively bind to plasma proteins resulting into delayed onset of action and long duration of action. It does not cross blood-brain barrier and does not disturb CNS catecholamine flux. It depresses heart functioning due to its hypertensive effect. During chronic administration, blood volume increases due to the sodium ions and water retention. Cumulative effects may give rise to complications when the dose of the drug is increased. Chlorpromazine and imipramine-like drugs may reverse the effects of guanethidine.

Side-effects include, postural hypotension, edema, generalised weakness and diarrhoea. The latter effect is probably due to guanethidine induced release of serotonin in intestine. A sudden withdrawal of the drug during chronic administration produces a supersensitivity of effector cells for norepinephrine. Guanethidine neither cause impotence nor it develops tolerance to the patient.

Other compounds like xylocholine, bethanidine, debrisoquin and guanadrel have similar actions to that of bretylium or guanethidine and are used as antihypertensive agents. Bethanidine has a rapid onset of action than guanethidine. While xylocholine has other actions like muscarinic and MAO inhibitory activity. It is not used clinically.

Drugs that degenerate sympathetic nerve endings :

6-Hydroxydopamine is an example of this class. Its degenerative action on the sympathetic nerve ending was first reported by Tranzer and Thoenon in 1967. Like bretylium, it employs the similar transport mechanism for getting entry into nerve terminals where it acts as both false neurotransmitter and destructor of nerve terminals. Its uptake into nerve endings can be efficiently blocked by desipramine.

During initial phase of its action, norepinephrine is released from the damaged synaptic vesicles, producing sympathomimetic effects. This phase is then followed by a prolonged decrease in the catecholamine concentration. It does not cross the blood-brain-barrier and affects most of the peripheral sympathetic nerves. In large doses, it also affects the storage vesicles of serotonin. Upon withdrawal of the drugs, the degenerated nerve endings get repaired almost completely.

Other compounds from this category include, 6-hydroxydopa, 6-aminodopamine, α-methyl hydroxydopamine and α-methyl-6-aminodopamine.

19.5 DRUGS THAT BLOCK THE INTERACTION OF NOREPINEPHRINE WITH THE RECEPTOR SITES OR ADRENERGIC ANTAGONISTS

The autonomic nervous system, which is concerned with the involuntary maintenance of a stable internal environment, is sub-divided into the parasympathetic and sympathetic nervous system. Norepinephrine is the principal neurotransmitter in the sympathetic division. In addition, in response to stress, the adrenal glands secrete into the blood stream a hormone, epinephrine which is responsible for the "flight or fight" syndrome. It stimulates the heart and dilates some blood vessels to supply the muscles with more blood. Norepinephrine has the same cardiac actions but constricts the blood vessels.

The adrenergic antagonists retain some of the structural features but lack intrinsic activity at the adrenoreceptors.

In 1948, Ahlquist observed that the tissues, he examined carried two kinds of adrenergic responses i.e. alpha and beta responses. The α-receptors are further subdivided into $α_1$ and $α_2$-receptors while β-receptors are sub-divided by Land et al into $β_1$ and $β_2$-receptors. With few exceptions, drugs that act on the β-adrenergic system, all possess some chemical elements of structural similarity with the endogenous agonist, epinephrine. While α-adrenoceptor blocking agents do not show such structural relationship. In general, the effects produced by adrenoceptor blockers are influenced upon by the existing sympathetic tone at the site of action.

The α-receptor blockers, in most cases, do not show selectivity of action and also inhibit presynaptic $α_2$-receptors. This causes an increase in norepinephrine release resulting into an intensification of the effects of reflex sympathetic stimulation on the heart (e.g., reflex tachycardia and augmented contractile force).

The β-receptors are involved in the action of norepinephrine on the heart, pulmonary vessels, blood vessels supplied to skeletal muscles, glycogenolysis and lipolysis. Thus, β-blockers would be useful in the management of cardiovascular disorders like hypertension, angina pectoris and cardiac arrhythmias. The side-effects of β-blockers mainly include, bradycardia, reduced cardiac output and bronchoconstriction. These agents prevent glycogenolysis and lipolysis resulting into a decrease in blood glucose level. Thus, they increase the patients sensitivity to insulin and other oral hypoglycemic agents.

19.6 α-ADRENOCEPTOR BLOCKING AGENTS

These agents can be categorised into:

(a) Some α-blockers act competitively and in reversible fashion. These agents do not follow a strict SAR pattern and enjoy wide structural variations. These drugs are relatively non-specific in their actions. Examples include phentolamine, tolazoline etc.

(b) Irreversible α-blockers antagonize specifically the responses mediated through either $α_1$-receptor or $α_2$-receptor. The blockade results by the formation of covalent bond between the drug and α-receptor site. For example, prazosin selectively blocks postsynaptic $α_1$-receptors while yohimbine possesses selectivity at $α_2$-receptors. Other examples include phenoxybenzamine, dibenamine etc.

Pharmacological Actions of α-receptor Blocking Agents :

1. Cardiovascular System :

These agents cause a reduction in blood pressure which is usually accompanied with reflex tachycardia. Inhibition of the compensatory circulatory reflexes gives rise to postural hypotension. Due to their quinidine like depressant action on myocardium, they have a beneficial effect in the cardiac arrhythmias.

2. Smooth Muscles:

Since both types (α and β) of adrenoceptors are present in the smooth muscle, complete blockade of the inhibitory effects of catecholamines on the smooth muscle cannot be achieved. The degree of adrenergic blockade is governed by relative potencies of the α-blockers. The overall effect is an increase in GIT tone and motility due to the action of unopposed parasympathetic innervation.

3. CNS:

The CNS effects vary with each drug. The intensity is governed by the nonpolar nature (and hence, the ability to cross, blood-brain-barrier) or lipophilicity of individual agent and the pattern of their CNS distribution.

Classification :

The agents which block α-adrenoreceptors, enjoy wide structural variations and a firm SAR cannot be framed out for these agents.

On the chemical basis, various α-receptor blocking agents can be classified as:

(i) Ergot alkaloids,
(ii) 2-Haloalkylamines,
(iii) Imidazolines,
(iv) Benzodioxans
(v) Dibenzapepines, and
(vi) Miscellaneous agents.

(i) Ergot Alkaloids :

These alkaloids are obtained from the fungus, Claviceps purpurea which is parasitic to rye and other grains. Such ergot affected grain if consumed by a person, the toxicity that develops is known as ergotism. Abortion, gangrene and mania are some of the important features of ergotism.

The constituents of ergot can be roughly divided into two groups. The first group is heterogenous in nature and consists of mainly bioactive amines like histamine, acetylcholine, tyramine, isoamylamine, ergosterone etc. While the second group consists of compounds which are derivatives of lysergic acid. It is this group which is termed as ergot alkaloids. It includes ergotamine, ergometrine, ergosine and ergotoxine. Ergotoxine is again found to consist of ergocryptine, ergocristine and ergocornine. All these three alkaloids have similar pharmacological action. Hence, it is usual practice to refer them collectively as ergotoxine.

Ergometrine (ergonovine) is an amide of lysergic acid while rest of the five naturally occurring alkaloids are amino acid type derivatives of lysergic acid. All natural alkaloids are optically active, the 1-isomer being pharmacologically active form. Di-hydro derivatives and a number of semisynthetic amides of lysergic acid have been prepared of which methyl-ergonovine and methylsergide are employed clinically.

1. **Lysergic acid :** $R_1 = H$; $R_2 = OH$

2. **Ergometrine:** $R_1 = H$;
    $R_2 = -NH-CH-CH_2OH$
    $\quad\quad\quad\quad\quad |$
    $\quad\quad\quad\quad\quad CH_3$

3. **Methylergonovine :** $R_1 = H$;
    $R_2 - NH-CH-CH_2OH$
    $\quad\quad\quad\quad |$
    $\quad\quad\quad\quad C_2H_5$

4. **Methylsergide :** $R_1 = CH_3$;
    $R_2 = -NH-CH-CH_2OH$
    $\quad\quad\quad\quad\quad |$
    $\quad\quad\quad\quad\quad C_2H_5$

Pharmacology of ergot alkaloids :

1. To varying degrees, these alkaloids act as partial antagonists at a adrenoceptor, tryptaminergic and dopaminergic receptor sites. Bromocriptine is a dopaminergic agonist that is useful in the treatment of Parkinson's disease.

2. All ergot alkaloids antagonize the action of 5-hydroxytryptamine. Hence, they are of value in the treatment of migraine headache which is due to the cranial vasodilation induced by endogenous 5-hydroxytryptamine release.

3. Naturally occurring alkaloids are powerful smooth muscle constrictors with weak to moderate α-receptor blocking activity. While dihydrogenated alkaloids possess a greater degree of α-receptor blocking activity and weak to moderate smooth muscle stimulant action. Dihydroergotoxine is extensively used α-blocker.

4. Both natural and semisynthetic amide derivatives of lysergic acid exhibit no significant α-receptor blocking activity. However, they evoke powerful contraction of uterine muscle.

5. The ergot alkaloids can reverse the pressor response to epinephrine to depressor. Some of them are used as a vasodilator and antihypertensive agents. In addition to their action on the cardiovascular centres in the medulla, mild hypertension and depression of reflex compensatory mechanisms also are reported to occur.

6. Some of these agents are used to stimulate contraction of uterus postpartum and to relieve the migraine pain.

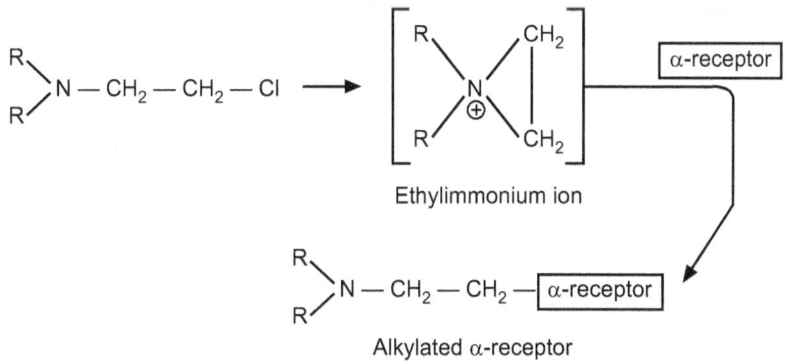

Fig. 19.2 : Mechanism of action of β-haloalkylamines

(ii) 2-Haloalkylamines :

These compounds resemble the nitrogen mustard antineo-plastic agents and may be represented by the following formula :

R – N – CH$_2$ – CH$_2$ – X
|
R

where, R = arylalkyl group
X = halogen

The effectiveness is dependent upon the nature of R.

Nitrogen mustards may antagonise some of the adrenergic responses but like nitrogen mustards, p-haloalkylamines have no cytotoxic effects.

The groups attached to the nitrogen are important for the transport of the drug to the receptor area and binding to the receptor surface. These agents cause a more complete and long-lasting blockade of adrenergic α-receptors through the formation of an immonium ion. This ethylimmonium intermediate then breaks to form a highly reactive carbonium ion (electrophile) which reacts with a nucleophilic group present in the β-receptor, forming a stable and perhaps only slowly reversible covalent bond as shown in the Fig. 19.2.

These agents have a delayed onset and long duration of action. The delayed onset of action is expected on the basis of a slow production of active ethyl immonium ion intermediate. Irreversible nature of the covalent bond formed at α-receptor and lipophilicity of these agents contribute to prolonged duration of action. They all block histamine, acetylcholine, and 5-hydroxytryptamine receptors in the CNS.

They are non-selective in their action. The inhibition of presynaptic α$_2$-receptors by these agents causes an increase in norepinephrine release resulting into an initial phase of rise in blood pressure. This is followed by a relaxant effect on the vascular bed resulting into a decrease in total peripheral resistance. Phenoxybenzamine inhibits both, neuronal and extraneuronal uptake of norepinephrine. They are also beneficial in the treatment of cardiac arrhythmias.

These drugs (e.g. dibenamine) are inadequately absorbed by oral route and hence are usually administered intravenously. Due to their lipophilic nature, most of the administered drugs may be retained in the body fat. It dealkylates to form N-phenoxyisopropylbenzylamine.

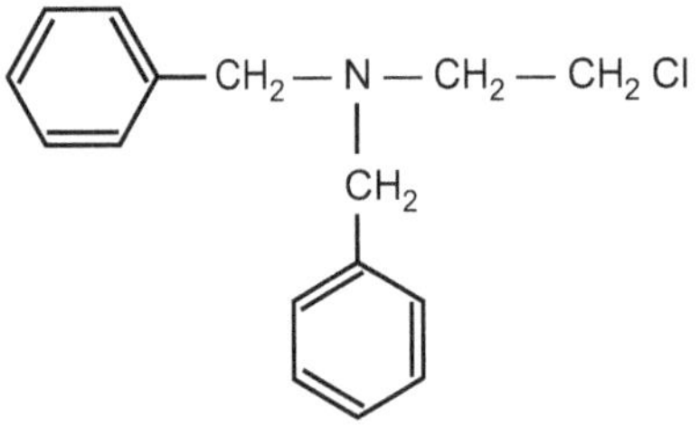

[Structures: Dibenamine and Phenoxybenzamine]

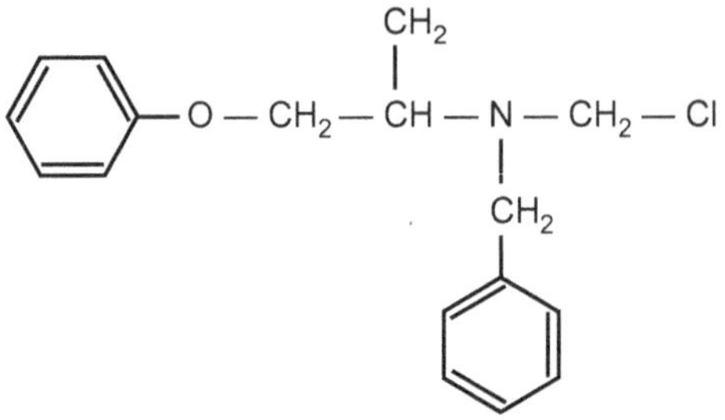

These drugs for example, phenoxybenzamine, can stimulate the CNS. Nausea, vomiting, motor excitability are some of its side effects which have central origin. Other side effects include, miosis, palpitation, nasal stuffiness, postural hypotension and reflex tachycardia. Local tissue irritation is reported to occur when they are parenterally administered.

(iii) Imidazolines:

The pharmacology of a large series of 2-substituted imidazolines was first studied by Hartmann and Isler in 1939. In addition to α-receptor blocking activity, these agents enjoy to varying degrees, sympathomimetic, parasympathomimetic, histamine-like, antihistaminergic, MAO and cholinesterase-inhibitory activities. The dominance of any of the above properties can be affected by structural changes in the basic skeleton. Phentolamine and tolazoline are the examples of clinically employed agents from this class, in the management of hypertension.

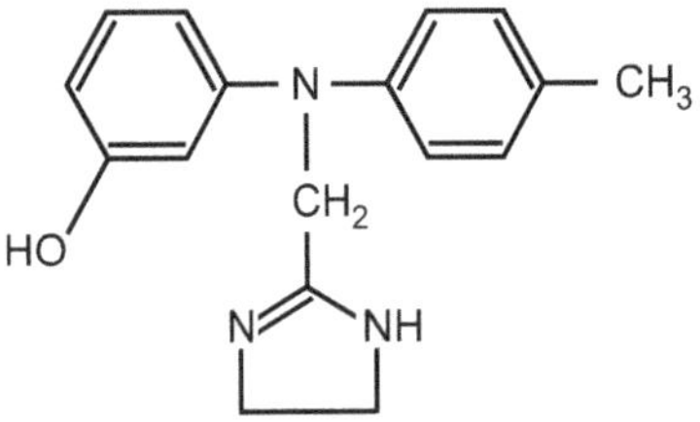

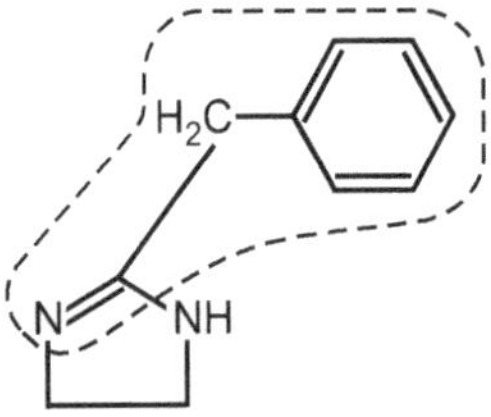

[Structures: Phentolamine and Tolazoline]

The encircled portion resembles structurally with norepinephrine. The blockade of α-receptors produced by imidazolines has a quick onset and of short duration. It can easily be reversed by large doses of norepinephrine. Hence, the α-receptor blockade caused by these agents is said to be of competitive or reversible type.

Due to its structural resemblance with histamine and $α_1$-receptor blockers, tolazoline acts as a powerful vasodilator. The peripheral vasodilation is counter balanced by reflex mediated increase in the cardiac rate and contractile force. In GIT, it exerts cholinergic responses resulting into an increase in gastric acid and other secretions from exocrine glands. These actions at muscarinic receptors can be blocked by atropine. It's non-selectivity inhibits α-receptors. An increased release of norepinephrine due to presynaptic $α_2$-receptor blockade, results in tachycardia, an increased cardiac stroke volume and coronary vasodilatation.

Phentolamine has similar actions to those of tolazoline except -

(i) It is more powerful α-receptor blocker, and

(ii) It does not stimulate the secretion of gastric acid.

In higher doses, phentolamine releases histamine and can block 5-HT receptors.

These drugs can be administered orally as well as parenterally. Imidazolines do not undergo major metabolism in vivo and get excreted largely in an unchanged form through the urine.

Side-effects arise mainly due to their stimulatory action at cardiac and GIT sites. They include, nausea, vomiting, diarrhoea, abdominal pain, headache, flushing, shivering, tachycardia, anginal pain and cardiac arrhythmias. Hence, these drugs should not be used in patients with peptic ulcer or having coronary arterial disease.

(iv) Benzodioxans :

Dioxane is a commercial solvent similar to the glycols. A number of aminoalkyl derivatives of benzodioxan are found to possess potent α-receptor blocking activity. They cause a reversible blockade of α-receptor which is of short duration. The effects of circulatory catecholamines are more effectively antagonized. In addition, they cause depression of myocardium through a direct action.

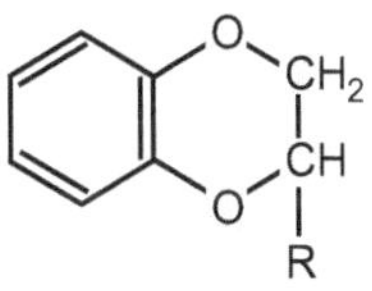

Benzodioxans

Piperoxan $\longrightarrow$ R = $-CH_2-N\bigcirc$

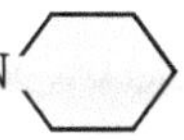

Side-effects include, nausea, vomiting, headache, anginal pain and tachycardia. In large doses, they depress the CNS functioning.

(v) Dibenzapepines:

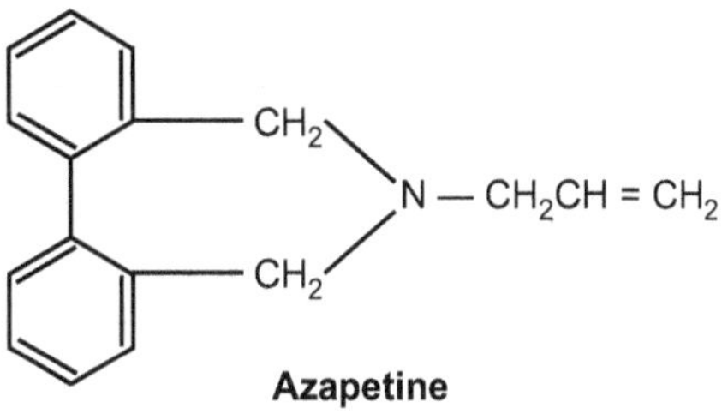

Azapetine

The compounds from this series possess similar properties of those of imidazolines. Azapetine is the most effective agent from this class.

It has prominent α-receptor blocking activity with weak histamine-like actions.

(vi) Miscellaneous Agents :

(a) Yohimbine : It is an alkaloid isolated from the bark of the West African tree Yohimbeche and shares some structural similarity with reserpine and lysergic acid.

Besides its α-receptor blocking action, it is also known to block peripheral 5-HT receptors. It can easily enter the CNS and block central α_2-adrenoceptors. At some places, it is marketed for the treatment of impotence.

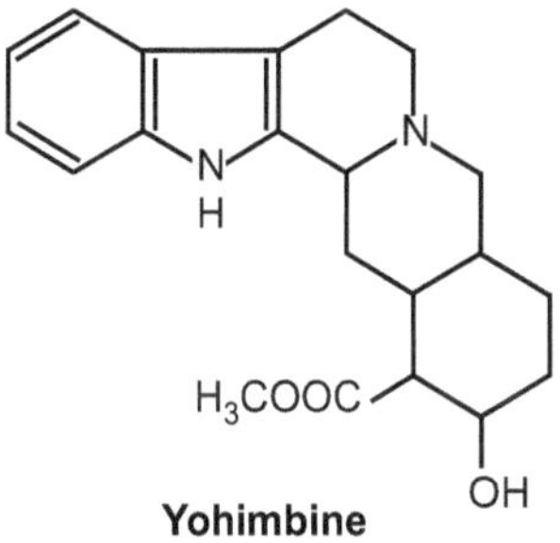

Yohimbine

(b) Quinazoline derivatives : Examples from this category include prazosin and trimazosin.

Prazosin, an anti hypertensive agent selectively acts on postsynaptic α_1-receptors, causing vasodilation of the arterioles. In therapeutic doses, it does not affect cardiac output and heart rate. No other pharmacological action is reported. Its use is accompanied by modest tachycardia and low level of renin release, probably due to its lack of ability to attack presynaptic α_2-receptors.

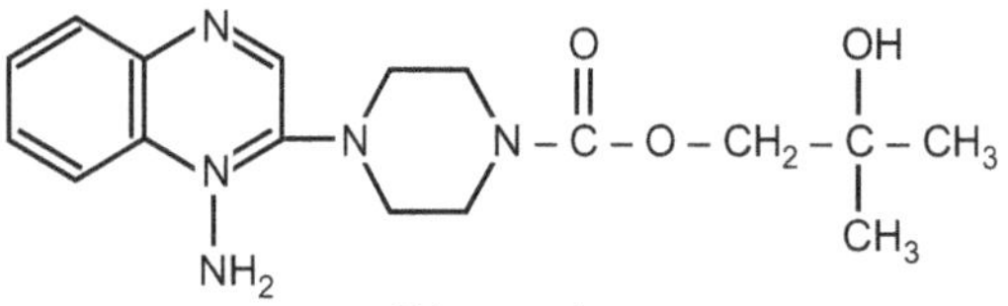

Trimazosin

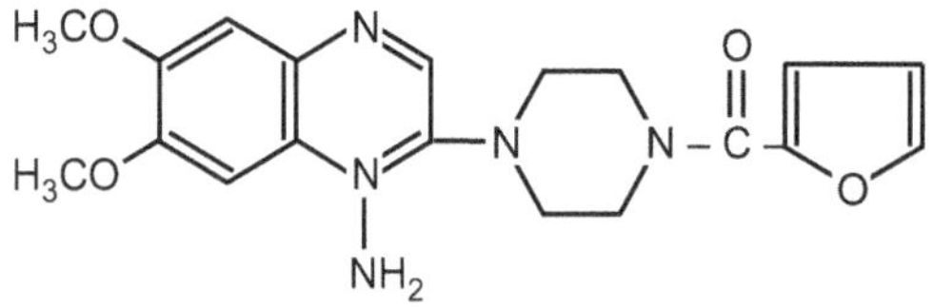

Prazosin

It is orally active and gets extensively metabolized in liver, through O-dealkylation and glucoronide conjugation. Side effects include, drowsiness, palpitation and fluid retention.

Trimazosin is less potent α-blocker than prazosin, otherwise pharmacologically similar to prazosin.

(c) Some drugs like hydrallazine, minoxidil, diazoxide and sodium nitroprusside can be clinically employed in the management of hypertension due to their vasodilatory activity on the arterioles. Their relaxation property on the vasculature is assigned to their ability to interfere with the action of calcium. Other agents like, chlorpromazine, haloperidol and many other neuroleptic drugs also exhibit α-receptor blocking activity and their side-effects to some extent can be explained on this basis.

(d) Clonidine : It is an imidazoline compound, structurally similar to tolazoline. It acts by inhibiting the sympathetic traffic from CNS. Cardiovascular activity and blood pressure are centrally governed mainly by hypothalamus and nucleus tractus solitaries. Catecholamines are the principal neurotransmitter in this region. Clonidine acts centrally and interfere with the adrenergic ganglionic functioning.

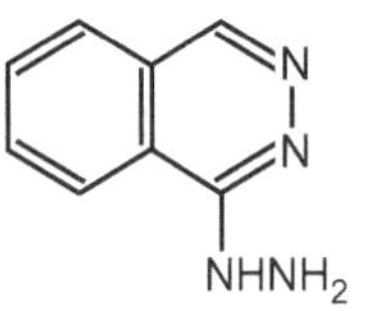

Hydrallazine

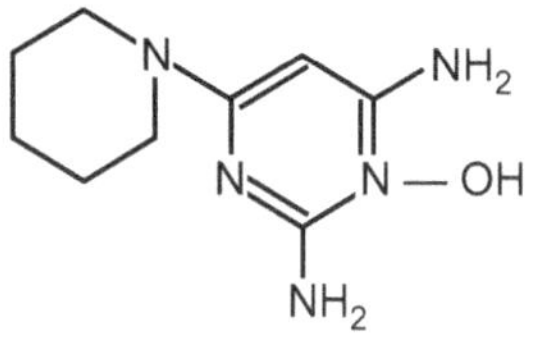

Minoxidil

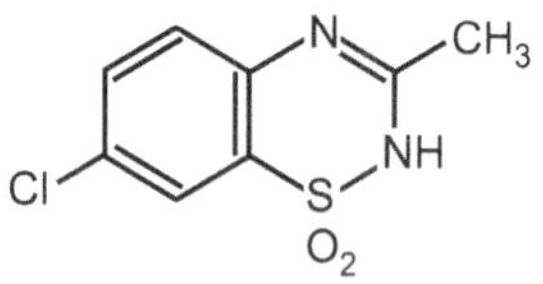

Diazoxide

$Na_2[Fe(CN)_5NO] \cdot 2H_2O$

Sodium nitroprusside

The cell bodies of preganglionic neurons are located in the spinal cord or the motor nuclei of the cranial nerves. The ganglion is located near the centre in the sympathetic autonomic system. Hence, the preganglionic fiber is very short. Adrenergic discharge raises the blood pressure, hence adrenergic neuron blocking agent decreases or lowers down the elevated blood pressure.

Table. 19.1: Daily oral dose for adrenergic blocking agents

Drug	Oral dose
Reserpine	0.25 mg
α-methyl dopa	750 mg - 2.0 g
Bretylium	5 mg/kg
Guanethidine	10 - 300 mg
Bethanidine	5 - 50 mg
Tolazoline	50 - 150 mg
Phenoxybenzamine	50 - 100 mg
Phentolamine	5 mg i.v.
Clonidine	5 - 20 mg
Prazosin	0.5 - 10 mg
Hydrallazine	25 - 100 mg
Minoxidil	10 - 40 mg
Propranolol	40 - 80 mg
Metoprolol	50 - 100 mg
Timolol	10 - 20 mg
Atenolol	50 - 100 mg
Practolol	300 mg
Nadolol	40 - 80 mg
Pindolol	10 - 20 mg
Bupranolol	120 - 240 mg

The inhibition of sympathetic function results in corresponding dominance of parasympathetic tone resulting into bradycardia.

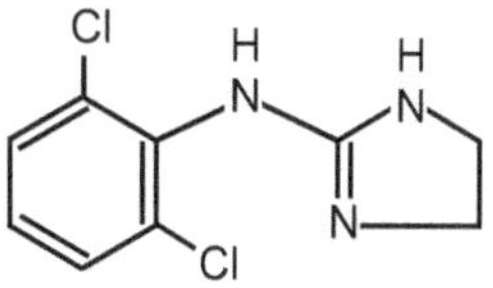

Clonidine

Clonidine is α_2-agonist. It stimulates both, central and peripheral α_2-receptors resulting into reduced norepinephrine release. It lowers down mild to moderate hypertension by reducing vasomotor tone. It has a number of chlorpromazine like actions.

Side-effects include, dry mouth, drowsiness, postural hypotension and rebound hypertension after abrupt withdrawal.

19.7 THERAPEUTIC USES OF α-RECEPTOR BLOCKING AGENTS

(i) Migraine : Migraine is characterised by periodic paroxysmal headache accompanied with nausea and emesis. The headache is sometimes preceded by visual and vasomotor disturbances. The localized pain in the head may shift to the face, shoulder and arms. The headache is often associated with vasodilation and edema.

The reason behind migraine is usually assigned to the local release of serotonin in the periarterial tissues. The cranial vasodilation in migraine can be reversed by the use of α-adrenoceptor blockers, e.g., ergotamine. Caffeine also constricts cerebral blood vessels and thus can potentiate the action of ergotamine.

(ii) With the exception of ergot alkaloids, α-receptor blocking agents can be used in the treatment of peripheral vascular spastic diseases.

(iii) Though blood volume replacement is most important treatment in any type of shock, phenoxybenzamine or phentolamine are used primarily as adjuncts to the main treatment of shock. Since vasoconstriction is a prominent feature of shock, the α-receptor blocking agents can increase the blood perfusion of important areas of the body.

(iv) α-receptor blockers, due to their ability to inhibit sympathetic tone, can be used in the treatment of hypertension.

(v) Phenoxybenzamine can be employed in the diagnosis of pheochromocytoma.

19.8 β-ADRENOCEPTOR BLOCKING AGENT

Unlike α-adrenoceptor blocking agents, the β-adrenoceptor blockers exhibit structural similarity with isoprenaline or norepinephrine. Hence, structural requirements for these agents have been fairly well established. This structural similarity imparts β-adrenoceptor blockers.

(i) These agents act more selectively on β-receptors and do not interfere with cholinergic, histaminergic or serotonergic actions.

AND

(ii) These agents, with some exceptions, still retain sympathomimetic properties and can be termed as partial agonists.

Similarly their structural resemblance with local anesthetics, enable these agents to exert a membrane-stabilizing effect or a quinidine-like action. This property justifies their use to treat cardiac arrhythmias.

Optical isomers exist due to the presence of asymmetric β-carbon atom. Levorotatory (–) forms are more potent β-antagonists than are the dextro (+) isomers.

β-receptor responses are largely relaxant. The major exception to generalization, is the cardiac $β_1$-receptors, stimulation of which, increases the rate and force of contraction of the heart. It is found that $β_1$-receptors are predominant in heart, alongwith few $β_2$-receptors.

Therefore, selective $β_1$-adrenoceptor blocking agents gained a high clinical importance as antihypertensive agents.

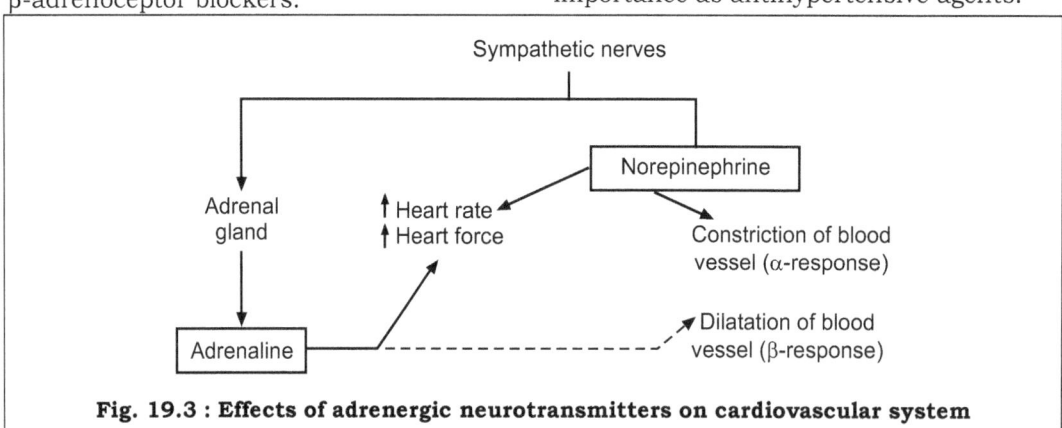

Fig. 19.3 : Effects of adrenergic neurotransmitters on cardiovascular system

Pharmacology :

1. By its tonic activity, sympathetic nervous system exerts an important control over the rate and force of heart beats. β-blockers hence cause reduction in the rate and force of heart contraction. Caution has to be taken therefore, in the administration of β-blockers in patients whose myocardial activity is already depressed.

2. β-blockers cause a fall in stroke volume, systolic blood pressure, cardiac work capacity and coronary blood flow.

3. β-blockers inhibit the renin release from the juxtaglomerular cells of the kidney which is thought to be mediated through β-receptors.

4. The cardiac effects of β-blockers are often reflected in an increased total body sodium and extracellular fluid volume. Postural hypotension is not prominent feature of β-blockers.

5. Some of the β-blockers have quinidine-like or membrane stabilizing activity due to the decreased inward sodium current.

6. β-blockers which have some degree of intrinsic adrenergic activity (partial agonists) can also stimulate β_2-adrenoceptors and lead to some degree of bronchodilation. If this property is associated with cardioselective β_1-blockers, such drugs would be helpful in the treatment of hypertension in asthmatic patients, e.g. atenolol.

SAR Studies :

It is an interesting fact that, with few exceptions, β-adrenoceptor blockers possess some structural similarity with norepinephrine. Placement of bulky substituents on the nitrogen atom in the side-chain, imparts selectivity of action on β-receptors. While agonistic or antagonistic feature of a drug is mainly governed by nature of the substituents on catechol nucleus. Selectivity on individual sub-types of β-receptors is also determined by these substituents. The aliphatic hydroxyl group is found to be necessary for both, agonists and antagonists of β-receptors.

On the basis of their relative affinity for β-receptor sub-types, β-blockers can be categorised into three classes.

(a) Non-selective β-blockers :

e.g. propranolol, pindolol, alprenolol, nadolol, bunolol, sotalol, timolol, oxprenolol, penbutolol etc.

(b) Selective β_1-blockers :

Acebutolol, atenolol, bevantolol, metoprolol, pafenolol, practolol, tolamolol etc. These agents can behave in a non-selective manner, if given in large doses.

(c) Selective β_2-blockers:

These agents do not find any clinical utility. Butoxamine is a somewhat selective β_2-antagonist.

The non-selective β-blockers bring about a blockade of both, β_1 and β_2-adrenoceptors. β_2-receptors are predominant present in lung, particularly bronchial muscles (alongwith few β_1-receptors). Cardioselective β-antagonists will have much greater affinity for the β_1-receptors of the heart than for β_2-receptors present in other tissues. But non-selective β-blockers, will also block β_2-receptors in the lungs, resulting into broncho-constriction, a case contraindicated in patients suffering from bronchial asthma. A patient suffering from obstructive airway disease should not be treated with a non-selective β-blocker because of possibility of aggravating bronchospasm. Hence, in such patients, cardio-selective β_1-blockers should be used with great care. β-blockers also inhibit glycogenolysis mediated by β-receptors in liver and skeletal muscles, thus reducing blood-glucose level. Hence, these agents should be used with great caution in patients undergoing the therapy with insulin or other oral hypoglycemic agents.

The selective β_1-blockers are widely employed as antihypertensive agents. They act through the following postulated mechanisms.

1. Inhibition of renin release.
2. Inhibition of cardiac output.
3. Inhibition of synaptic norepinephrine release, and
4. Restoration of vascular relaxation response.

Therapeutic Uses of β-blocking Agents:

Most of the therapeutic applications of β-blockers are based upon their ability to reduce the effects of catecholamines on the Heart. These uses include:

(a) In the management of hypertension, usually alongwith diuretics.

(b) In the treatment of angina pectoris and myocardial infarction.

(c) As adjunct with vasodilators to reduce the reflex tachycardia.

(d) In some arrythmias involving adrenergic stimuli.

(e) As prophylactic agent in migraine.

(f) These agents have limited application in pheochromocytoma, hypertropic subaortic stenosis, mitral stenosis and wide-angle glaucoma.

Metabolism:

All β-blockers are orally effective. In emergency conditions, intravenous administration is favoured. Some drugs like propranolol, alprenolol, metoprolol and oxyprenolol are metabolised mainly by hepatic microsonial enzymes. At least eight metabolites of propranolol have been isolated from the urine. Some of the metabolites of propranolol and alprenolol retain significant pharmacological activity and help to prolong their effects.

Practolol and sotalol are disposed almost entirely by glomerular filtration. Long-duration of action and central effects associated with propranol and alprenolol can be partly attributed to their high lipophilicity.

Toxicities :

1. Mild adverse reactions include nausea, vomiting, mild diarrhoea, insomnia, hallucination and muscle weakness.

2. Heart failure may develop suddenly or slowly in patients with myocardial insufficiency.

3. These agents cause impairment of conduction through A-V bundle, but the inotropic action of digitalis is not inhibited.

4. Non-selective β-blockers may lead to the attacks of bronchospasm due to an increase in airway resistance in asthmatic patients or in patients having a history of allergy.

5. These agents depress the carbohydrate metabolism and potentiate the action of hypoglycemic agents in diabetic patients. They also mask tachycardia which is an important sign of developing hypoglycemia.

6. Some of these agents cause withdrawal symptoms if abruptly withdrawn during long-term treatment. This is due to the supersensitivity of β-receptors induced by chronic blockade.

Classification :

On the chemical basis, clinically employed β-adrenoceptor blocking agents can be categorised into :

(a) Arylethanolamines, and

(b) Aryloxypropanol amines.

(a) Arylethanolamines : Isoproterenol is a basic structure to yield good β-adrenergic blocking compounds.

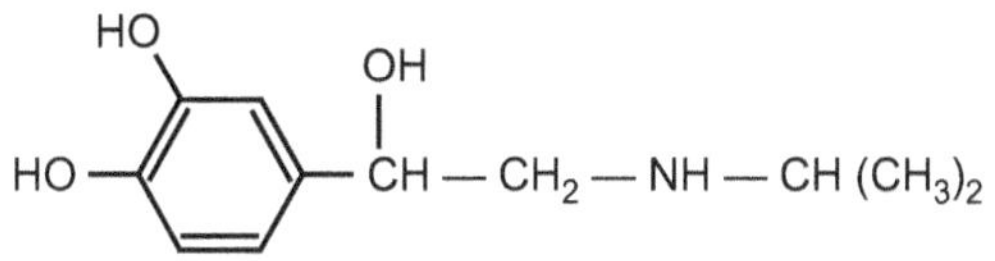

Isoproterenol

An evidence about the existence of subtypes (α and β) of adrenoceptors, put forward by Ablquist (1948) was confirmed by dichloroisoproterenol, a classic β-blocker. This agent was reported in 1958 by Mills from the Eli Lilly company and is commonly known as DCI.

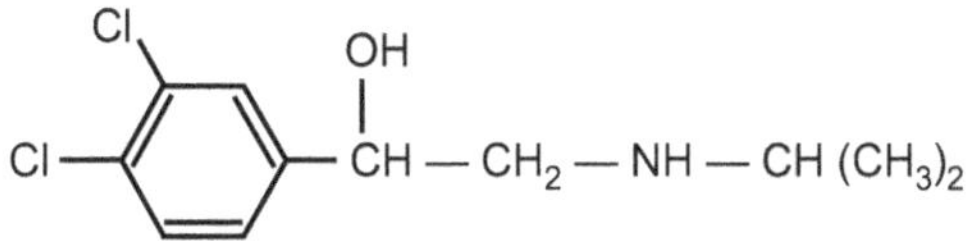

Dichloroisoproterenol

DCI, the first β-adrenoceptor blocking agent was found to inhibit both, the relaxation of bronchial smooth muscle and cardiac stimulant actions (β-responses) of isoprenaline. Replacement of the electron rich hydroxyl groups with an electron rich phenyl at 3-4 positions gives pronethalol (1962) which is even better β-blocker than dichloroisoproterenol.

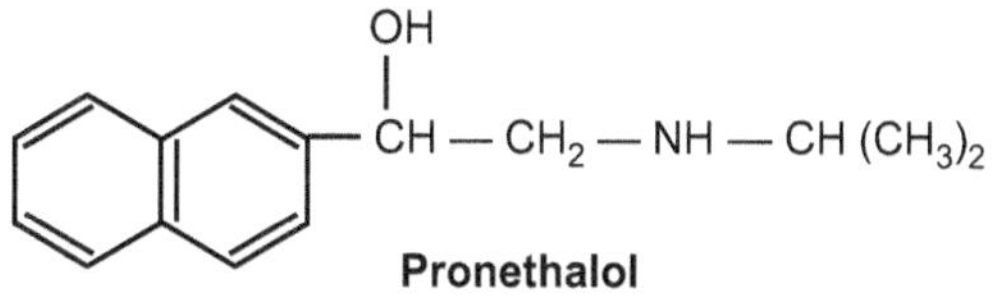

Pronethalol

Other derivatives in which the para hydroxyl group on phenyl ring is replaced by methylsulphonamide were also prepared, e.g. sotalol.

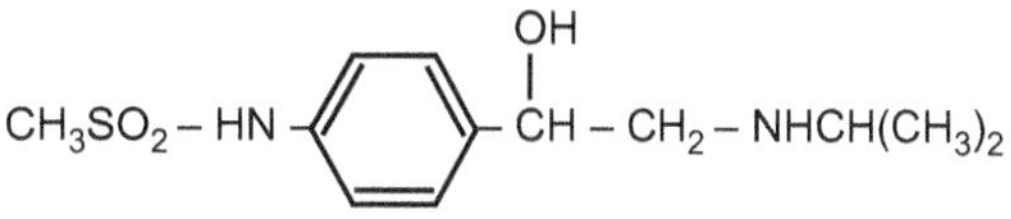

Sotalol

Other compounds from this category include :

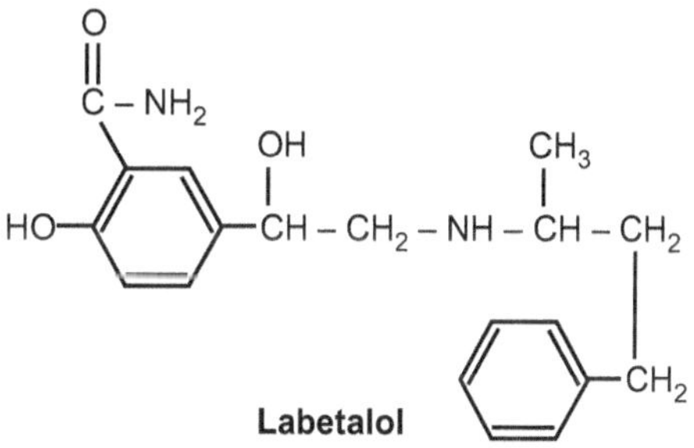

Labetalol

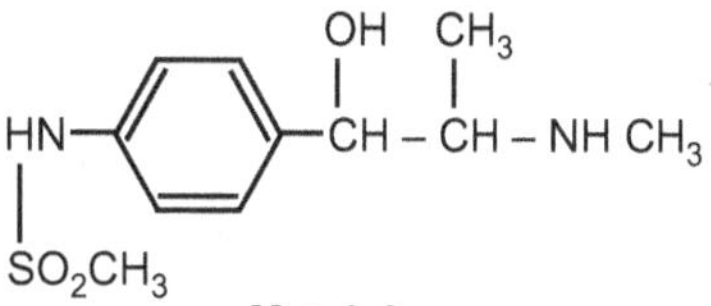

Metalol

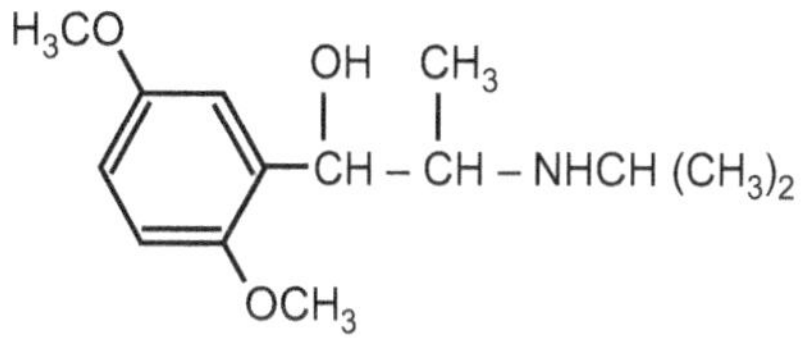

Butoxamine (selective β_2-blockers)

(b) Aryloxypropanolamines :

Pronethalol, an arylethonalamine, was withdrawn from clinical testing because of the report that it caused lymphosarcoma in mice. However, within two years of this report, Black and co-workers discovered a potent β-blocker, propranolol, a close structural relative of pronethalol.

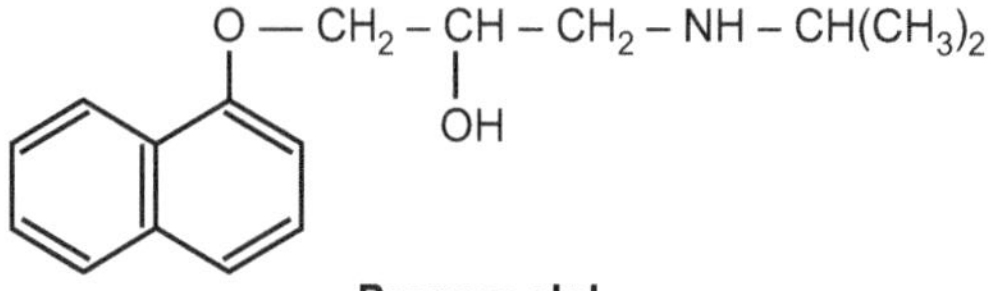

O — CH$_2$ – CH – CH$_2$ – NH – CH(CH$_3$)$_2$
            |
            OH

Propranolol

(i) Propranolol:

Propranolol is the prototype of the group of β-blocking agents known as aryloxypropanolamines. Since Prichard (1968) first used propranolol clinically, a series of compounds from this series have been prepared.

Propranolol, a non-selective β-blocker is the prototype drug and other agents from this series differ just quantitatively from it. Hence its pharmacology will be dealt here in detail.

Pharmacology :

Clinical uses of propranolol are mainly based upon its effect on cardiovascular system.

(i) It is an effective antihypertensive agent. This activity is specially beneficial when the drug is used in combination with vasodilators.

(ii) In therapeutic dose, it slows down the conduction in atria and A-V node and reduces sinus rate.

(iii) Its action in part, may be attributed to its ability to redistribute the intramyocardial blood flow.

(iv) In larger doses, it has quinidine-like, membrane stabilization effect on myocardium which qualifies it, to be used to treat arrhythmias.

(v) Its non-selectivity of action, causes that blockade of bronchial β$_2$-receptors. It results into an increase in air-way resistance. Hence, it is contraindicated in patients with asthma.

(vi) A major clinical problem with propranolol was its high lipid solubility, which allows it to penetrate nerve tissues and exert an undesirable cardio-depressant effect in addition to its β-blockade. Hence, it is to be used with caution in patients with disturbances of cardiac conduction. Other CNS-effects include, fatigue, headache, dizziness and insomnia.

(vii) It inhibits the glycogenolytic and lipolytic actions (β-mediated) of endogenous catecholamines and thus potentiates the activity of insulin and other oral hypoglycemic agents in diabetic patients.

Absorption, Fate and Excretion :

Propranolol is an orally effective agent. Due to extensive plasma protein binding (90-95%) of the drug, variations in plasma concentration of propranolol are quite usual after oral administration. In body, propranolol undergoes complete metabolism. A propranolol metabolite of particular interest is 4-hydroxypropranolol, which still retains short-acting β-antagonist activity.

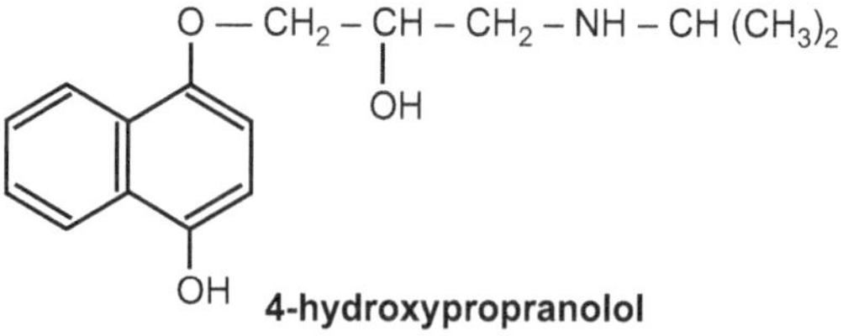

O — CH$_2$ – CH – CH$_2$ – NH – CH (CH$_3$)$_2$
            |
            OH

OH **4-hydroxypropranolol**

Naphthoxylacetic acid, isopropylamine, propranolol glycol etc. are some of the major metabolites of propranolol, isolated from human urine alongwith some glycuronide conjugates.

Side-effects of propranolol, associated with CNS, bronchial tract and metabolic system, prompted the search for cardioselective β_1-receptor blocking agents. The prototype of this new series of compounds was practolol, which is devoid of the depressant effect of propranolol. It was the first cardioselective β-antagonists. Oxprenolol and alprenolol then developed which are considered as the ring opened analogues of propranolol. These agents reduce the rise in plasma renin activity, normally induced by the cardiovascular effects.

(ii) Atenolol :

It is an example of long acting selective β_1-antagonist. It retains weak sympathomimetic activity and in high doses, exhibits membrane stabilising effect. If administered orally, its efficacy does not attain expected level due to incomplete absorption from GIT. No significant metabolism is reported and the major fraction of excreted drug remains unchanged in urine. Advantages over propranolol include its inability to enter the CNS and weak potentiation of insulin-induced hypoglycemia. Hence, it is comparatively safer antihypertensive drug in diabetic patients.

(iii) Labetalol :

It is both selective α_1-receptor and non-selective β-receptor blocking agent. On the quantitative basis, it is $1/10^{th}$ as potent as phentolamine as an α-blocker and 1/3 as potent as propronolol as β-blocker. The extent of β-receptor blockade appears to be more by parenteral than oral route.

Labetalol gets completely absorbed from GIT but due to high first pass hepatic metabolism about, only 1/3 of the administered dose reaches the circulation. It binds to plasma protein to the extent of about 50%. It acts mainly by decreasing the plasma renin activity and by its vasodilatory action. Most of the drugs undergo metabolism to form inactive glucuronide conjugates e.g. O-phenylglucuronide.

Other non-selective orally active β-blockers include nodolol, timolol and pindolol. They do not possess membrane stabilizing activity. Nodolol is a long-acting drug and lacks partial agonist activity while timolol is a moderate-acting agent. Pindolol is a short-acting β-blocker and retains partial sympathomimetic activity.

(iv) Butoxamine :

It is an example of selective β_2-antagonists. It blocks β_2-receptors in uterine and bronchial smooth muscles and in skeletal muscles. It is a useful research tool but it does not, at present, have any clinical use.

Table 19.2 : Clinically employed aryloxypropanolamines

Aryl–O–CH₂–CH(OH)–CH₂–NHR (general structure, with X substituent on ring positions 2–6)

Aryloxypropanolamine blockers

Sr. No.	Name	X	R	Selective
1.	Propranolol	2,3- (fused benzene ring)	isopropyl	Non-selective
2.	Pindolol	2,3- (fused pyrrole, NH)	isopropyl	Non-selective
3.	Alprenolol	2-CH₂–CH=CH₂	isopropyl	Non-selective
4.	Oxyprenolol	2-OCH₂CH=CH₂	isopropyl	Non-selective
5.	Bunitrolol	2-CN	t-butyl	Non-selective
6.	Nodolol	2,3- (fused ring with two HO groups)	t-butyl	Non-selective
7.	Tolamolol	2-CH₃	–CH₂CH₂O–C₆H₄–CONH₂	β_1-receptor
8.	Practolol	4-NHCOCH₃	isopropyl	β_1-receptor
9.	Metoprolol	4-CH₂CH₂OCH₃	isopropyl	β_1-receptor
10.	Atenolol	4-CH₂COCH₂	isopropyl	β_1-receptor
11.	Acebutolol	4-NHCOC₃H₇	isopropyl	β_1-receptor
12.	Timolol	morpholino-thiadiazolyl group	OCH₂–CH(OH)–CH₂–NH–C(CH₃)₃	Non-selective

SECTION - III : DRUGS ACTING ON CENTRAL NERVOUS SYSTEM

NEUROPHARMACOLOGY

20.1 INTRODUCTION

Therapeutic agents are administered in the body to bring about a definite biological response. Their absorption, distribution, metabolism and excretion are markedly affected by their physico-chemical parameters. Beside their sites of action, these drugs may be carried out to other body compartments where their actions are not desired. For example, drugs of sufficient lipophilic nature, may be carried into the CNS, thus give rise to desired or undesired effects. A wide variety of the CNS acting drugs includes therapeutic agents which are used to relieve pain, anxiety, depression, excitation and neurological disorders. These agents have their primary site of action in brain and the spinal cord. They may or may not alter the state of conciousness. Beside these agents, many drugs which primarily act at the peripheral systems, may influence the CNS functioning, if used in higher doses or during chronic administration. So before dealing with such drugs which act chiefly on the CNS, a glance at the cellular structure of the brain will definitely help us to understand better, the SAR, sites or mechanisms of action of these agents.

20.2 CELLULAR BIOLOGY OF BRAIN

The functional unit of the CNS is the neuron or a nerve cell. The pattern of neuronal transmission in the CNS remains essentially same as what we have seen in autonomic nervous system. The depolarization associated with an action potential developed at, presynaptic nerve terminal results in the mobilization and release of neurotransmitter in the synaptic cleft. The release of neurotransmitter is voltage dependent and requires the influx of extracellular Ca^{++} ions into the presynaptic terminals. It activates the postsynaptic receptor sites causing the depolarization of postsynaptic axon. Thus, similar procedure is involved which transmits information to, and receives it from, other neurons and peripheral end organs. The transformation of an immensely complex language of the external stimuli is done with the help of neurotransmitter, into a very simple language of ionic, electrical and chemical signals.

The mechanisms of impulse transmission in the CNS are characterised by

(i) The presence of interneuron or the nerve cell which originates and terminates at the same site and

(ii) The interconnection of nerve tracts which control different responses at distinct places. These nerve tracts regulate their own and each other's activity in a complex manner.

The interaction of neurotransmitter with the postsynaptic receptors may cause their activation resulting into depolarization of the post-synaptic membrane (i.e., excitatory post-synaptic potential, EPSP). While an inhibition of impulse transmission occurs due to hyperpolarization of post-synaptic membrane (i.e., inhibitory post-synaptic potential, IPSP). On the basis of effects caused by neurotransmitters on the postsynaptic sites, they can be categorized into excitatory neurotransmitters and inhibitory neurotransmitters. EPSP develops due to opening of ion-channels with a reduction in electrical resistance of the membrane while IPSP develops due to selective ion movement with increased membrane resistance. In normal CNS functioning, there exists a fine balance between excitatory and inhibitory nerve tracts in the important brain compartments. Predominance of either neurotransmitter in brain will cause diseases of mind.

More than one nerve tract may govern the functioning of a specific brain area. Consequently more than one neurotransmitter may be present in this area. For example, the caudate nucleus is rich in both dopamine and acetylcholine. However, cholinergic neurons exist primarily as interneurons. When such two transmitters coexists in a given synapse, no single agonist or antagonist would provide maximum agonism or antagonism.

Certain endogenous bioactive substances can influence the neuronal activity differently than do neurotransmitters. Depending upon the circumstances they may potentiate or depress the neuronal response to excitatory or inhibitory neurotransmitters. They are known as modulators. They do not show significant effect on ion conductance when tested in vitro. They originate from cellular and nonsynaptic sites and include carbon-dioxide, ammonia, prostaglandins etc.

Many therapeutic agents may influence the synthesis, breakdown and availability of the neurotransmitters either in facilitatory or inhibitory manner. In most of the cases, the undesired CNS-effect are due to the high tissue concentration developed due to the dose and route of administration choosen. These effects arise when the number of receptor sites (activated or deactivated) crosses the threshold required to generate the biological response. Chronic

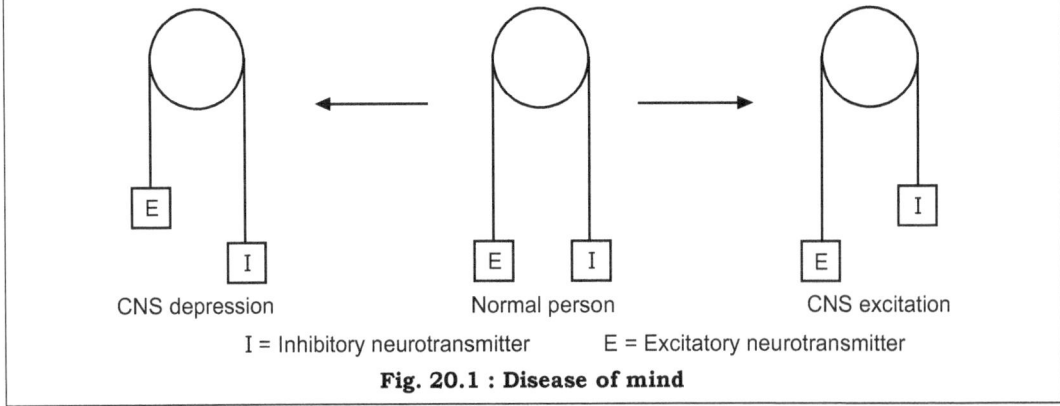

Fig. 20.1 : Disease of mind

administration of most of the CNS-acting drugs may cause adaptive changes in the receptor sites. The rates of synthesis, storage, release and re-uptake processes for the neurotransmitter concerned can be adjusted by these adaptive changes, so as to effect up or down regulation of the response.

The drugs which cause CNS-stimulation, do so either by the blockade of inhibition or by direct neuronal excitement due to drug-induced increase in the release of neurotransmitter. The stage of excitement which is observed during the induction of general anesthesia can be explained on this basis. Similarly CNS-depressant drugs exert their action by stabilization of the neuronal membrane resulting into decreased neurotransmitter release. Some drugs cause CNS stimulation, some cause CNS-depression. While some agents may exert both effects simultaneously on different areas of the CNS. A phase of depression which immediately follows after prolonged CNS excitation, is in part due to the exhaustion of stores of neurotransmitter. Similarly a chronic drug-induced depression may turn into hyper-excitability if the drug is abruptly withdrawn.

A CNS-acting drug usually affects several CNS functions to varying degrees due to the interconnection of the nerve tracts. The CNS excitatory effects are usually additive. Similarly CNS depressant effects are also additive in nature. The effect of antagonism between a depressant and stimulant drug is variable and is governed by lipophilicity and the potency of respective agents:

20.3 BRAIN COMPARTMENTS

Morphologically and on the functional basis, brain structure comprises of compartments shown in Fig. 20.2.

(i) Cerebral cortex : The entire surface of cerebrum is composed of gray matter and is known as cerebral cortex. It governs all the vital and higher centers like memory, consciousness, mental activities and many reflex acts. Centers which supervise the functioning of important systems like cardiovascular or GIT, are also located in it.

(ii) Basal ganglia (nuclei) : These are the masses of gray matter situated deep within the cerebral hemispheres. They are involved in the control of movement and posture.

(iii) Thalamus : It lies in the center of the brain, just beneath the cortex or above the hypothalamus. The neurons of thalamus act as relays between the incoming sensory impulses and the cortex region. They also interconnect neurologically different compartments of the brain. The thalamus and basal nuclei also regulate the visceral functions.

(iv) Hypothalamus : It is a vital organ of integration for autonomic nervous system. It regulates body temperature, blood pressure, intermediary metabolism, water balance, sleep and sexual cycle. It is a center for emotional responses.

(v) Pons : It is a relay station from-lower to the higher centers. It connects both halves of the cerebellum.

(vi) Mid brain : It is a short, constricted portion that connects the cerebral hemispheres and thalamus -

hypothalamus to the spinal cord. The major monoamine containing neurons of the brain are located within this region. The co-ordination centers for cardiovascular and respiratory systems are also present in the mid-brain region.

(vii) Cerebellum : It is a small region present behind the cerebral hemispheres and extends from posterior pons. It governs the body posture in the space and causes antigravity maintenance of blood flow.

(viii) Spinal cord : This term describes the slender cord-like region from the end of medulla oblongata to lower lumber vertebrae. It acts as both, relay center and co-ordination center for sensory and motor impulses.

(ix) Limbic system : It is often referred to as the visceral brain. It consists of hippocampus (near to the pons), amygdaloid complex (one of the basal ganglia), hypothalamus, mid-brain and part of the thalamus. This system is involved in –

(a) reception and integration of olfactory information.

(b) behavioural and emotional expressions, mainly due to its connections with hypothalamus and

(c) control of extrapyramidal motor system. This system helps in the functioning of voluntary (pyramidal) motor system. This system helps in the functioning of voluntary (pyramidal) motor system. Damage to extrapyramidal system results in disorders of involuntary movements e.g., tremors.

(d) Reticular activating system : This system is spread within the region of mid-brain pons and medulla oblongata. Its function is to link peripheral sensory and motor events with higher centers of integration.

Reticular activating system is completely characterized region of gray matter which helps in both integration and co-ordination of nerve impulses. It is thus responsible for wakefulness and the level of arousal. It alerts the cortex to a state of wakefulness. Depression of this system (e.g., by hypnotic drugs), naturally leads to induction of sleep. This system is also involved in the co-ordination of eye-movements.

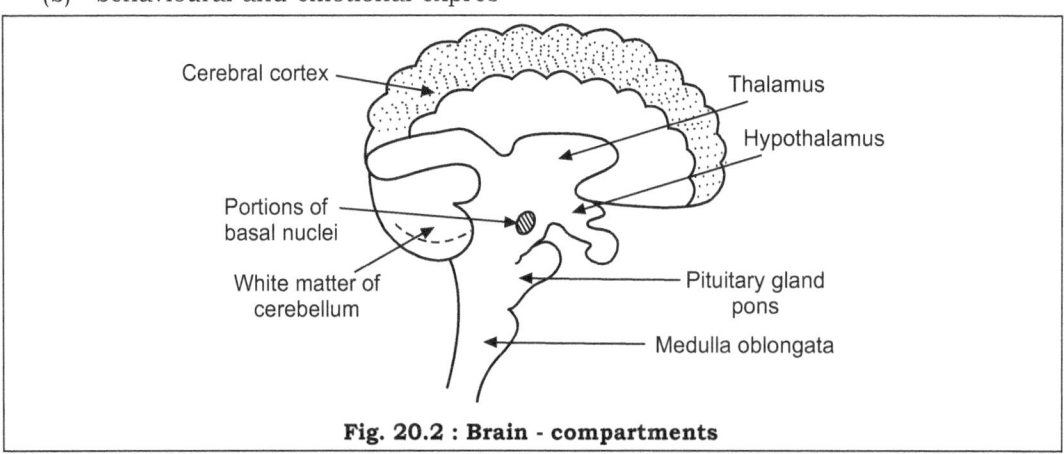

Fig. 20.2 : Brain - compartments

20.4 CENTRAL NEUROTRANSMITTERS

(a) Acetylcholine :

It is a neurotransmitter and is distributed in the irregular fashion within the regions of the mammalian CNS. The cerebral, limbic and thalamic regions are mainly dominant regions of cholinergic inter regional and local circuits.

(b) Norepinephrine :

The CNS contains all adrenoceptors (α_1, α_2, β_1 and β_2) and norepinephrine exhibits either excitatory or inhibitory responses depending upon predominance of receptor subtypes in a particular region. As in the autonomic nervous system, stimulation of α_2-adrenoceptors leads to marked inhibition of the release of norepinephrine.

Norepinephrine operates predominantly in the region of hypothalamus, in certain zones of the limbic system and in neurons of reticular formation.

From these neurons, the multiple branched axons interconnect the nerve tracts arising from cortical, subcortical and spinomedullary fields. For example, activation of α-adrenoceptors leads to the excitatory effects in diencephalic and mesencephalic regions. While activation of β-adrenoceptor causes hyperpolarization resulting into inhibition of cortical structures. Norepinephrine governs the CNS-functions that include feeding, sleeping, memory, learning and attention.

(c) Epinephrine :

Epinephrine containing neurons are relatively few and are present in medullary reticular formation in the mammalian CNS.

(d) Dopamine :

It is an inhibitory neurotransmitter and present in higher amounts in the basal ganglia, the olfactory tubercle and some region of the frontal cortex. In Parkinsonism, however, there appears a fall in concentration of dopamine in brain region.

(e) 5-Hydroxytryptamine :

Its presence in the brain region was first reported in 1957. The GIT enterochromaffin cells are supposed to be storage depots of 5-hydroxytryptamine. Minor amounts of 5HT are retained in the platelets and brain. In CNS, it governs mainly behavioural phenomena. It is mainly present in the regions of hypothalamus, limbic system, brain stem pituitary gland and raphe nuclei. It regulates sleep, pain perception, depression and aggressiveness and any disturbance in its turnover leads to mental illnesses and CNS dysfunction. For example, the hallucinogenic action of LSD is in part, attributed to its ability to reduce the turnover of 5 HT in brain. In addition, 5 HT also regulates body temperature and the release of pituitary hormones.

5-Hydroxyindoleacetic acid is the principal metabolite of 5-HT, excreted through urine.

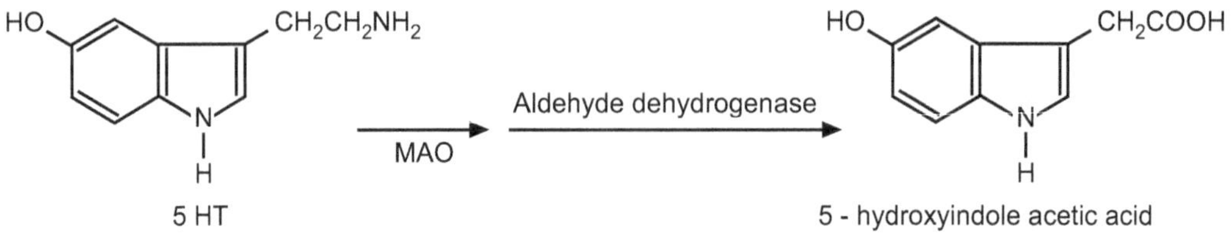

Fig. 20.3 : Metabolism of serotonin

(f) Amino acids :

The CNS contains considerably higher concentration of certain amino acids. In general monocarboxylic amino acids (e.g., GABA, glycine, taurine etc) act as inhibitory neurotransmitters while dicarboxylic amino acids (e.g., glutamate, aspartate etc.) act as excitatory neurotransmitters.

(i) **Gamma-amino benzoic acid (GABA) :** Its presence in the brain region was first reported in 1950. It causes inhibition of interneurons through the activation of chloride ionophore. Its inhibitory action is potentiated by benzodiazepines and is antagonized by the convulsant drugs. Valproic acid increases the brain GABA levels and thus calm down the CNS excitation seen in epilepsy.

(ii) **Glycine :** It is present in the ventral horn of the spinal cord and in the reticular formation where it acts as an inhibitory neurotransmitter. Its inhibitory actions are antagonized by strychnine.

(iii) **Dicarboxylic acids :** Glutamate and aspartate are the examples of dicarboxylic amino acids which act as excitatory neurotransmitters in virtually every region of brain.

(g) Histamine :

It is present in significant amounts in the hypothalamus and reticular formation where its actions are propogated through c-AMP. Unlike other neurotransmitters, no active re-uptake processes for histamine have been reported in the CNS.

In addition, other amino acids like alanine, cysteine, imidazole-4-acetic acid may qualify the status of neurotransmitter.

(h) Peptides :

Many endogenous peptide substances present in the CNS are suspected to bring out their own responses or to act in a supportive manner for other neurotransmitters. They include endorphins, substance P, vasoactive intestinal peptide (VIP), cholecystokinin, gastrin, vasopressin, oxytocin, Leutenizing hormone-releasing hormone, growth hormone-releasing factor etc. They are located in the specific neurons and their release process is Ca^{++} ion dependent. No active re-uptake mechanisms are so far reported for these peptides.

20.5 BLOOD-BRAIN-BARRIER

Not all the categories of drugs administered in the body, can reach the CNS area and cause CNS-effects. Their entry into the region of CNS is supposed to be governed by a permeable barrier, known as the blood-brain-barrier. This barrier operates to regulate the passive diffusion of both, macromolecules as well as micromolecules from the systemic circulation into the various regions of the CNS. Certain properties like, molecular weight, charge and lipophilicity of the molecules play an important role in controlling the passage of bioactive substances in the CNS.

In human body and other complex organisms a steady state concentration of hormones, amino acids, sugars and ions (like Na^+, K^+, Ca^{++}, etc.) is maintained in circulation. Frequent small fluctuations in their concentrations are expected after meal or exercire. These fluctuations do not affect the functioning of different organs of the body, leaving brain as an exception.

Table 20.1: Some central-neurotransmitters

Transmitter	Agonists	Antagonists
1. Acetylcholine	M_1 : Muscarine	Atropine
	M_2 : Bethanechol	Atropine
	N : Nicotine	Dihydro-β–erythroidine
2. Norepinephrine	$α_1$: Phenylephrine	Prazosin
	$α_2$: Clonidine	Yohimbine
	$β_1$: Dobutamine	Practolol
	$β_2$: Terbutaline	Butoxamine
3. Epinephrine	same as above	Same as above
4. Dopamine	D_1 : Dihydrexidine	Phenothiazine
	D_2 : Apomorphine	Butyrophenone
5. 5-Hydroxytry-ptamine	5 HT_1 : LSD	Methylsergide
	5 HT_2 : LSD	Spiroperidol
6. GABA	A : Muscimol	Picrotoxin
	B : Baclofen	Saclofen
7. Glycine	Taurine	Strychnine
8. Dicarboxylic amino acids	N-Me-D-aspartate	α-amino adipate

Brain is a highly specialized organ of the body. Even a slight fluctuation in the composition of blood supplied to brain, may affect nervous function. Since some hormones and amino acids serve as neurotransmitters, such fluctuation may lead to uncontrolled nervous activity. Hence, the brain must be kept rigorously isolated from such transient changes in the composition of the blood. The concept of Blood-Brain-Barrier, whose existence was first demonstrated conclusively in the 1960's has been put forward. It possesses the unique and specialized mechanisms by which, brain excludes unwanted substances presented to it by circulation. The barrier serves a critical function as stringent gatekeeper between blood and brain to create the unchanging environment, the brain needs.

Fortunately to receive the essential nutrients needed for brain functioning, there exists specialized transport systems that recognize and carry nutrients into the brain. There are several different types of transporter, each of which has a specific function. These transporters not only carry nutrients into the brain but also pump surplus substances out, in order to maintain a constant environment for neurons.

The first evidence for the existence of such barrier came out in 1913 through the observations of Edwin E. Goldmann when he showed that the central nervous system is separated from the blood by a barrier of some kind. With an introduction of Electron microscopy, it can be stated with certain surety that the endothelium of brain capillaries is the anatomic site of the blood-brain-barrier. These capillaries that supply blood to the tissues of the brain, has a unique structure. In contrast to any usual animal cell, the endothelial cells forming the tube of a brain capillary are locked by continuous tight junctions that prevent substances in the blood from diffusing freely into the brain. In addition, the brain capillaries are almost completely surrounded by processes of the brain cells, known as astrocytes. Previously it was thought that the astrocytes form the blood-brain-barrier. But now it is proved that the endothelial cells govern the transport across the blood and brain cells. Hence, they constitute the barrier site.

Lipophilicity is an important parameter which governs an ability of a molecule to reach the blood-brain-barrier. Lipid soluble substances easily cross the barrier and enter the brain. The reason lies in the lipophilic nature of cell-membrane of capillary endothelium. But certain substances which are of vital importance for brain function (e.g., glucose, certain amino acids) are not lipophilic. A special transport control system exists in capillary endothelium to recognize and to bring nutrients across the membrane. Recently S.I. Harik proved that each endothelial cell is richly supplied with such transport sites. Each transporter is undoubtedly composed of proteins that span the cell-membrane, thereby forming a channel through which nutrients and other substances needed for brain metabolism cross the barrier.

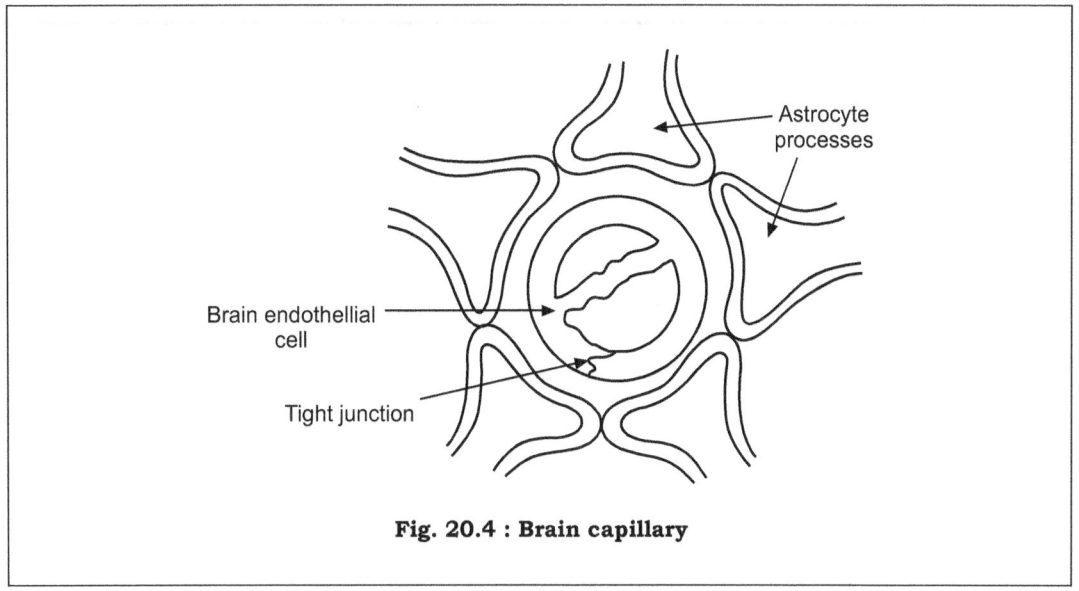

Fig. 20.4 : Brain capillary

If an unwanted substance enters the endothelial cells from blood, it can be modified through enzymatic steps into a chemical form, in the endothelium and rendered unable to enter the brain.

For example, L-dopa is converted in endothelium into dopamine and DOPAC in successive steps by the enzymes AADC and MAO. Hence the enzymatic conversions can serve as a means of controlling how much L-dopa reaches the brain.

An interesting experiment by Stanley I. Rapoport indicated that the concentrated sugar solution temporarily loosens the tight junctions between endothelial cells. When the sugar solution is removed, the barrier is re-established. This presents a more precise way of administering medicines which enter the brain slowly. e.g., penicillin. This technique is of clinical value in patients with brain tumors where the entry of drugs in brain can be facilitated using this procedure.

The operation of metabolic and physical barriers across blood and brain cells is collectively known as blood-brain-barrier. The term describes all the obstacles to the free passage of a substance from the blood stream to the brain cells.

The barrier is not equally strong in all parts of brain. It is relatively liberal in the hypothalamic region and in the area postrema.

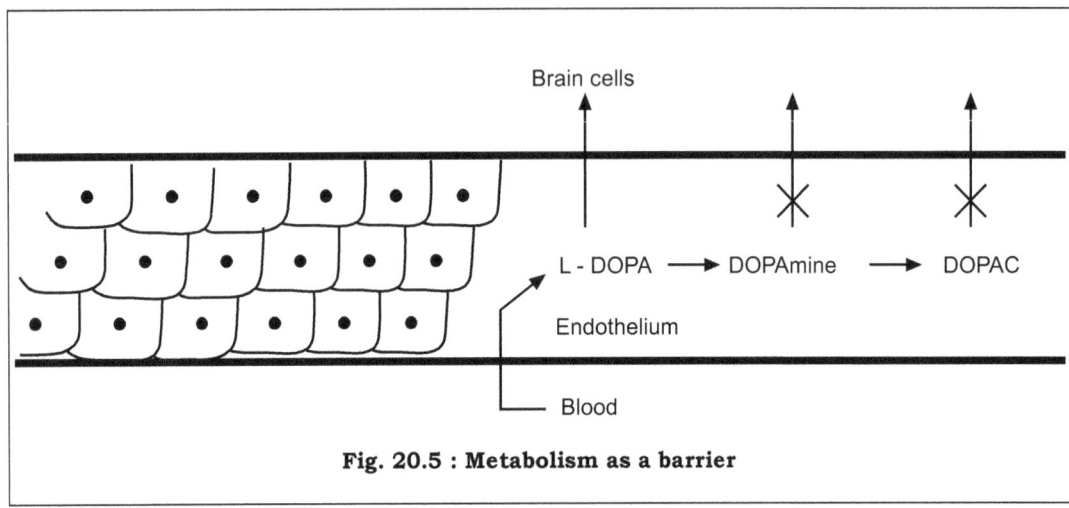

Fig. 20.5 : Metabolism as a barrier

GENERAL ANAESTHETIC AGENTS

21.1 INTRODUCTION

General anaesthetics is a class of CNS depressant drugs which produce a partial or total loss of the sense of pain with a controlled and reversible depression of the functional activity of the CNS. In order to perform more complicated surgical operations, the surgeon needs time and needs a patients whose muscles are relaxed. General anesthetics serve both these objectives. They also induce analgesia and suppress visceral reflexes to available extent.

These agents depress the cardiovascular (e.g., hypotension and arrhythmias may occur) and respiratory system. The respiratory depression usually demands the supplemental ventilation. The dose of an anaesthetic agents can be reduced by using other adjuvants like opioids, barbiturates, muscle relaxant or N_2O.

Characteristics of general anaesthetics:

(i) The agents in this class enjoy wide structural variation and hence strict SAR can not be framed out.

(ii) These agents are nonspecific in action., i.e., they do not interact with specific receptors. Hence, they are thought to be simple general cellular poisons.

(iii) They are used at high concentration and have access to all areas of the body.

(iv) Most of these agents contain bromine or fluorine atom. Hence, if oil-gas partition coefficient of the drug is of low value, it will leave the fatty tissues more readily in the post-operative period. The released drug is then exposed to metabolism for relatively short period of time resulting into the generation of less amount of fluorine or bromine atom. They in turn, cause less renal, hepatic or psychic toxicities.

(v) The intensity of GIT-side effects like, nausea and vomiting is influenced by other factors like premedication, disease state and duration of the surgery.

(vi) The term 'MAC' (i.e., minimum alveolar concentration) is used to define the potency of various anaesthetic agents. It is usually expressed as the percentage of inhaled gases that is represented by anaesthetic gas at one atmosphere. Lower the value of MAC, higher will be the potency of anaesthetic agent. For example, methoxyflurane (MAC = 0.16) is the most potent of the anaesthetic agents. MAC value is determined under non-premedication conditions because premedicated drugs lower down the dose of anaesthetic agent, needed to achieve adequate surgical anaesthesia. MAC value is an additive property.

(vii) General anaesthetic agents produce analgesia, unconsciousness, amnesia and muscular relaxation. They virtually affect almost every organ system due to their lipophilic character. Cardiovascular and respiratory system are usually depressed. Ionized or polar compounds can not exert anaesthetic activity.

(viii) The depth of anaesthesia depends upon the tension or partial pressure of a drug at brain tissue. This tension depends on the arterial tension which in turn, exists in equilibrium with the alveolar tension. It means, higher the tension in alveoli, more rapid will be the induction of anaesthesia. The alveolar tension primarily depends upon the pressure at which anaesthetic gas is administered and the solubility of anaesthetic agent in the blood.

If the anaesthetic agent is soluble in blood, sufficient tension at alveoli can not develop due to rapid elimination of anaesthetic agent. While quick induction of anaesthesia occurs due to development of higher alveolar tension which develops by insolubility or partial solubility of anaesthetic agent in the blood. At different organs, including brain, anaesthetic agent exists in equilibrium condition where the rate of entry and rate of exist of agent remains same. But the depressant effects of anaesthetic agent are exerted predominantly on the CNS due to its highly vascular structure. For example, CNS receives about 160 ml of blood per minute. The depressant effects are first exerted on cortical centers, then on spinal centers, followed by depression of medullary centers. The effect is directly proportional to its oil : gas partition

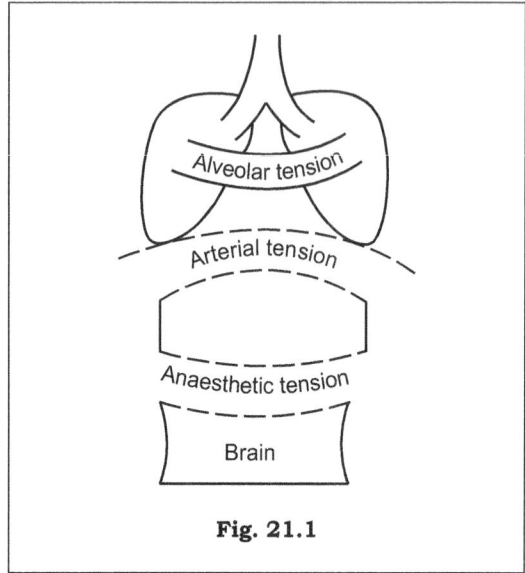

Fig. 21.1

coefficient. The greater its oil : gas partition coefficient, the more will be its capacity to get absorbed in the fatty tissues.

21.2 STAGES OF ANAESTHESIA

The concept of blood-brain-barrier has been put forward to explain the unique specialized mechanism by which, brain excludes many substances presented to it by circulation. In general, lipophilic and unionized molecules pass most readily into the CNS. In case of general anaesthetic agents, as the concentration is increased, penetration into CNS increases, resulting into increased depth of anaesthesia. A pattern of descending depression is seen where the higher cortical centers are attended first while the vital medullary centers are attacked at the last. For convenience, Guedel divided anaesthesia into four separate stages, with the third stage further subdivided into four planes.

Stage I : Analgesia

Consciousness is maintained and analgesia is produced. Since higher cortical centers are depressed, this stage is also called as cortical stage.

Stage II : Delirium or stage of excitement

Consciousness is lost. Further removal of cortical inhibition leads to excitement. Patient may move, salivate, cough, vomit, shout and struggle violently. Hypertension and tachycardia may also occur. To avoid this excitement stage, short-acting intravenous anaesthetics (e.g., thiopental sodium) may be given to the patient prior to anaesthetic agent that allows the patient to pass through this stage rapidly, thus reducing some of these hazards.

Stage III : Surgical anaesthesia

Skeletal muscles are relaxed. Hence most of the operative procedures are performed at this stage. It is further sub-divided into four planes representing progressive increase in the depth of anaesthesia and decreased respiration as follows :

Plane I : Cessation of eye movement.

Plane II : Beginning of paralysis of respiratory muscles.

Plane III : Paralysis of all the respiratory muscles except diaphragm.

Plane IV : Paralysis of diaphragmatic muscles. Hypoxia or a decreased cerebral blood flow is also reported. Respiration ceases altogether as stage IV is entered.

Stage IV : Respiratory paralysis or medullary paralysis (Apnea)

This is a toxic or overdose stage which begins with a complete respiratory paralysis and ends with the failure of the circulation or cardiovascular collapse. The tissues rapidly become anoxic.

The sequence of awakening events in the anaesthesized patient is essentially a reverse process to that of induction. Usually autonomic reflexes, like pupillary size, blood pressure and heart rate are good index to judge the depth of anaesthesia.

To minimize the toxic manifestations associated with the dose or slow onset of action of volatile or gaseous anaesthetic agents, short-acting potent anaesthetic agents are administered to the patient to cause a rapid, short-lived, loss of consciousness before a volatile or gaseous anaesthetic is given. The anaesthesia induced by them, is then maintained by volatile anaesthetic agent. Thus, intravenous, short-acting potent anaesthetics (basal anaesthetics or fixed anaesthetics) cause a rapid transition from a complete consciousness (stage I) to surgical anaesthesia (stage III) and complications associated with stage of delirium can thus be avoided.

21.3 PREANAESTHETIC MEDICATIONS

It is a routine practice to give premedication to the patient who is going to be anaesthesized.

(i) Generally a hypnotic is given on the night before to assure a good night sleep.

(ii) One or two hours before surgery, atropine or hyoscine is usually administered to prevent excessive secretion of saliva or mucus which might impede the work of anaesthetist. Atropine also prevents cardiac arrest due to the stimulation of vagal center.

(iii) Morphine (or pethidine) is also given to minimize fear and apprehension.

(iv) The use of sodium pentothal as an induction agent in 1930s promoted the use of intravenous anaesthetics, which induce a brief period of anaesthesia within seconds of being injected. This anaesthesia is often maintained with gaseous or volatile anaesthetic which is administered by various techniques.

(v) If the muscle relaxation achieved by anaesthetic agent itself is not sufficient, a muscle relaxant is usually administered. The introduction of muscle relaxants in the 1940s helped to minimize complications involved in surgery.

The simplest technique to administer a volatile anaesthetic involves, dropping the liquid anaesthetic on a guaze or other absorbing material supported over the patient's nose and mounted by a framework, forming a mask. But the vapours, often explosive (e.g., ether) may spread into the surrounding area. New techniques allow a controlled supply of oxygen, carbon-dioxide and anaesthetic agent by means of flowmeters.

21.4 MECHANISMS OF ACTION

All these agents are lipid soluble compounds of simple but diversified structures. Different theories stressing upon the relationship between the physical properties of the anaesthetic agents and their anaesthetic potency have been postulated. Prominent amongst them are –

(a) Meyer-Overton hypothesis : Meyer and Overton in the year 1901, independently correlates the potency of anaesthetic agents with their lipid solubility.

(b) Critical volume hypothesis : It is an extention of Meyer-Overtone theory. According to it, the hydrocarbon core of the lipid bilayer region of nerve membranes accomodates the anaesthetic molecules which expand the membrane by fluidizing resulting into disorganization of its functional components. Thus, anaesthetic agents inhibit the essential conformational changes of membrane proteins involved in

(i) ion conductance,

(ii) carrier transport system and /or

(iii) enzyme activity on the inner-membrane surface.

The membrane protein, itself may also be the site of action.

(c) Ferguson's principle : Anaesthetic agents distort the cell membranes or block ion-channels. The physical nature of anaesthetic activity prompted Ferguson (1939) to suggest a relationship between anaesthetic potency and thermodynamic activity of a drug. In the case of volatile anaesthetics administered with air or oxygen, thermodynamic activity is proportional to the relative saturation of a drug.

The relative saturation of a drug is defined as P_t/P_o for volatile drugs and gases.

$$\text{Relative saturation (a)} = P_t/P_o.$$

Where,

P_t = Partial pressure of the drug in the gaseous mixture.

P_o = Vapour pressure of the pure drug at same temperature.

Mullin in 1954, suggested that the thermodynamic activity increases as the series is ascended.

(d) Krnjevic hypothesis (1972) : Anaesthetic agents inhibit both the release and action of neurotransmitter by reducing the availability of free Ca^{++} ions in the sarcoplasm.

Reticular activating system is involved in the maintenance of consciousness. It contains a large number of synapses. By inhibiting the release of neurotransmitter, anaesthetic agents slow down the synaptic transmission in reticular activating system resulting into unconsciousness.

(e) According to some scientists, anaesthetic agents exert their action by affecting the energy yielding processes in the CNS. The target molecules appear to be either the cytochrome reductance or some flavoproteins.

21.5 CLASSIFICATION OF GENERAL ANAESTHETIC AGENTS

(I) Volatile or inhalational general anaesthetic agents :

(a) Inflammable and/or explosive agents e.g., cyclopropane, diethyl ether, ethylene etc.

(b) Noninflammable anaesthetic agents. e.g., nitrous oxide, halothane, enflurane, isoflurane, methoxyflurane, fluroxene, chloroform etc.

(II) Intravenous or basal general anaesthetic agents : e.g., thiopental sodium, methohexital, thiamylal etc.

21.6 VOLATILE GENERAL ANAESTHETIC AGENTS

The volatile or inhalational general anaesthetic agents are used to maintain the anaesthesia induced by basal anaesthetics. They exist either in gaseous form or as volatile liquids that are easily transformed into vapours. Inhalational anaesthetics in current use are relatively inert and nontoxic which interact with the nerve tissues physically. These agents mainly include nitrous oxide, halothane, enflurane, isoflurane and methoxyflurane. They are neither irritating to the respiratory system nor their odours are unpleasant. The popularity of other inhalational agents like, chloroform, ethers or cyclopropane varies geographically.

These disadvantages can be minimized by combining these agents with other anaesthetics of limited toxicity. This principle is adopted in the balanced anaesthesia.

[A] Gaseous Anaesthetic Agents :

Gyclopropane and nitrous oxide are the general anaesthetic agents which exist in gaseous form at room temperature and usual atmosphere pressure. In cylinder, due to high pressure applied, they exist in the liquid form which gasifies when the pressure is released.

(i) Cyclopropane (1929) : It is a dense, colourless gas with sweet odour and taste. About 15 - 20 % cyclopropane mixed with 80 - 85 % oxygen is sufficient to achieve a stage of surgical anaesthesia. Since it is most plasma insoluble of anaesthetic agents, it produces a rapid but smooth induction of anaesthesia. It forms an explosive mixture with air. It is rapidly excreted out by lungs in an unchanged form.

Table 21.1 : Currently used volatile general anaesthetics

Sr. No.	Anaesthetic agents	MAC	Blood-gas partition coefficient (37°C)	Limitations
1.	Cyclopropane (gas)	9.2	0.41	Flammable
2.	Diethyl ether	1.92	12.1	Flammable, slow induction
3.	Nitrous oxide (gas)	> 100	0.47	Weak anaesthetic
4.	Halothane	0.75	2.3	Myocardial depression, hepatotoxicity
5.	Enflurane	1.68	1.8	Respiratory and CVS depression
6.	Isoflurane	1.15	1.4	Respiratory and CVS depression
7.	Methoxyflurane	0.16	12.0	Renal toxicity

Other agents like diethyl ether, ethyl-chloride, divinyl ether and ethylene are less favoured anaesthetics due to their inflammable and/or explosive nature. Chloroform causes liver and nephrotoxicity while trichloroethylene is no longer used due to its decomposition to extremely toxic agents, like phosgene and carbon monoxide.

(ii) Nitrous oxide : Its preparation was first reported by Joseph Priestley in 1772 and Sir Humphry Davy (1800) was first to recognize its anaesthetic property. It is a useful analgesic and light noninflammable anaesthetic agent (MAC is > 100). It is used alone, it can not produce a stage of surgical anaesthesia within therapeutic dose-range. It is less depressant to both, cardiovascular and respiratory systems. Its onset of action is extremely rapid. It lacks irritation properties. These advantages qualify it as an ideal supplemental anaesthetic. e.g. N_2O-O_2 - halothane.

Anaesthesia occurs with a mixture of 80% N_2O with 20% O_2 which is acompanied by nausea, vomiting and excitement. Hence, this gas is often termed as laughing gas. It is reported to be teratogenic and bone marrow depressant. Megaloblastic changes in bone marrow occur due to its ability to oxidize cobalt atom in vitamin B_{12}. But since it is a good analgesic in subanaesthetic concentration (20 - 30 %), it is used for minor dental operations, and dressing of burns etc. It is rapidly excreted in unchanged form, mainly through lungs.

[B] Volatile Liquid General Anaesthetic Agents :

(i) Diethyl ether : It was introduced as an anaesthetic agent in 1840s. Ether gets oxidized rapidly upon exposure to air, light or moisture to form unstable peroxides and acetaldehyde which are of explosive nature. It has extremely slow induction time. Hence it is usually administered in N_2O-O_2 mixture. It has an unpleasant after taste and stimulates the brain stem respiratory centres. A small fraction of inhaled ether undergoes metabolism to ethanol and acetaldehyde.

(ii) Halothane (1956) : It is one of the most commonly employed agent (2-2.5 %), usually administered through N_2O-air mixture. Since it reaches equilibrium more rapidly due to its low solubility in blood, both the induction and emergence are smooth and rapid. It does not cause respiratory irritation. But circulatory depression occurs due to its action on vasomotor centers, autonomic ganglia and blood vessels. It is a poor analgesic and muscle relaxant. It also causes ventilatory depression. Shivering is common during recovery. If used in delivery process, it may increase the blood loss and delay the delivery due to the inhibition of uterine contractions.

About 15% of the inhaled drug undergoes metabolism to give trifluoroacetic acid, bromide and fluoride which appear in the urine. The drug is said to cause 'halothane hepatitis' which is preceded by fever, usually 5 - 10 days postoperatively due to autoimmune destruction. It should not be used in combination with barbiturates due to its hypotensive action.

(iii) Enflurane (1973) : It is similar to its properties with halothane except its irritating odour that leads to coughing and bronchospasm. It's administration is accompanied by a dose-dependent depression of cardiovascular and respiratory system. Seizures of short duration may also be seen which can be controlled by hyperventilation. Hence, enflurane is contraindicated in the patients having seizure disorder. Relaxation of uterine and skeletal muscles is reported. About 2 - 5% of the inhaled drug undergoes metabolism to give difluoromethoxy difluoroacetic acid and fluoride ions.

(iv) Isoflurane (1981) : Due to very low solubility in tissues, isoflurane has a more rapid induction and emergence than halothane. It has similar properties with halothane, except its actions on –

(a) cardiovascular system that is less pronounced. Hence, it is a safe drug.

(b) respiratory system that results into coughing and increased secretions.

Due to its very insignificant metabolism into the body, the concentration of fluoride ions generated, is too low to cause renal hepatic toxicity.

(v) Methoxyflurane (1960) : It has a large blood gas partition coefficient which explains its slow induction rate. Hence, stage of delirium can be easily seen. To eliminate the stage of excitement, a rapid acting intravenous anaesthetic is to be given prior to its use. The high blood : gas partition coefficient of drug causes its prolonged retaintion into the fatty tissue resulting into prolonged action and greater metabolism. It has a characteristic feature to constrict the pupil throughout all the stages of anaesthesia. Postoperative hepatic and renal toxicity, nausea, vomiting occurs due to toxic amounts of fluoride ions. It differs from halothane as follows.

(a) It has a higher analgesic potential and

(b) It does not cause the relationship of uterus. Hence, it can be used to produce analgesia during labour.

Major fraction of the inhaled drug undergoes metabolism to difluoromethoxy-acetic acid, dichloroacetic acid, oxalic acid and fluoride ions.

(vi) Fluroxene : It is a light anaesthetic agent with an inflammable and explosive nature. Nausea is quite common.

(vii) Chloroform (1840) : Once upon a time, it was a popular anaesthetic agent but is now seldom used. It has a good muscle relaxant activity. It is hepatotoxic and nephrotoxic alongwith dangerous effects on cardiovascular system.

21.7 INTRAVENOUS (BASAL) ANAESTHETICS

For rapid induction of anaesthesia, the sodium salts of ultrashort acting barbiturates are usually administered intravenously or by retention enema. The advantages associated with these agents are

(1) Smooth induction in lower doses.

(2) Fair muscular relaxation

(3) Control of visceral reflex responses

(4) Nonexplosive nature

(5) Short and uncomplicated recovery.

The potent respiratory depression is the risk generally associated with their use and hence they are used to produce rapid and pleasant anaesthesia which is then maintained with the volatile anaesthetics. Their high lipid solubility and rapid destruction of these drugs by liver, contribute to their short-duration of action.

(a) Hexobarbitone : It was introduced in 1932 followed by the introduction of thiopental in 1935 by Lundy. Thiopental is depressant of both CVS and respiratory system. Methohexital and thiamylal are the other barbiturates which are used as intravenous anaesthetic agents. All these agents are poor analgesics and produce signs of catecholamine and histamine release. Sympathomimetic responses accompanied with their use include dilated pupils, sweating, an increase in blood pressure and tachycardia.

Thiopental sodium crosses placenta and thus depresses fetus. For single injection, its concentration should not exceed 2.5% in aqueous solution. Methohexital is more potent anaesthetic than thiopental but produces even shorter period of anaesthesia.

(b) Ketamine hydrochloride : Ketamine was developed in 1970 as a structural analogue of phencyclidine, a parenteral anaesthetic agent. It has rapid onset and short duration of action and may be of value in short surgical procedures which do not require skeletal muscle relaxation. The side-effects include an increase in blood pressure, delirium, hallucinations and tachycardia. Diazepam, promethazine, or morphine are the drugs which reduce or abolish these untoward effects.

Table 21.2 : Intravenous anaesthetics

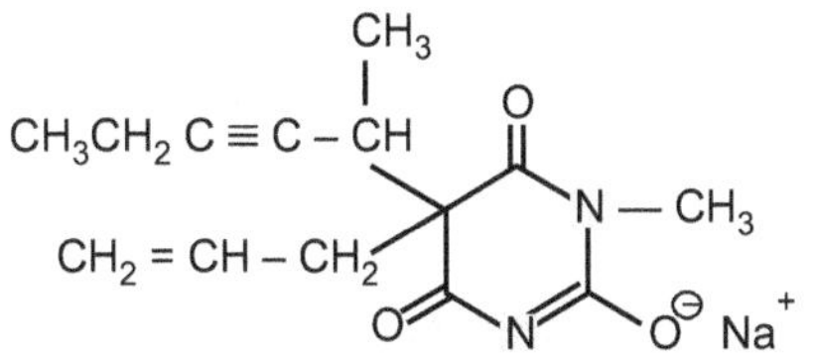

Methohexital sodium

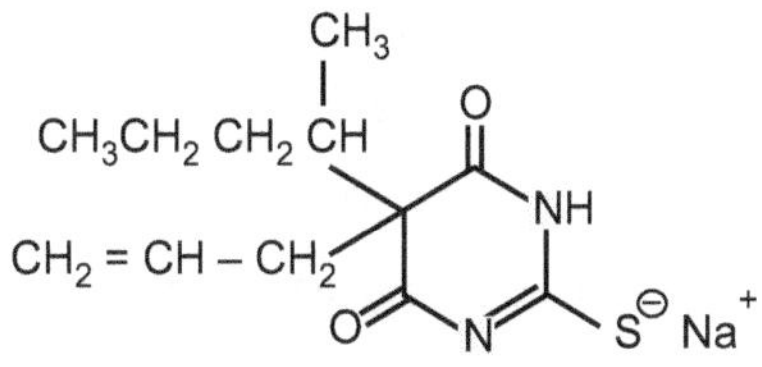

Thiamylal sodium

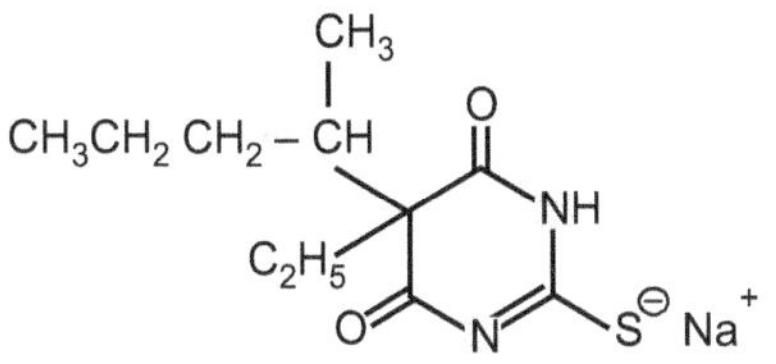

Thiopental sodium

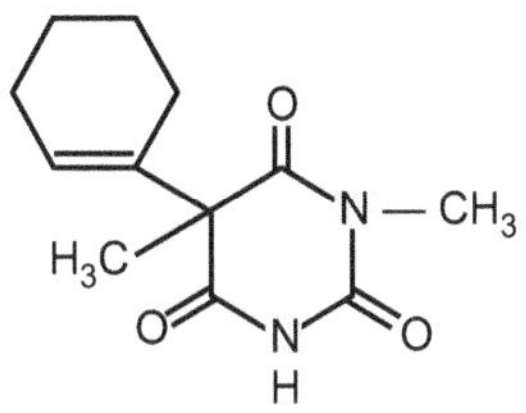

Hexabarbital

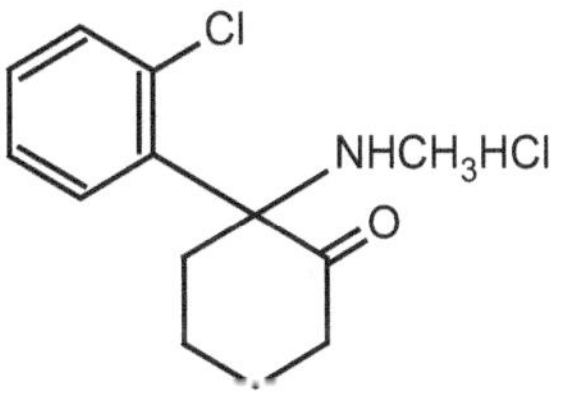

Ketamine hydrochloride

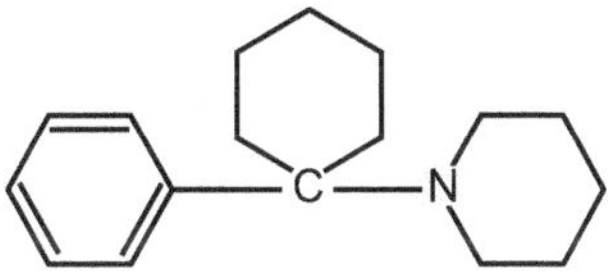

Phencyclidine

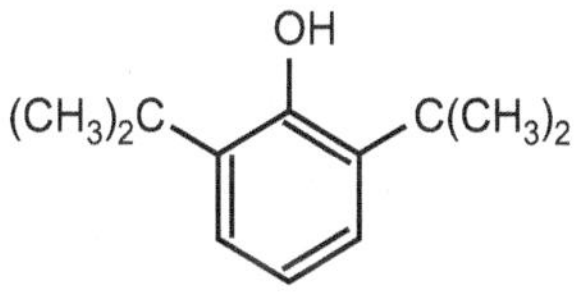

Propofol

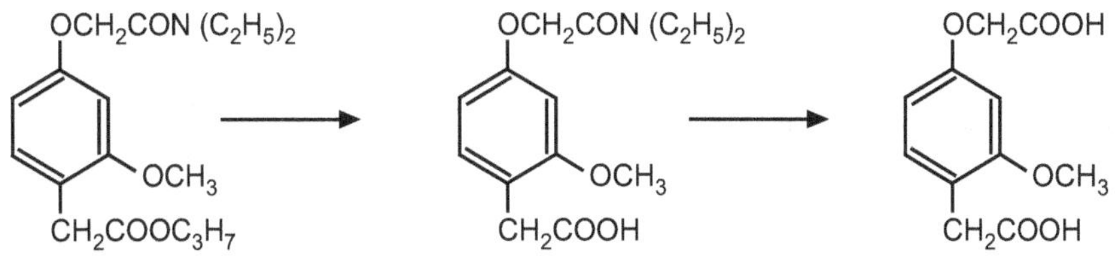

Propanidid → **Metabolite** → **Metabolite**

(c) Propanidid : It is a eugenol derivative. It is an oily liquid having anaesthetic action of very short duration when given intravenously. Unlike other anaesthetics, it has a stimulant action on respiration while depressant action on myocardium, resulting into hypotension. Respiratory stimulation may be due to a reflex response to the stimulation of peripheral chemoreceptors. The nausea and vomiting is more frequent with propanidid than any other I.V. anaesthetic. The cardiovascular collapse is frequent in hypertensive patients.

Propanidid is attacked at its ester linkage by the serum cholinesterase in plasma and liver. The resulting acid further undergoes metabolism with the loss of diethylamino group.

(d) Miscellaneous agents : Althesin is reported to possess anaesthetic activity. It is a mixture of alphaxalone and alphadolone acetate dispersed in polyoxyethylated castor oil.

(i) **Aliphaxalone**: R = – CH_3
(ii) **Alphadolone acetate:**
    R = –CH_2COCH_3

21.8 NARCOANALYSIS

In the persons with criminal background, to expose out his real thoughts and motives, intravenous barbiturates are given in subanaesthetic doses. The person looses his inhibition and feels free to talk the truth. Barbiturates which are used for this purpose include pentobarbitone, thiopentone and amylobarbitone. These agents are also of value in regaining the memory in the cases of neurotic amnesia.

21.9 DISSOCIATIVE ANESTHESIA

This is a stage of partial anaesthesia where some parts of the brain (specifically midbrain region) are anaesthesized by the drug while rest of the region remains unaffected. The person is detached from its surrounding and hence this state is known as dissociative anaesthesia. Ketamine and phencyclidine are the drugs which cause dissociative anaesthesia in order to carry out minor surgery and diagnostic investigations in very young children.

21.10 PREMEDICATIONS

Premedication is required to supplement the anaesthesia and to create suitable working conditions for the surgeon. The drugs which are commonly employed include.

(i) Tranquillizers like diazepam, lorazepam and midazolam.

(ii) Sedative-hypnotics like etomidate, etc.

(iii) Anticholinergic agents like atropine, hyoscine.

(iv) Opioid analgesics like morphine, meperidine, fentanyl, alfentanil and sufentanil.

(v) Neuroleptic compounds like droperidol.

LOCAL ANAESTHETIC AGENTS

22.1 INTRODUCTION

Local anaesthetic agents are the drugs which are applied in appropriate concentration (as close to the site of action as possible) to achieve a selective analgesia or anaesthesia of relatively restricted areas of the body. To be useful clinically, the action should always be reversible without any structural damage to the nerve fibers. Many potent local anaesthetics could not be used clinically due to their high systemic toxicities.

The sensitivity of a nerve fiber to a local anaesthetic is inversely related to its diameter and since pain fibers in general, are smaller in diameter than many other types of sensory and motor fibers, they are anaesthesized by concentrations of local anaesthetics which cause neither muscle paralysis nor abolition of the sense of touch. The intensity of activity is governed by both fiber size and anatomical fiber type. When applied locally, they reversibly block sympathetic fibers resulting into vasodilation except cocaine which leads to vasoconstriction.

These drugs are mainly used for the temporary relief of localized pain and itching due to minor burns, insect bites, allergic response, in dentistry and minor surgical procedures.

22.2 MECHANISM OF ACTION

These agents act by preventing the generation or propogation of the nerve impulse by inhibition of large transient, voltage-dependent rise in the permeability of the membrane to sodium ions.

The outer layer of connective tissue which wraps the sensory and motor nerve outside the spinal cord, is known as *epineurium*. In this, a nerve is itself enclosed in a membrane of dense, concentric layers of connective tissue, called as *perineurium*. Within the perineurium, the individual nerve fiber (axon) is embedded in longitudinally arranged strands of collagenous fibers called as *endoneurium*. If used in higher concentration, local anaesthetic agent can penetrate deep enough to block even the most centrally located nerve fiber. In this case, however, the duration of blockade of centrally located nerve will be less than that of peripherally located nerves.

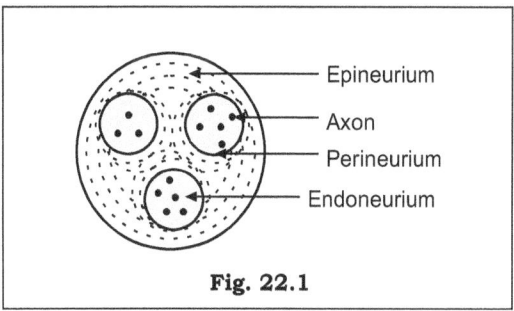

Fig. 22.1

Each axon has its own cell membrane (axolemma) tightly surrounded by (not in all axones) a myelin sheath. The myelin is not continuous along the fiber. The interruptions are called as the nodes of Ranvier. The axolemma serves as a barrier between the cytoplasm of the axon (axoplasm) and the endoneurium. The composition of the membrane is highly lipoidal with some protein fragments equal (or sometimes exceeding) to the quantity of lipids. It possesses selective permeability to ions and molecules. To understand the impulse generation and ion fluxes phenomenon, the concept of 'sodium channel' is put forward. It is supposed to be a macromolecular complex of glycosylated proteins having the molecular weight, exceeding 300,000 daltons. It is embedded in the matrix of the axonal membrane in non-uniform pattern and has an aqueous pore extending from interior of the matrix to the outer surface of nerve membrane. The concept is proposed to describe a mechanism for the controlled influx of cations which is achieved by the opening and closing of the aqueous pore of the sodium channel by constriction of the channel at two sites. The internal end of the channel resides within the membrane, while the external opening of the channel is said to be of 0.3 × 0.5 nm dimensions, surrounded by a ring of six oxygen atoms.

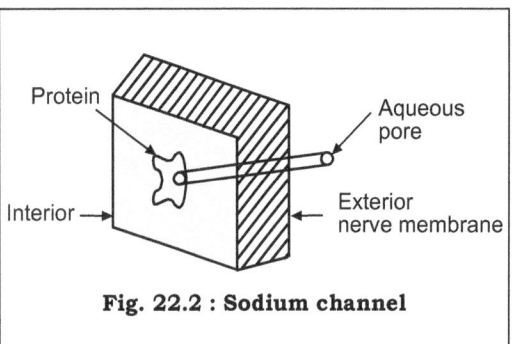

Fig. 22.2 : **Sodium channel**

I. Since the sodium channel is the sole route for the influx of sodium ions during nerve depolarisation, the simplest way to exert local anaesthetic action is to block these sodium channels thus preventing development of action potential without affecting the resting potential of the nerve. Thus, the basis of local anaesthetic action is to stabilize the nerve membrane, making it less excitable. The proposed local anaesthetic receptors are supposed to be situated in the vicinity of the sodium channels, either at inner or the outer gate which are acted upon by the charged form of the molecule. This hypothesis is termed as 'specific receptor theory'. It explains the voltage dependent binding of the charged form with its receptor sites.

The association of local anaesthetic molecules within the membrane may affect selective permeability characteristic of the nerve membrane by increasing the distortion of the lipids that constitute the nerve membranes. The increased degree of disorder of lipids will plug the membrane channels through which sodium enters the nerve. This action is mainly exhibited by unchanged, non-polar or lipophilic local anaesthetic agents by increasing the surface pressure of the lipid layer, and the hypothesis is known as membrane expansion theory.

II. Interaction with calcium : Calcium exists in the membrane in a bound state. It is the binding of this calcium with phospholipid which initiates the action potential and ion permeability changes. Local anaesthetic agents displace the bound calcium from these sites and compete with calcium for a phospholipid receptors. They may form more stable bonds with calcium, thereby inhibiting ionic fluxes.

III. Some local anaesthetic agents increase the threshold potential (a voltage essential to change the resting potential to the action potential), thereby the nerve cannot elicit the action potential and an impulse is not propogated.

IV. Immediately after an impulse propogation, the axon remains completely inexcitable (absolute refractory). Some drugs may extend or prolong this refractory period.

V. Some drugs may alter the velocity at which an impulse is conducted along the nerve. If conduction velocity is retarded, it may result into reduced impulse conduction. Some of these agents may also influence the working of Na^+—K^+—ATPase pump.

VI. Besides true local anaesthetic agents, many drugs like CNS depressants, reserpine, antihistaminics act by membrane stabilization. In vitro, all these agents retard impulse conduction. Many local anaesthetic agents antagonise the actions of histamine which acts as a neurotransmitter in atleast some peripheral nerves.

VII. According to Nachmansohn, due to structural resemblance of procaine with acetylcholine (acetylcholine antagonistic nature), local anaesthetics might owe their effectiveness to an interaction with acetylcholine receptors in the nerve fibers. Similarly atropine and many related anti-cholinergic and agents exhibit local anaesthetic activity.

The nerve membrane is lipophilic in nature. Hence for easy penetration into the nerve membrane, the local anaesthetic molecule should be uncharged or lipophilic e.g., benzocaine. Once it reaches to its sites of action –

Saxitoxin hydrochloride

(i) If it is still uncharged, it will get accumulated within the membrane and cause an expansion of the membrane (and thus narrow the sodium channel (B), by increasing the movements of the lipid molecules or by altering the conformation of the lipoprotein moiety as shown in the Fig. 22.3.

(ii) While anaesthetics that are effective only in the cationic form (e.g., cinchocaine and lignocaine), have their postulated receptors located in the vicinity of the gates, perhaps in the sodium channel itself (A and C). The production of charged cations is facilitated by the metabolic activity of the nerve cell.

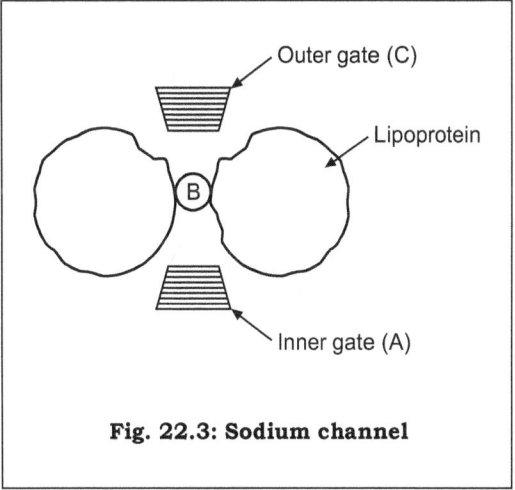

Fig. 22.3: Sodium channel

(iii) Some local anaesthetic exist at the sites of action in both, charged and uncharged form due to their characteristic pKa value. Hence, such agents (e.g., procaine) act by both the mechanisms. Since many local anaesthetic agents are amines, the proportion of the uncharged molecules will be more in alkaline medium.

All the local anaesthetics clinically available, have their site of action either within the lipoprotein moiety or at the inner gate of the sodium channel. Tetrodotoxin and saxitoxin are the probable exceptions, in the sense that they inhibit the development of action potential by acting chiefly on the external surface of the nerve membrane.

The drug-receptor interaction in local anaesthetic agents at the sodium channel, can be visualized in the manner quite similar to acetylcholine-receptor interaction.

22.3 STRUCTURAL FEATURES OF A LOCAL ANAESTHETIC AGENT

Most of the local anaesthetic agents, on the chemical basis, are characterised by the presence of hydrophilic and lipophilic moieties bridged by an intermediate alkyl chain. The lipophilic part may be attached to the alkyl chain through either an ester linkage or an amide linkage. Usually the amide local anaesthetic agents are chemically more stable, both in vivo as well as in vitro. Many local anaesthetics are the derivatives of para amino benzoic acid. The hydrophilic part consists of an amino group in the form of either tertiary or secondary amine. It is this part which imparts ionic charactertistics to the molecule. For the penetration into the nerve membrane, molecule should be present in an uncharged form while to act on the sodium channel-receptors, the positively charged substituted ammonium cation is important.

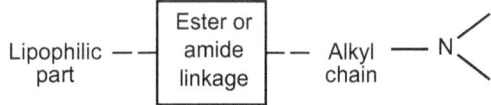

Local anaesthetic agent

The pKa value, lipid solubility and molecular size of the compound are the prominent factors (alongwith the pH at the site of action) which govern the potency of local anaesthetic agent. Most of them have pKa value in the range of 7 to 9 and are only sparingly soluble in water. Their water solubility may be increased by preparing their hydrochloride salts which when injected into the tissue, release the free base due to buffering effect of the tissue fluid. The clinical utility of all synthetic local anaesthetic agents is evaluated with reference to procaine.

Once a local anaesthetic agent is administered, it may take time to cause its effect. This time gap is known as a latent period. Usually the longer acting local anesthetic agents have longer latent periods.

To prolong duration of action and to reduce the risk of systemic toxicity, usually a vasoconstrictor (e.g., epinephrine) is added to the local anaesthetic solution. It helps to tie anaesthctic agent at desired site and decreases its rate of absorption. Vasoconstrictors can be used effectively when anaesthetic is infiltered around the nerve fibers and are not effective when local anaesthetic is applied to mucous membranes. They increase the contact time of an anaesthetic with the nerve fiber by increasing the duration of action. Commonly used vasoconstrictors include epinephrine, levonordefrin (α_1-adrenergic agonist), phenylephrine hydrochloride etc. Their use is accompanied with some side-effects of sympathomimetic origin. Repeated vasoconstriction due to prolonged use may produce gangrene.

22.4 PHARMACOLOGY

Local anaesthetics, principally act to interfere in Na^+ ion flux and thus prevent the depolarization of the nerve membrane. The degree of interference of initiation or propogation of an impulse is governed by dose of the drug and its site of action.

(i) CNS : Following absorption, all nitrogenous local anaesthetics may cause central stimulation followed by depression as blood level of drug, continues to increase. In toxic doses, the death may be caused due to respiratory failure. The high degree of CNS stimulation may sometimes cause chronic convulsions. The CNS excitation effect may be explained on the basis of selective depression of inhibitory neurons in the CNS.

(ii) Cardiovascular system : Myocardium is the primary site of action. Local anaesthetic agents cause the depression of the myocardium resulting into decrease in the conduction velocity and the force of contraction. With an exception of cocaine, most local anaesthetic agents lead to arteriolar dilation. This is reflected more in spinal and epidural anaesthesia where hypotension is a prominent sign. Due to the relaxant action on the cardiac muscles, some local anaesthetic amides (e.g., procainamide and lidocaine) are used as antiarrhythmic agents, in particularly ventricular arrhythmias. They act by raising the threshold for cardiac stimulation.

(iii) Neuromuscular system : Local anaesthetic agents are found to decrease the conductance in neuromuscular junction. They also potentiate the effect of other muscle relaxants. It is proposed that the local aesthetic agent forms a complex with nicotinic cholinergic receptor and thus depresses the ionic conductance.

(iv) Smooth muscles : Local anaesthetics also impair the ionic conductance in the smooth muscles and cause the relaxation of both, vascular and bronchial smooth muscles.

22.5 METABOLISM

Local anaesthetic agents having ester linkage are rapidly hydrolyzed by plasma cholinesterases and also in the liver. The amide local anaesthetics are bound to plasma proteins to a high degree and are almost completely metabolized by hepatic enzymes. The important points of attack are :

(i) Dealkylation of the aminoalkyl groups;

(ii) Hydrolysis of amide linkage;

(iii) Hydroxylation of the aromatic ring moiety;

(iv) *Conjugation* : Conjugation pro ducts of local anaesthetic agents are chiefly glucuronides.

22.6 ADVERSE REACTIONS

(i) On CNS : Uneasiness, shivering, tremors, convulsions.

(ii) On CVS : Myocardium depression, vasodilation, hypotension.

(iii) Allergic reactions : These reactions are frequently seen with the use of ester type local anaesthetics while amide local anaesthetics are free of allergic manifestations. In such cases certain antihistaminics can be used as local anaesthetics.

Most of the local anaesthetics can easily cross the placental barrier and affect the foetus by entering into the circulation. This property is least seen with chloroprocaine. Hence, it is a drug of choice in obstetrics. Amide type local anaesthetic agents should not be used during sulfonamide therapy.

22.7 SITES OF ACTION OF LOCAL ANAESTHETICS

1. Topical anaesthesia : It is used to relieve pain or itching at mucous surfaces, damaged skin surfaces, wounds or burns. Local anaesthetic agent is ineffective if it is applied directly to the unbroken skin. Absorption from the mucous membranes varies considerably. It is more rapid at tracheobronchial tree. For an application, the local anaesthetic agent may be dissolved in ointment.

2. Infiltration anaesthesia : In minor operations, a local anaesthetic is injected at sites in and around the area which is to be anaesthesized. The finer nerve endings are anaesthesized in the tissues which are to be incised. Lidocaine, procaine and bupivacaine are the drugs of choice in this category. Epinephrine, if used alongwith, as a vasoconstrictor, doubles the duration of infiltration anaesthesia.

3. Nerve block anaesthesia : A relatively higher concentrations of a local anaesthetic solution is injected in the close vicinity of the main nerve trunk supplying the area in which anaesthesia is required during surgery. Other nerves present in the nerve trunk are also anaesthesized. Duration of action is governed by lipid solubility and protein binding.

4. Surface anaesthesia : A superfacial anaesthesia can be achieved by applying the local anaesthetic solution directly to the mucous membranes of nose, mouth, throat, tracheobronchial tree and genitourinary tract. Examples of drugs used in this category include, cocaine, lidocaine and tetracaine.

5. Intravenous regional anaesthesia : A local anaestheic agent solution is injected into a vein. It is more effective in upper extremity (e.g. brachial plexus block) than in the lower extremity. Effective agents include lidocaine.

6. Spinal anaesthesia : In this case, a local anaesthetic is directly injected into the subarachnoid space where the nerves are not protected by perineurium. It results into blockade of the roots of those nerves, supplied to the site of operation. The order of anaesthesia is as follows :

(a) Sensory fibers,

(b) Sympathetic fibers, and

(c) Motor fibers.

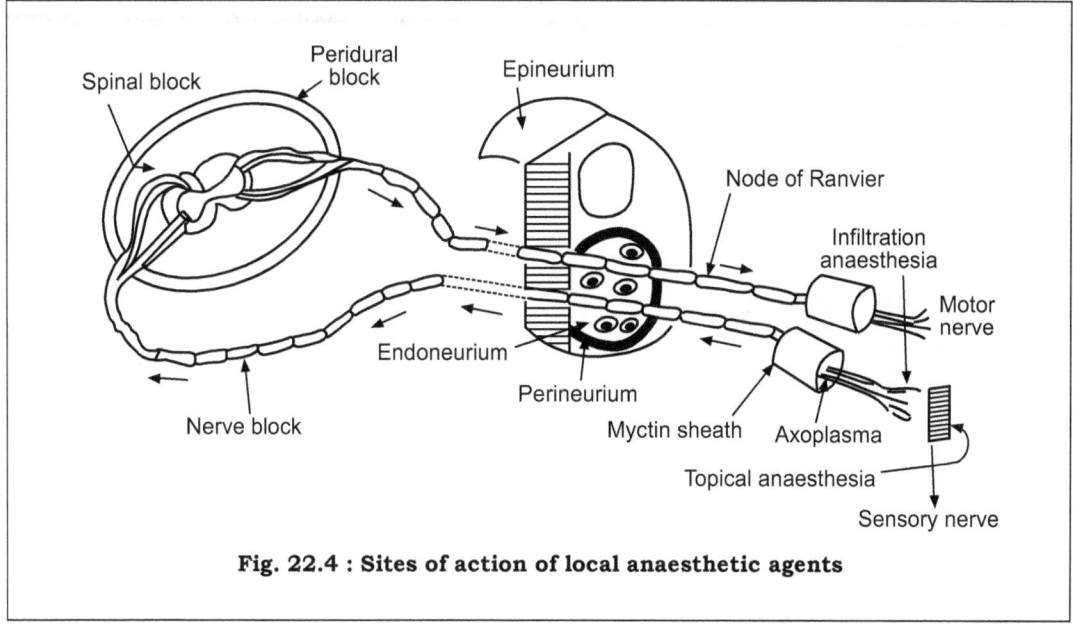

Fig. 22.4 : Sites of action of local anaesthetic agents

Motor fibers are last paralyzed by anaesthetic agent and are usually first to recovery. If the specific gravity of the local anaesthetic solution is equal to that of cerebrospinal fluid (isobaric) the solution will not move and will fix at the site of injection. Hence, for proper distribution of the agent, the solution should be either heavier or lighter than the cerebrospinal fluid. The hyperbaric solutions of local anaesthetic agent are more frequently used than are the hypobaric solutions. The regulation of the distribution of the agent in subarachnoid space can also be done by placing the patient either in the head-up or head-down position.

Spinal anaesthesia solutions are usually injected between the 3rd and 4th lumbar vertebrae. It slowly diffuses into the cerebrospinal fluid. Due to the differences in the sensitivity of individual nerves, zones of differential anaesthesia develop. Procaine, dibucaine, lidocaine, tetracaine and bupivacaine are the commonly used drugs.

Due to the blockade of sympathetic nerves, hypotension arises due to arteriolar dilation. Cardiac output is also reduced. This can be treated with ephedrine or mephentermine.

7. Epidural anaesthesia : An anaesthetic solution is injected into the epidural space below the second lumbar segment. It is a more favoured form of regional anaesthesia. No zone of differential sympathetic blockade is seen. Selective somatic sensory anaesthesia without muscle relaxation can be achieved by using intermediate concentrations. Cardiovascular complaints are less associated with epidural form. Commonly used agents include chloroprocaine, lidocaine and bupivacaine.

8. Peridural anaesthesia (extradural block) : A local anaesthetic solution is injected in the space immediately external to dura matter. As such, the solution does not enter the spinal canal, thus minimizing the risk of nerve damage. This type of anaesthesia is commonly employed in obstetrics, during thoracic and abdominal surgery and to reduce the intensity of post-operative pain.

22.8 CLASSIFICATION OF LOCAL ANAESTHETIC AGENTS

(A) On the chemical basis, local anaesthetic agents are classified as :

(i) Aminoalkyl esters of p-amino benzoic acids,

(ii) Alkyl esters of amino benzoic acids;

(iii) Esters of benzoic acid;

(iv) Aminoacylamides;

(v) Aminoalkylamides;

(vi) Urethanes;

(vii) Miscellaneous agents.

(B) Similarly Takman has proposed another classification of local anaesthetic agents, based on their site of action. Accordingly local anaesthetic agents are classified as :

(i) Those acting at the internal surface (gate) of the sodium channel.

(ii) Those acting by an independent physiochemical parameters, and

(iii) Those acting by a combination of a receptor (gate) and receptor independent mechanism.

(C) Another type of classification is based upon the duration of action of the local anaesthetic agents.

(i) Short acting agents (20-40 minutes) : e.g. procaine.

(ii) Intermediate acting agents (50-120 minutes): e.g. lidocaine, prilocaine.

(iii) Long acting agents (400-450 minutes): e.g. bupivacaine, etidocaine.

Epinephrine addition to the local anaesthetic solution prolongs the duration of action of the anaesthetic agent.

22.9 INDIVIDUAL LOCAL ANAESTHETIC AGENTS

1. Cocaine : Introduced in 1884, for clinical use in ocular surgery by Koller, cocaine is the prototype of local anaesthetic agent. This naturally occurring drug then provided the stimulus for the development of all currently employed local anaesthetics. This alkaloid is present in the leaves of several species of Erythroxylon in the concentration range of 0.4 - 1.8%. Chemically it is benzoylmethylecgonine, an ester of benzoic acid and ecogonine. Based upon these chemical features, molecular modification studies began in 1892, that resulted into synthesis of procaine in 1905.

Pharmacology :

CNS : Cocaine causes CNS excitation characterised by euphoria, restlessness, increased respiration and vomiting. It is immediately followed by a phase of CNS depression.

CVS : Effects on the heart are the manifestation of sympathomimetic effects of cocaine. There is an initial rise in blood pressure due to the tachycardia and vasoconstriction.

Cocaine also causes mydriasis and a rise in body temperature (pyrogenic).

It is mainly used in lower concentration in ocular surgery and in higher concentration to cause anaesthesia of nasal and pharyngeal mucosa. It is well absorbed from all sites. It is extensively hydrolysed by plasma esterases. Very minor amounts are excreted unchanged in the urine.

Cocaine is often abused for its effects on the CNS. Its chronic use leads to development of dependence.

2. Procaine : It is synthesized in 1905 by Einborn. Due to the poor penetration from mucous surfaces, it is not effective topically. It is readily absorbed if given parenterally. Hence, it is used for infiltration, nerve block and spinal anaesthesia. In body, like other ester-type drugs, procaine is rapidly hydrolysed by plasma esterases to produce para amino benzoic acid. Hence, sulphonamides should not be used simultaneously with ester-type local anaesthetics.

It leads to vasodilation but is devoid of CNS stimulant effect. Vasoconstrictors like epinephrine prolongs the duration of action of procaine. When combined with procaine, it prolongs the duration of action of other drugs, e.g., procaine penicillin G.

Chloroprocaine, a halogenated derivative of procaine, has a greater potency and less toxicity but has shorter duration of action due to rapid metabolism. It is a drug of choice in obstetrics.

3. Tetracaine : If given intraveneously, it is more active and more toxic than cocaine and procaine. It is mainly used for topical and spinal anaesthesia.

4. Lidocaine (1948) : It is an aminoethylamide. It is most widely used in topical, infiltration, regional nerve block and spinal anaesthesia to cause prompt, intense and long-lasting action. It is also a favourite dental anaesthetic agent. It is well absorbed from all sites and metabolises mainly through dealkylation to monoethylglycine and xylidide.

Adverse reactions are few and include sleepiness and dizziness.

5. Bupivacaine : It is a longer acting amide type local anaesthetic. It is commonly used in epidural and spinal anaesthesia.

6. Etidocaine : It is a longer acting derivative of lidocaine. It is mainly used for epidural, infiltration and regional block anaesthesia.

7. Mepivacaine : It is another derivative of lidocaine having more prolonged action and more rapid onset than lidocaine. Though ineffective topically, it is used for all other types of anaesthesia.

8. Prilocaine : It is an amide type agent having longer onset and duration of action. It is less toxic than lidocaine when used to produce infiltration, regional or spinal anaesthesia. During chronic adminstration, it may cause methemoglobinemia.

9. Dibucaine (cinchocaine) : Chemically it is a quinoline derivative having a potent and long-lasting action. Toxicity is considerable. Sometimes it is used as topical anaesthetic.

10. Benoxinate and proparacaine are the procaine type benzoate esters and share similar pharmacological properties. Unlike some topical anaesthetics, proparacaine is virtually devoid of irritation effect. Both these drugs are mainly restricted to ophthalmological use.

11. Hexylcaine, cyclomethylcaine and dyclonine are the examples of local anaesthetics which are commonly used to anaesthetize mucous membranes and the skin.

12. Benzocaine and butyl aminobenzoate have poor water solubility. They are applied to wound in the form of dusting powder to produce a sustained anaesthetic action. Benzocaine is also supplied in the form of ointments or lozenges due to its non-irritant property.

SEDATIVE – HYPNOTIC AGENTS

23.1 INTRODUCTION

Certain conditions like coma, anaesthesia resemble physically with the natural sleep, except the difference that the person does not lose the ability to be easily aroused, from natural sleep. Lack of sleep can readily develop a variety of serious neurotic and psychotic disorders. Ideally, a sedative-hypnotic drug should induce sleep that is similar in sleep pattern to the natural sleep.

A sedative drug decreases activity and excitement of the patient and calms the anxiety by producing mild depression of the CNS without causing drowsiness or sleep while a hypnotic drug produces drowsiness, compelling the patient to sleep by depressing the CNS, particularly the reticular activity, which characterizes wakefulness. Thus pharmacologically, sedatives, hypnotics and general anaesthetic agents can be regarded as the agents causing only increasing depths of the CNS depression.

It is proposed that (on similar grounds of endogenous opioids), a natural sleep is induced by some endogenous hypnogenic factors which are produced during a state of wakefulness. When these factors are accumulated to certain concentrations, they induce a slow wave of sleep. These factors are found to depress the activity of higher centers present in the cortex region. From cerebrospinal fluid of brains of goats and sheep, 'Factor S' has been isolated and characterised. It appears to be a peptide of low molecular weight. Another factor was isolated from cerebral venous blood by Monnier et al, which was termed as 'sleep factor delta'. It is non-peptide and produces more rapid induction of sleep than 'Factor S'.

Like hypnogenic factors, the presence of alarming factors has also been proposed. They are found to be polypeptides of considerably higher molecular weight.

Various sedative-hypnotic agents are employed as :

1. Anti-anxiety agents in the emotional strain and chronic tension state.
2. Anticonvulsant agents.
3. Muscle relaxants.
4. Basal anaesthetics.
5. Potentiation of analgesic drug effect.
6. Adjuvants to anaesthesia.
7. In hypertension.

The prolonged administration of these agents is not recommended because it may result into :

(a) Alteration of the pattern of naturally occurring sleep.
(b) Increasing tolerance and physical dependence to the drugs.
(c) Hangover effect, and

(d) Since death can be caused by respiratory collapse, if used in higher concentration, sedative-hypnotics are frequently used agents in attempting suicides.

23.2 CLASSIFICATION

Sedative-hypnotic drugs lack structural specificity. Since they are not characterised by common structural features, these agents appear to be non-specific in their action. Arbitrarily, the sedative-hypnotic agents may be classified as :

(i) Barbiturates,
(ii) Benzodiazepines,
(iii) Acyclic hypnotics containing nitrogen,
(iv) Cyclic nitrogen containing hypnotics,
(v) Alcohols and aldehydes,
(vi) Acetylene derivatives,
(vii) Miscellaneous agents

23.3 BARBITURATES

Barbiturates are often termed as prototypes of sedative-hypnotic category of drugs. In United Kingdom, nomenclature pattern of barbiturates adopt the ending -one while in United States, ending -al is preferred. The first agent from this class, i.e. barbital (5, 5-diethyl barbituric acid) was introduced in 1903 by Fischer and Von Mebring, followed by the introduction of phenobarbital in 1912. Since both these drugs turned out to be powerful hypnotic agents, over 2500 barbiturates were synthesized and evaluated, of which very few were proved of clinical utility. The parent compound in this series is Barbituric acid or 2, 4, 6-trioxohexa-hydropyrimidine which is devoid of central depressant activity. Chemically it is malonylurea.

Barbituric acid

The presence of alkyl or aryl groups at C-5 imparts central depressant activity to barbituric acid. Clinically used barbiturates are listed in Table 23.1 and they vary mainly in their potency, onset and duration of their action. Generally, an increase in the lipophilicity of the compound results in more rapid onset of action accompanied with an increase in the potency. But since metabolic degradation is also enhanced, highly lipophilic barbiturates exhibit shorter duration of action. For example, ultra-short acting barbiturates (thiopental sodium) are highly lipophilic and potent-CNS depressants having short duration of action. These thio-barbiturates are more lipid soluble than corresponding oxy-barbiturates. These properties disqualify them to be used as sedative-hypnotics. Instead they are preferentially used as basal anaesthetics. On the contrary, introduction of polar groups like hydroxyl, ketone, amino or carboxyl, into C_5 - alkyl side-chain makes the compound more hydrophilic in nature. Due to the polar nature, hydrophilic barbiturate do not dissolve well in microsomal membranes of liver and are excreted without significant metabolism. Branched, cyclic or unsaturated side chains at C_5-position generally reduce the duration of action due to an increased ease of metabolic conversion to a more polar, inactive metabolite. It is proposed that lipophilic agents get rapidly redistributed in the body compartments, resulting into quicker termination of their biological responses. The clinical utility of all barbiturates is partly paralysed by their addiction liability and withdrawal syndrome.

Barbiturates exhibit lactam-lactim tautomerism at C_2-position. Sodium salts of various barbiturates are preferred. Since barbiturate solution is strongly basic, upon parenteral administration, it may cause tissue necrosis. Hence care is needed to be taken while administering barbiturates by parenteral route.

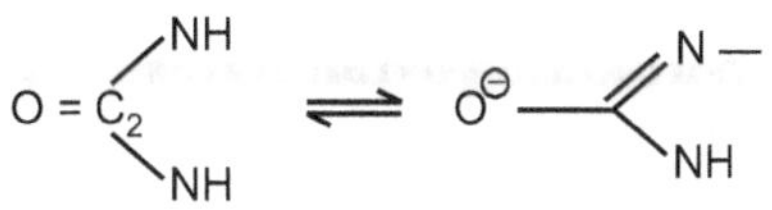

Tautomerism

Depending upon the duration of action, barbiturates are divided into four classes like :

(i) Long acting barbiturates (six hours or more)
(ii) Intermediate acting (3-6 hours)
(iii) Short-acting (less than 3 hours), and
(iv) Ultra-short acting (intravenous barbiturates)

Table 23.1 : Barbiturate classification

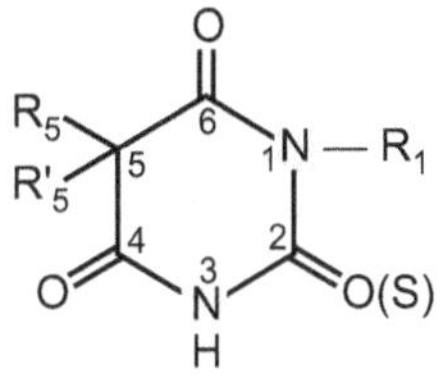

Name	R_1	R_5	R_5'	Sedative dose (mg)	hypnotic dose (mg)
I. Long-acting barbiturates :					
Barbital	H	C_2H_5	C_2H_5		300
Phenobarbital	H	C_2H_5	C_6H_5	15-30	100
Mephobarbital	CH_3	C_2H_5	C_6H_5	30-100	100
II. Intermediate acting barbiturates :					
Amobarbital	H	C_2H_5	$-CH_2CH_2CH(CH_3)_2$	20-40	100
Aprobarbital	H	allyl	isopropyl	30-40	100
Butabarbital	H	C_2H_5	$-CH-CH_2-CH_3$ | CH_3	15-30	100
Probarbital	H	C_2H_5	$-CH(-CH_3)_2$	50	150-400

Contd...

III. Short-acting barbiturates :

Name					
Cyclobarbital	H	C_2H_5	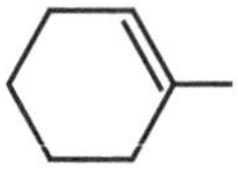 cyclohexenyl		100-300
Heptabarbital	H	C_2H_5	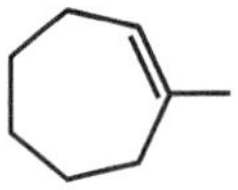 cycloheptenyl	100	200-400
Butalbital	H	allyl	isobutyl	50	150-300
Pentobarbital	H	C_2H_5	$-CH(CH_3)-CH_2CH_2CH_3$	30	100
Talbutal	H	allyl	sec-butyl	50	150-300
Secobarbital	H	allyl	$-CH(CH_3)-CH_3-CH_2-CH_3$	30	100

IV. Ultra-short acting barbiturates :

Name					
Hexobarbital	CH_3	CH_3	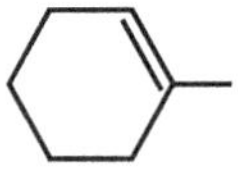 cyclohexenyl		400-500
Thiopentone	H	C_2H_5	$-CH(CH_3)\ CH_2\ CH_2\ CH_3$	C_2 – oxygen is replaced by sulphur	

Pharmacology of Barbiturates :

(a) CNS effects : These agents cause a nonspecific depression of the CNS. Reticular activating system and rhinencephalon are more sensitive to their action. The reversible depression of CNS is accompanied by little effect on cardiac, skeletal or smooth muscles in therapeutic doses. A dose dependent depression ranging from mild sedation to general anaesthesia is reported. These agents do not possess analgesic action. On the contrary they are found to be hyperalgesic in small doses. They may decrease REM sleep episodes which accounts for hangover experienced by the patient in terms of depression followed by nausea, dizziness and disorientation. Due to their CNS depressant activity, they may be used as :

(i) **Sedative-hypnotics :** e.g. amobarbital, butabarbital, pentobarbital, secobarbital etc.

(ii) **Anticonvulsants :** e.g. Phenobarbital, and

(iii) **Basal anaesthetics :** Pentobarbital.

(b) Cardiovascular effects : In larger doses, depression of myocardial muscles and decreased myocardial contractility and stroke volume are reported. In anaesthetic doses, they inhibit ganglionic transmission resulting into hypotension.

(c) Gastrointestinal tract : A decrease in tone and amplitude of muscle contraction is caused by the administration of oxybarbiturates.

(d) Respiratory system : If administered intravenously, these agents may cause laryngospasm.

(e) Liver : Barbiturates are found to induce hepatic microsomal enzyme system. They enhance the rate of metabolism of co-administered drugs alongwith their own metabolism. This partly explains the origin of tolerance development. Metabolism of both, exogenous drugs and endogenous substances is accelerated.

(f) Miscellaneous effects : Barbiturates decrease the urine flow and also cause a decrease in the tone and amplitude of uterine muscle contraction.

Metabolism of Barbiturates :

Barbiturates are well absorbed in the form of their sodium salts. Once absorbed, binding to plasma-proteins occurs to varying degrees. Lipophilicity is a governing parameter in deciding the extent of plasma-protein binding and metabolism of barbiturates. Barbiturates can easily cross placental barrier.

A few barbiturates (which already possess enough polar groups) having low-lipid solubility are largely excreted unchanged in urine. While barbiturates having high lipophilicity are metabolised. The metabolites may be conjugated with glucuronic acid or may be exerted as such.

Oxybarbiturates are metabolised only in liver. While for thiobarbiturates, besides liver, other organs like kidney, brain also stand as sites for metabolism. The metabolic pattern of barbiturates include :

(i) Oxidation of radicals on C_5 to yield hydroxy, keto or carboxyl derivatives.

(ii) Opening of the barbituratering by hydrolytic cleavage.

(iii) N-dealkylation and N-hydroxylation.

(iv) Desulfuration of 2-thiobarbiturates to oxybarbiturates is a common metabolic process.

Mechanism of Action :

1. Barbiturates may act on the macromolecular complex, composed of GABA-ergic receptor, chloride ionophore and benzodiazepine receptor sites.

2. The depressant effect is exerted mainly at polysynapses due to an increase in chloride ion conductance. The post-synaptic neurons, instead of being depolarized, are hyperpolarized. The inside becomes more negatively charged with respect to the outside. The nerve membrane is said to be stabilized. This results into depression of polysynaptic respons.

3. At higher concentrations, barbiturates decrease Ca^{++} dependent release of neurotransmitter.

4. GABA-ergic pathways are employed by barbiturate to induce the depression. Participation of glycinergic pathways is not witnessed.

Adverse Effects of Barbiturates :

Barbiturates, is one of the most widely used as well as abused series of drugs. All barbiturates share, to a greater or lesser degree, a similar set of disadvantages.

Short-acting barbiturates have lower incidences of adverse reactions than long-acting barbiturates and include, nausea, vomiting, diarrhoea, drowsiness, irritability, temper, restlessness, allergic reactions etc.

In some sensitive patients, due to mild barbiturate intoxication, a state of paradoxic excitement arises which is characterised by restlessness and delirium. This state can be compared with the state of delirium due to alcohol.

Hepatic microsomal enzyme system, upon induction may accelerate the production of very toxic substance which interferes in the heme metabolism. The condition is known as intermittent polyporphyria. Hence, barbiturates are contraindicated in patients who suffer from intermittent polyporphyria.

Chronic administration will lead to the development of addiction and tolerance. Tolerance to barbiturates confers tolerance to all general CNS-depressants.

Barbiturate Poisoning :

With a desire to attempt suicide, a person may consume toxic overdose of a barbiturate. Usually barbiturates with high lipophilicity are more toxic due to their rapid onset of action and increased potency. Symptoms include coma with depressed cardiovascular and respiratory functions. Pupils are first constricted but later dilated as hypoxia deepens. Patient develops a shock. The pulse becomes weak and rapid. Temperature drops alongwith kidney failure may occur.

Treatment may be based upon general supportive measures including ventilation, lavage or emesis. Alkalinization of urine by the administration of sodium bicarbonate, enhances barbiturate excretion. In renal failure, hemodialysis or hemoperfusion is preferred. In less severe cases to speed up the recovery, barbiturate antagonists like bemegride or amipbenazole, may also be tried.

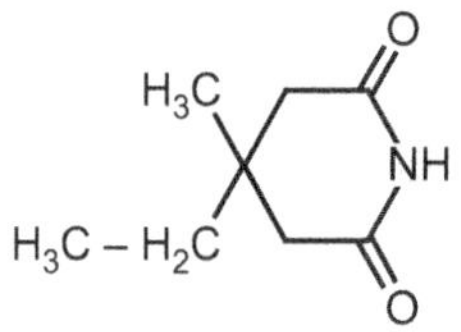

Bemegride

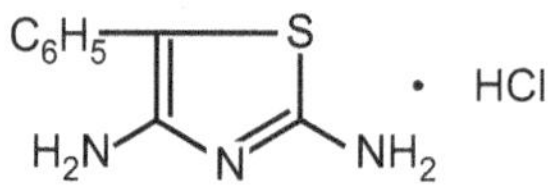

Amiphenazole

Therapeutic Uses of Barbiturates :

Depending upon their potency and duration of action, barbiturates may be clinically employed as :

1. Non-analgesic sedative-hypnotics.
2. Anticonvulsant agents.
3. Basal anaesthetic agents.
4. In pre-anaesthetic medication,
5. In psychiatric treatment, as diagnostic and therapeutic aid, and
6. In narcoanalysis.

23.4 BENZODIAZEPINES

An extensive research had been carried out on the benzodiazepine (i.e., benzene ring fused with a seven membered diazepine ring) series after the discovery, in 1960, that chlordiazepoxide displayed psychotropic activity, in experimental animals. Over 2000 compounds belonging to this series have been synthesized and pharmacological screening of these compounds has been carried out in the search of a better tranquilizer, muscle relaxant, anticonvulsant or a sedative-hypnotic drug.

All benzodiazepines exhibit hypnotic action to more or less extent with varying degree of metabolism in liver. Hence, only those benzodiazepines which are quickly metabolised and excreted, can be used as hypnotics in clinical practices. While long acting agents can be used as antianxiety agents.

Benzodiazepines do not induce hepatic microsomal enzyme systems. All possess low toxicity profiles and less abused potential. Due to these qualities, they are more favoured sedative-hypnotic agents than barbiturates.

On the basis of duration of action, they can be classified as :

1. Long-acting benzodiazepines : e.g. diazepam, flurazepam.
2. Intermediate-acting : e.g. Temazepam.
3. Short-acting : e.g. brotizolam.
4. Ultra-short acting : e.g. Triazolam, midazolam.

These drugs are being evaluated for their potential to act as basal anaesthetics.

In general, flurazepam, temazepam and triazolam have good margin of safety when they are employed as sedative-hypnotic agents. Flurazepam is basically a prodrug and its actions are due to its active metabolite, desalkylflurazepam. It is safest of all sedative-hypnotics available. Clorazepate has long duration action which can be partly explained by retention in plasm of nordiazepam, its active metabolite. Midazolam, a newer ultra-short acting benzodiazepine is recently introduced.

Midazolam

Except intravenously administered diazepam, all benzodiazepines neither possess analgesic effect nor exhibit hyperalgesia. Due to their fetal damage, they are contraindicated during pregnancy.

Pharmacology of Benzodiazepines :

1. The CNS depressant effect of benzodiazepines prompted their use as sedative-hypnotics, antianxiety, muscle-relaxant and anticonvulsant agents.

2. They do not induce anaesthesia when used alone. For this, they have to be combined with other CNS-depressants.

3. Most benzodiazepines decrease sleep latency.

4. Respiratory and cardiovascular functions are slightly depressed by benzodiazepines. In toxic doses, they may decease the blood pressure and increase the heart rate.

5. Gastrointestinal effects include a decrease in nocturnal gastric secretion in humans by diazepam.

6. Benzodiazepines do not exert peripheral effects in therapeutic doses. In toxic doses, coronary vasodilatation and neuromuscular blockade is reported. With some benzodiazepines, muscle hypotonia occurs.

Table 23.2 : Clinically used Benzodiazepines

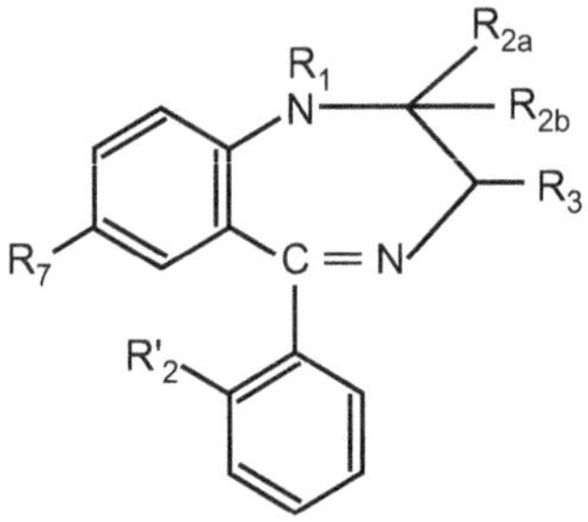

5-aryl-1, 4-benzodiazepine

Name	R₁	R₂	R₃	R₇	R'₂
Chlordesmethyl diazepam	H	= O	H	Cl	Cl
Fosazepam	$-(CH_2)-P(\uparrow O)-(CH_3)_2$	= O	H	Cl	H
Nitrazepam	H	=O	H	NO₂	H
Clonazepam	H	=O	H	Cl	NO₂
Nordiazepam	H	=O	H	Cl	H
Nimetazepam	CH₃	=O	H	NO₂	H
Demoxepam	H	=O	H	H	Cl
Halazepam	– CH₂CF₃	=O	H	H	Cl
Prazepam	– CH₂–◁	=O	H	H	Cl
Flunitrazepam	CH₃	=O	H	NO₂	F
Flurazepam	– (CH₂)₂N(C₂H₅)₂	=O	H	Cl	F
Quazepam	– CH₂CF₃	= S	H	Cl	F
Lorazepam	H	=O	OH	Cl	Cl
Temazepam	CH₃	=O	OH	Cl	H
Potassium chlorazepate	H	2a OH 2b OK	COOK	Cl	H

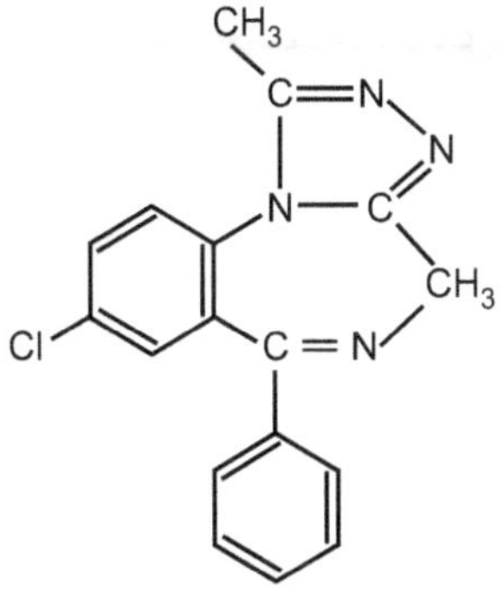

Alprazolam

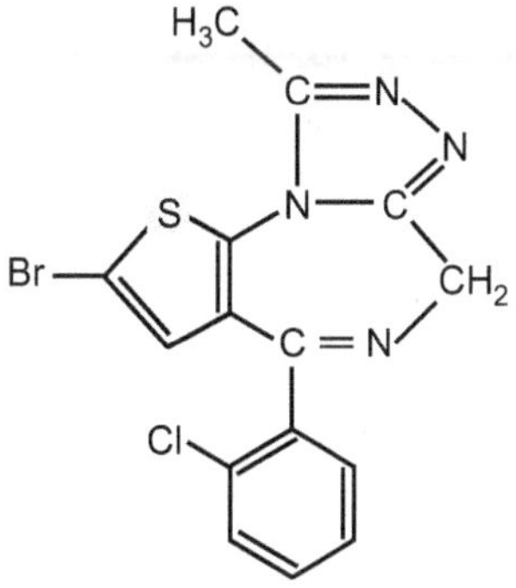

Brotizolam

Mechanism of Action of Benzodiazepines :

1. In CNS, benzodiazepines do not equally affect the activity of all levels and hence cannot be classified as general depressant of the CNS.

2. The midbrain reticular activating system, which is responsible for the maintenance of awakefulness, is depressed by benzodiazepines.

3. The term 'anxiety', is defined in terms of symptoms which include fear, apprehension, sweating, dizziness and difficulty in breathing. The anti-anxiety activity of benzodiazepines may be attributed to the depressant action of these drugs on the mechanisms that evoke anxiety and aggression.

4. In convulsions, these drugs act by just preventing the spread of the seizures.

5. Most of the actions of benzodiazepines result due to the potentiation of GABA-induced neuronal inhibition. GABA-ergic inhibitory interneurons regulate the activity of large neurons in the CNS. The potentiation of GABA-ergic inhibitory action induced by benzodiazepine, on either presynaptic or (in rare cases) postsynaptic membranes in polysynaptic neuronal pathways in CNS, results in the interference in the transmission processes.

6. The macromolecular complex of GABA receptor consists of benzodiazepine receptor sites. These benzodiazepine receptor sites have been discovered in 1977 in mammalian brain tissue. The multidimensional activities exhibited by benzodiazepines suggest the presence of functionally distinct sub-types of benzodiazepine receptor.

Absorption, Fate and Excretion of Benzodiazepines :

Except clorazepate, all benzodiazepines are well absorbed from GIT. Flurazepam and prazepam enter the circulation in the form of their active metabolites. All benzodiazepines have a strong binding affinity for plasma-proteins. Once absorbed, they are readily redistributed in various body compartments. They can cross the placental barrier.

Liver is the principal site for benzodiazepine metabolism. The major steps followed during their metabolism, include :

1. N-desalkylation : Atleast five clinically used benzodiazepines, including diazepam undergo this biotransformation to yield, an active metabolite, nordiazepam.

2. C_3-hydroxylation : For example, nordiazepam may be converted to oxazepam. The C_3 hydroxylated metabolite may undergo glucuronidation or may be oxidized further.

3. Reduction of C_7-NO_2 group : Benzodiazepines which possess C_7–NO_2 group (e.g., nitrazepam) may be inactivated by reduction of NO_2 group to amines. Acetylation of this amino function is reported to occur prior to the excretion.

4. Ring hydroxylation : Hydroxylation in the aromatic ring portion of benzodiazepines occurs to a limited extent.

Adverse Reactions of Benzodiazepines :

Benzodiazepines are relatively safer drugs. The side-effects include, nausea, vomiting, diarrhoea, weakness, headache, blurred vision, euphoria, restlessness, paradoxic excitement, and tachycardia. Development of tolerance and withdrawal symptoms are also reported. Withdrawal symptoms include rebound insomnia, dysphoria, headache and irritation.

Therapeutic Uses of Benzodiazepines :

1. As anti-anxiety agents.
2. As sedative or potentiates the action of a hypnotic drug.
3. Muscle relaxant and anti-convulsant agent.
4. Psychostimulant agent.
5. Preanaesthetic medication.
6. During withdrawal of alcohol in chronic alcoholics.

Table 23.3 : Benzodiazepines Versus Barbiturates

Benzodiazepines	Barbiturates
1. Are not general neuronal depressant.	Are general neuronal depressant.
2. Act on reticular activating system, thus reduce alertness and wakefulness.	They act by depressing the cortical response.
3. Do not cause hyperalgesia.	Cause hyperalgesia.
4. Do not cause true anaesthesia.	Can cause true anaesthesia.
5. Sleep induced by benzodiazepines, resembles much with neutral sleep.	Likely to produce hangover and psychomotor impairment.
6. Do not induce hepatic microsomal enzyme system.	Induce hepatic microsomal enzyme system.
7. In overdoses, less chances to cause unconsciousness and espiratory depression and hence relatively more safety.	Overdoses may result into a death due to respiratory and CVS collapse.
8. They get slowly eliminated from the body.	They get eliminated more readily than benzodiazepines.
9. Long-term use is rarely indicated.	Long-term use is rarely indicated.

23.5 ACYCLIC HYPNOTICS CONTAINING NITROGEN

There are many drugs, though structurally not related with barbiturates, can produce sedation and hypnosis. The time of onset, duration of action and untoward effects may be the probable points of difference. This class does not offer any advantage over other hypnotic classes besides, therapeutic efficacy and relative safety of some agents.

(a) Urethanes : These are the esters of monohydric alcohols with carbamic acid. Ethinamate is a clinically used example of this class. It is employed for the prompt treatment of simple insomnia, due to its rapid onset and short duration of action. In liver, the cyclohexyl ring is hydroxylated and glucuronidation occurs at the same position. Ethinamate is a quite safe agent. Side effects include, nausea, vomiting and skin rash. Prolonged use may result into tolerance and physical dependence.

(b) Ureides : Acylation of urea yields ureides. Cyclic diureides like, barbiturates, are powerful hypnotics while monoureides are quick acting light hypnotis. Examples include, capuride, carbromal and bromvalurea.

Bromvalurea and carbromal are in clinical use from long time due to their short acting, mild hypnotic action. They are considered to be relatively safe drug. Since both of these agents can release bromide ion in vivo, their prolonged use may lead to acute bromide toxication and hence, is not recommended.

(c) Carbamates : Meprobamate, a bis carbamate ester, was introduced in 1955 as an antianxiety agent. Its toxicity profile lies inbetween that of barbiturates and benzodiazepines. In larger doses (800 mg) it is sometimes used as hypnotic. In usual doses, it exhibits analgesic, antianxiety and muscle relaxant properties. The latter effect is due to depression of polysynaptic reflexes in the spinal cord. It does not cause anaesthesia. It is less toxic but exhibits some degree of addiction.

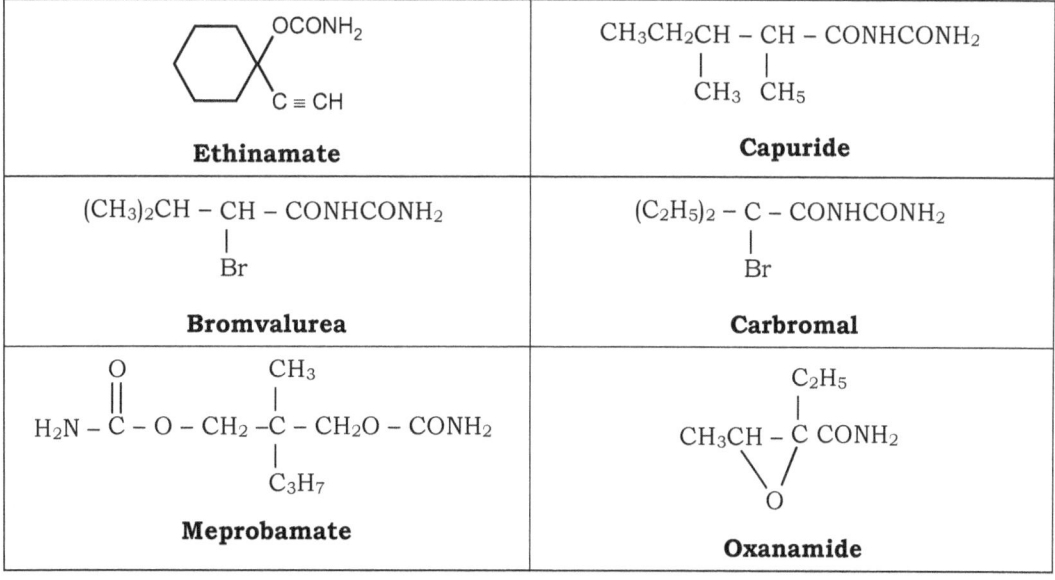

Table 23.4 : Clinically used Acyclic Hypnotics

Orally, it is well absorbed. About 90% of the administered dose undergoes metabolism in the liver, mainly to a side chain hydroxyl derivative which can further be glucuronidized. It may induce hepatic microsomal enzyme system. Side-effects include, drowsiness, hypotension, allergic reactions and ataxia. Addiction and tolerance development is also reported.

(d) Amides : Examples from this class include, oxanomide, valnoctamide, trimethobenz and diethyl allyl acetamide. All these agents are marketed as tranquillizers and muscle relaxants, having good sedative properties.

23.6 CYCLIC HYPNOTICS CONTAINING NITROGEN

After the success of barbiturates in sedative-hypnotic therapy, many heterocyclic ring structures bearing a close structural relationship with barbiturates were synthesized and screened for the CNS depressant activity. The clinically useful agents from this class are :

(a) Glutethimide : Structurally related to thalidomide and was introduced in 1954 as a hypnotic agent. It is more potent than any other non-barbiturate hypnotics, but does not offer any advantage over barbiturates. It has some anti-cholinergic activity.

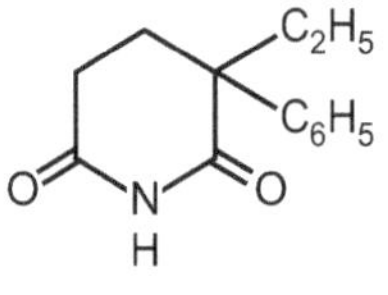

Glutethimide

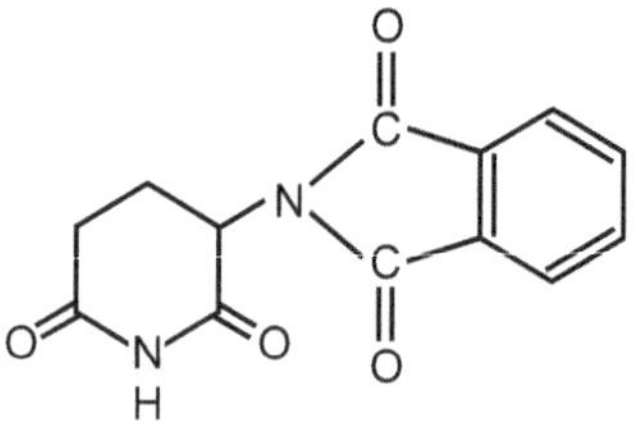

Thalidomide

About 95 - 97% of the administered dose of glutethimide undergoes metabolism in the liver and conjugated with glucuronic acid. The resulting glucuronide is excreted in urine as well as bile. It induces hepatic microsomal enzyme system.

Side-effects include, headache, blurring of vision, excitement, skin rashes and hangover. Prolonged administration leads to tolerance and dependence.

(b) Methyprylone : It does not exhibit analgesic, tranquillizing or muscle relaxant activities. Similar to barbiturates, it causes dependence. The pharmacokinetics and side-effects of methyprylone is similar to glutethimide. Ethypicone is one of the metabolite of methyprylone which still retains hypnotic activity.

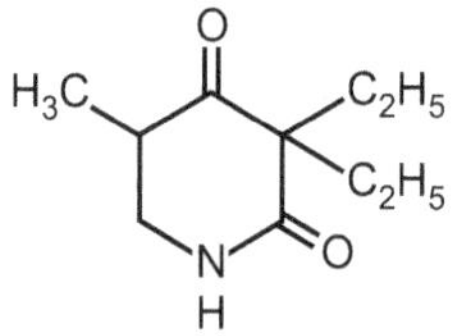

Methyprylone

(c) Methaqualone : Though similar to barbiturates in its hypnotic effects, methaqualone has analgesic, local anaesthetic, spasmolytic, and weak antihistaminic activities. It is also a potent antitussive agent. Orally, it is well absorbed. It is extensively metabolized in the liver mainly to 4'-hydroxy and N'-oxide metabolites. The fact that antihistaminic drug potentiates methaqualone's hypnotic action, encouraged the formulation of such combinations. Mandrax, for example, contains 250 mg methaqualone and 25 mg diphenhydramine.

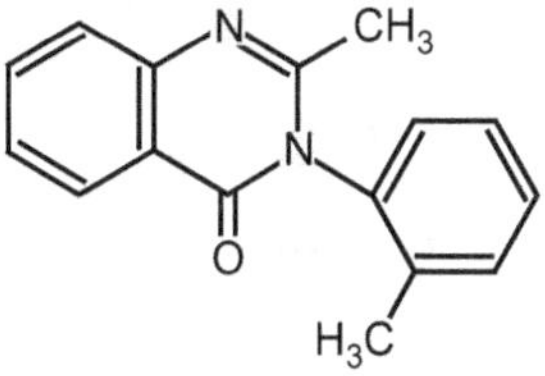

Methaqualone

In overdoses, methaqualone causes muscle spasms. Side-effects include, nausea, vomiting, diarrhoea, sweating, urticaria, hallucinations and convulsions.

Ethinazone and mecloqualone are other methaqualone analogues which exert a potent analgesic and antitussive activity in addition to hypnotic activity.

23.7 ALCOHOLS AND ALDEHYDES

The oldest sedative-hypnotic agents are alcohols, aldehydes, opioids and bromides. Since the branching of alkyl chain in alcohols, offers a greater resistance to metabolic inactivation, resulting in increased activity, hence all clinically useful alcohols are tertiary alcohols. Examples include, amylene hydrate, chlorobutanol, ethchlorvynol, methylpentynol, trichloroethanol and chloral hydrate.

(a) Despite a safe and reliable hypnotic agent (1.5 - 2.0 g), chloral hydrate possesses the following disadvantages :

1. Poor analgesic property.

2. Quite irritating to the mucous membrane and skin. Thus, may cause nausea, vomiting and diarrhoea.

3. In high doses, may cause marked respiratory depression.

4. Has an unpleasant taste and odour.

5. Causes physical dependence.

To overcome these problems, a number of derivatives, especially hemiacetals have been prepared, the important amongst them are :

$$Cl_3C - CH \begin{matrix} OH \\ OH \end{matrix}$$

Chloral hydrate

$$Cl_3C - CH(OH) - O - CH(CH_3) - CH_2 - C(CH_3)_2 - OH$$

Chloralodol

$$C(CH_2OCH(OH)CCl_3)_4$$

Petrichloral

$$Cl_3C - CH_2OH$$

Trichloroethanol

Dichloralphenazone is a complex of chloral hydrate and phenazone. All these compounds generate chloral hydrate in vivo and hence their pharmacological activities remain same.

In liver chloral hydrate is largely metabolized to trichloroethanol which may undergo further oxidation to trichloroacetic acid mainly in liver and kidney and excreted in the form of its glucuronide. (i.e., urochloralic acid) in urine.

Side-effects of chloral derivatives include, nausea, vomiting, flatulence, light headedness, allergic reactions and hangover. It is contraindicated in patients with hepatic or renal disfunctioning.

(b) Trichloroethanol : It is a principal metabolite of chloral hydrate retaining excellent hypnotic activity. Its properties are essentially same with that of chloral hydrate. Due to its irritative nature, it is used in the form of monosodium salt of its phosphate ester (Triclophos sodium, $CCl_3CH_2OPO_3$ H^-, Na^+) which in vivo, releases tri-chloroethanol.

(c) Ethchlorvynol : In addition to sedative-hypnotic properties, it has anticonvulsant and muscle relaxant properties. It has a rapid onset and short duration of action. It is extensively metabolised in liver. Side-effects include nausea, vomiting dizziness, and hypotension. It crosses placental barrier.

$$\begin{array}{c} CH = CHCl \\ | \\ C_2H_5 - C - C \equiv CH \\ | \\ OH \end{array}$$

(d) Paraldehyde : Chemically it is cyclic polyether. On exposure to light and oxygen, it undergoes decomposition to acetaldehyde. Introduced in 1882, it is one of the powerful and safest hypnotic drug having marked anticonvulsant properties. It has rapid onset of action and does not posess analgesic effects. Its unpleasant taste, pungent odour and mucous membrane irritating properties limited its widespread use and abused.

Orally it is well absorbed. Liver is the principal site of its metabolism where it is metabolised (about 70-80%) to acetaldehyde.

Paraldehyde → acetaldehyde → acetic acid → $CO_2 + O_2$.

Its use is recommended in psychiatric states characterised by excitement. Its use is contraindicated in the presence of pulmonary or hepatic disease.

23.8 ACETYLENE DERIVATIVES

Two analogues of ethinamate, hexapropymate and carfimate can be grouped under this class.

Hexapropymate

Carfimate

23.9 MISCELLANEOUS AGENTS

(a) Bromides : Though they were used as anticonvulsants and sedatives, due to their extremely low rate of excretion, they tend to accumulate in the body resulting into intoxication like, skin rash, hallucinations or CNS depression. Now they are no longer used clinically. Sodium bromide and potassium bromide are the examples of once popular sedative agents.

(b) Chlorpromazine : Its ability to antagonize the actions of dopamine in CNS, explains its hypnotic and antipsychotic actions.

(c) Some antihistamines and anticholinergic agents may exhibit CNS depressant action. Examples include doxylamine, diphenhydramine and pyrilamine.

(d) Sulfones : The agents from this class induce toxic effects at therapeutic doses and hence no longer used as sedative-hypnotic drugs.

(e) Plant extracts : A number of plant extracts are reported to possess sedative-hypnotic activity. Examples include, Radix valerianae, Rauwolfia serpentine, Avana sativa and Glandulae lupuli.

EPILEPSY AND ITS TREATMENT

24.1 INTRODUCTION

The term, epilepsy derived from the Greek word, 'epilambariein' which means 'to seize' or convulsion. A convulsion is a violent involuntary spasmodic contraction of the skeletal musculature.

Epilepsy is a collective designation for a group of chronic CNS disorders having in common the occurrence of brief and selflimited, sudden and transitory seizures of abnormal motor, sensory, autonomic or psychic origin resulting into a repeated neuronal discharge, causing an alteration in a state of consciousness.

All forms of epilepsy have their origin in the brain. Epilepsy results when many neurons in union, under a highly excited stage, deliver massive discharges abolishing a finely organized pattern of the integrative activity of the brain.

John Jackson proposed that these seizures are caused by occasional, sudden, excessive, rapid and local discharges of gray matter and once initiated by the abnormal focus, the seizures attack the neighbouring normal brain tissue resulting into generalized convulsions.

This abnormal focus may originate as the result of local biochemical changes, ischemia or the loss of vulnerable cell inhibitory system.

The normal inhibitory mechanisms generally restrict the spread of convulsive activity to the neighbouring normal cells. Hence, a seizure focus in man may remain normal over long period of time and may not cause signs and symptoms of epilepsy. However, certain physiological changes may trigger the focus and thus facilitate the spread of abnormal electrical activity to normal tissue.

Such factors include,

(i) Changes in blood glucose concentration

(ii) Blood gas tension

(iii) Plasma pH

(iv) Total osmotic pressure and electrolyte composition of extracellular fluids

(v) Fatigue

(vi) Emotional stress

(vii) Nutritional deficiency

Seizures, in fact, are nothing but electrical explosions of the brain. In an epilepsy, the hyperactivity is sustained due to re-circulation of excitatory impluse of low refractory periods. Once initiated, seizure pathway may not include the original seizure focus. They get terminated or controlled by

(a) either complete exhaustion of neurotransmitter, oxygen or high energy phosphate energy stores,

(b) or by gradual accumulation of carbon-di-oxide or adenosine.

An epileptic focus may encapsulate both normal and abnormal tissues. In abnormal tissues, local tissue organization may be disturbed due to cellular changes related with vascular supply and nature of local extra cellular spaces. In the seizure focus, neuronal hyperactivity is usually associated with the region of periphery of the focus.

In summary, epilepsy is a CNS malfunctioning which leads either to generalized hyperactivity (involving essentially all parts of the brain) or to hyperactivity of only a portion of the brain. This hyperactivity results due to either decreased concentration of inhibitory neurotransmitters (e.g., GABA, glycine) or an increase in the concentration of excitatory neurotransmitters (e.g., ACh, glutamic acid etc.). The involvement of Ca^{++} ions in epilepsy is suspected due to its role in transmitter release. For example, in hypocalcemia, the threshold for the release of neurotransmitter is lowered down. This increases the susceptibility of a patient to seizure attack. While in hypercalcemia, muscle weakness and lethargy are the symptoms due to an increased threshold for the release of neurotransmitter.

When an epileptic attack occurs due to unidentified cause, it is known as primary or idiopathic epilepsy. While certain known causes like, trauma, infection, meningitis, brain tumors, cerebrovascular disease or metabolic abnormalities are recognized in some epileptic attacks. These epilepsies are termed as secondary or symptomatic epilepsies.

Once initiated from the original seizure focus, the epileptic attack may become progressively intense and long-lasting. It gradually spreads up in the other neighbouring regions of the brain, covering the remote area from the point of stimulation. A hyperactive neurone naturally leads to increased after discharges in all neurones to which it is synaptically interconnected. If the process gets repeated for may times, adaptive changes take place into the neurones which participate in it, resulting in development of secondary seizure foci. Secondary foci either follow the instructions released by primary focus or may develop their independent capacity to initiate seizures by causing the synchronous firing at high frequency. The period for which an attack continues is known as 'ictal period'. Hence, the time gap between two successive seizure attacks is termed as inter-ictal period.

Epilepsy is a chronic condition which can be controlled by a long-term treatment. If a single-drug therapy is adopted, the long term use of that drug may result into the dose dependent side-effects. To avoid this, the therapy is usually initiated with two or more antiepileptic agents at reduced dose. In certain cases, however, a single drug is as effective as multiple drugs and is usually safer for the patient.

24.2 TYPES OF EPILEPSIES

In the experimental studies, convulsions can be produced either by an electric shock or by chemical. In electrically induced convulsions, there occurs a spontaneous, quick CNS excitation of highest magnitude while in chemically induced convulsions, this level of CNS stimulation can be attained steadily over a period of time as the drug is absorbed.

Electrically induced convulsions start with a tonic phase characterised by the powerful stimulation of all motor neurons in the brain and loss of consciousness. After some time, animal gradually relaxes. This is followed by comparatively weak and short-lived clonic phase. The neuronal storage sites are exhausted already by tonic spasm.

In it, flexor and extensor movements repeat alternatively and contraction of one set of muscles is accompanied by the relaxation of its antagonist muscles. At the end of clonic convulsions, consciousness reappears but the animal still seems to be depressed.

In chemically induced convulsions, tremors and hyperexcitability are seen first followed by clonic phase. As the chemical attains maximum plasma level, tonic phase is reached. The decline in plasma concentration results into reappereance of clonic convulsions. At the end of clonic phase, postictal depression is seen.

The CNS stimulants can be categorised as

(i) Mild general CNS stimulants : e.g., amphetamine, caffeine.

(ii) Analeptics : Powerful medullary stimulant but weak general CNS stimulants.

Convulsants : Powerful general CNS stimulants.

Strychnine, Picrotoxin, Leptazol and Nikethamide are some of the convulsant drugs.

Epilepsies of generalized hyperactivity originate in thalamus and midbrain and cover the cortex region of both cerebral hemispheres via reticular activating system. Examples include, grand mal, petit mal, infantile spasms and myoclonic seizures. While the partial or focal epilepsy may originate from a localized area of cerebral cortex or subcortex and has limited scope to spread. In cortex, epileptic foci are most often located in one or both temporal lobes.

[A] Generalized Epilepsy:

Once initiated, it spreads quickly into the entire or at least the greater part of the brain.

(i) Tonic-clonic seizures (grand mal) : It has a close resemblance with electrically induced convulsions where the mass stimulation of cortical neurons occurs. As the name indicates, initially there is a generalized tonic activity followed by a clonic phase. It results due to a potent cerebral excitation and is also known as major seizures. Its onset is pre-intimated to the patient by a warming sensation that is known as aura. Patient may become cyanotic. Heart rate and blood pressure increase and dilation of pupils also occur. These signs are characteristics of sympathetic nervous system stimulation. The total attack lasts for several minutes. After the attack, sleep prevails due to neuronal store-exhaustion.

(ii) Absence or minor seizures (petit mal) : It is reported to occur mainly in young children between the age of 6 to 14. Seizures frequently disappear spontaneously after adolescence. Seizures are usually of brief durations (in seconds) accompanied by a momentary loss of consciousness and originate due to synchronization of both, excitatory and inhibitory neurons within the brain stem and medial reticular activating system.

(iii) Myoclonic seizures : The attack is characterised by the jerky muscular movements of head, limbs or body as such. The duration of attack remains near about 1 second and it reappears at about 5 seconds intervals for a period of a minute. The etiology of attack is not clear and is supposed to be due to brain damage.

(iv) Infantile spasms : The attack, sometimes begins with a cry and is often associated with momentory unconsciousness. The structural or functional brain abnormalities or pyridoxine deficiency are some recognized causes responsible for infantile spasms.

[B] Partial or Focal Epilepsy :

In this type, the initial neuronal discharge originates from a specific, limited cortical area. In children, cortical dysplasias and low grade neoplasms are the most commonly identified causes. In adults the causes include various structural lesions (e.g. traumatic scars, neoplasms, vascular malformations, strokes, neuronal heterotopias.)

(i) Complex partial seizures (psychomotor or temporal lobe seizures) : It usually originates in the medial anterior temporal lobe or fronted lobe of the brain and is characterised by hallucinations, fear, hate or other emotional and behavioural abnormalities. Symptoms are extremely complex and varied and may sometimes be confused with psychotic disorder.

(ii) Motor epilepsy : Only one entire side of the body is affected. Consciousness is usually not lost. In severe cases, motor epilepsy is transformed into grand mal followed by paralysis of the hyperactive side of the body. Motor epilepsy is mainly withnessed in the childhood and is due to more limited cortical abnormalities.

(iii) Sensory epilepsy : Similar to motor epilepsy except the fact that it arises in the sensory cortex. Simultaneous attack of both, motor and sensory epilepsy in the patients, is also reported.

(iv) Akinetic seizures : Superficially no convulsions are seen. Patient may suddenly fall down on the ground without loss of consciousness.

Status epilepticus (acute repetitive seizures) : It is the condition in which one attack follows another without patients regaining consciousness. The attack may be of grand mal, petit mal or partial seizures. If it remains untreated, it may be fatal. Status epilepticus originates due to failure of the patient to follow therapeutic regimen prescribed for him. Diazepam, clonazepam, thiopentone or lignocaine may be administered intravenously to control this condition. If the treatment fails, general anaesthesia may be required. Precautions are to be taken if the patient suffers from cardiac arrhythmias, hypoglycemia, dehydration or electrolyte abnormalities. Multiple drug therapy is often required, since two or more seizure types may occur in the same patient.

It appears then, in the treatment of any type of epilepsy, abrupt discontinuation of therapy may develop status epilepticus. Hence dosage should always be reduced gradually when a drug is being discontinued. Withdrawal should be done gradually over a period of months.

24.3 MECHANISMS OF EPILEPTOGENESIS

If one neurone in the circuit is stimulated, it will, itself be able to pass a wave of excitation to the neurones which are synaptically interconnected to it. It results into development of paroxysmal depolarizing shift (PDS) which displays the characteristics of gaint excitatory postsynaptic potential. Thus, burst in the neuronal network begins.

Another mechanism relates epileptogenesis with the reduction in inhibitory components of neuronal circuits. Dopamine, 5-hydroxytryptamine, glycine and gamma amino butyric acid are the prominent inhibitory neurotransmitters present in brain. The spread of the hyperactivity from the seizure focus to its neighbouring region is prevented mainly by the local inhibitory loops. Certain factors like, ischemia, folic acid deficiency, endocrine changes, emotional stress etc. may paralyze these inhibitory mechanisms and thus facilitate the spread of the seizure. Excess of folate in the brain may cause an initiation of epileptic attack.

In addition to abnormalities in ionic channel conductance, epileptic discharges are also caused due to an impaired synaptic transmission.

24.4 MECHANISM OF ACTION OF ANTICONVULSANT DRUGS

(1) Many carbonic anhydrase inhibitors (e.g., acetazolamide) are found to possess anticonvulsant properties. Carbonic anhydrase plays a role in promoting the elimination of excess carbon-di-oxide from the brain and blood circulation. Since excess CO_2 decreases nerve conduction, these drugs are thought to exert their anticonvulsant action by decreasing the cerebral respiration.

(2) It has been postulated that excessive discharge of neurotransmitter is the cause of generation of seizures. Various anticonvulsant drugs (e.g., bromides, primidone, trimethadione) increase the levels of serotonin in brain which causes a nonspecific depression of the CNS function while phenytoin causes a decrease in the brain concentration of excitatory neurotransmitter (e.g., glutamic acid) and thus controls the spread of the seizure.

(3) Excess of folic acid cofactor in the brain may initiate the spread of epileptic attack. Inhibition of these cofactors may lead to an accumulation of dopamine (an inhibitory neurotransmitter) in the brain. Certain drugs like phenytoin and phenobarbital act by causing folic acid deficiency.

(4) The anticonvulsant activity of barbiturates is attributed to their ability to exert conformational rearrangement of oxidative enzymes essential for brain respiration.

(5) Gamma amino butyric acid level in brain is also important to prevent the spread of the seizures. Many anticonvulsant drugs are reported to operate by increasing brain levels of GABA. Pyridoxine deficiency hinders the production of GABA. Pyridoxine participates in tryptophan metabolism which is found to be disturbed in pyridoxine deficiency. This is more evidenced in hypsarrhythmia (infantile seizures).

24.5 CLASSIFICATION OF ANTI-CONVULSANT DRUGS

Since epilepsy primarily results through excessive stimulation of the brain neurons, anticonvulsant drug is principally, a CNS depressant drug. In the 1850s, bromide were introduced as effective anticonvulsant drug but bromides induce serious toxic problems. Bromides of sodium, potassium, ammonium, lithium, calcium and strontium were tried. Bromides mainly depress the cerebral cortex region. Bromides alongwith phenobarbital were the drugs of choice until 1938. Other structural relatives of barbiturates (malonylureas), were developed before 1965. These include hydantoins (glycolylurea), oxazolidinediones and succinimides. While diversified structural skeletons (e.g., benzodiazepines, iminostilbenes and valproic acid) were developed after 1965. Chlorazepate was approved for antiepileptic therapy in 1981. Current research trends are oriented to design antiepileptic agents on GABA skeleton e.g., progamide.

On the structural basis, the currently available anticonvulsant drugs are classified into following classes:

(i) Barbiturates
(ii) Hydantoins
(iii) Oxazolidinediones
(iv) Succinimides
(v) Phenacemide
(vi) Benzodiazepines
(vii) Sodium valproate

Table 24.1

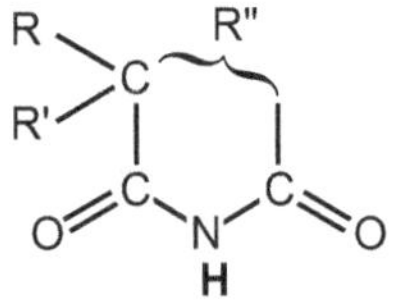

Ureide structure

Where

R"	Class	R'	Class
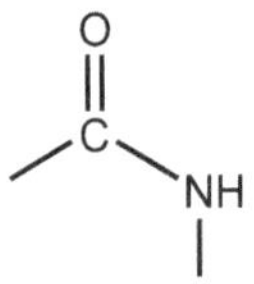 −C(=O)−NH−	Barbiturates	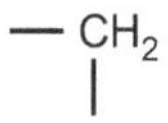 −CH₂−	Succinimide
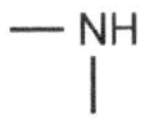 −NH−	Hydantoins	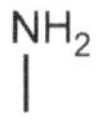 −NH₂	Phenacemide
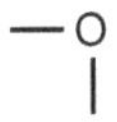 −O−	Oxazolidinediones	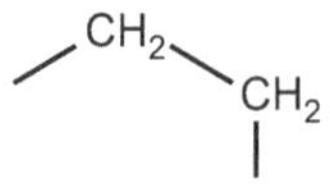 −CH₂−CH₂−	Glutarimides

A basic chemical structure common to most of the clinically used antiepileptic drugs is as shown in Table 24.1.

Though plasma concentration of anticonvulsant drug is usually related to its anticonvulsant activity, it may sometimes lead to wrong interpretation, since many antiepileptic drugs are highly bound to plasma proteins and the concentration of free drug is only a small fraction of the total plasma concentration of a drug. Usually, in long term treatment, anticonvulsant drugs may cause hematopoietic depression (folate deficiency) and hepatic and renal damage.

Table 24.2 : Drugs used clinically in the control of epilepsy

Types of epilepsy	Drug of choice
1. Grand mal	Phenobarbital
	Phenytoin
	Carbamazepin
2. Petit mal	Nitrazepam
	Clonazepam
	Sodium valproate
3. Myoclonic seizures	Phenobarbital
	Nitrazepam
	Clonazepam
	Sodium valporate
4. Infantile seizures	Nitrazepam
	Clonazepam
	Vitamin B_6
5. Psychomotor seizures	Phenytoin
	Carbamazepine
	Methsuximide

24.6 ANTICONVULSANT BARBITURATES

The clinically effective anticonvulsant barbiturates are :

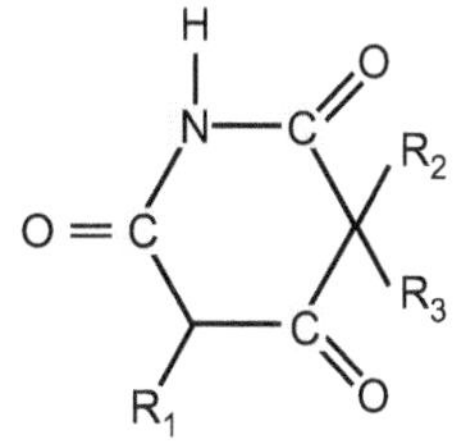

(i) Phenobarbarbital :
   $R_1 = H$, $R_2 = C_2H_5$, $R_3 = C_6H_5$

(ii) Mephobarbital :
   $R_1 = CH_3$, $R_2 = C_2H_5$, $R_3 = C_6H_5$

(iii) Metharbital :
   $R_1 = CH_3$, $R_2 = R_3 = C_2H_5$

Most of the barbiturates exhibit anticonvulsant activity at sedative-hypnotic doses. But phenobarbital revealed maximum anticonvulsant potency at sub-hypnotic doses. It was clinically employed in 1913 in the treatment of grand mal epilepsy. Though the above mentioned barbiturates (long acting) exhibit a high degree of effectiveness in grand mal seizures, phenobarbital is relatively non-selective.

Phenobarbital causes CNS depression by both mechanisms,

i.e.,(i) by exerting GABA - mimetic increase in conductance of chloride ions and

(ii) by reducing the Ca^{++} dependent release of neurotransmitters.

Phenobarbital is slowly but completely absorbed when given orally. About 50 - 60 % of the total phenobarbital administered is bound to plasma proteins. The major metabolite, p-hydroxyphenyl derivative (inactive) is obtained through oxidative hydroxylation by hepatic microsomal enzymes. Another is N-glucoside derivative. Both are excreted in urine partly as conjugates. Phenobarbital is a potent inducer of hepatic microsomal enzymes.

Adverse effects of phenobarbital therapy include, sedation, irritability, confusion, hypocalcaemia, tolerance and folate deficiency.

Mephobarbital and primidone in vivo, are converted into phenobarbital. Hence, their activity, mechanism of action and adverse effects are same as that of Phenobarbital. However oral absorption of mephobarbital is incomplete. Both these drugs are effective antiepileptic agents only due to the fact that, they serve simply as a source of in vivo phenobarbital.

Primidone is an example of deoxybarbiturates, effective for all except petit mal epilepsy. Orally, it is rapidly absorbed. Principle metabolites include phenobarbital and phenylethylmalonamide. Both metabolites retain antiepileptic activity. About 40% of administered dose is excreted unchanged in the urine. It is a potent inducer of hepatic microsomal enzymes.

24.7 HYDANTOINS

Phenytoin, in the form of its sodium salt, is the more widely used drug for all types of epilepsy except petit mal. It was first synthesized by Biltz in 1908 and was introduced into clinical practice by Merrit and Putnam in 1938. It is a nonsedative structural relative of phenobarbital. The hydantoins are most effective against grand mal while remain ineffective against petit mal. The clinically used antiepileptic hydantoins are

(a) Phenytoin : R_3 = H; R_5 = C_6H_5
   R'_5 = C_6H_5

(b) Mephenytoin : R_3 = CH_3, R_5 = C_2H_5

(c) Ethotoin : R_3 = C_2H_5; R_5 = H;
   R'_5 = C_6H_5

Phenytoin acts as antiepileptic agent by following mechanisms.

(a) By binding strongly with membrane proteins and phospholipids, it causes membrane stabilization. Stabilization effect is exerted on all neuronal membranes including those of peripheral nerves, resulting into an increase in the refractory period. The depressant action on the membranes accounts for its antiepileptic and antiarrhythmic properties.

(b) It prevents the firing of the neurones by decreasing norepinephrine release.

(c) Epileptic seizures cause an accumulation of Na^+ ions within the cerebral neurons which initiates enhanced synaptic transmission following rapid, repetitive presynaptic stimulation. Phenytoin decreases the intracellular Na^+ ion concentration.

Orally, phenytoin is slowly and incompletely absorbed. It is extensively bound to plasma protein. Daily dose in the order of 300 - 500 mg is required to produce effective plasma concentration. It is extensively (90 - 95%) metabolized by hepatic microsomal enzymes. Principal metabolites include, p-hydroxyphenyl derivative, dihydroxy catechol, dihydrodiol and 3-methoxy derivatives. They are conjugated mainly with glucuronic acid in liver prior to their excretion in urine.

Toxic reactions depend upon dose and route of administration and include skin rashes, gastric irritation, nausea, vomiting, folate deficiency, drowsiness, fatigue, confusion and hyperplasia and hypertrophy of gums. The latter effect may be due to an inhibitory effect of phenytoin on collagenase, an enzyme which breaks down the collagen of connective tissue. Hypocalcaemia is also reported to develop due to induction of vitamin D-metabolising enzymes.

Upon i.v. administration, cardiovascular collapse is most dangerous effect. Hence i.v. dose of phenytoin should not exceed 50 mg/minute.

Mephenytoin was introduced in 1945 for the treatment of epilepsy. On weight basis, it is twice as active as phenytoin. It was found to be more toxic than phenytoin due to the formation of arene oxide intermediates during its metabolism. While ethotoin (1957) has very low efficacy. Hence it is used as an adjunct to other agents in the treatment of generalized seizures.

24.8 OXAZOLIDINEDIONES

The oxazolidine-2,4-diones were originally developed as analgesics (Richards & Everelt, 1944) but were introduced into anticonvulsant therapy between 1946-48. Trimethadione and paramethadione are the clinically used examples from this class. They are effective against petit mal seizures but if used alone, are ineffective against other types of epilepsy.

(i) Trimethadione : $R_3 = CH_3$; $R_5 = CH_3$
 $R'_5 = CH_3$

(ii) Paramethadione : $R_3 = CH_3$;
 $R_5 = CH_3$; $R_5' = C_2H_5$

Trimethadione (tridione) is the prototype of the agents effective against petit mal. Orally, it is rapidly absorbed and uniformly distributed. It is insignificantly bound to plasma proteins. Dimethadione, a N-demethyl derivative (active) is a major metabolite. Delay in onset of antiepileptic activity is due to the slow accumulation of this metabolite which imparts anticonvulsant activity to trimethadione.

Adverse effects include skin rash, blurring of vision, hepatitis, nephrosis and sedation. The evidence for its teratogenic effect is gathering. Like ethosuximide, it may precipitate grand mal epilepsy.

Paramethadione is similar to trimethadione but less effective and less toxic.

The petit mal epilepsy involves low frequency discharges in the thalamus and cerebral cortex which are induced through reticular activating system. Oxazolidinediones are effective only against petit mal condition. This effectiveness is due to two fold action of these agents,

(i) By increasing the threshold for excitation, they prevent the spread of seizure into the thalamus and cerebral cortex.

(ii) By increasing the duration of refractory period in the neurons.

(iii) A slight inhibitory (sedative) action on the resting respiration of the brain cells is an additional effect.

24.9 SUCCINIMIDES

Though less potent, succinimides have enjoyed more success over oxazolidinediones since they possess less significant side-effects. These drugs are moderately effective against petit mal seizures but remain ineffective against grand mal.

The first drug from this series, phensuximide, introduced in 1951 (Chen et al) is the weakest and now is rarely used. It is followed by Methsuximide (1958) and ethosuximide (1960). Both these drugs are effective against petit mal seizures. Ethosuximide is orally well absorbed and gets evenly distributed. It is extensively (75%) metabolised through the oxidation of the side chain to give several metabolites including 2-(1-hydroxy ethyl)-2,-methyl succinimide (inactive) which is excreted partly as glucuronide in urine.

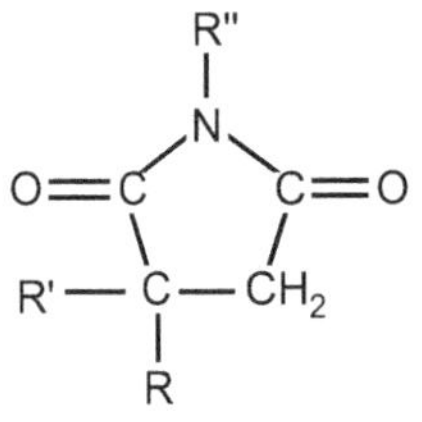

(i) Phensuximide R = C_6H_5; R' = H; R" = CH_3

(ii) Methsuximide : R = C_6H_5; R' = CH_3 R" = CH_3

(iii) Ethosuximide : R = C_2H_5; R' = CH_3 R"= H

Adverse reaction include :

(i) Gastrointestinal complaints like nausea, vomiting and anorexia,

(ii) CNS effects like drowsiness, euphoria, lethargy, headache, restlessness and

(iii) Agitation, skin reactions and tolerance.

Methsuximide is metabolized by hepatic microsomal enzymes to N-demethyl and various p-hydroxyphenyl derivatives. Adverse reactions are similar to ethosuximide. But it is much more toxic than phensuximide.

24.10 ACETYLUREAS

Acetylureas are a group of compounds structurally related with barbiturates and hydantoin. Phenacemide is an open chain analog of the hydantoins. Introduced in 951, it possesses a high anticonvulsant activity, associated with liver and bone marrow toxicities which limits its use. It inhibits the metabolism of other antiepileptic drugs if concomittanly administered and hence is used as adjunct in complex partial seizures. Orally, it is well absorbed. Upon metabolism, p-hydroxy phenyl derivative is obtained. As thought earlier, a ring closure to form hydantoin does not occur. Adverse reactions include skin rash, GIT complaints, nephritis and aplastic anemia.

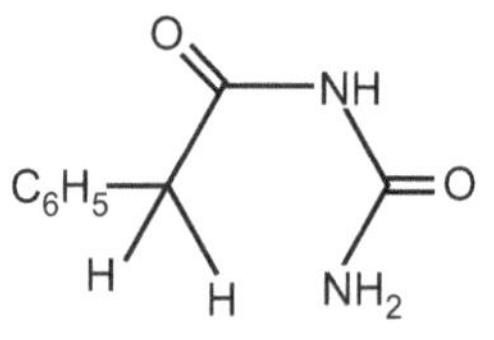

Phenacemide

24.11 BENZODIAZEPINES

Chlordiazepoxide was the first clinically used (1960) antiepileptic agent from this class, followed by diazepam, lorazepam, nitrazepam, clonazepam and clorazepate. They may be used as supplement in antiepileptic thereapy,

(i) Nitrazepam : R = H

(ii) Clonazepam : R = Cl

Benzodiazepines somehow increase the effectiveness of GABA, an inhibitory neurotransmitter by,

(i) Making easy the functioning of variety of GABA mediated synaptic systems linked with Cl^- ionophose system and

(ii) Increasing the affinity of GABA for receptor sites in brain tissues.

Two different binding sites for GABA in hippocampal pyramidal cells have been identified by Alger and Nicoll in 1982. Direct CNS depression is also induced by benzodiazepines by increasing k^+ conductance.

(a) Diazepam is mainly advised intravenously against status epilepticus. In other forms of epilepsy, diazepam is less effective than nitrazepam and clonazepam. It is rapidly absorbed and distributed. It is extensively bound to plasmaproteins. It undergoes metabolism to N-desmethyldiazepam (active) which gradually hydroxylates to oxazepam (active). A relatively high degree of tolerance is reported to develop.

(b) Clonazepam is the most potent benzodiazepine. It is effective by both, orally and intravenously. Side effects are few and mild.

(c) Nitrazepam is preferred against myoclonic and kinetic seizures. Both, clonazepam and nitrazepam are prinicipally metabolized to inactive 7-amino derivatives. Muscular inco-ordination, behavioural disturbances and increased salivary and bronchial secretions constitute less frequent side effects.

(d) Clorazepate is recommended in combination with certain other drugs in the treatment of partial seizures.

24.12 SODIUM VALPROATE (VALPROIC ACID)

Introduced in 1965, chemically it is n-dipropylacetic acid. It is a broad spectrum antiepileptic agent having minimal sedation and other CNS side-effects. It is more effective against petit mal seizures. Its daily dose is 1200 mg in divided doses. It metabolizes to several shorter chain fatty acid derivatives including 2-propyl-2-pentenoic acid and 2-propyl-3-oxo-pentanoic acid,

$$CH_3 - CH_2 - CH_2 \diagdown$$
$$CH - COOH$$
$$CH_3 - CH_2 - CH_2 \diagup$$

Valproic acid

Valproic acid inhibits GABA deactivating enzymes including GABA transaminase and retards re-uptake of GABA by glial cells and nerve endings and thus increases the synaptic concentrations of GABA.

It is one of the potent antiepileptic drugs having minimal sedation and other CNS effects. GIT disturbances are most commonly observed. Tolerance to its anticonvulsant effects is yet not reported. Due to teratogenic evidence in animals, it should not be used during pregnancy.

24.13 IMINOSTILBENES

First synthesized in 1953, carbamazepine is introduced in 1974 in clinical practice against all types of epilepsies except petit mal seizures. It is structurally related to tricyclic antidepressants. Hence it is also effective in manic depressive patients. Oral absorption is slow and erratic. Once absorbed, it gets readily distributed.

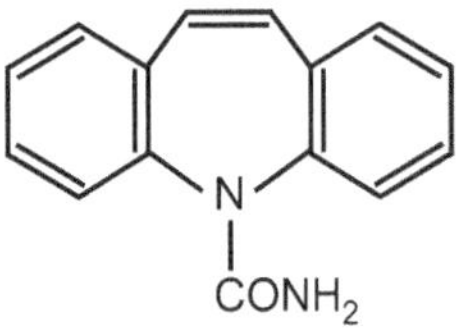

(Carbamazepine structure)

Carbamazepine is metabolised (70%) to 10, 11-epoxide, 10-11-dihydroxide and iminostilbene metabolites which are excreted as glucuronides in urine. In the treatment of epilepsy, it is effective alone or when used in combination with other drugs. It relieves pain associated with trigeminal neuralgia, a condition in which even slight CNS stimulation causes unbearable pain. Other actions include :

(i) Antidiuretic effect.
(ii) Useful in diabetes insipidus.
(iii) Induction of hepatic microsomal enzymes.
(iv) Acts as a partial agonist at adenosine receptors.

In majority cases, toxicity is relatively minor and includes drowsiness, blurred vision, ataxia, vertigo, skin rash and gastric irritation.

24.14 CARBONIC ANHYDRASE INHIBITORS

Acetazolamide, ethoxzolamide and sulthiame are effective anticonvulsants, used in the treatment of grand mal and petit mal seizures. Tolerance develops quite rapidly. Their anticonvulsant action is due to their direct inhibiting action on brain carbonic anhydrase enzymes, resulting into stabilization of membrane due to CO_2 accumulation in brain. In addition, sulthiame inhibits oxygen consumption by the brain.

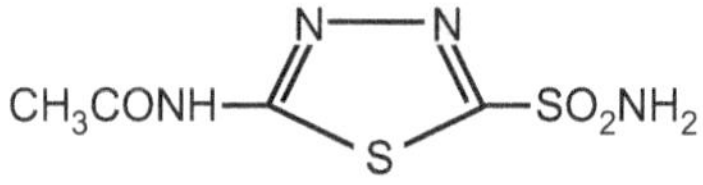

Acetazolamide

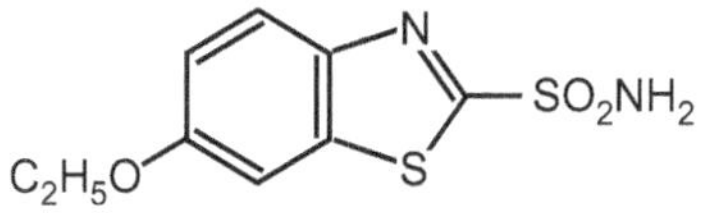

Ethoxzolamide

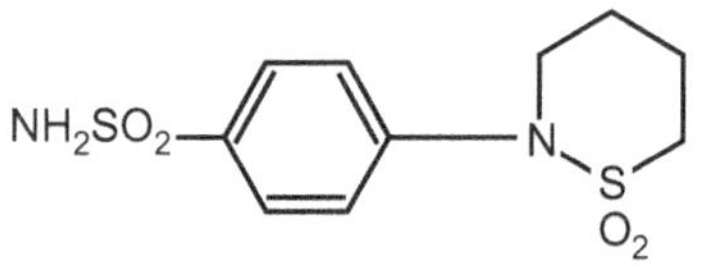

Sulthiame

Acetazolamide is the prototype drug in this series. Orally it is well absorbed and largely excreted unchanged in the urine. It is effective against absence seizures but tolerance is reported to develop quickly.

24.15 MISCELLANEOUS AGENTS

These agents include lidocaine, quinacrine, pyridoxine, and prostaglandin. Currently some derivatives of GABA have also been prepared and evaluated clinically. Progabide is one such agent which acts as agonist at GABA receptors.

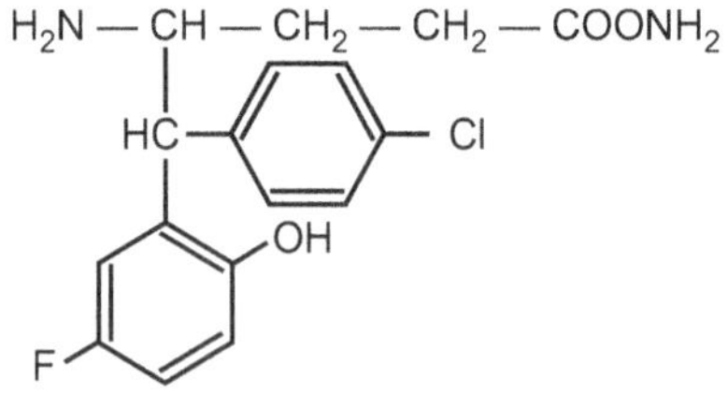

Progabide

ALIPHATIC ALCOHOLS

25.1 INTRODUCTION

The word alcohol is originally derived from the Arabic word, *alkahl*. It is used to describe the series of hydroxylated compounds. In pharmacology, if not specified, the term, alcohol refers to ethyl alcohol or ethanol. It is known as one of the most widely abused drug in the world. Fermentation is the primary source of getting ethanol. One can not get fermented beverages of high ethanol content due to self-limiting nature of fermentation. Fermentation does not proceed further when the alcohol content becomes high enough to inhibit the yeast.

Though alcohol is found to affect almost every vital organ of the body in appropriate concentration, its therapeutic value is much more limited.

25.2 ABSORPTION, FATE AND EXCRETION

Alcohol is absorbed by simple diffusion process across any mucosal surface. Absorption from GIT is extraordinarily rapid, particularly when the stomach is empty. Food of high lipid content slows down its rate of absorption. Thus, anything that delays gastric emptying will retard its absorption. Inhalation route can also be used due to volatile nature of alcohol.

After absorption, alcohol gets uniformly distributed to all tissues in the body. The extent of distribution to individual organ depends upon its degree of vascularization.

The metabolism of alcohol is carried out mainly in liver. Various dietary, hormonal and pharmacological factors alter the rate of its metabolism. Alcohol dehydrogenase is located in the soluble cytoplasm; whereas acetaldehyde dehydrogenase is located in mitochondria. These two enzymes are responsible for oxidative metabolism of major fraction (90 - 98%) of alcohol that enters the body. Alcohol dehydrogenase is a zinc containing enzyme having a molecular weight of about 85,000. The remaining

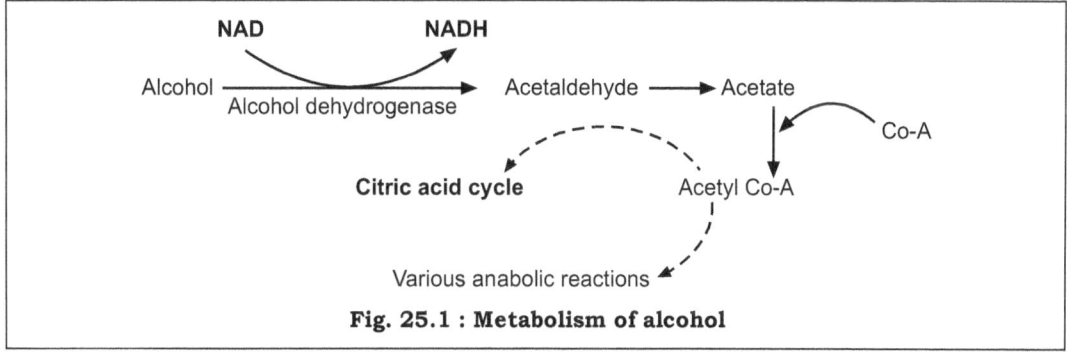

Fig. 25.1 : Metabolism of alcohol

minor fraction (2 - 5%) of unmetabolized alcohol leaves the body through kidneys or lungs. The oxidation of ethanol in the body releases 7 kcal energy per gram. The oxidation proceeds relatively independent of ethanol concentration (zero-order kinetics). The NAD can be regenerated from NADH either by the mitochondrial respiratory chain or by cytoplasmic redox reactions.

Microsomal mixed-function oxidase enzymes are also involved in the oxidation of minute quantity of alcohol to acetaldehyde. In acute alcohol intoxication, these enzymes may be induced resulting into interference with the metabolism of other drugs.

Minute amounts of alcohol are conjugated with sulfate or glucuronide. Most of the unchanged alcohol is excreted through urine and expired air. The quantification of ethanol in the expired air is the commonly used test in legal proceedings.

25.3 MECHANISM OF ACTION

Alcohol affects the working of almost every vital organ in the body. The diversity of its actions can be explained by its amphophilic nature due to which, it can easily penetrate into lipoidal layers, causing their disorganization. This membrane fluidizing effect results into disturbances in the electrical conduction and the release of neurotransmitters.

Some of the biological effects of alcohol are the consequences of increased NADH concentration in the tissues resulting due to the oxidation of alcohol. It modifies other NAD linked catalytic units.

25.4 PHARMACOLOGY

The more concentrated the alcohol, the more pronounced its effects. It is abused due to its prominent CNS effects.

(a) CNS : Administration of alcohol, results into first stimulation, followed by the depression due to the depression of inhibitory control mechanisms. The cortex is thus released from its integrating control. In low amounts, it causes the depression of midbrain and hypothalamus region. As the concentration of alcohol is increased, effect on sensory areas of the cortex extends to the motor areas. In larger amounts, respiratory centers in the medulla are depressed. The moderate CNS depression is characterized by euphoria, talkativeness, aggressiveness and behavioural activation. Due to rapid distribution, however, these effects are of relatively brief duration. Delirium tremens is a familiar alcoholic mental disease. Avitaminosis may be considered as one of the contributing factors in its production.

(b) Skin : For skin application, alcohol can be used for a variety of reasons. It has astringent, germicidal, counter irritant, rubefacient and cooling effect on skin. In trigeminal neuralgia, the relief of pain can be obtained through direct reversible damage to the sensory nerve by the injection of absolute alcohol in the close proximity to nerves or ganglia.

(c) CVS : In moderate amounts, alcohol causes cutaneous vasodilation and produces a feeling of warmness. A fall in body temperature is likely the result of both the central and peripheral actions of alcohol. Coronary blood flow does not increase. The blood pressure, cardiac output and force of muscle contraction remains unaffected. In larger quantities, however, alcohol causes cardiovascular depression alongwith rhythm disturbances.

(d) Respiration : In respiratory collapse, alcohol in moderate amounts, reflexly stimulate the respiratory centers in medulla by local irritation of receptors present in buccal, esophageal and gastric mucosa. Overdosage will antagonize this action.

(e) Skeletal muscles : Alcohol, in small amounts, accelerates and sharpens the functioning of skeletal muscles. Larger amounts of alcohol lead to CNS depression resulting into a decrease in the overall muscular work.

(f) GIT : Due to the mild irritation to the sensory endings present in the mucosa of GIT, alcohol stimulates the secretion of salivary and gastric juices. In low concentration alcohol hence, stimulate the appetite. In intoxication, alcohol impedes the actions of digestive enzymes and relaxes GIT secretory and motor functions. Chronic gastritis and gastroenteritis often result. Vomiting may result due to local irritation. The lack of absorption from the tract of a varied diet, frequently results in an autaminosis. Upon oxidation, alcohol releases 7 kcal energy per gram of alcohol. Hence, alcohol can be considered of nutritional value but it does not act as a reserve food as does the glucose.

(g) Liver : Chronic alcohol intoxication is manifested by the accumulation of fat and protein in the liver which may become irreversible and may promote the appearance of characteristic cirrhosis. Malnutrition and vitamin deficiency, further may contribute to cirrhosis.

(h) Kidney : The diuretic effect exerted by alcohol can be accounted by

(i) the large amount of fluid normally consumed with ethanol and

(ii) decrease in the renal tubular reabsorption of water due to inhibition of the secretion of antidiuretic hormones.

(i) Sexual functions : During chronic administration, alcohol reduces blood testosterone levels resulting into impotence, sterility and testicular atrophy.

(j) Chronic administration of alcohol results into the development of tolerance and physical dependence.

(k) Teratogenic effects of alcohol have also been reported due to its free access to fetus, circulating through placenta. This results into development of immunological, morphological and neurological abnormalities in the newborn.

25.5 ADVERSE REACTIONS

The ethanol withdrawal syndrome is characterized by headache, tremors, hallucinations and autonomic hyperexcitability. In acute reactions, hangover represents a mild withdrawal syndrome. Usually the blood ethanol concentration of 100 mg/dl can be considered as an index of intoxication. Patient may become unconscious which prevents further intake of ethanol.

The cases of cross tolerance have been reported between ethanol and other CNS depressants, like barbiturates, paraldehyde etc. While alcohol potentiates the action of phenothiazines and butyrophenone antipsychotic agents.

25.6 TREATMENT OF ALCOHOLISM

The treatment of chronic alcoholism is based upon the consequences and causes of alcohol intoxication. It involves

(i) complete withdrawal of alcohol, supported by psychiatric treatment.

(ii) use of benzodiazepines for the suppression of withdrawal symptoms.

(iii) use of multivitamin preparations to correct dietary deficiencies and

(iv) treatment with disulfiram.

Disulfiram:

It is a vulcanizing agent mainly used in rubber industries. It exists in the form of colourless or slightly yellow crystals which are nearly insoluble in water. Chemically, it is tetraethylthiuram disulfide.

$$(C_2H_5)_2N-\underset{\underset{S}{\|}}{C}-S-S-\underset{\underset{S}{\|}}{C}-N(C_2H_5)_2$$

Disulfiram

It appears relatively nontoxic when given alone. But in the presence of alcohol, it produces acetaldebyde syndrome characterized by intense throbbing in the head and neck region due to vasodilation, nausea, vomiting, sweating, thirst, chest pain, respiratory difficulties, hypotension, blurred vision and confusion. It interferes in the metabolism of alcohol by reacting with the sulfhydryl groups present in aldehyde dehydrogenase enzyme, thus preventing further oxidation of acetaldehyde. As a result, there occurs 5 - 10 fold increase in the blood acetaldehyde concentration. Beside this, disulfiram also causes an irreversible inhibition of other enzymes containing sulfhydryl group. It also interferes with the catecholamine synthesis by inhibiting dopamine - β - hydroxylase enzyme. Thus, it stands as an illustrative example of drug interactions.

It is well absorbed from GIT but rapidly undergoes decomposition to two units of diethyldithiocarbamates in blood, mainly by glutathione reductase enzymes. The metabolites undergo glucuronidization in liver. Part of the diethyl-dithiocarbamate further metabolizes to carbon disulfide and excreted through lungs.

Adverse reactions of disulfiram include fatigue, tremors, headache, mild GIT disturbances, reduced sexual ability and allergic dermatitis. Due to its teratogenic nature, it should not be used during pregnancy. In other patients, it should be given under strict medical supervision due to the chances of occurance of cardiovascular collapse, respiratory failure, convulsions and coma. Similarly the medical preparations containing ethanol as a constituent should be avoided during its administration.

Other drugs like, calcium carbamide, phenylbutazone, sulfonylureas, metronidazole etc. are capable of exerting a similar effect to that of disulfiram on ethanol metabolism. But the duration of action of such effect may be brief. Citrated calcium carbimide has less severe side-effects.

25.7 METHANOL (Methyl Alcohol)

It is the simplest member from the series of aliphatic alcohols. It was formerly, known as 'wood alcohol' since it was obtained by the destructive distillation of wood. Its activity spectrum is quite similar to that of ethanol but methanol is only about half as potent as to ethanol. It is mainly used as a solvent and as an agent to 'denature' in various industries. This, being tax free, is considerably less costly than ethanol containing beverage.

Its absorption from GIT is quite rapid. After absorption, it is uniformly distributed into the body. Its toxicity appears to be primarily due to the formation of toxic metabolites (like, formaldehyde and formic acid), through its oxidation in liver and kidney. The rate of metabolism is slow and usually takes several days. A severe acidosis then develops which is followed by optic nerve damage leading into partial or total blindness. Signs of methanol intoxication include, headache, vomitting, vertigo, severe upper abdominal pain, motor restlessness, blurring of vision etc.

Treatment of methanol intoxication involves neutralization of acidosis by the infusion of sodium bicarbonate until the urine pH attains 7.5 and removal of remaining unoxidised methanol by hemodialysis.

Withdrawal symptoms of methanol include, sweating, loss of appetite, sleeplessness, hallucinations, tremors and tachycardia.

Other alcohols of non-therapeutic value include, propanols, butanols and pentanols. All these alcohols are not consumed by humans and are more toxic than ethanol.

ANXIOLYTIC AGENTS

26.1 INTRODUCTION

Anxiety is an unpleasant symptom of many psychiatric disorders, usually associated with the feelings of fear and apprehension. The antianxiety agents or anxiolytic drugs are the chemical agents which are used to control the effects of stress and the discomfort, tension and dysphoria associated with neuroses and mild depressive states. In addition to the disturbance in mood, other symptoms result due to changes in sleep, GIT and autonomic nervous system.

The limbic system of the brain is the primary generative site for the emotions. The reticular formation of the brain is involved in anxiety states since the weakening of its inhibitory action leads to overstimulation and anxiety. Behavioural symptoms like fear, anger, pleasure and continuous restlessness result due to the direct stimulation of hypothalamus.

Most of the antianxiety agents, in addition, have sedative, anticonvulsant and muscle relaxant properties in a dose-dependent fashion and share at least some of the properties of traditional sedatives. Their chronic use may induce tolerance which is sometimes followed by physical dependence.

Depending upon the source and symptoms, anxiety states can be classified mainly as

(a) Panic anxiety which is characterised by sudden and unpredictable attacks of anxiety. Alprazolam is a preferred drug for the treatment of panic disorders and

(b) Somatic anxiety which, at least to some extent, results due to participation of somatic elements. When anxiety can not be categorised in either of these two classes due to coexistance of other bodily symptoms, it can be called as mixed anxiety state.

26.2 TREATMENT OF ANXIETY

Though the treatment of anxiety disorders should always involve non-drug approaches, in certain cases, drug treatment becomes necessary. Alcohol and barbiturates act as antianxiety agents, mainly due to their CNS-depression effects. Alcohol causes an irregular descending depression of the CNS and may cause medullary paralysis in toxic doses. Various antianxiety drugs which can be used in the treatment of anxiety disorders can be listed as below.

(a) Barbiturates
(b) Propanediols
(c) Diphenylmethane derivatives
(d) Antidepressant agents
(e) Adrenergic-β-receptor blocking agents
(f) Benzodiazepines
(g) Miscellaneous agents.

The wide diversity of compounds used to treat anxiety disorders makes it difficult to frame out a firm SAR pattern. Hence important SAR correlations will be discussed in individual classes.

26.3 BARBITURATES

All barbiturates can act as effective antianxiety agents due to their sedative property. But their liability to produce tolerance, physical dependence and severe withdrawal symptoms, restricted their widespread acceptance as antianxiety agents. Pentobarbital, amobarbital and phenobarbital can be sometimes used to treat anxiety disorders due to a lesser degree of sedation and other adverse effects associated with them. They can induce hepatic microsomal enzymes and may enhance the metabolism of other drugs. These long acting barbiturates are now rarely prescribed to treat anxiety.

26.4 PROPANEDIOLS

Mephenesin, a centrally acting muscle relaxant was developed from aliphatic polyalcohol series. In addition, it has sedative property. Its very short duration of action led to the studies of mephenesin derivatives. Some mephenesin derivatives have more psychotropic and less muscle relaxant activity. Meprobamate is one such drug, first synthesized in 1951 in order to develop a long-acting analog of mephenesin. It is an example of propanediol carbamate and has anxiolytic, muscle relaxant and sedetive/hypnotic activities.

Meprobarate is well absorbed from GIT. It has intermediate duration of action. It is extensively metabolized (90%) mainly to hydroxymeprobamate which undergoes glucuronide conjugation. The resulting glucuronide is excreted through urine. The remaining unmetabolized drug is eliminated as such in urine. Meprobamate induces hepatic microsomal enzymes. Hence, it is contraindicated in intermittent polyporphyria.

Meprobamate neither activates GABA-ergic response nor it causes synaptic depression. It acts by selectively depressing the thalamus and limbic system. In therapeutic doses, it does not affect peripheral autonomic function.

Adverse effects include, nausea, vomiting, diarrhoea, slurred speech, drowsiness, weakness, aplastic anemia, allergic reactions and hypotension. Chronic use may result into development of tolerance and physical dependence. Withdrawal symptoms, in extreme cases, may be accompanied by convulsions.

Other propanediol carbamates include, tybamate and carisoprodol. Both these agents share many of the properties of meprobamate. Tybamate has a shorter duration of action while carisoprodol is more effective as muscle relaxant.

$$CH_3-\underset{\underset{CH_2O-\underset{\underset{O}{\|}}{C}-NH_2}{|}}{\overset{\overset{CH_2O-\overset{\overset{O}{\|}}{C}-NH_2}{|}}{C}}-CH_2CH_2CH_3$$

Meprobamate

$$CH_3-\underset{\underset{CH_2-O-\underset{\underset{O}{\|}}{C}-NH-C_4H_7}{|}}{\overset{\overset{CH_2OCONH_2}{|}}{C}}-CH_2CH_2CH_3$$

Tybamate

$$CH_3-\underset{\underset{CH_2-O-\underset{\underset{O}{\|}}{C}-NH-CH(CH_3)_2}{|}}{\overset{\overset{CH_2O-\overset{\overset{O}{\|}}{C}-NH_2}{|}}{C}}-CH_2CH_2CH_3$$

Carisoprodol

These drugs have a narrow margin of safety, a number of adverse reactions and a significant abuse potential. Hence, they are not much favoured in the treatment of anxiety disorders.

26.5 DIPHENYLMETHANE DERIVATIVES

Hydroxyzine is an effective antianxiety agent from this class which is used to treat anxiety states induced by drug-withdrawal. Besides anxiolytic activity, it has antihistaminic, anticholinergic and antidepressant activities. It acts by depressing reticular activating system.

26.6 ANTIDEPRESSANT AGENTS

Doxepin is an example of anxiolytic agent from this class. It has tricyclic ring structure which is quite similar to imipramine skeleton. It has antidepressant activity and also possesses anxiolytic activity. Hence, it may be used in the treatment of anxiety induced depression.

Doxepin

26.7 ADRENERGIC β-RECEPTOR BLOCKING AGENTS

Many of the symptoms associated with anxiety are due to the activation of adrenergic nervous system. These include sweating, palpitation, tremors and tachycardia. Hence, adrenergic-β-blockers can be used to treat chronic anxiety and stressful situation. These agents cause anxiolytic effect, independent of their established mode of action. For example, propranolol glycol, a metabolite of propranolol, has been reported to induce CNS depression in experimental animals. β-blockers are sometimes administered in combination with diazepam in chronic anxiety cases. β-blockers commonly used for this purpose include propranolol and slow release formulations of oxprenolol hydrochloride.

Propranolol glycol

However, these agents should not be used to treat anxiety disorders in patients suffering from heart disease, asthma and diabetus mellitus.

26.8 BENZODIAZEPINES

The anxiolytic agents discussed prior to this, can induce tolerance and physical dependence. Their withdrawal symptoms and adverse reactions may prove lethal. This prompted the search for a better anxiolytic agent having a wide margin of safety. The first member of the series, i.e., chlordiazepoxide, was synthesized in the late 1950s at Roche laboratories. Benzodiazepines due to their low toxicity and high clinical effectiveness, are the most widely used anxiolytics. In addition, they also have anticonvulsant, muscle relaxant and sedative/hypnotic properties at high dose-level. For antianxiety use, generally long-acting benzodiazepines are employed because more stable blood concentrations can be maintained during chronic use.

In benzodiazepines, there exists a wide separation of antianxiety and sedative actions. In clinical practise, presently, chlordiazepoxide, diazepam, oxazepam, clorazepate, lorazepam, prazepam, alprazolam and halozepam are employed as anxiolytic agents. Chlordiazepoxide is the first clinically introduced agent from this series. It has anticonvulsant and muscle relaxant properties. It can be administered by orally, intravenously and also intramuscularly. Chlordiazepoxide and diazepam have been used extensively in children. While in patients suffering from hepatic dysfunction, oxazepam, lorazepam and alprazolam are advised.

SAR studies revealed that an electronegative group at position 7 is necessary for anxiolytic activity and presence of a nitro or a halogen group at C-7 in most of the structures of benzodiazepines seems to fulfill this requirement.

In recent modifications, the C_5-phenyl ring is replaced by heterocyclic ring to get newer benzodizepines.

Pharmacology :

(a) CNS : Benzodiazepine causes a mild CNS depression by potentiating the inhibitory effects of γ-amino butyric acid. They cause an increase in conductance of GABA-activated chloride channels and depress the spinal reflexes. They do not affect significantly the REM sleep but increase the seizure threshold value. Some of their inhibitory effects proceed via the mechanism different from GABA-ergic potentiation. Anxiolytic action is exhibited at doses that do not have pronounced hypnotic or ataxic effects.

(b) Skeletal muscle : Since muscle relaxation is an inherent property associated with most of the CNS-depressants, benzodiazepines cause relaxation of skeletal muscles, through an induced depression of spinal and supraspinal motor reflexes.

(c) Peripheral effects : Benzodiazepines, in therapeutic doses, do not affect much the respiratory and cardiovascular systems. In an intravenous dose, diazepam may cause a slight decrease in respiration. The minimal peripheral effects of benzodiazepine may be due to the lack of peripheral GABA-ergic neurons.

Mechanism of Action :

The presence of benzodiazepine receptors in the mammalian brain tissues was first reported in 1977 by Mohler and Okada. Cerebellar and cerebral cortices are the regions of higher density benzodiazepine receptors. These receptor sites are both centrally and peripherally located. The peripheral receptors are present in mast cells, liver, heart, lymphocytes and platelets. The receptor site is a macromolecular complex which is comprised of GABA receptors, benzodiazepine receptor and a chloride ionophore.

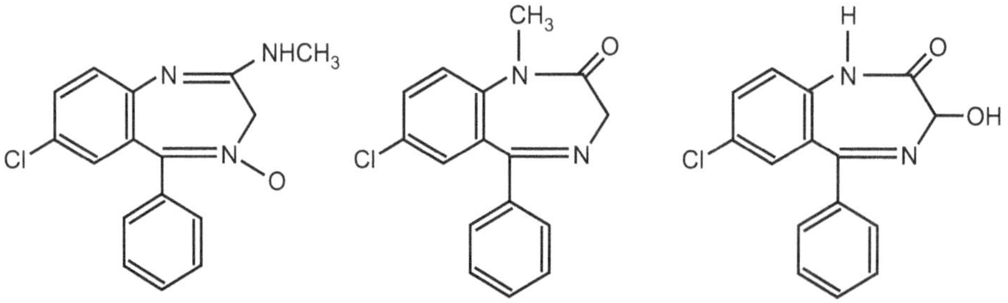

Chlordiazepoxide   Diazepam   Oxazepam

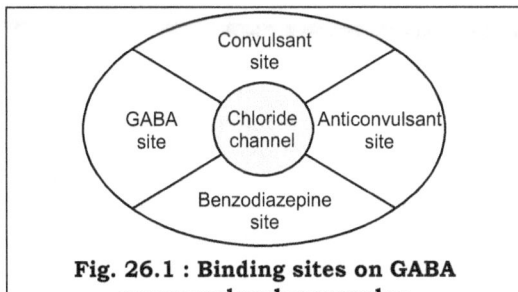

Fig. 26.1 : Binding sites on GABA macromolecular complex

Drugs that inhibit GABA ergic transmission are convulsants and anxiogenics, while drugs that enhance GABA-ergic transmission are anxiolytics, anticonvulsants, muscle relaxants and sedative-hypnotics.

The multiplicity of actions associated with benzodiazepines can be explained in terms of functionally distinct sub-binding sites at GABA macromolecular complex. For example, BZ_1-binding sites for benzodiazepine are mainly responsible for anxiolytic action and are present in the brain, while BZ_2-binding sites are mainly responsible for the anticonvulsant and hypnotic effects of benzodiazepines and are located in cerebral cortex.

The various sites on GABA macromolecular complex bear a relationship with each other in an allosteric manner. The spontaneous increased activity of the limbic neurons is inhibited by benzodiazepines, probably by allosteric interaction with either GABA or glycine (the major inhibitory neurotransmitters in brain) resulting into presynaptic inhibitory processes in both, brain and spinal cord.

Absorption, Metabolism and Excretion :

Except diazepam, most of the benzodiazepines are absorbed relatively slowly from GIT. Clorazepate is absorbed in the form of its metabolite, nordiazepam (N-desmethyldiazepam) which is obtained due to a decarboxylation of clorazepate due to gastric acid secretions.

Most of the benzodiazepines are irregularly absorbed from intramuscular sites.

Once absorbed, due to their high lipophilicity, benzodiazepines uniformly distribute in most of the tissues and are extensively bound to plasma proteins. They usually have a large apparent volume of distribution.

Most benzodiazepines yield similar metabolites in the liver, leading to Ndealkylated or hydroxylated products. For example, nordiazepam is the principal active metabolite of diazepam, halazepam, chlordiazepoxide and prazepam. In some cases, nordiazepam may be further metabolized to demoxepam (another active metabolite) or is hydroxylated to oxazepam which is further inactivated by conjugation with glucuronic acid. Since chlordiazepoxide and diazepam lead to the formation of active metabolites, their duration of action is extended. While lorazepam, oxazepam, temazepam and triazolam do not form active metabolites. These drugs can be directly conjugated at C_3 hydroxyl group and thus get rapidly inactivated and excreted.

The metabolism of benzodiazepines may be induced by rifampin and may be inhibited by drugs like cimetidine, isoniazid and disulfiram. Most of the benzodiazepines are excreted in the form of their oxidized and glucuronide metabolites in the urine.

Adverse Reaction :

Benzodiazepines are the agents with wide margin of safety. The acute overdosage rarely results in lethal effects. The adverse effects associated with benzodiazepine therapy include, nausea, headache, vertigo, weight gain, metallic taste, irritability, paradoxical delirium, confusion and impaired motor functions. Benzodiazepines depress the CNS functioning in neonate. Hence, their use, especially during the first trimester in pregnancy should be contraindicated. Some imidazobenzodiazepines have selective, antagonistic action against benzodiazepines and can be used to treat acute overdose poisoning by benzodiazepines.

Chronic administration of high doses of benzodiazepines may lead to tolerance and physical dependence. Abrupt withdrawal of drug after chronic administration may lead to rebound insomnia. The severity of withdrawal symptoms is governed by the biological half-life of the compound. The withdrawal of benzodiazepines with a relatively short duration of action may result in an intense form of withdrawal symptoms while long-acting benzodiazepines are associated with relatively mild withdrawal symptoms.

Therapeutic Uses :

Though various benzodiazepines differ only in the potency and duration of action, the one given below are usually preferred to others in the specific situations.

(a) Acute and chronic anxiety : Chlordiazepoxide
(b) Generalized anxiety states : Alprazolam
(c) Status epilepticus : Diazepam
(d) Insomnia : Flurazepam, nitrazepam and triazolam.

The benzodiazepines should be used with caution in patients with respiratory insufficiency, hepatic failure, obstetrics and pregnancy.

26.9 MISCELLANEOUS AGENTS

(a) Antihistaminics : Some of the H_1-receptor blocking agents (e.g., diphenhydramine, hydroxyzine) can be used in mild anxiety states due to their sedative property. Hydroxyzine can potentiate the effects of most CNS depressants. Advantage associated with their use, is the lack of abuse potential.

(b) Thioxanthenes : These agents share many properties with phenothiazines due to their structural similarity. Thiothixene is the most potent and the most commonly used member of this series.

(c) Chlormethiazole : It is a nonbenzodiazepine agent having many activities similar to diazepam.

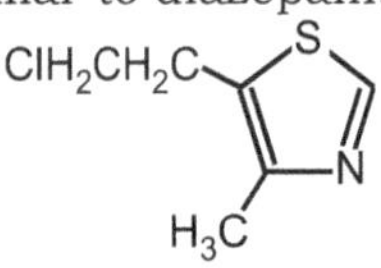

In chronic administration, chlormethiazole may induce tolerance and physical dependence.

(d) Buspirone hydrochloride : It is a member of azaspirodecanedione series and is devoid of usual sedative, anticonvulsant and muscle relaxant properties. It is an effective antianxiety agent which lacks abuse potential.

Adverse reactions are few and include dizziness, headache and nervousness.

(e) Other miscellaneous CH_3 agents include :

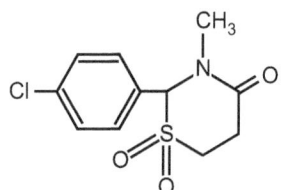

Chlormezanone

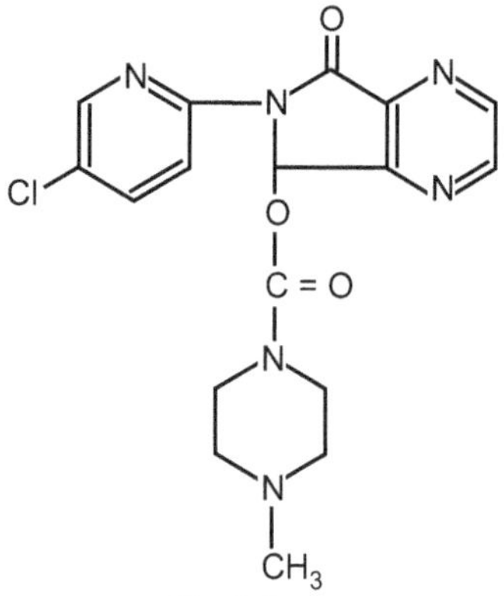

Zopiclone

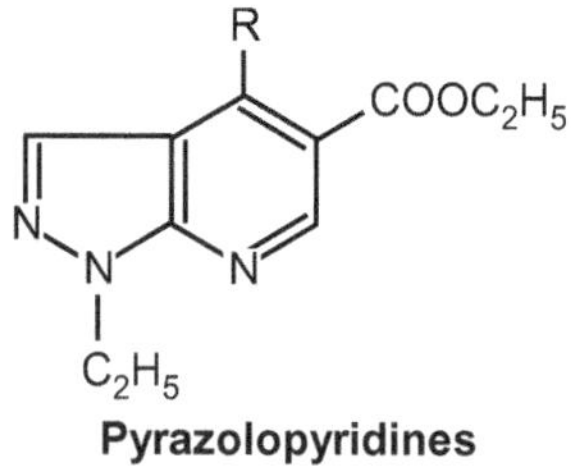

Pyrazolopyridines
(e.g., etazolate and cartazolate)

Chlormezanone is a structural relative of chlorzoxazone and possesses anxiolytic and muscle relaxant activities.

CENTRAL NERVOUS SYSTEM STIMULANTS

27.1 INTRODUCTION

The drugs acting on CNS are generally classified as specific and non-specific which are characterised by the dose-response relationship of that particular drug. The specific drugs (either CNS stimulants or depressants) do usually affect several CNS functions to varying degree at high concentrations. These effects other than desired action are regarded as limitations in selectivity or untoward effects e.g. some drugs exhibit prominent central stimulation at toxic level and others produce mild stimulation as a side-effect. Examples are found in the local anaesthetics (cocaine), parasympatholytics (atropine), sympathomimetics (amphetamine) and salicylates.

Thus, the drugs having the main activity (and not as the side-effect) to increase the activity of various portions of the central nervous system, are collectively called as 'central nervous system stimulants'.

27.2 THERAPEUTIC APPLICATIONS OF CNS STIMULANTS

(1) Analeptics : Certain stimulants act upon the sensory areas of the brain. These agents find their use in elevating the CNS activity in order to increase alertness and to lessen mental fatigue and narcosis brought about by the excess of depresessant drugs. e.g., caffeine.

(2) Respiratory stimulants : The respiratory stimulation may be brought about by either :

(a) direct stimulation of respiratory centre of the medulla by the clinically used CNS stimulants, or

(b) by acting reflexly by changing the pH of the blood which is supplied to the centre, e.g., carbonic acid, carbon-dioxide, ammonia etc. These agents are of value in the treatment of narcotic poisoning and in conditions of threatened collapse of respiratory mechanisms.

Since emetic centre is also located in the medulla, at therapeutic doses, a few CNS stimulant drugs exert an effect on this emetic zone and may be used as emetics in the treatment of poisoning.

27.3 LIMITATIONS OF CNS STIMULANTS

(1) Since these agents lack selectivity of action, very few of these agents are employed therapeutically.

(2) Unfortunately, the margin of safety of CNS stimulant drugs is generally very narrow and unpredictable because a balance between excitatory and inhibitory influences in CNS is normally maintained within relatively narrow limits. For examples, most analeptics, at higher concentration may lead to the generation of convulsions. While no selectively acting respiratory stimulant is presently available.

(3) Since on molecular level, the basic elements involved in CNS stimulation are similar to those in CNS depression, it is not possible to stimulate the nervous system over a long period of time. This is because the drug induced CNS excitability is followed by depression, proportional in depth to the intensity and duration of the stimulation.

Most of the CNS stimulant drugs act either by :

(a) blocking the inhibition of CNS activity induced by CNS depression of any origin, or

(b) enhancing neuronal excitation (which may involve increased neurotransmitter release, more prolonged transmitter action, stabilization of the post-synaptic membrane or decrease in synaptic recovery time etc.)

27.4 CLASSIFICATION

1. Drugs which are mainly used as analeptics.
2. Methylxanthines.
3. Central stimulant sympatho-mimetics.
4. Miscellaneous agents.

27.5 ANALEPTICS

Both inspiratory and expiratory centres are located in the reticular formation of the medulla and together are responsible for spontaneous respiration.

Many physiological factors like temperature, blood flow, (change in the amount supplied, decrease in pH and oxygen content and increase in CO_2 content, irritation of respiratory passages, vomiting etc. alter the rate and depth of respiration.

Analeptics (take up) stimulate the entire nervous system (particularly medulla), thereby counteracting the respiratory depression resulting from overdose of CNS depressant drugs. These agents act as competitive antagonist (strychnine) of the inhibitory neurotransmitters at post-synaptic inhibitory sites. Amongst inhibitory neurotransmitters, γ-amino butyric acid (GABA) predominates in the brain while glycine is more important in the spinal cord. For example, picrotoxin acts on the regulatory sites of GABA receptors while strychnine antagonizes the inhibitory actions of glycine.

Large doses of an analeptic is necessary to overcome a highly depressed state of respiration. These agents may produce convulsions due to their ability to stimulate all parts of the brain and hence these agents act as an analeptic (rather than a convulsant), better in the presence of slight depression. An additional benefit is gained due to adrenal catecholamine release resulting into brochodilation which helps to improve air flow in the lungs. As in the light of current knowledge, the terms analeptic and convulsant are virtually synonymous, the respiratory depression is best treated by other supportive measures like artificial respiration, oxygen administration, peritoneal dialysis and forced diuresis for the treatment of patients poisoned by depressant drugs.

[I] Strychnine :

It is the main active alkaloid present in the seeds of Strychnos nux-vomica in the range of 1.1-1.3% concentration. Considerable amount of brucine, another less potent alkaloid is also present. Strychine is a powerful CNS stimulant. It is nonselective in its action.

Strychnine is well absorbed from almost all routes of administration. In liver, it is extensively metabolized. About 10 - 15% of administered dose may be excreted in urine in an unmetabolized form.

Strychnine brings about its CNS stimulant effect by selective, competitive antagonism of glycine. Glycine is the principal inhibitory neurotransmitter to motor neurons and interneurons in the spinal cord. Strychnine is also reported to inactivate choline-esterase enzymes.

Adverse reactions include, stiffness of face and neck muscles, hypoxia, convulsions followed by medullary paralysis. The adverse effects of strychnine are dose-dependent and may be corrected by treatment with diazepam.

[II] Picrotoxin :

It is a nonnitrogenous compound, naturally obtained from the seeds of Anamirta cocculus. It may decompose into picrotoxinin (active component) and picrotin (a neural component). Picrotoxin is a potent CNS stimulant. It lacks selectivity of action. It mainly acts by blocking the inhibitory responses mediated through GABA-ergic neurons.

Adverse effects of picrotoxin are the extension of its CNS stimulating action. Convulsions may be produced at higher concentrations which are of tonic-clonic type and are unco-ordinated. Diazepam and clonazepam are effective antidote for the treatment of its toxicity symptoms.

[III] Pentylenetetrazol :

This synthetic compound causes the activation of all levels of cerebrospinal axis by antagonizing the GABA-induced inhibitory mechanisms. It is rapidly absorbed from almost all routes of administration and gets uniformly distributed to all body compartments. In liver, pentylenetetrazol undergoes metabolism and thus deactivated. It is a useful screening device for anticonvulsant activity.

[IV] Nikethamide and Doxapram :

These are the powerful CNS-stimulant drugs. They have a considerable selectivity of action on medullary region. In large doses, both these agents may produce convulsions. However, doxapram is more safe CNS-stimulant drug having lesser side effects unlike above discussed analeptics. Potentiation of excitatory mechanisms in the CNS is the mechanism of action for these agents. Adverse effects include, vomiting, sweating, sneezing, coughing, hypertension, tachycardia, arrhythmias and tremors.

Whatever may be the analeptic agent used, it should be contraindicated in epilepsy, hypertension, cardiac disease and hyperthyroidism.

27.6 METHYLXANTHINES

It is a usual experience that beverages like tea, coffee and cocoa cause diuresis. All these beverages contain methylxanthines, like caffeine, theophylline and theobromine. These are closely related alkaloids which differ only in the potency and have a mild CNS-stimulant effect.

Xanthine is the 2, 6-dihydroxylated purine, where

$R_1 = R_3 = R_7 = H$

Derivative	R_1	R_3	R_7
Caffeine	CH_3	CH_3	CH_3
Theophylline	CH_3	CH_3	H
Theobromine	H	CH_3	CH_3

Tea contains about 30 - 40 mg/cup of caffeine, coffee contains about 100 - 150 mg/cup of caffeine, and cocoa contains about 15 - 18 mg/cup of caffeine. Methylxanthines are effective mood elevators and increase the muscle strength. They combat the mental fatigueness and cause medullary stimulation resulting into increased rate and depth of respiration. In this regard, they are less potent than analeptics.

Other effects of methylxanthines include, diuresis, positive inotropic effect, relaxation of bronchial smooth muscles (hence useful in bronchial asthma) and increased gastric secretion. In most of these actions, the order of potency is

Theophylline > Caffeine > Theobromine

Most of these actions can be explained on the basis of their ability to

(i) increase the intracellular concentration of cyclic nucleotides by inhibiting phosphodiesterase enzymes.

(ii) selectively antagonise adenosine mediated actions,

(iii) mobilize intracellular calcium ions, and partly by

(iv) antagonizing the inhibitory mechanisms mediated by GABA-ergic neurons.

Caffeine is the most potent xanthine, producing cortical and medullary stimulation while theobromine stands last in the list. Caffeine helps to combat fatigue and sleepiness and stimulates mental alertness. In higher doses methylxanthines produce signs of CNS-stimulation of increasing depth resulting into nausea, vomiting, restlessness, insomnia, tremors and tachycardia.

Caffeine and theophylline have cardiovascular effects in moderate doses. Vasodilation and positive inotropic effects are seen due to an increase in the catecholamine release. Theophylline may be useful in the treatment of congestive heart failure.

Due to an effective bronchodilatory action, theophylline may be indicated in the treatment of bronchial asthma. It causes an increase in the vital volume. It also augments the contractility of striated muscle and increase the capacity to work. The muscle stimulant effect is brought about by inhibition of muscle adenosine triphosphate and nerve cholinesterase enzymes. Methylxanthines increase the secretory capacity of most of the endocrine and exocrine tissues. They play an important role in suppressing the signs and symptoms of inflammation, probably by interferring the prostaglandin synthesis.

Caffeine is well absorbed from GIT. While to increase oral absorption of theophylline, it is presented in the form of soluble derivatives or mixtures. For example, in aminophylline, ethylenediamine component facilitates the absorption of theophylline from GIT. These theophylline derivatives cause GIT distress except the mixture of theophylline and sodium glycinate. The latter preparation, being less alkaline, does not produce any discomfort in GIT. Since intra-muscular injection leads to prolonged local pain sensation, this route needs to be avoided.

Sodium acetate is usually used with theobromine to accelerate its oral absorption. Theobromine lacks prominent cerebral and cardiovascular stimulant effects of methylxanthines and better acts as a diuretic.

Once absorbed, methylxanthines are readily distributed to all tissues. The extent of protein binding is reported to be more for theophylline. They can readily cross the placental barrier. Liver stands as a principal site for their metabolism where methylxanthines are converted mainly into uric acid derivatives. For example, 1-methyluric acid and 1-methylxanthine are the main metabolic products of caffeine while 1,3-dimethyluric acid is the principal metabolite of theophylline which are excreted through urine. About 1 - 2 % of caffeine, in comparison to 10 - 12 % of theophylline (administered dose) appears in urine in unmetabolized form. Most of the actions of methylxanthines, at least in part, have their origin in their anti-adenosine effects. Adenosine is an inhibitory autacoid in the CNS. It depresses cardiac function and dilates the coronary and cerebral vasculature by acting centrally. Methylxanthines act as selective adenosine antagonist.

Therapeutic Uses of Methylxanthines :

(i) Mainly as CNS-stimulant to treat drug-induced depressive states.

(ii) Theophylline is one of the most effective bronchodilating agent. It is used in the form of aminophylline in the treatment of bronchial asthma, chronic obstructive pulmonary disease and congestive heart failure.

(iii) Caffeine is sometimes combined with aspirin to neutralize headache.

(iv) Due to its constrictor action on cerebral blood vessels, caffine alongwith an ergot alkaloid may be used in the treatment of migraine.

Adverse effects of methylxanthines are mild and include nausea, emesis, restlessness, insomnia and seizures. Certain degree of tolerance and psychic dependence develops to beverages containing methylxanthines. Diazepam is the drug of choice to treat their toxicity symptoms.

27.7 CENTRAL STIMULANT SYMPATHOMIMETICS

The phenylethylamine derivatives with potent adrenergic activity, by virtue of structural features and physical properties, exert a significant effect on the CNS, which is useful in the treatment of various psychogenic disorders related to depressive states. Hence, they are also known as psychomotor stimulants. Amphetamine is the prototype drug from this series. However, due to the toxicity and tolerance liability these agents have been largely replaced by tricyclic antidepressants, MAO inhibitors and the derivatives of 2-benzylpiperidine and 2-phenylmorpholine.

Phenethylamine derivatives are generally prescribed in the management of obesity, narcolepsy, minimal brain dysfunction and in cases of mild depression. These agents exert their action through following mechanisms :

1. Inhibition of re-uptake mechanisms for several bioactive amines.
2. Enhancement of neuronal release of catecholamines.
3. Direct α-adrenergic receptor stimulation and
4. Inhibition of monoamino oxidase enzymes usually at higher concentrations.

The prototype amphetamine, combats drowsiness seen in narcolepsy and depresses the appetite. Its dextro-isomer (Dexedrine) is more potent CNS stimulant. A chemically dissimilar but possessing amphetamine like actions, is the drug methylphenidate. Both, amphetamine and methylphenidate are readily absorbed by oral route. The prototype amphetamine, may be metabolized in human to give norephedrine, para hydroxynorephedrine (which accounts for the tolerance developed after repeated amphetamine administration), phenyl acetone, benzoic acid and hippuric acid. A significant amount of unchanged drug also appears in the urine.

Since amphetamine is a base, in amphetamine toxicity, the chloride induced ionisation of amphetamine prevents its tubular reabsorption and thus accelerates its excretion through urine.

Table 27.2 : Sympathomimetics with CNS stimulant activity

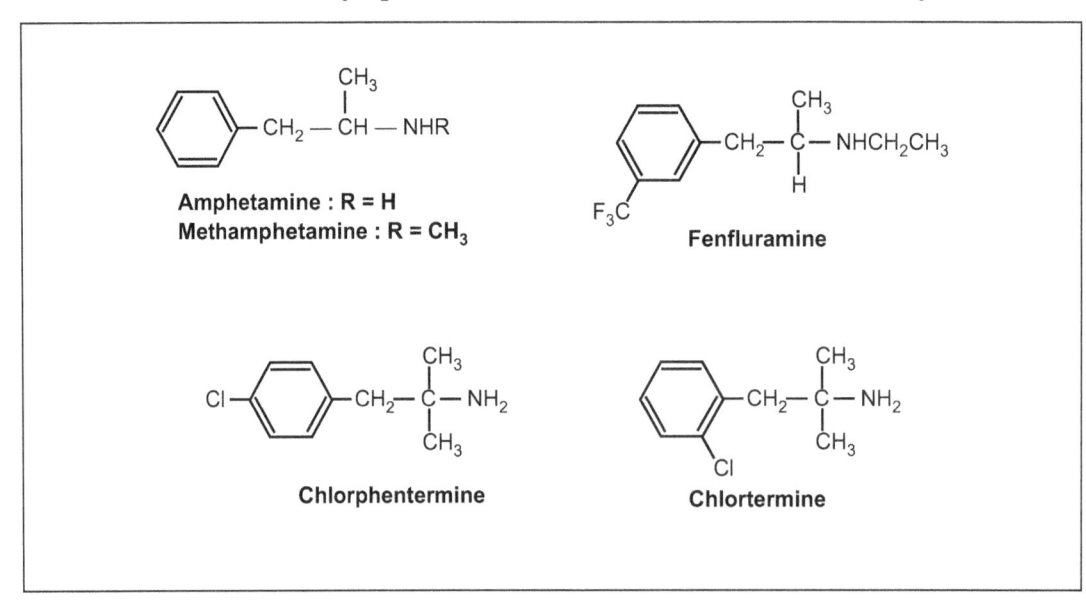

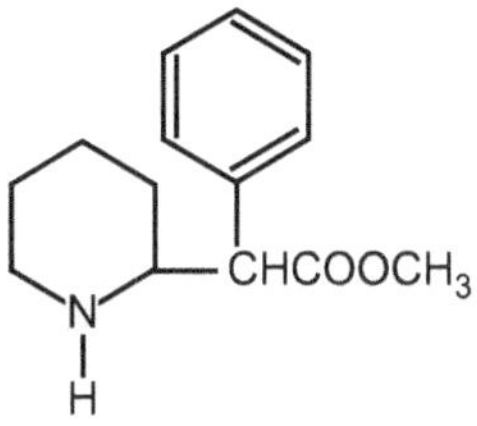

Methylphenidate

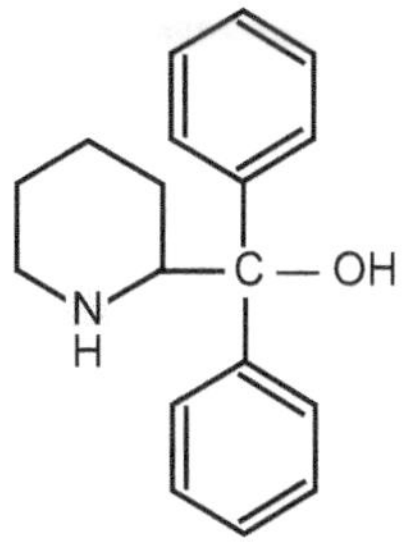

Pipradrol

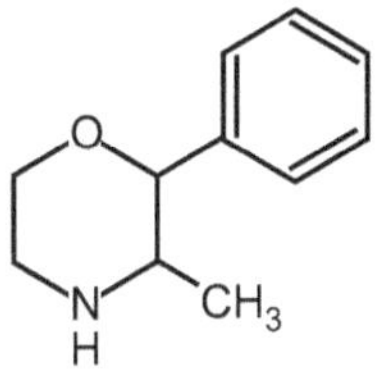

Phenmetrazine

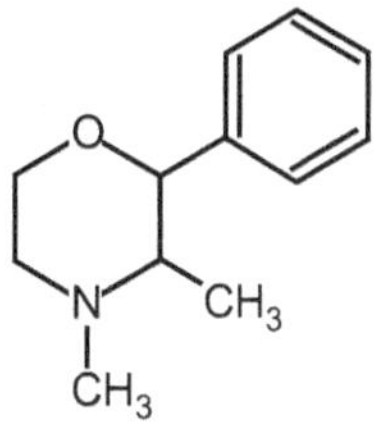

Phendimetrazine

Since amphetamine is a base, in amphetamine toxicity, chloride-induced ionization of amphetamine prevents its tubular reabsorption and thus accelerates its excretion through urine.

Methylphenidate is a mild CNS stimulant with more prominent effects on mental activity, due to which it is listed as a drug of abuse. Its principal metabolite is ritalinic acid, a product of ester-cleavage.

These agents are effective in the treatment of minimal brain dysfunction (hyperkinetic syndrome) which is a disease of childhood and of narcolepsy which is mainly characterized by sleepiness. Due to their appetite-reducing effect, they may sometimes be used in the treatment of obesity.

Amphetamine congeners, if used as anorexigenic (to decrease appetite), leads to insomnia and restlessness due to their CNS stimulant properties. Other adverse effects include, nervousness, irritability, anorexia and possibility of cardiac irregularities. They are reported to cause tolerance and physical dependence, if administered for prolonged period of time. They are contraindicated in patients with cardiovascular disease of any origin.

27.8 MISCELLANEOUS AGENTS

(1) Pemoline Magnesium :

Though structurally dissimilar, pemoline shares many of the pharmacological properties of methylphenidate. It is a useful drug in the treatment of minimal brain dysfunction (which is defined in 1963 by the Task Force of the National Institute of Blindness and Neurological diseases as a syndrome affecting "Children of near average or above average intelligence with mild to severe disabilities of learning or behavioural type of CNS origin").

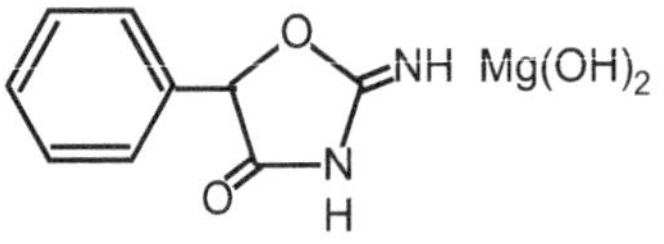

Pemoline magnesium

(2) Deanol Acetamidobenzoate :

It has been proposed that deanol penetrates the central nervous system where it serves as a precursor to choline and acetylcholine. The drug is considerably safe for use and is indicated in the treatment of a variety of mild depressive states and for alleviation of behaviour problems and learning difficulties (minimal brain dysfunction) of school-going children.

27.9 HALLUCINOGENS OR PSYCHODELICS OR PSYCHOTOMIMETICS

The word hallucinogenic (feeling of exhilaration or realistically erotic dreams) runs parallel in meaning with the word psychoses (i.e. psychotomimetics = mimicking of psychosis).

Psychotomimetics are the agents which induce temporary changes in mood, perception or behaviour that may result into vivid dreams, hallucination or nightmares.

These agents are classified mainly into :

1. True psychotomimetics : Examples include, phenylethyl amines, indole ethylamines and some miscellaneous compounds.

2. Psychodelics : These agents are highly effective in altering mood and perception and are used illegally for this purpose e.g. lysergic acid diethylamide, mescaline etc.

There is a state of heightened awareness of sensory input but a diminished control over what is experienced. Changes in sensory perception are a prominent features of drug action. The patient receives vivid visual illusions. A series of adrenomimetic responses occur. The LSD-like drugs bear CNS-stimulant action which makes it difficult for the patient to differentiate the boundaries of one object from another. In higher doses, convulsions may occur. All these effects are better represented by the term, "mind-expanding" drugs.

Examples of the series include LSD, psilocybin, psylocin, dimethyl tryptamine and diethyl tryptamine.

Mescaline is one of the alkaloids of peyote cactus, Lophophora williamsi. Chemically it resembles closely with epinephrine. It shares CNS-stimulant activity with LSD. The drug treatment is associated with usual side-effects like, nausea, vomitting and hyper-reflexia of limbs.

In general, all psychotomimetics exhibit the full range of psychic alterations (like psychic state, autonomic and somatomotor activities, metabolic effect and direct action on bronchi and uterus) with only quantitative differences. All these agents cross the blood brain and placental barriers. Many theories have been proposed to explain psychotomimetic effects.

Deanol acetamidobenzoate

1. Signs of sympathetic stimulation occur after the administration of lysergide which suggests that it may accelerate or induce the production of hallucinogenic metabolites from noradrenaline.

2. These agents may cause :

(a) changes in cerebral blood flow and permeability of cerebral capillaries,

(b) alterations in levels of adrenal corticoidal and thyroid hormones, or

(c) changes in synthesis or metabolism of serotonin, norepinephrine, acetylcholine or other potential transmitter in brain. For example, the raphe nuclei activity is governed by serotonergic neurons. The suppression of raphe neurons caused by LSD-like drugs, results into hallucinations during REM sleep. Thus, disturbed serotonin neuronal activity manifests itself as a hallucinatory experience.

(d) Cerebral funciton is extremely depedent on the utilisation of energy in the form of ATP. Psychotomimetics may disrupt cerebral energy production or utilization in such a fashion that it alters the behaviour.

Metabolism :

The psychotomimetic drugs after administration, are rapidly removed from the blood and distributed to various body tissues. The major metabolism takes place in liver but some detoxification of LSD is also reported to occur in muscle and brain. In general, hydroxylation followed by glucuronidation constitutes the fate of these agents.

Adverse Effects:

These include psychic toxicity, paranoia and confusion. Tolerance develops quite rapidly. Overdosage may result into a death of the patient due to respiratory depression. Cross-tolerance amongst various hallucinogens is also reported. These drugs do not produce physical dependence and naturally then, withdrawal symptoms.

(a) Indole derivatives :

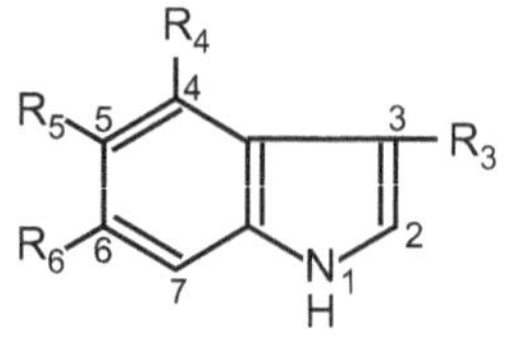

Name	R_3	R_4	R_5	R_6
1. Dimethyltryptamine	$(CH_2)_2N(CH_3)_2$	H	H	H
2. Diethyltryptamine	$(CH_2)_2N(C_2H_5)_2$	H	H	H
3. Bufotenine	$(CH_2)_2N(CH_3)_2$	H	OH	H
4. Psilocybin	$(CH_2)_2N(CH_3)_2$	$OPO(OH)_2$	H	H
5. Psilocin	$(CH_2)_2N(CH_3)_2$	OH	H	H
6. 6-hydroxydiethyl-tryptamine	$(CH_2)_2N(C_2H_5)_2$	H	H	OH
7. 5-Methoxydimethyl-tryptamine	$(CH_2)_2N(CH_3)_2$	H	OCH_3	H

(b) Carboline derivatives :

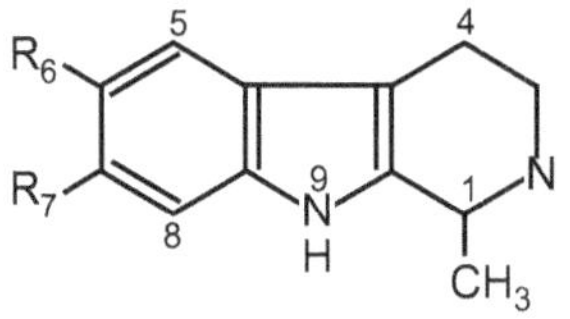

Name	R_6	R_7	Position of double bond
1. Harmine	H	CH_3O	1, 3
2. Harmaline	H	CH_3O	1
3. 6-Methoxyharmalan	CH_3O	H	1
4. 6-Methoxytetrahydroharman	CH_3O	H	–

(c) Polycyclic derivatives :

(i) Yohimbine and Ibogaine :

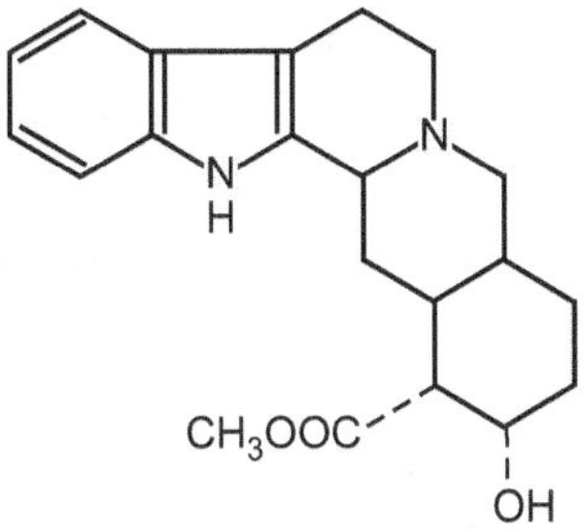

Yohimbine

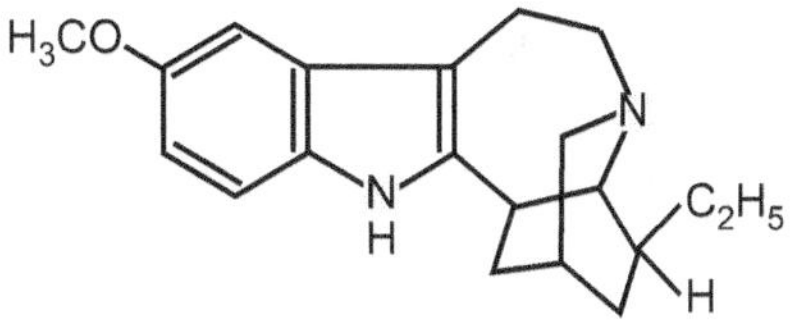

Ibogaine

(ii) Lysergic acid derivatives :

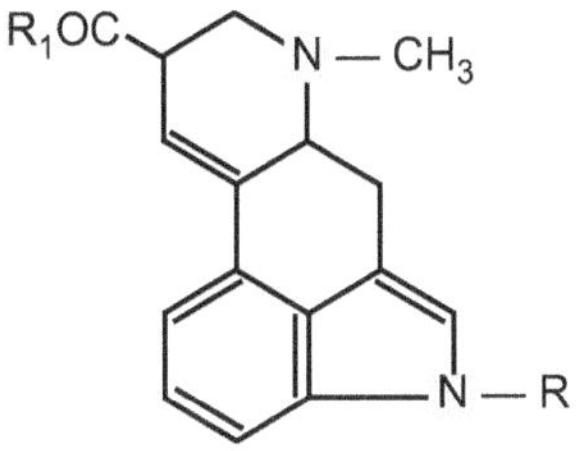

Name	R	R_1
1. d-Lysergic acid amide	H	NH_2
2. d-Lysergic acid ethylamide	H	NHC_2H_5
3. dl-Methyllysergic acid ethylamide	CH_3	NHC_2H_5
4. dl-Acetyllysergic acid ethylamide	$COCH_3$	NHC_2H_5
5. d-Lysergic acid dimethylamide	H	$N(CH_3)_2$
6. d-Lysergic acid diethylamide	H	$N(C_2H_5)_2$
7. dl-Methyllysergic acid diethylamide	CH_3	$N(C_2H_5)_2$
8. dl-Acetyllysergic acid diethylamide	$COCH_3$	$N(C_2H_5)_2$

(d) **Phencyclidine** : It is a psychotomimetic agent, previously tried for its anaesthetic effect. It causes delinking of the thoughts and hallucinations. It has anticholinergic activity and in CNS, it potentiates the dopaminergic responses in an indirect way.

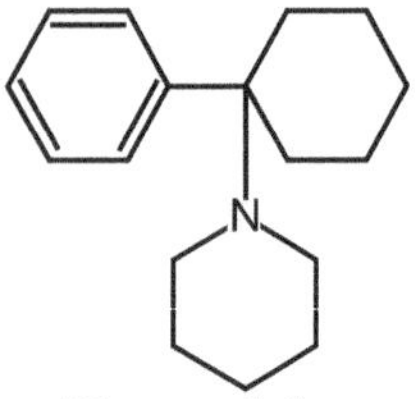

Phencyclidine

It is potentially dangerous and toxicity symptoms include, respiratory depression, motor seizures, cardiac arrest and coma.

Its structural relative, ketamine shares many of these effects and is used as an anaesthetic agent to produce dissociative anaesthesia. Diazepam is an effective antidote to control phencyclidine-induced seizures.

(e) Δ - nine - trans-tetrahydro-cannabinol (Δ^9 - THC) : Δ^9 - THC is the psychoactive constituent of marijuana which is obtained from the species, *Cannabis sativa*. It causes sleepiness, euphoria and hallucination and a tension-free sensation.

The cardiovascular effects include peripheral vasodilation and an increase in the heart rate.

In body, Δ^9 - THC is biotransformed to the active metabolite, 11-hydroxy- Δ^9 - THC which is converted into 8,11-dihydroxy - Δ^9 -THC, an inactive urinary metabolism.

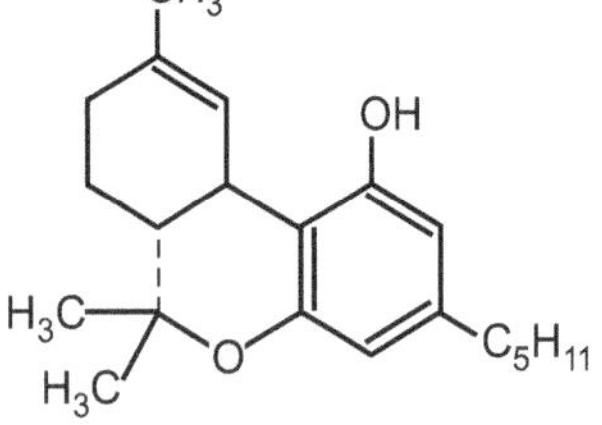

(–) Δ^9-trans-Tetrahydrocannabinol

Δ^9 - THC has bronchodilatory action and may be used in the treatment of asthma. It can also be used as an antiemetic and in the treatment of glaucoma.

(f) Miscellaneous hallucinogens : Many compounds, though not belonging to any definite family or a class, do exhibit hallucinogenic actions in man. Research is still continued to define the structure-activity relationship and molecular features essential for hallucinogenic activity.

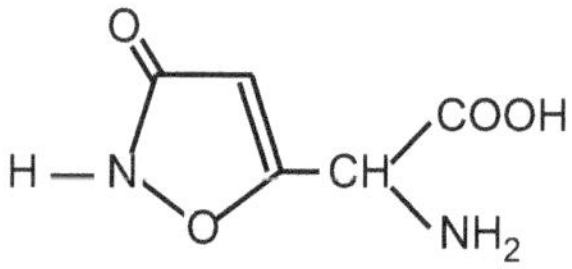

Ibotenic acid

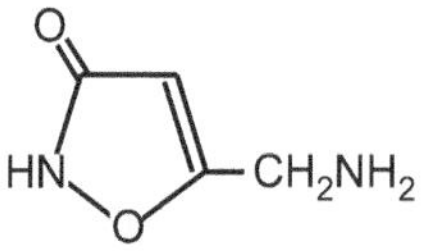

Muscimol

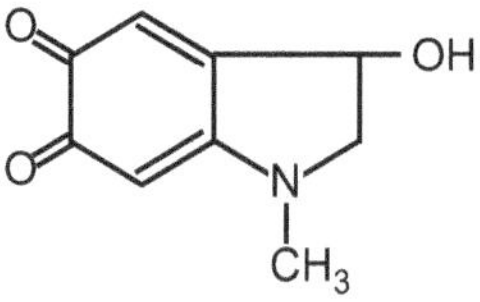

Adrenochrome

PSYCOTROPIC DRUGS

28.1 INTRODUCTION

Human brain is an extraordinarily-complex, highly co-ordinated and delicately functioning center for telecommunication, created yet ever. Various nerve tracts, of both monophasic and biphasic nature, smoothly carry out their assigned duty either in a restricted areas or by interconnecting various brain compartments and important centres of integration, amplification and implimentation. Both sensory and motor messages are carried out within a fraction of a second by super fast impulse trains through these nerve tracts. These impulse-trains are driven, in part or to complete distance by a variety of neuro chemical transmitters. Synaptic cleft is a halting station where the same neurotransmitter may continue to drive the impulse train or other neurotransmitter may take over the charge. Acetylcholine, noradrenaline, dopamine, GABA and serotonin are the major neurotransmitters whose balanced interrelations in brain, constitute a normal healthy mind. Disfunctioning in any one of these systems may cause an interference in the performance of other transmitter system resulting into emotional, behavioural and motor abnormalities, which are collectively known as psychiatric reactions. At some occasions, under certain circumstances, even a normal man also diplays some signs of 'diseases of mind' due to spontaneous but temporary fluctuations in the interrelationship of these biogenic amines. Hence, if we learn some basic information about these biogenic amines, it will be both, convenient and beneficial for us to understand the mode of action of psychotropic drugs.

(a) Acetylcholine :

It is an important mediator in cortex, reticular formation, limbic system and basal ganglia. It regulates the sensory functions, motor activity, a short term memory and classical phase of sleep.

(b) Noradrenaline :

It has been discovered in reticular formation, hypothalamus, medulla oblongata and locus coeruleus. Beside thermo regulation, it governs memory, paradoxical sleep, adaptation capacity, motor activity and vegetative symptoms.

(c) Dopamine :

Unlike acetylcholine and noradrenaline (which are excitatory neurotransmitters), dopamine, GABA and serotonin have inhibitory roles to play on in vivo screen of the brain. Dopamine is an important neurotransmitter in limbic system and basal ganglia (which control the posture and muscle movement). It regulates motor activity, memory and emotional tone of the person.

(d) Serotonin:

It is present mainly in Raphe nuclei, limbic system, hypothalamus and spinal cord. It is involved in the control of sensory function, emotional tonus, learning habit, sleep pattern, and thermoregulation.

(e) GABA :

It is the principle inhibitory neurotransmitter present in the brain that relaxes and cools down overall brain activity. Most of the CNS-depressant agents, for example, bring out their actions due to prolongation and potentiation of central GABA-ergic responses.

The relative importance of these neurotransmitters in various mental illnesses, varies from species to species. Psychosis involves a disorder of higher functions and thought process. It involves abnormalities of mental, behavioural and emotional processess and is characterized by dementia, delirium, delusions, memory disturbances and hallucinations. Besides psychoactive agents, some drugs from the classes like, cardiac glycosides, antihypertensive, sedatives, steroids and CNS-stimulants possess psychiatric side-effects. Before dealing with the drugs used in the treatment of psychotic disorders, let us briefly summarise, the characterstics of individual disorder. These diseases of mind can be categorised as under :

(i) Psychoses result due to chronic thinking and emotional impairment associated with auditory hallucinations. The most common form of psychoses is schizophrenia which means 'to split mind'. These disorders retard the intellectual and emotional growth of the patient. Antipsychotic agents nulify these discrepancies and bring the patient to the normal condition.

(ii) The affective psychoses include endogenous depression, acute mania and manic-depressive states. Depression is associated as a symptom with many psychiatric disorders. Mania is an exactly opposite condition than the depression. It is characterised by CNS excitement, euphoria, insomina, slurred speech, irritability and an increase in physical activity. Lithium salts and antipsychotic agents can be employed in the treatment of manic disorders. In it's milder form, mania is often termed as hypomania.

(iii) When recurrent episodes of depression occur alongwith mania in a bipolar fashion, the condition is termed as major affective or manic-depressive disorder. Main symptoms include, insomnia, anorexia, worry, sadness, decreased physical and mental activity, confusion and alternative waves of excitation followed by depression. The treatment involves the use of antidepressant drugs or a shock treatment. Unlike amphetamine, these antidepressant drugs do not produce CNS excitation in normal subjects.

(iv) Neuroses are less severe psychiatric disorder having many things common with psychosis. Symptoms of neuroses include anxiety, tension, depression, thinking and emotional impairment.

28.2 CLASSIFICATION

Various psychotropic drugs, depending upon their selectivity of action in different diseases of mind, can be divided into three major categories, namely

(i) Antipsychotic agents

(ii) Antimanic agents

(iii) Antidepressant drugs.

28.3 ANTIPSYCHOTIC AGENTS (Major Tranquillizers or Neuroleptics)

These drugs are used in the treatment of psychoses. Clinically these agents counteract hallucinations and delusions and facilitate the social adjustment of the patient by reducing dopaminergic activity in the CNS. These agents have their effectiveness due to

(a) A calming effect to reduce hyper-activity (tranquillizing).

(b) A reduction and meaningful co-ordination of nerve impulse propogation (neuroleptic) and

(c) A reduction in dopaminergic hyperactivity in specifically midbrain region.

Antipsychotics or neuroleptics, are the most frequently used terms for this class. The drugs from this class, are used primarily for the treatment of schizophrenia and mania though many of them have anxiolytic actions too. The prominent symptoms of schizophrenic patients (like, delusions, hallucinations, immobility, perceptual disturbance and thinking and behavioural impairment) can be treated well by these drugs. While haloperidol and chlorpromazine can be effectively used in the treatment of mania alongwith lithium salt.

Due to the wide structural variations, it is not possible to link different classes of antipsychotic agents on the basis of a single rational concept. However in terms of physical properties, they are found to be extremely lipophilic, highly surface active substances that accumulate readily at cell-membranes. Their ability to stabilize membranes or inhibit certain membrane bound enzyme is governed by their conformational and steriochemical factors.

In addition to neuroleptic activity, these drugs have a bunch of other clinically useful activities which include, antiemetic, antipyretic, antihistaminic, gangliolytic, and ability to prolong and potentiate the effects of analgesic and CNS depressant drugs.

Serotonin and noradrenaline are the mediators of thermoregulation in the hypothalamus. They lower down the body temperature probably by their antiserotonin and adrenolytic effects in hypothalamus. Due to same reason, they may increase appetite resulting into weight gain. Certain side effects (miosis, hypotension) result due to their antagonistic effect at α-adrenoceptor sites. Their antiemetic effect is due to the blockade of dopamine receptors in chemoreceptor trigger zone of medulla. The most serious side-effect is depression which arises probably due to the depletion of serotoninergic neurones in the CNS. Due to their surface active nature, they can easily stabilize nerve-membranes, resulting into a local anaesthetic action, especially at high concentration. This property imparts them an ability to exert an antiarrhythmic effect on heart. Due to the sedative effect, these drugs normalize sleep irregularities seen in many psychoses. Various antipsychotic agents have cholinergic blocking (dry mouth, constipation, urinary retention) and adrenolytic activity. Beside this, these agents influence the rate of secretion of various endocrine glands due to their action on hypothalamus and pituitary regions.

The major side-effects are shared by all neuroleptic agents. These side-effects are the extension of their pharmacological actions. These include –

(a) Akathesia :

This is an inability to lie or to sit due to motor restlessness.

(b) Dyskinetics:

Neuroleptic agents primarily act by antagonising the activation of dopamine receptors on post-synaptic neurons in the limbic system. Upon chronic administration of neuroleptic agents, these dopamine receptors become supersensitive due to prolonged blockade. This results into dyskinesia which is characterized by rhythmic involuntary muscle movements occuring over face, mouth and tongue.

(c) Dystonic Reactions :

They involve impairement of muscular tone resulting into decrease in spontaneous motor activity.

(d) Extrapyramidal Symptoms :

Due to such a high risk of these side-effects, neuroleptic agents are rarely indicated for neuroses.

28.4 MECHANISM OF ACTION OF NEUROLEPTIC AGENTS

(1) In 1958, Carlsson suggested that dopamine, besides a precursor of noradrenaline and adrenaline, might also function independently, as a neuro-transmitter in the CNS.

(2) The highest concentration of dopamine have been found in the thalamus, hypothalamus, basal ganglia and the limbic portions of the forebrain.

Dopamine usually has a depressant action, on the basal ganglia (i.e., caudate nucleus, putamen and globus pallidus), which are involved in the control of posture and involuntary (extrapyramidal) aspects of movement. In schizophrenia, there may be a state of functional overactivity of dopamine in cortex or in limbic system. While in mania, there may be an excess of monoamines in cortical region.

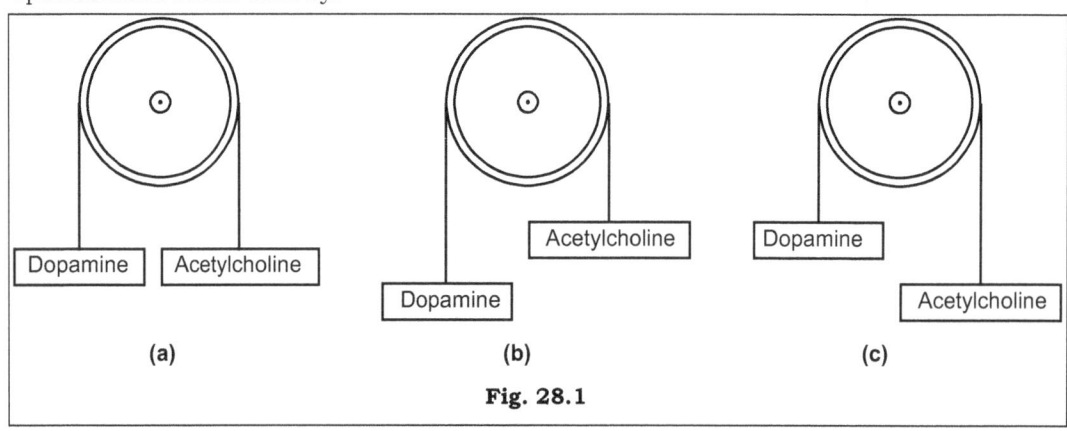

Fig. 28.1

(4) In the control of emotional responses, the hypothalamus is closely associated with the reticular system, the latter incorporates a balanced complex of excitatory (ACh) and inhibitory (dopamine) components. Dopamine exerts its central actions by activation of adenylate cyclase enzymes. Antipsychotic agents antagonise the actions of dopamine by inhibiting the activation of adenylate cyclase enzyme.

(5) There is an evidence which suggests that schizophrenia is associated with the presence of greater than normal amounts of dopamine (inhibitory component) at central synapses. This results into the hyper activation of adenylate cyclase by dopamine in the limbic system.

(6) The antipsychotic drugs e.g., chlorpromazine acts by

(a) Increasing metabolic rate of dopamine,

(b) Blocking dopamine receptors.

While reserpine-like drugs cause depletion of dopaminergic neurons. This results in an increase in concentration of excitatory component (ACh) and decrease in the concentration of inhibitory component (dopamine). Thus, all the antipsychotic drugs increase the turnover of dopamine in the brain.

(7) Dual dopaminergic-cholinergic hypothesis, (picturized in figure 28.1) in which the blockade of dopamine receptors by antipsychotic agents, shifts the balance (a), in the favour of ACh (c). The predominance or over activation of cholinergic interneurons leads to an increase in extrapyramidal effects (posture and the involuntary aspects of movements). Hence, all antipsychotic drugs are always associated with a varying degree of extrapyramidal effects. Exception is clozapine which has clearly antipsychotic and has little extrapyramidal action. Antiparkinsonism agents are often given alongwith antipsychotic agents to prevent the appearance of extrapyramidal symptoms. The extrapyramidal effects appear due to the blockade of dopamine receptors in the corpus striatum whereas blockade of dopamine receptors in the limbic and frontal cortices is responsible for antipsychotic effect. Hence antiparkinsonian agents block extra-pyramidal effects by acting selectively at corpus striatum and without interfering with antipsychotic efficacy. Similarly drugs that combine dopamine blocking and anticholinergic properties are the efficacious antipsychotics with low extrapyramidal effects.

(8) Beside this, some of the antipsychotics may also inhibit cholinergic and adrenergic transmission, as well as interfere with the regulation of cyclic nucleotide phosphodiesterase by Ca^{++} - calmodulin.

Thus, all neuroleptic agents bring about

(a) Psychomotor slowing

(b) Emotional quieting and

(c) Affective indifference and may be indicated occassionly in the treatment of depression or severe anxitey. They are best classified in terms of their chemical structures into

(i) Phenothiazines

(ii) Rauwolfia alkaloids

(iii) Butyrophenones

(iv) Miscellaneous agents

28.5 PHENOTHIAZINES

These compounds are chemically constituted by a lipophilic, linearly fused tricyclic system having a hydrophilic basic amino alkyl chain. The majority of aminoalkylated tricyclic compounds with a central '6' membered ring, produce predominantly neuroleptic effects. They do not cause anesthetic effect. However their ability to promote sleep and lack of interest in what was going on was found to be beneficial, in the treatment of psychiatric patient. Presently more than 30 phenothiazines are being used in various psychiatric conditions.

Chlorpromazine, the prototype drug of this series is most widely used antipsychotic agent. Since it is the most extensively studied agent from this class, for pharmacological details, it has been choosen as a representative of this class.

Synthesized at Rhone Poulenc Laboratories in France, chlorpromazine was first introduced into clinical practice in 1951 by Laborit. Beside antipsychotic effect, it has antihistaminic, antiadrenergic, anticholinergic, antidopaminergic and antiserotoninergic actions. Due to these multi antiautacoidal actions it has been marketed under the name, Largactil, which means large (number of) actions. These actions help it to play the role of antipsychotic, antiemetic, antipyretic, antihypertensive, motordepressive or local anaesthetic agent to varying degrees. Beside these actions, by depression of the activity of reticular activating system, it prolongs and potentiates the actions of analgesics and CNS depressants. Due to accumulation into the cell-membrane, phenothiazines cause a depressant effect on certain membrane bound enzymes.

Chemistry :

The potency of antipsychotic phenothiazines is mainly influenced by both, the location and nature of the substitution on tricyclic nucleus. For example, presence of Cl or OCH_3 group at position 2, enhances muscle relaxant activity while substitution of a trifluoromethyl, or chloro group at 2-position and replacement of dimethylamino group with a piperazino group in R_{10} substituent, greatly increase antipsychotic, antiemetic and local anaesthetic activities of the compound.

Table 28.1 : Clinically useful thioxanthenes

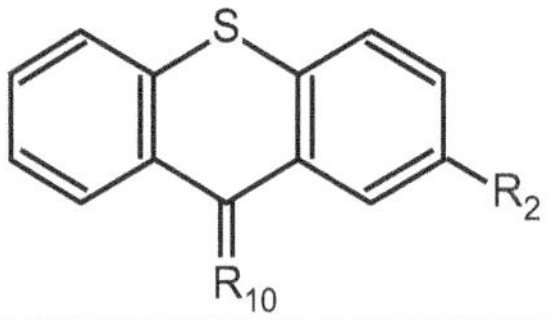

Generic name	R_2	R_{10}
Chlorprothixene	Cl	$-CH(CH_2)_2N(CH_3)_2$
Thiothixene	$-SO_2 N (CH_3)_2$	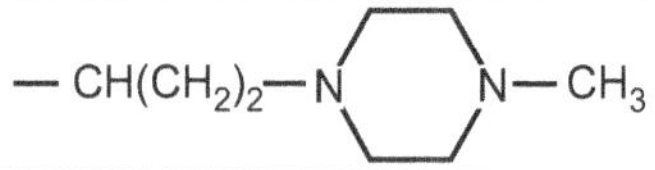 $-CH(CH_2)_2-N\underset{}{\frown}N-CH_3$
Clopenthixol	Cl	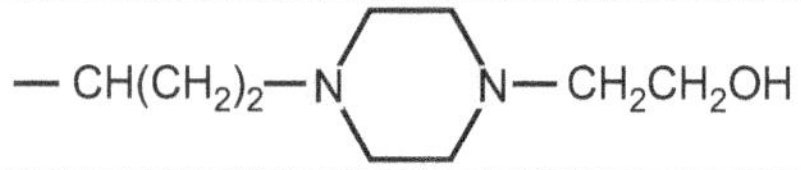 $-CH(CH_2)_2-N\underset{}{\frown}N-CH_2CH_2OH$

Table 28.2 : Clinically useful phenothiazines

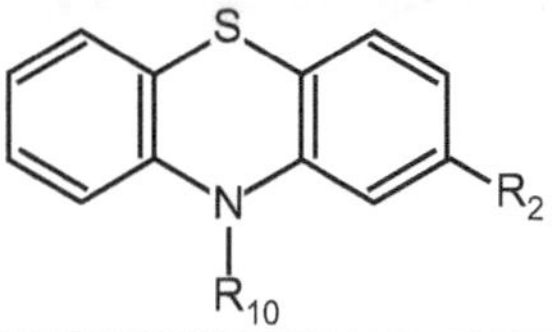

Generic name	R₂	R₁₀
(A) Propyl dialkylamino side chain :		
(i) Promazine	H	$-(CH)_3N(CH_3)_2$
(ii) Chlorpromazine	Cl	$-(CH_2)_3N(CH_3)_2$
(iii) Triflupromazine	CF_3	$-(CH_2)_3N(CH_3)_2$
(B) Alkyl piperidyl side-chain :		
(i) Thioridazine	SCH_3	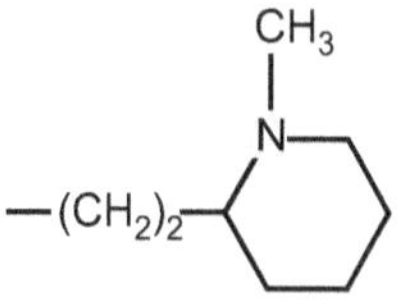 $-(CH_2)_2-$ (2-methylpiperidyl)
(ii) Mesoridazine	$O \leftarrow SCH_3$	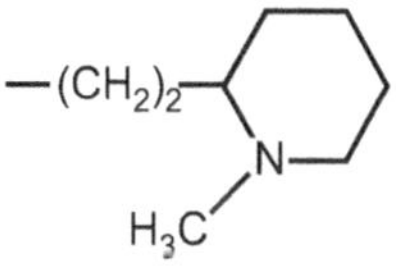 $-(CH_2)_2-$ (N-methylpiperidyl)
(C) Propyl piperazine side-chain :		
(i) Prochlorperazine	Cl	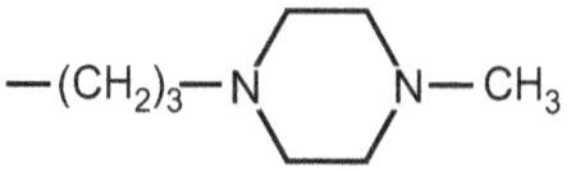 $-(CH_2)_3-N\underset{}{\frown}N-CH_3$
(ii) Trifluperazine	CF_3	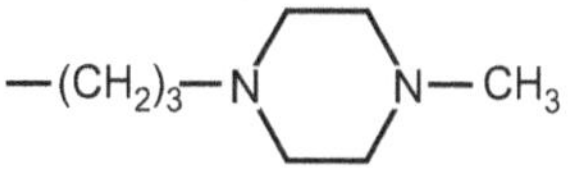 $-(CH_2)_3-N\underset{}{\frown}N-CH_3$
(iii) Perphenazine	Cl	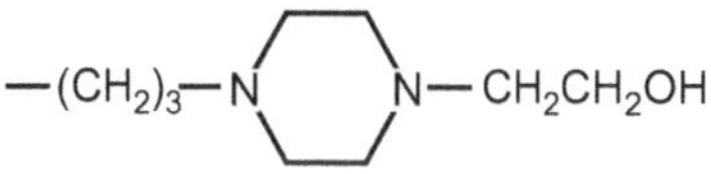 $-(CH_2)_3-N\underset{}{\frown}N-CH_2CH_2OH$
(iv) Fluphenazine	CF_3	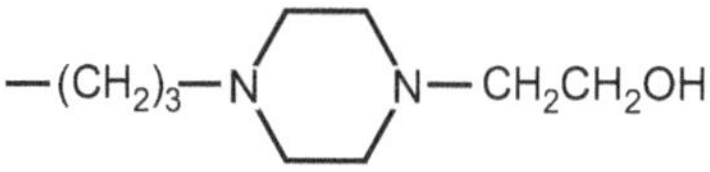 $-(CH_2)_3-N\underset{}{\frown}N-CH_2CH_2OH$
(v) Carphenazine	$\underset{\parallel}{O}$ $-C\ CH_2\ CH_3$	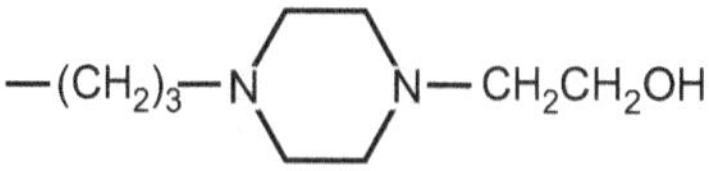 $-(CH_2)_3-N\underset{}{\frown}N-CH_2CH_2OH$

The piperazine phenothiazines may be esterified with long chain fatty acids to produce slowly absorbed, long-acting, lipophilic pro-drugs. For example,

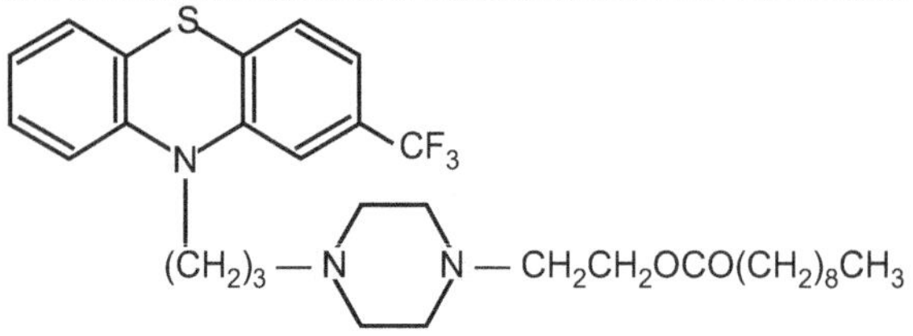

Fluphenazine decanoate

Thioxanthene series result when the nitrogen atom at 10 position in phenothiazine structure, is replaced by carbon atom and a side chain is attached to C_{10} by a double bond. For example, chlorprothixene is a structural relative of chlorpromazine.

The introduction of piperazine ring in the side chain at 10th position in both, phenothiazine or thioxanthene series, leads to an increase in potency of antipsychotic activity as well as in intensity of extrapyramidal effects.

In Both the Series :

(a) A three carbon atom separation between position 10 and amino nitrogen atom of the side-chain, imparts antipsychotic activity.

(b) When an ethylene chain is interposed between position 10 and amino nitrogen atom of the side-chain, it results into increase in anticholinergic or antihistaminic property, while.

(c) Further increase in this connecting bridge, is associated with diminished anti-psychotic activity.

(d) In all the clinical useful examples, the amino nitrogen atom is always tertiary. In body, this 3° nitrogon may be converted (through metabolism) to either 2° or 1° size nitrogen, in order to increase hydrophilicity (and hence the rate of excretion) of the compound.

(e) Thioridazine is the most potent antimuscarinic agent.

These agents have antiemetic action primarily due to the suppression of central dopaminergic stimulation of chemoreceptor trigger zone. Chlorpromazine, prochlorperazine, promethazine, triflupromazine and perphenazine may be selectively used for antiemesis purpose. Surprisingly enough, thioridazine has poor antiemetic activity.

As we know, the extrapyramidal effects are always associated with the use of neuroleptic agents, due to overactivation of cholinergic interneurons in corpus striatum. To prevent the appeareance of these effects, an effort to incorporate anticholinergic fraction into phenothiazine nucleus was made. Some quaternary salts of certain phenothiazines have been prepared. This modification, no doubt, results into suppresion of extrapyramidal effects but it fails to protect the original antipsychotic activity too.

Pharmacology :

(i) CNS : The prominent CNS effects of chlorpromazine include, behavioural activation, detachment from the surrounding, antianxiety action, and normalization of muscle tone. The frequency and intensity of hallucinations tend to decrease. For example, most of the pharmacological actions of LSD-like hallucinogens are antagonised by chlorpromazine. Anorexogenic effect is observed. Tolerance to sedative like effect develops during due cource of time. Unlike other phenothiazines, prochlorperazine and fluphenazine are devoid of sedative effects.

(ii) CVS : Chlorpromazine has a direct depressant action on the myocardium. A mild hypotension and reflex tachycardia can be seen due to α-adrenoreceptor blockade at peripheral region.

(iii) Hormone release : Chlorpromazine inhibits the release of growth hormone. The reduction in the concentration of gonadotropins, estrogens and progesterone may result into amenorrhea.

(iv) Miscellaneous effects : These include,

(a) Chlorpromazine may cause diuresis, probably by inhibition of the release of antiduretic hormone.

(b) Chlorpromazine interferes with energy yielding processes in the body.

Absorption, Metabolism and Excretion :

Chlorpromazine is well absorbed from GIT but slightly in erratic fashion. Due to the high lipophilicity, it is extensively bound to plasma proteins or accumulates into various cell-membranes in the body. It can easily cross the placenta and can enter fetal circulation.

Phenothiazines are primarily metabolized by oxidative processes, resulting into introduction of hydroxyl groups at 3 or 7 position of phenothiazine ring. These inactivated hydroxylated metabolites are excreted in urine, mainly in the form of glucuronide conjugates. For example, chlorpromazine appears in the urine, in the form of glucuronides of 7 hydroxylated metabolite. During metabolism, the 3° amino nitrogen of the side-chain may be converted to 1° nitrogen. In thioxanthenes, sulfoxide formation is a prominent route of metabolism.

These metabolites and their conjugates are excreted out mainly through urine and faeces.

Adverse Reactions :

Phenothiazines are remarkably safe drugs having their lethal dose extraordinarily high. The usual adverse reactions include, dry mouth, constipation, urinary retension, hypothermia, palpitation, mild hypotension, and extrapyramidal effects. Thioridazine has greater antimuscarinic action (and hence low tendency to produce extrapyramidal effects).

28.6 RAUWOLFIA ALKALOIDS

Reserpine and its analogues (rescinnamine, deserpidine) had been widely used in Hindu medicines, in the treatment of serious mental and emotional disorders which are characterized by varying degree of CNS excitement. They are less effective than phenothiazines and are rarely used for this purpose. Today, reserpine and related compounds are used mainly as antihypertensives or in cases where a combined antihypertensive and sedative effect is desired.

Table 28.3 : Clinically useful butyrophenones

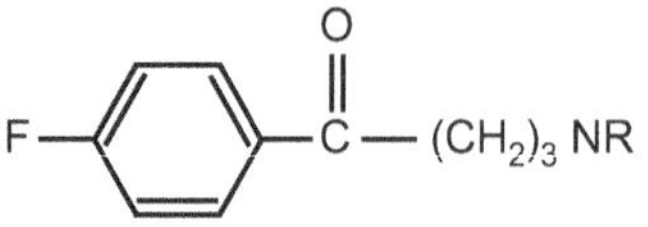 Butyrophenones: F—C₆H₄—CO—(CH₂)₃—NR	
(a) Haloperidol NR 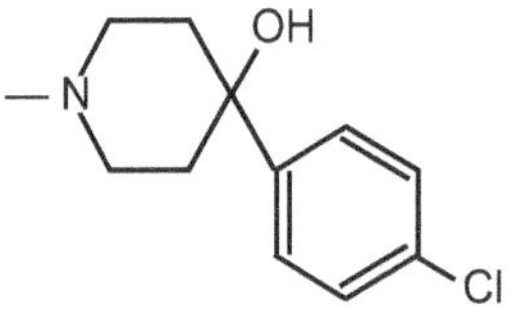 = piperidine with OH and 4-chlorophenyl	**(d) Trifluperidol** NR 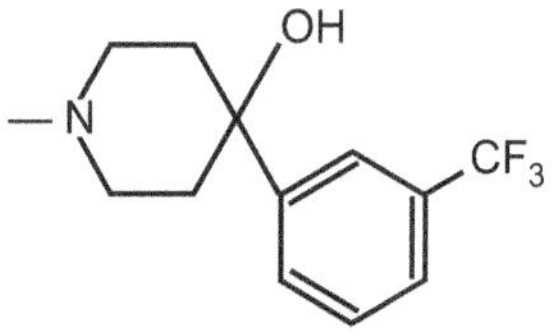 = piperidine with OH and 3-CF₃-phenyl
(b) Benperidol NR 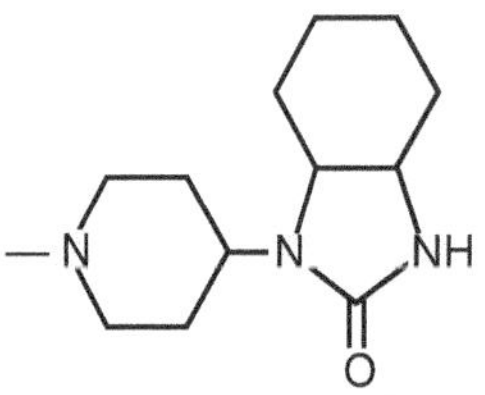 = piperidine linked to benzimidazolinone	**(f) Paraperidide (Amiperone)** NR 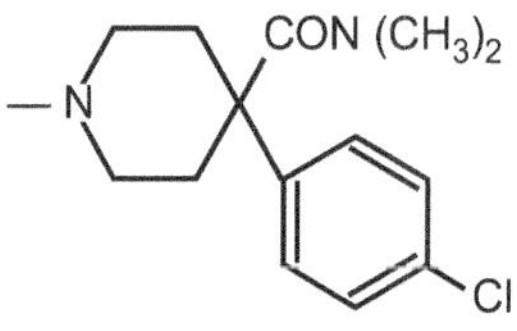 = piperidine with CON(CH₃)₂ and 4-chlorophenyl
(c) Droperidol NR 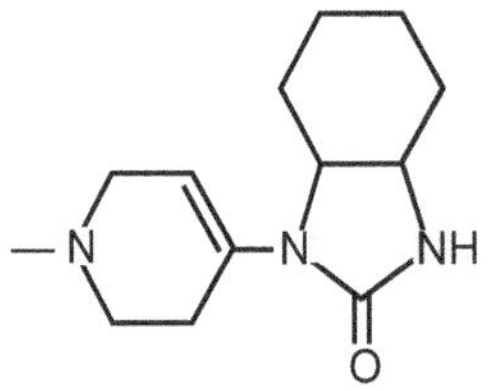 = tetrahydropyridine linked to benzimidazolinone	**(g) Spiroperidol** NR 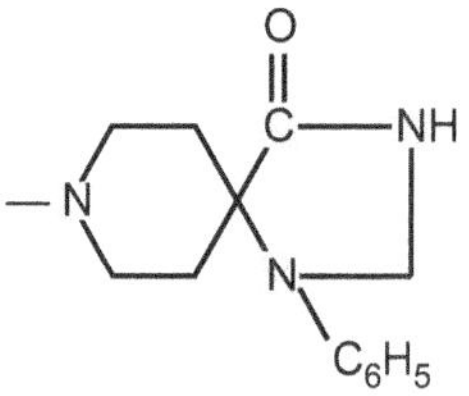 = spiro piperidine with phenyl-substituted imidazolidinone

Reserpine was first isolated and identified in 1950, from extracts of Rauwolfia serpentina. Its pharmacologic effects are due to its ability to cause depletion of monoamine (catecholamines GABA, histamine, serotonin) neurotransmitters from their storage sites. This action is exerted at both central and peripheral nerve terminals.

The depletion of catecholamines results into exposure of the organ to unopposed parasympathetic nervous system. This is reflected in the association of bradycardia, hypotension and constriction of pupil, with the use of reserpine.

Reserpine exerts hypothermia through its action over hypothalamus. It also lowers down threshold for the appearence of seizures. Its antipsychotic action is mainly due to its ability to cause depletion of dopamine from the neurones in the brain.

The metabolism of reserpine involves an enzymatic cleavage of the molecule into trimethoxy benzoate, and methyl reserpate. Adverse reactions of reserpine includes, salivation, insomnia, diarrhoea, vivid dreams, depression, hypotension and bradycardia.

28.7 BUTYROPHENONES

A number of compounds from a series of fluorobutyrophenones were found to be effective in the treatment of major psychoses, during structure-activity studies on analgetics of meperidine analogues. Haloperidol stands as a prototype of this series, whose antipsychotic properties were first discovered by Janseen in 1958. Butyrophenones are quite different from phenothiazines in structure, but possess pharmacological actions, uses and adverse effects, similar to phenothiazines. They differ from phenothiazines in following points.

(a) They have a tendency to cause insomnia.

(b) They do not cause postural hypotension.

(c) No risk of jaundice upon chronic administration.

(d) They have less pronounced antimuscarinic and adrenolytic actions.

(e) They enjoy longer duration of action due to relatively low rate of metabolism.

Like phenothiazines, they provoke extrapyramidal effects upon chronic administration. They undergo metabolism primarily through N-dealkylation. The inactive metabolites may be excreted in the urine in the form of conjugates of glucuronic acid. Due to low rate of metabolism haloperidol has more prolonged action. Its metabolites are excreted mainly through bile and urine. Besides its neuroleptic activity, haloperidol can block hallucinogenic actions of LSD and mescaline.

Trifluperidol is more potent antipsychotic agent. While droperidol, a short acting tetrahydropyridine derivative, is mainly used in anaesthesia. It can also be given parenterally to control acute psychiatric reactions.

Butyrophenones are commonly used drugs in psychiatry and veternary medicines.

28.8 MISCELLANEOUS AGENTS

Various compounds which are structurally distinct from the phenothiazines and from butyrophenones have been successfully used in the treatment of major psychoses. These include dihydroindolones (e.g. molindone), dibenzoxazepines (e.g. loxapine), dibenzodiazepines (e.g. clozapine), diphenylbutyl-piperidines (e.g. pimozide). Carbamazepine combined with haloperidol has shown good neuroleptic activity with lesser incidence of side-effects.

(a) Molindone :

Molindone and oxypertine are the dihydroindolones which have moderate antipsychotic activity. Molindone is rapidly absorbed after oral administration. In liver it is extensively metabolized to inactive products which are excreted in urine.

Adverse reactions include, skin rashes, sedation, mild hypotension, reflex tachycardia and extrapyramidal symptoms.

(b) Loxapine :

It is a useful agent in the treatment of schizophrenia and belongs to dibenzoxazepine class. Upon oral administration, it is readily absorbed and rapidly distributed in the body. Liver is the principal site for its metabolism. Its inactive metabolites are excreted through urine. It causes less severe sedation and extrapyramidal symptoms are also less pronounced.

Adverse reactions include, mild hypotension, photosensitivity, dryness of mouth, constipation, urinary retention and lowering of seizure threshold.

(c) Clozapine :

It is an example of dibenzodiazepines which, like dibenzoxazepines, structurally resemble with imipramine-like antidepresants. Clozapine is an antipsychotic agent with high degree of antimuscarinic activity (which accounts for extremely low incidences of extrapyramidal symptoms). It is an excellent example where antipsychotic activity is clearly dissociated from extrapyramidal effects. Clozapine has a multiple receptor interactions which include action at muscarinic, α-noradrenergic and histaminergic receptors. Fluperlapine is a new antipsychotic that is structurally and biologically quite similar to clozapine.

Unfortunately, clinical use of clozapine was paralyzed by incidence of blood dyscrasias, and especially agranulocytosis.

(d) Pimozide:

It is an effective antipsychotic agent from the class, diphenylbutylpiperidine which has close structural resemblance with butyrophenones. Pimozide analogues are highly potent and long-acting antipsychotic agents.

(e) Propranolol :

It's ability to block serotonin function in the areas of CNS controlling behaviour, qualifies it to be used in the treatment of schizophrenia. There is a possibility that dopaminergic mechanisms may be interlinked with serotonergic functions. In addition it also exerts nonspecific membrane stabilization action.

28.9 ANTIMANIC AGENTS

Mania or psychotic excitement is thought to be caused by excessive activity of monoamine neurotransmitters in the brain. The excitement is often accompanied by fluctuations in the mood and behaviour of the patient. Cade published the first report about the use of lithium salts (mood stabilizing agents) in the treatment of mania, in 1949. Lithium carbonate is the most effective drug currently used in the treatment of mania and manic-depressive disorders. It is highly specific for the manias; normalizes mood and minimizes thinking and motor behaviour without causing sedation. It is also effective in depressive states which are not associated with manias. Lithium carbonate however remains ineffective in the treatment of schizophrenia. In contrast to this, antipsychotic agents like chlorpromazine or haloperidol can be used alongwith lithium carbonate to constitute a short-term treatment of mania.

Lithium Carbonate :

Lithium is usually taken in the form of its carbonate salt. Upon oral administration, absorption occurs rapidly. Lithium does not bind to plasma proteins and gets uniformly distributed in the body. It is excreted almost quatitatively in unchanged form through the urine. Due to the delayed onset (6 - 10 days) of action, the acute manic attacks can be controlled by using phenothiazine or butyrophenone antipsychotic agent.

Lithium brings about its antimanic action by exerting diversified effects upon monoamine neurotransmitter. These include :

(a) Decreases the release of norepinephrine from the presynaptic terminals.

(b) Most of the norepinephrine is then, destroyed within the neurones.

(c) Enhances norepinephrine reuptake processes in the synaptic cleft and minimizes its concentaration within the synapse.

(d) It reduces both, the release and action of dopamine.

(e) It inhibits the functioning of adenylate cyclase enzyme and thus normalise the overactive norepinephrinergic neurones in the brain. This is the basis of its antimanic effect. While its effectiveness in the treatment of depressive states, may be related to its ability to modify synthesis, release or action of dopamine.

By decreasing the release of norepinephrine (catecholamine is presumed to increase during manic attacks) lithium reduces motor activity, diminishes euphoria and acts against insomnia. As far as CNS is concerned, it has actions opposite to those of the tricyclic antidepressants. While lithium is effective in an acute manic attack, neuroleptic agents are more preferred in the treatment of severe manic attacks.

Due to the inhibition of the action of antidiuretic hormone, its administration may cause polyuria and polydipsia, due to alteration in the electrolyte metabolism.

Lithium is a safe drug provided, a close watch on the blood level is kept. Occasional side-effects which usually occur, include, GIT discomforts, abdominal cramps, headache, muscular weakness, muscle twitches, tremors, ataxia, slurred speech, blurred vision, polyuria, polydipsia, mental confusion, insomnia and weight gain. These symptoms occur during first 2 to 4 weeks of therapy and disappear there after. In a few cases, lowering of the dose is required.

Lithium is contraindicated in renal disease, decompensated heart pathology and in early pregnancy.

It has been reported that verapamil, a calcium antagonist is effective in acute manic attacks. Other calcium antagonist, like, nifedipine may also have antimanic properties.

28.10 ANTIDEPRESSANTS

Depression is an intense normal response but usually of relatively brief duration to loss and disappointment. It may either appear itself as an illness or as a prominent feature of several mood disorders (affective disorders). A depressed person experiences disturbances of sleep, appetite motor activity and sex drive. Usually it results due to an increased metabolism (with diminished synthesis) of monoamine neurotransmitters in brain. This is accompanied by related imbalances in functioning of other neurohumoral systems. Short-term use of antianxiety drugs rather than antidepressant is usually effective in cases of moderate depression associated with anxiety. While lithium salts or antidepressant agents are generally reserved for more severe disorders of mood. Antidepressant agents affect only the pathologically depressed emotional sphere. Some of them influence mainly the depressed motor activity. The subject then feels more energetic, less sleepy and more fresh. They also elevate the depressed mood and hence also called as mood elevators. In severe reacting depressions, a combined therapy of a tricyclic antidepressant and an antianxiety agent is more preferred. All antidepressant drugs have a delayed onset of action. Their action begins after a latent period of 2-3 weeks.

The antidepressant drugs are classified as –

(i) Tricyclic antidepressants,

(ii) Monoamine oxidase inhibitors,

(iii) Miscellaneous agents.

In severe or treatment resistant cases, electroconvulsive shock treatment may give beneficial results. In actual practice of medicines, besides drug therapy, social and psychological treatments are also employed for better results.

It is an early observation that reserpine evokes depressive reactions by causing a depletion of biogenic amines. The depression thus, can be overcome by increasing the concentration of biogenic monoamines in the central synapses. This can be acheived by

(a) Either inhibiting the reuptake of neurotransmitter back to the storage granules of presynaptic nerve terminal.

(b) Or by inhibiting the metabolic degradation of neurotransmitter by synaptic and intraneuronal mono amine oxidase enzymes.

In fact, most of the antidepressant agents are found to increase the amount of aminergic neurotransmitters in the synapses by either of above mechanisms. Both α-adrenergic and serotoninergic activity postsynaptically are enhanced by a wide range of chemically dissimilar antidepressant agents. However the action of some of the newer drugs has raised the possiblity that dopamine may also play a role.

Most of the tricyclic antidepressants inhibit the uptake mechanisms for norepinephrine and serotonin. Mono amine oxidase (MAO) inhibitors irreversibly block the metabolic action of MAO enzymes on the biogenic amines. Most of the recently developed antidepressants act by one or another of these mechanisms, as well as by acting as a direct receptor agonists or antagonists. The presence of a sedative component in some antidepressants is associated with their antagonising action at histamine H_1-receptors. Similarly most of the clinically used antidepressants lead to desensitization of β-adrenoceptors upon chronic administration.

Table 28.4 : Some commonly used tricyclic antidepressants

(a) $R_1 = -(CH_2)_3 N (CH_3)_2$
$R_2 = -H$
Imipramine

(b) $R_1 = -(CH_2)_3 NHCH_3$
$R_2 = -H$
Desipramine

(c) $R_1 = -(CH_2)_3 N (CH_3)_2$
$R_2 = -Cl$
Clomipramine

(d) $R_1 = -CH_2 - CH - CH_2 - N (CH_3)_2$
           $|$
          CH_3
$R_2 = -H$
Trimipramine

(a) $R = -CH (CH_2)_2 N (CH_3)_2$
Amitriptyline

(b) $R = -CH (CH_2)_2 NHCH_3$
Nortriptyline

(c) $R = -CH - CH$
         $\quad\quad\quad |$
         $\quad\quad\quad CH_3$
         $\quad |$
         $CH_2 - N (CH_3)_2$
Butriptyline

$R_1 = -(CH_2)_3 NHCH_3$
Protriptyline

$R = CH(CH_2)_2 N(CH_3)_2$
Doxepin

28.11 TRICYCLIC ANTIDEPRESSANTS

It is a class of compounds, structurally related with phenothiazine agents. Imipramine and amitriptyline are most widely employed members of this class. In phenothiazines, a 7 membered central ring results due to replacement of sulfur by an ethylene linkage. This is imipramine nucleus which was first synthesized in 1948 while amitriptylene is the structural homolog of thioxanthene antipsychotic agents. Both are devoid of antipsychotic activity probably due to difference in the three dimentional molecular conformation. Similarly clomipramine is the homolog of chlorpromazine.

Primarily developed as a sedative-antihistaminic agent, imipramine was later tested for antipsychotic activity due to the structural resemblance with phenothiazines. It is due to the efforts of Kuhn that its antidepressive potential was reported in 1958. Its various derivatives have then been synthesized. Retaintion of antidepressive activity is another point of difference with phenothiazine antipsychotic agents.

These tricyclic antidepressants vary in their ability to inhibit the reuptake mechanisms of norepinephrine and serotonin in central synapses. Depending upon the nature of nitrogen atom in the dimethylamino group present in the side-chain, they can be categorized into –

(a) Tertiary amine tricyclic antidepressants which include imipramine, amitriptyline, trimipramine and doxepine. These anti-depressants primarily inhibit reupake mechanism for serotonin and are associated with sedative effects, and

(b) Secondary amine tricyclic antidepressants which include desipramine, nortriptyline and protriptyline. They can be considered as active metabolic products of tertiary amine tricyclic agents. These antidepressants primarily inhibit reuptake processes in noradrenergic central synapses and cause a degree of central stimulation.

Clomipramine is the most selective inhibitor of serotonin uptake mechanism while maprotiline is found to be most selective inhibitor for noradrenergic uptake processes.

Pharmacology :

Since imipramine is the most extensively studied example of this series, it will be considered as a prototype drug while discussing the pharmacological properties of tricyclic antidepressants.

(i) CNS : In normal persons, these agents do not behave as antidepressants. They do not elevate mood and motor activity. On the contrary, sedation and unpleasant anticholinergic effects are exerted. Motor activity is also depressed.

While in depressed person, antidepressant effects appear but with slow onset (about 2 - 3 weeks). The blockade of reuptake mechanisms for biogenic monoamines results into elevation of mood and motor activity (i.e., hypomania). The release of neurotransmitter is further enhanced by their antagonistic action at central presynaptic autoreceptors, present on nerve terminals. An antagonistic effect is also exerted on muscarinic cholinergic, α_1-adrenergic and histaminergic receptors present in brain which accounts for the emergence of side-effects. Due to the sedative effect, tertiary amine tricyclic antidepressants are drugs of choice, in the treatment of anxiety induced depression.

Imipramine reverses depressive actions of reserpine and also has marked anticonvulsive property. This observation led to the testing of carbamazepine (an anticonvulsant) for antidepressant activity.

(ii) CVS : Tricyclic antidepressants have significant cardiovascular effects. Postural hypotension results, probably due to peripheral α-adrenergic blockade. The elevated norepinephrine level in cardiac cells is responsible for induction of cardiac arrhythmias. While tachycardia can result from muscarinic receptor blockade. In addition, imipramine, itself has an ability to depress myocardium. Among tricyclic antidepressants, only doxepine exerts minimal CVS effects and is a safe drug to be used as an antidepressant in patients with cardiac abnormalities.

Beside these agents, the second generation antidepressants having similar pharmacological actions have recently been synthesized.

(a) Amoxapine:

It is a demethylated metabolite of loxapine, which is an antipsychotic agent. Unlike other tricyclic antidepressants, amoxapine antagonises the effects of activation of central dopamine receptors and gives rise to extrapyramidal symptoms. It also causes sexual disturbances in men. It has comparatively an early onset of action.

(b) Buproprion :

Its structure closely resembles with the structure of amphetamine. It inhibits the uptake mechanisms for dopamine.

(c) Doxepine :

It has a weak ability to inhibit the uptake mechanisms for biogenic amines. Both geometric isomers of doxepine possesses considerable antidepressant activity.

Table 28.5 : Second generation antidepressants

(A) Tetracyclic antidepressants :

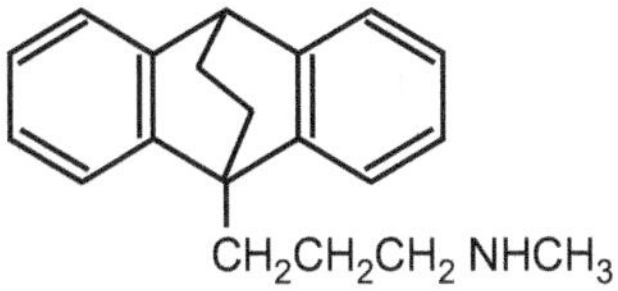

Maprotiline

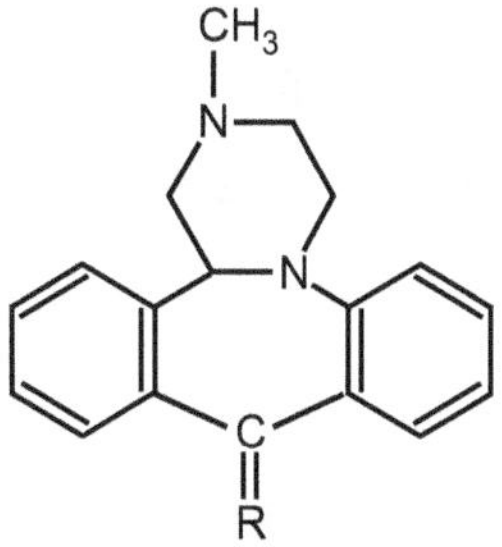

Mianserin

(B) Bicyclic antidepressants :

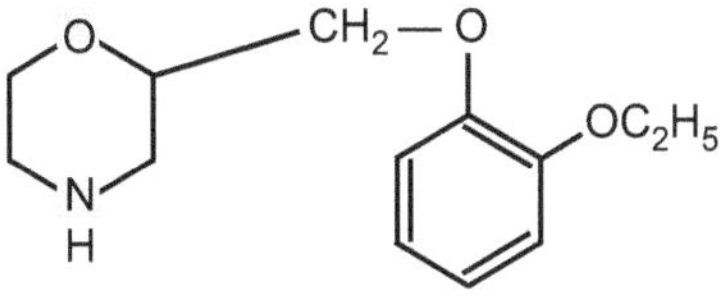

Viloxazine

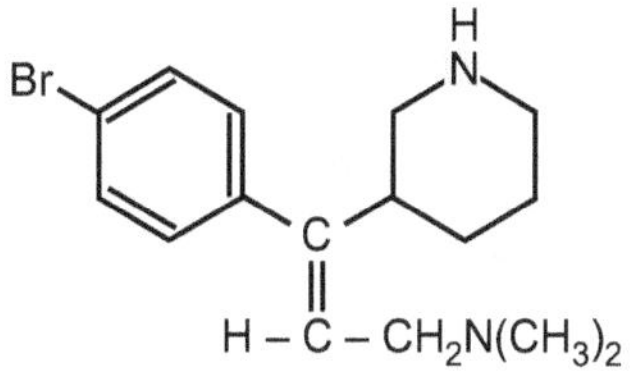

Zimelidine

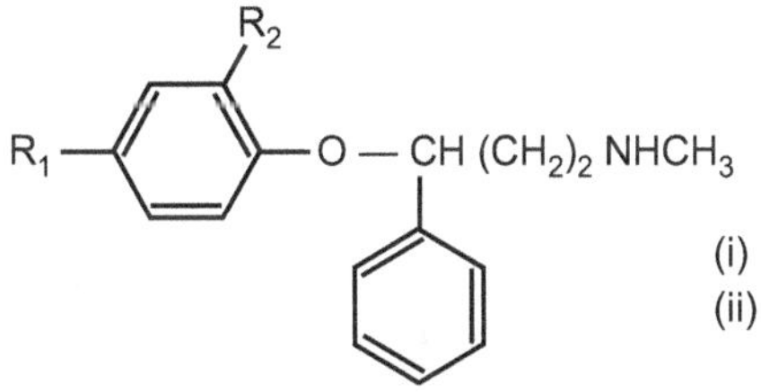

(i) Nisoxetine : $R_1 - H$; $R_2 = OCH_3$
(ii) Fluoxetine : $R_1 = -CF_3$; $R_2 = H$

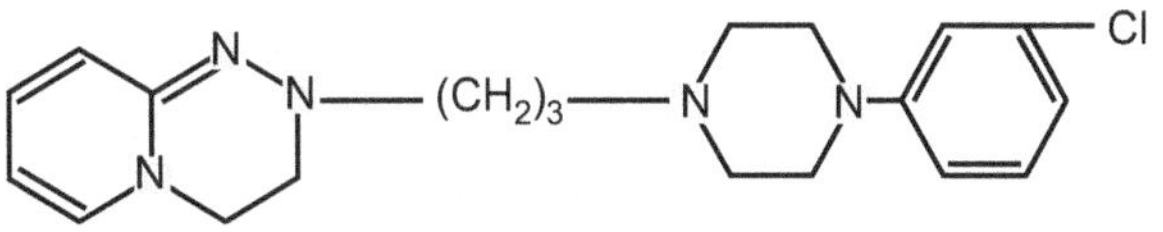

Trazodone

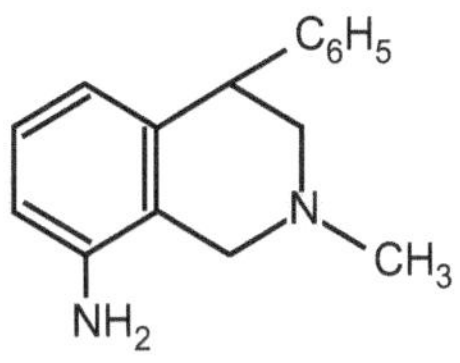

Nomifensine

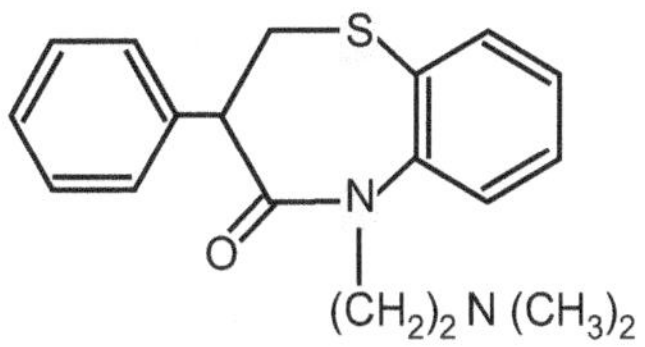

Thiazesim

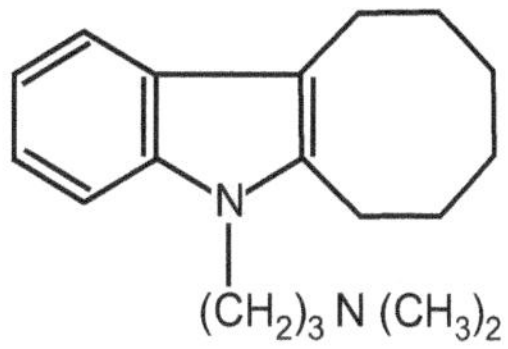

Iprindole

(C)   Tricyclic antidepressants :

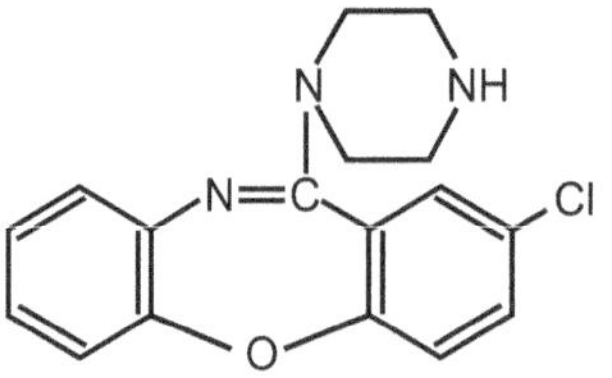

Amoxapine

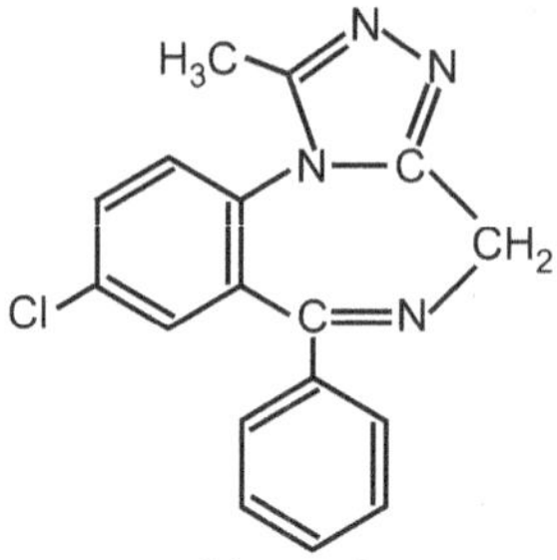

Alprazolam

(D)   Monocyclic antidepressants :

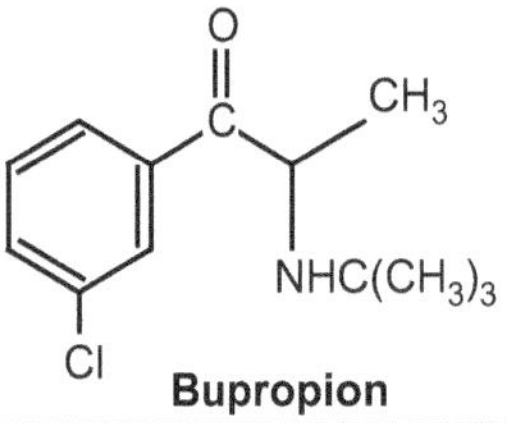

Bupropion

(d) Maprotiline :

It is a tetracyclic antidepressant agent. Its action is due to inhibition of reuptake mechanism for norepinephrine. Its metabolite, oxaprotiline is also effective antidepressant agent.

(e) Mianserin and Iprindole :

Both these drugs exert antidepressant activity through mechanisms which do not involve either the inhibition of uptake mechanisms for biogenic amines or by inhibition of their destruction by MAO enzymes.

(f) Nomifensine :

Chemically it is a phenylisoquinoline derivative. It is equally effective inhibitor of uptake mechanisms for both, norepinephrine and dopamine.

(g) Protriptyline :

Being a secondary amine tricyclic anti-depressant, it exerts its activity by inhibition of uptake mechanism for noradrenaline. Unlike other tricyclics, it has minimal anticholinergic activity.

(h) Trazodone :

Being a phenylpiperazine derivative, it resembles closely with oxypertine (an antipsychotic agent) in structure. But it lacks antipsychotic activity. It works mainly on serotonergic mechanisms and exerts antidepressant action, coupled with anxiolytic effect.

Absorption, Metabolism and Excretion:

When adminstered orally, tricyclic antidepressants are well absorbed. Due to their lipophilic nature, they get readily distributed throughout the body and are extensively bound to plasma proteins and to constituents of tissues.

Most of tricyclic antidepressants are metabolized in the body primarily through N-demethylation and hydroxylation.

For example, mono N-demethylation of imipramine, amitriptyline and doxepine generates active metabolites (like, desipramine, nortriptyline and nordoxepin) which upon further N-demethylation, get converted into inactive products. N-oxidation of imipramine also occurs and this metabolite is excreted in the urine.

Apart from, N-demethylation, hydroxylation by hepatic microsomal enzymes at position 2 of the ring, stands as another principal metabolic pathway for these agents. The products obtained, undergo conjugation with glucuronic acid and are excreted in urine.

The slow rate of inactivation and elimination of tricyclic antidepressants results into considerably long duration of their antidepressant action.

Adverse Effects :

The adverse effects include, dry mouth, cycloplegia, epigastric distress, constipation, urinary retention, blurred vision, palpitation, tachycardia, postural hypotension, weight gain, fatigue, weakness, muscle tremors and manic excitement.

Most of the above effects arise due to the anticholinergic and α-adrenolytic properties of tricyclic antidepressants. The peripheral anticholinergic effects of these agents can be potentiated by the use of other anticholinergic drugs and can be antagonized by administration of neostigmine. After chronic use of these agents, some degree of tolerance to peripheral anticholinergic effects may be developed.

Beside this, imipramine may lead to agranulocytosis while amitriptyline is found to produce excessive drowsiness after continued administration. In few instances, physical or psychic dependence may develop.

28.12 MONOAMINE OXIDASE INHIBITORS

According to the current concept, norepinephrine is biosynthesized within the nerve cells and is stored in the intraneuronal granules at presynaptic nerve endings from which, it is released by nerve impulse into the synaptic cleft. Here it interacts with the receptors present on the post synaptic cell body. The released norepinephrine is inactivated mainly through its conversion to normetanephrine by the enzyme, catechol - o - methyl transferases while norepinephrine released intraneuronally either spontaneously or by the depleting action of reserpine-like drugs, appears to be inactivated by monoamine oxidase (MAO) enzymes.

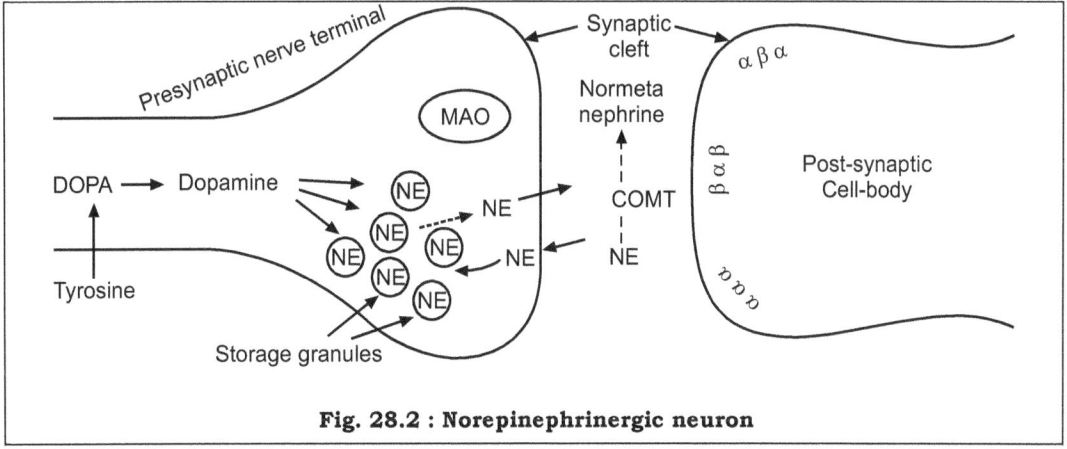

Fig. 28.2 : Norepinephrinergic neuron

MAO refers to a family of isoenzymes located primarily in the outer membranes of mitochondria. They are scattered throughout the body. In the peripheral region, they metabolize the circulating monoamines in blood and liver. In central region (CNS), beside inactivating norepinephrine which is released intraneuronally, they also attack on the monoamine which is taken up back to storage granules through reuptake mechanism.

Structurally it is a flavin containing enzyme that is closely linked functionally with an aldehyde reductase in all tissues. Depending upon the substrate specificity, these enzymes can be sub-categorised as–

(a) MAO - A isoenzymes who preferentially attack on serotonin.

(b) MAO - B isoenzymes who preferentially attact on sympathomimetic amines.

These enzymes inactivate the biogenic amines by conversion into aldehydes followed by subsequent oxidation or reduction to an acid or alcohol. For example,

MAO-inhibitors which are therapeutically used can equally inhibit both subtypes of MAO-isoenzymes. This inhibition is of irreversible nature. After discontinuation of the treatment, MAO-metabolic system takes time to re-establish since new enzyme molecules are to be biosynthesized. Hence, the antidepressant effect of MAO-inhibitors can be observed even after the treatment is discontinued.

Due to the less effectiveness of MAO-inhibitors, they are less preferred over tricyclic antidepressants. The clinically used agents from this class are chemically dissimilar but hold a common ability to inhibit the functioning of MAOs. They include phenelzine, isocarboxazid and tranylcypromine. Both phenelzine and tranylcypromine can also inhibit the amine uptake to some extent. In anxiety-induced depressions, they elevate the mood and correct the sleep disorders. Though effective centrally, they fail to protect the actions of endogenous catecholamines at peripheral effector sites. Hepatotoxicity is a prominent feature that paralyze their wide-spread acceptance.

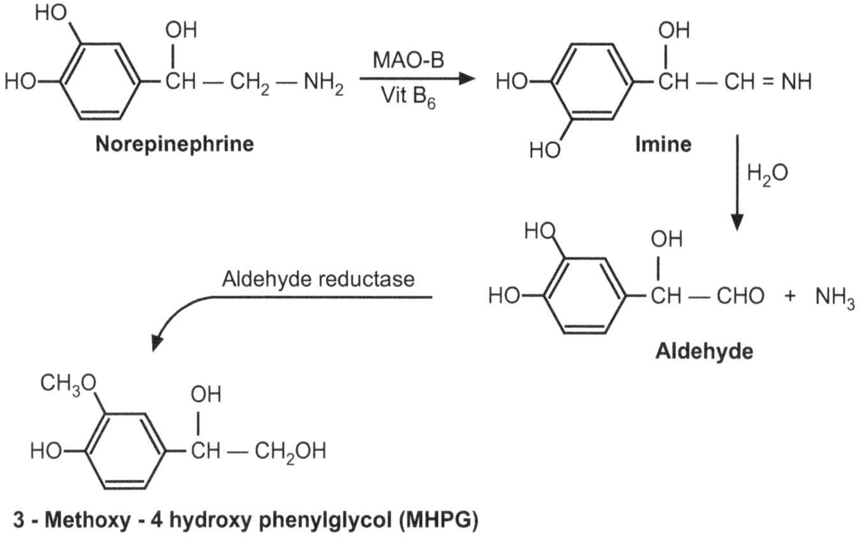

Fig. 28.3 : Inactivation of norepinephrine by MAO

Beside these drugs, many compounds like, cocaine, mescaline, chlorpromazine, hormoline and p-chloromercury benzoate display MAO-inhibitory activity.

Iproniazid, an isopropyl derivative of isoniazid, is the first MAO-inhibitor used therapeutically. Initially developed as an antituberculosis agent, its antidepressant activity was first noted by Zeller and co-workers during its clinical studies. In 1957, then, it was employed for the treatment of depressive disorders. Subsequently various substituted hydrazines and hydrazides were prepared and tested for their clinical utility. Iproniazid and its congeners possess severe hepato-toxic potential and they had been withdrawn from the clinical use.

Isocarboxazid is hydrazide derivative while tranylcypromine is a nonhydrazide compound which results due to the cyclization of side-chain of amphetamine. A long-lasting antidepressant effect can be seen with isocarboxazide due to its in vivo conversion to active hydrazine. Thus, it can be considered as a prodrug. Both phenelzine and isocarboxazid inactivate flavin prosthetic group in enzyme on the cost of their own oxidation to reactive intermediates which bind to enzyme surface through covalent bond. While tranylcypromine causes an irreversible inhibition of MAO, probably by an interaction with its sulfhydryl group. Like isoniazid, phenelzine-like hydrazine antidepressants interact with pyridoxal phosphate and thus interfere in the biosynthesis of GABA, an inhibitory neurotransmitter in the CNS. Hence, chronic administration of relatively high doses of these drugs lower down threshold for seizures.

Pharamacology:

(i) CNS : Like tricyclic antidepressants, MAO-inhibitors reverse the reserpine induced depression and potentiate the actions of biogenic monoamines in the CNS, especially norepinephrine and serotonin. Unlike, tricyclic antidepressants, MAO-inhibitors increase the psychomotor activity in both, normal as well as depressed persons.

Due to the blocking action at sympathetic ganglia, these drugs cause postural hypotension. They also lead to hypothermia and correct the sleep disorders accompanied with anxiety induced depression.

(ii) CVS : Due to their hypotensive action, they may be useful drugs in the management of hypertension. e.g. pargyline which is basically a MAO-inhibitor, but is used clinically as antihypertensive. They may also be used in the treatment of angina.

Table 28.6 : Clinically used MAO-inhibitors

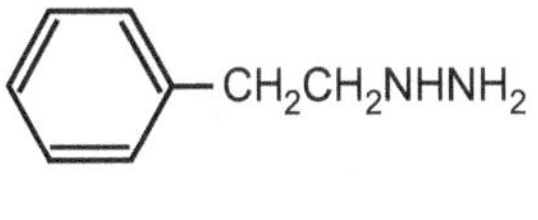

Phenelzine (Hydrazine): Ph–CH$_2$CH$_2$NHNH$_2$

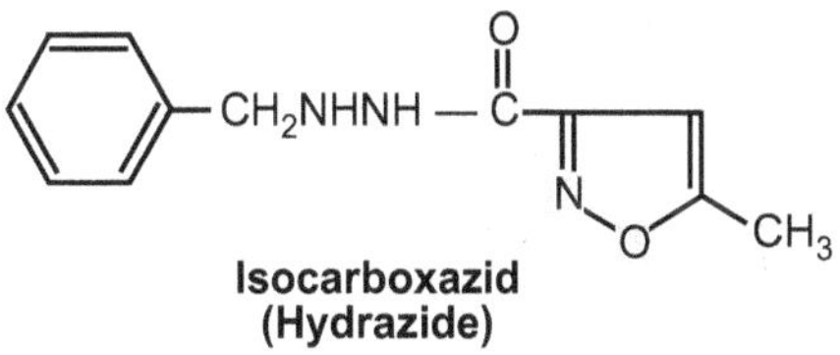

Isocarboxazid (Hydrazide): Ph–CH$_2$NHNH–C(=O)–(5-methylisoxazol-3-yl)

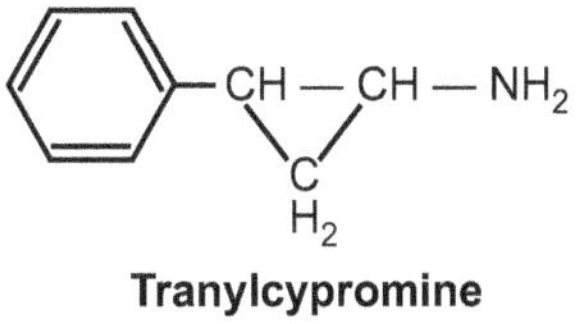

Tranylcypromine: Ph–CH–CH–NH$_2$ with CH$_2$ bridge (cyclopropane)

Beside inhibiting the functioning of MAOs (monoamine metabolizing enzymes, they may also inhibit nonspecifically the functioning of other drug metabolizing enzymes and thus may alter the pattern of metabolism of concurrently administered drugs.

These drugs are well absorbed from GIT. Due to irreversible inhibition of MAO enzymes, caused by these drugs, the antidepressant action emerges quite slowly but once appeared, it remains for prolonged period.

Adverse effects include, dry mouth, blurred vision, headache, weakness, insomnia, hypomania, postural hypotension and tremors. The hydrazine MAO-inhibitor may cause deficiency of vitamin B_6 resulting into peripheral neuropathy. Similarly hydrazine MAO-inhibitors are relatively more hepato-toxic than non-hydrazine MAO-inhibitors. Since the MAO-inhibition is irreversible, late toxic effects may appear.

The combination therapy of MAO-inhibitor with a tricyclic antidepressant was proposed to increase the therapeutic effectiveness. The effectiveness or potency of antidepressant action definetly increased but together with that of adverse effects. Toxicity profile also runs parallel. Hence, to avoid toxic complications, both these categories of antidepressant drugs should not be used together. If however, in some circumstances, even if it is used, the patient should be kept strictly under supervision of the experts.

28.13 MISCELLANEOUS AGENTS HAVING CONSIDERABLE MAO-INHIBITING ACTIVITY

A large variety of compounds like alcohols, amidines, guanidines, isothioureas, xanthines, amphetamines inhibit MAO in vitro. These compounds, however are essentially devoid of in vivo MAO inhibitory activity.

Other compounds of interest, are

(a) Harmala Alkaloids :

Harmine and Harmaline, both possess considerable MAO inhibitory activity.

(b) Indolealkylamines:

Both α-methyltryptamine and α-ethyltryptamine inhibit MAO enzymes present in guinea pig liver.

(c) Propargylamine Derivatives :

$$\text{C}_6\text{H}_5\text{-CH}_2-\underset{\underset{\text{CH}_3}{|}}{\text{N}}-\text{CH}_2-\text{C}\equiv\text{CH}$$

Pargyline

Pargyline is a powerful inhibitor of MAO enzymes.

28.14 THERAPEUTIC USEFULNESS OF MAO-INHIBITORS

These drugs are used in the treatment of psychotic patients with mild to severe depression. The treatment results into an increased sense of well being, increased desire and ability to communicate, elevation of mood, increased physical activity and mental alertness and improvement in appetite.

Antianxiety agents can also be employed on many occassions, in treatment of depressive disorders. They have been dealt separately in another chapter.

The tricyclic antidepressants have largely replaced MAO-inhibitors for the treatment of depression. The use of tricyclic antidepressants alongwith or shortly after discontinuation of MAO-inhibitors may prove to be dangerous due to emergence of hyperexcitation, hyperpyrexia, seizures and severe atropinism.

DRUG THERAPY IN PARKINSONISM

29.1 INTRODUCTION

In 1958, Carlsson suggested that dopamine, besides acting as a precursor of noradrenaline and adrenaline, might also function independently as a neurotransmitter. The highest concentration of dopamine has been found in the basal ganglia, mostly in the caudate nucleus, pallidurn and corpus striatum (Putamen). It has usually a depressant action, particularly on cells that have been excited by glutamate. The control of voluntary movements is mainly exercised by striated tracts which incorporate a balanced complex of excitatory (acetylcholine) and inhibitory (dopamine) components. If by chance, due to certain reasons, if the concentration of acetylcholine predominates over the concentration of dopamine, it leads to an increase in the extrapyramidal effects (i.e., posture and the involuntary aspects of movements) Parkinsonism is such a chronic disease of extrapyramidal origin for which there is no cure. It was, described first by James Parkinson in 1817 by four major symptoms. These include,

1. Involuntary tremors of the limbs.
2. Rigidity of muscles (stiffness).
3. Slow initiation of all voluntary movements (akinesia).
4. Dementia and speech difficulties.

These symptoms appear in a quite progressive manner. As one might expect, the signs of cholinergic nervous system activation (e.g. profuse salivation) can be seen. The old aged people are more likely get attacked by this disease where etiology remains undefined in most of the cases (idiopathic Parkinsonism).

A lot of research has been carried out to define the etiology of the disease. The disease could not be related to any way to hereditary characteristics. In most of the patients, due to the old age, degeneration of dopamine containing neurons in the brain occurs. Since a threshold number of neurons are required for smooth functioning of muscles, the loss of dopaminergic neurons (aging process) may lead to predominance of cholinergic activity. Recently MPTP (N–methyl-4 phenyl-1, 2, 3, 6 – tetrahydropyridine), an intermediate in meperidine synthesis, is reported to cause the loss of dopaminergic neuronal activity. The environment may be polluted with several MPTP like substances. In such environment, due to prolonged exposure, a person may get attacked by Parkinsonism and related disorders.

It is believed that dopamine (an inhibitory neurotransmitter) constitutes more than 50% of the brain catecholamines. It is biosynthesized by large pigmented nigral neurons which are synaptically connected to striatum (i.e., caudate nucleus and putamen). The striatum is also innervated from the cortex, thalamus and the raphe nucleus of midbrain.

The GABA-ergic neuronal loops originating from the striatum is projected to substantia nigra. GABA is an inhibitory neurotransmitter which controls the rate of impulse flow from nigral neurons and thus provides smooth and co-ordinated motor movements. Once the impulse from nigral neuron reaches to striatum, dopamine is released from various post-synaptic terminals and acts to form a balanced complex with an excitatory component (ACh) to initiate motor movement. Thus, one nigral neuron can govern the activity of several striatal neurons through multiple branching of dopaminergic axon. These dopaminergic terminals end on medium-sized spiny neurons which constitute about 96% of the striatal cells. At these synapses, cholinergic interneurons are present. There is a possibility that the dopaminergic mechanisms may be intimately tied up with the serotonergic functions exercised by raphe nuclei of mid-brain. The striatum, as we know possesses the significant amount of ACh, an excitatory neurotransmitter. This balanced complex of ACh and dopamine may be shifted in favour of ACh, in Parkinsonism, due to,

(a) aging process in old-aged people,

(b) repeated exposure to MPTP - like toxins,

(c) treatment with butyrophenone and phenothiazine antipsychotic drugs which may cause either increased metabolic rate of dopamine or may block dopamine receptors, resulting into an increase in concentration of excitatory component (ACh) and decreasing the concentration of inhibitory component (dopamine). All antipsychotic drugs increase the turnover of dopamine in the brain.

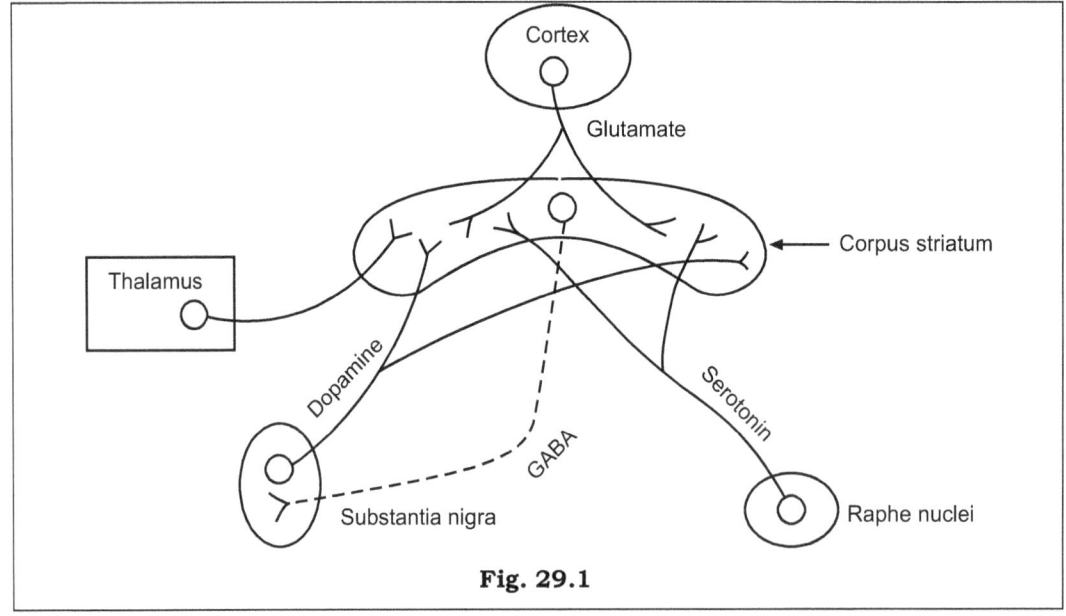

Fig. 29.1

(d) reserpine like drugs cause depletion of dopaminergic neurons in basal ganglia.

In fact, the dopamine content in the striatum and nigra are found to be very low in Parkinson's disease. This decreased dopamine level may allow striatal acetylcholine interneurons to be relatively overactive, resulting into the signs and symptoms of Parkinsonism. Thus, the treatment will be effective if the drug decreases the overactivity of cholinergic neurons in basal ganglia or elevates the inhibitory activity of dopaminergic neurons. Of the several drugs employed for the treatment of Parkinsonism, levodopa serves as a prototype of central dopa-agonist agents while trihexyphenidyl represents central anticholinergic agents. While dantrolene acts directly on the skeletal muscles.

29.2 LEVODOPA

Since Parkinsonism is characterized by dopamine deficiency in the brain, the most rational approach would be to make up that deficiency by the administration of exogenous dopamine. Unfortunately dopamine, itself, does not cross the blood-brain-barrier when administered systemically. Hence, dopa, its immediate precursor, was tried. It is taken up in the brain by specific amino acid transport system. Due to higher activity, levodopa, an active isomer, is preferred over the recemic mixture. In brain, levodopa is converted to dopamine by pyridoxine dependent, aromatic amino acid decarboxylase enzymes. This conversion takes place in the cell bodies and synaptic terminals of the nigrostriatal neurons.

Only about 1 - 2% of orally administered levodopa can reach the CNS due to its extensive degradation in stomach and liver. Hence, to get desired therapeutic effects, levodopa is to be administered in larger doses. This also potentiates the spectrum of its adverse effects. This degradation of orally administered levodopa can be effectively inhibited by the concurrent administration of peripherally acting dopa decarboxylase inhibitors. This allows a 70 - 90% reduction in the required dose of levodopa and naturally, also in the intensity of adverse effects. Carbidopa and benserazide are the examples of clinically used inhibitors of dopa decarboxylase enzymes.

Levodopa is a prodrug which is converted in the brain into dopamine. 3, 4 - dihydroxyphenylacetic acid and 3-methoxy-4-hydroxyphenyl acetic acid are the major metabolites of dopamine which are excreted in urine either unchanged or in the form of their glucuronide, or sulfate conjugates. Minute amount of dopamine is also biotransformed to norepinephrine and epinephrine which account for cardiovascular effects of dopamine. Dopamine, itself has agoniot effect on α- and β-adrenoceptor.

Levodopa

Levodopa corrects the extra-pyramidal defects and improves speech, posture and gait. Due to β-adrenoceptor agonist activity, levodopa may cause cardiac arrhythmias in higher doses. Hence, its use in the patients with cardiac problems or having major psychosis, may prove fatal.

The adverse effects of levodopa are usually reversible and dose-dependent.

These include nausea, vomiting, dyskinesia, chloreoathetosis (i.e., involuntary pulling of the head to one side), postural hypotension and confusion. They may result either due to accumulation of newly formed dopamine in basal ganglia (e.g., choreoathetosis) or due to presence of hypersensitive dopamine receptors (dyskinesia). Levodopa is contraindicated in following conditions :

(a) narrow-angle glaucoma
(b) major psychosis
(c) cardiac arrhythmias and
(d) pregnancy

29.3 INHIBITORS OF AROMATIC L-AMINO ACID DECARBOXYLASE

The orally administered levodopa is extensively metabolized to dopamine by l - aromatic amino acid decarboxylase enzymes in GIT, liver and kidney. Dopamine can not cross blood-brain-barriers. Hence, large doses of levodopa were needed to achieve desired central effects. This naturally then invites the adverse effects of high intensity and frequency. The problem could be solved by administering levodopa alongwith decarboxylase.

Due to their ionization at physiological pH, they fail to enter the CNS and their enzyme inhibitory action remains peripherally restricted. Deorenil and fusidic acid do not inhibit decarboxylase enzymes. They enter the CNS and prolong the duration of action of dopamine by preventing its metabolism. For example, deprenil inhibits mono amino oxidase isoenzyme-β (MAO-β) which predominates in certain regions of CNS while fusaric acid inhibits the conversion of dopamine to norepinephrine, catalyzed by dopamine β-hydroxylase.

The decarboxylase inhibitors are pharmacologically inert when given alone. In presence of levodopa, these inhibitors make fast, the appearance of both, therapeutic as well as adverse effects.

29.4 DOPAMINE AGONISTS

It was revealed that dopamine is present in relatively large amounts in localized areas of the brain where it acts on its specific receptor sites. Spano in 1976 classified these multiple dopamine receptor sites in.

(a) D_1-receptor Sites :

D_1-receptor sites are characterized by sensitivity to micromolar concentration of dopamine as well as micromolar concentration of spiperone, a selective D_1-antagonist. Their activation result in the stimulation of adenylate cyclase activity. Thioxanthines and certain phenothiazines selectively bind to these sites.

(b) D_2-receptor Sites :

These receptor sites have much higher affinity and selectivity than the D_1-receptor sites, for all neuroleptic agents. Their activation by certain agents (e.g., butyrophenones) result into inhibition of adenylate cyclase activity.

In the treatment of Parkinsonism, a relief can be brought about by using drugs which act directly on postsynaptic dopaminergic receptors. Bromocriptine, pergolide mesylate, lisuride and apomorphine are the drugs that have strong dopaminergic activity.

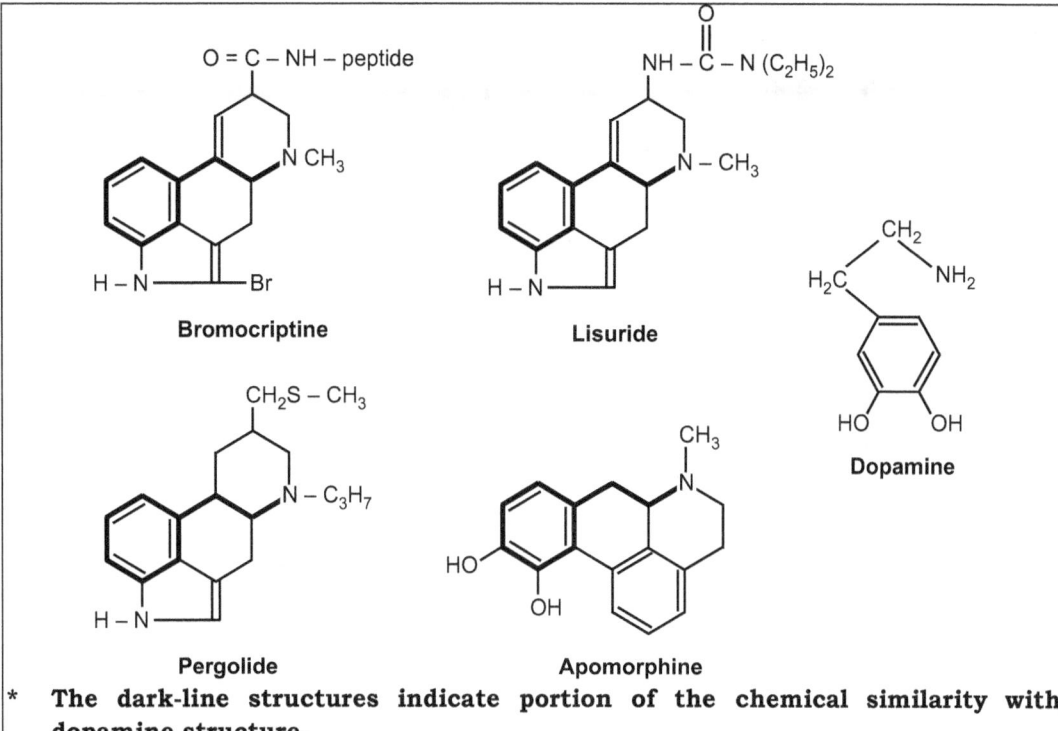

* The dark-line structures indicate portion of the chemical similarity with dopamine structure.

Bromocriptine, lisuride and pergolide are the examples of ergoline class. All they can be considered as derivatives of lysergic acid, of which bromocriptine has been proved very effective. It mainly acts on dopaminergic receptors present in CNS, cardiovascular and GIT system.

When administered orally, bromocriptine is readily absorbed. In body, it undergoes extensive metabolism to several inactive products, most of which are excreted mainly in bile. Often it is administered in combination with levodopa. Such combination allows a reduction in the required dose of levodopa and also in its side-effects. In therapeutic doses, bromocriptine can induce nausea, vomiting, constipation, psychiatric reactions, postural hypotension and hallucinations.

Pergolide and lisuride have similar pharmacological actions to that of bromocriptine except longer duration of action of pergolide.

Apomorphine, an emetic agent was the first dopaminergic agonist, clinically used in the treatment of Parkinsonism. It causes dopaminergic effects by activating dopamine receptors in the corpus striatum. In comparison with other dopamine agonists, apomorphine has shorter duration of action. If given in higher doses, it acts on the presynaptic dopamine autoreceptors and may inhibit dopamine synthesis and release.

Renal damage is reported in patients receiving apomorphine for prolong period of time.

Other side-effects induced by apomorphine include, vomiting, hormonal changes and hypotension. Sometimes it is administered with domperidone (a peripherally acting dopamine antagonist) to limit its peripheral side-effects.

29.5 AMANTADINE

HYDROCHLORIDE

Originally amantadine was developed as an antiviral agent in the treatment of A_2 influenza. Later accidently, it was found to possess good activity in Parkinsonism and since then, it is used in combination with levodopa.

It is readily absorbed from GIT and possesses longer duration of action. It undergoes insignificant metabolism and is excreted in urine mostly in unchanged form. Its effectiveness in Parkinsonism may be due to its ability to release dopamine from the dopaminergic terminals in nigrostriatum. It may also inhibit the reuptake of dopamine back to neuronal cells and also possess some anti-cholinergic properties.

Side-effects are mild and may include insomnia, dizziness, dry mouth (due to decreased salivation) and urinary hesitancy. In overdoses, it may cause grand mal convulsions. Due to the development or tolerance to its therapeutic effects, its use in Parkinsonism is less favoured.

29.6 ANTICHOLINERGIC AGENTS

Parkinsonism is characterized by a decreased concentration of dopamine and over activation of cholinergic interneurons in the basal ganglia. So treatment with anticholinergic agents offers one of the direct approaches to normalise the disturbed balance of excitatory and inhibitory components in brain. Trihexyphenidyl stands as a prototype of clinically used anticholinergic agents in parkinsonism. Other examples include, benztropine, procyclidine and ethopropazine. Out of these trihexyphenidyl and benztropine are the most favoured agents. They cause mild to moderate improvement in parkinsonism. Side-effects include, delirium, constipation, urinary retention, dry-mouth, confusion, hallucinations and cycloplegia.

Antihistamines, amitriptyline and the tricyclic antidepressants also have anticholinergic activity of certain degree. In addition, their sedative effect may add to their clinical qualification in the treatment of Parkinsonism. Though they are less effective anticholinergic agents, the side-effects associated with their use are also of mild nature.

29.7 PROPRANOLOL

Propranolol, the β - adrenoreceptor blocking agent, has been reported to be beneficial in the treatment of parkinsonism. It mainly acts to reduce down the intensity of involuntary muscle activity in Parkinsonism, probably by interfering with the serotonin function in the areas of the brain, that control behaviour.

Domperidone

Amantadine

OPIOID ANALGESICS AND ANTAGONISTS

30.1 INTRODUCTION

The propagation of the pain impulse is an alarming event in the body which indicates damage to the tissues (noxious stimuli). The spinal cord, thalamus and cerebral hemispheres are the brain compartments which are involved in the integration and perception of pain impulses. The spinal cord acts as a receiving center for pain impulses from which, they are sent to the cerebral hemispheres through the thalamus. These pain impulses run separately from those which carry other sensations like, touch, pressure, heat and cold. But activation of these sensory impulses may reduce the intensity of pain. The intensity of pain sensation is governed by the cerebral cortex which has a control over the inflow of impulses through the thalamus. Hence, the impulse strength in the thalamo-cortical system, when crosses a critical threshold value, pain is realised. The pain sensation is usually accompanied with emotional trauma which is characterized by depression, fear, anxiety and sometimes with anorexia. The locus ceruleus contains both, nor-adrenergic neurons and high concentration of opioid receptors and is intimately involved with the generation of emotional trauma. Besides noradrenaline, other neurotransmitters such as serotonin and histamine are also involved in the modulation of nociception in the brain.

Analgesia may be defined as 'a state of relative insensitivity to pain, where the capacity to tolerate pain is increased without the loss of consciousness'. The term, 'analgesic' is generally applied to the agents or actions required to produce analgesia. It can be produced by :

(a) Changing the perception of the pain by increasing the pain threshold value, and

(b) By reducing the intensity of emotional trauma.

In fact, many analgesic drugs lower down the intensity of emotional trauma to a varying degree. The patient thus feels mentally strong. Even if the pain intensity is not altered, the patient can tolerate it much comfortably, without any physical discomfort or disagreeable sensation.

Analgesics are divided into two main classes:

(I) Opioid analgesics (centrally acting drugs), and

(II) Non-opioid (non-narcotic) analgesics (peripherally acting analgesic agents).

Minor aches and pains are treated usually with non-opioid analgesics while opioid analgesics are strong drugs that afford the relief from severe and more intense pain. Besides this, many CNS-depressant drugs can bring about analgesic effects by their sleep-inducing ability. Anaesthetics block all forms of sensory impulses including that for pain.

30.2 NARCOTIC OR OPIOID ANALGESIC AGENTS

Friedrich W.A. Serturner in 1805, first isolated and discovered the potent analgesic activity of morphine, from the juice of unripped seed capsule of the poppy plant, Papaver somniferum. Morphine was the first, of all the alkaloids isolated from plant sources. Its chemical synthesis was first reported in 1952, by Gates and Tshudi. Opium (the Greek name for juice) contains more than 20 distinct alkaloids. Of these, codeine was isolated in 1832, by Robiquet followed by isolation of papaverine by Merck in 1848.

Morphine relieves pain without blocking the motor activity, and without interfering with consciousness at therapeutic doses. The term opioid, is used to designate collectively the drugs (natural or synthetic) which bind specifically to any of the sub-species of receptors of morphine and produce, to varying degrees, morphine-like actions. They are often known as the narcotic analgesics due to their ability to produce drug dependence. With the development of many analgesics which are morphine derivatives but with little tendency to produce physical dependence, the term narcotic is rapidly losing its popularity.

Besides a central analgesic effect, opioids relieves the emotional component of the painful experience. The other actions that are associated with opioids are sedation, euphoria, reduced anxiety, respiratory depression, cough suppression, a decreased gastrointestinal motility (constipation) and effects on hormonal and cardiovascular system. In therapeutic doses, morphine sometimes, produce nausea or vomiting. The related compound apomorphine, for example, is a powerful emetic agent. If the administration is continued, opioids can also produce tolerance, physical as well as psychological dependence. In order to reduce these side-effects, an orally effective opioid analgesic agent can be combined with non-narcotic (aspirin-like) analgesic agent. In all, clinically used opioid agents (whether agonist or antagonist) usually laevo enantiomers are pharmacologically effective.

Table 30.1 : Optium alkaloids

Opium Alkaloid	Main effect	% w/w in opium
I. Phenanthrenes :		
Morphine	Analgesic	10
Codeine	Analgesic and antitussive	0.5
Thebaine	CNS stimulant	0.2
II. Benzylisoquinolines :		
Papaverine	Spasmolytic	1.0
Noscapine	Antitussive	6.0

Opium contains about 25% by weight, alkaloidal compounds. These opium alkaloids can be divided chemically into two distinct classes, as shown in the table 30.1.

Morphine is a prototype of all clinically employed opioid drugs. Depending upon the nature of the response obtained, these morphine-like drugs are categorised as :

(a) Morphine-like opioid agonists.

(b) Opioids with mixed actions (partial agonists), and

(c) Opioid antagonists.

30.3 MORPHINE-LIKE OPIOID AGONISTS

Morphine is a pentacyclic compound that contains N-methyl piperidine moiety. Though morphine itself is a potent analgesic agent, the serious side-effects like sedation, respiratory depression, emesis, addiction and tolerance, associated with morphine, initiated the attempts for modification of this structure, in order to increase the therapeutic usefulness and to maximise analgesic potency at the expense of its side-effects.

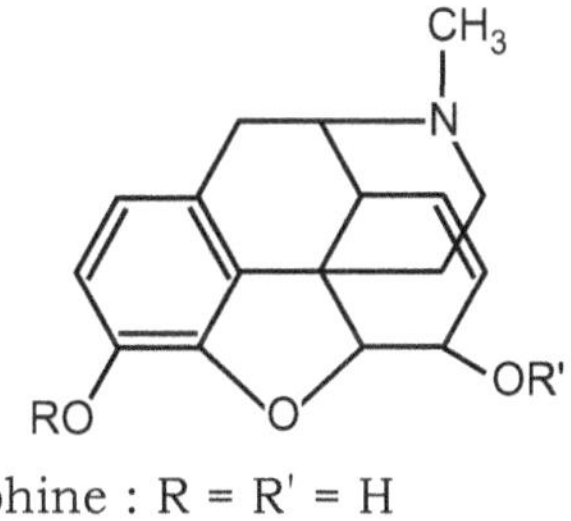

(a) Morphine : R = R' = H

(b) Codeine : R = CH$_3$; R' = H

(c) Heroin : R = –COCH$_3$; R' = –COCH$_3$

Like other simple semi-synthetic analogues of morphine (like, codeine, heroin, hydromorphone, hydrocodone), many other classes of chemically distinct opioid agonists have been prepared through the concept of molecular dissection. These include, morphinan, benzomorphan, meperidine, methadone and propoxyphene. These opioids are highly lipophilic agents and get widely distributed in the body.

(a) Morphine :

Since the chemical synthesis of morphine is a costly affair, the alkaloid is still obtained from the natural source. Most of the semi-synthetic and synthetic analogues of the morphine share their pharmacological actions with morphine. All opioid agonists produce analgesia, respiratory depression, gastrointestinal spasm, tolerance and physical dependence. They vary in their relative potencies due to differences in their receptor-affinity, intrinsic activity, lipophilicity, plasma-protein binding and metabolic pattern. While discussing their pharmacological actions, morphine is considered as the prototype compound. Mention will be made about differences, whenever they exist.

CNS :

Unpleasant response comprised of anxiety, light headedness and uneasiness is observed in normal persons (not suffering from pain), if morphine is given. Whereas in patients who need analgesic effect, morphine relieves pain with some sedation and euphoria. Besides suppressing the pain perception, it elevates mood and relieves the symptoms of emotional trauma accompanied with the pain sensation. Patients can comfortably tolerate the pain even if the pain intensity is not altered. This effect results due to inhibition of activity in locus ceruleus which is involved in the feelings of fear, anxiety, panic and alarm.

In higher doses, other side-effects like, nausea, vomiting, respiratory depression, restlessness, and perhaps convulsions may become pronounced. This may be accompanied by disturbances in the muscle movements (like, catalepsy, muscular rigidity) due to interference of functioning of dopaminergic neurons in striatum and substantia nigra. Morphine acts on the vital centers present in the medulla to cause.

(i) Respiratory depression due to depressant action on respiratory centers in the pons and medulla.

(ii) Cough suppression.

(iii) Stimulation of vomiting centers in chemoreceptor trigger zone, and

(iv) Depression of vasomotor centres.

Morphine also exerts its effects on the hypothalamus to cause several centrally mediated endocrinological effects which include :

(i) Inhibition of the release of gonadotropin releasing hormone and corticotropin releasing factor, This is reflected in turn, in the lowering down of the concentration of LH, FSH, ACTH and β-endorphin.

(ii) Increase in the plasma concentration of growth hormone, prolactin and vasopressin.

(iii) Increase in the release of antidiuretic hormone.

(iv) Hyperglycaemia that results due to hypothalamic stimulation.

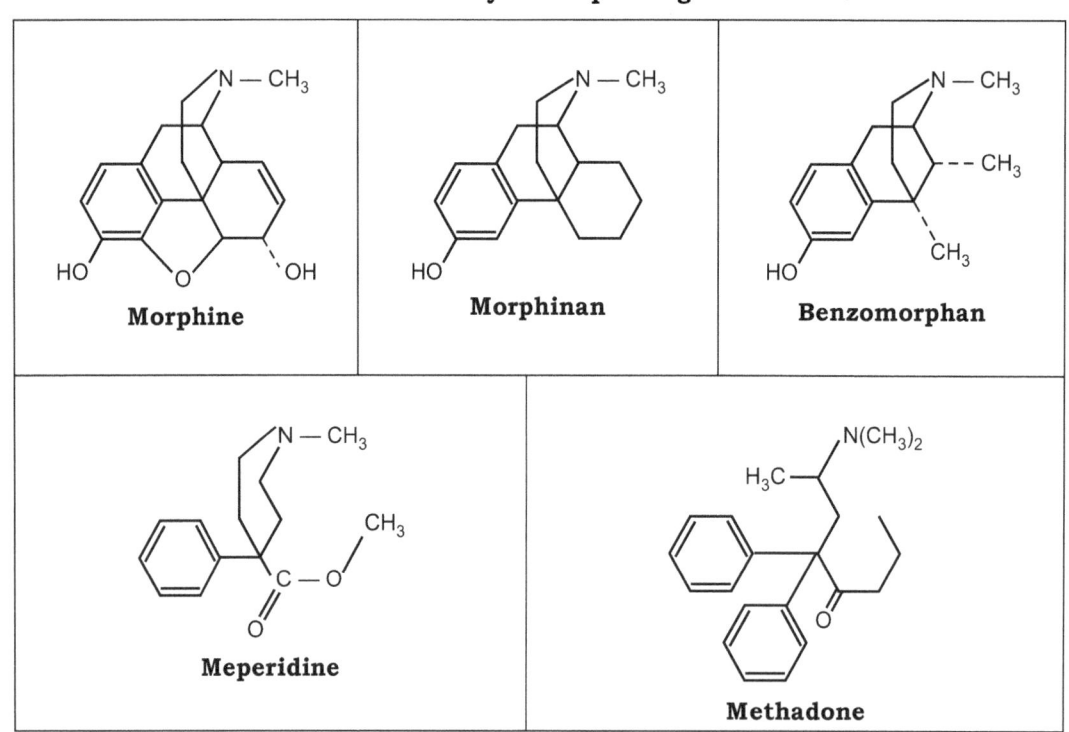

Table 30.2 : Clinically used opioid agonist classes

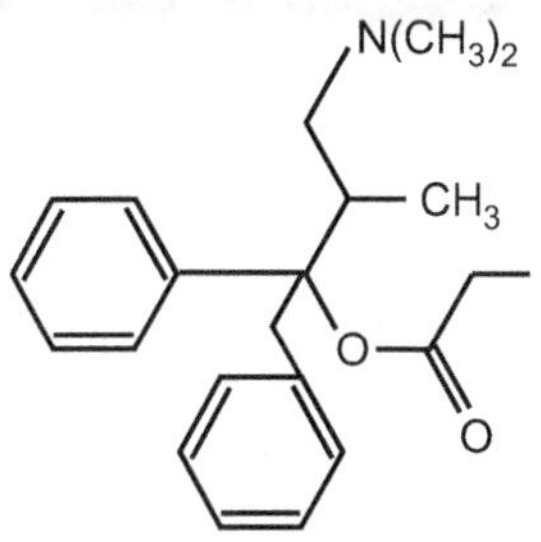

Propoxyphene

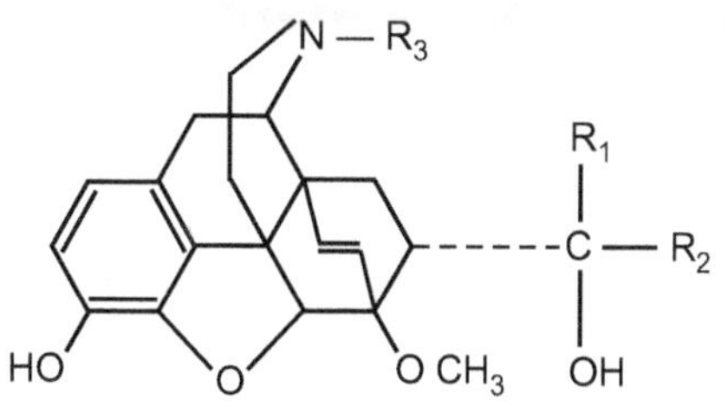

Oripavines

Respiratory system :

Morphine depresses all phases of respiratory activity, by virtue of a direct effect on the brain stem respiratory centers. The responsiveness of these centers to the alveolar carbon dioxide tension (P_{CO_2}) also decreases. Besides an increase in the threshold to CO_2 stimulation, an antitussive effect is also seen due to atleast in part by a direct effect on cough center in the medulla.

Emetic effects :

Opioid agonists are known for their emetic effect due to the direct stimulation of chemoreceptor trigger zone. This effect probably mediates through the over-activeness of dopaminergic neurons. The emetic effect of morphine hence, can be best antagonised by phenothiazine antipsychotic agents.

Pupil :

Morphine produces a pin point constriction of pupil resulting into miosis. A decrease in the intraocular tension is also seen with therapeutic doses of morphine.

Cardiovascular effects :

Peripheral vasodilatation and reduction in the peripheral resistance are the major effects exerted by morphine due to the diminished central sympathetic outflow. The opiod-induced histamine release is the prime factor involved in the hypertension observed during the treatment. Both, central and peripheral mechanisms are involved in producing variable and complex cardio-vascular effects in patients with acute myocardial diseases.

Gastrointestinal tract :

Opioids lead to an increase in tone that is associated with the decreased motility. The overall effects are delayed gastric emptying, increased fluid absorption and constipation. In general, gastric, biliary and pancreatic secretions are somewhat decreased. The pressure in the biliary tract increases resulting into epigastric distress. These effects are mediated in part, by a local direct action on the myenteric plexus and partly by the CNS.

In therapeutic doses, morphine does not affect normal uterine contractions during labour. Uterine hyperactivity however, is depressed. Morphine itself, should not be given to women in labour due to its respiratory depressant action. Pethidine is more preferred agent in such cases due to its weak respiratory depressant effect.

Absorption, Metabolism and Excretion :

Morphine is well absorbed by almost all routes. Intravenous route permits a quick but short-lived action and hence, is preferable in emergencies. While duration of action is somewhat longer with oral route. In comparison to morphine, the oral effectiveness of codeine is much higher. Morphine moderately binds (about $\frac{1}{3}$ of plasma concentration) to plasma-proteins. All opioids cross the placental barrier. Since morphine is the least lipophilic of opioids used clinically, it crosses the blood-brain-barrier at relatively lower rates.

N-demethylation is an important metabolic pathway for clinically used opioid. Morphine to some extent, is also converted to normorphine in the liver. Due to high first pass metabolism, it is less active orally than parenterally. Both, morphine and normorphine undergo conjugation either to monoglucuronide or diglucuronide. Four other minor metabolites are also identified. All these metabolites are inactive. Among them, the principal metabolite is morphine-3-glucuronide. Minute amount of morphine is also excreted in urine in unchanged form. Bile and urine are the routes employed for the excretion of morphine and its metabolites.

Adverse effects :

These include nausea, vomiting, constipation, epigastric distress, respiratory depression, dysphoria and allergic skin reactions due to morphine-induced release of histamine.

The development of tolerance and physical as well as psychological dependence with repeated use is the characteristic feature of all opioid drugs. Drug dependence is less likely to occur when morphine is given orally rather than parenterally. Because acute withdrawal symptoms may be precipitated in addicts, opioid antagonist should be administered cautiously in the treatment of morphine poisoning. Withdrawal symptoms may consist of hyperactivity, chills, increased respiratory rate and increased blood pressure. Essentially, no cross tolerance or dependence exists between opioids and barbiturates, alcohol, amphetamines or cocaine.

The pinpoint pupils, depressed respiration and coma, are the three prominent features of opioid poisoning. Opioid antagonists are the drugs of choice to reverse the severe respiratory depression associated with opioid poisoning. The pure opioid antagonists like, naloxone or naltrexone do not exert any (therapeutic or adverse) effect of opioid.

They are usually given by slow intravenous injection and are useful as :

(i) restorative agents in cases of opioid poisoning, and

(ii) diagnostic agent for opioid-addicts.

(b) Codeine :

It is known for its analgesic, antitussive, and constipation producing ability. Due to high oral to parenteral potency ratio, it is usually combined with aspirin or paracetamol for oral use. In contrast to morphine, poisoning by codeine occasionally leads to production of seizures.

(c) Thebaine:

The replacement of hydrogen atom in the hydroxyl groups of morphine by methyl groups results in the thebaine or dimethylmorphine nucleus. Thebaine, itself is devoid of analgesic and other central depressant actions of morphine. On the contrary, it has excitatory activity that sometimes leads to convulsions. Thebaine derivatives (oripavines) are semisynthetic analogues of morphine and are powerful analgesics.

Etorphine is a pure agonist, buprenorphine is a partial agonist while diprenorphine is a potent opioid antagonist. Due to the high lipophilicity but complexed molecular structure, buprenorphine exerts pharmacological action that is slower in onset and last longer than morphine. It is well absorbed from most of the sites and is extensively bound to plasma-proteins. Its action is terminated by N–dealkylation followed by glucuronidation.

Nausea, vomiting, drowsiness are some of its side-effects. The psychotomimetic side-effects are suppressed due to the presence of a cyclopropylmethyl groups (which imparts antagonistic potency) at N–atom. (Though tolerance and physical dependence develop with its prolong use, buprenorphine is the less abused drug.)

(d) Benzylisoquinoline Opioid Alkaloids:

Besides morphine, codeine and thebaine, benzylisoquinoline alkaloids (like, papaverine, noscapine) are also present in considerable amounts in opium. They have less marked CNS depressant effects. In addition, papaverine has a spasmolytic or relaxing effect on cardiac and smooth muscle. It is used as a vasodilator and antispasmodic drug, while noscapine is a cough suppressant.

(e) Heroin :

It is diacetylmorphine. It has an rapid onset and shorter duration of action than morphine. In body, it gets rapidly hydrolyzed to morphine. Hence, its pharmacological actions are quite similar to that of morphine. However due to greater lipophilicity, it produces greater euphorigenic effect. In the brain, heroin is deacetylated first to 6-monoacetylmorphine and then to morphine. In this sense, heroin carries morphine rapidly into the brain.

Prior to 1929, many analogues of morphine had been prepared by attempting simpler molecular modifications. All these simple derivatives (which include dihydrocodeine, dihydromorphine, hydromorphone, hydrocodone, oxycodone, ethyl morphine, methylhydromorphone) have similar pharmacological properties to morphine, Except hydromorphone and hydrocodone, which remain in the clinical use, none were found to be superior to morphine.

Synthetic Opioid Agonists:

Many new opioid series of totally synthetic origin were developed during 1930's to 1950's in an attempt to dissect the drug dependence ability from its analgesic activity. These include morphinans, benzomorphans, meperidine, methadone and propoxyphene type compound.

The structural elements which are almost essential for analgesic activity in opioidal agents are shown in the following figure.

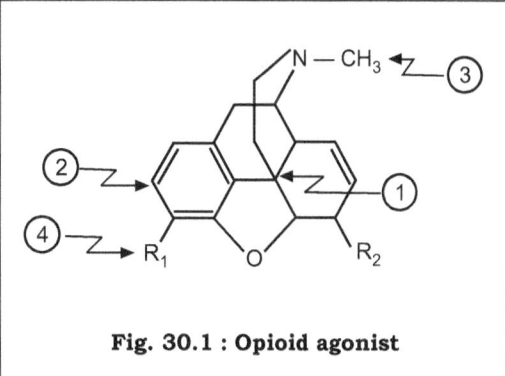

Fig. 30.1 : Opioid agonist

Structural requirements :

1. A quaternary carbon atom.

2. An aromatic nucleus linked directly to quaternary carbon atom.

3. A tertiary amino group, two saturated carbon atoms away from the quaternary carbon.

4. A phenolic hydroxyl group meta to the quaternary carbon if the tertiary nitrogen is the part of heterocyclic ring.

In the early 1940's, it led to the discovery of the first totally synthetic opioid analgesic agent, meperidine (i.e. pethidine). A more distinct analogue of morphine, methadone was introduced into medical use shortly after the end of second world war. Propoxyphene was introduced in 1957.

(a) Meperidine (pethidine) :

Primarily developed for antispasmodic use, meperidine was found to produce good analgesia. Qualitatively it has similar pharmacological action to that of morphine. However, due to its shorter duration of action, side-effects are less pronounced. Unlike other opioids, meperidine is not useful in exerting constipation or antitussive effect.

It is well absorbed by almost all routes. Usually, it is less effective by oral route. Significant amount of administered drug binds to plasma-proteins. N-demethylation and hydrolysis are the principle routes of metabolism. Upon N-demethylation, normeperidine is obtained which is responsible for excitatory (nervousness, muscle twitches, hallucinations) side-effects of the drug. While meperidinic acid is obtained upon hydrolysis which is excreted through urine in partly conjugated form. Meperidine is also excreted unchanged in urine in trace amount.

Adverse effects are less intense but similar to morphine. Some side-effects are associated with its atropine-like properties.

Alphaprodine and anileridine are opiates having actions just similar to meperidine. Alphaprodine is principally used in obstetrics and minor surgical procedures.

(b) Fentanyl :

It is a structural relative of meperidine having a very high analgesic potency. It has a shorter duration of action. In therapeutic doses, it may produce muscular rigidity and apnea. It has a widespread acceptance as an intravenous anaesthetic in surgical anaesthesia, for which it is usually combined with droperidol.

(c) Methadone :

The further simplification of morphine nucleus by opening of the N-atom containing ring resulted into methadone series. It is a more potent analgesic and antitussive agent than morphine. Of the optical isomers, *l*-methadone has a more potent analgesic activity while d-isomer acts as antitussive agent. It is the most efficacious opioid for oral use. Due to its longer duration of action, it is a drug of choice for patients with cancer pain.

Orally, it is well absorbed. In the body, it is extensively bound to plasma proteins. The drug is inactivated by N-demethylation followed by cyclization. Rifampin induces its metabolism. Methadone is also excreted in unchanged form in traces. Bile and urine serve the function of vehicle for excretion of methadone and its metabolites.

Adverse effects are just similar to that of morphine. A more powerful depression of respiratory centers is produced. The drug can develop tolerance, physical dependence and withdrawal symptoms. Though of a mild nature, the withdrawal symptoms are more prolonged.

Other clinically used members, like dextromoramide, dipipanone and phenadoxone have similar properties to that of methadone.

(d) Dextropropoxyphene :

It is a less analgesic, structural relative of methadone. The laevo isomer retains some antitussive activity. It is readily absorbed by almost all routes. It is metabolized by N-demethylation to norpropoxyphene, its major metabolite.

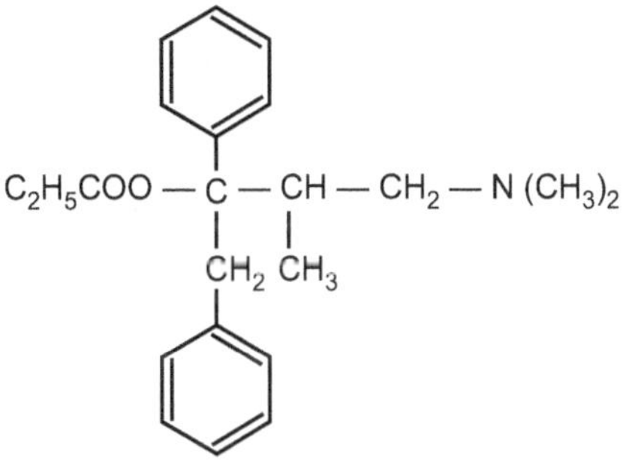

$C_2H_5COO - \overset{\underset{|}{CH_2}}{\underset{|}{C}} - \overset{|}{\underset{CH_3}{CH}} - CH_2 - N(CH_3)_2$

(with phenyl group attached to central C and phenyl group attached to CH)

Adverse effects include, marked respiratory depression, delusions, hallucinations, seizures and cardiotoxicity. The excitatory and cardiotoxic effects may be due in part to norpropoxyphene. Opioid antagonist may be used to treat the severe toxicity accompanied with overdose of the drug.

(e) Morphinan and Benzomorphan :

Morphinan lacks the ether bridge between the carbon atoms 4 and 5. The laevo form of morphinan (levorphanol) possesses the analgesic activity and is also used as adjunct to nitrous oxide induced anaesthesia. While the dextro form (dextromethorphan) is having cough depressant activity.

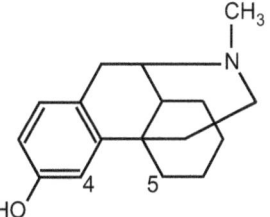

N-methylmorphinan

In fact, the removal of ether bridge and all the peripheral groups in the alicyclic ring of the morphine did not destroy its analgesic activity, encouraged May and Murphy to synthesize a new series of compounds known as benzomorphans (in which the alicyclic ring was replaced by one or two methyl groups). Benzomorphan itself is devoid of analgesic activity.

The clinically used opioids from morphinan series include, butorphanol (partial agonist) and opioid antagonists like, oxilorphan, levallorphan and cyclorphan. While pentazocine and cyclazocine are the potent opioid partial agonists from benzomorphan series. These drugs have a low tendency to produce dependence due to partial opioid antagonistic property. Unlike morphine, increase in the heart rate and blood pressure is reported with pentazocine due to increase in the peripheral catecholamine release.

30.4 THERAPEUTIC USES OF OPIOID AGONISTS

(a) They are used to relieve intense post-operative pain and discomfort.

(b) Due to their sedative effect, they cool down the emotional trauma (anxiety, fear, panic symptoms), and are beneficial in patients who suffer insomnia due to pain or cough attacks.

(c) They induce a decrease in the intestinal motility and can be used in the treatment of some forms of diarrhoea. Loperamide, diphenoxylate and difenoxin are the drugs which cause constipation effect.

(d) In general, the dextro isomers of opioid agonists retain analgesic effect while the laevo forms exhibit antitussive activity.

(e) Due to their vasodilatory and respiratory depressant effects, they are useful in the treatment of pulmonary edema.

30.5 MECHANISM OF ACTION OF OPIOID AGONISTS

Opioids act as agonists of endogenous substances known as endorphins (a group of endogenous morphine like peptides), interacting with steriospecific binding sites or opiod receptors located in brain and other tissues. The activation of opioid receptors which are irregularly distributed in different regions of CNS explains various therapeutic as well as adverse effects of opioids.

For example :

(a) Activation of opioid receptors in spinal cord, thalamus and cortex region results in suppression of pain impulses.

(b) Activation of opioid receptors in reticular activating system and medullary region plays an important role in the processes of sleep and vomiting respectively, and

(c) The muscle movement is affected due to the activation of opioid receptors in the limbic system.

Enkephalins represent the simplest members of endorphins. They are located in the short interneurons, predominantly in the areas of the CNS which are related to the perception of pain, mood, behaviour and to the regulation of neuro-endocrinological functions. Enkephalinergic neurons present in sensory and related pathways are stimulated by trauma.

The released enkephalin then increases tolerance to pain by suppressing the conduction of pain impulse. Their principal site of action is the terminals of pre-synaptic neurons where they interfere in the release of neurotransmitters ('like acetylcholine, norepinephrine and dopamine). The opioid mediated fall in the cyclic AMP levels also contributes to produce analgesia.

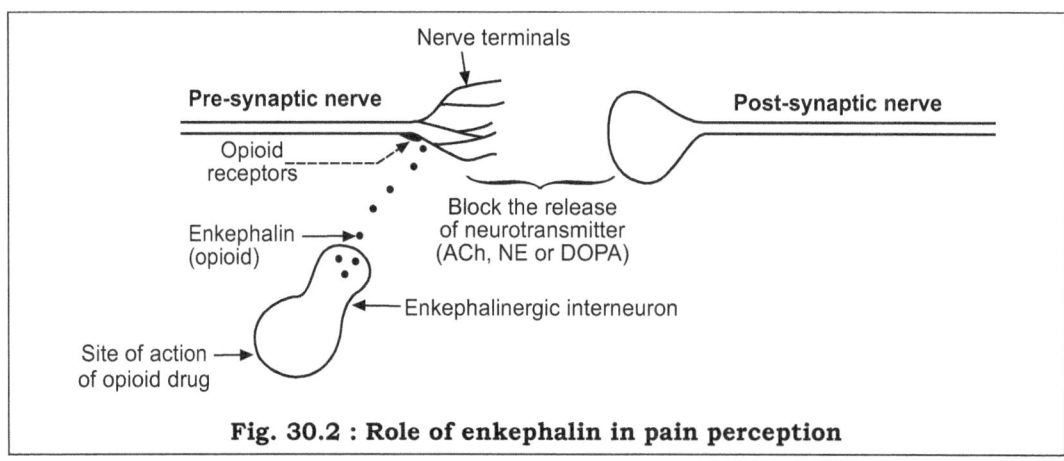

Fig. 30.2 : Role of enkephalin in pain perception

Thus under the influence of enkephalin, presynaptic terminals fail to release the neurotransmitter in the synaptic cleft and the pain impulse is not received by the post-synaptic nerve.

The opioid analgesic agents bring about the detachment of the pain sensation by two fold mechanisms. Thus, they :

(a) Inhibit the propagation of the pain impulse, and

(b) Depress the limbic system and frontal lobes of the brain and relieves the symptoms (anxiety, fear, discomfort) of emotional trauma, associated with the pain sensation.

It is assumed that all opioid agonists produce their effects by mimicking the actions of endogenous enkephalins. Disorder of enkephalin function, thus may be reflected by some forms of mental illness. In normal persons, enkephalins appear to function as neurotransmitter, modulators of neuro-transmission or neurohormone at various sites in the CNS and peripheral regions. They are supposed to be the degradation products of endorphins, obtained through proteolysis.

Endorphins have potent morphinomimetic activities and may induce respiratory depression and addiction liabilities.

The actions of both endorphins and morphine-like drugs can be reversed by opioid antagonists. The details about their biosynthesis, bio-availability and degradation pattern are yet to be confirmed.

The anterior pituitary hormone, β-lipotropin is a polypeptide consisting of about 91 aminoacid residues. It was first isolated from sheep pituitary in 1964 by Choh Hao Li, of Hormone Research Laboratory, University of California and was later recognised as one of the precursor of endorphins. For example, in the β-lipotropin structure,

(i) aminoacid residues 61 - 76

$$= \text{endorphin } \alpha$$

(ii) aminoacid residues 61 - 96

$$= \text{endorphin } \beta$$

(iii) aminoacid residues 61 - 77, and

$$61 - 86 = \text{endorphin } \gamma$$

This was confirmed by the isolation of α and β-endorphins by Roger Guillemin from pig posterior pituitary and hypothalamus extract in 1976. As we know, the term enkephalins (which means, "in the head"), is usually applied to low molecular peptides which are supposed to be the degradation products of endorphins. They are involved in both, the enhancement and inhibition of the perception of pain.

In 1975, Hughes first reported the presence of enkephalins in the brain extract. Two such endogenous pentapeptide enkephalins have been isolated and characterized. They include :

(i) H – Tyr – Gly – Gly – Phe – Met – OH
   Methionine enkephalin

(ii) H – Tyr – Gly – Gly – Phe – Leu – OH
    Leucine enkephalin

They are metabolised very rapidly in vivo by carboxypeptidase A and leucine amino peptidase. The active portion of the morphine nucleus, present in the enkephalin structure retains the same conformational feature.

Thus, when properly folded, enkephalins show a good topographical relationship with morphine.

Based upon the structures of these endogenous enkephalins and endorphins, attempts are being done to get synthetic potent endorphin analogues.

For example, D-ala-ala-D-(leu)^5-enkephalin, methionine carbinol and metkephamid are some of the synthetic peptides developed.

30.6 OPIOID RECEPTOR

Morphine-like drugs exert their effects by selectively acting on receptors situated both in the higher centers and in the spinal cord. They are also present in several peripheral tissues. The diversified actions and side-effects of opioids can only be explained on the basis of existence of several receptor sub-types. At least eight subtypes of opioid receptors have been recognized in the brain and other tissues, of which four subtypes exist predominantly in the CNS.

Martin and Gilbert in 1976 have postulated the existence of three sub-types of opioid receptors, designated as :

(i) mµ (morphine is the prototype agonist).

(ii) kappa (k), where ketocyclazocine is prototype agonist.

(iii) σ (N–allylnormetazocine is prototype agonist).

While Lord et al, in 1977 designated the fourth sub-type as :

(iv) δ (delta), where leu-enkephalin is prototype agonist.

It is thought that :

(i) µ sub-species are involved in producing : analgesia, respiratory depression, euphoria, emesis and addiction liability.

(ii) k sub-species are involved in producing : spinal analgesia, miosis and sedation.

(iii) σ sub-species are involved in producing : dysphoria, hallucinations, respiratory stimulation.

(iv) δ sub-species activation may lead to alterations in affective behaviour.

An agonist or antagonistic activity of opiod agents depends upon their relative affinity for these receptor sub-types.

The functional moieties of opioid receptor, responsible for drug-receptor interactions have also been characterized. Beckett and Casy (1954) proposed that an opioid receptor is composed of four reactive sites. These include :

(i) A flattened part which holds the aromatic portion of an opioid drug through the Vander Waals forces.

(ii) A cavity or a hollow disk which entraps the ethylene bridge between the quaternary carbon and tertiary nitrogen atom, and

(iii) An anionic site which interacts with the tertiary nitrogen (at physiological pH, 3° nitrogen gets quaternized) through ionic bonding.

(iv) A binding site for the hydroxyl group.

The receptor facilitates binding with drug by accommodating the opioid molecule in its irregular T-shaped pouch. However, by changing this favourable conformation of opioid receptors, sodium ions are reported to reduce its affinity for opioid agonists and to increase the affinity for opioid antagonists. These antagonists also differ in their relative affinities for different receptor subtypes which govern their observed biological response. For example, naloxone (opioid antagonist) is more potent in antagonizing the effects of µ agonists than k or σ agonists. Depending upon their relative affinities for different sub-types of opioid receptors, they can be classified as -

(a) Partial opioid agonists, and

(b) Pure opioid antagonists.

30.7 PARTIAL OPIOID AGONISTS

Opioid antagonists competitively antagonize the effects of opioid analgesics by binding at several sub-species of opioid receptor. The first opioid antagonist, N-allylnorcodeine was discovered in 1915. The key to antagonistic activity appears to reside in the alkylation of the piperidine nitrogen of the morphine. The structural features which impart antagonistic activity to the molecule includes :

1. N–allyl or N–cyclopropylmethyl group.

2. 14–Hydroxy group in morphines and morphinans and 9-hydroxy or methyl group in β-configuration in 6, 7-benzomorphans.

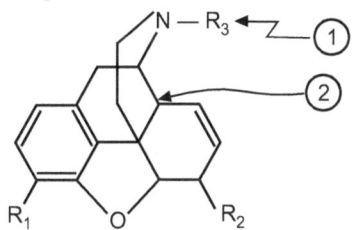

At piperidine nitrogen, as the chain-length increases to amyl or hexyl, agonistic activity is restored. All the above discussions are not strictly followed in the thebaine (oripavine) derivatives.

In general, an allyl or methyl cyclopropyl group at piperidine nitrogen imparts antagonistic property to the molecule. If such antagonistic feature of the molecule is dominated by agonist feature, the compound acts as partial agonist and demonstrates its dual, agonist and antagonistic properties. Such a dual nature may be due to its ability to activate some receptor subtypes and to inhibit the other sub-types. The discovery of morphine antagonist, Nalorphine (N-allylnormorphine) in the 1940's, and subsequent demonstration of its dual agonist and antagonistic properties opened new avenues for the development of agents with reduced dependence liability.

Cyclazocine, pentazocine, buprenorphine, nalbuphine and butorphanol are some of the examples of well-known dualists in the clinical use. They behave like morphine and exert analgesic effect in patients who were not in touch recently with opioid agonists. While a mild withdrawal syndrome may be precipitated, if they are given insufficient dose to the opioid-addict patients. Tolerance develops to agonistic and not to antagonistic effects of these drugs.

Out of these, nalorphine, cyclazocine and nalbuphine have antagonistic action at μ receptor sub-type while buprenorphine, propriam and pentazocine are relatively weak antagonists at μ sub-type.

(a) Nalorphine :

Its synthesis was first reported in 1941. It displays all the morphine-like actions but in less intense form. The respiratory depression, miosis and cough suppressant action of morphine are retained. Though it is a good analgesic agent, it could not be used clinically due to its ability to cause more intense dysphoric reaction. Tolerance is reported and withdrawal symptoms are milder.

(b) Levallorphan :

It has quite similar properties to nalorphine.

(c) Cyclazocine :

Both, cyclazocine and pentazocine are the benzomorphan derivatives. They retain all the pharmacological actions of opioid agonists in less intense form. Analgesic effects in part, are due to the agonist action at k opioid receptor sub-type. While by their antagonistic action, they reduce the intensity of euphoric, miosis, respiratory depression and physical dependence properties of opioid agonists. Cyclazocine is orally effective (the cyclopropylmethyl substitution at N-atom slow down the rate of metabolism by N–dealkylation) and has a longer duration of action. The cross-tolerance between nalorphine and cyclazocine is reported.

(d) Pentazocine :

It elevates the plasma catecholamine concentration resulting into an increase in heart rate and blood pressure. It retains analgesic action but does not antagonize the opioid-induced respiratory depression. It is well absorbed by all routes. It has a shorter duration of action due to the rapid first pass metabolism in the liver.

Adverse effects associated with pentazocine therapy include, nausea, anxiety, sweating, hallucination, marked respiratory depression, increased blood pressure and tachycardia. Psychotomimetic effects are reported to occur at therapeutic dose-level. With repeated use, tolerance and physical dependence are reported to develop.

(e) Nalbuphine :

It has a structural resemblance with both, oxymorphone (opioid agonist) and naloxone (opioid antagonist). Its activity spectra is quite similar to that of pentazocine. But due to its ability to antagonize μ receptor activation, it is less likely to produce dysphoric effects and respiratory depression.

(f) Butorphanol :

It is a member of morphinan series, having actions similar to pentazocine. It has less intense psychotomimetic and cardiovascular side-effects. But like pentazocine, it has respiratory depressant activity. Since it is available only in parenteral form, the treatment of acute rather than chronic pain is possible.

(g) Buprenorphine :

It is a semi-synthetic thebaine derivative having higher lipophilicity. It is a potent analgesic agent without psychotomimetic effects. The additional alkyl substitution at C_7 suggests an evidence for an additional lipophilic binding site in opioid receptor. It has similar but less intense pharmacological effects to that of morphine. Its bulky and rigid structure (near the tertiary nitrogen atom), sterically hinders the ionic interaction between the positively charged nitrogen atom and anionic receptor site. But once the interaction occurs, the molecule gets very slowly dissociated from the receptor surface due to close and compact fitting. This is reflected in its effects which are slower in onset and last longer than morphine.

30.8 OPIOID ANTAGONISTS

In particular, the pure agonist molecule can be converted into a partial agonist or a pure antagonist by relatively minor changes in the structure. The most common such substitution is that of a large moiety (like an allyl or a n-methylcyclopropyl group) at the nitrogen atom of the piperidine ring in the structure. For example, morphine can be converted to nalorphine, levorphanol to levallorphan and oxymorphone to naloxone or naltrexone. The large moiety at nitrogen atom, imparts antagonistic (lack of intrensic activity) property to the structure by sterically hindering the ionic interaction between positively charged N-atom and anionic receptor site. In certain structures (i.e., nalorphine, levallorphan), however intrinsic activity does not vanish completely, resulting into partial antagonism. Such agents still retain agonistic actions at k and σ receptor sub-types. While naloxone and naltrexone are the examples of pure antagonists which are completely devoid of agonist activity. They antagonise the activation of all the sub-types of opioid receptor.

Opioid antagonists are devoid of any pharmacological action when they are administered alone to the patient. However, they reverse the pharmacological or subjective effects of opioid agonists and can precipitate the withdrawal symptoms in opioid addicted persons. They antagonise euphoretic, miotic, respiratory depressant and physical dependence properties of opioid agonists. The withdrawal symptoms of opioid antagonists are very few and of mild nature.

Naltrexone is structurally related to naloxone except that a cyclopropylmethyl rather than an allyl group is present at the piperidine nitrogen of oxymorphone moiety. Naloxone is more effective parenterally than orally due to its extensive first pass metabolism in the liver. While naltrexone has a longer duration of action than naloxone, probably due to the bulky cyclopropyl methyl group at N-atom which sterically hinders its metabolism. In addition, naltrexone upon metabolism is converted to 6–naltrexol which still retains opioid antagonistic activity.

Both these agents reverse the opioid-induced respiratory depressant effect. But relatively high doses may be needed, particularly for naloxone. They have very few side-effects. Naloxone therapy may be associated with drowsiness.

30.9 THERAPEUTIC USES OF OPIOID ANTAGONIST

1. In the treatment of respiratory depression seen in the opioid poisoning.

2. Chronic administration of nalorphine alongwith morphine prevents or minimizes the development of physical dependence.

3. Reduce the intensity of various untoward effects of opioids, like euphoria, drowsiness, vomiting and muscular inco-ordination.

4. Therapeutic agents in the treatment of shock and certain stress conditions characterized by an elevated endorphin or enkephalin levels.

5. Therapeutic agents in the treatment of opioid-addiction.

30.10 ANTITUSSIVE AGENTS

The cough reflex is initiated by either chemical or mechanical stimulation of cough receptors located in tracheobronchial passages. Their activity is governed by the cough centers present in the medulla. Thus, both the central as well as peripheral mechanisms are involved in the generation of cough reflex. Naturally it follows then, both centrally acting (opioids) as well as peripherally acting (β–adrenergic agonists) agents may be effective in the treatment of cough reflex.

Excessive tracheobronchial secretion and bronchoconstriction are the major cough symptoms. Bronchodilation induced by β-adrenergic agonists thus may be beneficial, while opioids may act centrally to exhibit an antitussive effect by elevating the threshold for coughing. Most of the antitussive opioids (i.e., dextro isomers) are devoid of analgesic and addiction properties. Hence it is proposed that their antitussive effect may be propogated through the receptors other than the recognised sub-types (mμ, σ, k, and δ) of opioid receptor.

At recommended doses, opioid antitussive agents produce mild adverse effects which include, nausea, drowsiness, urticaria, dizziness, and gastrointestinal disturbances.

Other centrally acting non-opioid antitussive agents include, benzonatate, chlophedianol, diphenhydramine, carbetapentane, caramiphen and glaucine.

SECTION - IV : DRUG TREATMENT OF RHUMATIC DISEASES

DRUGS FOR RHEUMATIC DISEASES

31.1 INTRODUCTION

Inflammation can be defined as a defensive but exaggerated local tissue reaction in response to exogenous or endogenous insult. It is a complex phenomenon, comprising of biochemical as well as immunological factors. It is recognised by the following symptoms :

1. Calor (Heat)
2. Rubor (Redness)
3. Tumor (Swelling), and
4. Dolor (Pain).

Tissue damage initiates or activates the local release of various chemotactic factors that provoke directly or indirectly the appearance of the mediators of pain and inflammation. These factors include :

(a) Amines : Histamine, serotonin.

(b) Polypeptides : Plasmakinins.

(c) Proteases : Kallikrein, plasmin. Release of lysosomal enzymes usually occurs from mast cells, macrophages, polymorphonuclear leucocytes and platelets.

(d) Prostaglandins.

(e) Hageman factor : This factor is activated when it comes in contact with a foreign surface. Once activated, it initiates the production and release of plasma kinins. They are capable of causing vasodilation and increased capillary permeability. One of such plasmakinins, bradykinin was first described and named by Rocha and Silva et al (1949).

(f) Other factors : These include leucotoxin, leucocytosis promoting factor and lymph node permeability factor.

All these mediators cause local vascular response, which is characterised by :

1. Increased blood flow to the affected area.

2. Increased vascular permeability which may cause edema.

3. Cellular infiltration of platelets and macrophages from the capillaries into the tissue spaces.

So in brief, the sequence of early events in inflammation may be summarised as :

(a) Initial injury which causes the release of inflammatory mediators.

(b) Vasodilation.

(c) Increased vascular permeability, resulting into cellular infiltration.

(d) Migration of phagocytic cells to the inflamed area, resulting into release of lytic enzymes due to rupturing of cellular lysosomal membranes.

An inflammation may be either a primary or a secondary response to the tissue damage. A primary inflammation consists of direct and generally acute defence reaction while in the secondary inflammation, it is an indirect consequence of the exaggerated cell physiology, arising due to pathological condition, e.g., rheumatoid arthritis.

The anti-inflammatory analgesic agents, also popularly known as non-steroidal anti-inflammatory drugs are associated with analgesic and antipyretic activities. The peripheral nerve fibres which conduct pain impulses may be categorised as :

(a) The large myelinated A fibers that conduct fast, more intense and precise pain.

(b) The myelinated B fibers that conduct pain impulses of intermediate intensity, and

(c) Unmyelinated C fibers that conduct slow and diffused pain.

The drugs covered in this chapter, have an ability to inhibit the synthesis of thromboxane and prostaglandins. This fact was first discovered by Vane in 1971. He assigned the therapeutic as well as adverse effects of aspirin-like drugs to their ability to prevent prostaglandin biosynthesis.

Considerable evidence has supported the concept that non-steroidal anti-inflammatory analgesic drugs act by inhibiting the biosynthesis of prostaglandins which are the basic cause behind pain, fever and inflammatory conditions. They have the ability to sensitize the pain receptors to mechanical and chemical stimulation. The biosynthesis of prostaglandins is catalysed by microsomal enzymes present in almost every mammalion cell type, except erythrocytes.

Prostaglandins are a group of cyclopentane derivatives formed from polyunsaturated fatty acids by most mammalion tissues. The basic structure of all prostaglandins contains about 20 carbon atoms having a cyclopentane ring with two adjacent side-chains.

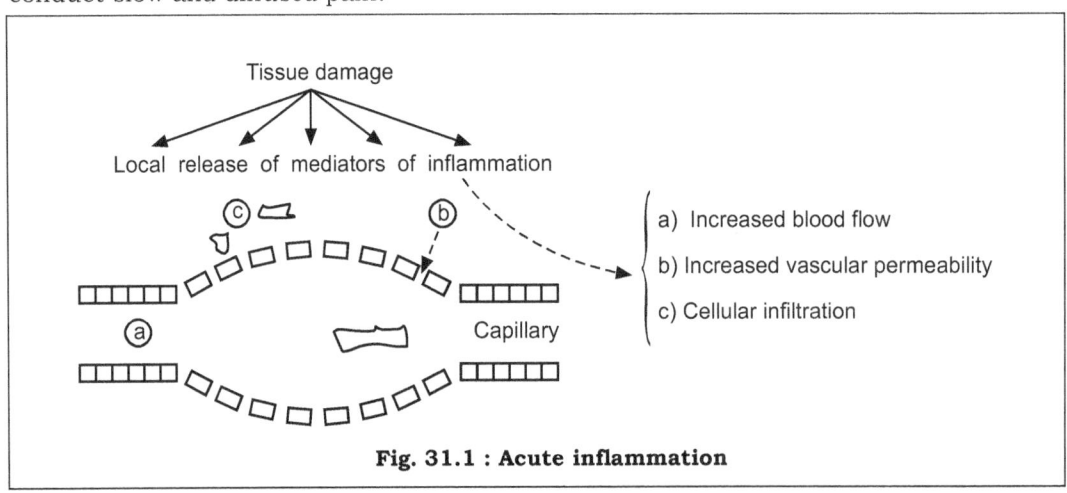

Fig. 31.1 : Acute inflammation

Arachidonic acid serves as a precursor for biosynthesis of prostaglandins in humans. Arachidonic acid is probably stored in the phospholipid fraction of the cell. The biosynthetic route for the formation of various prostaglandins is shown in Fig. 31.2.

Prostaglandins potentiate the early inflammatory response, causing vasodilation, increased permeability, facilitating cellular infiltration and sensitizing the pain receptors. The non-steroidal anti-inflammatory analgesics do not act centrally to intervene in the perception of the pain. They act peripherally to inhibit both, the synthesis and release of prostaglandins. Thus, they have minimum CNS side-effects. They neither induce mood alterations nor have a tendency to cause drug dependence. Thus, morphine like drugs act on CNS while these drugs act mainly peripherally at the site of origin of pain.

Prostanoic acid (Basic structure)

An elevation of body temperature is usually seen in many infectious diseases, It is also often associated with the inflammatory process. The center for control of body temperature is located in the hypothalamus. An elevation of the body temperature occurs due to the attack of pyrogenic substances on this regulatory center. Pyrogens are the metabolic products of bacteria and leucocytes. They induce changes in the normal regulatory process of body temperature resulting into reduced heat loss by peripheral vasoconstriction associated with an increase in the heat production. The net result is a rise in body temperature.

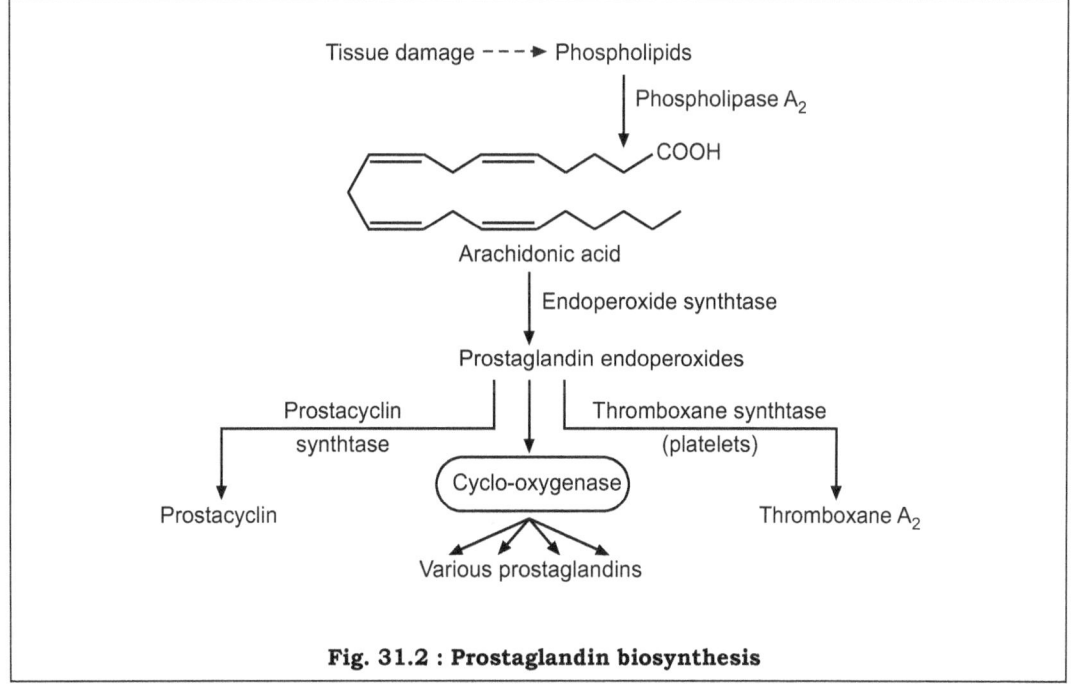

Fig. 31.2 : Prostaglandin biosynthesis

In an inflammatory disorder, the endogenous pyrogen appaeently passes into the CNS and stimulates the release of prostaglandin-like substances from some specific sites within the brain. The non-steroidal anti-inflammatory analgesic agents have antipyretic activity. They block the synthesis and release of these substances, followed by peripheral vasodilation and increased sweating, resulting into considerable heat loss from the body. This brings down the body temperature to its normal.

Inflammation is a major symptom of various connective tissue diseases. These include,

(a) *rheumatic fever* : It is characterised by arthritis, swelling, immobility of joints and fever.

(b) rheumatoid arthritis, ankylosing spondylitis and osteoarthritis.

(c) systemic lupus erythematosus and polyarteritis nodosa.

The non-steroidal anti-inflammatory agents are clinically employed in the treatment of all above mentioned conditions. They also provide relief to the patient from the emotional trauma of fever, pain and insomnia. Besides inhibiting the cyclooxygenase enzymes involved in prostaglandin biosynthesis they also interfere with a variety of other enzymes.The adverse effects, in part, can be accounted on this basis. The major adverse-effects common to different classes of these drugs include.

(a) Except para amino phenol derivatives, these drugs produce gastrointestinal side-effects. In the untreated normal person, the GIT-membrane is protected from mucosal damage by prostaglandins like PGI_2 and PGE_2. These drugs inhibit the synthesis of gastric prostaglandins and expose the mucosal membrane to increased gastric acid attack resulting into gastric or intestinal ulceration.

(b) Their ability to inhibit the biosynthesis of prostaglandins entitles them to prevent the formation of thromboxane A_2, a potent platelet aggregating agent. Thus, treatment with non-steroidal anti-inflammatory drugs leads to increase in the bleeding time.

(c) The gestation or spontaneous labour is found to be prolonged.

(d) Due to their higher affinity for plasma proteins, these agents cause easy displacement of other plasma protein-bound drugs. This may lead to a sudden, unexpected rise in the plasma concentration of co-administered drug resulting into potentially dangerous effects.

(e) In some individuals, hypersensitivity reaction may be seen during therapy which is characterised by edema, generalised urticaria and sometimes bronchial asthma. Epinephrine is usually used to control such hypersensitivity reaction.

The anti-inflammatory analgesics also popularly known as non-narcotic analgesic agents are also associated with antipyretic property. The prototype of this class is aspirin, and hence, though this class comprises the chemically unrelated heterogeneous group of compounds, it is often referred to as 'aspirin-like' drugs. They are valuable for the non-specific relief of pain of mild to moderate intensities, like headache, arthritis, neuralgia, dysmenorrhea etc. Due to their ability to inhibit the synthesis end release

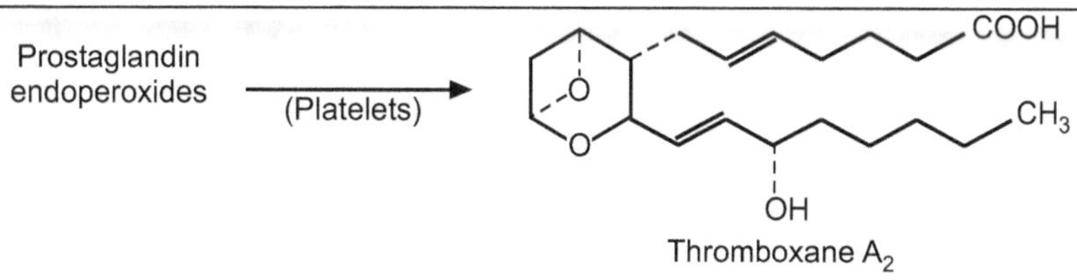

```
Prostaglandin
endoperoxides  ──(Platelets)──▶  [structure]
                                  Thromboxane A₂
```

Fig. 31.3

of thromboxane A_2 (platelet aggregating agents), some of these agents are also useful in the treatment of diseases characterized by platelet hyperaggregability such as, coronary artery disease, myocardial infarction etc.

Their effectiveness in various inflammatory conditions is due to their ability to inhibit the biosynthesis of prostaglandins. Aspirin itself inactivates the cyclo-oxygenase enzyme by acetylating serine group at its active site. With the exception of indomethacin, the aspirin-like drugs irreversibly inhibit the cyclo-oxygenase enzymes.

Besides this, some of these agents may have an ability to speed up the breakdown of mucopolysaccharide, in addition to inhibiting its synthesis. They also stabilize the lysosomes and cool down other mediators of inflammation.

Some of 'aspirin-like' drugs have uricosuric effect (i.e., promote excretion of uric acid) and hence may be useful in the treatment of gout.

31.2 CLASSIFICATION

The various analgesic-antipyretic anti-inflammatory agents can be classified as :

   I. Salicylic acid derivatives.
   II. Para amino phenol derivatives.
   III. Pyrazolon derivatives.
   IV. Indole acetic acid derivatives.
   V. Propionic acid derivatives.
   VI. Fenamates (N-arylanthranilic acid derivatives).
   VII. Miscellaneous agents.

31.3 SALICYLIC ACID DERIVATIVES

The salicylic acid derivatives are most widely employed to treat arthritis.

Salicin is a glycoside which was isolated from the bark of the white willow (Salix alba). It has analgesic and antipyretic activities. Upon hydrolysis, it yields salicylic acid and glucose. Salicylic acid could not be used internally due to its irritating property. Its use is restricted for the topical region, as a keratolytic agent. In an attempt to reduce its irritation property, several derivatives of salicylic acid have been synthesized. These derivatives can broadly be divided into :

(a) Esters of salicylic acid: These agents, have very little value as analgesic agents. They are used externally mainly as counter-irritants. Example is methyl salicylate.

(b) Salicylate esters of organic acids: These compounds vary in their stomach irritation property. Few of these compounds have been employed as analgesic agents. Examples include that of aspirin.

(c) Inorganic salicylates : The following salts of salicylic acid may be used internally as analgesics.

(i) Sodium salicylate

(ii) Magnesium salicylate

(iii) Choline salicylate

(iv) Ammonium salicylate

They are of limited clinical utility.

(d) Several derivatives of salicylic acid are synthesized by altering substituents on the carboxyl or hydroxyl group in the molecule. They all differ both, in potency as well as toxicity. The clinically used derivatives of salicylic acid include salicylic acid, methyl salicylate, sodium salicylate, phenyl salicylate, acetyl salicylic acid etc.

Diflunisal is an anti-inflammatory analgesic agent introduced into the market in 1971. While benorylate is an ester of aspirin and paracetamol. The gastrointestinal side-effects of benorylate are milder than that of the aspirin. It is mainly indicated for the treatment of rheumatoid arthritis. Similarly salsalate is the ester formed between two salicylic acid molecules. It is said to cause less gastric irritation.

Aspirin is probably still the most extensively employed analgesic-antipyretic and anti-inflammatory agent associated with fewer side-effects. In moist air, it gradually undergoes decomposition to salicylic acid and acetic acid. The name aspirin was derived from Spiraea, the plant species from which salicylic acid was once obtained.

Pharmacology :

(a) Analgesic Effect :

Salicylates relieve the low to moderate intensity pain through both, central and peripheral mechanisms. It inhibits the cyclo-oxygenase enzymes involved in the biosynthesis of prostaglandins which are the main mediators of pain and inflammation. Since it does not act on the cortex region, it does not produce major CNS–adverse effects during chronic administration.

(b) Antipyretic Effect :

In therapeutic doses, salicylates lower down an elevated body temperature by their action in the hypothalamus region. Its antipyretic effect results due to cutaneous vasodilation that is associated with increased rate of sweating. In toxic doses, it causes uncoupling of oxidative phosphorylation resulting into increased heat production (hyperthermia). The overall effect is elevation of the body temperature. Besides hyperthermia, higher doses of salicylates may cause minor CNS–disturbances that include dizziness, confusion, delirium and tinnitus aurium. Nausea and vomiting may occur due to the activation of both, central (chemoreceptor trigger zone in medulla) as well as peripheral (local gastric irritation) mechanisms. These symptoms led to the condition, known as salicylism. These symptoms are readily reversible when the drug is withdrawn.

(c) Respiratory System :

In therapeutic doses, salicylates directly stimulate the respiratory centers present in the medulla. They uncouple oxidative phosphorylation resulting into an increase in oxygen consumption primarily in skeletal-muscles followed by an increase in CO_2 production. This increased P_{CO_2} – blood gas tension then acts as a hyper-ventilatory stimulus to the respiratory centers in the medulla. Thus salicylates increase both, rate and depth of respiration through direct and indirect mechanisms.

(d) Metabolic Effect :

Salicylates reduce the blood glucose concentration either by inhibiting glucose production or by increasing its rate of utilization. In diabetic patients, salicylates thus potentiate the action of hypoglycemic drugs.

Salicylates also cause an accumulation of glutamic acid. The convulsions seen sometimes in salicylate poisoning are thus due to the accumulation of glutamate in the cerebral region.

(e) Acid-base Balance :

Salicylates uncouple oxidative phosphorylation resulting into an elevated plasma CO_2 level (respiratory alkalosis). The renal adjustment to these respiratory changes like, increased bicarbonate, sodium and potassium ion excretion leads to acidosis. Potassium ion depletion is also found to occur during the chronic administration of salicylates.

(f) Cardiovascular Effect :

Salicylates do not influence the cardiovascular function in ordinary doses. However, they directly depress the circulation in toxic doses. They cause the inhibition of the synthesis of thromboxane A_2, the platelet aggregation factor. The fibrinogen in the plasma is also reduced by the salicylates. Hence, salicylates can be used to treat coronary artery thrombosis due to their anticoagulant action. However, for a person undergoing surgical procedure, salicylate therapy should not be used.

(g) Gastrointestinal System :

The prostaglandins, locally released from the mucosa of GI–membrane are responsible for the inhibition of the gastric acid secretion and formation of cytoprotective mucous layer. Salicylates inhibit the synthesis of these prostaglandins, resulting into various adverse effects ranging from nausea, vomiting, epigastric distress, dyspepsia to erosive gastritis and peptic ulcer. These effects may be minimized by formulating salicylates in the buffer solution. Gastric hemorrhage sometimes occur due to local damage to submucosal capillaries, when larger doses of salicylates are administered.

(h) Endocrine Effect :

The functioning of endocrine glands like, adrenal and thyroid gland is influenced by salicylates during long term treatment.

(i) Other Effects :

1. During chronic treatment, salicylates may cause dose-dependent hepatic and renal toxicities.

2. Local irritant effects on skin and gastric mucosa are also observed.

3. Excess prostaglandin production is responsible for increased frequency and force of uterine muscle contractions. This results into decreased uterus blood flow leading to ischemic condition (associated with menstrual pain) that is seen in dysmenorrhoea.

Aspirin-like drugs due to their inhibitory action on prostaglandin biosynthesis, are useful to relieve menstrual pain in dysmenorrhoea.

Absorption, Distribution, Metabolism and Excretion :

Salicylates are well absorbed from GIT. Salicylic acid and methyl salicylate can also be absorbed from the skin when applied in the form of ointments. The absorption from rectal route is slow and incomplete.

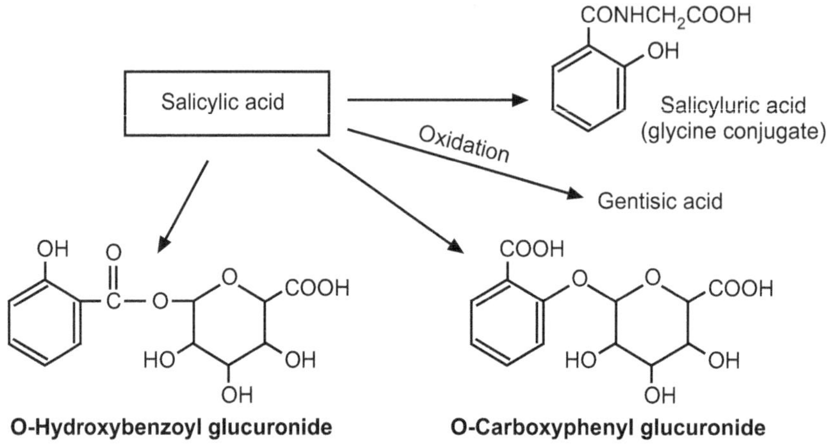

Fig. 31.4 : Bio-transformations of salicylic acid

After absorption, salicylates are readily distributed through most of the body compartments except CNS where less amount of drug reaches due to their ionic nature.

They are known to cross placental barrier. In plasma, salicylates are extensively bound to plasma-proteins, more particularly to albumin.

Salicylates undergo metabolism primarily by the enzymes present in hepatic endoplasmic reticulum and mitochondria. The absorbed salicylate is rapidly biotransformed to salicylic acid in plasma, liver and erythrocytes which then undergoes metabolism as shown in the Fig. 31.4.

These metabolites alongwith small amounts of unchanged salicylic acid are excreted mainly through urine. The rate of excretion can be altered by changing the urine pH.

In case of diflunisal which is not biotransformed to salicylic acid, the drug is mainly excreted in the form of its glucuronide conjugate.

In certain patients, aspirin-like drugs may cause hypersensitivity reactions. Idiosyncratic reactions may occur due to inhibition of prostaglandin biosynthesis. These include, skin rashes, angioneurotic edema and asthma. In case of toxicity arising due to overdosage of salicylates, gastric lavage, alkalinization of urine coupled with diuresis may be some of the means to relieve toxicity symptoms.

31.4 PARA-AMINO PHENOL DERIVATIVES

Since p-amino phenol is the metabolite of dye aniline, these analgesic agents are also called as "coal tar analgesics". The only agents of interest from this class are :

Acetanilide (1886) is probably one of the oldest of analgesic antipyretic agents. It is metabolised into paracetamol and aniline.

Due to the toxicity of the latter compound, acetanilide, is no longer used in therapeutics. The reduction in the toxicity profile of acetanilide occurs if a hydroxyl group is attached to it at para position. This observation was confirmed by the use of paracetamol, which has less overall toxicity and is most widely used agent from this category.

The p-amino phenol derivatives are all analgesic-antipyretic agents. They possess very weak anti-inflammatory activities. They lack the gastric irritation property of salicylates. They neither have uricosuric effect nor they have any action on respiratory system or on bleeding time. Phenacetin was introduced in 1887 followed by paracetamol in 1893. Paracetamol is the major active metabolite of both, acetanilid and phenacetin. Metabolism occurs primarily by hepatic microsomal enzymes.

The metabolites, aniline and p-phenetidine induce the conversion of haemoglobin into methaemoglobin. Small amount of sulphaemoglobin also forms. This results into toxic reactions, like cyanosis, anemia, weakness, dyspnoea, respiratory depression and in toxic overdose, cardiac arrest.

While paracetamol has very low toxicity potential. In large doses, it may cause renal and hepatic necrosis. Hence it is more preferred agent over phenacetin.

31.5 PYRAZOLON DERIVATIVES

On the chemical basis, these derivatives can be categorized as :

Antipyrine is the parent drug from this category, introduced in 1887 by Knorr. It has analgesic and antipyretic activity. Its name has been derived from its antipyretic activity. Its structural modifications further resulted into the introduction of aminopyrine (amidopyrine) and dipyrone into clinical use. Aminopyrine is more effective analgesic than antipyrine. Fatal agranulocytosis caused by dipyrone and aminopyrine has limited their usefulness. Aminopyrine is no longer used-clinically.

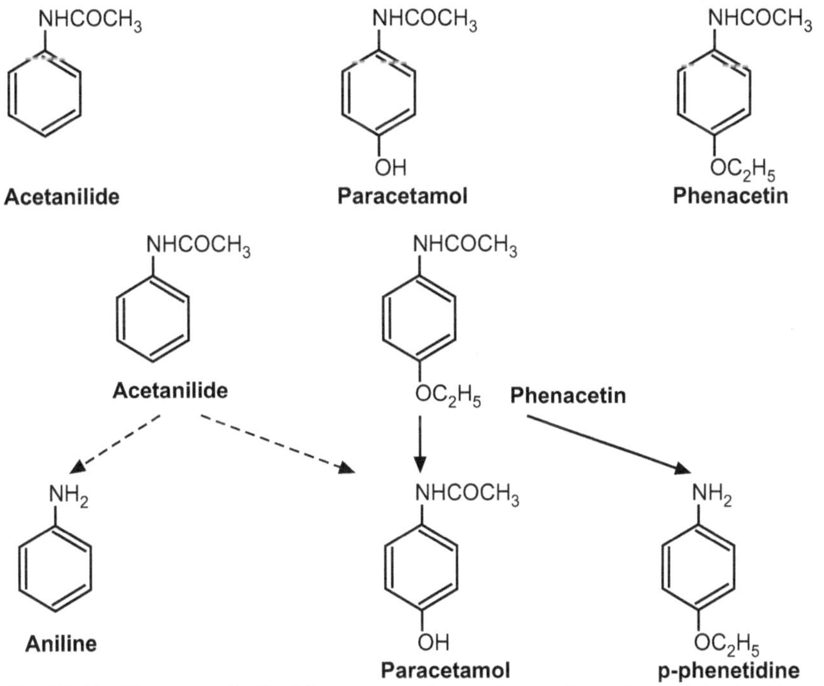

Fig. 31.5 : The metabolic bio-conversions of p-amino phenol derivatives

These derivatives have been introduced in 1949 for the treatment of rheumatoid arthritis. They have good anti-inflammatory activity with weak antipyretic action. Their toxicity precludes their long term use.

Both these derivatives are well absorbed from GIT and rectum. In plasma, they are extensively bound to plasma-proteins. Phenylbutazone has considerably longer duration of action due to production of active metabolite (oxyphenbutazone). The other metabolite, γ-hydroxyphenylbutazone, (though devoid of antirheumatic activity) retains uricosuric activity. Minute quantity of phenylbutazone also appears in urine in the unchanged form. Both, the parent drug and its metabolites partly are excreted as conjugates and partly in the free form.

Oxyphenbutazone when administered, it is mainly excreted in the form of its O-glucuronide conjugate.

Phenylbutazone is one of the powerful inducers of hepatic microsomal enzymes. Like salicylates, it uncouples oxidative phosphorylation.

Adverse effects include, nausea, vomiting, skin rashes, epigastric discomfort, edema, insomnia, blurred vision, aplastic anemia, agranulocytosis and thrombocytopenia. Due to such a wide range of side-effects, these drugs should not be used routinely and for long term. They are contra-indicated in patients with cardiac, hepatic and renal dysfunction.

A new drug, azapropazone has good analgesic, antipyretic and anti-inflammatory activities. Chemically it is pyrazolobenzotriazinedione having less toxic effects. Its potent uricosuric activity entitles it to be used in the treatment of acute gout. Unlike other pyrazolon derivatives, it does not cause agranulocytosis.

Azapropazone

31.6 INDOLE ACETIC ACID DERIVATIVES

Serotonin plays an important role in inflammatory conditions. In the hope that antiserotonergic compounds may be having anti-inflammatory activity, laboratory evaluation of many new synthetic indole derivatives have been carried out that led to the discovery of indomethacin. Indomethacin and sulindac, the clinically used agents from this class, are indene derivatives. Introduced in 1964, indomethacin is found to possess powerful anti-inflammatory activity associated with weak analgesic-antipyretic activity. It is sometimes also used to treat menstrual pain seen in dysmenorrhoea. The toxicity associated with indomethacin therapy precludes its use for long-term treatment. While, sulindac is basically a prodrug which is converted in vivo to a highly active anti-inflammatory metabolite that inhibit prostaglandin biosynthesis. Sulindac is relatively a safer drug than indomethacin.

Indomethacin

Sulindac

Indomethacin is one of the powerful inhibitors of prostaglandin biosynthesis. It is a potent anti-inflammatory agent with mild analgesic antipyretic activities. Like salicylates, indomethacin uncouples oxidative phosphorylation.

Indomethacin is rapidly and completely absorbed from GIT. In plasma, it is extensively bound to plasma-proteins. O-demethylation and N-deacylation are the prominent metabolic pathways for the drug. The free and glucuromide conjugates are primarily excreted through urine, bile and faeces. Small fraction of indomethacin also appears unchanged in urine.

The most frequent adverse effects of indomethacin therapy include, severe frontal headache, GIT disturbances, peptic ulceration, dizziness, mental confusion, hallucinations, aplastic anaemia and thrombocytopenia. The drugs ability to inhibit the prostaglandin biosynthesis and its antiserotonergic structural features contribute much for the appearance of most of these side-effects. In some patients salicylate like hypersensitivity reactions may be seen. It is contraindicated in patients with epilepsy, parkinsonism, psychotic diseases and in pregnancy.

Sulindac, another clinically used member of this series is relatively safer. The lower incidence of gastro-intestinal side-effects is due to its prodrug nature, due to which it remains silent at the sites of absorption in GIT. It is converted in vivo, to its active sulfide metabolite, which then acts as a potent inhibitor of cyclooxygenase enzymes. It may interfere with the platelet function to increase bleeding time by inhibiting thromboxane A_2. It does not cross the placental barrier. The metabolites (sulfone and sulfide forms) may be excreted in urine and faeces in the free and conjugated forms.

31.7 PROPIONIC ACID AND PHENYLACETIC ACID DERIVATIVES

Numerous phenylacetic acid and propionic acid derivatives have been synthesized and are found to possess anti-inflammatory activity. The first agent of the series was ibufenac which could not be introduced clinically due to its hepatotoxicity. Its derivatives, like ibuprofen, fenoprofen, ketoprofen, indoprofen, flurbiprofen, naproxen, fenbufen, alclofenac, fenclofenac, diclofenac are free of hepatotoxicity and are better tolerated. They all have good analgesic antipyretic and anti-inflammatory activities.

Since they all have an ability to inhibit prostaglandin biosynthesis, they can prolong bleeding time. The gastro-intestinal side-effects are milder than that of salicylates.

Ibuprofen was clinically introduced in 1969. It is well absorbed from GIT. It is extensively bound to plasma-proteins. Its metabolic changes involve hydroxylation and carboxylation in the side-chain alkyl radical followed by glucuronide conjugation. They are excreted in urine in both, free and conjugated forms.

Adverse effects include nausea, vomiting, heart burn, abdominal discomfort, headache, edema, skin rashes, dizziness, blurred vision, depression, and thrombocytopenia. It is contraindicated during pregnancy.

Ketoprofen and flurbiprofen are much more potent than ibuprofen. Naproxen is the best tolerated agent having longest half-life. It is naphthalene acetic acid derivative. It is also equally effective in the treatment of acute gout due to its prominent inhibitory effect on leukocyte migration. It is also effective to treat the menstrual pain seen in dysmenorrhoea. While diclofenac is a hybrid nucleus of both, phenylacetic acid and fenamate skeletons. It is contra-indicated in first three months of pregnancy.

31.8 FENAMATES

Fenamates is a family of N–arylanthranilic acids. The clinically used agents from this series include, mefenamic acid, meclofenamic acid, flufenamic acid, tolfenamic acid and etofenamic acid. They have moderate anti-inflammatory activity and mainly used as a short term analgesic. Diarrhoea, drowsiness and headache are among the side-effects. They are usually used for relieving pain and discomfort associated with dysmenorrhoea. Meclofenamic acid can also be used to treat rheumatoid arthritis.

All these agents are well absorbed orally. Mefenamic acid and its dicarboxylic acid metabolite appear in the urine in free and conjugated forms.

The adverse effects are few and mild. They include dyspepsia, diarrhoea, skin rashes, drowsiness, dizziness, and inflammation of the bowel.

31.9 MISCELLANEOUS AGENTS

(a) Piroxicam and tolmetin are recently developed promising agents having good analgesic-antipyretic and anti-inflammatory agents. Both these agents have an ability to inhibit cyclooxygenase enzyme. They are rapidly and completely absorbed from GIT, and get extensively bound to plasma-proteins.

Piroxicam

Tolmetin

Piroxicam is metabolized mainly by hydroxylation in the pyridyl ring followed by glucuronide conjugation, while tolmetin metabolism occurs by the oxidation of methyl group para to carbonyl group. The metabolites are excreted in urine in both, free and conjugated forms. Piroxicam is better tolerated agent, having long half-life.

Both these drugs cause gastric erosions and increase in the bleeding time. The most frequent adverse effects include nausea, vomiting, epigastric pain, anxiety, skin rash, gastric and peptic ulceration.

(b) Gold compounds : The clinically used agents from this category include, aurothioglucose, auranofin and gold sodium thiomalate. In all these agents, the gold is directly attached to sulfur. Hence these compounds are supposed to act by the inhibition of vital sulfhydryl systems in the body. Gold gets accumulated in the lysosomes where it inhibits the activity of acid phosphatase, β-glucuronidase and cathepsin enzymes which have catalytic role in various inflammatory disorders.

In addition, gold compounds inhibit the synthesis of mucopolysaccharide which are necessary for the formation of connective tissues. Hence, they can be used in the treatment of rheumatoid arthritis in patients who do not respond well to the therapy with aspirin-like drugs.

They are usually administered by intramuscular route, since the absorption from oral route is erratic and incomplete. They are extensively bound to plasma-proteins. Their onset of action is slow and signs of inflammation are reduced in intensity gradually. The slow rate of excretion of gold compounds can be enhanced by concomitant administration of sulfhydryl agents like, penicillamine and dimercaprol. They are primarily excreted in urine and faeces.

The adverse effects associated with gold therapy include, cutaneous reactions, aplastic anemia, leucopenia, agranulocytosis, thrombocytopenia, nephrosis, hepatitis and peripheral neuritis. They are contraindicated in patients with anemia, renal disease, hepatic dysfunction and in pregnancy.

(c) D-penicillamine : Only D-isomer is clinically used in the treatment of rheumatoid arthritis because L-penicillamine is reported to cause optic neuritis due to its anti-pyridoxine activity. Being a metabolite of penicillin, it has a structural resemblance with cysteine. In certain cases, combination of D-penicillamine with aspirin-like drugs may give better results. It, alongwith a disulfide metabolite is excreted in urine and faeces. Due to its high toxicity, it should not be used frequently or for a long-term treatment.

(d) Other clinical agents which have beneficial effects in the treatment of inflammatory disorders include :

(i) *Antimalarial agents :* Chloroquine and hydroxy chloroquine.
(ii) *Glucocorticoids*
(iii) *Immunosuppressive agents :* Azathioprine, cyclophosphamide.
(iv) *Sulfonamides :* Diflumidone.

31.10 TREATMENT OF GOUT

Once the uric acid is filtered by renal glomeruli, it is almost completely reabsorbed into circulation from proximal tubules. In normal circumstances, some of the reabsorbed uric acid is again driven back into the urine by distal tubules. Due to low solubility of undissociated form of urates, the crystals of sodium urate (the end product of purine metabolism) get deposited in the joint cavities and on articular cartilages. Their deposition initiates inflammatory reactions which involve local infiltration of phagocytes that, after ingestion of urate also release chemotactic substances and probably lactic acid. Lactic acid further lowers down the pH of the surrounding medium, resulting into further deposition of uric acid. The phagocytosis of urate crystals releases a glycoprotein which is responsible to produce acute gouty arthritis. An acute attack of gout occurs as a result of an inflammatory reaction. Usually small joints are affected before larger ones.

Aurothioglucose	Auranofin	Gold sodium thiomalate

Uricosuric agents enhance the rate of excretion of uric acid by reducing the rate of its tubular reabsorption. They thus relieve the signs and symptoms of acute attack of gout and afford symptomatic relief in this condition. Phenylbutazone is such a uricosuric agent.

(a) Colchicine :

It is an alkaloid obtained from colchicum autumnale. It was clinically introduced for the treatment of acute attacks of gout in 1763 by Von Storck.

It does not possess analgesic activity. In inflammatory disorders, it is effective only against acute gouty arthritis. It neither effectively inhibit the prostaglandin biosynthesis nor it influences the tubular reabsorption of uric acid. It probably acts to inhibit the release of lactic acid during phagocytosis of the urate crystals. Its central effects include, depression of the respiratory centers, central vasomotor stimulation and antipyretic action.

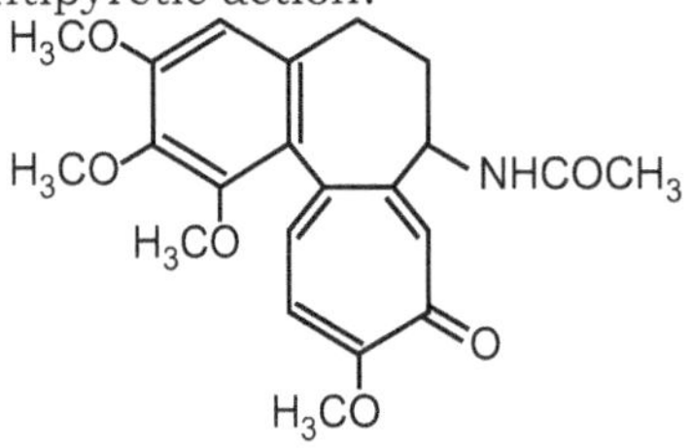

Colchicine

The alkaloid is readily absorbed from GIT and by intravenous route. The drug alongwith its metabolites are mainly excreted through urine and faeces.

The adverse effects are mild and include nausea, vomiting, diarrhoea, abdominal pain and leucopenia. These effects appear in the dose-dependent fashion and are reversed if the treatment is discontinued. In severe toxicity death usually results due to respiratory arrest.

(b) Allopurinol :

Chemically, it resembles in structure with hypoxanthine. It inhibits the formation of uric acid by competatively antagonising xanthine oxidase enzyme which catalyzes the conversion of hypoxanthine to xanthine, the precursor for uric acid synthesis.

Thus due to the structural similarity, it competes with hypoxanthine which is the substrate for xanthine oxidase enzyme. At higher concentration, due to the non-specific nature of the enzyme, it acts as non-competitive inhibitor. Instead of hypo-xanthine, allopurinol is attacked by xanthine oxidase and is converted primarily to oxypurinol which is also effective enzyme inhibitor. Thus by inhibiting the uric acid formation, it lowers down hyperuricemia and prevents the formation of uric acid stones. In order to enhance therapeutic effectiveness, allopurinol may sometimes be combined with uricosuric agent.

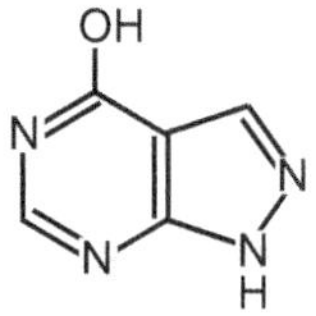

Allopurinol

The adverse reactions include, nausea, vomiting, diarrhoea, gastric irritation, headache, fever, drowsiness, and cutaneous reactions. In some patients, hypersensitivity reactions may also be seen.

The pKa of uric acid is 5.6. The solubility of undissociated urates is usually low. Hence, their solubility can be increased by inducing their ionisation. Hence alkalinization of urine is one of the effective ways to minimize the intra-renal urate deposition.

Probenecid and sulfinpyrazone also mobilize the uric acid. They are also useful agents in the treatment of chronic gout disorders though they lack analgesic and anti-inflammatory activities.

SECTION - V : AUTACOIDS

PROSTAGLANDINS

32.1 INTRODUCTION

The name, prostaglandin was originally given to a lipid factor in human seminal plasma. In the mid-1930's, Goldbatt and Van Euler independently remarked that a humoral principle present in human seminal fluid leads to both smooth muscle contraction and vaso-constriction. Euler identified the lipid soluble nature of that component; the name prostaglandin was given to these substances after their putative source, the prostate gland. In 1964, the Swedish Scientist Bergstrom, reported the synthesis of PGE_2 from arachidonic acid using homogenates of sheep seminal vesicle. The work of Bergstrom developed the keen interest of other scientists in the prostaglandins which resulted into identification of thromboxane A_2 (a platelet aggregating factor) in 1975, followed by Prostacyclin or PGI_2 in 1976. In 1971, Vane assigned the therapeutic effectiveness of 'aspirin-like' drugs to their ability to inhibit prostaglandin biosynthesis.

Prostaglandin is a family of naturally occurring hormone like vaso-active substances that play a key role in regulating cellular metabolism when present even in minute quantities. They are characterised by :

(a) Very rapid rate of metabolism and hence low oral activity, and

(b) Complex set of bio-activities exhibited by each of the naturally occurring compounds.

In the body, the circulating plasma concentration of these substances are very low in the normal person, due to prominent pulmonary degradation. Prostacyclin however, escapes pulmonary metabolism and therefore may act as the circulating hormone. It may be metabolized by platelets, the kidneys and other tissues to the biologically active, 6–keto PGE_1.

The enzymes that catalyze the biosynthesis of prostaglandins are present in almost every tissue, with the probable exception of erythrocytes. Thus, they can be biosynthesized by almost every tissue. Hence, they have extensive and varied activities in the mammalian system. Some of them having clinical significance, include,

1. Stimulating or relaxing uterine smooth muscle.
2. Constriction of bronchi.
3. Inhibiting gastric acid secretion.
4. Mediating inflammatory responses.
5. Promoting sodium ion excretion.
6. Inducing labour.

The occurrence of prostaglandins in humans is widespread. But like, neurotransmitters, they are not stored in the tissues. In tissues, they are biosynthesized locally, only when they are required. Thus, they qualify to be called as local hormone. The only exception to this is probably the seminal fluid, in which, atleast 15 different prostaglandins have been identified. Besides mammals, they have been detected in insects, shell fish and corals.

Structurally, they are derivatives of prostanoic acid and have a cyclopentane ring to which two side-chains are associated at adjacent carbon atoms. Prostanoic acid, itself does not occur naturally but it can be chemically synthesized.

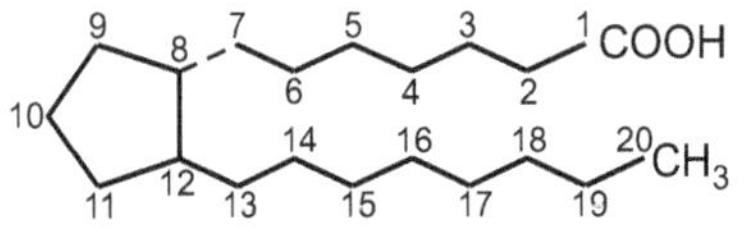

Prostanoic acid

Two side-chains are attached to the cyclopentane ring at carbon atom 8 and 12. The, upper side-chain, having carboxyl (–COOH) group at its terminal, is termed as carboxylhexyl or α-side chain while the lower side-chain (attached to C_{12}) having hydroxyl function at C_{15} is called as hydroxyoctyl (ω) side-chain.

32.2 NOMENCLATURE OF PROSTAGLANDINS

The present classification is based upon the nature of :

(a) The cyclopentane ring.

(b) Two adjacent side-chains, and

(c) Configuration of newly introduced functional group.

(a) Nature of the Cyclopentane Ring :

Depending upon the functional groups present, the cyclopentane ring may be called as :

Thus in other words,

(i) A-type cyclopentane ring contains α, β-unsaturated ketone system or more specifically 10, 11—unsaturated ketone function.

(ii) B-type cyclopentane ring contains 8, 12-unsaturated ketone system.

(iii) E-type cyclopentane ring contains β-hydroxy ketone system.

(iv) F-type cyclopentane ring contains 1, 3-diol system.

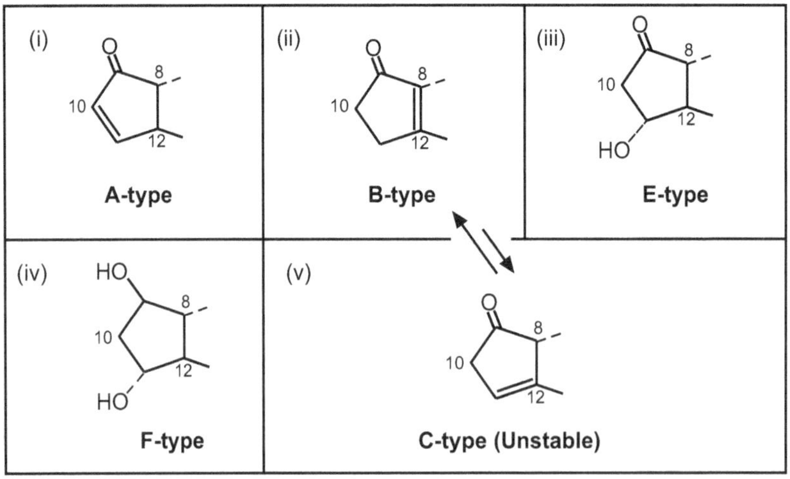

(i) A-type
(ii) B-type
(iii) E-type
(iv) F-type
(v) C-type (Unstable)

(b) Nature of Adjacent Side-chains :

The further division within each type (i.e. A, B, C, D, E, F etc.) can be made according to the extent of unsaturation in the side-chains, resulting into different series, like :

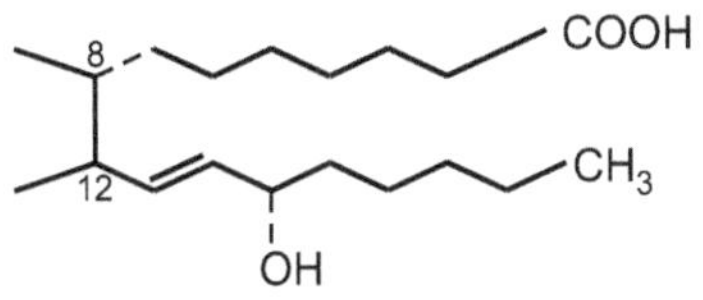

Series 1

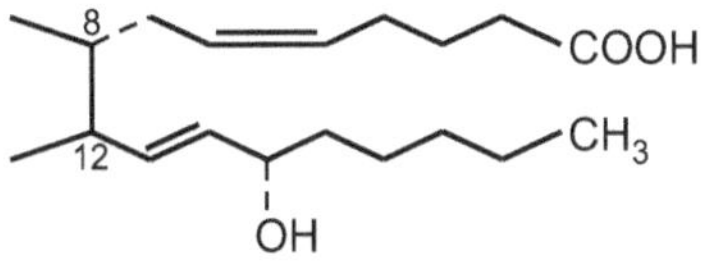

Series 2

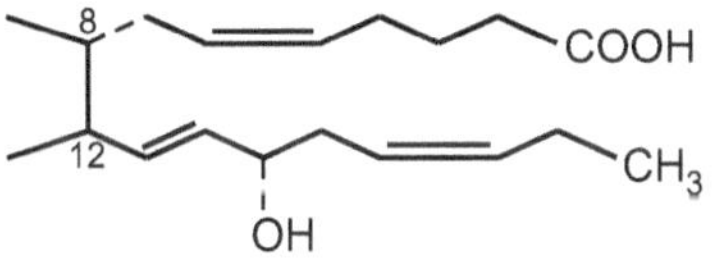

Series 3

The side-chains may contain as many as three or four double bonds. The number of such double bonds, appear as a numerical (i.e., 1, 2, 3 etc.) subscript in the name of prostaglandin. For example, PGA_2 (prostaglandin A_2) contains cyclopentane ring of the type-A and the subscript 2, indicates the presence of two double bonds in the adjacent side-chains (i.e. series 2).

(c) Nature of the Configuration :

This function is needed to define the configuration of newly introduced functional group in the molecule. For example, PGE can be converted to PGF by reducing the C_9 ketone function to a hydroxyl group. The reduced compound will be named as either $PGF_{1\alpha}$ or $PGF_{1\beta}$ depending upon the configuration (α or β) of newly introduced C_9-hydroxyl function.

In all naturally occurring prostaglandins, upper side-chain is attached to the cyclopentane ring at C_8 through an α-bond (i.e., projecting behind the plane) and is shown by a dotted line. Similarly, the natural prostaglandins possess an α–hydroxyl group at C_{15} atom.

32.3 BIOSYNTHESIS OF PROSTAGLANDINS

In man, arachidonic acid acts as the principle precursor for the biosynthesis of endogenous prostaglandins. It is obtained mainly from dietary linoleic acid. In the body, arachidonic acid is stored in the phospholipids of the cell membranes in the esterified form with membrane phosphatidyl choline. During injury or tissue damage, arachidonic acid is released due to the hydrolysis of this ester linkage by phospholipase A_2 enzymes which are members of the class, acylhydrolases. Since arachidonic acid contains four double bonds, chemically it is termed as eicosatetraenoic acid. It serves as the precursor for the biosynthesis of prostaglandins having two double bonds in their alkyl side-chains (i.e., compounds with 'series 2'). Other polyunsaturated fatty acids may also be released which include eicosatrienoic acid (ETA) and eicosapentaenoic acid (EPA) that serve as the precursor for the biosynthesis of prostaglandins having one and three double bonds in their alkyl side-chains, respectively, (i.e. compounds with 'series 1' and 'series 3').

Phospholipase A_2 is a membrane-bound enzyme which is activated mainly by calmodulin alongwith Ca^{++} ions. That partly explains the effectivity of nifedipine (calcium channel blockers) in inflammatory reactions. The activity of released phospholipase A_2, appears to be under hormonal control. For example, plasmakinins activate tissue phospholipases.

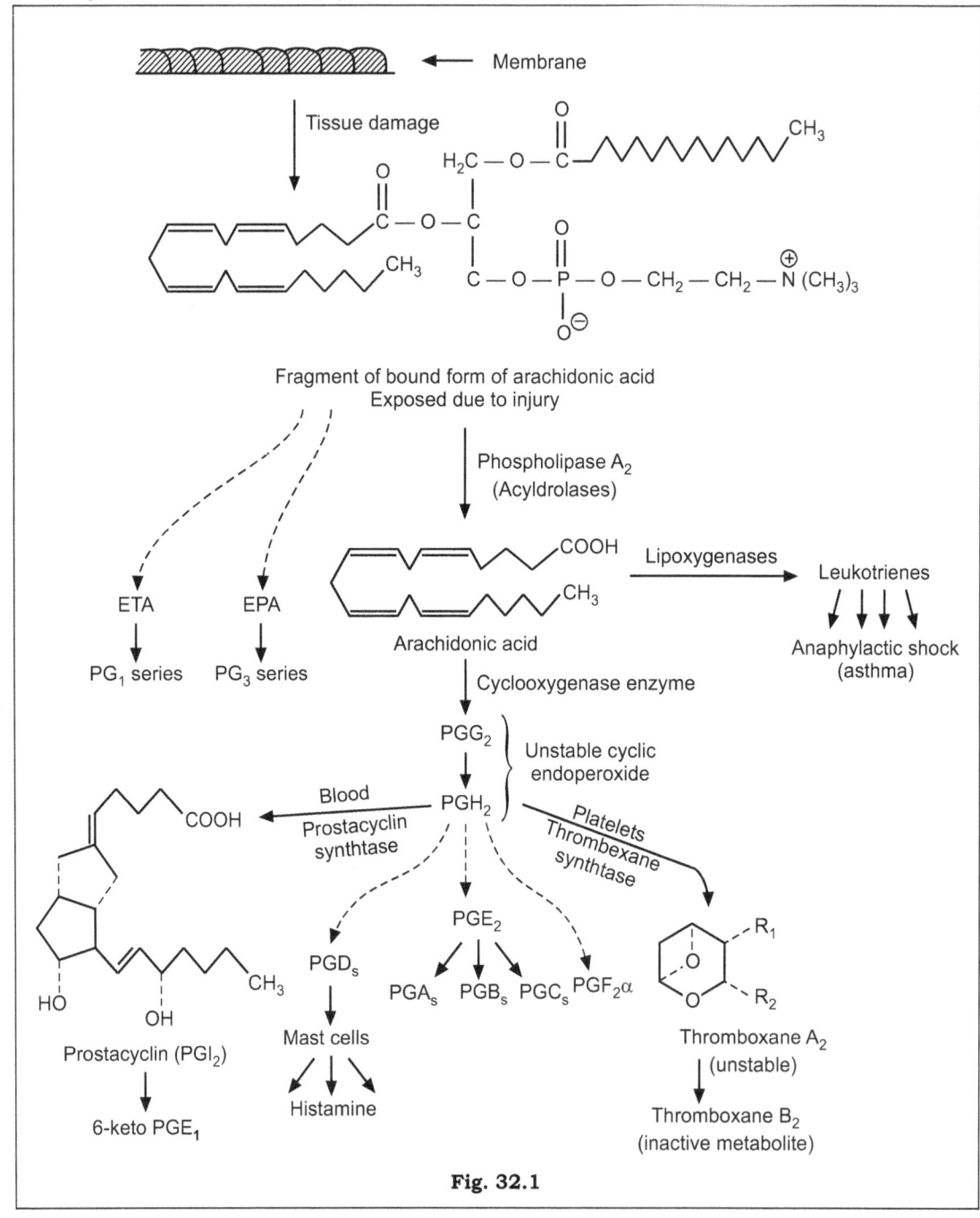

Fig. 32.1

Arachidonic acid is partly converted into several non-prostaglandin compounds, known as leukotrienes (LTs). The reaction is catalyzed by lipoxygenases. Leukotrienes are oxygenated products of straight-chain, fatty acids. Hydroperoxy-eicosatetraenoic acid (HPETE) is obtained first which is then reduced to hydroxyeicosatetraenoic acid (HETE) by lipid peroxidases. They are known as leukotrienes mainly because of their conjugated triene structure and their occurrence in leukocytes. The most important amongst lipoxygenases, is 5-lipoxygenase enzyme. The leukotrienes have been implicated in the inflammatory responses. They have an ability to induce bronchospasm and peripheral vascular permeability and have important functions as mediators of asthama, For example, the slow reacting substance of anaphylaxis (SRS-A) is found to be closely associated with the release of leukotrienes.

Rest of arachidonic acid is acted upon by cyclooxygenase enzyme. The enzyme, first oxidises and then cause cyclization of arachidonic acid to give unstable cyclic endoperoxide derivatives like PGG_2 and PGH_2. The PGG_2 contains –OOH group at C_{15} position, instead of the usual –OH group. They are relatively unstable with half-lives of about 5 minutes. Cyclooxygenase utilizes heme as a co-factor for this reaction. The PGH_2 acts in reality, the precursor for different endogenous prostaglandins in all tissues. The type of prostaglandin to be biosynthesized, is governed by the cell-type and demand of the situation.

For example, PGH_2 is mainly converted into PGI_2 (prostacyclin) in the blood vessel wall by prostacyclin synthtase. It is a unstable-agent having a half-life of about 2 minutes. It has strong anti-platelet aggregation property. It is hydrolyzed non-enzymatically to 6-keto PGE_1, a relatively stable metabolite.

The PGH_2 is also converted to thromboxane A_2 (a platelet aggregation inducing factor) by thromboxane synthtase. Since they are formed in platelets (thrombocytes) and have oxane ring in their structure, the name thromboxane is given. Thromboxane A_2 is also unstable compound, having a half life of about 30 seconds. It is nonenzymatically converted into thromboxane B_2, a more stable metabolite.

PGH_2 is also used as a substrate for the biosynthesis of specific endogenous prostaglandins like PGD_2, PGE_2 and $PGF_{2\alpha}$. The prostaglandins from E series are then converted to PGAs, PGBs and PGCs through dehydration and isomerization. These conversions are catalyzed by different isomerases.

Aspirin-like drugs inhibit the biosynthesis of endogeous prostaglandins, by acetylating the serine residue in cyclooxygenase enzymes. This results into their inactivation. Since cyclooxygenase enzymes catalyze the formation of prostaglandin endoperoxide from arachidonic acid, the synthesis of all the compounds beyond this step is inhibited by 'aspirin-like' drugs. But the biosynthesis of nonprostaglandin substances (e.g., leukotrienes) from arachidonic acid is not inhibited by these drugs. The rate of leukotriene synthesis increases due to the inhibition of cyclo-oxygenase enzyme. The increased concentration of leukotriences may be then, responsible for the hypersensitivity reaction seen for 'aspirin-like drugs' in certain patients.

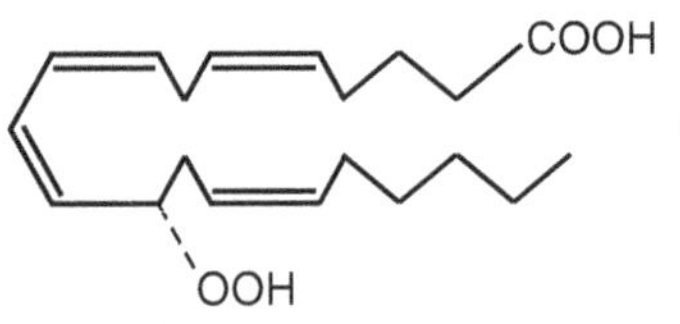

12-HPETE → **12-HETE**

32.4 CATABOLISM

Prostaglandins are potent vasoactive substances. They are primarily metabolised in the liver and pulmonary vascular bed. The initial and relatively rapid enzymatic catabolism of prostaglandins take place in the lungs.

In the lungs, they are attacked by :

(i) 15-hydroxy dehydrogenase that oxidises-15-α–OH group to the corresponding ketone function, and followed by

(ii) Δ^{13} – reductase that reduces the double bond present between C_{13} and C_{14}.

The modifications significantly affect the biological activity of the resulting prostaglandin, which is then attacked by a second phase of catabolism in the liver. This phase proceeds at a slow rate and includes :

(i) the subsequent oxidation in the α-side chain (i.e. carboxyhexyl) at C_2 and C_4 respectively.

(ii) This is followed by oxidation in the ω-side chain (i.e., hydroxyoctyl) at C_{20} position.

The final structure that appears after these four attacks is of a dicarboxylic acid, that is excreted in urine.

The enzymes which catalyze the prostaglandin degradation are mainly present in the lung, liver, kidney, intestine, testicles, spleen and adipose tissues.

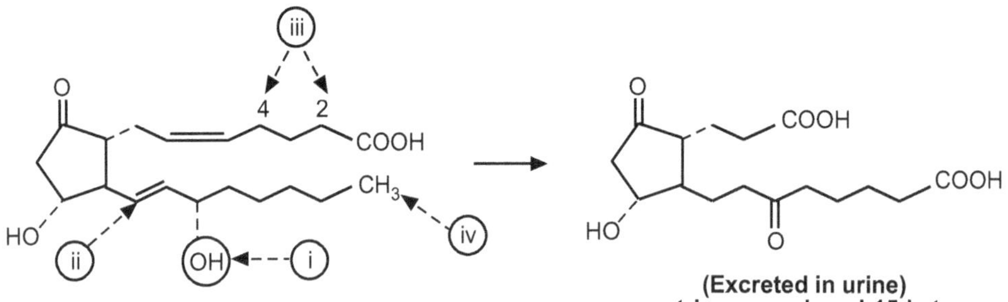

PGE$_2$ → (Excreted in urine)
α-trinor-ω-carboxyl-15-keto-13, 14-dihydro PGE$_2$

32.5 PHARMACOLOGY

Prostaglandin-synthesizing enzymes are present in almost every tissue of the body except erythrocytes. Hence, prostaglandins can be locally synthesized everywhere in the body as per the need of the situation. This explains the wide range of biological activities associated with the release of prostaglandins.

(a) CNS :

Prostaglandins regulate the neuronal transmission in the CNS through feedback systems. They, themselves do not act as neurotransmitters and act as the modulators of transmission and control the CNS activity as per the situation. Hence, the CNS effects of all prostaglandins are quite complex and sometimes opposing each other. Usually they cause sedation, stupor, catatonia and other behavioural changes.

PGEs, in general, inhibit the release of catecholamines from nerve endings resulting into depression of CNS activity. Thus, they are effective against chemically induced convulsions at higher concentration. During inflammation, fever is induced due to the release of pyrogen. The release of PGE_2 is linked with the endogenous pyrogen activity. PGEs may also cause dilatation of extracranial blood vessels and thus are involved in the migraine.

(b) ANS :

The pharmacological activity (i.e., in intact animal, or in vivo) of any drug need not always be the extension of its physiological activity (i.e., on isolated tissue or in vitro). Qualitative as well as quantitative differences may occur either due to the drug induced release of active substances in the blood or due to the production of active metabolites of the drug. This is more true for prostaglandins. They control the release of both noradrenaline and acetylcholine through negative feedback mechanism. Their inhibitory effect on the rate of neurotransmitter release is sometimes compared with autoregulation caused by the activation of the presynaptic α_2-receptors.

(c) Body Temperature :

The temperature-controlling centers are located in the hypothalamus. The body-temperature is maintained at the normal value by the balanced functioning of oppositively acting noradrenergic and serotonergic neuronal systems. The set point in the temperature-controlling centers is disturbed by an endogenous pyrogen, a 14,000 daltron protein, released during inflammation. The pyrexia thus produced is linked with the release of prostaglandin in the preoptic area of the hypothalamus.

(d) CVS :

The peripheral vasodilation is induced by PGAs, PGEs and PGI_2. A decrease in blood pressure occurs due to a fall in total peripheral resistance. The cardiac stimulant action of PGE is linked with the increase in the c-AMP concentration. While $PGF_{2\alpha}$ and thromboxane A_2 elevate the blood pressure by acting as a powerful vasoconstrictor. An initial increase in blood pressure, followed by prolonged hypotension is usually observed with leucotrienes.

(e) Blood :

PGE$_2$ and PGI$_2$ promote erythropoiesis by enhancing erythropoietin release. Prostaglandins, in general (except PGI$_2$, PGE$_1$, and PGD$_2$) is a very powerful inducer of platelet aggregation. During inflammation, thromboxane A$_2$ and platelet factor 4 are released that have platelet aggregating and vasoconstricting action. This results into ischemia and thrombosis. Number of factors like, serotonin, ADP and noradrenaline-release, contribute to the ischemia induced by vasoconstriction and coagulation. This condition in part, may be responsible for the development of some diseased states like myocardial infarction. The vasoconstrictory and platelet aggregating activity of thromboxane A$_2$ is antagonised by prostacyclin (PGI$_2$) that is released by vascular endothelium.

(f) Respiratory System :

PGA and PGE$_2$ act as bronchodilators while PGF$_{2\alpha}$, prostaglandin endoperoxides and thromboxane A$_2$ are powerful bronchoconstrictors. PGI$_2$ is a weak bronchodilator and dilates pulmonary blood vessels. Though the actions of both vasoconstrictor or vasodilatory prostaglandins is antagonized by aspirin like drugs, they cannot inhibit the release of leukotrienes. Thus hypersensitivity in certain patients, may be seen during the therapy with 'aspirin-like' drugs due to the unopposed actions of leukotrienes on the lung tissue.

(g) Pain :

The afferent nerve-endings of pain-impulse carrying nerve tract, act as receptors for pain-producing substances. During inflammation, bradykinins and histamine act as pain-producing substances. They induce the synthesis and release of prostaglandins (PGEs and PGI$_2$, more specifically) which then amplify the pain sensation by sensitizing the pain-nerve endings to bradykinins. The leukotrienes induce the release of histamine from basophils which then acts as a mediator of itch and pain sensation.

Prostaglandins are also involved in oedema formation and allergic reaction. For example PGI$_2$ and PGE$_2$, both cause vasodilation resulting into increased blood flow in the inflamed area. However, their actions are potentiated by other autocoids like, histamine and serotonin.

(h) Endocrine Glands :

Prostaglandins, in part, are responsible for increased concentration of ACTH, growth hormone, prolactin, gonadotropin and insulin in plasma. However, PGF$_{2\alpha}$ causes degeneration of corpus luteum and thus cuts down the source of progesterone during menstrual cycle.

(i) GIT :

Various prostaglandins like PGD$_2$, PGE$_2$, PGF$_{2\alpha}$, and thromboxane A$_2$ are locally synthesized and released in the GIT membrane. They protect the mucosal membrane of GIT by

(i) inhibiting excess gastric acid secretion, and

(ii) promoting the formation of cytoprotective mucous layer.

With the exception of PGE$_2$ and PGF$_{2\alpha}$ other prostaglandins increase the accumulation of water and electrolytes in the intestinal lumen. Nausea, vomiting, diarrhoea are the side-effects, frequently associated with oral prostaglandin therapy. Usually methylated derivatives of natural prostaglandins are more effective by the oral route.

(j) Reproductive System :

The seminal fluid contains about 15 different types of prostaglandins. The testis can synthesize PGE_1, $PGF_{1\alpha}$ and $PGF_{2\alpha}$. Prostaglandins are found to be involved in the production and secretion of testosterone, the male sex hormone. These facts indicate that, prostaglandin-deficiency may be responsible for male infertility. Besides this, prostaglandins may also influence fallopian tubal motility, ovum transport and formation of cervical mucous. They also regulate some processes in ovulation. In fact, PGE_2 and $PGF_{2\alpha}$ have been identified in menstrual discharge.

The effect of prostaglandins on the uterus is governed by the type of prostaglandin used and the physiological state of the uterus. For example, PGA, PGE and PGB in vitro cause relaxation of strips of uterine myometrium while PGF_1 and PGI_2 and leukotrienes in general cause the contraction of uterine muscles. $PGF_{2\alpha}$ is the main causative factor involved in dysmennorhea and causes degeneration of corpus luteum.

(k) Metabolic Effects :

Prostaglandin E_1 is found to potentiate the effect of insulin on carbohydrate metabolism. It also increases the rate of lipolysis and mobilizes the calcium ions from bone into the tissues.

(l) Kidney :

Prostaglandins, in general, dilate the renal vasculature except $PGF_{2\alpha}$ that causes vasoconstriction. Many prostaglandins are locally synthesized in the medulla region while the cortex region is rich in the enzymes that catabolize these prostaglandins. Prostaglandin E_2 and prostacyclin induces diuresis while thromboxane A_2 reduces the rate of glomerular filtration. Certain vaso-active substances like, noradrenaline, vasopresin and angiotensin-II may promote the prostaglandin synthesis. The release of renin is then stimulated by certain prostaglandins like, PGE_2, PGD_2 and PGI_2, resulting into diuresis and increased sodium excretion.

32.6 MECHANISM OF ACTION

Prostaglandins possess the actions of a wide variety and complexity. Such a wide diversity of actions of conflicting nature cannot be explained by proposing the existence of specific receptor sites for prostaglandins. Still some binding sites for prostaglandins and leukotrienes in some tissues have been claimed to be identified.

In most of the cases, prostaglandins act as the modulators of tissue functions. For example, c-AMP acts as a second messenger in most of the excitatory actions of sympathetic nervous system while c-GMP propagates most of the inhibitory actions of parasympathetic nervous system. The biological activities of prostaglandins arise due to interference of prostaglandins in the biosynthesis of these cyclic nucleotides. In some cases, the release of intracellular Ca^{++} is also responsible for appearance of biological activity.

32.7 THERAPEUTIC USES OF PROSTAGLANDINS

Different disease conditions are characterized by either an increase or decrease in the plasma prostaglandin levels. For example, in rheumatic disorders, excess prostaglandin plasma levels are observed. Similarly cardiac ischemia and atherosclerosis in part occur due to excessive thromboxane A_2 activity. 'Aspirin-like' drugs inhibit the prostaglandin synthesis, leading to higher incidences of development of :

(i) ischemia of the renal medulla, resulting into nephropathy.

(ii) higher fluidity of blood, due to unopposed action of prostacyclin, and

(iii) hypersensitivity reactions in some patients due to increase in the leukotriene synthesis.

Due to their modulating action on the functioning of various tissue activities, prostaglandins at least on the theoretical grounds, may be useful for :

(a) Induction of midtrimester abortion and as the contraceptive agents.

(b) Because of their cytoprotective action, they may be used to heal peptic ulcer and ischemic heart diseases. In the latter, prostaglandins act mainly by exerting vasodilatory effects.

(c) Some prostaglandins have anti-aggregating effect on platelets. Hence, they are useful to treat advanced peripheral vascular diseases.

(d) They also increase pulmonary blood flow. Hence they can also be used in infants with congenital heart defects, in order to increase the oxygen content of the blood.

(e) Dipyridamole potentiates the anti-aggregating action of prostacyclin in blood. While aspirin can inhibit the synthesis of both, prostacyclin and thromboxane A_2. Hence in order to maintain platelet level in blood, dipyridamole may be concomitantly administered with aspirin-like drugs.

POLYPEPTIDES OF PHARMACOLOGICAL IMPORTANCE

33.1 INTRODUCTION

The endogenous polypeptides play an important role in the human physiology. By acting directly or indirectly at different points of regulatory mechanisms, they exercise a fine control upon variations in normal body mechanisms. Through different points of contact, they also co-ordinate (and reciprocate) changes brought about in their own functioning by different disease conditions. As per the need of the moment, their actions may be propagated through central or peripheral feed-back systems. Among them, oxytocin and vasopression, are the true hormones while angiotensin, plasmakinins, substance P and vasoactive intestinal polypeptide (VIP) are mainly vasoactive polypeptides. In certain conditions characterized by inflammation, anaphylactic reactions or shock, they influence the cell physiology and homeostatic mechanism of the body. Lung is the principle site for the catabolism of these vasoactive polypeptides.

33.2 ANGIOTENSINS

Renin (molecular weight 42,000) is a proteolytic enzyme that catalyzes the formation of active pressor hormone, the angiotensin. Its presence in the kidney was first discovered in 1898. It was named 'renin' by Bergman due to its renal origin. Kidney is the rich source of renin where it is stored in the granular juxtaglomerular (J G) cells in the walls of the afferent arterioles, in the form of prorenin (a zymogen with a molecular weight of 63,000). The prorenin, in turn, is obtained by intracellular proteolysis of an inactive precursor, preprorenin. Both, prorenin and preprorenin are also present in plasma.

Upon release into the renal arterial blood stream, renin catalyzes the conversion of angiotensinogen (inactive precursor) into angiotensin-I. Angiotensinogens are glycoproteins, present in the plasma α_2 - globulin fraction. They are synthesized in liver and transported to plasma in the bound form with α_2-globulin, from which they are cleaved off and acted upon by renin, to produce angiotensin-I (decapeptide). Angiotensin-I, which has a less intrinsic activity is converted to more active form, angiotensin-II (octapeptide) by angiotensin converting enzyme. This enzyme also catabolizes bradykinin to inactive fragments and hence it is also known as kininase-II.

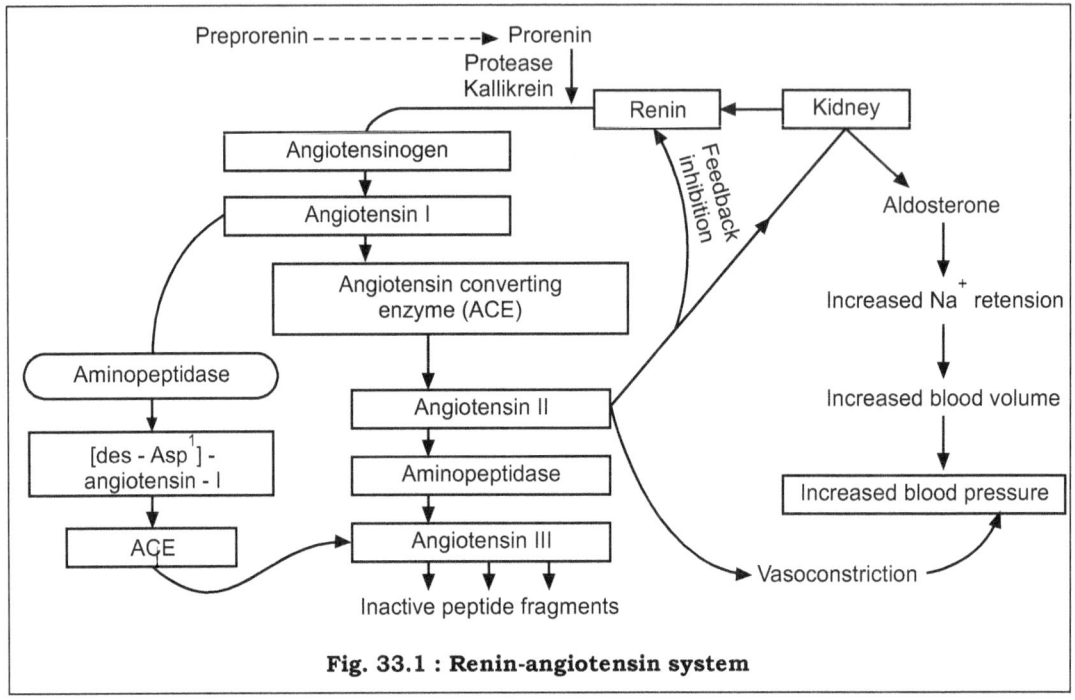

Fig. 33.1 : Renin-angiotensin system

Angiotensin-II is one of the most potent vasoconstrictor agent. Its action may be terminated by aminopeptidase enzyme through its conversion into angiotensin-III (heptapetide) which still retains some activity. The heptapeptide is then further degraded into various inactive fragments by some nonspecific enzyme systems.

As shown in the Fig. 33.1, angiotensin-I can be directly converted into angiotensin-III by another pathway which is of minor importance.

The renin-angiotensin system is an important part of the homeostatic mechanisms in the body. It works to maintain the blood-pressure at the normal level. It also regulates the electrolyte balance by controlling aldosterone secretion by adrenal cortex.

Renin has a half-life of about 15 minutes in the circulation. The components of renin-angiotensin system get activated by decreased blood volume, low renal pressure (baroreceptors in renal afferent arterioles) and low sodium ion concentration in the plasma (chemoreceptors in renal afferent arterioles). Similarly the JG cells are directly innervated by central sympathetic nerves. Hence under the conditions of strain and stress, the sympathetic stimulation may lead to the hypertension due to the activation of renin-angiotensin system. Beside these factors, prostaglandins also are found to stimulate the release of renin in response to inflammatory stimuli. For example, PGI_2 (prostacyclin), through its vasodilating action, activates the baroreceptors and stimulates the renin release. The components of renin-angiotensin system are also present in many other tissues.

The angiotensin converting enzyme (dipeptidyl carboxypeptidase) specifically catalyzes the conversion of angiotensin-I to angiotensin-II. The enzyme is metallo enzyme (Zn^{++}) that requires chloride ion and is inhibited by hypoxia. It is released from endothelial cells of the vasculature. The same enzyme also nonspecifically catalyses the catabolism of bradykinin alongwith other enzymes. The angiotensin-I is also converted directly to angiotensin-III through [des-Asp^1] – angiotensin-I, a nonapeptide derivative. It is a pathway of minor importance. The renin-angiotensin system regulates the blood pressure and plasma sodium at normal level by exerting generalized vasoconstriction and inducing aldosterone release.

33.3 PHARMACOLOGY

1. CNS : The vasoactive polypeptides poorly penetrate the blood-brain-barrier and angiotensins are no exception to them. However some amounts of angiotensin reach the brain region through the membrane which is not protected by BBB. It stimulates the central sympathetic transmission. The feeling of thrust is potentiated. It also activates the central mechanism for the release of anti-diuretic hormone. The resultant increase in the water intake and efferent sympathetic activity may lead to the hypertensive state. Angiotensin also exerts a direct stimulant action on sympathetic ganglia and adrenal medulla.

2. Peripheral autonomic nervous system : Angiotensin directly stimulates the peripheral sympathetic nervous system, resulting into vasoconstriction. Cyclic-AMP is expected to be involved in the increased outflow of norepinephrine from sympathetic nerve terminals.

3. Adrenal medulla : The increase in the rate of release of catecholamines is reported due to the direct stimulant action of angiotension on chromaffin cells. The rate of synthesis and release of aldosterone is also augmented, resulting into increased retention of sodium and exertion of potassium and hydrogen ions. Both these effects ultimately result into the rise in peripheral resistance into the vasculature.

4. CVS : Angiotensins are potent pressor substances. Acting by both, direct and indirect mechanisms, angiotensin causes vasoconstriction. The effect is less pronounced in the skeletal muscles and brain vessels. Angiotensin also exerts a positive inotropic (increased force of contraction) and chronotropic (increased rate of contraction) effect on the cardiac muscles. These effects which propagate due to increased Ca^{++} - influx can be antagonized by calcium channel blockers.

The ultimate results on the cardiac functioning are difficult to interpret due to occurrence of reflux responses mediated through the activation of baroreceptors by elevated systemic blood pressure. If these reflex responses are inhibited (either by vagotomy or atropine treatment), cardiac acceleration may be seen which sometimes lead to coronary insufficiency.

Angiotensin causes an increase in the vascular permeability in large arteries resulting into oedema formation. The fluid containing high molecular weight substances escapes into extracellular space through the gaps between arterial endothelial cells. The widening of gap results due to the angiotensin-induced contraction of endothelial cells.

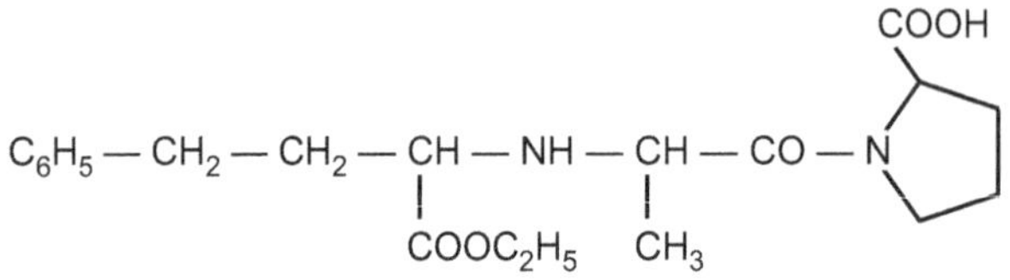

$$C_6H_5-CH_2-CH_2-\underset{\underset{COOC_2H_5}{|}}{CH}-NH-\underset{\underset{CH_3}{|}}{CH}-CO-N\underset{}{\diagup}\overset{COOH}{|}$$

Enalapril (monoethyl ester of enalaprilic acid)

5. Extravascular smooth muscles : The diversified effects ranging from contraction to relaxation on various smooth muscles are exerted by angiotensin by both, direct as well as indirect (influencing the functioning of autonomic nervous system) mechanisms.

6. Kidney and urine formation : In normal person, angiotensin has antidiuretic action due to the decrease in the rate of glomerular filtration. The angiotensin-induced release of aldosterone also affects tubular reaborption of sodium ions. However in hypertensive patients, both, the renal vasoconstriction (i.e., increased perfusion pressure) and the activation of baroreceptor lead to an increase in the rate of glomerular filtration.

33.4 MECHANISM OF ACTION

The presence of specific receptor sites for angiotensin in certain tissues (chromaffin cells in adrenal medulla) has been suspected. There is an evidence that the actions of angiotensin on heart and smooth muscle, may involve calcium-dependent mechanism. In some cases, the activation of cyclic nucleotides is responsible for angiotensin-induced responses. Angiotensin may also augment the synthesis of arachidonic acid and its endogenous catabolic products by the activity of phsopholipase enzymes.

33.5 ANGIOTENSIN ANTAGONISTS

Angiotensins are the potent vasoconstrictor. They tend to increase the peripherial vascular resistance. The angiotensin-induced release of aldosterone increases the sodium ion retention in plasma, resulting into an increase in plasma volume. The overall result of all these effects is hypertension. Hence, one can expect that angiotensin atagonists would be effective antihypertensive agents. This expectation was proved to be correct by the development of captopril and saralasin.

(a) Captopril : The angiotensin converting enzyme (dipeptidyl carboxypeptidase) catalyses the conversion of less active, angiotensin-I to highly active, angiotensin-II. Captopril is an example of angiotensin converting enzyme inhibitors (ACE-I). It was developed in 1977 from a series of mercapto alkanoyl derivatives.

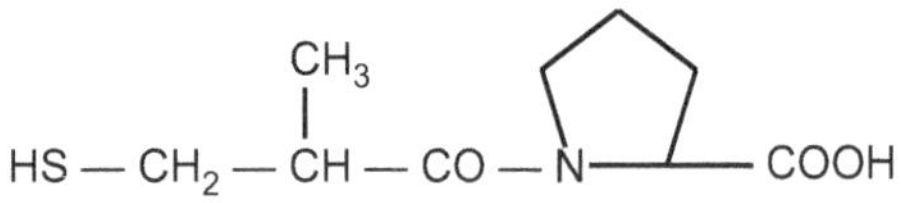

$$HS-CH_2-\underset{\underset{CH_3}{|}}{CH}-CO-N\diagup\!\!-COOH$$

(mer) captopril

Captopril inhibits ACE in highly specific fashion. It thus lowers down the synthesis and release of angiotensin-II. The actions exerted by angiotesin-II (vasocontriction and aldosterone release) are also inhibited. This results into the arteriolar dilatation, decreased cardiac force of contraction and less fluid retention (diuresis). Though angiotensin mediated aldosterone release is inhibited, an adequate aldosterone level is maintained by other mediators like ACTH and plasma potassium ion concentration. The ACE-inhibition leads to elevated levels of circulating renin and angiotensin-I which may, in part, be responsible for terminating the action of captopril.

Captopril is orally effective agent. The parent drug and its metabolites (disulfide dimer and cysteine disulfide) are mainly excreted through urine.

The adverse effects may be due to the presence of –SH group in the structure and its ability to inhibit angiotensin converting enzyme (kininase-II). The same enzyme also catalyzes the degradation of bradykinin. Hence, captopril potentiates the actions of endogenous bradykinin.

Frequent adverse effects include, headache, fever, loss of taste, vertigo, minor gastrointestinal disturbances and severe hypotension. These effects are dose-dependent and may disappear upon drug-withdrawal.

Captopril is mainly used in the treatment of

(i) mild - to - moderate essential hypertension.

(ii) chronic congestive heart failure.

Its effectiveness in the therapy may be increased by the concurrent administration of either a diuretic agent or adrenergic blocking agent.

(b) Enalaprilic acid (enalapril) : It has similar pharmacological effects, mechanism of action and therapeutic uses to that of captopril. Like captopril, it does contain a "proline surrogate".

Due to poor oral absorption, enalaprilic acid is administered in the form of its monoethyl ester, enalapril. Enalapril acts as prodrug and release enalaprilic acid in vivo. It differs from captopril in having higher potency, slower onset of action (due to the release of enalaprilic acid from its prodrug) and longer duration of action.

(c) Saralasin : It is a substituted analog of angiotensin-II and acts by competitively blocking the angiotensin receptor sites.

Sar – Arg – Val – Tyr – Val – His – Pro – Ala

Saralasin

In the structure of angiotensin-II, the phenylalanine at position 8 is replaced by alanine (results into decreased intrinsic activity) and sarcosyl is substituted at NH_2-terminal (in order to increase the resistance to enzymatic hydrolysis by amino-peptidases), to yield saralasin molecule. It does not cross BBB and is retained in the vascular and extracellular fluid compartments to block angiotensin receptor sites. This results into decrease into peripheral vascular resistance and blood pressure. An increase in blood pressure during initial stage of therapy may be seen which is due to increased plasma renin concentration.

The adverse effects of saralasin include severe hypotension, rebound hypertension and acute hypertension.

The antihypertensive action of saralasin is potentiated by the concurrent administration of directly acting vasodilators.

Since β_1-adrenergic agonists and endogenous release of prostaglandin potentiate the release of renin, the administration of β_1-adrenergic blocking agents and aspirin-like drugs also inhibit some of the responses mediated by renin-angiotensin system.

33.6 PLASMAKININS

Bradykinin and kallidin are the extensively studied members of the family, plasmakinins. These vasoactive polypeptides are obtained from pharmacologically inactive precursor, kallidinogen which, like angiotensinogen, is a member of α-2-globulin fraction of plasma proteins. The enzyme, kallikrein catalyzes this conversion. The enzyme is named as kallikrein due to its higher concentration in pancreas, the organ known as kallikreas in Greek terminology. Besides pancreas, the enzymes are also found in saliva, plasma and in urine. Accordingly it can be termed as plasma kallikrein and tissue kallikrein.

The plasma kallikrein has a molecular weight of about, 1,00,000 and acts mainly on the high molecular weight kininogen. It is obtained from a precursor (prekallikrein) by an activator that is induced by Hageman factor, plasmin and kallikrein itself. While tissue kallikrein differs from plasma kallikrein in that it has a low molecular weight and hydrolyzes both, a low and high molecular weight kininogens.

Kallidin (decapeptide), is the product of hydrolysis of low molecular weight kininogens by tissue kallikrein enzymes. While bradykinin is the product of hydrolysis of high molecular weight kininogen by plasma kallikrein. It is a nonapeptide, missing the lysine amino acid from the terminal of kallidin molecule. Blood contains enzyme systems capable of destroying both, kallikrein and kallidin.

The name, bradykinin is derived from the Greek words, bradys (slow) and kinin (to move), since it induces slowly developing contraction of the gut.

Bradykinin is a potent arteriolar vasodilator. It may induce venous vasoconstriction. The effects of plasmakinins are complex and variable due to the involvement of reflex responses mediated through sympathetic nervous system. They are found to be an important factor in

(i) homeostasis

(ii) coagulation and fibrinolysis (Hageman factor)

(iii) inflammatory responses (prostaglandin release), and

(iv) control of organ blood supply.

Their role in defense mechanisms of the body appears to be due to their ability to cause the accumulation of leukocytes.

Plasmakinins potentiate the release of catecholamines from the adrenal medulla. The mechanism of action of plasmakinins is not yet clear but may involve the participation of cyclic nucleotides, calcium ion fluxes and protein phosphorylation. Plasmakinins also augment the release of prostaglandins which then sensitize the nerve terminals of pain-nerve to the action of bradykinin. Bradykinin is most potent mediator of pain sensation.

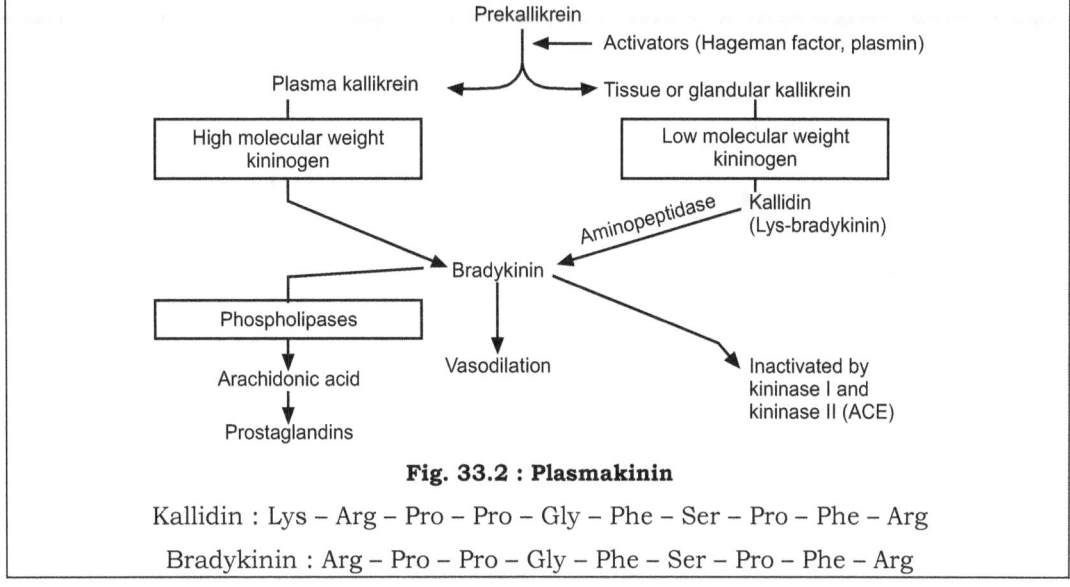

Fig. 33.2 : Plasmakinin

Kallidin : Lys – Arg – Pro – Pro – Gly – Phe – Ser – Pro – Phe – Arg

Bradykinin : Arg – Pro – Pro – Gly – Phe – Ser – Pro – Phe – Arg

The plasmakinins have extremely short half-life of about 15 seconds. Lung is the principal site of catabolism. They are inactivated by kininase-I and kininase-II (angiotensin converting enzyme) in the lung as well as in other vascular beds.

The plasmakinins are potent arteriolar vasodilator. They increase vascular permeability resulting into edema formation. A fall in the total peripheral resistance leads to a decrease in the blood pressure. Due to venous vasoconstriction, the cardiac rate may be increased reflexly.

The plasmakinins cause contraction of various smooth muscles with some exceptions. In asthma, kinin release is involved in the bronchoconstriction. Bradykinin is also released during anaphylactic shock and in inflammatory responses. Aspirin-like drugs may antagonize the bronchoconstriction brought about by bradykinin. While its effects are potentiated by captopril (kininase-II inhibitor).

Plasmakinins are of little therapeutic value due to their extremely short biological half-lives. No specific kinin antagonist exists at the present time.

33.7 NEUROPEPTIDES

(a) Substance P : It is undecapeptide, first detected in the extracts of brain and gut by Euler and Gaddum, in 1931. It has the following structure.

Arg – Pro – Lys – Pro – Gln – Gln – Phe – Phe – Gly – Leu – Met – NH_2

It is localized within nerves in the CNS and periphery and hence also termed as neuropeptide. In CNS, it is present along with serotonin in certain neurons.

It exerts a powerful hypotensive effect and promotes diuresis. It has a stimulant action on salivary secretion. It acts directly on the muscle cells and causes contraction of intestinal, bronchial and other smooth muscles. It is also involved in propagation of pain impulses to the CNS.

(b) Vasoactive intestinal polypeptide (VIP), is yet another peptide which is widely distributed in both, CNS and peripheral nervous system. Its presence in the body was first reported by Said and Mutt in 1972. It is a polypeptide of 28 amino acid. In certain neurons, it is present alongwith acetylcholine.

VIP has similar actions on blood pressure and on salivary secretions as that of substance P. Unlike latter, it relaxes many smooth muscles and exerts bronchodilatory action. It also promotes glycogenolysis.

Beside the salivary secretions, other exocrine secretions are also stimulated.

33.8 OTHER POLYPEPTIDES

Other polypeptides of pharmacological significance include endorphins, enkephalins, neurotensin, bombesin, somatostatin, cholecystokinin and secretin. They have regulatory activities mainly in brain and gut.

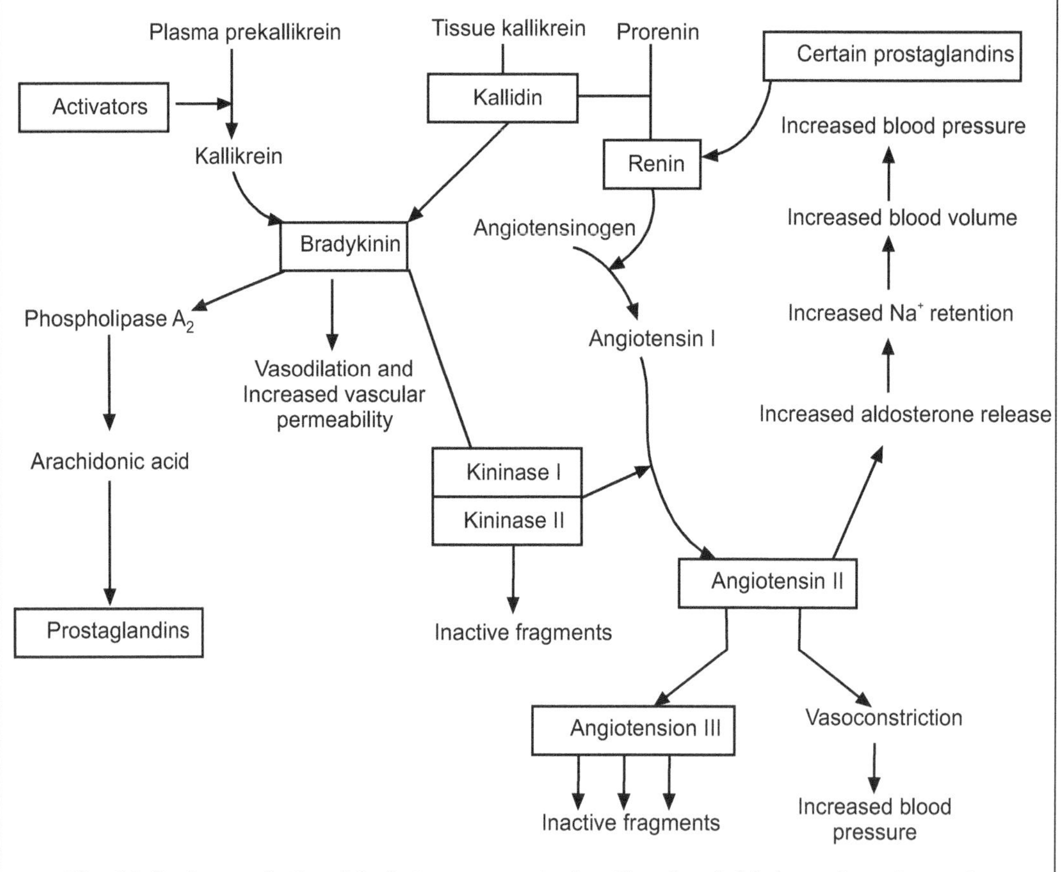

Fig. 33.3 : Interrelationship between prostaglandins, bradykinin and angiotensins

CYCLIC NUCLEOTIDES

34.1 INTRODUCTION

Nucleotide is characterised by the presence of either purine or pyrimidine base attached to a pentose sugar which in turn, is esterified with phosphoric acid. In ribose sugar moiety, esterification occur at the free hydroxyl groups present on carbon 2', 3' and 5'.

The cyclic nucleotides of pharmacological importance include,

(a) Cyclic adenosine–3', 5', monophosphate or cAMP.

(b) Cyclic guanosine–3', 5' monophosphate or c-GMP.

As the name indicates, both these cyclic nucleotides are monophosphates. Many hormones, neurotransmitters and autacoids bring about their effects, at least in part, by altering the intracellular levels of cyclic nucleotides. For example, epinephrine is unable to penetrate the cell-membrane. Hence the biological effects of hormone are mediated inside the cell through an accumulation of c-AMP. Due to their intermediary function, these cyclic nucleotides are often termed as second messengers.

34.2 CYCLIC-AMP

Earl W. Sutherland and co-workers were first to identify the presence of c-AMP in body tissues in 1957. Epinepherine induces the conversion of glycogen to glucose in both, liver and muscles. The glucose is then utilized in the energy production under stressful conditions. The enzyme, phosphorylase catalyzes the rate-limiting step of glucogenolysis to produce glucose-1-phosphate. Sutherland proposed that c-AMP acts as an immediate activator for converting inactive dimeric phosphorylase (b) into active tetrameric phosphorylase (a). Later the structure for c-AMP has been elucidated which was found to be a cyclic nucleotide. The phosphoric acid residue is esterified at carbons 3' and 5' to give cyclic monophosphate structure. In addition to its role in hepatic glycogenolysis, c-AMP also plays a role in the production of lactic acid by activating phospho-fructokinase, an enzyme that catalyzes the conversion of fructose - 6-phosphate to fructose - 1, 6-diphosphate.

34.3 BIOSYNTHESIS, RELEASE AND METABOLISM

Receptors for a number of hormones and autacoids function by regulation of the concentration of intracellular second messenger, cyclic adenosine - 3', 5'- monophosphate through the activation or inhibition of intracellular adenylate cyclase. Adenylate cyclase is incorporated into all membranes. In adrenergic system, stimulation of β-receptors results in an activation of adenylate cyclase (i.e., increased formation of c-AMP), while α-receptor stimulation inhibits the formation of c-AMP.

ATP - Mg^{++} ion complex serves as a precursor for the biosynthesis of c-AMP. The biosynthesis is induced by the activation of adenylate cyclase and is catalyzed by guanosine triphosphate (GTP).

Pyrophosphate is the byproduct of this reaction. The subsequent hydrolysis of pyrophosphate serves as a stimulus for biosynthesis of c-AMP.

Once formed, c-AMP is utilized in two different ways. It is inactivated by phosphodiesterase enzyme to 5'-AMP. Like adenylate cyclase, the enzyme phosphodiesterase also needs Mg^{++} ion for its activation. Many drugs potentiate the effect of c-AMP by inhibiting phosphodiesterase activity. These include, papaverine, methylxanthines etc. Thus, the positive inotropic effect of methylxanthines is mainly due to an accumulation of c-AIMP by inhibition of phosphodiesterase enzymes in cardiac muscles. The phosphodiesterase inhibitors, in general are effective only at relatively higher concentration and may antagonise enzymes and or receptors which are necessary for action of other drugs.

Similarly c-AMP utilizes an ATP molecule to bring about an activation of a specific protein kinase which consists of two subunits (Fig. 34.1). The activation involves detachment of a regulatory unit (R) from the catalytic unit (C), thus relieving an inhibitory effect of regulatory unit on catalytic unit. The catalytic unit, in free form in association with ATP, modulates the activities of different proteins in different cells by phosphorylating them and bringing about diversified physiological responses.

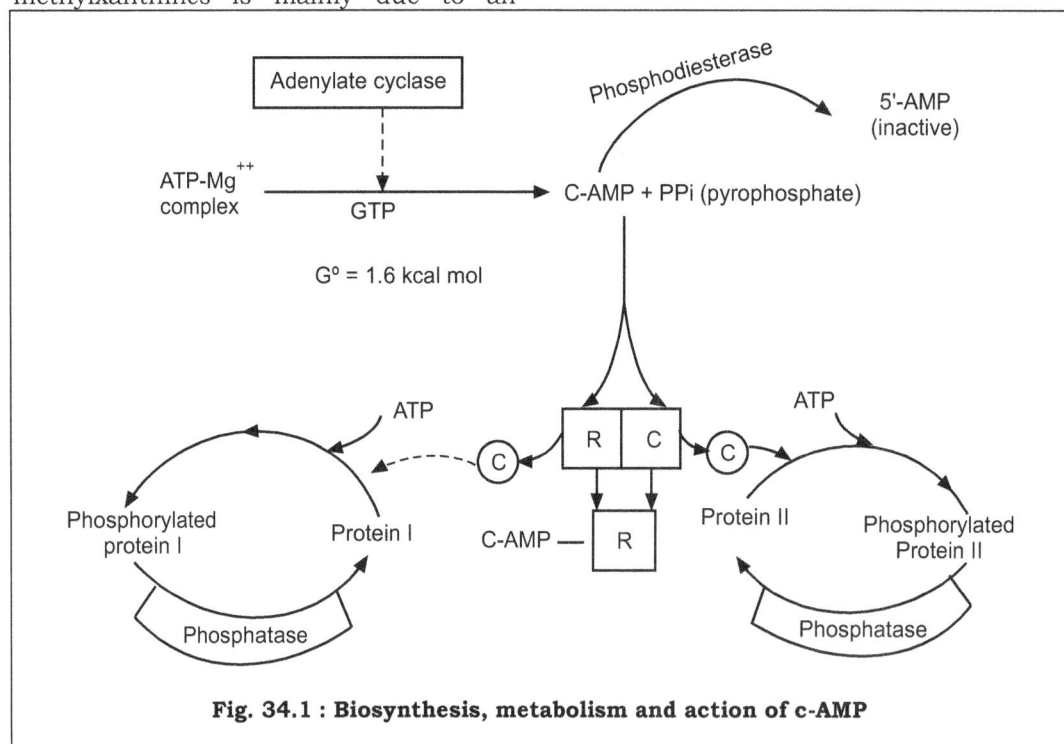

Fig. 34.1 : Biosynthesis, metabolism and action of c-AMP

Thus, the activation of new protein kinase by already activated protein kinase produces a further amplification of the responses. Different cells contain different substrates for protein kinases, which upon activation evoke the responses, characteristic of that particular cell.

Adenylate cyclase also consists of catalytic sub-unit which is activated by receptor subunit of the enzyme structure through guanyl nucleotide binding protein fraction of adenylate cyclase.

Beside phosphodiesterase inhibitors, certain proteins may also potentiate the effects of c-AMP by inhibition of phosphatase enzyme which catalyzes dephosphorylation process. Thus, both, an increase in the rate of phosphorylation and decrease in the rate of dephosphorylation prolongs the duration of responses mediated through c-AMP.

An interference in the accumulation of intracellular c-AMP level, serves as a basis for mechanism of action of many hormones. Thus hormones which lead to an increase in the c-AMP concentration include, epinephrine (on β - receptor), glucagon, vasopressin, prostaglandins, ACTH, LH and thyroid stimulating hormone. While some hormones are reported to lower down the intracellular c-AMP concentration. These include, norepinephrine (α - receptors), insulin, PGF_2 and melatonin.

C-AMP is also involved in the activation of receptors present at both, presynaptic and/or postsynaptic sites. The presynaptic receptor activation (e.g., α_2 - adrenergic receptors) by c-AMP may result into inhibition of transmitter release.

At certain sites, c-AMP accumulation is also coupled with an activation of membrane phosphatidyl inositol system resulting into an influx of extracellular calcium ions. In fact, certain c-AMP induced responses can not mediate in the absence of Ca^{++} ions. While in few cases, Ca^{++} ions and c-AMP act as alternative rather than as complementary activators.

Certain disease conditions are characterized by an increase in the intracellular c-AMP level. These include, cholera, diabetis, epilepsy and mania. While in hypertension, intracellular c-AMP level is found to be lowered down. Similarly certain side-effects of the drug therapy may be due to their interference in the c-AMP turnover in the cell. For example,

(i) Isoproterenol may facilitate the synthesis of c-AMP, while lithium may inhibit its synthesis,

(ii) Insulin may activate phosphodiesterase enzymes while methylxanthines inhibit their metabolizing action on c-AMP, and

(iii) Dibutyryl c-AMP is an agonist of c-AMP, while tolbutamide antagonizes phosphorylation of protein kinases.

34.4 CYCLIC - GMP

Like c-AMP, cyclic GMP is also widely distributed in tissues but in relatively smaller concentration. Cerebellum and retina are particularly rich in c-GMP amounts. The GTP serves as a precursor for c-GMP and the conversion is catalysed by a membrane-bound enzyme, guanylate cyclase.

The responses of epinephrine which are mediated through the activation of β-receptors are mainly due to an accumulation of c-AMP. Similarly ACh brings about its many muscarinic responses through an accumulation of c-GMP. In fact, at several occassions, the overall response of drug on a particular tissue or organ is due to its ability to alter the ratio of intracellular concentration of these two cyclic nucleotides which act exactly opposite to each other. For example, in anaphylaxis reaction, the release of various mediators from the sensitized mast cell is governed by opposing effects of these nucleotides on each other. An activation of adenylate cyclase (i.e., an increase in c-AMP level) results into inhibitor of degranulation while activation of guanylate cyclase (i.e., an increase in c-GMP level) promotes exocytosis.

Some of the effects which are mediated through an activation of guanylate cyclase include,

(a) The muscarinic cholinergic effects on the heart, the vas deferens and intestinal smooth muscles.

(b) The estrogenic effects on uterus.

(c) The effects of oxytocin, $PGF_{2\alpha}$ and serotonin on uterine muscles.

All these effects can be blocked or reduced in intensity by drugs which lead to an increase in intracellular c-AMP levels. Just like c-AMP, the action of c-GMP, at certain sites is coupled with the membrane phosphatidyl inositol system.

In cerebellum, c-GMP is present at much higher concentration. In brain, three distinct c-GMP systems have been identified. Many CNS-acting drugs may utilize these systems to bring about their desired and undesired effects.

Besides anaphylaxis, cyclic nucleotides are also involved in contraception, diuresis, immune response, inflammation, hypertension and Parkinson's disease.

34.5 PURINOCEPTORS

Adenosine, an integral part of c-AMP, itself acts as a modulator in both, central as well as peripheral nervous system. It mediates depressant responses, by acting on purinoceptors. Many centrally acting drugs utilize purinoceptors for propagating their CNS effects. Adenosine and its analogues are found to possess multidimensional activities which include, vasodilatory, antiarrhythmic, sedative, analgesic, anticonvulsant and hypothermic effects. These effects are mediated through the activation of purinoceptors which are linked to adenylate cyclase. These receptor sites are categorized as :

(i) P_1-purinoceptors (adenosine receptors) and

(ii) P_2-purinoceptors (ATP – receptors).

The P_1 – receptor site is linked to adenylate cyclase and hence can be antagonized by methylxanthines, while P_2 - receptor site is not blocked by methylxanthines and is activated only by relatively higher concentrations of adenosine.

Purinoceptors are involved in many central effects like, sedation, motor changes and respiratory depression and thus help to explain mechanism of action of some CNS-acting drugs. e.g., morphine.

SEROTONIN AND ITS ANTAGONISTS

35.1 INTRODUCTION

In simple words, autacoids can be defined as 'the endogenous bioactive substances that are locally biosynthesized and are released to act on the local tissues'. Serotonin or 5-hydroxytryptamine is one of such autacoids. The entero-chromaffin cells of the gastrointestinal mucosa store major amounts of the body's serotonin content. Remaining minor but considerable amount of serotonin is held by platelets and the CNS region. Tryptophan serves as the precursor for the biosynthesis of serotonin. Synthetically it was first prepared in 1951.

Chemically it is 3 – (β-ethylamino) 5-hydroxyindole

35.2 BIOSYNTHESIS, METABOLISM AND ELIMINATION

The enterochromaffin cells of GIT, platelets, bone marrow and CNS region are the principal sites for serotonin storage. In the CNS, higher concentrations of serotonin are present in thalamus, hypothalamus and raphe nuclei of the brain stem. It serves the function of neurotransmitter in the central serotoninergic neurons. In pineal gland, serotonin is present in highest concentration where it serves as the precursor for the pineal hormone, molatonin.

The biosynthetic route involves :

(a) Conversion of tryptophan to 5-hydroxy tryptophan by the enzyme, tryptophan-5-hydroxylase. It is a rate-limiting step and is interfered by p-chloro phenylalanine. Pineal gland contains highest concentration of both, serotonin and tryptophan - 5 - hydroxylase enzyme.

(b) The 5-hydroxytryptophane is immediately then decarboxylated to serotonin by a non-specific aromatic - L - amino acid decarboxylase (i.e., 5 - hydroxytryptophan decarboxylase). Platelets can not synthesize serotonin due to the lack of this enzyme. In the enterochromaffin cells, serotonin is stored into the secretory granules in the form of a nondiffusible complex with ATP and other substances. Platelets receive preformed serotonin during their circulation through tissues. They store it into the granules in an inactive form. The same biosynthetic pattern is also followed into the CNS.

The GIT smooth muscles are innervated by both cholinergic and adrenergic nerves. Certain factors like, acidity, hypertonicity, activation of cholinergic as well as adrenergic nerves may facilitate the serotonin release from enterochromaffin cells of the GIT. Part of the released serotonin into the circulation may be taken up by an active energy dependent process into the platelets while rest is inactivated mainly by catabolic processes in hepatic and pulmonary vascular beds. The efflux of serotonin from platelets is involved in hemostatis and blood coagulation. Reserpine has an ability to impair such energy dependent uptake processes and promotes the release of serotonin from the platelets. Besides this, serotonin is also released during thrombin-induced release reactions and platelet destruction.

The serotonin released into the circulation is metabolized by enzymes present mainly in the liver and tissues that contain serotonin. The Fig. 35.1, illustrates various routes by which serotonin is inactivated in the body.

Alongwith the metabolites, serotonin also appears in urine (in minute amounts) in both, free and conjugated form. In certain conditions, (when the person takes MAO – inhibitor drug or suffers from tumors of enterochromaffin cells of GIT), serotonin is also inactivated by N-methylation, N-acetylation, O-methylation followed by conjugation. In fact, these deactivating mechanisms are routinely employed in pineal gland. Thus the metabolic pattern of serotonin in the pineal gland differs from that seen in the peripheral sites. In pineal gland, serotonin is mainly converted into 5-methoxytryptamine, 5-methoxyindole acetic acid, 5-methoxytryptophol and N-acetyl serotonin. The latter metabolite serves as the precursor for melatonin synthesis in pineal gland.

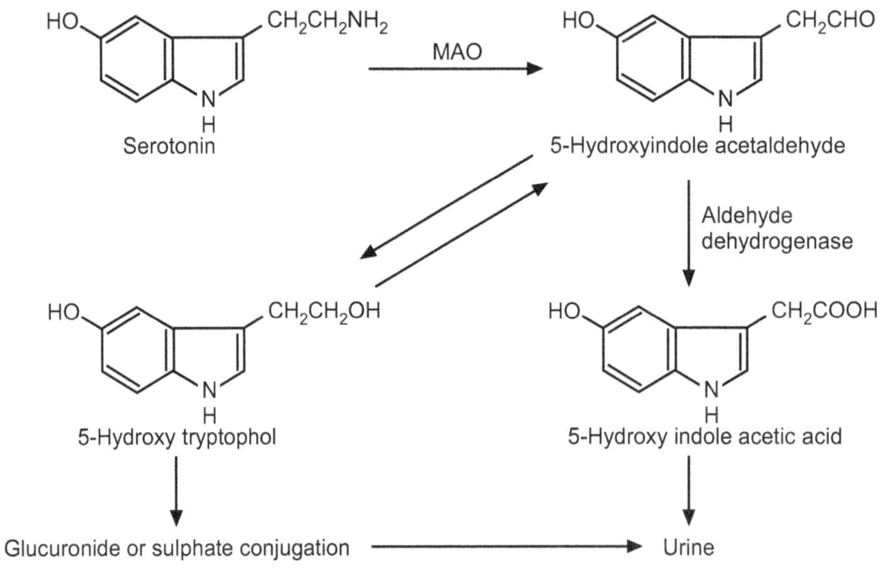

Fig. 35.1 : **Inactivation of serotonin in body**

35.3 PHARMACOLOGY

Serotonin possesses a broad spectrum of activities and affects almost every vital system in the body. The main pharmacological actions include.

(a) CNS :

It acts as a neurotransmitter in the serotoninergic neurons whose activation leads to mostly depressive effects. Serotonin is mainly involved in sleep, thought, pain perception, mood and behavioural states. The interference in the functioning of serotoninergic neurons is the probable cause involved in the mental illnesses which may result into hallucinatory activity. Besides this, the regulation of blood pressure, body temperature and neuroendocrine function is also exerted by serotonin. Thus, the central effects of serotonin resemble quite closely to the central effects of adrenaline. Many antidepressant drugs may augment both, α - adrenergic and serotoninergic activity at post-synaptic sites. Serotonin is a vasoconstrictor agent that exerts a control on dilatation of extra cranial blood vessels. The rapid metabolism of central serotonin leads to dilatation of these vessels resulting into migraine attack. Similarly the potentiation of central serotonin effects may result into hallucinatory effects. The hallucinogens like, psilocin, psylocybin and LSD may act through this mechanism due to their structural similarity with serotonin.

(b) Peripheral Actions :

At peripheral sites, serotonin mainly acts in the histamine-like manner. Most of its effects at peripheral sites are due to local nerve reflexes coupled with its own direct actions. This results sometimes into complex responses which are not easy to interpret.

(i) CVS : The effects of serotonin on cardiovascular system are invariably complex due to involvement of direct and reflex mechanisms. The reflex mechanisms include the release of noradrenaline from the sympathetic nerve terminals and a direct stimulant action on the vagus centre. This may result into fluctuating changes in the blood pressure. In general, vasoconstriction, tachycardia and positive inotropic and chronotropic effect on the heart are some of the prominent CVS effects of serotonin. This is followed by bradycardia and hypotension due to the activation of baroreceptors in the coronary bed.

In low doses, serotonin leads to vasodilation in skeletal muscles while at higher doses it may activate ganglionic transmission, adrenal medullary secretion and sympathetic nerve terminals. In high doses, it may also interfere in the hemostatic mechanisms and promotes fibrosis at various organ sites.

(ii) Respiratory system : Due to the activation of carotid and aortic chemoreceptors, an increase in respiratory minute volume and rate is seen. Serotonin also leads to the constriction of bronchial smooth muscles. This effect is more potentiated in asthmatic patients. In carcinoid patients, excessive release of serotonin may lead to pulmonary stenosis.

(iii) GIT : Serotonin has a stimulant action on the gastrointestinal smooth muscles, resulting into an increase in the peristaltic activity. Thus, excess local serotonin release (as in the carcinoid tumor condition) in GIT, may produce favourable environment for peptic ulcer attack.

(iv) Exocrine glands : Due to the direct and reflex actions, serotonin alters the exocrine secretion in a variable manner. The secretion of pepsin and gastric acid are found to be suppressed.

(v) Endocrine glands : At higher doses, serotonin increases the rate of release of catecholamines (from adrenal gland), ACTH, FSH, LH, prolactin, growth hormone and thyroid-stimulating hormone. It is also involved in the regulation of sexual activity.

35.4 SEROTONIN RECEPTORS

Serotonin is well absorbed when given orally as well as parenterally. However it is ineffective by oral route due to its rapid inactivation. The endogenous as well as parenterally administered serotonin brings about its effects by acting on serotonin receptors present in the cell-membrane. Three distinct receptor sub-types have been identified for serotonin. These include,

(a) 5-HT$_1$ Receptor Sub-type :

These receptors are located at both, central and peripheral sites. Their activation may result into inhibition of transmitter release, behavioural changes, fall in blood pressure through peripheral vasodilatation and at certain sites, vasoconstriction.

(b) 5-HT$_2$ Receptor Sub-type :

Like 5-HT$_1$ type, these receptors are also located in both, central and peripheral region and are linked with behavioural effects, smooth muscle constriction and platelet aggregation.

(c) 5-HT$_3$ Receptor Sub-type :

These receptor sub-types are mainly associated with the ion-channels present in the peripheral neurons and govern the transmitter release. More particularly their presence in the nicotine/GABA/glycine channel system is proposed.

Thus the pharmacological actions due to serotonin release, are the outcome of direct and indirect activation of these receptor sub-sites coupled with reflex mechanisms. A substance effective as an antagonist at one of 5-HT receptor sub-type, may act as agonist at other 5-HT receptor sub-types e.g., LSD.

In mid-brain region, dopaminergic mechanisms are intimately tied up with serotoninergic functions, and inhibition of serotoninergic receptor activation by antipsychotic agents may indirectly attack on the predominance of dopaminergic component in the schizophrenia.

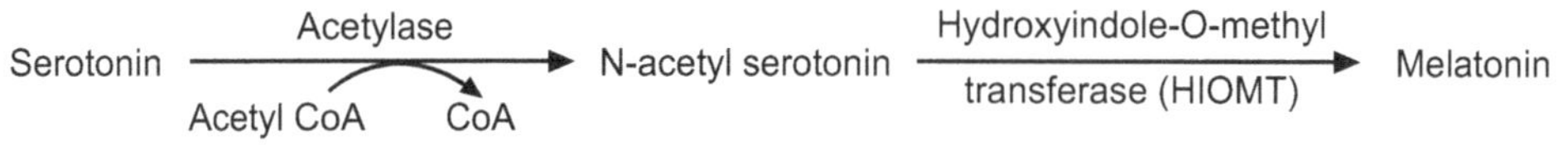

$$\text{Serotonin} \xrightarrow[\text{Acetyl CoA} \quad \text{CoA}]{\text{Acetylase}} \text{N-acetyl serotonin} \xrightarrow{\text{Hydroxyindole-O-methyl transferase (HIOMT)}} \text{Melatonin}$$

35.5 MELATONIN (N-Acetyl-5-Methoxy Tryptamine)

Pineal gland biosynthesizes serotonin and melatonin, both from dietary tryptophan. Melatonin is exclusively biosynthesized in the pineal gland. Serotonin serves as a precursor for its synthesis.

Adenylate cyclase induced accumulation of c-AMP causes an increase in the activity of HIOMT enzyme. In mammals, melatonin biosynthesis is activated by the exposure to darkness and is depressed by light. Melatonin is associated with many physiological processes like, puberty, ovulation, sleep etc. Since the release of LH is inhibited by melatonin, an excess melatonin release (as in the case of pineal tumour) may cause a diminution of gonadal function. Thus melatonin governs the functioning of reproductive processes and other endocrine functions.

35.6 SEROTONIN ANTAGONISTS

In certain conditions like, tumors of enterochromaffin cells of intestinal mucosa (carcinoid tumor), the demand for dietary tryptophan (which is the precursor for serotonin biosynthesis) is increased. The chromaffin cells consume more tryptophan for the serotonin synthesis. This results into a decrease in niacin synthesis leading to development of pellegra symptoms. Besides this, the increased level of serotonin may exert several undesired responses, more particularly by acting on the central regions (e.g., behavioural changes, mood fluctuation, increased melatonin formation etc.). In such conditions, to counteract responses due to excessive serotonin release the use of antagonists may be of clinical utility. These agents may antagonize serotonin actions through direct, indirect or physiological antagonism. Unfortunately these agents lack the selectivity of action and also affect the activity at receptors for other autacoids. They include,

(a) Structural Relatives of Serotonin :

Many indole derivatives to varying degrees, exert serotonin antagonistic action. LSD, 2-bromo LSD, methylsergide are some of the examples of such drugs which act as competitive antagonist of serotonin, particularly on smooth muscles. Many hallucinogens (psilocine, psilocybin) and psychotropic agents also have some degree of antiserotonin activity. Ergot alkaloids also are no exception. Methylsergide is one of such synthetic analogues of ergot alkaloid which is devoid of hallucinogenic activity. Due to its antiserotoninergic activity, it is useful in the treatment of migraine, mania and diarrhoea, caused due to excessive serotonin release. It may bring out vasoconstriction of extracranial blood vessels by acting as partial agonist of serotonin and thus relieves migraine pain.

(b) Drugs Structurally Unrelated to Serotonin :

Many drugs which are structurally unrelated with serotonin may exhibit antiserotonin action. Some of them have highly selective action at certain 5-HT receptor sub-type but also influence the functioning of receptors for other autacoids. These includes chlorpromazine phenoxybenzamine, cyproheptadiene and ketanserin.

Cyproheptadine : Basically, cyproheptadine is an example of classic antihistaminic class. Beside this, it has a weak anticholinergic activity and significant antiserotonin action on various smooth muscles. It also exerts central antidopaminergic activity.

Ketanserin : It is a selective $5\text{-}HT_2$-receptor antagonist. It is devoid of any blocking action on other receptor sub-types of serotonin. Beside this, it also exerts blocking action on dopaminergic, H_1 histaminergic and α_1-adrenergic receptors. It also depresses sympathetic activation from CNS.

Due to its selective $5\text{-}HT_2$-receptor blocking activity, its potential as antihypertensive agent is being evaluated.

HISTAMINE AND ITS ANTAGONISTS

36.1 INTRODUCTION

A number of substances with widely differing structures and with diversified pharmacological activities are normally present in the body. These include histamine, serotonin, prostaglandins, angiotensin, bradykinin, kallidin etc. Since their pharmacological activities do not permit to call them as hormones or neurohormones, they are grouped together in a class, known as autacoid [Greek word : autos (self) and akos (medicinal agent or remedy)]. Though autacoids play an important role in the body's economical system, their physiological functions can not be stated with assurance.

Histamine is widely distributed in plant and animal tissues. Due to its widespread occurrence in body tissues, it was named histamine which means 'tissue amine'. It was first discovered in 1907 by Windaus and Vogt. Its vasodepressor effect was reported in 1910 by Dale et al. In 1927, it was first isolated from liver and lung tissues. It is found to be involved in the diversified physiological processes. It is released in body usually, in response to tissue injury, inflammation, and allergic or hypersensitivity reactions.

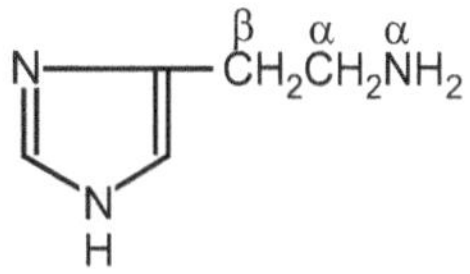

$$\text{Imidazole-}CH_2CH_2NH_2$$

Histamine

Histamine is comprised of an imidazole ring connected to an amino group through ethylene bridge. Both, imidazole ring and amino group are basic and get protonated under acidic condition. Chemically, it is β–imidazolyl ethylamine. The structural features of histamine permit it to exist in ionic, tautomeric and conformeric forms which constantly get interconverted to each other. These forms differ mainly in the electronic charge distribution and in the position of hydrogen atoms.

There are many drugs with histamine like properties. These drugs may contain the following molecular fragments.

$$-N = C - CH_2 - CH_2 - NH_2$$

OR

$$= N - C - CH_2 - CH_2 - NH_2$$

(36.1)

These fragments seem to be necessary for attack of histamine on receptor centers of target cells.

36.2 BIOSYNTHESIS, STORAGE AND CATABOLISM

The major source of histamine in body appears to be the decarboxylation of the naturally occurring amino acid, histidine, under the influence of L-histidine decarboxylase. It is highly specific enzyme whose activity is governed by histamine itself, through negative feedback inhibition mechanism. This conversion utilizes pyridoxal-5-phosphate as a coenzyme. Histidine is also converted to histamine by a pathway of minor importance that is catalyzed by non-specific enzyme, aromatic-L-amino acid decarboxylase (dopa decarboxylase). Almost all mammalian tissues contain varying amounts of histamine, L-histidine decarboxylase and enzymes that metabolize histamine. The higher concentration of histamine, however, is found in the skin, intestinal mucosa, lungs and bone marrow. These are the organs which are exposed to external environment. In brain, histamine is present in significant amount.

The tissue fixed mast cells and blood basophils (circulating counterparts of mast cells) are the principal cells where histamine is synthesized and is stored in secretory granules. Besides mast cells, histamine is also present in skin, gastric mucosa and CNS where it is biosynthesized and stored in non-mast cells. Here histamine usually undergoes rapid turnover and is released, rather than stored. It is this histamine which is probably of greater physiological importance.

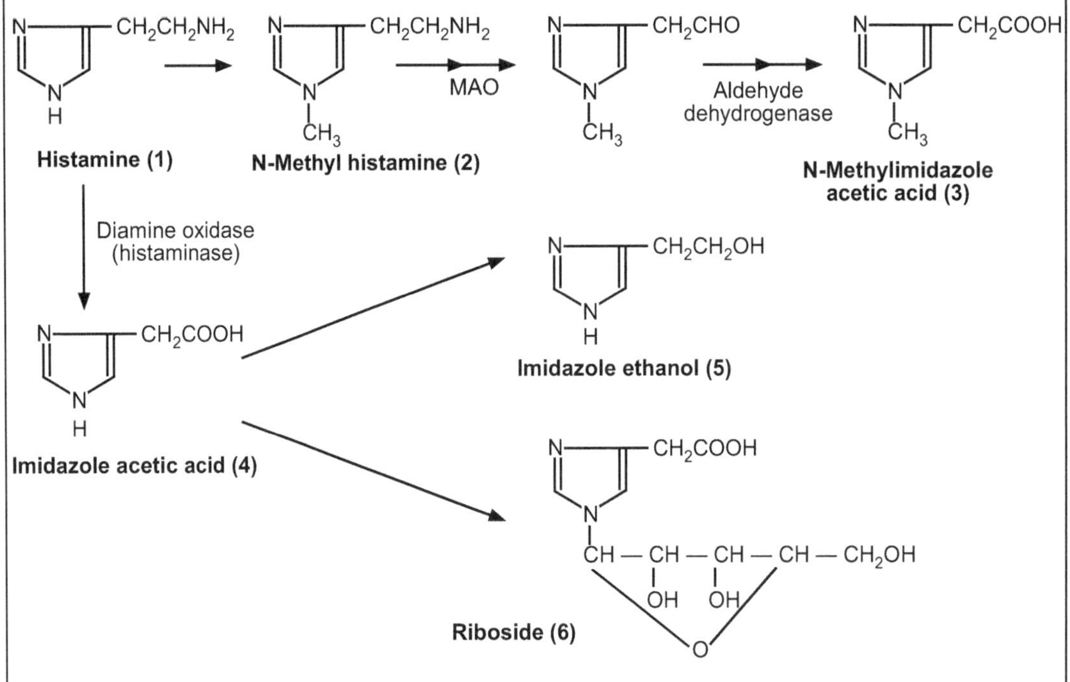

Fig. 36.1 : **Histamine inactivation in body**

Some histamine is also synthesized in the gut lumen by bacteria. But most of it, is inactivated during absorption in the gastrointestinal mucosa, liver and lungs to N-acetyl histamine.

Figure 36.1 shows the principal pathways by which histamine is inactivated in the body.

Except (1) and (2), rest of the metabolites of histamine retain little or no physiological activity. In general, conjugation reactions rarely utilize ribose as a substrate. Histamine seems to be among such rare compounds, which are biotransformed through the conjugation with ribose moiety. Acetylation and N-demethylation are other metabolic pathways of minor importance. Urine serves as the principal vehicle for the excretion of these inactive products.

Specific as well as non-specific enzymes are involved in the inactivation of liberated histamine into the body. Imidazole-N-methyl transferase is present in the tissues but not in blood whereas diamine oxidase is present in high concentration in intestine, kidney, liver and thoracic duct lymph. It also utilizes other diamines as its substrates. It is mainly inhibited by antimalarial drugs.

36.3 HISTAMINE RELEASE

At almost every site of action, histamine is biosynthesized locally and is then stored in subcellular organelles. Under normal conditions, much of the body's store of histamine remains in an inactive form within the tissues. The tissue bound mast cells and basophils are the principal cells for histamine storage. Thus almost every organ is supplied with blood containing histamine, released by basophils. Within the secretory granules of mast cells and basophils, histamine is stored with a heparin-protein complex, to which it is loosely bound with ionic forces. The sensitization of mast cell is caused by an antigen when it interacts (through bridge formation) with two membrane-bound antibody (immunoglobin) molecules resulting into initiation of a chain of events that ends into an expulsion of the contents of secretory granules by the process of exocytosis. It is Ca^{++} and Mg^{++} ion dependent and energy required metabolic process. Histamine is released from its heparin-protein complex by an exchange program, probably involving calcium ions. Cyclic AMP inhibits the release of histamine, presumably by closing the calcium channels while c-GMP facilitates the calcium influx and induces histamine release.

The concentration of c-AMP is governed by the membrane-bound adenylate cyclase enzyme which is activated by norepinephrine (α-adrenergic agonist), epinephrine (β-adrenergic agonist), prostaglandins and by histamine (negative feedback inhibition by activation of H_2-receptor) itself, while the concentration of c-GMP is governed by another membrane bound guanylate cyclase enzyme which is activated by cholinergic agonists. Both these second messengers control the breakdown of phosphatidylinositides and the generation of phosphorylated derivatives of inositol which are involved in the regulation of calcium channels.

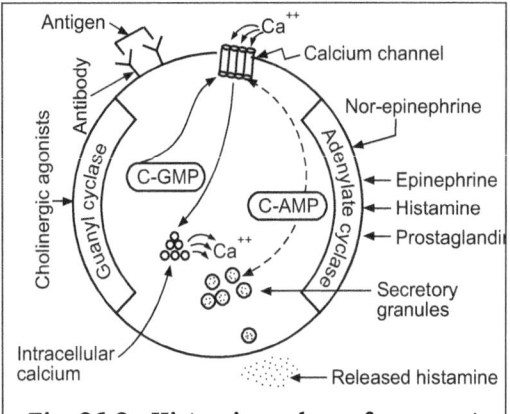

Fig. 36.2 : Histamine release from mast cells

The intracellular concentration of free calcium is important for the exocytotic release of histamine. In certain cases, non-exocytotic mechanism may also be involved in the release of histamine. These include morphological changes in the mast cells resulting into mast cell lysis or physical displacement of histamine. Chlorpromazine may cause the histamine release from mast cells by a cytotoxic mechanism.

Since activation of H_2-receptor sites on mast cell membrane, results into elevation of c-AMP, all physiological actions of histamine that are initiated by H_2-receptor activation, will be associated with elevated intracellular c-AMP level. Similarly, the physiological actions of histamine that are due to H_1-receptor activation in general may then be associated with elevated intracellular c-GMP levels.

In hypersensitivity reaction, the mast cell is sensitised by an interaction of specific antigen with the cell bound antibody (IgE or reagin), resulting into degranulation and subsequent release of granular contents. Histamine is released along with other autacoids like, plasmakinins, angiotensin, prostaglandins, serotonin, platelet activating factor, slow releasing substance of anaphylaxis (SRS-A) and eosinophill chemotactic factor.

36.4 HISTAMINE LIBERATION

Histamine release may be increased in urticarial reactions, mastocytosis and basophilia. Similarly in certain patients, many drugs may produce hypersensitivity reactions by sensitizing mast cells. In some cases, these drugs or their metabolic products may act as antigen while few of them can directly or indirectly activate the calcium ion channel. This may result into an eventual expulsion of the granular contents of the mast cells which include heparin and other mediators of anaphylaxis alongwith histamine.

Chlortetracycline, morphine, pethidine, amphetamine, tolazoline, d-tubocurarine and atropine are some of the drugs which cause the histamine release. Hence, these drugs are termed as histamine liberators. They do not deplete histamine stores from non-mast cells.

36.5 HISTAMINE RECEPTORS

Histamine is orally ineffective due to its inactivation by the intestinal bacteria. It is also inactivated by its 'first pass' through the liver. When given parenterally, it is readily absorbed.

$$\underset{H}{\underset{|}{N}}\!\!\overset{\pi}{\underset{}{\diagdown}}\!\!\!\overset{}{\underset{}{\diagup}}\!\!\overset{\beta}{CH_2}-\overset{\alpha}{CH_2}-\overset{\alpha}{NH_2}$$

Histamine is a highly polar hydrophilic molecule. The imidazole ring and the amino group are both basic and are protonated in acidic solution.

Unchanged form ⇌ **Monocationic form**

All the nitrogen atoms in the histamine molecule are negatively charged while all the hydrogen atoms in the molecule are positively charged. In solution, histamine exists in an equilibrium mixture of ionic, tautomeric and conformer forms. Histamine has a strong ability to form H-bonds due to the presence of H-donars like, ammonium and imidazole cations.

At physiological pH, histamine may get pronated at α-nitrogen resulting into monocationic N_r-H tautomer. The uncharged form might be required for access to the sites of action while the monocationic form is needed for its physiological activity in the body.

Histamine has a wide range of diversified pharmacological actions. On the similar line of the Ahlquist experiment (who proposed in 1948, the existance of α and β receptor for adrenergic drugs), the existence of two distinct receptor sites (i.e., H_1 - and H_2 - receptor) for histamine has been proposed, to explain these diversified actions. Both these receptor sites are scattered throughout various body tissues.

H_1-receptor activation has been found to be associated with the accumulation of c-GMP which is induced by the activation of guanylate cyclase enzyme. It is involved in histamine induced, vasodilatation, bronchoconstriction, itch and pain sensation, increase in vascular permeability and some of the central responses of histamine.

While accumulation of c-AMP brings about the activation of H_2-receptor sites. H_2-receptors are predominantly present in the heart muscles, parietal cells, plasma basophils and brain tissues. The H_2-receptor mediated effects of histamine include,

(a) inhibition of sympathetic transmission.

(b) secretion of gastric acid, pepsin and instrinsic factor.

(c) +ve ionotropic and +ve chronotropic effect on the heart.

(d) relaxation of uterine muscles, and

(e) control of histamine release through feedback inhibition mechanism.

Certain tissues may possess both receptor sites. Hence the effects of histamine observed may be due to activation of both, H_1- and H_2-receptor sites. Such effects include,

(a) emetic effect,

(b) increase in the coronary blood flow,

(c) relaxation of small arteries, and

(d) hypotension resulting from vascular dilatation, mediated by receptor of both H_1 and H_2-receptors.

In general, the effects mediated through H_1-receptors predominate when activation of both receptor sites occurs in the same tissue. The presence of a third receptor subsite (H_3-receptor) for histamine is also proposed in 1979 by Tepperman et al.

The monocationic form of histamine appears to be involved in the activation of both, H_1- and H_2-receptor sites. This physiologically active form of histamine may form H - bonding with the basic moiety of the receptor. The imidazole ring remains coplaner with the side-chain. At the H_1-receptor, imidazole tautomerism is not the basic requirement but the presence of the N-atom ortho to the ethylamino side chain seems to be necessary for receptor activation while in H_2-receptor activation tautomeric property of imidazole ring appears to be of special significance.

At these receptor sites, histamine may exist in two distinct and preferred conformations.

Trans (extended) **Gauche (folded)**
conformation **conformation**

In the extended conformation, the charged ammonium group remains maximal apart (5.1 A°) from the N^π - nitrogen atom. It is proposed that for the H_1-receptor activation, histamine should be present in the trans conformation while gauche conformation is involved in the H_2-receptor activation.

Beside histamine, 2-methyl histamine selectively acts as H_1-receptor agonist while 4-methyl histamine acts selectively as H_2-receptor agonist. Betazole has a potent gastric secretagoque activity. It is an isomer of histamine which possesses a pyrazole, rather than imidazole ring. Betazole has little or no systemic activity. The adverse effects of betazole are mainly due to its H_1-receptor activity and include headache, weakness and flushing. Clonidine, tolazoline and some antidepressant agents act like partial H_2-agonists.

Betazole **Betahistine**

Similarly betahistine is relatively selective H_1-receptor agonist drug. It acts as a vasodilator and is mainly used for investigational purposes. Histamine itself has limited diagnostic use due to its poor oral effectiveness and distressing side-effects associated with its use. Hense these selective H_1- and H_2-receptor agonists received more attention.

36.6 PHYSIOLOGICAL ACTIONS OF HISTAMINE

Most of the actions of histamine are mediated through the activation of H_1 - and H_2-receptor sites. Sometimes, the nature of the response becomes complicated due to the involvement of reflex mechanisms.

(a) CVS : Blood vessels : An ability of histamine to dilate the capillaries and to increase their permeability may result into decrease in the peripheral resistance, a fall in systemic blood pressure, a reddening of the skin of the face (flushing) and edematous swelling of the tissues. These actions suggest the basic role of histamine in the beginning of the inflammatory reactions.

Capillary dilatation involves both, H_1- and H_2-receptor activation. A throbbing headache is often experienced due to histamine-induced dilatation of cerebral vessels, while H_1-receptors are involved to increase capillary permeability. The capillary permeability is increased by contraction of the endothelial cells, resulting into exposure of freely permeable basement membrane to the plasma. This effect is further augmented due to capillary dilatation.

In larger doses of histamine, death may result due to asphyxia which arises by low blood supply to lungs through constriction of pulmonary artery. Unlike capillaries, larger blood vessels are thus constricted by histamine to compensate the decrease in the total peripheral resistance. Thus, an elevation of blood pressure may be seen.

Heart : The cardiac effects of histamine are mainly mediated through H_2-receptors. Histamine exerts an increase in the rate and force of contraction of the heart muscles, probably by promoting calcium flux. In toxic doses hence, it may produce arrhythmias. In recommended doses however, cardiac stimulant effects of histamine may be potentiated by increase in catecholamine release brought about by baroreceptor reflexes. These reflexes may be activated by decreased blood pressure due to vasodilation.

(b) Extravascular smooth muscles : Histamine stimulates or more rarely relaxes - various smooth muscles. For example, bronchial and GIT smooth muscles get contracted while those of fine blood vessels get relaxed. In normal persons, the functioning of extravascular smooth muscles is little affected. However in asthmatic patients, bronchospasm may result due to the activation of H_1 - receptors. The lumen of the airways is restricted and breathing becomes more difficult. Prostaglandins may get locally released and bronchial secretory activity may be increased.

Histamine causes contraction of smooth muscles of GIT. This action, coupled with its stimulatory action on the gastric acid secretion causes nausea, vomiting, diarrhoea, abdominal cramps and epigastric distress. In human uterus, the responses are less significant.

(c) CNS : Histamine is unevenly distributed in the brain and may also act as a central neurotransmitter where its functions may relate to the endocrine regulation specifically of anterior pituitary gland.

The exogenous histamine does not cross the blood brain barrier and parenterally administered histamine is devoid of any CNS effect. However, the sensitization of sensory nerves in the skin by histamine may provoke an axon reflex which, when propogated to the CNS results into itching or pain sensation.

Behavioural responses, cardiovascular effects and lowering of body temperature may be observed due to histamine - induced alterations in the functioning of midbrain and cerebellum region. The activation of both, H_1 and H_2 - receptor sites is responsible for these central effects of histamine.

(d) Glandular tissues : Histamine is a potent gastric secretagoque. The cells containing histamine, are located in close proximity to the parietal cells in the gastric mucosa. The histamine released, act on the H_2-receptors, resulting into accumulation of c-AMP through an activation of adenylate cyclase enzyme. The c-AMP then activates $H^+ - K^+$ - ATPase pump (which exchanges a proton for K^+-ion which works on the same principle to that of $Na^+ - K^+$ - ATPase pump. This results into gastric secretion. Histamine works in combination with Ach and gastrin (a hormonal secretagogus) to increase gastric acid and pepsin release. It also induces the release of intrinsic factor.

The salivary, bronchial, pancreatic, intestinal and lacrimal secretions are also found to be increased by histamine. The baroreceptor reflex mechanism, stimulated by histamine-induced vasodilatation induces catechol release from the adrenal gland. Thus, excessive histamine release may cause peptic ulceration and may aggrevate asthmatic condition.

Pentagastrin : Gastrin (heptadecapeptide) is a hormonal gastric secretagogue. The secretions of gastric acid, pepsin and instrinsic factor are also found to be increased by pentagastrin which is a synthetic pentapeptide derivative of gastrin.

Its gastric secretagogue activity is comparable to those induced by histamine or betazole and it causes fewer and milder side-effects which include nausea, flushing, dizziness and tachycardia. It has relatively shorter duration of action (about 10 minutes).

$(CH_3)_2HC - H_2CO - C - NHCH_2CH_2C - NH - CH$

$H_2N - C - CH - NH - C - CHNHC - CH - NH - C$

(with side chains: $CH_2-C_6H_5$, CH_2-COOH, $CH_2-CH_2-S-CH_3$, and indole ring)

Pentagastrin

(e) Intradermal tissues : Histamine stimulates sensory nerve endings in the skin. This sensitization results into itch (nerve endings in epidermis) and pain (nerve endings in dermis) sensation. The pigmented cutaneous lesions may be observed due to the local release of histamine in the upper corium, in urticaria.

Histamine, when injected intradermally, it produces dilatation of both, the capillaries and neighbouring arterioles resulting into appearance of localized red spot around the site of injection. The vascular permeability is increased in this area resulting into increased exudation of the tissue fluid, giving rise to a wheal formation. These three effects i.e., dilatation of capillaries, formation of wheal and dilatation of arterioles, collectively termed as Lewis triple response.

(f) Hypersensitivity reactions : Due to genetic predisposition, certain persons may get sensitized by antigens derived from a variety of sources. This sensitization induces the disturbances in the body's immuno-inflammatory system, resulting into allergic reactions. Allergic responses may cause chronic and acute illnesses and include sinus problems, conjuctivitis, urticaria, hay fever, bronchial asthma or in extreme cases, anaphylactic shock. For example, when nasal mucosa is involved, allergic rhinitis or/and conjunctivitis may occur.

These allergic or hypersensitivity reactions involve an interaction of a specific antigen with the cell-fixed antibody resulting into release of autacoids. Mast cells and basophils are the principle target cells of hypersensitivity reactions. Besides histamine, other autacoids (like, plasma kinins, serotonin, prostaglandins, slow reacting substance of anaphylaxis etc.) are also liberated from the mast cells, which play a role to varying degree, in the allergic phenomenon.

Hence treatment of hypersentitivity reactions with histamine antagonists is only partially effective. For example, in human asthma, SRS - A plays a major role, whose actions can not be antagonized by histamine antagonists. Hence the use of physiological antagonist, like adrenergic drugs and theophylline would be more effective. These drugs inhibit the degranulation process by inducing an accumulation of c-AMP which then acts through feedback inhibition mechanism and they also exert responses of an opposing nature to counteract the effects of already released autacoids.

(g) Histamine shock : Histamine dilates the capillaries and also increases vascular permeability. The increased permeability promotes plasma to leave the circulation, resulting into decreased blood volume. Similarly vasodilatation in the finer vessel results into retaintion of large amount of blood in the tissues. The overall effects are decreased blood volume, reduced venous return and lower cardiac output. These effects are more pronounced when histamine is present in larger doses and give rise to condition, known as histamine shock.

(h) Histamine may also play a role in anabolic processes. Histamine is orally ineffective. When given parenterally, it unselectively activates both, H_1- and H_2-receptors, giving rise to diversified range of pharmacological effects. Hence, clinical use of histamine is limited due to adverse effects produced by histamine because of unselectivity of action.

Clinically, histamine may be used

(i) to diagnose pheochromocytoma, and

(ii) in distinguishing pernicious anemia from other forms of anemia.

36.7 HISTAMINE ANTAGONISTS

Histamine antagonists would be effective in the treatment of pathological conditions developed due to excessive histamine release or to exaggerated sensitivity to histamine. They may either exert opposite physiological responses or may antagonize the responses to histamine by competition for its receptor sites. Agents which interfere in the biosynthesis of histamine are not of clinical utility due to involvement of histamine in some of the vital biochemical reactions of the body.

(a) Physiological antagonists : This class includes sympathomimetic agents (e.g., adrenaline, isoprenaline), xanthine derivatives (e.g., aminophylline) and anticholinergic agent (e.g., atropine-like agents), all of which antagonize the bronchoconstrictor effect of histamine by producing bronchodilation, an exactly opposite response. Hence these agents may be of value in the treatment of asthmatic condition and anaphylactic shock.

Sympathomimetic amines, for example do not interfere in the biosynthesis, release and other pharmacological actions of histamine. In histamine shock, they effectively reverse the symptoms by virtue of their peripheral vasoconstrictor action. The pharmacogical responses induced by both, sympathomimetic amines and xanthine derivatives are mainly due to an accumulation of c-AMP, while anticholinergic agents exert beneficial effects in hypersensitivity reactions mainly due to their antagonizing effect on ACh responses. Due to their antisecretory effects on the bronchial tract, they are less favoured than other physiological antagonists in asthmatic condition.

(b) Competitive antagonists : These drugs, due to their structural similarity with histamine, antagonize the responses to histamine by competition for its receptor sites. These are categorized as

(i) H_1-receptor blocking agents

(ii) H_2-receptor blocking agents.

All the clinically used antagonists from this class, are reversible competitive inhibitors of the actions of histamine. Hence they are also termed as antihistaminic agents. They share following structural features, in common, with histamine.

(i) charged or quaternerized ammonium ion in the side-chain, and

(ii) a flat aromatic or heterocyclic ring.

Histamine is highly polar hydrophilic compound. It has a strong ability to form H-bonds with the receptor surface. It may thus, interact with the strongly hydrophilic region in the receptor surface. It is proposed that these hydrophilic regions may be located in less specific lipoidal region that has strong affinity for bulky groups present in the antihistaminic agents. The competitive antagonists may then interact with this lipoidal region and inhibits the attack of histamine molecule on its binding site on the receptor through umbrella-like covering effect. It seems logical then, to assume that both, histamine and antihistamine may not interact with precisely the same binding sites at the receptor surface.

Upon chronic administraction, some antihistamines may gradually loose their effectiveness. This may be due to their ability to induce their own metabolizing enzymes resulting into their rapid inactivation. In such cases, switch over to another antihistamine is advisable rather than to increase the dose in order to maintain effectiveness of the drug.

Thymoxyethyldiethylamine was the first antihistamine reported in 1937. It was soon followed by a number of other antihistamines. They do not interfere in the biosynthesis, release or metabolic processes of histamine. The clinical failure of these agents to inhibit some of the histamine responses (e.g., gastric acid secretion) favoured an idea about the presence of two distinct receptor-sites for histamine viz, H_1- and H_2-receptors. The responses mediated through H_2-receptors could not be inhibited by the antihistamines which were clinically used at that time. The first selective H_2-receptor blocker was first reported in 1972 by Black et al. Presently cimetidine and ranitidine are the clinically used selective H_2-receptor blocking agent.

In general, for selective H_1-receptor blocking activity, the presence of ethylamino side-chain in the structure is essential while imidazole ring is not required. While for selective H_2-receptor blocking activity, the ethylamino side-chain can be modified without any restriction. Imidazole ring, however is necessary which, in certain cases may be replaced by other bioisosteric heterocyclic ring.

36.8 H_1-RECEPTOR BLOCKING AGENTS

Since these agents are mainly used in the treatment of allergic reactions, they are also termed as antiallergic or classic antihistamines. Antergan was the first clinically employed classic antihistaminic drug. Most of these compounds possess substituted ethylamine (–CH–CH–N=) moiety which seems to be necessary for antihistaminic activity. In some compounds, the part or whole of this ethylamino side-chain is incorporated within a ring structure. However many compounds which possess this moiety, may not have antihistaminic activity while agents from other therapeutic classes may exhibit considerable antihistaminic activity. These include, phenoxybenzamine (α-adrenergic blocking agent), many local anaesthetics, tranquillizers (phenothiazines), atropine like drugs and antiparkinsonian agents.

Like histamine, most of the classic antihistamine, retain ethylamino side-chain and may be represented by following general formula.

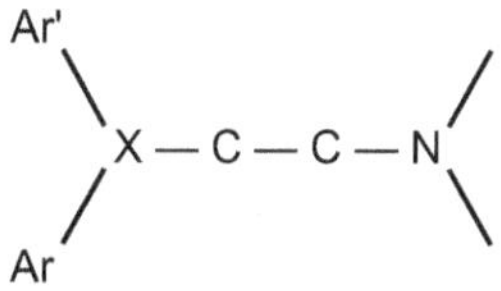

$$\begin{array}{c} Ar' \\ \diagdown \\ X-C-C-N \\ \diagup \\ Ar \end{array}$$

Classic antihistamine

where,

(i) X = nitrogen (i.e., ethylene diamine derivatives)

(ii) X = oxygen (i.e., aminoalkyl ether analogues), and

(iii) X = carbon (i.e, monoamino propyl derivatives)

While the incorporation of ethylamino side-chain into ring structure may result into cyclic basic chain analogue. Sometimes the two aromatic rings are bridged, which constitutes tricyclic ring derivatives.

The general formula for classic antihistamines offer many sites for modification. The substitutions on the aryl rings, replacement of the aliphatic dimethylamine group by smalll basic heterocyclic rings (e.g., triprolidine), increased branching on ethylene chain and the substitution between 'x' and aliphatic nitrogen, all modify the potency, metabolism, ability to reach the site of action, toxicities or adverse reactions of the antihistamines.

Since the structures of classic antihistamines have a close resemblance with structures of cholinergic blocking agents, most of the classic antihistamines do exhibit anticholinergic activity. The reverse is also true.

According to the chemical features they share, classic antihistamines are classified as :

1. Ethylene diamine derivatives
2. Aminoalkyl ether analogues
3. Cyclic basic chain analogues
4. Monoaminopropyl analogues
5. Tricyclic ring systems
6. Miscellaneous agents

Pharmacology :

(i) CVS : These agents do not afffect cardiac stimulant effect of histamine which is mediated through H_2 - receptors. They antagonise, however, the effects of H_1-receptor activation on vascular muscles and adrenal chromaffin cells. They antagonize histamine induced vasodilation and increased permeability of capillaries. Thus, the symptoms seen in Lewis triple response are suppressed. They also inhibit the release of epinephrine from adrenal chromaffin cells and activation of autonomic ganglia.

(ii) Respiratory smooth muscles : Bronchoconstriction is one of the major symptoms seen in hypersensitivity reactions. These agents inhibit histamine-induced bronchoconstriction. Unfortunately classic antihistamines are of limited clinical utility in the treatment of hypersensivity reactions seen in humans. This is mainly because of two reasons :

(a) Histamine is only one of many such autacids released by sensitized mast cells in hypersensitivity reactions. Antihistamines therefore will only inhibit the histamine responses which are not important in human hypersensitivity reactions. For example, in humans, leukotrienes (i.e., metabolic products of arachidonic acid) is main mediator of allergic bronchoconstriction. These agents do not inhibit responses to other autacoids. However other symptoms e.g., hypotension, itch and pain which are mainly mediated through H_1 - receptors are well controlled.

(b) Since they are competitive antagonists, they would not exert immediate effects if given after an anaphylactic shock has begun. In such condition, physiological antagonists (e.g. epinephrine) are much more useful.

(iii) **CNS** : Due to their own direct effects and effects related with their anticholinergic property, classic antihistamines can both, stimulate and depress the CNS. Some agents may produce insomnia, restlessness and nervousness while others may produce sedation. In CNS, these drugs antagonize the effects of stimulation of histaminergic neurons. Some of these agents are effective in the treatment of nausea, vomiting and motion sickness. These include, promethazine, dimenhydrinate, diphenhydramine and other piperazine derivatives.

Due to their central anticholinergic property, some of these agents may be used as antiparkinsonian drugs e.g., promethazine. Similarly the ethanolamine derivatives are particularly prone to sedation and hence be used as tranquillizers. In higher doses, some of them exert local anaesthetic activity e.g., pyrilamine and promethazine.

(iv) Glandular secretions : Due to their anticholinergic action, they may suppress the secretions of salivary, lacrimal and other exocrine glands. However they failed to inhibit gastric acid secretions. Since acetylcholine is also involved in the gastric acid secretion, some antihistamines may interfere in the secretion of gastric acid due to their atropine-like activity.

(v) Skin : They may evoke allergic reactions, if applied topically. Hence their topical use should be avoided. Antazoline, being least irritant, may be used in eye drops.

Absorption, Distribution, Metabolism and Excretion :

Classic antihistamines are orally well absorbed. Some of these agents exhibit much longer duration of action. Upon absorption, these agents get widely distributed throughout various body compartments. Liver is the principal site for their metabolism. Metabolite formation depends upon the chemical nature of antihistamines and it is influenced by age, sex and animal species in which the drug is studied. Metabolism occurs through typical metabolic reactions like, N-dealkylation, deamination, side-chain degradation, ring hydroxylation and oxidation. In chronic administration, many antihistamines induce metabolizing enzymes, resulting into increased metabolism of the antihistamines. Urine is the main vehicle through which these metabolites and little unchanged parent compound is excreted. Being weak bases, their gastrointestinal absorption and renal excretion is influenced by the pH of the medium.

Adverse Effects :

Prominent side-effects include sedation, drowsiness, restlessness, irritability, muscular twitching and convulsion. The sedation induced by antihistamines is potentiated by the concomittant use of alcohol. The anticholinergic activity associated with some of these agents may produce dryness of mouth, blurred vision, urinary retention, constipation and some atropine - like side-effects. Most of the adverse effects of antihistamines disappear with continued therapy. The chronic administration of phenothazine-type antihistamines may sometimes lead to agranulocytosis, hemolytic anemia or hepatitis. Topical application of these agents may provoke allergic manifestations. Although no evidence about teratogenic effects in humans, has been received, these agents are contraindicated in the first trimester of pregnancy. In chronic administration, these drugs may develop tolerance to their effects.

Therapeutic Uses :

(i) These agents are used in the treatment of various allergic reactions, which include, contact dermatitis, hay fever, urticaria, vasomotor rhinitis, asthma, erythema multiform and drug sensitization.

They are more useful in acute rather than chronic form of urticaria. These agents may suppress the antigen-antibody interactions and may be used alongwith glucocorticoids.

(ii) Diphenhydramine and pyrilamine possess weak anxiolytic activity and are often combined with atropine-like drugs to exhibit marked sedative activity in the treatment of insomnia.

(iii) Some of these agents are also used in suppressing vertigo and motion sickness.

(iv) Due to their atropine-like action, they have been used in cough mixtures and in the treatment of Parkinsonism.

(v) Antazoline and diphenhydramine may be useful in cardiac arrhythmias due to their quinidine-like effects.

(vi) Some of them may be used as antiemetic in cases where, vomiting is caused by histamine liberated from the damaged cells.

However these agents are less favoured in the treatment of allergic reactions of eyes and nose, acute anaphylactic shock and common cold of viral origin due to their low effectiveness.

36.9 CROMOLYN SODIUM

Cromolyn belongs to a completely novel class of compounds which brings about its antihistaminic effects by the suppression of the release of autacoids from secretory granules during antigen - antibody interaction. It bears neither a structural relationship to other commonly used antihistamines nor it possesses a smooth muscle relaxant or bronchodilatory activity.

It is highly water soluble synthetic analogue of Khellin (bronchodilator), an ingredient of plant origin. Chemically it is a disodium salt of 1,3-bis (2-carboxychromone-5-yloxy) -2-hydroxy-propane.

The drug, usually given through inhalation, attacks on pulmonary mast cells and inhibits the release of all autacoids including histamine and leukotrienes, from IgE-sensitized pulmonary mast cells by preventing the degranulation process. Its effectiveness in the treatment of hypersensitivity reactions, apppears to be due to its 'membrane-stabalizing' action through the phosphorylation of mast-cell protein. It also inhibits the influx of Ca^{++} ions by increasing the concentration of c-AMP.

Cromolyn sodium

Cromolyn sodium is poorly absorbed from GIT. Hence it is given by inhalation in order to act immediately on the sensitized mast-cells present in bronchi and lungs. About 10% of the inhaled dose is found to be absorbed into the circulation. It is mostly excreted in unchanged form, principally through urine and bile.

Adverse effects are few and of mild nature. These include, nasal congestion, wheezing, cough, pharyngeal irritation and headache.

It is mainly used in the treatment of allergic reactions induced by antigen-antibody interactions. However it is not used in the treatment of acute asthmatic attack.

Aqueous solutions are also developed to treat various nasal and ophthalmic conditions resulting by airborne allergens.

36.10 H$_2$-RECEPTOR BLOCKING AGENTS

Some of the histamine responses are exclusively mediated through H$_2$-receptor subsites. These responses include-

(a) dilatation of arterioles, capillaries and small veins.

(b) increase in the rate and force of heart contraction.

(c) increase in the c-AMP accumulation that inhibits the histamine release through feedback inhibitory mechanism.

(d) increase in gastric acid, pepsin and intrinsic factor secretions.

(e) reduced release of lysosomes and antibodies.

The classic antihistamines failed to inhibit these responses which are mediated through H$_2$-receptors. Hence, the search for effective and selective H$_2$-antagonists begun. The first success in this direction was reported in 1972 through the intellectual efforts of Black et. al. They carried out stepwise modifications of the histamine molecule to yield, burimamide, which was first selective H$_2$-antagonist. It was soon followed by other agents like metiamide, cimetidine and ranitidine.

Unlike H$_1$ receptor blocking agents, these drugs retain imidazole (or other bioisosteric ring) ring but may possess a much bulkier side-chain. In ranitidine, instead of imidazole ring, a substituted furan ring is incorporated. Similarly the side-chain amino group remains uncharged at physiological pH. Unlike H$_1$ - antagonists, these drugs are polar and hydrophilic compounds, just like histamine.

Though burimamide is a potent H$_2$ - antagonist, it could not be used clinically due to its oral ineffectiveness and toxic reactions seen in animal testing. Better absorption and increase in the potency were achieved by introducing a methyl group in the ring to yield metiamide. In the side-chain of burimamide, the methylene group is bioisosterically replaced by sulfur to give metiamide. It also could not survived clinically due to the reports of metiamide developed agranulocytosis. The thiourea group, present in the metiamide-side chain was suspected to be the cause of agranulocytosis. Hence, thiourea group is replaced by cyanoguanide group which is bioisosteric with thiourea to give cimetidine. Cimetidine is the first clinically used H_2-receptor blocking agent.

Ranitidine, is a nitroethane derivative of furan and on the molar basis, it is five times more potent than cimetidine.

The extensive studies of different ionic, tautomeric and conformational forms of histamine helped the scientists to identify minimum structural requirement for H_2-agonist activity. This then results into the development of burimamide, metiamide, cimetidine and ranitidine. New compounds, structurally related with ranitidine have been prepared. These compounds contain different polar groups instead of imidazole ring, which include diaminofurazan moiety, 3-amino-4-methyl furanzan or a 3-amino-4-phenyl furazan moiety.

Lamtidine is the lead compound of a new series of H_2 - receptor antagonists, containing a dialkylamino alkylphenoxy moiety.

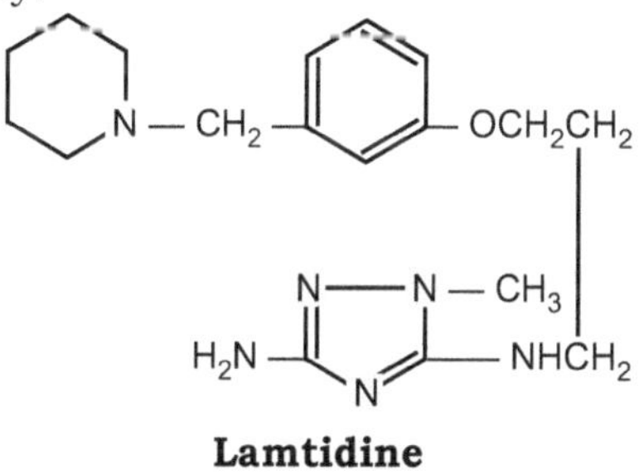

Lamtidine

The diaminofurazan moiety may be considered as a bioisoster of the diamino-nitroethane group, present in the ranitidine structure.

Pharmacology :

H_2-receptor blocking agents are reversible competitive antagonists of histamine on H_2-receptors. They do not have significant blocking action on H_1- or other autacoid receptors. Their prominent antagonistic action is centered mainly on the H_2-receptors present in gastric mucosa, resulting into a dose-dependent suppression of gastric acid secretion. They also antagonise gastric acid secretion induced by physiological agents other than histamine. They may also interfere in the release of intrinsic factor required for absorption of vitamine B_{12}. These drugs do not have any direct effect on serum gastrin and gastric emptying rate.

Sexual dysfunction in men during chronic administration may result due to peripheral antiandrogenic effects of these drugs. Hypospermia and diminution of seminal vascular size are the main symptoms.

Mechanism of Action :

Gastrin, histamine and acetylcholine are the three most important mediators of gastric acid secretion. Receptors for all these secretagogues, are present in the gastric mucosa, near parital cells. Of these, histamine has a direct action on gastric mucosa to increase acid secretion by activating the H^+ - K^+ - ATPase pump. While gastrin or acetylcholine do not possess intrinsic efficacy. They can thus only potentiate the effect of histamine on gastric acid secretion (i.e., a potentiating efficacy).

The current hypothesis states that the H_2-antagonists simply inhibit the direct actions of histamine (by forming some sort of reversible complex with the H_2-receptors) on acid secretion.

The responses to stimulation of histamine H_2-receptors are mediated through the activation of adenylate cyclase, providing yet another analogy between histamine H_2- and adrenergic β-receptors.

36.11 ABSORPTION, FATE AND EXCRETION

Famotidine and ranitidine are the clinically used agents from this category. By oral route, they are rapidly and completely absorbed. However, the presence of antacid may interfer in their absorption pattern. Both these drugs get widely distributed in the body. Famotidine was developed by replacing imidazole ring of cimetidine by a 2-guanidinothiazole ring. It has poor bioavailability as it is poorly soluble in the low pH of the stomach. Unlike cimetidine, famotidine has no effect on the cytochrome p450 enzyme system. Less than 30% of dose gets metabolized in the liver. It is principally excreted unchanged in urine. While N-oxide, S-oxide and desmethyl derivatives are obtained upon ranitidine metabolism. Most of the administered dose of ranitidine appears in the urine as the mixture of unchanged (free and conjugated) and its metabolite forms. Minor quantity may be eliminated in stool.

Adverse effects are few and of mild nature. These include nausea, diarrhoea, constipation, headache, skin rashes and dizziness. Due to their antiandrogenic effect, they may cause sexual dysfunction. Ranitidine is devoid of this effect.

36.12 THERAPEUTIC USES

These drugs have inhibitory effect on gastric acid secretion. Hence they are highly effective in treating conditions characterized by hypersecretion of gastric acid. Thus, they create a favourable environment for rapid healing of gastric and duodenal erosions.

Antacids are commonly used along with H_2-receptor blocking agents in the treatment of peptic ulcer.

Famotidine has also been used in combination with an H_1-antagonist to treat and prevent urticaria caused by an acute allergic reaction.

36.13 INHIBITORS OF H^+-K^+-ATPase PUMP

The gastric acid secretion is regulated by the functioning of H^+ - K^+ - ATPase pump present in the parietal cell membrane. It works just similar to Na^+-K^+- ATPase pump and exchanges proton for K^+- ions. Recently some agents from benzimidazole class were developed which appear to selectively inhibit the functioning of this pump by getting accumulated in the parietal cell-membrane. One such agent is omeprazole which effectively inhibits, both basal and enhanced gastric acid secretion.

Omeprazole

It is effective orally as well as parenterally and inhibits ATPase pump in the reversible fashion. Its clinical usefulness promoted further the development of lansoprazole, pantoprazole, rabeprazole and other drugs from this category.

❖ ❖ ❖

INDEX

A

Absence seizures, 24.3
Absorption, 2.1, 2.3, 15.3
Acebutolol, 19.20
Acetaldehyde dehydrogenase, 25.1
Acetanilide, 31.9
Acetazolamide, 24.12
Acetylcholine, 11.7, 13.1, 14.1, 20.5, 28.1
Acetylcholinesterase, 13.7
Acetyl-β-methylcholine, 13.4
Acetylation, 4.17
Acetylureas, 24.10
Active transport, 2.5
Acyclic hypnotics, 23.11
Addiction, 7.1
Additive response, 1.3
Adenosine, 34.4
Adenylate cyclase, 6.4, 34.1
Adrenaline, 18.1, 17.2
α-adrenergic agonist, 36.3
α-adrenergic blocking agents, 36.11
β-adrenergic agonists, 18.18, 36.3
β-adrenoceptor blockers, 19.1
Adrenergic receptors, 18.17
Adrenergic responses, 18.9
Adrenergic synapse, 18.4
Adrenoceptors, 18.7
Adrenochrome, 27.12
Affinity, 5.7
Ageing process, 14.14
Agonist, 6.3
Akathesia, 28.4
Akinetic seizures, 24.4

Albumin, 5.2, 5.6
Alcohol dehydrogenase, 25.1
Alcohol, 7.13, 25.1
Alcuronium chloride, 16.9
Aliphaxalone, 21.10
Allergen, 9.2
Allergy, 1.4, 5.9, 9.2
Allopurinol, 31.14
Alphadolone, 21.10
Alpha adrenergic receptor, 18.20
Alpha adrenoceptor blocking agent, 19.7
Alphaprodine, 30.8
Alprazolam, 23.9, 28.18
Alprenolol, 19.15, 19.20
Althesin, 21.10
Amantadine, 29.6
Ambenonium, 14.3, 14.6
Aminopyrine, 31.9
Amiphenazole, 23.6
Amitriptyline, 28.15
Amobarbital, 23.3
Amoxapine, 28.16
Amphetamines, 7.8, 7.12, 18.1, 18.2, 27.6
Analeptics, 27.2
Analgesia, 8.3, 21.3, 30.1
Anaphylaxis, 9.6
Angiotensins, 33.1
Angiotensin antagonists, 33.4
Anileridine, 30.8
Antagonism, 1.3, 10.6
Antagonist, 6.3, 9.2
Antiallergic antihistamines, 36.10
Antianxiety agents, 13.1, 26.1

Anticholinergic agents, 21.10, 29.6, 36.9
Anticholinesterases, 14.1
Anticonvulsant agents, 23.1
Antidepressant agents, 26.3, 28.13, 36.6
Antigen-antibody interaction, 9.2
Antigens, 9.1
Antihistaminic agents, 36.10
Anti-inflammatory agents, 31.2
Antimanic agents, 28.12
Antimuscarinic agents, 15.1, 15.9
Antiparkinsonian agents, 28.5
Antipsychotic agents, 28.3
Antipyrine, 31.9
Antipsychotic agents, 35.4
Antitussive agents, 30.16
Anxiety, 23.9, 26.1
Anxiolytic agents, 26.1
Apnea, 30.8
Apomorphine, 29.5
Apparent volume of distribution, 2.9
Aprobarbital, 23.3
Arachidonic acid, 31.3, 32.3
Arecholine, 13.10
Aromatization, 4.10
Arsenic poisoning, 10.7
Aspirin, 31.4, 31.6
Asthma, 9.9
Atenolol, 19.19, 19.20
Atopic diseases, 9.9
Atracurium, 16.8
Atropine, 5.7, 15.1
Auranofin, 31.13
Aurothioglucose, 31.13
Autacoids, 32.1, 36.1
Autoimmunity, 9.3
Autonomic ganglia, 17.1
Autonomic nervous system, 12.4

Autonomic profile, 8.2
Axolemma, 22.2
Azapetine, 19.11
Azapropazone, 31.10

B

Baclofen, 16.10, 20.7
Barbiturate poisoning, 23.6
Barbiturates, 7.12, 11.4, 23.2, 24.6, 26.2
Barbituric acid, 23.2
Basal anaesthetics, 21.8
Basal ganglia, 20.3
Beclomethasone, 9.12
Behavioural profile, 8.2
Bemegride, 23.6
Benorylate, 31.6
Benoxinate, 22.10
Benperidol, 28.10
Benserazide, 29.3
Benzilylcholine, 13.4
Benzocaine, 22.10
Benzodiazepine receptor, 23.5
Benzodiazepines, 7.8, 16.10, 23.6, 23.10, 24.11, 26.3
Benzodioxans, 19.7
Benzomorphan, 30.4, 30.9
Benzpyrene, 4.20
Benztropine, 29.6
Beta adrenergic receptor, 18.23
Beta adrenoceptor blocking agent, 19.14
Betahistine, 36.6
Betazole, 36.6
Bethanechol, 13.8, 20.7
Bethanidine, 19.4
Bioavailability, 1.6
Biological half-life, 4.1
Biological membrane, 2.1

Biotransformation, 4.1
Blind screening, 8.2
Blood-brain-barrier, 20.7
Body proteins, 5.2
Botulinum toxin, 16.4
Bradykinin, 9.6
Brain capillary, 20.8
Brain compartments, 20.3
Bretylium, 18.20, 19.4
Bromides, 23.14
Bromocriptine, 29.5
Bromvalurea, 23.11
Brotizolam, 23.7
Bufotenin, 27.10
Bunitrolol, 19.20
Bunolol, 19.15
Bupivacaine, 22.9
Buprenorphine, 30.14
Buproprion, 28.16
Burimamide, 36.14
Buscopan bromide, 15.4
Buspirone hydrochloride, 26.7
Butabarbital, 23.3
Butorphanol, 30.14
Butoxamine, 19.17, 19.19
Butriptyline, 28.15
Butyrocholinesterases, 13.7, 14.1
Butyrophenones, 28.5, 28.11

C

Caffeine, 7.5, 7.11, 27.4
Calcium carbimide, 25.4
Calmodulin, 1.5, 6.5
Captopril, 33.5
Capuride, 23.11
Carbachol, 13.8
Carbamazepine, 24.12, 28.11

Carbamates, 14.5, 23.11
Carbidopa, 29.3
Carbolonium bromide, 16.7
Carbromal, 23.11
Carcinogenicity, 10.3
Carfimate, 23.14
Carisoprodol, 16.13, 26.3
Carphenazine, 28.7
Cartazolate, 26.7
Catechol-O-methyl transferase, 18.5
Catecholamines, 18.5, 28.10
Cellular immunity, 9.1
Central neurotransmitters, 20.5
Central nervous system stimulants, 27.1
Cerebellum, 20.4
Cerebral cortex, 20.3
Chemical antagonism, 6.17
Chemotherapy, 1.3
Chloral hydrate, 4.6, 23.13
Chloralodal, 23.13
Chlordesmethyl diazepam, 23.8
Chlordiazepoxide, 26.4
Chlormethiazole, 26.7
Chlormezanone, 16.14, 26.7
Chloroform, 21.8
Chloroprocaine, 22.9
Chlorphentermine, 27.6
Chlorpromazine, 19.5, 23.14, 28.3, 28.7
Chlorprothixene, 28.6, 28.8
Chlorzoxazone, 16.14
Choline acetyl transferase, 12.7
Cholinesterase enzyme, 12.9, 14.2, 16.1
Cholinergic agonists, 13.1
Cholinergic blocking agents, 13.1
Cholinergic nervous system, 13.1
Cholinergic receptor, 6.4, 13.5
Cholinesterase inhibitors, 14.2

Cholinesterase reactivators, 14.13
Cholinomimetics, 13.7
Cimetidine, 36.14
Cinchocaine, 22.10
Clomipramine, 28.15
Clonazepam, 23.8
Clonidine, 7.6, 19.13
Clopenthixol, 28.6
Clorazepate, 23.9
Clortermine, 27.6
Clozapine, 28.12
CNS stimulants, 27.1
Cocaine, 22.8
Codeine, 30.3, 30.6
Colchicine, 31.14
Competitive antagonism, 6.15
Complement, 9.3
Complexation, 3.1, 3.8
Conjugation, 4.10
Covalent bonding, 6.9
Cromolyn sodium, 9.7, 36.13
Cross tolerance, 7.3
Cyanide poisoning, 10.8
Cyclazocine, 30.14
Cyclic AMP, 6.6, 9.7, 34.1
Cyclic GMP, 9.7, 34.3
Cyclic nucleotides, 13.4, 34.1
Cyclooxygenase, 32.5
Cyclopentamine, 18.24
Cyclopropane, 21.5
Cyproheptadine, 35.6
Cytochrome P-450, 4.3

D

Dantrolene sodium, 16.10
Dealkylation, 4.9
Deanol acetamidobenzoate, 27.8

Deanol, 13.10, 27.8
Debrisoquine, 19.4
Decamethonium, 16.6
Delayed hypersensitivity, 9.5, 9.10
Delirium, 21.3
Demecarium, 14.4, 14.6
Demoxepam, 23.8
Depolarizing blocking agents, 16.12
Deprenil, 29.4
Depression, 26.2, 28.10
Desensitization, 6.11
Desipramine, 28.15
Dextromethorphan, 6.14
Dextropropoxyphene, 30.9
Diacylglycerol, 6.5
Diazepam, 26.4
Diazoxide, 19.12
Dibenamine, 19.10
Dibenzapepines, 19.11
Dibenzodiazepines, 28.11
Dibenzoxazepines, 28.11
Dibucaine, 22.10
Dichloroisoproterenol, 19.17
Diclofenac, 31.11
Dicyclomine, 15.4
Diethyl ether, 21.6
Diethyl tryptamine, 7.11
Diethylcarbamazine, 9.9
Diethylpropion, 18.22
Diflunisal, 31.6
Diffusible drug, 3.8
Dihydro-β-erythroidine, 16.9
Dimethyltryptamine, 27.10
Dipole-dipole interaction, 6.10
Diprenorphine, 30.7
Dipterex, 14.9
Dipyrone, 31.9

Dissociative anaesthesia, 21.10
Distribution, 2.8, 15.3
Disulfiram, 4.21, 7.8, 19.3, 25.3
Dobutamine, 18.17
Domperidone, 29.6
Dopamine receptor, 29.4
Dopamine, 18.1, 20.5, 28.1
Doxapram, 27.3
Doxepin, 26.3, 28.16, 28.15
Droperidol, 28.10
Drug, 1.3
Drug allergy, 5.9
Drug addiction, 7.1
Drug antagonism, 1.5, 6.14
Drug dependence, 7.1
Drug distribution, 5.6
Drug elimination, 5.7
Drug-food interactions, 3.14
Drug interactions, 11.1
Drug metabolism, 4.1, 5.7
Drug persistance, 5.9
Drug-protein complex, 5.4
Drug-receptor interactions, 1.4, 6.9
Dyskinetics, 28.4
Dystonic reactions, 28.4

E

Echothiophate, 14.7
Edrophonium, 14.4, 14.6
Efferent nerves, 12.2
Efficacy, 6.2
Eicosapentaenoic acid, 32.3
Eicosatrienoic acid, 32.3
Electrostatic bonding, 6.10
Emylcomate, 16.13
Enalapril, 33.4
End plate region, 17.3

Endoneurium, 22.1, 22.2
Endoperoxide synthtase, 31.3
Endorphins, 30.10
Enema, 1.8
Enflurane, 21.7
Enkephalins, 30.10
Enzyme perturbation theory, 6.9
Ephedrine, 18.10
Epidural anaesthesia, 22.7
Epilepsy, 24.1
Epinephrine, 12.4, 18.1, 18.10, 18.13, 20.5
Epineurium, 22.1
Ergometrine, 19.8
Ergot alkaloids, 19.7
β-erythroidine, 16.8
Etazolate, 26.7
Ethanol, 4.21
Ethchlorvynol, 23.14
Ethinamate, 23.11
Ethopropazinc, 29.6
Ethosuximide, 24.10
Ethoxzolamide, 24.12
Etidocaine, 22.9
Etofenamic acid, 31.12
Etorphine, 30.7
Eucatropine hydrochloride, 15.4
Excretion, 2.11, 15.3
Extrapyramidal symptoms, 28.4

F

Facilitated diffusion, 2.4
Famatidine, 36.16
Fenamates, 31.12
Fenbufen, 31.11
Fenclofenac, 31.11
Fenfluramine, 18.23, 27.6

Fenfluramine, 27.6
Fenoprofen, 4.12, 31.11
Fenoterol, 18.18
Ferguson's theory, 3.5
Ferguson's principle, 3.5, 21.4
Fentanyl, 30.8
Fibrinogen, 5.2
Filtration, 2.7
Flufenamic acid, 31.12
Flunitrazepam, 23.8
Fluphenazine, 28.7
Flurazepam, 23.8
Flurbiprofen, 31.11
Fluroxene, 21.8
Focal epilepsy, 24.4
Fonazine, 16.11
Formulation factors, 3.15
Fosazepam, 23.8
Functional antagonism, 6.17
Fusaric acid, 29.4

G

GABA, 12.13
Gallamine triethiodide, 16.9
Gamma amino benzoic acid, 20.6
Gamma amino butyric acid, 6,4, 12.13, 24.2, 26.5, 27.2, 28.2, 29.2
Ganglionic blockers, 17.6
Ganglionic stimulants, 17.4
Ganglionic transmission, 17.1
General anaesthetics, 21.1
Generalized epilepsy, 24.3
Genotoxic effects, 10.1
Glaucoma, 14.11
Globulins, 5.2
Glucuronic acid, 4.10
Glutamic acid, 12.13

Glutathione, 4.13
Glutethimide, 23.12
Glycine, 12.13, 20.6
Glycopyrrolate, 15.4
Gold sodium thiomalate, 31.12
Gout, 31.13
Grand mal epilepsy, 24.4
Guanadrel, 19.4
Guanethidine, 19.4, 19.5
Guanylate cyclase, 34.3, 36.3
Guthion, 14.9

H

H_2-receptor antagonists, 36.14
Hageman factor, 9.8, 31.1
Halazepam, 23.8
Hallucinogens, 7.11, 27.8
Haloperidol, 28.3, 28.10
Halothane, 21.6
Harmala alkaloids, 28.22
Harmaline, 27.10, 28.22
Harmine, 27.10, 28.22
Hay fever, 9.9
Heavy metal poisoning, 10.6
Hemicholinium, 16.4
Heparin, 9.7
Heroin, 30.3
Hexamethonium, 17.7
Hexapropymate, 23.14
Hexobarbitone, 21.8
Hexoprenaline, 18.19
Hexylcaine, 22.10
Histamine antagonists, 36.9
Histamine liberation, 36.4
Histamine receptor, 36.4
Histamine shock, 36.9
Histamine, 6.17, 11.8, 20.6, 36.1

Histidine, 36.2
L-histidine decarboxylase, 36.2
Homatropine, 15.4
Humoral immunity, 9.1
Hydantoins, 24.6
Hydrallazine, 19.12
Hydrazine, 28.22
Hydrogen bonding, 3.9, 6.10
H^+-K^+-ATPase-pump, 36.16
Hydrolytic reactions, 4.8
Hydrophobic bonding, 5.3
Hydrophobic forces, 6.10
6-Hydroxyclopamine, 19.5
4-Hydroxypropranolol, 19.18
5-Hydroxytryptamine, 7.11, 19.3, 20.5
Hydroxyzine, 26.3
Hyoscine, 15.1, 15.9
Hyoscyamine, 15.2
Hyperreactivity, 6.19
Hypersensitivity, 1.4, 6.18, 9.5
Hypnotic, 21.3
Hyporeactivity, 1.4
Hypospray, 1.10
Hypothalamus, 20.3

I

Ibogaine, 27.11
Ibotenic acid, 27.12
Ibuprofen, 31.11
Ictal period, 24.2
Idiopathic parkinsonism, 29.1
Idiosyncrasy, 1.4, 10.2
Iminostilbenes, 24.12
Imipramine, 28.15
Immune mechanisms, 9.3
Immunity, 1.4, 9.1
Immunoglobulins, 9.2, 9.5
Immunostimulants, 9.11
Immunosuppressants, 9.11
Immunotoxicity, 10.2
Impulse transmission, 12.1
Incompatibility, 11.2
Indole derivatives, 27.10
Indolealkylamines, 28.22
Indomethacin, 31.10
Indoprofen, 31.11
Induced-fit theory, 6.9
Inducers of drug metabolism, 4.20, 11.5
Infantile spasms, 24.4
Infiltration anaesthesia, 22.6
Inflammation, 31.1
Inhalation, 1.6
Inhibitors of metabolism, 4.20, 11.5
Inositol triphosphate, 6.5
Interferon, 9.5
Interneuron, 17.2, 20.6
Internuncial neurons, 12.5
Intra-arterial injection, 1.10
Intracellular receptor, 6.6
Intramuscular injection, 1.9
Intraperitoneal injection, 1.10
Intrasternal injection, 1.10
Intrathecal injection, 1.10
Intravenous injection, 1.9
Intravenous anaesthetics, 21.8
Intravenous regional anaesthesia, 22.6
Intraventricular injection, 1.10
Intrinsic activity, 6.2
Ion-dipole interaction, 6.10
Ionization, 3.6
Ipratropium, 15.4
Iprindole, 28.17
Ipronaizid, 28.11
Irreversible anticholinesterases, 14.3

Isoantibodies, 9.2
Isocarboxazide, 28.21
Isoetharine, 18.18
Isoflurane, 21.7
Isoprenaline, 18.1, 18.10
Isopropamide, 15.5
Isoproterenol, 19.17
Isosterism, 6.11
Isosystox, 14.9
Isoxsuprine, 18.18

K

Kallidin, 9.8, 33.6
Kallikrein, 9.8
Ketamine, 21.8
Ketanserin, 35.6
Ketoprofen, 31.11
Ketotifen, 9.7
Kininogen, 9.8
Krnjevic hypothesis, 21.5

L

Labetalol, 19.17, 19.19
Lamitidine, 36.15
Leukotrienes, 32.5
Levallorphan, 30.14
Levodopa, 29.3
Levonordefrin, 32.5
Lidocaine, 22.6, 24.12
Limbic system, 20.4
Lipophilicity, 3.2
Lipoxygenases, 32.5
Lisuride, 29.5
Lithium carbonate, 28.12
Lobeline, 17.5
Local anaesthetic agents, 22.1
Lorazepam, 23.8
Loxepine, 28.11

Leukotrienes, 32.5
Lysergic acid, 19.8, 27.11

M

Mandrax, 23.13
Mania, 28.2
Manic–depressive disorder, 28.2
Maprotiline, 28.17
Mast cell, 9.6, 36.2
Mazindol, 18.23
Mecamylamine, 17.7
Meclofenamic acid, 31.12
Mefenamic acid, 31.12
Melathion, 14.9
Melatonin, 35.5
Membrane expansion theory, 22.2
Membrane stabilization, 22.3
Meperidine, 30.4
Mephenesin, 16.13, 26.2
Mephobarbital, 23.3
Mepivacaine, 22.9
Meprobamate, 16.13, 23.11, 26.2
Mercapturic acid, 4.10
Mercury poisoning, 10.7
Mescaline, 27.8
Mesoridazine, 28.2
Metabolism, 4.1
Metalol, 19.17
Metaraminol, 18.10
Metaprotorenol, 18.18
Metoprolol, 19.20
Methacholine, 13.7
Methadone, 30.4, 30.8
Methantheline bromide, 15.5
Methaqualone, 23.12
Methocarbamol, 16.13
Methohexital sodium, 21.9

Methoxamine, 18.17
Methoxyflurane, 21.7
6-methoxyharmalan, 27.10
Methscopolamine bromide, 15.8
Methsuximide, 24.10
Methyl alcohol, 25.4
α-methyl dopa, 19.3
Methyl salicylate, 31.6
α-Methyl-m-tyrosine, 19.3
Methylation, 4.10
Methylergonovine, 19.8
Methylphenidate, 27.7
Methylsergide, 19.8
Methylxanthines, 27.8
Methyprylone, 23.12
Metiamide, 36.14
Metoclopramide, 13.10
Metocurine chloride, 16.8
Metoprolol, 19.20
Meyer–Overton hypothesis, 21.4
Mianserin, 28.17, 28.18
Mid brain, 20.3
Midazolam, 23.7, 23.9
Migraine, 19.13
Minoxidil, 19.12
Miotine, 14.4
Mipafox, 14.9
Molindone, 28.11
Mono amino oxidase, 12.11, 18.5, 28.14
Monoamine oxidase inhibitors, 28.19
Morphinan, 30.4, 30.9
Morphine, 30.3
Motor epilepsy, 24.4
Muscarine, 12.9, 13.2
Mascarinic blocking agents, 15.2
Muscarinic receptors, 6.3, 13.2, 15.3
Muscimol, 27.12

Mutagenesis, 1.4
Myasthenia gravis, 14.11
Myoclonic seizures, 24.4

N

Nadolol, 19.13
Nalbuphine, 30.14
Nalorphine, 30.13
Naloxone, 11.8, 30.6
Naltrexone, 30.6
Naproxen, 31.11
Narcoanalysis, 21.10
Narcotic analgesics, 11.8, 30.2
Neostigmine, 14.4, 14.6
Nerve block anaesthesia, 22.6
Nerve cell, 12.2
Neuroleptics, 28.3
Nervous system, 12.2
Neurohumoral transmission, 12.1
Neurological profile, 8.2
Neuromuscular blockers, 16.1
Neuromuscular junction, 16.3
Neuromuscular transmission, 16.1, 17.3
Neuropeptides, 33.7
Neuroses, 28.2
Neurotransmitters, 18.3
Nicotine, 7.10, 12.9, 16.1, 17.5
Nicotinic cholinergic receptor, 6.2, 13.3, 16.2,
Nikethamide, 27.3
Nimetazepam, 23.8
Nitrazepam, 23.8
Nitrogen mustards, 19.9
Nitrous oxide, 21.6
Nodes of Ranvier, 22.2
Nodolol, 19.20
Nomifensine, 28.17, 28.18
Non-competitive antagonism, 6.16

Non-narcotic analgesic agents, 30.1, 31.4
Norepinephrine, 12.4, 18.4, 20.5
Norepinephrinergic neuron, 28.19
Normetanephrine, 18.5
Nortriptyline, 28.15
Noscapine, 30.2
Nucleoside formation, 4.19
Nucleotide formation, 4.19
Nucleotide, 34.1
Nylidrin, 18.18

O

Obidoxime, 14.14
Occupation theory, 6.8
Omeprazole, 36.16
Opioid agonist, 30.3
Opioid analgesic agents, 20.2, 30.1
Opioid antagonists, 30.15
Opioid receptor, 30.12
Opioids, 7.1, 30.1
Optical isomers, 6.13
Organ failure, 10.2
Organophosphorus compounds, 14.8
Oripavines, 30.5
Oxanamide, 23.11
Oxazepam, 26.4
Oxazolidinediones, 24.6
Oxidation, 4.6
Oxidation-reduction potential, 3.10
Oxotremorine, 13.10
Oxprenolol, 19.20
Oxymetazoline, 18.24
Oxymorphone, 30.15
Oxyphenbutazone, 31.10
Oxyphenonium, 15.5

P

Pancuronium bromide, 16.8
Papaverine, 30.2, 34.2
Para amino phenol, 31.8
Paracetamol, 31.9
Paraldehyde, 23.14
Paramethadione, 24.9
Paraoxon, 14.9
Parasympathetic nervous system, 12.6
Parasympatholytic agents, 15.2
Parathion, 14.9
Parenteral administration, 1.9
Pargyline, 28.22
Parkinsonism, 18.24, 29.1
Partial agonist, 6.3
Partial vapour pressure, 3.4
Partial seizures, 24.4
Partition coefficient, 3.3
Pemoline magnesium, 27.7
D-Penicillamine, 31.13
Pentagastrin, 36.8
Pentazocine, 30.14, 31.13
Pentolinium, 17.7
Pentylenetetrazol, 27.3
Pergolide, 29.5
Peridural anaesthesia, 22.7
Perineurium, 22.1
Perphenazine, 28.7
Pethidine, 30.5
Petit mal epilepsy, 24.3
Petrichloral, 23.13
Phagocytosis, 2.8
Pharmacodynamics, 1.3
Pharmacokinetics, 1.3
Pharmacology, 1.3, 25.2, 33.3
Pharmacotherapeutics, 1.3

Phenacemide, 24.10
Phenacetin, 31.9
Phenaglycodol, 16.13
Phencyclidine, 7.12, 21.9, 27.11
Phendimetrazine, 18.22, 27.7
Phenelzine, 28.21
Phenmetrazine, 18.22, 27.7
Phenobarbital, 4.20, 23.3
Phenothiazines, 28.6
Phenoxybenzamine, 19.10
Phenoxyphosphoryl dicholine, 14.9
Phensuximide, 24.10
Phentermine, 18.20, 18.22
Phentolamine, 19.10
Phenylbutazone, 4.20
Phenylephrine, 18.10, 18.17
Phenyramidol, 16.14
Phenytoin, 24.8
Phosphatidylcholine, 4.4
Phosphodiesterase, 6.5, 34.2
Phospholipase A_2, 32.3
Phototoxicity, 10.1
Physicochemical parameters, 3.1
Physiological antagonists, 12.10
Physostigmine, 14.5
Picrotoxin, 27.3
Pilocarpine, 13.9
Pimozide, 28.12
Pindolol, 19.20
Pinocytosis, 2.8
Piperoxan, 19.11
Pipradrol, 27.7
Piroxicam, 31.12
Plasmakinins, 33.6, 9.6
Poisoning, 10.5
Poldine methylsulfate, 15.4
Polypeptides, 33.8

Polypharmacy, 1.1
Pons, 20.3
Pore transport, 2.3
Potency, 1.5
Practolol, 19.20
Pralidoxime, 14.14
Prazepam, 23.8
Prazosin, 19.12
Preanaesthetic medications, 21.3
Prednisone, 9.9
Prilocaine, 22.9
Primidone, 24.8
Probarbital, 23.3
Procaine, 22.9
Progabide, 24.12
Programmed screening, 8.3
Promazine, 28.7
Promethazine, 36.12
Pronethalol, 19.17
Propanidid, 21.9
Propantheline, 15.9
Proparacaine, 22.10
Propoxyphene, 30.3, 30.5
Propranolol, 19.18, 28.12, 29.6
Propranolol glycol, 26.3
Propylhexedrine, 18.20
Prostacyclin synthtase, 31.3, 32.5
Prostaglandin biosynthesis, 31.3, 32.3
Prostaglandins, 9.6, 32.3, 36.1
Prostanoic acid, 32.2
Protein binding, 4.22, 5.1, 11.4
Protriptyline, 28.15
Pseudocholinesterases, 14.1
Psilocin, 7.11, 27.10, 35.3
Psilocybin, 7.11, 27.10, 35.3
Psychodelics, 27.8
Psychomotor epilepsy, 24.7

Psychoses, 28.2
Psychotomimetics, 27.8
Psychoactive agents, 28.2
Psychotropic drugs, 28.3
Purinoceptors, 34.4
Pyrazole, 4.21
Pyrazolon derivatives, 31.9
Pyridostigmine, 14.4, 14.6
Pyrogallol, 18.6
2-Pyridine aldoxime methiodide, 14.13

Quazepam, 23.8

Ranitidine, 36.14
Rate theory, 6.8
Rauwolfia alkaloids, 28.9
Reagin, 36.3
Receptor site theories, 6.8
Receptor, 1.4, 5.6, 6.1
Rectal administration, 1.7
Reduction, 4.7
Refractory period, 22.3
Relative saturation value, 3.5
Renin, 33.1
Reserpine, 19.3, 28.10
Respiratory stimulants, 27.1
Reticular activating system, 20.4
Reversible anti-cholinesterases, 14.3
Rhumatism, 31.1
Ritodrine, 18.18
Routes of administration, 1.6

S

Salbutamol, 18.10, 18.18
Salicylic acid, 31.5
Salsalate, 31.6

Saralasin, 33.5
Saxitoxin hydrochloride, 22.3
Schradran, 14.9
Scopolamine, 15.1
Screening, 8.3
Second messenger, 18.25
Sedative–hypnotic agents, 23.1
Seizures, 24.1
Sensitization, 7.3
Sensory epilepsy, 24.4
Serotonin antagonists, 35.5
Serotonin receptor, 35.4
Serotonin, 28.2, 35.1
Serum sickness, 9.10
Silent receptors, 6.11
Simple diffusion, 2.3
Sleep factor delta, 23.1
Sodium ion channel, 22.2
Sodium nitroprusside, 19.12
Sodium valproate, 24.6, 24.11
Sodium–potassium–ATPase pump, 2.5
Sotalol, 19.17
Soterenol, 18.18
Spare receptors, 6.10
Specific receptor theory, 22.2
Spinal anaesthesia, 22.6
Spinal cord, 20.4
Spiperone, 29.4
Spiroperidol, 28.10
Stages of anaesthesia, 21.2
Status epilepticus, 24.4
Steric features, 6.12
Storage depots, 2.11
Strychnine, 27.3
Styramate, 16.14
Subcutaneous administration, 1.9
Sublingual administration, 1.7

Substance P, 12.13, 33.7
Succinimides, 24.6
Succinylcholine bromide, 16.5
Sulfate conjugation, 4.10
Sulfones, 23.14
Sulindac, 31.11
Sulthiame, 24.12
Supersensitivity, 6.18
Suppositories, 1.8
Surface anaesthesia, 22.6
Surgical anaesthesia, 21.5
Suxethonium bromide, 16.6
Sympathomimetic agents 36.9
Sympathetic nervous system, 12.4, 18.1
Sympathomimetic agents, 18.7, 36.9
Sympathomimetic amines, 18.1, 36.9
Synapse, 18.3
Synergistic response, 1.3, 4.22
Systemic toxicity, 10.2

T

Tachyphylaxis, 6.17, 7.3, 18.8
Talbutal, 23.4
Taurine, 12.13
Tautomerism, 23.3
Tazolol, 18.10
Temazepam, 23.8
Teratogenicity, 10.3
Terbutaline, 18.18
Testing of drug, 8.1
Tetracaine, 22.6
Tetracyclic antidepressants, 28.17
Tetraethyl pyrophosphate, 14.9
Tetrahydro cannabinol, 27.12
Tetrahydrozoline, 18.24
Tetrodotoxin, 22.4

Thalidomide, 23.12
Thebaine derivatives, 30.6
Theobromine, 27.4
Theophylline, 9.9, 27.4
Therapeutic index, 1.3
Thermodynamic activity, 3.4
Thiazesim, 28.17
Thiamylal sodium, 21.9
Thiopental sodium, 21.9
Thioridazine, 28.7
Thiothixene, 28.6
Thioxanthenes, 26.7
Threshold potential, 22.3
Thromboxane A_2, 31.3, 32.5
Timolol, 14.11, 19.20
Tolamolol, 19.20
Tolazoline, 19.10
Tolerance, 1.4, 6.17
Tolfenamic acid, 31.12
Tolmetin, 31.12
Tonic-clonic seizures, 24.3
Topical administration, 1.8
Topical anaesthesia, 22.6
Toxicity testing, 10.3
Toxicology, 10.1
Toxogenin, 14.14
Tranylcypromine, 28.21
Trazodone, 28.18
Triazolam, 23.7
Trichloroethanol, 23.13
Tricyclic antidepressants, 28.15
Triethylcholine, 16.4
Trifluperazine, 28.7
Trifluperidol, 28.10

Triflupromazine, 28.7

Trihexyphenidyl, 29.3, 15.4

Trimazosin, 19.12

Trimethadione, 24.9

Trimethaphan, 17.8

Trimipramine, 28.15

Triptamine, 35.5

Tropicamide, 15.5

Tropolone, 18.6

Tropylcholine, 13.4

Tuaminoheptane, 18.24

d-Tubocurarine chloride, 16.7

Tybamate, 26.2

Types of receptor, 6.4

U

Urecholine, 13.8

Uricosuric agent, 31.14

Urethanes, 23.11

Ureides, 23.11

Urticaria, 9.9

V

Vaginal administration, 1.9

Valproic acid, 24.11

Vander Waals forces, 5.3, 6.10

Vasoactive intestinal polypeptide, 33.8

Vecuronium bromide, 16.8

Viloxazine, 28.17

Volatile anaesthetics, 21.5

W

Withdrawal symptoms, 6.18, 7.1

X

Xanthines, 27.4

Xanthine derivatives, 36.9

Xylocholine, 19.5

Y

Yohimbine, 18.8, 19.11, 27.11

Z

Zimelidine, 28.17

Zopiclone, 26.7

SAMPLE QUESTIONS

1. What are advantages of bioassay? Give an experimental design for the bioassay of insulin.

2. (a) Mention the toxic manifestations and management of poisoning from organophosphorus compounds and solanaceous drugs.

    (b) Describe in general the treatment of poisoning.

3. (a) How do barbiturates affect their own metabolism and that of other drugs? What are the consequences of this?

    (b) Is it true that β-adrenoceptor agonists are beneficial in the treatment of angina? Justify.

4. Define and classify analgesics. Describe pharmacology of morphine and compare it with that of pethidine.

5. Classify sympathomimetic drugs. Explain the pharmacology of epinephrine.

6. Mention the therapeutic uses and toxic manifestations of,
    (a) Barbiturates
    (b) Atropine
    and suggest antidote treatment.

7. Describe mode of action, uses and side-effects of,
    (a) Disodium chromoglycate
    (b) Phenytoin
    (c) Propranolol.

8. Compare the pharmacological actions of,
    (a) Morphine and aspirin
    (b) Digitalis and quinidine
    (c) Adrenaline and noradrenaline
    (d) Succinyl choline and d-tubocurarine

9. Discuss the effects of following drugs on CNS.
    (a) Alcohol
    (b) Chloropromazine
    (c) Benzodiazepine
    (d) Amitriptyline.

10. Compare the advantages and disadvantages of bioassay as against those of physical and chemical assay. Describe briefly the bioassay methods for acetylcholine.

11. Define and classify poisons. Write the manifestations and management of,
    (a) Morphine poisoning
    (b) Insecticide poisoning

12. Write briefly the adverse effects and uses of,
    (a) Atropine
    (b) Chlorpromazine
    (c) Digoxin
    (d) Imipramine

13. Compare the pharmacological actions
    (a) Benzodiazepines and barbiturates as hypnotics
    (b) Furosemide and hydrochlorothiazide
    (c) Adrenaline and ephedrine
    (d) Ether and halothane

14. Write pharmacological actions of
    (a) Propranolol (b) Clonidines
    (c) Methyldopa
15. Define bioassay. Describe with examples the different designs of bioassay.
16. Write notes on :
    (a) Chronic toxicity test.
    (b) Bioassay of digitalis.
    (c) Insecticide poisoning.
17. Describe mechanism of action, therapeutic uses, and untoward symptoms of,
    (a) Adrenaline
    (b) Chloropromazine
    (c) Furosemide
18. Mention the pharmacodynamic actions and clinical significance of tricyclic antidepressants. In what way do they differ from the CNS stimulants ?
19. Describe the mechanism of action, uses and substitutes for,
    (a) Physotigmine
    (b) Aspirin
    (c) Nitroglycerine
    (d) Isoprenaline
20. Describe the bioassay procedure for tubocurarine.
21. What are tranquillizers ? Name some important tranquillizers and explain the pharmacology and therapeutic uses of chlorpromazine.
22. Answer the followings :
    (a) Why is reserpine no longer widely used as tranquillizer ?
    (b) How does alcohol influence the body temperature ? Is it wise to administer alcohol to person suffering from cold exposure ?
    (c) What are the actions of amphetamine ? Why it is liable to abuse ?
    (d) Does salbutamol have any advantages over isoprenaline in asthma therapy and how are they administered ?
23. Classify antihypertensive agents ? Write down the mechanism of action of
    (a) Methyl dopa
    (b) Reserpine
    (c) Guanethidine.
24. Describe various factors modifying drug action giving suitable examples.
25. Describe the major features of a lipid bilayer membrane. How drugs are transported across this membrane ?
26. Give the pharmacological actions of histamine. Describe the clinical uses of histamine.
27. Write short notes on (Any three) :
    (a) Rate theory of drugs action
    (b) Disadvantages of oral route
    (c) Diagnostic agents
    (d) Dose-response relationship.
28. (a) Give advantages and disadvantages of sublingual and intravenous routes of administration.
    (b) Explain graded dose-response relationship.
29. (a) What are different factors which modify dose of a drug ?
    (b) What is the significance of plasma-protein binding ?

30. Write short notes on :
    (a) Drug synergism and antagonism
    (b) Mechanism of action of classic antihistaminic agents.
    (c) Peritoneal dialysis.
    (d) Factors modifying absorption of a drug.

31. Describe in brief, the different phases of drug trials in man.

32. Explain the following terms and their implication in drug use.
    (a) Affinity and efficacy of a drug
    (b) Abstinence syndrome
    (c) Carrier state
    (d) Margin of safety

33. Discuss in brief, advantages and disadvantages of protein binding of drugs.

34. (a) Give mechanism of action of antihistaminics and describe their uses.
    (b) List with examples, the routes for drug excretion and explain how excretion determines dosing.

35. Write notes on,
    (a) Allergic reactions to drugs
    (b) Drug dependance
    (c) Conjugation of drugs
    (d) Parenteral routes of drug administration.

36. Describe briefly, with suitable examples, the various dosage forms of the drug.

37. Define biotransformation and mention the different chemical processes with examples. State the necessity of this phenomenon in the body.

38. Write notes on :
    (1) Ferrous sulphate
    (2) Inhalation route of drug administration
    (3) Placebo
    (4) Drug antagonism
    (5) Loading and maintenance dose of a drug

39. Describe in brief, the different phases of drug trials in man.

40. Explain the terms :
    (1) Teratogenicity
    (2) Drug dependance
    (3) Sensitization
    (4) Blood - brain - barrier

41. Discuss :
    (1) Dose - response relationship.
    (2) Mechanism of drug action including receptor concept.
    (3) Biological variation.

42. Explain the following terms and their implications in drug use,
    (a) Tolerance
    (b) Receptors
    (c) Placental barriers
    (d) Therapeutic index.

43. Define autacoids. Mention various autacoids and their antagonists. Write in short therapeutic uses of H_1 - blockers.

www.ingramcontent.com/pod-product-compliance
Lightning Source LLC
Chambersburg PA
CBHW080721300426
44114CB00019B/2452